THE ENCYCLOPEDIA
OF ALCOHOLISM

by
Robert O'Brien and Morris Chafetz, M.D.

Facts On File Publications

New York, New York

EDITORIAL STAFF

Editors

Robert O'Brien   Morris E. Chafetz, M.D.

Associate Editor

Joan Harvey

Contributing Editors

Marion C. Chafetz, Lynne M. Constantine, Charlotte Cross,
John P. Harrington, Joyce Lautens O'Brien, Lynn Prindle

THE ENCYCLOPEDIA OF ALCOHOLISM

by Robert O'Brien and Morris Chafetz, M.D.

© Copyright 1982 by Green Spring, Inc.

Library of Congress Cataloging in Publication Data

Main entry under title:

Encyclopedia of alcoholism

  Bibliography: p.
  Includes index.
  1. Alcoholism—Dictionaries. I. O'Brien, Robert,
1932-
HV5017.E5   362.2′92′0321   81-12562
ISBN 0-87196-623-9   AACR2

Printed in the United States of America
10 9 8 7 6 5 4 3 2 1

TABLE OF CONTENTS

Scientific advances are made in discrete steps, each of which must be duplicated and repeated many times before we are certain that it is valid, how it should be used.... It is an ethical imperative to caution here about the limitations of applying broad findings based on statistical populations to specific decision making by individuals.

A scientific truth concerning a population, represented by statistical average, may be inapplicable or even invalid for many individuals within that population.

> Morris E. Chafetz, M.D.
> Founding Director
> National Institute on Alcohol Abuse
> and Alcoholism
> Introduction to the Second Special
> Report to the Congress of the United
> States on Alcohol and Health

PREFACE

A staff member of a major government agency suggested that *The Encyclopedia of Alcoholism* be published in 100 volumes—one volume of basic information and 99 volumes of caveats, disclaimers, qualifications, special cases and contradictory material. Despite his advice (only partly in jest), we have designed *The Encyclopedia of Alcoholism* as a concise desk reference in dictionary format covering a myriad of topics relating to alcoholism. The more than 500 entries provide extensive information on the substance alcohol itself, on the social institutions, customs, and socioeconomic interrelations that have an impact on alcoholism, and on the physical and psychological manifestations of alcoholism.

The *Encyclopedia* can be of great use to the lay person and the professional alike. For the lay person we have tried to describe the subject as clearly and simply as possible, without resorting to jargon or other unfamiliar language. At the same time we have tried to avoid being simplistic. When a technical term appears repeatedly in the literature of alcoholism and has a precise meaning that must be understood to ensure accurate comprehension, we have taken the time to define and explain it.

For the professional we have tried to provide concise and clear statements of familiar material as well as a handy reference in which he or she can quickly find an elusive fact, date or statistic. Obviously, no article in a volume this concise will always fit the needs of the professional working in that particular area. The usefulness of the book will increase, however, as the professional moves beyond the immediate area of his or her expertise. To assist both the professionals and the lay people who may need more information than we can provide in our limited space, we have appended a short list of references to each of the major articles as well as a substantial bibliography.

To our knowledge this volume is the first A to Z encyclopedia to appear in the field of alcoholism. This distinction has both advantages and disadvantages. On the one hand, it has allowed us to approach the subject with a fresh eye and to select topics for articles because we felt that they should be included and not because they had been traditionally dealt with in volumes of this kind. On the other hand, since the guidelines are largely of our own creation, we may have omitted articles that should have been included or given some subjects insufficient treatment. We expect that some readers will disagree with us (and among themselves) about what should or should not have been included in *The Encyclopedia of Alcoholism* and about the amount of space devoted to individual topics.

Some of the volume's limitations are inherent in its concise format. In the interest of saving words, unfortunate impressions can sometimes be created. Where "alcoholic" is used as a noun, for example, it ideally should read "alcoholic person," lest anyone assume that we are reducing those who suffer from the condition of alcoholism to that single part of their life experience. Similarly, where the pronoun "he" appears (unless the context clearly suggests the male of the species), we intend the reader to understand that women are being spoken of as well.

In a book of this length and scope, it is inevitable that minor errors have crept in during successive steps in the editorial process. We have taken great pains, however, to avoid significant errors of fact or interpretation, though we cannot guarantee that some egregious flaw has not escaped our notice.

Undoubtedly as communication continues to improve within the alcoholism field, we shall be able to fill gaps and clarify cloudy areas in the present volume in future editions of *The Encyclopedia of Alcoholism*. This volume is a beginning in a field in which the end is still nowhere in sight.

Robert O'Brien   Morris E. Chafetz, M.D.
Sharon, Conn.   Washington, D.C.

ACKNOWLEDGMENTS

In a venture of this kind, the editors' debts are enormous. The burden of the project was, of course, borne by the tireless efforts of the staff members whose names appear on the copyright page.

It would be an impossible task to thank each and every one of the individuals and agencies who assisted us in the preparation of the manuscript, but we owe particular debts to the following: the staffs of the National Institute on Alcohol Abuse and Alcoholism and the National Clearinghouse for Alcohol Information, the National Council on Alcoholism, the World Health Organization, the League of Red Cross Societies, Alcoholics Anonymous, the Addiction Research Foundation (Canada), the various state and provincial (Canadian) agencies, as well as the embassies and agencies of other nations who responded to our requests for information.

Robert O'Brien would like to thank those without whose personal help this book would not have been possible: Dr. Robert Schurtman, Ms. Ruth Lassoff, Dr. Michael S. Bruno, Dr. Frank Herzlin and, particularly, Joyce O'Brien.

HISTORY OF ALCOHOL AND MAN

There is no period in recorded history free from references to production and consumption of alcoholic beverages. Even in prehistoric times it seems likely that Stone Age cultures made fermented meads by using honey as a base. Since fermentation can occur naturally, with airborne yeasts converting any sugary mash into ethyl alcohol and carbon dioxide, man's first discovery of an alcoholic brew was probably accidental. Thereafter prehistoric man probably began to attempt deliberate production of alcoholic beverages, and such beverages have retained an important and problematic role in most human societies since that time.

When the earliest literate societies sought to explain the origins of the alcoholic beverages they inherited from their ancestors, they recorded these legends on stone tablets and papyrus scrolls. One of the earliest of such mythologies is the pre-Christian epic of Gilgamesh, recorded by the Babylonian civilization. According to this creation myth, the powers of evil fought the powers of good in bloody combat for control of the earth. The powers of good were ultimately victorious, but these gods suffered many casualties in the struggle. Where the benevolent gods fell, their bodies were consumed by the earth to produce vines that memorialized their sacrifice. This myth is one example of the age-old association between wine and sacrificial blood that has been preserved as a symbol by a variety of religious cultures.

In Biblical legends the discovery of wine is also related to creation stories. Many have equated the tree of knowledge in Genesis with a grape vine. Eating the fruit of this tree led to Adam and Eve's awareness of their nakedness and their subsequent expulsion from the Garden of Eden. In Genesis, after the human race was nearly obliterated by the flood, Noah fell victim to the same sin. Having landed the Ark following the recession of the flood waters, "Noah began to be a husbandman, and he planted a vineyard. And he drank of the wine, and was drunken." Noah was discovered naked in his tent by his sons, an incident that was treated as a very serious matter. The Bible is full of similar incidences of drunkenness, involving warnings, denial and remorse.

Not all accounts of the discovery of wine stress the dangers of consumption. In the ancient Persian tale of King Jamshid, the king was so fond of grapes that he stored them in large earthernware containers to maintain a supply beyond the harvest season. Discovering that one batch had spoiled and fearing that it might be dangerous, he set the jar aside and labeled it "poison." One of the king's concubines, suffering from headaches, decided to kill herself by eating from this "poisonous" batch of grapes. Delighted that the juice relieved her malady, she induced the king to sample it. After tasting it, Jamshid too was delighted, and he immediately ordered production of the beverage in years to come, naming it *zeher-e-koosh* ("the delightful poison").

In addition to such legends, there exist many records of actual consumption of alcoholic beverages in early societies. The oldest are Mesopotamian, dating from 4000 B.C., although actual production may have begun 2000 years earlier. Clay tablets from this culture contain recipes for using wine as a solvent in medicines, a practice that would continue in other cultures for many centuries. The importance of wine for the Mesopotamians is suggested by the fact that a personal drinking cup accompanied most of their wealthy citizens to the funeral pyre. In the nearly contemporary Egyptian societies, however, the predominant alcoholic beverage was a beer fermented from barley. Called *hek,* the drink was important enough to early Egyptian commerce that, according to papyrus documents unearthed since, government officials were appointed to supervise and control its production. In addition to these early medicinal and commercial roles, alcoholic beverages also became important in religious rituals. Records of early Hebrew society define eight different types of wine to be used for distinct ceremonial occasions. Although the records are less precise, there are indications that fermented beverages also had well-established medicinal and religious functions in early civilizations further east, especially in China and India.

Not surprisingly the history of alcohol is inseparable from the history of alcohol abuse. Legislative codes intended to limit consumption of alcoholic beverages were required as soon as production of such beverages became efficient and widespread. The Code of Hammurabi of Babylonia, which dates from 1700 B.C., contains a variety of restrictions on the sale and consumption of alcohol. The code also documents the early existence of public drinking houses, which it regulated with laws that sometimes called for the execution of offenders. Equally old records from the reign of the Chinese Emperor Chung K'iang note the execution of drunkards as a demonstration to the public of governmental disapproval of alcohol, and one of his successors, Emperor Tei-Tsung, is known to have established, or "licensed," the number of places where the sale of alcohol was permitted.

Perhaps the most dramatic example of governmental restrictions on alcohol consumption was in ancient Persia. Possibly because of the unofficial approbation of alcohol implicit in the legend of King Jamshid, the aristocratic classes in ancient Persia habitually consumed alarming quantities of wine. In response the rising Islamic culture there adopted a complete prohibition of alcohol to combat widespread health problems, now known to be the result of nutritional deficiencies. Like all bans on alcohol consumption, this first known example had only limited success. The aristocratic classes in Persia continued to drink to excess, an aspect of the culture that inspired the hedonistic attitudes associated with the poet Omar Khayyam. Nevertheless, to this day fundamental Islamic religions have maintained a total ban on alcoholic beverages. Similarly Buddhist sects originating in India in the fifth century B.C. have maintained to this day a complete prohibition on consumption of alcohol.

The original temperance movements also date from pre-Christian times. The dynastic Egyptian tract called *Wisdom of Ani* opens with the command, "Take not upon thyself to drink a jug of beer." The consequences of excess are then listed in this document as advice for coping with a substance that the prevailing government was unwilling to ban entirely. A similar attitude is found in the Chinese *Canon of History,* written around 650 B.C. Noting that "men will not do without beer," and that "to prohibit it and secure total abstinence from it is beyond the power even of sages," the *Canon of History* provides a series of warnings about alcohol with the intention of fostering moderation.

The single most successful temperance document in history is the Bible, with its more than 150 references to alcohol. Although alcohol is deeply rooted in Jewish culture and granted an important role in religious celebrations, the Hebrew people have enjoyed a relative freedom from alcoholism that must in part be attributed to the many warnings about excess found in the Old Testament. The specifically cultural controls on alcohol consumption are suggested by Proverbs: "Wine is a mocker, strong drink is raging: and whosoever is deceived thereby is not wise." While the "strong drink" mentioned is simply undiluted wine, the warnings against abuse of it in Proverbs are sterner than those found in the writings of most cultures troubled by abuse of distilled alcoholic beverages; as evidenced in the 23rd Chapter:

> Who hath woe? who hath sorrow?
> who hath contentions? who hath babbling?
> who hath wounds without cause?
> who hath redness of eyes?
>   They that tarry long at the wine;
> They that go to seek mixed wine.
>   Look not thou upon the wine when
> it is red, when it giveth its color in
> the cup, when it moveth itself aright.
>   At the last it biteth like a serpent,
> and stingeth like an adder.

These sorts of warnings about the dangers of excess, deeply ingrained in the society's behavior patterns, created such effective cultural controls that carefully regulated consumption could be condoned and even encouraged without great danger of alcohol abuse.

European and, hence, American cultural attitudes, including those toward consumption of alcohol, derive more from the classical Greco-Roman civilizations than from the older cultures of the Middle East. The history of alcoholic beverage consumption in these classical ages can be described as a shift from the relatively formal and ceremonial use of libations associated with the Greek symposium toward the more excessive and self-indulgent feasts and drunken orgies common under the later Roman emperors. This same shift can be seen on the level of cultural archetypes in the transformation of Dionysus into Bacchus.

The Greek god Dionysus, identified with both wine and natural fertility, is a benevolent presence in the Homeric Hymns, dating from about 800 B.C. Expelled from Greece by Lycurgus, Dionysus embarked on travels to Thrace and India, spreading the cult of the vine as a potent blend of good in moderation and evil in excess. Greek society was notable for both temperance and thorough knowledge of wine-making techniques. Governmental regulations provided for wine inspectors, fines for drunkenness and specific dilutions of wine with water. In Greek culture undiluted wine was considered barbarous. Greek histories retell many stories of military confrontations won because of the drunkenness of the enemy, and moderation was also stressed in the medical tracts of the time. Even Plato, sternly ascetic in many matters, approved of festival libations and the designation of limited farmlands for the growing of wine grapes only.

The symposium was at the heart of Greek culture, and during it wine drinking was both essential and carefully regulated. Two courses were served, one of meats and one of fruits, followed by the drinking of diluted wine out of vessels with regulated capacities. The philosophical discussions at the symposium were thought to have been enriched by this shared and uniform libation.

In Roman society, however, Dionysus gave way to Bacchus and the intellectual symposium became a gluttonous feast. In the Ovidian *Metamorphoses* of the first century A.D., Bacchus is associated less with wine than with excessive consumption of it. In these poems, for example, Midas and Silenus, "filthy drunken good old friends," drink competitively for 10 days and 10 nights. Bacchus is so pleased by this display that he offers the winner the wish that results in the Midas touch. The social reflection of this literary reference was public feasting of gross proportions at which drinking ceremonies overwhelmed conversation. Life for the upper class was more leisurely in Rome than in Greece, and the Romans enjoyed better agricultural conditions for vine propagation, factors that abetted the general social permissiveness in regard to wine consumption. Intellectual support for this attitude was also abundant; Pliny the Elder, for example, devoted an entire volume of his *Historia Naturalis* to wines and wine making and the poet Martial made wine drinking an exception to his otherwise stern philosophy. The Roman culture, of course, gave us the adage *in vino veritas* and the term "bacchanalia."

As a result of the consequences of their excesses, the ancient Romans also instituted some historically important controls on drinking. The symposiums eventually degenerated to the point that the Roman Senate felt constrained to ban them entirely for a period beginning in 186 B.C. In 81 A.D. the Emperor Domitian ordered half the nation's vineyards destroyed and the Senate prohibited planting of new vines until 276 A.D. Having long witnessed the evidence of alcoholism that abounded in Rome a jurist named Domitius Ulpinus was the first to suggest the possibility that habitual drunkenness might be a disease. This cultural ambivalence, this coexisting excess and concern, was the primary characteristic of Roman attitudes toward alcohol and an important aspect of the legacy handed down to western European cultures.

The Middle Ages were a time when enormous improvements were made in the production of wine in Europe. The single greatest contribution was made possible by the Crusades, for when the Europeans returned from battling with the Moslems for control of the Holy Land, they brought with them the sirah grape from Persia. This was the beginning of a series of successful plantings of foreign grapes along the river valleys of France which has made that country world famous for its vineyards and its wine.

An even more important development in the production of alcoholic beverages in general during this period was the introduction of the distillation process, which also was imported. While distillation of seawater had been practiced in Europe since pre-Christian times, it was not until the eighth century A.D. that an Arabian alchemist known as Geber perfected a method of purifying the essence of wine.

Distillation of spirits is possible because alcohol boils at a lower temperature than water. As vapors rise from a heated alcoholic beverage, they can be drawn off, and after cooling, the vapors condense into liquid again. While naturally fermented beverages can attain a strength of only 14% alcohol, distillation of purified, or rectified, alcohol enables production of beverages with a much higher alcohol content. Because of the consequences of more potent alcoholic drinks, the first widespread distillation of potable alcohol in Europe during the Middle Ages brought about new attempts to control consumption of the substance.

Since rectified alcohol was considered to be of great medicinal value, distillation processes gained widespread acceptance in Europe. Belief in the value of alcohol as medicine emanated from Montpellier, Switzerland at the end of the 13th century, when the chemists Arnaldus de Villanova and Raymond Lully, both of whom reached the unheard-of age of 70, published testimonials to the powers of this apparent cure-all: "We call it *aqua vitae,* and this name is remarkably suitable, since it is really a water of immortality." Two hundred years later the German physician Hieronymus Brunschwig was proclaiming that distilled alcohol could cure everything, including jaundice, colds, deafness, baldness and much more. "It gives also young courage in a person," Brunschwig declared, "and causes him to have a good memory." This faith in alcohol as a panacea for all ills led the European religious orders of the Middle Ages to begin dispensing drinks to weary travelers. The practice survives in the image of the St. Bernard dog rescuing a snowbound traveler from certain death with a flask of brandy.

Brandy, a fortified beverage made by distilling wine, was in fact a rather late invention. The first distilled alcoholic beverage was whiskey, the "water of life," or *uisce beathadh,* of the Gaelic-speaking natives of Ireland. The origins of this distillation of alcohol by fermenting a mash of grain are obscure, but it seems certain that whiskey production was widespread in Ireland by the 12th century. In Scotland the mash used was slightly different, primarily malted barley rather than a mixture of grains. The reason why distillation processes proliferated in these countries was that the climate would not permit cultivation of vines. Hence, for a time in the British Isles, whiskey was even used for the religious functions that in other cultures traditionally called for wine. At the Battle of Culloden in 1746 "John Maitland, a Presbyter of the Episcopal Church of Scotland, administered the Holy Eucharist to the mortally wounded Lord Strathallan with oatcake and whiskey."

These new and more potent alcoholic beverages made society's susceptibility to drunkenness even more obvious, and as a result temperance regulations were instituted. In 1226 Switzerland introduced the first closing-time laws and in 1285 England followed suit. By 1436 such laws had been adopted in even relatively lenient Scotland. Germany in 1496 banned the sale of alcoholic beverages on Sundays and holy days. Norway decided in 1586 to forbid the sale of liquor during the hours of church services only.

Around this time a variety of often conflicting local regulations on alcohol sale and consumption began to proliferate, and organizations devoted to combating the problem of increasing public drunkenness emerged. The first formal temperance societies started in Germany. The order of St. Christopher was formed in Dietrichstein in 1517 with the aim of reducing excessive drinking, and it was followed in 1524 by a similar organization in Heidelberg. Temperance societies stressing moderation rather than complete abstinence soon began to spring up in other countries, particularly in those areas where the popularity of distilled liquors over wines and beers increased the dangers of relatively limited consumption.

In the years leading to the industrial revolution the patterns of increasing availability of alcoholic beverages and increasing concern about the ensuing alcohol-related problems established during the Middle Ages continued, with Britain becoming the leader in both respects. A typical example of the intertwining of political history with the history of alcohol use in Britain was the defeat of Bonnie Prince Charlie, pretender to the throne, at Culloden in 1746. During his flight after the battle the prince was hidden by a family named MacKinnon. In return he gave them a recipe for his favorite liquor, a blend of brandy and Scotch whisky. The drink, called *an dram budheach* by the Gaelic-speaking Scots, was then produced in huge quantities and its name corrupted into the present "Drambuie."

A similar series of coincidences resulted in the introduction of that most English of all alcohols: gin. In the 17th century a Dutch chemist named Franciscus Sylvius succeeded in producing a competitor for Arnaldus de Villanova's alcoholic aqua vitae. As enthusiasm for extramedicinal imbibing of the liquor grew, the new drink was flavored with juniper to disguise the taste of raw spirit. In France the flavoring ingredient gave rise to the generic name *genievre,* but the ready availability of wine there restricted its commercial possibilities. In England in 1690 Parliament passed the historically important Act for Encouraging the Distillation of Brandy and Spirits from Corn to appease its business community. Since Sylvius' aqua vitae was the most profitable distillation procedure available, the English adopted it and corrupted the French name for the flavoring ingredient into the term "gin." In its spread to the east, Sylvius' process was subject to a similar adoption and received another name, the Russian term "vodka."

Because of the English government's decision to encourage distillation, however, improved methods of production of alcoholic beverages had their most disastrous results in that country. The act of 1690 resulted in the production of a million gallons of gin by 1694, and that figure doubled within 20 years. Later restrictions had little effect, for by 1742 production had reached 20 million gallons a year. Despairing of finding a way to control the flow of gin through the nation, the English government then introduced the measure since imitated by almost all governments: in 1743 it began to levy high and unprecedented taxes on specifically potable alcohols. Henceforth all alcohols not intended for consumption could escape this tax only by being "denatured," or rendered unfit for consumption.

By the beginning of the 19th century, improved technology was conspiring against the government's delayed reaction to the proliferation of alcoholic beverages. Aeneas Coffey of Dublin invented the "continuous still," which was to be instrumental in the mass production of Scotch whisky. Although economically efficient, the continuous still seemed innocuous at first because it produced a distilled alcohol with a raw taste that resisted aging. After some years of mediocre success as a rectifier of gin, however, the still was discovered to work wonders with a malt mash fermented in small amounts in the Scottish Highlands, and Scotch whisky for the first time eclipsed Irish whiskey as the favorite alcoholic beverage of the British Isles.

The rise of British concern about alcohol abuse parallels the country's sudden growth in the availability of alcoholic beverages. In the Age of Enlightenment philosophical warnings about the dangers of excess, like those in ancient Greek society, appeared. "A man may choose," Boswell was told by Johnson, a famous abstainer, "whether he will have abstemiousness and knowledge, or claret and ignorance." Even more important was the growing awareness by London's leading social critics of the dangers of widespread alcoholism among the lower classes. The two most influential spokesmen for this new concern were William Hogarth, illustrator of such horrific images as *Gin Lane* and *Beer Street,* and Charles Dickens, whose novels are full of warnings about the dangers of habitual intoxication. These two men also represented different sides in a basic disagreement among social reformers on the issue of alcoholism: in Hogarth's illustrations it is liquor that brings poverty and misery but in Dickens' novels it is poverty and misery that drive people to drink. However disparate these views on the country's alcohol problem may have been, they combined to provoke the British government's carefully engineered and ultimately successful shift of national drinking habits from distilled alcohols to beer and ale.

At this time even more important changes of attitudes toward alcohol were occurring on the Continent, although they would go largely unheeded until modern times. In 1786 a town physician in Bratislava became the first medical doctor to call for government action against alcohol abuse. An even greater symbolic breakthrough came in 1849, when a Swedish physician named Magnus Huss wrote a tract called *Alcoholismus Chronicus,* which introduced the word "alcoholism" to the world. The prevailing climate of alcohol abuse and concern about it was such that only 20 years after the publication of this rather obscure medical essay newspapers in England were attributing deaths to "alcoholism." A precise definition of alcoholism as a disease syndrome, however, was formulated by another physician 3,000 miles away, in America.

Given its prominence in Europe, alcohol quickly found a place in the New World. In 1609, only two years after they had established the first English settlement in America, the inhabitants of Jamestown, Virginia ran an advertisement in London for brewers. By 1640 the first distillery, designed to manufacture gin, was erected by the Dutch settlers of New York. It was soon converted to produce rum, however, for it was that drink that dominated early American commerce in alcohol. "Rumbullion," as it was called, was a rectified alcohol produced from fermented molasses. The rum distillers, located mostly in New England, imported molasses from the West Indies, the best source of this raw material. They shipped some of their product to Africa, where it was bartered for slaves. The slaves were then brought to the West Indies to be traded for molasses, which in turn was shipped to New England. Thus a "triangle trade" was established. Since taxation could not be enforced in such distant lands, the trade remained lucrative and the price of rum was low enough to make it the favorite alcoholic beverage in America until the Revolutionary period, after which an abundance of grain supplies increased the availability of whiskey. In 1808 Congress outlawed slave trading and the rum industry was demolished.

The ban on slave trading was the final step in the rise of the indigenous American whiskeys: rye, bourbon and corn whiskey. These alcoholic beverages no doubt first came into use as substitutes for rum in isolated areas, perhaps as a result of the presence of Irish and Scottish settlers familiar with the whiskey-distilling techniques of their home countries. Because it was easier and more profitable to produce rye whiskey from grain than to transport the grain to market, Pennsylvania farmers, in particular, found rye a convenient medium for exchange, and thus production of the drink increased. A government tax on whiskey resulted in the Whiskey Rebellion of 1794, which was an attempt by distillers in Pennsylvania to resist the tax. Although short-lived, the revolt strengthened local insistence on the right to distill whiskey. A similar attitude prevailed farther south, in what is now Kentucky. Revenue inspectors there eventually despaired of ever adequately taxing local distilleries, thought to number more than 2,000 as early as 1810.

Against this background of burgeoning production and consumption of alcohol, Dr. Benjamin Rush of Philadelphia began his pioneer work on the pathological processes of alcoholism in 1785. His particular innovation was a scientific assumption that alcoholism was a disease and the subsequent study of it in terms of disease complexes like those that had resulted in the formulation of useful therapy for other disorders. Rush was open to the alternative positions on alcohol stressed by temperance societies, however, and these attitudes combined with public outrage over the increasing incidence of drunkenness caused his ideas to be abandoned for the "moral" approach that dominated America's attempts to curb alcoholism in the 19th century.

Early temperance organizations in the United States were closely aligned with religious groups and enjoyed great popularity in rural regions. By 1830 there were over 1,000 local groups affiliated with the American Temperance Society, whose philosophy had progressed from avoidance of alcoholic beverages to total abstinence. In the process, the organization also changed its focus from assisting habitual drunkards to petitioning state governments to prohibit the sale of alcohol in any form. Assisted by popular songs, plays and novels, such as T. S. Arthur's *Ten Nights in a Bar-Room,* the temperance societies had great success during the late 1800s. By 1912 seven states had enacted prohibition laws, others were close to ratifying similar legislation and agitation for a national ban on alcoholic beverages had begun.

In 1919 a national prohibition on beverages with an alcohol content of more than 0.5% went into effect and lasted until 1933. However well-intended, the Eighteenth Amendment to the Constitution and the Volstead Act, which provided for the amendment's enforcement, are now considered to have failed in their attempt to outlaw the use of alcoholic beverages. Heavy drinkers were unaffected, for an enormous illegal production of alcohol immediately replaced the regulated and taxed trade. Moderate drinkers were denied the social outlet of the saloons and then encouraged into general disregard for the law when speakeasies became a fashionable substitute for those meeting places. Teetotalers became even more entrenched in their belief that alcoholism was a sin and undeserving of professional medical treatment. The failure of Prohibition, however, discredited the moral approach to alcohol problems and so allowed the introduction of an alternative approach—a serious study of the issues, in the form of scientific investigation, surrounding alcohol consumption.

This "serious study of the issues" became the modern study of alcoholism. Still in its infancy before World War II, it progressed enormously in both scope and depth during the postwar years. It is to the wealth and variety of approaches and information gained during this most recent period that the bulk of this volume is devoted.

INTRODUCTION TO ALCOHOL

The term "alcohol" dates back at least to the first millennium B.C., and the current use of the word results from a long history of figurative usages and changing chemical definitions. The etymological source of the word has nothing to do with liquids, for "alcohol" is derived from the Arabic term *al-kol'l,* meaning a fine cosmetic powder made by pulverizing iron ore and worn as a mascara. The term did not enter European languages until the 16th century, when chemists applied it to any fine, impalpable powder produced by crushing a rougher crystalline substance.

In a series of etymological extensions that have become obscure, the word "alcohol" was eventually used to describe fluids as well as powders produced by a pulverizing process. Hence distilled, or rectified, fluids thought to be the essence, quintessence or "spirit" of another liquid were generally termed alcohols. However, there is a long history in the English language, in particular, of use of the term to describe the essential spirit of anything, including abstract qualities. It was in this sense that Samuel Taylor Coleridge, in his *Lectures on Shakespeare,* for example, described "intense selfishness" as "the alcohol of egotism."

Rectified alcohols were first produced by distilling wine, and when potable alcohols were eventually produced by distilling the fermented mash of other substances, they were called "alcohol" because they shared the essential property of being able to induce intoxication. In the early days of organic chemistry, "alcohol" was the name given to the entire class of compounds sharing the same chemical structure as the "spirit" of wine, even if such compounds were not intended for consumption or could not be consumed without fatal consequences. In popular usage the term "alcohol" has for the past 300 years been synonomous with spirituous liquids.

Alcohols are a remarkably diverse family of organic compounds. Potable alcohols appear relatively insignificant when compared with the immensely valuable industrial alcohol compounds, most of which are produced synthetically. The single distinct chemical feature that all alcohols have in common is the presence of an oxygen atom and a hydrogen atom bonded together to form a single unit known as a hydroxyl group, denoted by the symbol OH. An alcohol molecule occurs when this hydroxyl group appears in combination with a carbon atom or hydrocarbon chain. Alcohols therefore differ according to the number of carbon or hydrocarbon units present in their molecular structure, but all alcohols remain distinct from the hydrocarbon family because of the presence of the hydroxyl group. In fact the molecular polarity created by the presence of the hydroxyl group gives alcohol its most important chemical properties, extreme solubility and a low boiling point. The degree to which alcohols of various sorts possess these important properties is determined by the number of hydrocarbon units occurring in combination with the single, all-important hydroxyl group.

Since the hydroxyl group defines the alcohol molecule and determines its behavior in any chemical reaction, alcohols are usually classified according to the number of hydrocarbon units attached to the hydroxyl group. Hence, according to one standard classification, alcohols are primary if the hydroxyl is attached to a single carbon chain, secondary if the hydroxyl is attached to a carbon chain bearing two others and tertiary if the hydroxyl is attached to a carbon chain bearing three others. A more precise classification names alcohols according to the number of carbon units attached to the hydroxyl group; a hydroxyl group with one carbon unit is called a methyl alcohol; with two carbon units, an ethyl alcohol; with three carbon units, a propyl alcohol; and with four carbon units, a butyl alcohol. The most important propyl alcohol is known as isopropyl alcohol because of the position of the hydroxyl group in the molecule, but with that single exception these categories may be considered to include most common alcohols. Although in 1957 an even more specific and sophisticated system of classification was adopted at a congress of the International Union of Pure and Applied Chemistry in Paris, the classifications of methyl, ethyl, isopropyl and butyl alcohols are sufficient for a general discussion of the basic properties of simple alcohols.

Methyl Alcohol (Methanol)

Methyl alcohol is commonly termed "wood alcohol" because it was once produced by destructive distillation of hard woods. A primary alcohol, it is highly soluble because of its low carbon content, and it has a low boiling point, about 65°C. Consumption of this highly toxic alcohol, which is sometimes produced by moonshiners in remote areas of the southern United States, often results in blindness or death. Commercially its primary use is in the production of formaldehyde and other organic chemicals. Other commercial products made from methyl alcohol include antifreeze and industrial solvents. Because distillation processes can produce only limited amounts of varying purity, methyl alcohol is now synthetically manufactured by combining carbon monoxide and hydrogen at high temperatures with oxides of zinc or chromium as a catalytic agent.

Ethyl Alcohol (Ethanol)

Commonly called "grain alcohol" for the material from which it has traditionally been distilled, ethyl alcohol is highly soluble and has a boiling point of about 78° C. This type of alcohol is produced commercially by fermentation and used to make alcoholic beverages. Since potable alcohol is heavily taxed, ethyl alcohol intended for other purposes is denatured, or rendered unfit for consumption, by treatment with a variety of toxic or nauseous chemical substances that cannot be removed. In denatured form ethyl alcohol is used as an industrial solvent and as raw material for acetaldehyde and a variety of other important chemical compounds and tinctures. Some ethyl alcohol intended for industrial use is produced by fermentation of sugars and starches, but most commercial denatured alcohol of this variety is manufactured by combining the petroleum by-product ethene with sulfuric acid.

Isopropyl Alcohol (Propanol)

Known as "rubbing alcohol" because of its popular uses, isopropyl alcohol is a tertiary alcohol that has less solubility than either methyl alcohol or ethyl alcohol and a boiling point of about 82°C. In addition to its use as a rubbing compound, isopropyl alcohol is an ingredient in many hand and shaving lotions. Industrially it is an important additive in antifreeze, shellac and lacquer. Like ethyl alcohol isopropyl alcohol is manufactured mostly from a petroleum by-product, in this case propene.

Butyl Alcohol (Butanol)

Butyl alcohol has limited solubility and a relatively high boiling point, about 117°C. Nevertheless, of all classes of alcohols the butyl class has perhaps the broadest range of commercial uses. In various forms it is an essential ingredient in many types of lacquer, photographic film and dye. Butyl alcohol is also used in the manufacture of plastic, artificial leather and safety glass. It is produced by both fermentation and synthesis. When fermented, butyl alcohol is often made from sterilized molasses and the active enzymes found in certain soil bacteria. It is also produced by synthesizing the petroleum by-product butene in a similar procedure to those employed in the manufacture of ethyl and isopropyl alcohols.

Beyond these basic types there exists a variety of high-carbon alcohols produced in smaller quantities for more specialized uses. A range of alcohols possessing six to 10 carbon units in varying structures is essential to the manufacture of many synthetic plastics. Some complex alcohols with more than 10 carbon units are used to produce biodegradable detergents. Polyester cords for automobile tires, jet fuels, nitroglycerin explosives, inks and numerous other products are all manufactured by exploiting the properties of specific alcohols. In addition glycerol is a sweet-tasting, easily digestible alcohol sometimes used in medicinal syrups, and sterol is a chemically complex crystalline alcohol that exists in some plant tissues without known function.

Common Alcohols

Common Name	Chemical Name	Formula	Carbon Atoms	Melting Point C°	Boiling Point C°
methyl alcohol	methanol	CH_3OH	1	−93.9	64.96
ethyl alcohol	ethanol	CH_3CH_3OH	2	−117.3	78.5
isopropyl alcohol	2-propanol	$(CH_3)_2CHOH$	3	−89.5	82.4
butyl alcohol	butanol	$CH_2(CH_2)_2CH_3OH$	4	−89.53	117.25

THE ENCYCLOPEDIA
OF ALCOHOLISM

A

absenteeism   Absenteeism is a major problem among employed alcoholics. One study reported that male alcoholics had three times the number of sick absences as a matched control group (Maxwell). In addition to normal off-the-job absences, alcoholics often report to work but later disappear from the work place. Another problem is "on-the-job" absenteeism, which occurs when a worker is physically present but not mentally alert. In 1975 the largest cost to the United States resulting from alcoholism was that of lost production, an estimated $19.63 billion, compared with $12.74 billion in health and medical costs and $5.14 billion in motor vehicle accident-related costs.

EMPLOYEE ASSISTANCE PROGRAMS have been developed to help workers with alcohol problems.

John R. DeLuca, ed., *Fourth Special Report to the U.S. Congress on Alcohol and Health* (Rockville, Md.: National Institute on Alcohol Abuse and Alcoholism, 1981), p. 93.

Observer and M. A. Maxwell, "A Study of Absenteeism, Accidents, and Sickness Payments in Problem Drinkers in One Industry," *Quarterly Journal of Studies on Alcohol* 20 (1959):302–307.

Harrison M. Trice, *Alcoholism in America* (New York: Robert E. Krieger Publishing Co., 1978), pp. 70–72.

absinthe   A flavored spirit with a dry, bitter taste, absinthe is too potent to be drunk straight. It is usually diluted with water, which changes its yellowish-green color to milky white. The name "absinthe" comes from the botanical designation of the plant *Artemisia absinthium,* more commonly known as wormwood, the basic flavoring ingredient in this beverage.

In addition to wormwood, absinthe is flavored with angelica root, star anise, dittany leaves, licorice, hyssop, sweet flag and other aromatics. These ingredients are macerated and steeped in alcohol. The final product is between 60% and 80% (usually 68%) alcohol.

The effects of absinthe are worse than those associated with excessive use of other forms of alcohol. Not only is it habit forming, but it has a harmful effect on the nerves, causing delirium and, sometimes , a permanent mental deterioration known as absinthism.

Absinthe was invented by a Dr. Ordinaire, a Frenchman living in Switzerland. His recipe was later bought by Henri-Louis Pernod (see PERNOD), who in 1797 became the first to produce absinthe commercially. Because of its severe health hazards, absinthe was banned in most Western countries during the early years of the 20th century. It was outlawed in Switzerland in 1908 and in the United States in 1912. In France, where absinthe houses had been very popular in Paris during the late 19th century, it was banned in 1915.

Although these prohibitions have remained in effect, absinthe may still be consumed legally in some countries, including Spain.

absolute alcohol   The pure alcohol in a beverage, obtained by brewing followed by fractional distillation. (There is always a slight amount of water in alcohol; commercial absolute alcohol, used only for medical or industrial purposes, contains up to 1% of water.)

The term "absolute alcohol" is used to refer to the amount of pure alcohol in a substance. For example, three 1-oz drinks of

100-proof whiskey, four 8-oz glasses of beer and a half bottle of wine all contain approximately the same amount of pure alcohol, about 1½ ounces.

abstainer   Strictly defined, one who abstains completely from the consumption of alcoholic beverages. The application of the term or concept depends on the context in which it is being used and the philosophy of the person or organization using it. For example, many agencies reporting on alcohol abuse group abstainers with moderate or social drinkers, since all are considered nonabusers of alcohol. ALCOHOLICS ANONYMOUS, using a strict interpretation, insists upon complete abstinence. In cultures where the use of alcohol is proscribed or barely tolerated, such as in INDIA, abstention is the norm of social behavior and any use of alcohol is considered abuse.

abstinence   A complete refraining from the use of alcoholic beverages; also called total abstinence. (See also ABSTAINER.)

abuse   Alcohol abuse is a general term applied to the misuse of alcohol, resulting in one or more problems for the drinker. These problems can be psychological, such as loss of control over drinking or depressive states (see DEPRESSION); medical, involving either an acute or chronic illness (see DISEASES); or social, such as problems with family or work. Alcohol abuse does not necessarily involve alcoholism; for example, a person may go on drinking binges and become destructive without necessarily developing the kind of dependency usually associated with alcoholism. The act of getting drunk is itself a form of alcohol abuse.

Since alcohol is itself a drug, alcohol abuse can be classified under drug abuse (see DRUGS). In fact alcohol abuse is the major form of drug abuse in the United States. Both alcohol abuse and drug abuse are types of substance abuse. Food, for example, is a substance that is abused by many people, leading to the establishment of such groups as Overeaters Anonymous.

Substance abuse is subject to individual patterns. Some people may abuse more than one drug, such as those who use both alcohol and marijuana. In addition the amount of a substance that might constitute abuse for one person might be a safe level for another. A large man might be able to consume several drinks in a sitting with no ill effect, while a small woman consuming the same amount might become very drunk. Some countries, such as Sweden, have a low per capita intake of alcohol but a high incidence of alcoholism. Certain drinkers can consume large quantities of liquor day after day without ever developing social problems, yet they may gradually become victims of CIRRHOSIS or ALCOHOLIC HEPATITIS because of the amount they consume. This too is a form of alcohol abuse, although not one that is noticeable on a daily or even a yearly basis. (See also ADDICTION, ALCOHOLISM, COMPULSION, PROBLEM DRINKER.)

accidents   The role of alcohol consumption in the occurrence of accidents is receiving increasing attention today. In a national survey in the United States, 36% of those who said they drank regularly, compared with 8% of nondrinkers, reported two or more accidental injuries in the previous year (Brenner et al.). Furthermore the rate of death is considerably higher for alcoholics than for the rest of the population.

Falls

Apart from automobile accidents, the majority of accidents occur in the home or in public places, and of these, falls are the most prevalent. Falls account for more accidental deaths than any other cause except automobile accidents and for over 60% of all accidental injuries. A 1978 study of accidental deaths found that almost 50% of those who died from falls had been drinking (Haberman and Baden). Other studies have shown that alcoholics are more likely to suffer falls and resulting death than the general population.

Occupational Accidents

Occupational accidents affect a significant portion of the working population. The role of alcohol in such accidents has not been well documented to date. Drinking-related industrial accidents may be lower than expected because of a high rate of absenteeism among those who might otherwise be involved (Trice). However, in simulated industrial work, alcohol was shown to inhibit coordination and judgment, lengthen reaction time, and decrease motor performance and sensory skill. Experiments demonstrated that alcohol intoxication could alter a normal person's performance up to 18 hours after the ingestion of alcohol (Wolkenberg et al.). A study of railroad workers by T. A. Mannello and F. J. Seaman estimated that 30,000 workers drank on duty on 90,000 occasions during one year.

Fires and Burns

Use of alcohol appears to be significantly involved in fires and burns, with alcoholics particularly vulnerable to fire. One study found that alcoholics were 10 times as likely to die in a fire as members of a standard comparison population (Schmidt and de-Lint). In a study that compared fire deaths with other deaths, it was found that alcohol was involved in 52% of adult fire deaths (Halpen et al.). Alcohol lowers oxidation in the cells, increasing an individual's risk of being overcome by smoke inhalation. The incidence of alcohol involvement is nearly three times greater in deaths from cigarette-caused fires then in deaths from fires resulting from other causes.

Drownings

Alcohol is reported to play a significant contributory role in drownings. During such recreational activities as boating and swimming, alcohol may be consumed frequently and in quantity. Higher consumption can lead to poor judgment, faulty coordination and lack of attention. Alcohol may also depress the swallowing and breathing reflexes and turn a normal situation into a dangerous one. After drinking swimmers may take more risks, and the "warming" effect of alcohol may cause people to stay in cold water too long.

Aviation Crashes

In pilots alcohol may encourage risk taking and daredevil stunts as well as inhibit psychomotor performance. A large percentage of pilots involved in general aviation crashes were found to have a high BLOOD ALCOHOL CONCENTRATION (Lacefield). (See also DRIVING WHILE INTOXICATED.)

B. Brenner, I. H. Cisin and C. Newcomb, "Drinking Practices and Accidental Injuries" (paper presented at a session on Alcohol Use and Accidents of the Society for the Study of Social Problems, Miami, Fl., 1966).

John R. DeLuca, ed., *Fourth Special Report to the U.S. Congress on Alcohol and Health* (Rockville, Md.: National Institute on Alcohol Abuse and Alcoholism, 1981), pp. 81–83.

P. W. Haberman and M. M. Baden, *Alcohol, Other Drugs and Violent Death* (New York: Oxford University Press, 1978), passim.

B. M. Halpen et al., "A Fire Fatality Study," *Fire Journal* 5 (1975): 11–13.

D. J. Lacefield, "Alcohol Continues to Play a Big Part in Plane Crashes," *Journal of the American Medical Association* 233 (1975): 405.

T. A. Mannello and F. J. Seaman, *Prevalence, Costs and Handling of Drinking Problems on Seven Railroads*, U.S. Department of Transportation, Federal Railroad Administration (Washington, D.C.: University Research Corporation, 1979), passim.

Joy Moser, *Prevention of Alcohol-Related Problems* (Toronto: World Health Organization, 1980), pp. 45–46.

W. Schmidt and J. deLint, "Cause of Death of

Alcoholics," *Quarterly Journal of Studies on Alcohol* 33, no. 1 (1972): 171–185.

Harrison M. Trice. "Work Accidents and the Problem Drinker," *I. L. R. Res,* 3, p.2

R. C. Wolkenberg, C. Gold and E. R. Tichauer, "Delayed Effects of Acute Alcoholic Intoxication on Performance with Reference to Work Safety," *Journal of Research Safety* 7 (1975): 104.

acetaldehyde   The first step in the METABOLISM of alcohol results in its conversion to acetaldehyde. Acetaldehyde is even more toxic to the body than ethyl alcohol, although in the second step of metabolism acetaldehyde is converted into acetate, most of which is oxidized to carbon dioxide by the MITOCHONDRIA. Nevertheless some escapes into the bloodstream, especially at high levels of consumption, and is thought to play a central role in the toxicity of alcohol. Alcoholics have been found to have significantly higher levels of acetaldehyde in the blood than nonalcoholics, even when both groups received the same amounts of alcohol and the BLOOD ALCOHOL CONCENTRATION of both was the same. Apparently alcoholics metabolize acetaldehyde less effectively, probably because of LIVER damage caused by excessive consumption of alcohol. Dr. Charles Lieber of the Mount Sinai School of Medicine in New York postulates that the alcoholic may be the victim of a vicious circle: mitochondrial function in the liver is impaired by acetaldehyde, which leads to diminished acetaldehyde metabolism, an accumulation of acetaldehyde and, consequently, further liver damage.

Acetaldehyde has been shown to affect the HEART muscle adversely and may affect other muscles as well. It may also be a contributing factor in ADDICTION to alcohol, by combining with amine neurotransmitters in the brain, which send nerve impulses from one cell to another, to form psychoactive compounds similar to certain morphine derivatives and known for their ability to promote DEPENDENCE. This theory has yet to be confirmed.

Acetaldehyde also plays an important part in ANTABUSE (disulfiram) reactions. Normally acetaldehyde, produced as a result of the initial oxidation of ethanol by the alcohol dehydrogenase of the liver, does not accumulate in the tissues because it is oxidized almost as soon as it is formed, "most likely primarily by the enzyme aldehyde dehydrogenase. In the presence of disulfiram, however, the concentration of acetaldehyde rises because disulfiram seems to compete with NAD [co-factor nicotinamide adenine dinucleotide] for the active centers of the enzyme aldehyde dehydrogenase and thereby reduces the rate of oxidation of the aldehyde" [Ritchie]. When someone taking Antabuse consumes alcohol, his or her blood acetaldehyde concentrations increase five to 10 times higher than normal, resulting in a toxic reaction. The degree of intensity of the reaction depends on the concentration of disulfiram in the body, the quantity of alcohol ingested and the patient's degree of sensitivity to acetaldehyde. The consumption of only 7 milligrams of alcohol (0.24 ounces) has produced a mild reaction in some people and even such products as rubbing alcohol have caused reactions. The Antabuse reaction is sometimes referred to as the acetaldehyde syndrome.

Charles S. Lieber, "The Metabolism of Alcohol," *Scientific American* 234, no. 3 (March 1976): 25–33.

J. M. Ritchie, "The Aliphatic Alcohols," in L. S. Goodman and A. Gilman, *The Pharmacological Basis of Therapeutics,* 5th ed. (New York: Macmillan Publishing Co., 1975), pp. 148–149.

Ackoff's model   The assignment of alcoholic patients to treatment facilities is often determined on the basis of where vacancies exist rather than where particular patients would receive the most effective type of treatment. Such assignments are made under "uncertainty conditions," in which the action leads to any one of a number of possible outcomes but the probability of success of the outcome is unknown.

Ackoff's model describes a method of problem solution for an "evaluative" problem (such as that of placing patients in treatment) where there are alternative courses of action, all of which are specified before the research begins. The problem is to select the best of the alternatives. When Ackoff's model is used, "uncertainty conditions" of assigning patients to the most effective treatment facilities can be changed to "risk conditions," in which the probable outcome of treatment can be determined for specific types of patients.

acne rosacea   (From the Greek *achne* efflorescence via New Latin + the New Latin *rosacea* rosy, reddish.) A facial skin condition usually characterized by a flushed appearance and often accompanied by puffiness and a "spider-web" effect of broken capillaries. Acne rosacea is frequently caused by excessive consumption of alcohol over a prolonged period. (See also RHINOPHYMA.)

acute   A term used to describe a disease or condition that develops quickly into a crisis, as distinguished from a CHRONIC disease or condition.

acute alcohol intoxication   Severe alcohol intoxication or poisoning. The term is also used to refer to a circumscribed episode of alcohol intoxication as distinguished from a chronic, or prolonged, state of intoxication.

acute alcoholic state   A physical or mental disorder of an alcoholic that is associated with and immediately follows a prolonged bout of drinking. This condition can take such forms as acute KORSAKOFF'S

PSYCHOSIS or DELIRIUM TREMENS. The term "acute alcoholic state" is also used, more generally, to refer to alcohol intoxication.

acute alcoholism   This term may refer to alcohol intoxication or poisoning, to the state of intoxication of an alcoholic or to a temporary disturbance caused by excessive drinking. Because alcoholism is generally recognized as a CHRONIC disease, the term is considered ambiguous and is thus seldom used.

adaptive cell metabolism   After a prolonged period of steady drinking, the tissue cells of an alcoholic adapt to the constant large quantity of alcohol consumed. This conditioning leads to increased tissue TOLERANCE, with the consequent onset of WITHDRAWAL. If a person's cells have adapted to high quantities of alcohol and alcohol is not supplied, a CRAVING may develop resulting in LOSS OF CONTROL or the INABILITY TO ABSTAIN. Adaptive cell metabolism is one factor in GAMMA ALCOHOLISM. (See also METABOLISM.)

addiction   The use of the term "addiction" has changed over the years, and even today there is considerable variation in (and often confusion about) its usage. In the early 20th century the term "drug addiction" simply referred to the illicit use of drugs, without any distinction between different patterns of drug use and the effects of various drugs. Beginning in 1931 drug HABITUATION was distinguished from drug addiction (Tatum and Seevers). Drug addiction came to mean physical dependence on the effects of a drug, with illness, or WITHDRAWAL, occurring if the intake of the drug was severely reduced or stopped completely. Habituation was viewed as psychological dependence on a drug after repeated use; withdrawal from a habituating drug might involve emotional distress but not physiological illness.

In 1957 the Expert Committee on Addiction-Producing Drugs of the World Health Organization defined drug addiction as

a state of periodic or chronic intoxication, detrimental to the individual and society, produced by the repeated consumption of a drug (natural or synthetic). Its characteristics include: 1. An overpowering desire or need (compulsion) to continue taking the drug and to obtain it by any means; 2. A tendency to increase the dose; 3. A psychic (psychological) and generally a physical dependence on the effects of the drug.

Drug habituation was defined as

a condition resulting from the repeated consumption of a drug. Its characteristics include: 1. A desire (but not a compulsion) to continue taking the drug for the sense of improved well-being which it engenders; 2. Little or no tendency to increase the dose; 3. Some degree of psychic dependence on the effect of the drug, but absence of physical dependence and hence of an abstinence syndrome; 4. Detrimental effects, if any, primarily on the individual.

The definitions did not clear up all the confusion surrounding these terms; for example, someone who took a large quantity of a stimulant drug might assault others, thereby invalidating the fourth part of the definition of habituation. The word "addicted" (or "addiction" or "addict") was used both benignly, as in "He's addicted to jazz," and pejoratively, as in "He's been addicted to drugs for years."

In 1965 the World Health Organization abandoned these terms and adopted the more neutral term "drug dependence." This term was defined in a very general way:

A state, psychic and sometimes also physical, resulting from the interaction between a living organism and a drug, characterized by behavioral and other responses that always include a compulsion

to take the drug on a continuous or periodic basis in order to experience its psychic effects, and sometimes to avoid the discomfort of its absence. Tolerance may or may not be present. A person may be dependent on more than one drug.

Still used frequently today, the term "addiction" is generally employed to refer to a known physical dependence on the effects of a drug. JELLINEK, for example, uses the following terms in describing an addiction to alcohol: an increased tissue TOLERANCE, ADAPTIVE CELL METABOLISM, WITHDRAWAL SYMPTOMS, CRAVING, and LOSS OF CONTROL or INABILITY TO ABSTAIN.

Physical dependence, or the adaptive consequences of taking certain chemicals repeatedly, is clearly not the only aspect of addiction, however. As Dr. Vincent P. Dole has pointed out, physical dependence does not explain the drug-seeking behavior characteristic of addiction. People can be physically dependent on drugs without being addicted to them. For example, drugs prescribed for medicinal purposes, such as steroids, can give rise to physical dependence without causing a desire for the substance. When intake is optional, most users stop or reduce consumption. On the other hand, addicts who have been freed of their dependence through DETOXIFICATION usually relapse. Unfortunately those definitions that include some concept of psychological dependence are unable to explain such behavior.

Dole, who has worked extensively as a physician and an administrator in the methadone program in New York and in addiction research, found that former heroin addicts stabilized on methadone did not have the pleasure-seeking, reality-escaping traits generally associated with addicts. Addicts with a history of two or more years of addiction to heroin seemed to be quite willing to sacrifice the occasional euphoria produced by the drug for a continued feeling of normality. For Dole this finding suggested that the addictive behavior of chronic users of narcotics stemmed less from pleasure seeking than from a need to relieve a recurring discomfort. The same need may also be true for people who are unable to stop smoking or excessive drinking.

Vincent P. Dole, "Addictive Behavior," *Scientific American* 243, no. 6 (December 1980):138–154.

Frederick G. Hofmann, *A Handbook on Drug and Alcohol Abuse: The Biomedical Aspects* (New York: Oxford University Press, 1975), pp. 21–27.

Jerome Jaffe, Robert Petersen and Ray Hodgson, *Addictions: Issues and Answers* (London: Harper and Row, 1980), pp. 7–9.

E. M. Jellinek, *The Disease Concept of Alcoholism* (New Jersey: Hillhouse Press, 1979), pp. 69–77.

A. L. Tatum and M. H. Seevers, "Theories of Drug Addiction," *The Physiological Review* 11 (1931):187.

addictive drinker   See ADDICTION.

addictive drinking   See ADDICTION.

additive effect   See SYNERGY.

advertising   In many countries advertising of alcoholic beverages is considered at least partially responsible for increases in alcohol consumption levels. There are wide differences in opinion on the effect of such advertising, from the belief that a free-enterprise system should impose no restrictions on advertising to the view that government (in the public interest) should ban all alcohol advertising, as Sweden has done. The middle position holds that trade associations should impose their own restrictions to ward off government regulation. The Wine Institute, the Distilled Spirits Council of the United States and the United States Brewers Association have adopted codes for advertising. The middle viewpoint is also reflected by bills in the Michigan legislature and the U.S. Congress that favor allocation of a set percentage of commercial time to explain the dangers of alcohol abuse.

In the United States, advertising of distilled spirits on radio and television is prohibited. Beer and wine advertisements must be "presented in the best of good taste and discretion" and are subject to federal, state and local laws. One generally accepted restriction on television advertising is that all beer and wine commercials avoid any representation of drinking on the screen. Although frowned upon, sexual appeals, appeals to youth etc. are common in much alcohol advertising, but the alcohol industry and television producers appear, reluctantly, responsive to tightening up self-imposed regulations.

Beer, wine and liquor advertisements, including prices, are allowed in all print media. Each state has its own regulations on the type and size of storefront and billboard signs advertising alcoholic beverages. State regulations may be further restricted by local ordinances (Moser).

Advertising expenditures and liquor sales volume have risen proportionally since the 1950s, even when consumption is adjusted for increases in the total U.S. population or the legal-age drinking population *(The Liquor Handbook)*. Whether increased advertising causes increased sales or increased sales cause increased advertising or both is open to debate. Many factors besides advertising may account for the rising consumption of alcohol, and these may interact with whatever effects advertising has on consumption behavior. Such factors include the decreasing relative price of alcohol, growing affluence, a youth market created by the postwar baby boom, women's liberation, an increasing trend in communities from DRY to WET and the lowering of legal minimum-age requirements.

Advertising aims at achieving higher sales by attracting three types of purchasers: completely new buyers, new-to-the-brand buyers and brand-loyal buyers. There are also attempts to increase the level of purchasing among brand-loyal buyers and to decrease the number of buyers who switch to other products.

Most advertising is directed at drinkers, especially heavy drinkers, rather than nondrinkers. Heavy drinkers are the most important consumers of alcoholic beverages and account for a disproportionate share of product purchases and usage.

From 1974 to 1977 advertising expenditures for alcohol jumped from $310 million to $492 million. A 1977 analysis found that alcohol advertising in women's magazines increased dramatically from 1970 to 1974. For example, in 1970 *Glamour* contained three alcohol ads annually. By 1974 it had 61 pages devoted exclusively to alcohol advertising. The liquor industry accounts for one out of every 10 dollars spent on magazine advertising. (Such expenditures are tax-deductible business expenses.) In 1981 *Playboy* had the largest number of pages per issue devoted to alcohol advertising and *Psychology Today* was second.

Following a precedent set by the antismoking campaign, such groups as the National Safety Council and the National Council on Alcoholism have sponsored some counteradvertising. Studies by the Federal Trade Commission have shown that counteradvertising has had a significant impact both on reducing the number of people who started smoking and those who quit. For countercommercials to be effective they must be aired during prime time—frequently and repeatedly— either through revision of regulations now governing public service announcements or through purchase of airtime. As with regular commercials segmentation of the market according to drinking patterns, behavioral tendencies, value patterns and media behavior is essential for the creation of messages with maximum impact (Blane and Hewitt). When messages are not aired properly or targeted at specific populations, the results may backfire. A recent San Francisco counter-commercial attempt failed because a high proportion of the audience thought the ads were promoting consumption.

The liquor industry has been fairly active in public education campaigns that stress moderate and responsible use of alcohol. In 1980 Sam D. Chilcote, president of the Distilled Spirits Council of the United States, testifying before a Senate Subcommittee on Alcoholism and Drug Abuse on the issue of consumer warning labels, stated that in 1980 distilling companies would spend $50 million on advertising a message of moderation.

Howard T. Blane and Linda E. Hewitt, "Alcohol, Public Education, and Mass Media: An Overview," *Alcohol Health and Research World* 5, no. 1 (Fall 1980): 2–13.

The Liquor Handbook, 1975 (New York: Gavin-Jobson Associates, 1975).

Joy Moser, *Prevention of Alcohol Related Problems* (Toronto: World Health Organization, 1980), p. 123.

Bonnie Orr, "The Unselling of Alcohol," *Alcoholism* 2, no. 1 (September/October 1981): 36–38.

aging   See ELDERLY.

Al-Anon   Al-Anon, officially known as the Al-Anon Family Groups, is an organization designed to help the relatives and friends of alcoholics. Its philosophy, program and structure correspond to the related organization ALCOHOLICS ANONYMOUS, although the two operate independently.

History

During the early days of Alcoholics Anonymous family members of alcoholics used to attend the regular AA meetings. In 1951 relatives of AA members in and near New York City formed a Clearing House Committee; one of the founders was Lois Wilson, wife of Bill Wilson, who started

AA. The original staff members were volunteers. The committee adopted the name Al-Anon Family Groups and slightly modified the 12 Steps and 12 Traditions of AA as principles for Al-Anon members (see "The Twelve Steps" and "The Twelve Traditions" under ALCOHOLICS ANONYMOUS). By 1954 Al-Anon had grown enormously; it was publishing a monthly newsletter, *The Forum,* and had affiliated groups abroad. It was incorporated as a nonprofit unit under the title The Al-Anon Family Group Headquarters, Inc.

In 1967 delegates from Al-Anon groups across North America attended the first World Service Conference, which has become an annual event. In 1970 Twelve Concepts of Service, explaining the structure of Al-Anon, were adopted. Today the headquarters' office is known as the World Service Office (WSO), which assists more than 13,600 registered Al-Anon and ALATEEN groups. Over 2,600 of these groups are in other countries. Al-Anon literature is available in 17 languages and there are nearly 2,000 Spanish-speaking Al-Anon groups worldwide.

Organization

The only requirement for membership in Al-Anon is to have a relative or friend who is an alcoholic. The alcoholic may belong to AA, may still be drinking, or may be no longer drinking and not in AA. (Alcoholics may be members of Al-Anon if they have friends or relatives who are alcoholic.) Some members of Al-Anon may have stopped living with the alcoholic but may feel that their lives have been so strongly affected by their former association that Al-Anon can help them. Both men and women attend Al-Anon meetings, but in some cities there are special groups: some composed solely of women, others of homosexuals.

Al-Anon meetings are structured in the same way as AA meetings. A chairman or leader opens and closes the meeting and generally leads discussion on a central theme. There are no dues; groups are self-supporting through voluntary contributions.

Philosophy

Al-Anon members are taught that they are responsible only for their own reactions and responses to what the alcoholic does and not for the actions of the alcoholic. The primary purpose of the organization is not to stop the alcoholic from drinking but to help his or her family or friends. Members are taught neither to interfere actively with the alcoholic's drinking nor to protect the alcoholic from the consequences of drinking. The assumption is that the alcoholic will be forced to a point where the effects of his or her drinking have become so severe that he or she will be motivated to stop voluntarily. Meanwhile Al-Anon members focus on their own needs in their relationships with other family members.

Comments and Criticisms

Al-Anon may not be acceptable to those who object to its implicitly religious orientation or those who are not willing to attend many meetings and participate in a formal group discussion. While Al-Anon does provide peer counseling and support and an opportunity to see that others share the same problems, GROUP THERAPY can also provide the same things and may be more suited to some people. Critics have complained about the rigidity of the concepts taught at Al-Anon meetings. Members have been severely chastised because they mentioned interfering directly with a spouse's drinking or undergoing professional counseling (Lavino and Kay). Al-Anon teaches a program of "detachment with love," which can sometimes serve as an excuse for walking away from a situation rather than effectively dealing with it. The organization also emphasizes keeping the family together at all costs rather than looking after the health of individual family members.

The almost complete separation of Al-Anon from AA can sometimes create isolated approaches to family problems. It has also been pointed out that Al-Anon and Alateen have not adequately met the needs of people aged 18 to 25 who are single or recently married with no children. Another source of criticism is that over the years most Al-Anon groups have been primarily composed of women and little has been done to attract the husbands of alcoholic women.

Al-Anon Family Group Headquarters, *Al-Anon Faces Alcoholism* (New York, 1977).
Al-Anon Family Group Headquarters, *Living with an Alcoholic with the Help of Al-Anon* (New York, 1978).
John Lavino and Mary Ellen Kay, "The Kemper/Al-Anon Program," *Alcoholism* 1, no. 3 (January/February 1981):46–47.

Alateen   Alateen was started in 1957 by a boy in California whose father was an alcoholic in ALCOHOLICS ANONYMOUS (AA) and whose mother was in AL-ANON. Alateen was patterned after Al-Anon and shares with it the same Twelve Steps and Twelve Traditions, but it is designed for teenagers from 12 to 20 who have been affected by someone, usually a parent, with a drinking problem. It is not necessary that the drinker be in AA.

Alateen meetings are conducted by teenagers, although an active adult member of Al-Anon acts as a sponsor. The sponsor, who is generally not a parent of any of the Alateen members, guides the group and shares knowledge of the Twelve Steps and Twelve Traditions. Emotional detachment is stressed—the teenager is taught to suspend emotional involvement with the alcoholic's problems. When older, Alateen members are encouraged to join Al-Anon.

There are now over 2,000 Alateen groups. They have their own bimonthly newsletter, *Alateen: Hope for Children of Alcoholics*. They also have conventions and Alateen Loner's Service for teens who live where there are no groups.

alcohol abuse   See ABUSE.

alcohol addict   A person addicted to alcohol (see ADDICTION).

alcohol addiction   See ADDICTION.

alcohol amblyopia   (From Greek *amblys* dim + *ops* eye.) A rare disorder of the eye, alcohol amblyopia usually occurs in alcoholics with a lengthy history of severe drinking problems. The disease begins slowly with a slight vision impairment that becomes progressively worse. The visual failure is not caused by lesions of the eye or refractive error but is believed to be due to a toxic reaction in the orbital portion of the optic nerve. The typical complaint is a painless blurring of vision over a period of several weeks with reduced sharpness for both near and distant objects. Generally changes are relatively symmetrical in both eyes and, if not treated adequately, may be followed by optic nerve degeneration. Treatment consists of administration of VITAMINS AND MINERALS. With proper care and NUTRITION the symptoms are usually reversible. The disease is most common in male alcoholics who are also smokers.

alcohol as medicine   See MEDICATION.

alcohol concentration   The proportion of alcohol in a tissue or fluid expressed as volume or weight of alcohol per volume or weight of fluid or tissue. (See also BLOOD ALCOHOL CONCENTRATION.)

alcohol discharge rate   For a given hospital subpopulation or category, the alcohol discharge rate is the number of alcohol-related discharges divided by the total number of discharges multiplied by

100,000. (Discharge is the formal release of a patient from a hospital.) An alcohol discharge is classified by the National Center for Health Statistics as a discharge given to a person who has at least one of the following diseases: a type of alcoholic psychosis, such as DELIRIUM TREMENS, KORSAKOFF'S PSYCHOSIS, or other alcoholic hallucinosis, alcoholic paranoia or other, unspecified psychosis; CIRRHOSIS of the LIVER (alcohol); ALCOHOLISM manifested by episodic excessive drinking, habitual excessive drinking or alcoholic ADDICTION or other, unspecified alcoholism; toxic effect of ethyl alcohol; or acute or chronic pancreatitis (see PANCREAS).

The alcohol discharge rate is a significant index of alcohol abuse and alcoholism and, when used in conjunction with other indices, can be used to determine the approximate alcoholic population at any given time. However, it has limitations: only those who have gone for treatment are counted,

and some patients may go for more than one treatment. The following graphs, compiled by the National Institute on Alcohol

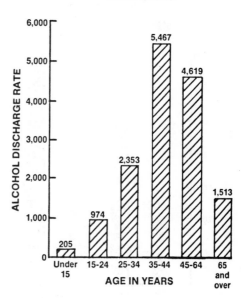

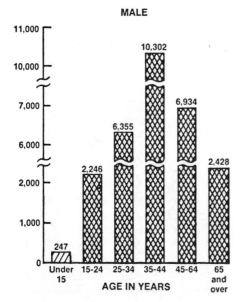

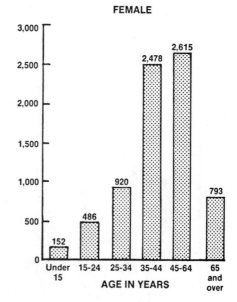

Alcohol Discharge Rate by Age: United States, 1976

Abuse and Alcoholism, are based upon 223,000 sample discharges from 511 short-stay nonfederal hospitals that mainly serve the civilian noninstitutionalized population.

U.S. Department of Health and Human Services, *Utilization of Short-Stay Hospitals by Persons Discharged with Alcohol-Related Diagnoses, United States, 1976* (Hyattsville, Md., 1980), pp. 1–34.

alcohol impairment   See IMPAIRMENT.

alcohol intoxication   See INTOXICATION.

alcohol pathology   Any morbid physical damage caused by the direct or indirect effects of alcohol consumption. This term is sometimes used to refer to individual harm caused by the ABUSE of alcohol.

alcohol tolerance   See TOLERANCE.

alcoholic beverage   Any beverage containing alcohol. (See individual entries for WINE, BEER, GIN and other specific beverages.)

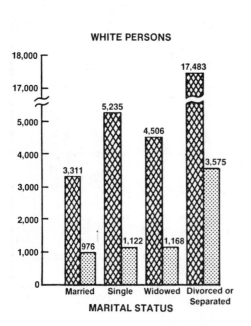

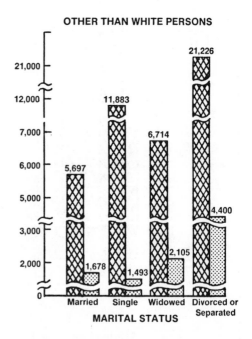

Alcohol Discharge Rate by Sex and Marital Status: United States, 1976

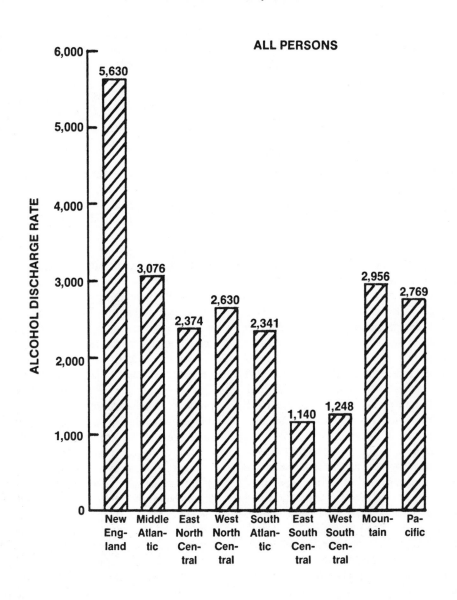

Alcohol Discharge Rate by Census Division: United States, 1976

alcoholic beverage control laws (ABC laws)   Society's control of the availability of alcohol dates back many thousands of years. The Code of Hammurabi, for example, formulated almost 4,000 years ago, contained four articles on the topic. The usual purpose of such laws was to prevent the fraudulent sale of alcohol, to assure availability and to secure revenue for the state.

In the United States, after the repeal of PROHIBITION, the emphasis was changed to prevention of alcohol abuse and promotion of temperance. But gradually alcoholic beverage control agencies again became primarily concerned with maintaining an orderly market and collecting revenue for government treasuries. Concern over the effects of regulation on consumption gave way to questions about the impact of regulation on the economics of the industry. However, because of the recognition that in the past 30 years there has been an increase in per capita consumption of alcoholic beverages in conjunction with liberalized control laws, more attention today is being paid to the possible preventative aspects of ABC laws. A debate has arisen in the field between those who believe that more stringent controls are necessary to curtail alcohol abuse and those who believe that these laws are not very effective and ignore the complex cultural, psychological, biological and social forces involved in problem drinking.

Supporters of increased legislation point to a number of studies that present evidence of a connection between an increase in the overall level of consumption in a population, the prevalence of heavy consumption and the rate of long-term health consequences of drinking, such as CIRRHOSIS. These findings, which show a direct relationship between the per capita consumption for all drinkers and the proportion of heavy users, seem to contradict the DISEASE CONCEPT, which holds that alcoholism affects only people who have some particular underlying physical or psychological problem. Studies in Norway, Finland, Canada and other nations have shown that when consumption of alcohol was suppressed (for instance, during a period of prohibition or a war), the rate of alcohol-related mortality and morbidity sharply decreased. Advocates of regulation feel that vulnerability to alcohol dependence is a widely shared trait. While controls on alcohol are not popular, supporters of regulation believe that it will result in a healthier life for those who might otherwise be addicted and thus promote individual freedom. They cite examples of governments intervening to safeguard public health in such areas as food, drugs and water.

Opponents of stricter restraints claim they will lead to increased costs for the state, resentment of the system by nonproblem drinkers, increased use of toxic substitutes by at least some heavy users of alcohol, and the growth of illicit alcohol trade with attendant criminality, expense and difficulties for law enforcement agencies, loss of revenue by producers, sellers and government, loss of respect for the law through widespread evasion, and loss or substantial reduction of personal benefits derived from alcohol use (Aldoory). In spite of some of the toughest drinking laws in the world, the United States has a growing alcoholism problem, which, according to opponents of increased regulation, casts doubt on the effectiveness of local control laws in altering or controlling established drinking habits. Overly restrictive laws, they point out, work in opposition to primary prevention programs based on the promotion of responsible use of alcohol by individuals. Some suggest that educating the public and providing the information needed for responsible decisions about drinking are more effective measures than controlling availability.

A large number of agencies at the federal, state and local levels are responsible for making regulations and enforcing laws relating to drinking. Laws vary a great deal from state to state and from county to county within individual states. To date there has been little data on whether or not restrictions governing alcoholic beverage sales have any significant local effects.

In the United States there are two major types of control system: the monopoly system and the license system. Under the monopoly system the state operates all or part of the wholesale and retail sale of alcohol; under the license system the state creates a partial monopoly for private enterprises by restricting competition. Control is exercised through the threat of license revocation. Comparisons of the two systems have found few significant differences in the area of alcohol consumption and alcohol-related problems, but so far no study has been able to reach significant conclusions about the comparative effects of the two systems.

Outlets

The most frequently employed means of controlling availability throughout history has been regulation of the number of places where alcoholic beverages can be purchased. Particularly targeted have been outlets for on-premise consumption. There are two divergent opinions on the effects of controls on places permitted to sell alcohol: an increase in opportunities to drink results in more drinking and drunkenness; and a widespread availability will promote moderate and civilized drinking. Some studies have concluded that the prevalence of drunkenness is not dependent on the number of outlets, but this conclusion does not hold where there is either extremely low accessibility or where a low accessibility situation changes to one of high accessibility.

States also have regulations that specify the location and kind of outlet which can be operated, that require food to be served with alcohol, that allow only wine and beer to be served and so on. These regulations vary widely from area to area. Limits on closing time, which also vary, have been shown to affect the time when motor vehicle accidents occur, but total consumption and the frequency of consumption generally seem to remain unaffected by closing-hour regulations. Early closing times may simply make the home a more attractive place in which to drink.

Age

States also regulate age limits. Many states have lowered their legal drinking age to 18 or 19, while others have kept it at 21. Richard L. Douglass, senior researcher at the University of Michigan, found that after Michigan reduced the legal drinking age to 18 in 1972, alcohol-related casualties increased significantly for 18- to 20-year-olds. Total consumption of alcohol also rose. Michigan's drinking age has since been restored to 21.

Pricing and Taxation

Economic considerations may affect drinking behavior. There are many advocates of such economic measures as increased prices and taxation of alcoholic beverages as a means of controlling and preventing alcohol problems. Data on the impact of pricing and taxation of alcoholic beverages have been inconclusive, but it is evident that they do have some effect. There are federal, state and local taxes on alcohol. The federal excise tax on liquor in the United States is $10.50 per gallon. Some support a doubling of the excise tax and use of the funds for the prevention and treatment of alcoholism. Regulation through pricing and taxation is unpopular with the public and the liquor industry.

Other Controls

Other regulatory controls include laws prohibiting sales to obviously intoxicated persons (known as DRAM SHOP LAWS), laws governing DRIVING WHILE INTOXICATED and PUBLIC DRUNKENNESS and laws protecting

the rights of alcoholics. (See also LEGAL AS-
PECTS OF ALCOHOL ABUSE.)

"Alcohol Controls Unfashionable but Neces-
sary," *The U.S. Journal of Drug and Alco-
hol Dependence* 5, no. 9 (October 1981):8.
Shirley Aldoory, "ABC Laws: An Overview,"
Alcohol Health and Research World 4, no. 2
(Winter 1979–80):2–10.
Richard L. Douglass, "The Legal Drinking Age
and Traffic Casualties," *Alcohol Health and
Research World* 4, no. 2 (Winter 1979–
80):19–25.
John R. DeLuca, ed., *Fourth Special Report to
the U.S. Congress on Alcohol and Health*
(Rockville, Md.: National Institute on Al-
cohol Abuse and Alcoholism, 1981), pp.
105–107.
Ralph O. Lidman and Jean Shields, "Upping
the User Ante," *Alcoholism* 2, no. 3 (Janu-
ary/February 1982):38–39.
David Joshua Pittman, *Primary Prevention of
Alcohol Abuse and Alcoholism: An Evalua-
tion of the Control of Consumption Policy*
(St. Louis, Mo.: Social Science Institute,
Washington University, 1980), passim.
Robin Room and James F. Mosher, "Out of the
Shadow of Treatment: A Role for Regula-
tory Agencies in the Prevention of Alcohol
Problems," *Alcohol Health and Research
World* 4, no. 2 (Winter 1979–80):11–18.

alcoholic cirrhosis   See CIRRHOSIS.

alcoholic disease   Any disease, mental or physical, caused by the effects of excessive alcohol consumption, including CIR-
RHOSIS, DELIRIUM TREMENS, KORSAKOFF'S
PSYCHOSIS. (See also DISEASES.)

alcoholic hepatitis   A disease of the
liver characterized by inflammation and ne-
crosis (cell death), alcoholic hepatitis can
develop abruptly in alcoholics after a severe
drinking bout. Its appearance may be accompanied by fever, jaundice and abnormal
accumulation of fluid in the abdominal cavity. Fatty infiltration and increased FIBRO-

SIS of the liver are frequent but not constant
symptoms of this disease.

The mortality rate for those with severe
alcoholic hepatitis is high, ranging from
10% to 30%. Some pass rapidly from alcoholic hepatitis to CIRRHOSIS and others recover normal liver function. Most in danger
are alcoholics with few or no symptoms who
continue to drink. Treatment of alcoholic
hepatitis consists of bed rest, a high-protein
diet and a multivitamin regimen.

Alcoholic hyaline, a clear glassy substance, is often found in the livers of patients with alcoholic hepatitis. Hyaline deposits may be a result of the degenerative
effects of alcohol on subcellular structures
called microtubules, which are important to
the secretory activity of the liver cells.

alcoholic liver disease   A general
category that encompasses a number of alcohol-induced liver diseases. The *Merck
Manual* defines alcoholic liver disease as "a
variety of syndromes and pathologic
changes of the liver caused by alcohol."
There is still some debate on exactly how
alcohol damages the liver, but both nutritional factors (see NUTRITION) and direct
toxicity are known to play a role. The development of alcoholic liver disease has
been directly related to the quantity and duration of drinking, although there is a variation in the susceptibility of different
individuals.

In its initial and milder form, alcoholic
liver disease is characterized by an accumulation of excess fat on the liver, called,
appropriately, FATTY LIVER. This is the most
common disease of the liver found in hospitalized alcoholics. A more serious form of
liver disease, which may or may not be
linked with a fatty liver, is known as ALCO-
HOLIC HEPATITIS, which has a mortality rate
ranging from 10% to 30%. This disease occurs when a number of liver cells die and
cause inflammation.

The most severe form of liver injury is
CIRRHOSIS, which is irreversible (though not

always fatal). It is characterized by scarring of the liver with fibrous tissue and breakdown of the liver structure. While the progression from hepatitis to cirrhosis is generally accepted, the relationship between alcoholic fatty liver and alcoholic hepatitis and cirrhosis is still under debate. Not all alcoholics with fatty liver develop cirrhosis, and fat buildup is not always present with cirrhosis. However, fatty infiltration is frequently seen in association with more advanced alcoholic liver diseases, and the ultrastructural changes found in the early stages of alcoholic fatty liver are identical to those evident in more severe alcoholic liver diseases.

There are a number of misconceptions concerning alcoholic liver disease. One is that liver damage must be accompanied by symptoms of illness after drinking. Another is that drinking is safe provided an individual does not have a physical DEPENDENCY on alcohol. Development of liver disease is directly related to the abuse of alcohol as measured by duration and dosage. Social drinking, particularly heavy drinking short of alcoholism (see HEAVY DRINKER), can result in damage to the liver. A third misconception is that cheap wine and liquor are more harmful to the liver than beer. The important factor is the amount of alcohol consumed. The toxic impurities that may be present in cheap alcoholic beverages are minute in relation to the ethanol content. The belief that an adequate diet will protect a heavy drinker from liver injury is also fallacious. While malnutrition may contribute to liver damage, many individuals with more than adequate diets have had severe liver disease.

It is essential that the diseased patient stop drinking alcohol. Much of alcoholic liver disease is completely reversible, and patients with a more advanced form of the disease who stop drinking have a better chance of survival than those who continue. This may be particularly true for women. A study conducted in 1977 in Britain showed that after five years 72% of male patients with alcoholic hepatitis or cirrhosis who continued to drink were alive but only 30% of female patients with those diseases who continued to drink were still alive.

In 1981 a team of researchers funded by the Addiction Research Foundation and headed by Dr. Yedy Israel found that when large amounts of alcohol are consumed over a long period of time, the individual liver cells expand, squeezing the fine blood vessels that form a network throughout the liver. This squeezing can block the flow of blood, causing stress on these vessels and can sometimes lead to rupture and internal bleeding. The researchers also suspect that the pressure of the swollen liver cells may trigger the formation of fibrous tissue around the blood vessels, which would prevent the exchange of materials between the bloodstream and liver cells. This presents a whole new concept of the cause of mortality from liver disease, because it suggests that it is the size of the liver cells and condition of the blood vessels that indicate the health of the organ, not the presence or absence of a diagnosed liver disease, such as cirrhosis or alcoholic hepatitis. This theory also offers some hope, for while cirrhosis is not reversible, the swelling of the cells and blood vessels is, provided the alcoholic stops drinking. Researchers are continuing their studies to determine why liver cells enlarge.

alcoholic muscle disease   See ALCOHOLIC MYOPATHY.

alcoholic myopathy (alcoholic muscle disease)   A condition recognized only in the past 25 years, alcoholic myopathy is associated with changes in muscle tissue. Although the cause of the disease, which occurs in several forms, is unknown, it is clear that alcohol is the primary factor in its development. Generally, if the patient stops drinking, the prognosis for all forms of alcoholic myopathy is good, and improvement occurs even in the most severe cases.

Subclinical Myopathy

It has been estimated that subclinical myopathy affects more than one-third of the alcoholic population. Because patients with this disease may not complain of muscular symptoms, it is difficult to detect. Subclinical myopathy is indicated by increased levels of the enzyme creatine phosphokinase (CPK), which is considered to be of muscle cell origin, in the blood. In addition there is frequently a rise in lactic acid. Alcoholic patients may be otherwise asymptomatic, although some may have a history of muscle cramps. Subclinical myopathy may progress to more severe forms of myopathy.

Acute Alcoholic Myopathy

This disease usually appears abruptly in chronic alcoholics. It is characterized by severe muscle cramps that vary in frequency or by muscle pain and swelling. The cramps usually occur in the arms and legs. Acute alcoholic myopathy is usually localized and relatively benign, and recovery is possible if the patient abstains from alcohol.

Chronic Alcoholic Myopathy

Associated with heavy drinking over many years, chronic alcoholic myopathy is a slowly progressive disease characterized by weakness and muscle atrophy, most often in the legs, although the symptoms may appear anywhere in the body. It can be alleviated if the patient abstains from alcohol.

alcoholic poisoning   An abnormal condition resulting from an extreme state of alcohol INTOXICATION, from which it differs only in degree. Dr. Mark Keller of the Rutgers Center of Alcohol Studies suggests that a BLOOD ALCOHOL CONCENTRATION above 0.4% indicates the occurrence of poisoning.

alcoholic polyneuropathy (peripheral neuritis)   (From *poly-* many + *neuro-* nerve + *-pathy* disease.) A disease of the nervous system, alcoholic polyneuropathy is thought to be caused by a thiamine deficiency, although its origin is still undetermined. It develops slowly, over months and years, affecting first and most severely the lower legs, where numbness and pain may develop. In some cases these symptoms are absent, and diagnosis is made on the basis of muscle wasting, tenderness of the calves of the legs and signs of impaired motor function. In time these symptoms may progress to the upper extremities as well. Partial recovery from this disease may take years and some permanent physical impairment is frequent.

alcoholic psychosis   Any mental disorder caused by the effects of alcohol consumption on the system, including DELIRIUM TREMENS, KORSAKOFF'S PSYCHOSIS and WERNICKE'S ENCEPHALOPATHY. (See also DISEASES.)

Alcoholic Treatment Center (ATC) Funded by the National Institute on Alcohol Abuse and Alcoholism, these centers offer treatment in three major settings: hospital, intermediate and outpatient. The system allows DETOXIFICATION to be followed up by longer outpatient or halfway-house care. Having different modes of treatment in the same place enables a center to fit the type of treatment to the client's needs.

David J. Armor, J. Michael Polich and Harriet B. Stambul of the Rand Corporation Social Science Department divide the types of treatment into 10 major categories, as follows:

Hospital Setting

1. *Inpatient hospital:* traditional 24-hour service based on a medical model but often including psychotherapy.

2. *Partial hospitalization:* partial service that allows the patient to go home or to work at appropriate times.
3. *Detoxification:* a short "drying out" period for patients with serious toxic symptoms.

Intermediate Setting

4. *Halfway house:* living quarters and services, such as job counseling, psychotherapy etc., for patients who need extended care but do not require hospital treatment.
5. *Quarterway house:* similar to a halfway house but offering more intensive, often physical care under more structured conditions.
6. *Residential care:* living quarters but little or no other therapy.

Outpatient Setting

7. *Individual counseling:* treatment sessions given by a paraprofessional (someone without a graduate degree in psychology, medicine, social work or a similar relevant field).
8. *Individual therapy:* treatment sessions given by a professional.
9. *Group counseling:* group sessions given by a paraprofessional.
10. *Group therapy:* group sessions given by a professional.

Most clients at an ATC receive a combination of treatments. Usually hospital care is quite short and intermediate care extends over a much longer period.

David J. Armor, J. Michael Polich and Harriet B. Stambul, *Alcoholism and Treatment* (New York: John Wiley and Sons, 1978), pp. 124–126.

Alcoholics Anonymous (AA) Alcoholics Anonymous is an international nonprofessional organization of alcoholics devoted to the maintenance of the sobriety of its members through self-help and mutual support; it was founded in the United States in 1935. The organization defines its purpose as follows:

> Alcoholics Anonymous is a fellowship of men and women who share their experience, strength and hope with each other that they may solve their common problem and help others to recover from alcoholism.
>
> The only requirement for membership is a desire to stop drinking. There are no dues or fees for AA membership; we are self-supporting through our own contributions. AA is not allied with any sect, denomination, politics, organization or institution; does not wish to engage in any controversy, neither endorses nor opposes any causes. Our primary purpose is to stay sober and help other alcoholics to achieve sobriety.

This "desire to stop drinking" is at the core of the AA program. Membership in a group is voluntary but AA groups, despite their loose organizational structure and concern for anonymity, are remarkably cohesive and able to provide substantial support for (or exert strong pressure on) members in order to maintain their SOBRIETY

Estimated Drug Addiction Among Members of Alcoholics Anonymous (1980)

	Those 30 Yrs. or Less	Those Coming to A.A. Since Last Survey	Total Sample
Women	63%	35%	34%
Men	51%	24%	20%
All	55%	27%	24%
(1977)			
Women	55%	29%	28%
Men	36%	15%	14%
All	43%	19%	18%

Source: General Service Office, Alcoholics Anonymous.

Alcoholics Anonymous Membership

	Reported Membership of U.S. and Canadian Groups	Size of Sample
1968	170,000	11,355
1971	210,000	7,194
1974	331,000	13,467
1977	404,000	15,163
1980	476,000	24,950

Source: General Service Office, Alcoholics Anonymous.

and ensure continued attendance at meetings. (For this purpose, as in many other areas, AA has a slogan: "Don't drink and go to meetings.")

A new member is asked if he has admitted to himself that he is "powerless over alcohol" and if he is ready to accept his problem. "Surrender" is a word often used in this regard, not in the sense of capitulating to the influence of alcohol or alcoholism but of surrendering to the fact that he cannot cope with alcohol and that he must stop pretending that he can (see DENIAL).

New members are urged to come to 90 meetings in 90 days, a crash program designed to provide maximum support during what is regarded as a dangerous time. They are exhorted to immerse themselves thoroughly in AA participation and are warmly received for having admitted past pride and failure. They are led to recognize their need for AA and to embrace its principles enthusiastically. Skepticism, questioning of AA methods and stories about those who have stayed sober without the help of AA are discouraged.

Each new member is urged to select a "sponsor," an experienced AA member in whom the newly sober beginner can confide on a continuing, individual basis. Members often contact their sponsor on a daily basis, seeking advice or, of even more immediate importance, asking for help when the temptation to drink becomes intense. Another form of AA counseling is known as "twelve-

stepping." Two AA members—always two to provide mutual support—will visit someone who is drinking, either a member or nonmember, and try to persuade him to seek help, which may or may not include medical help and professional therapy. The ultimate goal is to bring the individual into, or back into, AA and into sobriety.

Meetings are generally informal sessions. After customary business, announcements and voluntary collections are taken care of, a speaker addresses the group on some aspect of alcoholism, usually from an autobiographical point of view. The talk is followed by a period in which those who wish to be heard have an opportunity to speak. Sometimes all or part of the meeting is run like an "Australian meeting," in which everyone in attendance is called upon to either speak or "pass."

Living "the AA way" includes not only regular attendance at meetings and close contact with one's sponsor but a relationship with the "higher power." In the early days of AA (and in the Twelve Steps), this higher power was identified as God ("as you understand Him"). However, as AA has grown to include those whose religious beliefs range from strict fundamentalism to atheism, the concept of the higher power has been broadened, for some members, to include a rather general sense of spirituality or some spiritual resource within the individual. For others this new concept of the higher power has been extended to an entity outside of the normal religious organizations, such as a therapy group or, particularly, AA itself.

The AA member is encouraged to keep his problem as simple as possible and to avoid blowing it up to unmanageable proportions. He does not promise to stop drinking for all time but to "stay away from just one drink for just one day at a time." This stress on simplicity is reflected in the variety of slogans—"easy does it," "first things first," "stick to the program"—designed to help the alcoholic stay out of situations that might hurt him or cause him anxiety or anger. New members are urged not to make serious changes in their lives, except in the case of those aspects that would endanger their sobriety if continued. Major career changes, possibly stressful new relationships with the opposite sex and situations where alcohol is served or even available are to be avoided. The new member is encouraged to focus his social activity on AA and, whenever possible, to place strict limits on his outside social contacts. At the end of each successful day, he is urged to thank his higher power.

AA and Its Critics

Within AA there is mistrust, sometimes considerable, of professionals and others who work with alcoholics outside the organization. It is felt that professionals who are not alcoholics do not know what alcoholism is really about. Even professionals who are themselves alcoholics are sometimes resented for failing to recognize that the only successful cure for alcoholism is AA.

The organization views alcoholism as a permanent state that can only be controlled, not corrected. The heavy emphasis placed upon this philosophy promotes a prolonged, even permanent group dependency. All life situations are recast in terms of a member's sobriety or alcoholism. A preoccupation with nondrinking is substituted for a preoccupation with drinking. For example, *The Grapevine,* AA's monthly publication in the United States, is filled with jokes about the stupidity of people in a drunken state. Simple formulas and slogans, supplemented by an abundant variety of AA literature, are used to combat negative feelings that may lead to a resumption of drinking. Perhaps most important is the emphasis on the AA "program" centered around "doing the steps"—the Twelve Steps (see box). This progress, from one step to another, is the es-

sence of the program and entire meetings are often devoted to the study and analysis of one of the steps. Doing the steps gives the AA member a sense of participation and progress.

Critics have pointed out that this ingrown aspect of AA can lead to conflict in the mind of the member. Alcoholics Anonymous not only helps maintain sobriety—it *is* sobriety and, without it, sobriety is unattainable. The individual may not learn to cope with his disease or gain self-reliance because the program encourages dependency and discourages outside interests that would in any way diminish the central place of AA in the life of the member. Even the name—Alcoholics *Anonymous*—diminishes individual identity. (At meetings, members traditionally identify themselves as follows: "Hello. My name is [first name], and I'm an alcoholic.") The anonymity was originally justified as a way of protecting members against a society hostile to alcoholics and accustomed to discriminating against them. Even with more widespread acceptance of alcoholism as a disease, there is still some hostility and discrimination today. But in the eyes of its critics, AA perpetuates itself by maintaining this gulf; by stripping members of their names and, hence, their identities and leaving them with only the label "alcoholic," AA increases their dependence on the organization. Since there is no known cure for alcoholism and since AA does not consider itself a treatment program with an eventual end, the "fellowship" is therefore permanent and self-perpetuating. Dropping out is, in the eyes of many AA members, almost tantamount to the resumption of drinking. Nevertheless relatively few members remain in AA for 10 years or more.

Alcohol is seen as the alcoholic's "solution" to an uncomfortable state. This discomfort stems from a sense of failure caused by unrealistic goals and expectations and, often, a tendency to fantasize. The inevitable failures lead to a loss of self-esteem and then to uncontrolled drinking. This view is not unique to AA, but others feel that to focus exclusively on this aspect of a problem that is broader oversimplifies it.

There are other criticisms of AA. Meetings have been called exclusionary and their tone conventional and middle class; to some they are offensively inspirational and anti-intellectual. AA also claims that those who drop out are "failures" who were "not motivated"; thus the blame is placed upon the individual and the organization is absolved.

However, most critics recognize the success that Alcoholics Anonymous has had. While pointing out that neither the achievements nor failures of AA can be proven because there are no membership records to document them, they agree that the organization helps and sustains large numbers of alcoholics who would otherwise be without support or hope.

History

The history of AA begins with the story, raised almost to the level of myth, of its founder, Bill Wilson, or, as he came to be known, Bill W. Born in 1895 and raised in a broken home, Wilson found that alcohol relaxed him socially and gave him a new sense of freedom. After a brief stint in the Army and marriage, Wilson went to work on Wall Street, where he had some success. He gradually became an alcoholic and later described the years from 1930 to 1934 as an "alcoholic hell." In 1934 an old drinking friend who had sobered up introduced him to the Oxford Group, headed by the Episcopal clergyman Dr. Samuel Shoemaker. The nondenominational group stressed the importance of taking stock of oneself, confessing one's defects and a willingness to make up for past wrongs. A member also could choose his own concept of God or a "higher power." It is easy to see in these principles many of the ideas that form the basis of AA.

After attending a meeting, Wilson decided to try to dry out. He went back to his doctor, Dr. Robert Silkworth, who had dried him out several times before. Silkworth, somewhat ahead of his time, believed alcoholism was a disease and a hopeless one. He described it as an "obsession of the mind that condemns one to drink and an allergy of the body that condemns one to die." This idea of alcoholism as a disease became an important concept in AA. Wilson sank into a profound depression during his sobering up process and subsequently had a "conversion" experience. From his experience grew the idea of the hopelessness of the condition of alcoholism, "hitting bottom" as a prerequisite for changing, experiencing a conversion (this is not stressed in AA, though there is a conversion from drinking to sobriety) and realizing the importance of interaction with others, which had first impressed Wilson when his newly sober friend came to talk to him.

Wilson joined the Oxford Group and tried preaching his theories to other alcoholics with no appreciable results. On a business trip to Akron, Wilson met another member of the group, Dr. Bob (Dr. Robert Holbrook Smith), an alcoholic who was still drinking. Wilson told his story, without preaching, and stressed the disease aspect of alcoholism. Dr. Bob sobered up and Alcoholics Anonymous was founded, although not formally under that name. (AA dates its "birth" as June 10, 1935, Dr. Bob's first day of "permanent sobriety.") Wilson and Dr. Bob began talking to alcoholics in Akron. Later Wilson returned to New York and continued work there. He and his followers eventually split from the Oxford Group, rejecting their notions of absolutism and aggressive evangelism. In 1939 a third group was formed in Cleveland. At the time membership was about 100.

In 1938 and 1939 Wilson put together a collection of articles that generally reflected the ideas which formed the basis of the fledgling organization. Published by AA and entitled *Alcoholics Anonymous,* it has been more commonly referred to as "the Big Book." In the process Wilson developed the Twelve Steps for recovery. The book also contained case histories of recovered members. Although it did not do well at first, it gradually gained publicity and sales increased. (As of December 31, 1981 the book had sold 3,171,654 copies.) For some the Big Book has been the basic textbook of AA, for others almost a bible. Different conflicts among the groups, such as those related to religious status, organization, and anonymity, were resolved, and certain practices were formalized in 1946 in the Twelve Traditions (see box). Headquarters were established in New York, and AA began publishing books and a monthly magazine, *The Grapevine*. In 1958 there were 6,000 groups with about 150,000 members; by 1980 estimated worldwide membership had grown to over a million.

Organization

AA is incorporated as a nonprofit organization run by two operating bodies, AA World Services, Inc. and the AA Grapevine, Inc., which are responsible to a board of trustees. Each year there is a conference attended by 91 delegates from AA areas in the United States and Canada; the trustees; the directors of World Services, Inc., and the Grapevine, Inc.; and the staff of the General Service Office and *The Grapevine* in New York.

On the local level, group organization is kept to a minimum, generally a few officers who arrange programs for meetings and maintain contact with the General Service Office. In all AA organizations responsibility for leading groups is rotated.

New groups are started where there is a demand, usually by an experienced member who helps with the initial setting-up process.

Meetings

All AA meetings are open to all alcoholics, whether or not they have ever attended a previous meeting. "Open" meetings are open to everyone, alcoholics and nonalcoholics. "Closed" meetings are limited to alcoholics only so that members will feel more free to discuss particularly difficult or intimate problems. "Step" meetings are conducted like study groups, devoted to one of the Twelve Steps. They are less spontaneous than other meetings and members are encouraged to prepare themselves beforehand.

Leadership of meetings is often self-perpetuating, since leaders are usually chosen from a nucleus of those who have successfully maintained sobriety for a long time and who are willing to serve. (Length of sobriety is of major importance in AA and anniversaries of the date when a member first became sober are important events and are celebrated at appropriate meetings, often accompanied by a small party. Conversely, if a member resumes drinking, he loses all seniority and his sobriety begins from scratch, no matter how many years of previous sobriety he may have achieved.)

Speakers at AA meetings are usually drawn from within the group itself or from other groups—seldom from outside AA. Often members of one group will hold meetings for members of another group.

Membership

The membership of AA is primarily middle aged, middle class, married, white and male. The percentage of women is rising, however, from 22% in 1968 to 31% in 1980. Between 1977 and 1980, 34% of the new members were women. During the same period the number of members 30 years and younger increased from 11.3% to 14.7%. Along with the increase in these two populations there was a growth in the number of members addicted to another drug besides alcohol: 18% in 1977 to 24% in 1980. Among those joining AA since 1977, 27% report DUAL ADDICTION, indicating a continually rising proportion.

Only 5% to 10% of the alcoholics in the United States use AA. The organization claims a success rate of 75%, 50% on the first approach to AA and half of the first-time failures on their later return to the organization. Some studies corroborate AA's claims of success for about 50% to 60% of the alcoholics who use it.

The Twelve Steps

The Twelve Steps stress faith, disavowal of personal responsibility, passivity in the hands of God or a higher power, confession of wrongdoing and response to spiritual awakening by sharing with others. The first step involves the idea of despair and a breakdown of denial concerning alcohol. Second is the idea of hope, or seeing the light. Third, responsibility is shifted from oneself to a higher authority figure, and a dependent stance is taken. The next steps involve confessing, making amends, continuing confirmation of a new image of oneself and redirecting energy to help others. Much

emphasis is put on this 12th step, since in the history of AA it was Bill W.'s carrying of the message to Dr. Bob that saved both of them and made the founding of AA possible. Thus attempts by AA members to help individuals who are drinking are known as "twelve-stepping."

The Twelve Traditions

The Twelve Traditions specify that the unity of AA is paramount, that leaders serve but not govern, that all who desire help be accepted as members, and that groups are autonomous. The AA message is to be spread, but other enterprises are not endorsed and no sides are taken in controversies. Groups are self-supporting and nonprofessional, with as little formal organization as possible. Personal ambition is discouraged and anonymity is protected. However, anonymity is not required on a personal level or in small groups.

THE TWELVE STEPS
OF
ALCOHOLICS ANONYMOUS

1. We admitted we were powerless over alcohol—that our lives had become unmanageable.

2. Came to believe that a Power greater than ourselves could restore us to sanity.

3. Made a decision to turn our will and our lives over to the care of God *as we understood him.*

4. Made a searching and fearless moral inventory of ourselves.

5. Admitted to God, to ourselves, and to another human being the exact nature of our wrongs.

6. Were entirely ready to have God remove all these defects of character.

7. Humbly asked Him to remove our shortcomings.

8. Made a list of all persons we had harmed, and became willing to make amends to them all.

9. Made direct amends to such people whenever possible, except when to do so would injure them or others.

10. Continued to take personal inventory and when we were wrong promptly admitted it.

11. Sought through prayer and meditation to improve our conscious contact with God *as we understood Him,* praying only for knowledge of His will for us and the power to carry that out.

12. Having had a spiritual awakening as a result of these steps, we tried to carry this message to alcoholics, and to practice these principles in all our affairs.

THE TWELVE TRADITIONS
OF
ALCOHOLICS ANONYMOUS

1. Our common welfare should come first; personal recovery depends upon AA unity.

2. For our group purpose there is but one ultimate authority—a loving God as He may express Himself in our group conscience. Our leaders are but trusted servants; they do not govern.

3. The only requirement for AA membership is a desire to stop drinking.

4. Each group should be autonomous except in matters affecting other groups or AA as a whole.

5. Each group has but one primary purpose—to carry its message to the alcoholic who still suffers.

6. An AA group ought never endorse, finance, or lend the AA name to any related facility or outside enterprise, lest problems of money, property, and prestige divert us from our primary purpose.

7. Every AA group ought to be fully self-supporting, declining outside contributions.

8. Alcoholics Anonymous should remain forever nonprofessional, but our service centers may employ special workers.

9. AA, as such, ought never be organized; but we may create service boards or committees directly responsible to those they serve.

10. Alcoholics Anonymous has no opinions on outside issues; hence the AA name ought never to be drawn into public controversy.

11. Our public relations policy is based on attraction rather than promotion; we need always maintain personal anonymity at the level of press, radio, and films.

12. Anonymity is the spiritual foundation of all our Traditions, ever reminding us to place principles before personalities.

Alcoholics Anonymous World Services, *Alcoholics Anonymous,* 3rd ed. (New York, 1978).

General Service Office of Alcoholics Anonymous, *Analysis of the 1980 Survey of the Membership of AA,* 1981.

Margaret Bean, "Alcoholics *Anonymous,*" *Psychiatric Annals* 5, no. 3 (March 1975), pp. 3–64.

Ernest Kurtz, *Not-God: A History of Alcoholics Anonymous* (Center City, Minn.: Hazelden Educational Services, 1979).

Robert Thomsen, *Bill W.* (New York: Popular Library, 1975).

alcoholism　　A chronic disorder associated with excessive consumption of alcohol over a period of time. There has been a continuing discussion over the cause, nature and characteristics of this disorder and, consequently, a variety of definitions. (See accompanying box for a sampling of these definitions.) Most authorities recognize alcoholism as a "disease," although this position has been challenged in some medical circles on the ground that a self-inflicted condition cannot properly be designated a disease.

The earliest known use of the term "alcoholism" was by a Swedish scientist, Magnus Huss of Stockholm. Huss published a treatise, *Chronische Alkohols-Krankheit* ("Chronic Alcohol Disease," Sweden, 1849. Germany, 1852), in which he identified a condition involving abuse of alcohol and labeled it *Alkoholismus chronicus.* However, the disease concept of alcoholism is much older. References to it have been found in the works of the 18th century American physician Benjamin Rush, Chaucer and the Roman philosopher Seneca. Perhaps the first official recognition of alcoholism as a disease was a resolution by the American Medical Association in 1956. This landmark resolution, along with a similar one by the American Bar Association, has had a profound impact upon alcoholism-related state and federal laws, program financing, insurance coverage and hospital admissions policies, and the legal status of alcoholics.

A number of groups oppose the acceptance of alcoholism as a disease. Certain religious groups, particularly fundamentalist Protestants, continue to view alcoholism as drunkenness and, therefore, a "sin." Some social scientists believe the term "alcoholism" inadequately describes a social dysfunction. They claim that to call it a disease is to label it nothing more than a medical-psychiatric problem and that the medical approach is constricted and, often, ineffective. The counter argument is that the solution to the problem, if there is one, is not to reject the medical-psychiatric approach but to supplement it.

There are a variety of other arguments against the disease concept: alcoholism cannot be a disease because there is no anatomic structural abnormality; irresponsible persons will abuse the legal and medical benefits given them as "sick" people; alcoholism is a label that stigmatizes patients; the symptoms of alcoholism vary so widely that they defy definition as a disease; the concept dignifies and excuses drunkenness; the concept does not satisfactorily deal with a wide variety of categories, including heavy drinking nonalcoholics, borderline alcoholics, periodic alcoholics etc.

(Since this entire encyclopedia is devoted to alcoholism, every article in it deals directly or indirectly with the subject. However, there are several articles that may be particularly useful in their coverage of the concepts and aspects of alcoholism: ADDICTION, DEPENDENCY, DISEASES, DISEASE CONCEPT, ETIOLOGICAL THEORIES OF ALCOHOLISM, INABILITY TO ABSTAIN, LOSS OF CONTROL, RELEASE, RELIGION, TOLERANCE.)

DEFINITIONS OF ALCOHOLISM

An "alcoholic" is defined as one who is unable consistently to choose whether he shall drink or not, and who, if he drinks, is unable consistently to choose whether he shall stop or not. "Alcoholics with complications" are those who have developed bodily or mental disorders through prolonged excessive drinking.

Statistical Abstract (1979).

Alcoholism is a chronic disease manifested by repeated implicative drinking so as to cause injury to the drinker's health or to his social or economic functioning.

Mark Keller, *Quarterly Journal of Studies on Alcoholism* (March 1960).

Alcoholism is an illness characterized by significant impairment that is directly associated with persistent and excessive use of alcohol. Impairment may involve physiological, psychological or social dysfunction.
American Medical Association, *Manual on Alcoholism,* 3rd ed., 1977.

Alcoholism is a disease characterized by the repetitive and compulsive ingestion of any sedative drug, ethanol being just one of these, in such a way as to cause interference in some aspects of the subject's life, be it in the area of interpersonal relationships, job, marriage, or physical health. It is absolutely critical to appreciate that this definition does not in any way specify which sedative agent is used, the frequency of its use, or the amount ingested.

Stanley E. Gitlow
Mount Sinai School of Medicine, New York

**Summary of Prevalence Estimates for Alcoholism and
Problem Drinking in the United States**

Source	Population	Total	Male	Female
Chambers & Griffey, 1975. Survey-based estimate.	Heavy Drinkers[1]	18 million[2]	13,860,000	4,140,000
Johnson, Armor, Polich and Stambul, 1977. Survey-based AEDS estimate.[3]	Problem Drinkers[4]	14.4 to 9.3[5] million (1975)*	10,562,250 to 7,041,500	3,843,500 to 2,306,100
Cahalan & Cisin, 1976. Survey-based AEDS estimate.	Problem Drinkers[6]	13.7 million[5] (1975)	9,858,100	3,843,500
Keller, 1975. Estimate.	Problem Drinkers and Alcoholics	10.5 to 9.5 million (1972)	Not Available	
Summary of State Plans, 1976. AEDS estimate	Alcohol Abusers and Alcoholics	10.3 to 9.7 million (1975)	Not Available	
Creative Socio-Medics, 1977.		7.0 million (1974)	4,400,000	2,600,000
Flow Model Estimates.	Alcohol Abusers[7]	7.2 million (1975)	4,500,000	2,700,000
Keller & Gurioli, 1976. Modified Jellinek Formula.	Alcoholics	5.75 million (1975)	4,800,000	950,000

*Year for which estimate was made

Notes:

[1]Heavy Drinkers: persons who typically drink every day and often consume 5 to 6 drinks at each sitting.

[2]Prevalence estimate is based on U.S. population age 14 and over (no year specified).

[3]Estimate is based on rates suggested by Rand Corporation's re-analysis of results from a 1975 national survey conducted by Opinion Research Corporation.

[4]A problem drinking index was defined by combining various scores on a symptoms and consequences of problem drinking scale with a quantity-frequency index of consumption.

[5]Prevalence estimates based on U.S. population age 18 and over in 1975 (male: 70,415,000, female: 76,870,000).

[6]Problem drinkers: persons who indicate a high number of alcohol-related problems, such as psychological dependence, frequent intoxication, and financial or health problems, on a national probability survery.

[7]Alcohol abusers: persons whose drinking patterns have progressed to the point where they would be accepted by a treatment facility with a diagnosis of alcoholism.

Source: Judy F. Coakley and Sandie Johnson, *Alcohol Abuse and Alcoholism in the United States,* Working Paper #1 (Washington, National Institute on Alcohol Abuse and Alcoholism, 1978).

alcoholism in industry   See EM-
PLOYEE ASSISTANCE PROGRAMS.

alcoholist   Although rarely used in
the United States, the term is common in
some Scandinavian countries, where it is
generally employed to refer to a person
whose drinking results in abuse of alcohol.
The definition of the term varies; it is used
to denote both an alcoholic and a person
who uses alcoholic beverages but is not an
alcoholic.

alcoolisation   A term used by the
French to describe a pattern of large daily
consumption of alcohol with harmful effects
on health and a shortening of the life span
but without the development of either physical or psychological DEPENDENCE.

alcoolist   A term used by the French
to describe someone who drinks daily and
heavily to the extent that his or her life span
may be shortened but who is not physically
or psychologically dependent upon alcohol.

ale   A beer brewed by TOP FERMENTA-
TION that has a more bitter taste and a
slightly higher alcohol content than lager
beer. The name is derived from the Old
Norwegian *ol* and has been transformed by
English dialectical usage. In Britain ale and
beer are synonymous; elsewhere ale has a
variety of popular usages not strictly related
to beers or malt liquors produced by top
fermentation.

Fermentation of ale in Britain, the country with which it has been traditionally associated, was a common practice by the
time of the Roman invasions during the first
century A.D. At that time, however, ale was
less popular than fermented meads and ci-
ders, both of which were more easily produced by the predominantly nomadic
inhabitants. The Roman influence encouraged permanent settlements, which had
the effect of encouraging permanent *taber-
nae,* or alehouses, where fermented malt li-

quors were both produced and sold. The
Anglo-Saxon invasion in the fifth century
brought Britain under the control of a people already familiar with brewing techniques, and it was at this point that ale first
became a prominent feature of daily British
life.

Thereafter ale became the subject of
early legal legislation in Britain. The first
alehouses in the country to be licensed were
those authorized during the reign of King
Edgar, who ruled until 975. By 1100 Henry
II had levied the first taxes on malt liquor,
the term by which ale was then known, and
by 1300 Richard II had required all licensed alehouses to display identifying
signs. The first brewery to receive a royal
charter was the City Brewing Company of
London, which was given its commission in
1437 and retained an official monopoly on
ale production for some time. However,
most ale brewing remained a cottage industry, one presided over by women, who
closely oversaw the drawn-out fermentation
process. The product was a beer brewed exclusively from malt barley and commonly
mixed with spices to counteract its extremely sweet taste. As one dietary book of
1542 noted, "Ale is made of malt and
water; and they the which do put any other
thing to ale than rehersed . . . doth sofysti-
cate their ale."

A major change in ale brewing came in
the late 16th century, when hops were first
imported from Bavaria to flavor the sweet
brew produced by grains and natural sugars. Hops, or the female flowers of the *Humulus lupus* vine, probably arrived in Britain via Flemish immigrants to Kent during
the reign of King Henry VIII. Since that
time they have remained an essential ingredient in the mash from which ale is brewed.
Their use was first exploited by the large
family brewers, such as the Whitbreads, the
Barclays and the Courages, who for a time
competed with the brewers chartered by the
crown and have since replaced them.

Because of top fermentation true ale is

generally more bitter and "heavier" to the taste than lager beer, which is made by BOT-TOM FERMENTATION. This process employs a different yeast than that used in bottom fermentation, and takes place at higher temperatures and for a shorter period of time than the lager-making process. Today three principal types of ale are produced commercially in Britain. Mild ale is generally dark and very "hoppy" in taste; pale ale is lighter in color and drier in taste; and bitter, the most common type, is a compromise between the other two in both appearance and taste.

allergy   The question of whether alcoholism can be due to an allergy to alcohol has been raised at various times in the past, most notably by William D. Silkworth of the Charles B. Towns Hospital, a drying out facility in New York, in 1937. Silkworth's theory that alcoholism was due to an allergy to alcohol was published in ALCOHOLICS ANONYMOUS literature, and AA still uses it as part of the explanation of alcoholism. However, there is no medical evidence to support such a theory. While a person may be allergic to some constituent of an alcoholic beverage, such as a CONGENER, the American Medical Association states, "There is no similarity between the signs and symptoms of alcoholism and those of known allergies."

Alpha alcoholism   The first of five categories of alcoholism defined by JELLI-NEK. "*Alpha alcoholism* represents a *purely* psychological *continual dependence* or reliance upon the effect of alcohol to relieve bodily or emotional pain." Alpha alcoholism does not lead to LOSS OF CONTROL, and the damage it causes may be limited to a disturbance in the subject's family and/or social relationships. There are no WITH-DRAWAL effects and no signs of a progressive process. Alpha alcoholism is not an illness per se, but it signifies some other underlying disturbance. Alpha alcoholism

can develop into GAMMA ALCOHOLISM, but it is often seen for years without any signs of progression. Alpha alcoholism is sometimes known as problem drinking, but that term is also used to indicate physical dependence upon alcohol (PROBLEM DRINKER).

American Indians   Alcoholic beverages were unknown in most of North America before the arrival of the European colonists, although some Indians made alcohol from corn and cactus to use for spiritual purposes. White people utilized alcohol to enhance their treaty-making and trading sessions with the Indians and as an item of exchange. The practice of intoxicating the Indians and then cheating them out of their land and goods became so serious that tribal leaders themselves requested the enactment of federal laws to prohibit the sale of alcoholic beverages to Indians. These laws, passed in 1832, not only banned the sale of liquor to the Indians but made it illegal for them to be seen drinking in public; they remained in effect until 1953. Today 408 out of 482 tribes still prohibit the sale of liquor or other alcoholic beverages on their reservations.

It is not known how many Indians drink, since the population is diverse and scattered around the country—on reservations, in cities and in nonreservation rural areas. Therefore figures on Indian drinking are generally estimates and are not precise.

At present alcoholism is the number one health problem among Indians and Alaskans. In 1972 the National Center for Health Statistics reported that the three fastest rising causes of death among Indians, in order of frequency, were CIRRHOSIS of the liver, suicide and homicide, all of which can be traced to alcoholism. The same report estimated that alcohol consumption was related to a significantly larger percentage of traffic accidents, suicides, homicides, acts of violence and other crimes committed by Indians than the percentage perpetrated by the general popula-

Age Specific Mortality Rates per 100,000 Population for Indians and Alaska Natives in Reservation States, U.S. All Races and U.S. Other than White

	Indians and Alaska Natives (Indian Health Service[IHS])			U.S. All Races 1977	U.S. Other than White 1977	Ratio IHS 76–78 to U.S. All Races	Ratio IHS 76–78 to U.S. Other than White
	1976–78[1]	1975–77[1]	1974–76[1]				
Under 1	—	—	—	—	—	—	—
1–4	—	—	—	—	—	—	—
5–14	0.1	0.1	0.0	0.0	0.0	—	—
15–24	9.8	11.1	11.2	0.5	1.1	19.6	8.9
25–34	72.4	76.3	74.7	3.2	12.8	22.6	5.7
35–44	150.0	152.9	162.5	11.9	37.3	12.6	4.0
45–54	165.8	166.6	172.2	23.0	48.3	7.2	3.4
55–64	136.4	123.9	124.2	26.9	45.1	5.1	3.0
65–74	58.9	57.6	68.2	19.8	23.7	3.0	2.5
75–84	34.0	35.2	33.8	8.5	10.8	4.0	3.1
85+	8.0	24.8	43.2	3.1	4.6	2.6	1.7

1. Estimated population methodology revised in 1976.

2. Includes alcoholism, alcoholic psychosis and cirrhosis of the liver with mention of alcohol.

Source: Indians and Alaska Natives—Indian Health Service, Public Health Service (PHS). U.S. All Races and U.S. Other than White, 1977—National Center for Health Statistics, PHS (unpublished).

tion and that the incidence of drinking among Indians was double that among the general population. From 1976 to 1978 the suicide rate for Indians age 15 to 24 was more than three times the national rate for that age group and in 1977 the homicide rate for Indians age 25 to 34 was 3.3 times the national rate (Indian Health Service). In 1960, 76% of all Indian arrests were alcohol related, and between 1952 and 1967, 89% of all arrests of Indians by the Los Angeles police department were for intoxication. The proportion of convictions for driving-while-intoxicated (DWI) among Indians in Los Angeles County was seven times greater than the proportion of Indian drivers in the county. On a reservation in Maine, 47% of all deaths over a 20-year period were alcohol related, and every Indian in the state prison was there for an alcohol-related offense.

The proportion of Indians arrested for drunkenness far exceeds the drunkenness arrest rates of all other ethnic groups. The rate of alcoholic cirrhosis among Indians is more than five times the national average and accidental deaths (often alcohol related) of Indians are almost three times the national average. It has been estimated that 30% of the male Indian population and 15% of the female Indian population may be alcoholic (Jones). From 1976 to 1978 Indians age 25 to 34 experienced alcoholism mortality rates that were 23 times the national average; age 35 to 44, 13 times the national average; and age 45 to 54, seven times the national average.

For Indians the overall alcohol discharge rate (ADR) from Indian Health Service and contract general hospitals is three times higher than the U.S. all-races ADR and double the U.S. other-than-white ADR.

There have been numerous attempts to explain why the problem of alcoholism is so great among American Indians, and in these attempts there has been a tendency to ignore the diversity of the population. North American Indians comprise a large number of distinct peoples with unique cultures and world views. There are several myths about Indian drinking, such as that once an Indian has tasted liquor he has an uncontrollable craving for it. No proof exists that the psychological or physiological reactions of Indians to alcohol are different than those of other racial groups. While genetic differences may exist, there is thus far no conclusive evidence of differences in ethanol metabolism by racial group. However, the pattern of drinking among Indians

Homicide, Suicide and Alcoholism Death Rates by Age for Indians & Alaska Natives, U.S. All Races and U.S. Other Than White

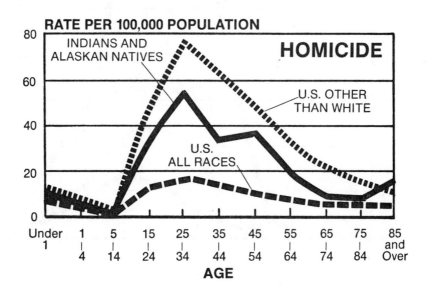

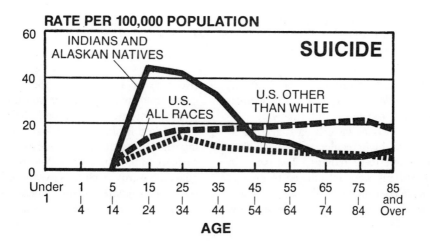

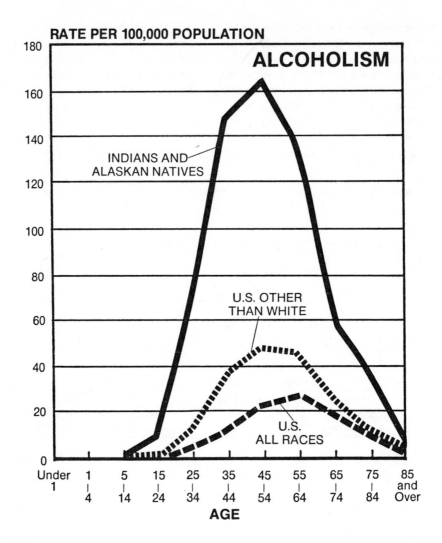

RATE PER 100,000 POPULATION

ALCOHOLISM

INDIANS AND
ALASKAN NATIVES

U.S. OTHER
THAN WHITE

U.S.
ALL RACES

AGE

Indians & Alaska natives are based on 3-year average, 1976–1978. U.S. all races rates are single year 1977. U.S. other than white rates are single year 1977.
Source: U.S. Indian Health Service

is generally either very heavy or abstinent, and the Indians themselves are concerned about their problems with drinking.

Several reasons have been suggested to explain the high incidence of alcoholism among American Indians. The way in which Indians were introduced to alcohol may have contributed to the way in which they drink, often rapidly and excessively.

(Because of variations in the supply of game from hunting and the constraints of frequent intertribal wars, many tribes consumed food in similar ways—at feasts during which large quantities were eaten in one sitting.) In the Passamaquoddy Indian language no words or phrases exist to describe social or moderate drinking. There are only terms to describe someone on a drinking binge—*sputsuwin*—or someone who is habitually drunk—*kotuhsomuin*—(Stevens).

Because alcohol was an entirely new factor in Indian society, with no external controls or socially established norms for its use, its destructive powers were not fully perceived at first. Furthermore drinking was encouraged by the traders. When Indians were later prohibited from drinking, they had to gulp quickly to avoid being seen. The laws against drinking also created a fatalistic attitude towards alcohol—"If it is prohibited to me, it must be because I have no control."

Indians generally do not condemn the drinkers among them, as they believe a drunk person is not himself and, therefore, not responsible for his behavior. Consequently Indians are often unwilling to testify against someone accused of committing a crime while drunk, creating problems for law enforcement officials. There is also heavy peer pressure to drink, and as with food, it is polite to share alcohol and to accept what is offered. Abstainers are sometimes accused of trying to be better than the rest.

The main cause of drinking problems among American Indians is probably sociocultural stress. There is a lack of identification with the ways of white society and a rejection of its goals. Indian traditions have been weakened and family relations have been disturbed; the elderly no longer have the same prestige and guiding role they once held. Indians experience strong feelings of powerlessness and anxiety because of conflicts between their ways and the ways of the white man. They have been placed on reservations, their religions and cultures have been undermined and their children have been placed in schools where they learn non-Indian traditions. Drink tends to loosen tribal social constraints and to blur the differences between Indian and white culture.

Drinking begins early, sometimes as early as age 10. Indian children are often raised on a reservation in one culture until school age, when they are sent to boarding school, where they must give up that style of life. The most problematic age is between 15 and 25, when adolescents are the most conformist and the least occupied. Many drop out of school and are either too young to work or unable to find jobs. The prevalence of drinking among older Indians sets an example for the youth.

Urban Indians have special problems, living in a setting where they are generally economically, educationally and socially disadvantaged and where they do not have the support systems, such as families and familiar customs, found on reservations. The Seattle Indian Health Board estimates that 60% (4,500) of the adult Indian population of Seattle are excessive drinkers. The arrest rate for urban Indians is over 40 times higher than that for the nation as a whole (38,461 per 100,000 vs. 930 per 100,000).

Another group with special problems is Indian women. A report by the National Center for Health Statistics showed that in 1975 women accounted for almost half of the total deaths from liver cirrhosis among American Indians, compared with one-third of cirrhosis deaths among both blacks and whites. Indian women were also more likely to die of liver cirrhosis at a younger age than either white or black women; between the ages of 35 and 54 Indian women died of cirrhosis at nine times the rate of white women, and between the ages of 15 and 34 they died at 37 times the rate of white women (Sandmaier).

The Inter-Tribal Alcoholism Center in Sheridan, Wyo. reports that approximately 25% to 35% of its clients are women. The center suspects that because of the family responsibilities held by Indian women, many are afraid to seek help. Indian fathers normally will not do housework or take care of the children, since these tasks are considered to be unmanly and/or counter to Indian tradition. A common fear is that while the Indian mother seeks help, the children are neglected and might be taken by the social welfare department and placed in foster homes.

Indian women with drinking problems can receive help from the North American Indian Women's Council on Chemical Dependencies (Box 188, Spooner, Wis. 54876).

The Indian Health Service (IHS) has been the primary resource for handling alcoholism-related problems of American Indians. IHS provides direct health service through 50 hospitals, 101 health centers and several hundred health clinics.

The most promising methods of treatment include Indians in the planning and implementation of their own programs on a community basis. It is important for therapists and counselors to be sensitive to tribal cultures and variations from tribe to tribe. Some specifically Indian Alcoholics Anonymous groups have integrated elements of their traditional cultures into the AA setting, and they have achieved more success than standard AA programs.

Edith Lynn Hornik, *The Drinking Woman* (New York: Association Press, 1977), passim.

Bruce Johansen, "The Tepees Are Empty and the Bars Are Full," *Alcoholism* 1, no. 2 (November/December, 1980):33–38.

Ernest P. Noble, ed., *Third Special Report to the U.S. Congress on Alcohol and Health* (Rockville, Md.: National Institute on Alcohol Abuse and Alcoholism, 1978), pp. 55–58.

Marian Sandmaier, *The Invisible Alcoholics* (New York: McGraw-Hill Book Company, 1980), pp. 145–146.

Susan M. Stevens, "Alcohol and World View: A Study of Passamaquoddy Alcohol Use," *Journal of Studies on Alcohol,* supplement no. 9 (January 1981):122–142.

Dale R. Walker, "Treatment Strategies in an Urban Indian Alcoholism Program," *Journal of Studies on Alcohol,* supplement no. 9 (January 1981):171–184.

amethystic   (From the Greek *amethystos* not drunken.) The Greeks believed that the gem amethyst could prevent intoxication. The term "amethystic" is now used to describe a substance or treatment method that could accelerate the normal sobering process or offset the effects of alcohol on the body. A number of researchers, particularly Ronald L. Alkana and Ernest P. Noble of California, have been looking for an agent that would counteract the effects of alcohol on the CENTRAL NERVOUS SYSTEM, but progress has been slow. Of primary concern to those engaged in research are the possibilities of such an amethystic agent in treating medical emergencies caused by an overdose of alcohol and its potential uses in the prevention of automobile accidents.

Unfortunately there are presently no effective antidotes for acute intoxication. In addition to being effective in combating the effects of alcohol, such an agent would have to be fast acting, free of toxic side effects, inexpensive, and capable of being stored and administered conveniently.

Since it is doubtful that any drug now known could be developed to hasten the METABOLISM of ethanol the 10 to 20 times needed to achieve rapid sobriety in an intoxicated person, research efforts have been focused on finding agents that counteract the effects of ethanol on the central nervous system. Recent findings indicate that chemical stimulation of noradrenalin (a neurotransmitter substance in the brain) can reverse some of alcohol's depressive effects.

amnesia   One of the typical warning signs of alcoholism is a period of temporary amnesia during which a person is conscious but later cannot recall what transpired. Memory is lost temporarily. (See also BLACKOUT, MEMORY.)

amphetamines with alcohol   Some people may take amphetamines in combination with alcohol to try to counter the depressant effects of alcohol or in the mistaken belief that amphetamines will increase the brief high produced by alcohol. While there may in fact be some possible antagonism of the depressant effects of alcohol on the central nervous system, there is no improvement of impaired motor coordination resulting from alcohol consumption, and the combination may produce a false sense of security. Another danger is that high levels of both alcohol and amphetamines may produce gastrointestinal upset, and if amphetamines are taken with a beverage containing tyramine (a white crystalline base derived from the amino acid tyrosine), such as Chianti wine, an excessive rise in blood pressure may occur. (See also DRUGS.)

amyl alcohol   A colorless liquid with a burning taste, amyl alcohol is the chief constituent of fuel oil and is used as a source of amyl compounds, such as amyl nitrite. This term should not be confused with ETHANOL, the principal chemical in alcoholic beverages.

animal   models   of   alcoholism
Many alcohol-related problems cannot be closely studied in humans. Alcoholics have numerous biomedical and psychosocial problems in addition to their alcoholism that can interfere with studies of the causes and consequences of excessive alcohol consumption. Factors such as poor nutrition, liver damage, psychiatric illness and drug abuse can make it difficult to determine what factors are caused by alcohol consumption and what are the result of these other problems. Animal models may be the only way that the effects of alcohol use can be isolated and examined.

Thoedore J. Cicero of the Department of Psychiatry, Washington University School of Medicine in St. Louis has made an extensive review of existing animal models. He states four main objectives of animal studies in the field of alcoholism: to examine the biomedical complexities associated with chronic alcohol consumption, such as LIVER damage and BRAIN dysfunction; to evaluate therapeutic methods that may be useful in the management of the alcohol WITHDRAWAL syndrome; to study the mechanisms underlying TOLERANCE to and physical DEPENDENCE on alcohol; and to investigate the factors that lead to and maintain excessive consumption of alcohol.

To be a true analogue of human alcoholism, an animal must meet a number of criteria. It must self-administer alcohol in pharmacologically significant amounts; TOLERANCE should be demonstrable following a period of continuous consumption; and dependence should develop. Psychological dependence cannot really be examined in an animal. Physical dependence is defined by those responses expressed during withdrawal.

At present no animal meets all the criteria for a true analogue of human alcoholism. For example, there are difficulties in many cases with self-administration. However, for studies of the neurobiological mechanisms underlying tolerance and dependence, forced administration of alcohol is usually sufficient to meet criteria.

Theodore J. Cicero, "A Critique of Animal Analogues of Alcoholism," in *Biochemistry and Pharmacology of Ethanol,* vol. 2, ed. Edward Majchrowicz and Ernest P. Noble, (New York: Plenum Press, 1979), pp. 533–560.

anisette   A liqueur produced from the mixture of aniseed (the seeds of anise) and other herbs, such as cinnamon and coriander, with alcohol. The result is a clear liquid of approximately 60 proof with a sweet, licorice flavor, which comes from the aniseed.

Anisette is primarily a French liqueur;

the best known variety originates in Bordeaux.

Anstie's Law   In 1862 Sir Francis Anstie, a British psychiatrist who established the first women's medical school in Britain, made public Anstie's Law of Safe Drinking. Anstie set 1½ ounces of absolute alcohol per day as the upper limit of safe drinking. Today, even after years of research, this law is still viewed as a good general guideline for the average drinker. Of course, it is not applicable to everyone; some individuals cannot tolerate any alcohol. One and a half ounces of absolute alcohol is equivalent to half a bottle of wine, four 8-oz glasses of beer or three 1-oz drinks of 100-proof liquor.

Antabuse   The brand name of the generic drug disulfiram, Antabuse is used to deter consumption of alcohol by persons being treated for alcoholism. By itself Antabuse has little effect in the body. However, if a patient taking Antabuse consumes alcohol, he or she will have a severe reaction to it, exhibiting such symptoms as headache, vomiting, breathing difficulty, and, occasionally, collapse and coma. Reaction to Antabuse begins within five to 10 minutes after ingesting alcohol and may last from 30 minutes to several hours, depending on the amount of alcohol in the body.

Antabuse interferes with the METABOLISM of alcohol in the liver by causing a toxic buildup of ACETALDEHYDE. Its real value is the knowledge of what will occur if a drink is taken. The drug's action often continues to be effective even after treatment is discontinued, and some patients may have had a reaction 14 days after taking their final dosage. Use of Antabuse is far from a complete answer, but it can be a major aid in the treatment of alcoholics.

Care should be taken when prescribing Antabuse for alcoholics who have such physical conditions as arteriosclerotic heart disease, hypertension, diabetes mellitus, cir-

rhosis or any other illness that might prevent their ability to tolerate acetaldehyde poisoning. In addition the action of Antabuse may alter the metabolism of some other medicines.

Antabuse is prescribed with the patient's full knowledge and understanding. The dosage is 500 milligrams a day for five to seven days and 250 milligrams a day thereafter. Patients have been treated for 17 years without bad effect (unless they drank). However, some people have experienced certain adverse reactions, including slight drowsiness, headache, and even temporary impotence and psychotic reactions. Since the safe use of this drug during pregnancy has yet to be established, it should not be given to pregnant women.

Anti-Saloon League   The Anti-Saloon League of America was founded in 1895 by a number of men interested in a political approach to what they perceived were the problems of the saloon and of liquor traffic, such as drunkenness, violence and the disintegration of family life. The league worked as a political pressure group, collecting money from church congregations and using it for launching publicity against saloons, for electing political candidates who supported the anti-saloon cause and for running local prohibition campaigns. It gained support in the early 1900s and between 1905 and 1915 the number of churches cooperating with it increased from 19,000 to 40,000. The Anti-Saloon League emphasized the economic advantages of prohibition and argued that alcohol made the working man inefficient and careless.

Larry Engelmann, *Intemperance: The Lost War against Liquor* (New York: The Free Press, 1979), pp. 10–19.

anxiety   One of the primary psychological causes of alcoholism is anxiety. Alcohol is known as a quick tension reducer, and according to some behavioral scientists, the potential alcoholic quickly learns that the immediate effect of drinking is a calming of anxieties. A drinking pattern is then established and alcohol is used as a means of managing disturbing feelings. Of course, many anxious people do not become alcoholics. Social factors and other learned responses to stress may have some effect in determining if an individual turns to alcohol or to some other means of coping. Alcohol's abilities to reduce anxiety may vary from individual to individual, depending on the amount of alcohol consumed and whether or not the subject is an alcoholic. JELLINEK and other researchers have found that drinking to the point of intoxication may increase rather than decrease anxiety. Jellinek concluded that for an alcoholic on a drinking bout, as LOSS OF CONTROL progressed, anxiety increased and was relieved for only very short periods by renewed alcohol intake.

aperitif   (French, *aperitif,* appetizer.) In its broadest sense an aperitif is any drink taken before a meal to stimulate the appetite. Among the more popular alcoholic beverages used for this purpose are champagne, vermouth, gin, sherry, mild whiskey, and cognac and water. These are usually referred to as cocktails.

Certain beverages are manufactured specifically as aperitifs. Such drinks are intended to be drunk slowly, in sips, and are often associated with moderation. They are usually strong in alcoholic content and may have a bitter taste, the degree of bitterness depending on the type of plant used as a flavoring. Among the more bitter of the plants utilized in the making of aperitifs are roots of parsley, fennel, asparagus and butcher's broom. Those with a milder bitter flavor include roots of maidenhair, couch grass, thistle and strawberry plant.

Four well-known French wines manufactured as aperitifs are Dubonnet, St. Raphael, Byrrh (pronounced beer) and Lillet. Although sometimes used in mixed drinks, they are usually drunk by themselves. The flavor of these wines is more pronounced than that of ordinary wines because of the special flavorings (i.e., the roots, barks and flowers of bitter plants) added to them. Dubonnet, for example, is red wine with bitter bark and quinine added. Byrrh and St. Raphael are also flavored with bitter bark and quinine but are fortified with brandy as well.

ABSINTHE, now illegal because of the severe health hazards it poses, was a popular aperitif in France during the late 19th and early 20th centuries. It was flavored with wormwood.

apomorphine   A chemical used in AVERSION THERAPY to produce nausea. Shortly after apomorphine is administered, the patient consumes alcohol; the nausea produced by the apomorphine subsequently becomes associated with the alcohol.

applejack   The American name for apple brandy, applejack is essentially the equivalent of French CALVADOS, although the term is sometimes used loosely to refer to hard cider. It ranges from 80 to 100 proof.

Applejack is usually made by distilling hard or fermented cider or fermented apple pomace. Another method, now rarely used, consists of freezing hard cider, concentrating the alcohol in the center, where it remains unfrozen; removing the ice; and pouring off the alcoholic center.

Applejack was one of the most popular drinks among the early settlers in North America, who sometimes referred to it as "essence of lockjaw." It is still very popular in rural areas and in the South.

It has been suggested that the risk of cancer of the esophagus from daily consumption of alcohol is increased if the beverage has an apple base (Tuyns et al).

A. J. Tuyns, G. Pequignot and J. S. Abbatucci, "Oesophageal Cancer and Alcohol Consumption," *International Journal of Cancer* 23 (1979):443–447.

aquavit   An alcoholic beverage distilled in Scandinavia from grain or potatoes and flavored with caraway seeds. The name "aquavit" (also spelled *akuavit, akvavit* and *akavit*) is the Scandinavian form of aqua vitae (WATER OF LIFE), the Latin term that was used in the late Middle Ages to refer to any distilled spirit.

Aquavit is particularly associated with Denmark, where it is also sometimes referred to as *schnaps* (see SCHNAPPS); in Sweden it is also known as *snaps*. *Linie Aquavit* ("equator aquavit") is a Norwegian variety which gets its name from the fact that it is shipped south from Norway and across the equator twice while it is still in casks. The exposure to the high temperatures of the equatorial zone is supposed to improve its flavor, much as the heating process used in the making of MADEIRA wine.

Aquavit is generally between 86 and 90 proof. Since it is usually not aged, it is normally colorless. Aged aquavit has a light brown color.

Aquavit is most often drunk straight as an aperitif. It is customarily gulped from a small glass, sometimes with beer as a chaser.

Argentina   Second to Brazil among South American countries in both size and population, Argentina is a predominantly Catholic, Spanish-speaking country largely peopled by Caucasians of European descent. The majority of this Caucasian population is descended from Spaniards and Italians, and the country as a whole has to some extent adopted the drinking habits of those nationalities.

Argentina produces more than four times as much wine as beer and distilled spirits combined, and of this diversified wine production, representing 2.5 million liters of ABSOLUTE ALCOHOL yearly, more than two-thirds is reserved for domestic consumption. The overall national drinking pattern is characterized by toleration of daily consumption of alcoholic beverages with effective cultural admonition of public drunkenness. Most drinking takes place in the home, usually in conjunction with meals, and the effective inhibition of drunkenness is thus provided by the family structure. Drinking outside the home generally takes place in family-oriented restaurants, which have the same inhibitory effect on drunkenness. The modern trends affecting this established pattern are heavier drinking among the middle and upper classes, increased acceptance of drinking by females and higher rates of alcohol abuse in rural areas than in urban areas. The country has few legal restrictions on advertising of alcoholic beverages, hours of sale or minimum age for purchase.

Argentina's estimates of the extent of the alcohol abuse problem in the country are based on a definition of alcoholism as a disease characterized by social, psychological or physical dependence on ethanol demonstrated by an inability to stop drinking after initial consumption. Based on this definition, the overall alcoholism rate has been estimated at about 5%, with extremes of about 12% in rural areas and 3% in urban areas. The reason for the higher rate in rural areas has not been determined. It is not related to illegal brewing or distillation, and may be due to the fact that in remote districts where most of the country's grape crops are grown, wine is readily available and other social opportunities are not.

The cost of alcoholism to the country has not yet been statistically researched, but authorities acknowledge the presence of rising job absenteeism, family problems and social aberrations related to alcohol abuse. Existing data on the problem reveal a cirrhosis mortality rate of 18.5 per 100,000 population, with most known cases affecting males between the ages of 40 and 65. In addition the Argentine government medical authorities estimate that up to 15% of all general hospital admissions and up to 30% of all psychiatric hospital admissions are related to alcohol use. Statistics on the cost of alcohol abuse in traffic fatalities are not available because Argentina has no law requiring a maximum BLOOD ALCOHOL CONCENTRATION for drivers.

It was not until 1977 that Argentina formed a national body, known as the Advisory Technical Committee on Alcoholism (CO.TE.SAL.), to study alcohol problems and their effects. Its authority to plan programs for prevention, treatment and rehabilitation, however, has been limited by the country's constitution, which grants virtual autonomy to each of the 22 provinces, and by its recent history of severe economic and political problems. Furthermore the Argentine wine industry, which is completely in private hands, is a powerful opponent of legislative restrictions on alcohol production and distribution. As a result treatment facilities for alcohol problems mostly consist of small general medical and psychiatric centers in the major cities of individual provinces. A major concern is the general lack of cooperation between these facilities and most of the country's nonpsychiatric physicians. But an equally important problem is the general reluctance to diagnose maladies as alcohol-related or to seek specific antialcoholism treatment. The principal efforts to combat this attitude are provided by the ALCOHOLICS ANONYMOUS, ALANON and ALATEEN organizations in most of Argentina's largest cities.

Armagnac   The best known French brandy after Cognac, it takes its name from the Armagnac region, located in the *departement* of Gers in southwest France. Armagnac is somewhat stronger and drier in taste than Cognac. It is also distilled by a different method. Whereas Cognac is distilled by a two-part process, the distillation of Armagnac is one continual operation. It comes from the still at approximately 104 proof (Cognac is between 140 and 150 proof at this stage) with less of the raw product distilled out than is the case with Cognac. Armagnac is aged in casks made of black Gascon oak and marketed at around 80 proof.

Asian Americans   Asian Americans comprise a number of diverse groups, making generalizations about them difficult. They are one of the less visible populations in the United States because of their comparatively small numbers (though this is changing as a result of increased immigration), geographic distribution (heavy concentration on the West Coast and in Hawaii), housing pattern (segregated) and low-profile life style.

Traditionally there has been a low incidence of alcohol abuse among Asian Americans, although their use of alcohol may be increasing as a result of assimilation and acculturation. Nonetheless the amount of drinking among them is lower than that among other ethnic groups. Asian Americans have some cultural taboos against drinking, which are reinforced by allergic and toxic reactions to alcohol. Recent studies have indicated that many Orientals develop a skin flush after drinking very small amounts of alcohol. This flush is sometimes associated with feelings of discomfort and a strong wish to stop drinking. One study by John Ewing and Beatrice Rouse (Rutgers Center for Alcohol Studies) found that Orientals exhibited marked flushing of the face, increased heart rate and a drop in blood pressure in response to a measured dose of alcohol. In the same study non-Orientals reported feeling happy, confident and alert after a dose that caused Oriental subjects to feel dizziness, pounding in the head and tingling sensations.

While it is believed that Asian Americans display only minor problem behavior when they drink, both Chinese Americans and Japanese Americans (who as groups have minimal arrest records, according to FBI statistics) are most likely to be charged with an alcohol-related violation if arrested. These offenses, such as driving under the influence or drunkenness, accounted for 27.8% of Japanese-American arrests in 1978.

Asian Americans have a low rate of use of alcohol treatment facilities mainly because of a philosophy that the family can best take care of its members. Other reasons include a cultural sensitivity to stigma, fear of losing face, unawareness of existing services, and cultural and language problems. Most Asian Americans do not recognize alcoholism as a problem except when it occurs in their own families, and then there is a tendency to hide or deny it.

John R. DeLuca, ed., *Fourth Special Report to the U.S. Congress on Alcohol and Health* (Rockville, Md.: National Institute on Alcohol Abuse and Alcoholism, 1981), p. 88.

John A. Ewing and Beatrice A. Rouse, "Drinks, Drinkers, and Drinking," in *Drinking,* ed. John A. Ewing and Beatrice A. Rouse (Chicago: Nelson Hall, 1979), p. 21.

H. L. Kitano, *Asian American Drinking Patterns,* National Institute on Alcohol Abuse and Alcoholism, Special Population Issues, Alcohol and Health Monograph no. 4 (Rockville, Md., in press).

P. H. Wolff, "Ethnic Differences in Alcohol Sensitivity," *Science* 175 (1972):449–50.

Australia   As acknowledged by its Alcohol and Drug Addicts Treatment Act of 1961, Australia is a country with enduring serious problems because of widespread alcohol abuse throughout a diversified population. The single most important cause of the alcohol problem, according to several government reports on the subject, is that excessive consumption of alcoholic beverages, usually in the form of beer, is not only accepted by most of the population but actually expected and encouraged. Although there is significant variation of the drinking pattern in urban and rural areas of the country, the nation as a whole is prone to associate heavy drinking with civil liberty, a pioneer identity, and other images of pride

and freedom embedded in the Australian concept of "mateship." While these characteristics are most dominant among the population descended from English and Irish settlers of the country, the condition of the native aboriginal population in regard to alcohol is, in its own respect, even worse because of the poverty and lack of opportunity affecting these people.

There was a 25% increase in per capita consumption of beer between 1962 and 1972, and in roughly the same period personal expenditure on alcohol rose 89%, second only to the percentage increase in rent in the national economy. As in many other countries this enormous growth in the consumption of alcohol has resulted in a certain dilemma for the government, which must balance its concern over the problem with the fact that by 1972 its revenues from alcohol production and sale had reached A $500 million ($390 million).

Extrapolations from limited surveys suggest that 5% of the male population, or about 215,000, and 1% of the female population, or about 43,000, are alcoholics, defined as consumers of 80.7 grams of beer per week. Surveys in Perth indicated that 11.4% of the aboriginal population were suffering from "chronic" drinking problems and that another 29% were suffering indirectly from "environmental" problems associated with alcoholism.

The cost of alcoholism to the country is staggering. It has been estimated that 4% of the Australian labor force is alcoholic and that productivity losses of A$30 million ($33.9 million) are attributable to absenteeism related to alcohol. Such a figure does not include years of labor lost because of alcohol-related diseases or fatalities. Furthermore it has been suggested that 30% of all crime, 50% of assaults and 55% of wife desertion in Australia are related to alcohol abuse. The Alcohol and Drug Services Commission of Victoria found that 17% of the 15-year-old boys and 5% of the 15-year-old girls under its jurisdiction admitted to frequent drunkenness, defined as more than once a month. Of the male adults admitted to hospitals in Victoria, 16% to 20% were found to be suffering from alcoholism in addition to their primary complaint. In 1973 in South Australia 329 traffic fatalities and 12,625 injuries were caused by drunk driving and 50% of the drivers arrested had a BLOOD ALCOHOL CONCENTRATION that was at least double the legal amount, 0.08%. Another limited survey revealed that in Perth, as a result of the introduction of alcohol sales on Sundays in 1970, the number of traffic fatalities occurring on that day of the week rose 5.9%, from 11% to 16.9%. In 1971 one person in 200 in West Australia was sentenced for drunkenness and disorderly conduct violations.

Treatment of alcoholism in Australia is complicated by the difficulty of operating a centralized program in a country of continental proportions. The Alcohol and Drug Addicts Treatment Board operates one major detoxification unit, three clinics for alcohol problems and various social work centers. It also coordinates the work of the different volunteer organizations around the country devoted to rehabilitation of alcohol abusers. Beyond these efforts, however, establishment of treatment centers is the responsibility of the individual states of the commonwealth, and treatment facilities and philosophies vary considerably throughout the country.

aversion therapy   A behavior therapy based on the experiments of Ivan Pavlov (1849–1936), a Russian scientist who worked extensively in the field of conditioned reflexes. Typically in aversion therapy, after detoxification a patient might be given a powerful nausea-producing drug, such as emetine or APOMORPHINE, and then a shot of liquor. The liquor must be drunk just before the drug-induced nausea occurs in order for the therapy to be successful. Once a patient undergoes this therapy a few times, he or she grows to associate the nau-

sea with the liquor. Conditioning sessions last 30 to 60 minutes and are given on alternate days for a total of four to six treatments. Reinforcement is given any time a patient develops a desire to drink.

Electric shock may sometimes be applied in the same way, a jolt of electricity given with a shot of liquor. However, this procedure has gradually become discredited and is not much used today. Another variation is the verbally induced aversion.

It has been stressed that alcoholics treated by aversion therapy must also be provided with alternative ways of securing gratification while sober if abstinence is to be maintained (Bandura).

There is disagreement over whether aversion provides any long lasting cure. It seems to be more effective with some personality types than with others; Robert S. Wallerstein feels that the best results are achieved with depressed patients because the "punishing aspect helps to alleviate guilt and externalize aggressive charge." He suggests that patients who are paranoid, antisocial or hostile passive-aggressive are not helped by aversion therapy. There is also the danger that a patient will have a serious physical reaction if the treatment is not carefully supervised by medical specialists. Many patients drop out of this type of treatment just because it is quite unpleasant. Aversion therapy is popular in some Eastern European countries, but it is not widely used in the United States.

David J. Armor, J. Michael Polich and Harriet B. Stambul, *Alcoholism and Treatment* (New York: John Wiley and Sons, 1978), pp. 33–34.

Albert Bandura, *Principles of Behavior Modification* (New York: Holt, Rinehart and Winston, 1969), passim.

Morris E. Chafetz and Harold W. Demone, Jr., *Alcoholism and Society* (New York: Oxford University Press, 1962), pp. 204–207.

John Langone, *Bombed, Buzzed, Smashed, or . . . Sober: A Book About Alcohol* (Boston: Little, Brown and Company, 1976), pp. 132–133.

Robert S. Wallerstein, "Comparative Study of Treatment Methods for Chronic Alcoholism: The Alcoholism Research Project at Winter V.A. Hospital," *American Journal of Psychiatry* 113 (1956):228–233.

aversive conditioning   See AVERSION THERAPY

B

BAC   See BLOOD ALCOHOL CONCENTRATION.

Bacchus   In Greek and Roman mythology the god of wine, identified with the Greek god Dionysus. A "son of Bacchus" is a hard drinker or drunkard.

BAL   Blood alcohol level. See BLOOD ALCOHOL CONCENTRATION.

bar   In its broader usage, a bar is a shop where alcoholic beverages are sold and drunk. Meals are not usually served. In this sense, bar is synonymous with SALOON. More specifically a bar is the counter over which drinks are served. (See also BAR DRINKER.)

bar drinker   One who habitually consumes alcoholic beverages in public establishments rather than at social functions or at home. A pronounced tendency to drink solely in bars, saloons and other public places can be caused by any of a number (or combination) of reasons: because drinking in the home is discouraged or prohibited for religious or other reasons; because the drinker is a minor and does not have parental approval to drink; because the drinker is trying to hide a drinking problem or the nature of his or her behavior while drinking.

Characteristic of bar drinking is the convivial anonymity. Most bar relationships are transient, limited to the confines of the bar and unscheduled (that is confined to chance encounters or "normal" routines of bar socializing). There is little peer pressure beyond the call to continuous or ever greater consumption. Most bar relationships are conducted in an atmosphere of at least mild intoxication and alcohol is therefore central to them. For this reason it has been suggested that recovering alcoholics with past patterns of bar drinking are most receptive to help from support groups, such as ALCOHOLICS ANONYMOUS, which stress anonymity, group support and a preoccupation with alcohol. (See also SOLITARY DRINKER.)

barbiturate   One of a number of generalized central nervous system depressants belonging to a class of drugs that includes alcohol. The most commonly abused barbiturates are short acting agents, such as pentobarbital (Nembutal) and secobarbital (Seconal). Because there is CROSS-TOLERANCE between alcohol and barbiturates, physicians sometimes prescribe them during WITHDRAWAL to achieve a gradual reduction of the physical dependence on alcohol. In such cases barbiturates are given in small quantities and gradually decreasing doses so that the patient does not in turn develop a dependence on them. Physicians also often prescribe barbiturates for alcoholics to help combat nervousness and insomnia stemming from abstinence, but instead of curing alcoholism, this practice can bring about a pattern of multiple drug use.

Alcoholics sometimes use barbiturates with alcohol in order to achieve an enhanced degree of intoxication. The combination increases central nervous system depression, possibly resulting in coma and respiratory arrest (see SYNERGY). (See also SEDATIVE.)

B & B   A dark-colored 86-proof liqueur, B & B consists of one part BENEDIC-

TINE and one part brandy (often Cognac). It is a drier version of straight Benedictine and is often preferred in the United States.

Beaujolais   A French wine that takes its name from the Beaujolais region in southern Burgundy, where it is produced. Although there are several varieties and qualities of Beaujolais wine, 99% of them are red and have a fruity taste. These wines are intended to be drunk when they are young and fresh (i.e., by the time they are three years old). Their alcoholic content is usually 12% or more, although it is sometimes as low as 10%.

beer   An alcoholic beverage produced by fermenting and aging a mash of malted cereal grain and hops (see BREWING). Alterations in the proportion of cereal and hop ingredients and variations in the fermentation process account for the wide variety of different beers. These include lager, ale, stout, porter, malt beer ("malt liquor"), bock beer and pilsner beer.

Beer's origins date back to prehistoric times. It was undoubtedly among the first alcoholic beverages known to man. The first recorded producers of beer were the Egyptians and Mesopotamians, both of whom are known to have fermented some forms of "barley-water" long before 2000 B.C., with one Mesopotamian record dating back to 4000 B.C. The Babylonian Code of Hammurabi in 1800 B.C. included an injunction against drunkenness that in all likelihood was provoked by overconsumption of beer.

From Egypt beer traveled to Greece, where it was produced in substantial quantities as early as 600 B.C., and, later, to Rome. In both the classical Greek and Roman societies, however, beer was considered a rather crude and even barbaric beverage in comparison with wine. It was left to the Gauls, in their colder climates, to pursue the refinement of brewing techniques. They began to do so, according to Tacitus, as early as the first century A.D.,

and this to a large extent reinforced the association of beer with barbarism and wine with culture, which, in muted forms, survives today.

During the same time span knowledge of beer brewing passed south from Egypt throughout most of Africa and north and east to regions that became part of Russia, where beer was called *quass;* China, where it became known as *samshu;* and Japan, where it was named *sake.* Beer's movement north and west to Europe, however, proved to be the most important. Just as the early history of beer began in regions that were too warm and dry for widespread cultivation of wine grapes, its later evolution occurred in lands too cold and damp for such cultivation, particularly Germany and Britain, where the greatest quantitative and qualitative advances in brewing were achieved. Originally done in homes and monasteries in western Europe, brewing became commercialized during the 16th century. For a short time, before the introduction of coffee and tea, some form of beer was one of the few available and affordable alternatives to water or milk for most of the population. Beer consumption was a habit easily transported to the New World by its western European settlers. With only brief interruptions by enthusiasm for other alcoholic beverages, beer has remained a prominent feature of life in western Europe as well as the United States, Commonwealth nations and a number of other countries.

Today the alcohol content of most beers varies from 3% to 6%, with malt beers ("malt liquors") slightly exceeding that proportion. The caloric value of beer depends on the variety, but in most cases it falls between 12 and 14 calories per ounce. Nutritionally beer is high in carbohydrates and low in fats and has a comparatively low proportion of B vitamins.

behavior modification   In behavior modification, also known as behavior modification therapy, the focus is on the behavior of the individual alcoholic rather than on underlying and perhaps deeply buried causes of the behavior. After it is determined what types of behavior are not useful to the individual, techniques are used to manipulate these in a manner that will benefit the alcoholic and possibly prevent future deviations.

There are two main goals of behavior therapy in the treatment of alcoholism. The first is to eliminate excessive alcohol consumption as a primary response to stress or other uncomfortable situations. The second is to establish alternative methods of coping with stressful situations. Initially the addiction cycle must be broken and then new habits must be established. Since most approaches today concentrate only on the first goal, they constitute only partial treatment.

The best known behavior modification technique is that of AVERSION THERAPY, in which a negative value is associated with the consumption of alcohol. Another technique is blood alcohol discrimination training, based on internal cues, although this type of training is being questioned because of doubts about the ability of alcoholics to estimate their blood alcohol level. Other techniques include assertiveness training and biofeedback.

Some behavior therapies employ a number of techniques. Individualized behavior therapy (Sobell and Sobell) for instance, has four major components: shock avoidance procedures; videotaped self-confrontation with drunken behavior; availability of alcohol as part of the treatment program; and individualized talk therapy focused on training in problem-solving skills. Unfortunately with this program there is no way of knowing which therapy contributes most to the outcome of the treatment.

One of the most recent trends in behavior modification is an attempt to teach controlled drinking as an alternative to alcoholic drinking. This approach is highly controversial since it directly contradicts the traditional LOSS OF CONTROL model of alcoholism. Because excessive consumption is viewed as learned behavior rather than an irreversible process, controlled drinking is seen as a viable alternative for some alcoholics. This is flatly denied by most opponents of CONTROLLED DRINKING.

Advocates of behavior modification point out that it is a much more efficient mode of treatment than psychoanalytic approaches, which often take years or may never be able to uncover the deep-seated causes of alcoholism. Opponents of behavior modification feel that it is a superficial treatment which does not really solve the problem, that its record to date is unimpressive and that symptoms frequently reappear. Moreover, in 1982, the methods and validity of the Sobell research have come under sustained attack.

David J. Armor, J. Michael Polich and Harriet B. Stambul, *Alcoholism and Treatment* (New York: John Wiley and Sons, 1978), passim.

John R. DeLuca, ed., *Fourth Special Report to the U.S. Congress on Alcohol and Health* (Rockville, Md.: National Institute on Alcohol Abuse and Alcoholism, 1981), pp. 152–153.

Cyril M. Franks, "Behavior Modification and the Treatment of the Alcoholic," *Alcoholism: Behavioral Research, Therapeutic Approaches,* ed. Ruth Fox (New York: Springer Publishing Company, 1967), pp. 186–203.

M. B. Sobell and L. C. Sobell, *Behavioral Treatment of Alcohol Problems* (New York: Plenum Press, 1978), passim.

behavioral learning theory   A psychological model of alcoholism that focuses on observable behavior and on the environmental conditions that serve to cause or maintain excessive drinking. It is thought that drinking patterns can be unlearned through modification of environmental stimuli and situations that reinforce negative behavior.

On the most basic level, the cause and continuation of alcoholic behavior are attributed to the association of alcohol consumption with a positive experience. To change such behavior, drinking is lined with aversive consequences, so that alcohol is given a negative rather than a positive value (see AVERSION THERAPY). As more is understood about alcoholism, however, the behavior model has become more complicated. Alcoholic behavior is broken into separate components and each is viewed as subject to modification through a number of different possible techniques.

Albert Bandura asserts that excessive drinking is acquired and maintained by a two-stage conditioning process. The positive value of alcohol derives first from the CENTRAL NERVOUS SYSTEM depressant and anesthetic properties of the drug that provide relief from stress. The behavior of drinking is reinforced by the reduction of unpleasant experience. When excessive use of alcohol becomes a habit, it begins to have consequent aversive effects on the individual, such as guilt or loss of a job, that in turn set up renewed stimulus for drinking. Eventually prolonged heavy alcohol usage produces alterations in the metabolic system creating physiological ADDICTION. Once addiction occurs, the second stage of the conditioning mechanism is reached. In this stage WITHDRAWAL symptoms (such as tremulousness, nausea, vomiting etc.) become the stimuli for alcohol consumption. Drinking is then reinforced automatically and continually through the termination of withdrawal symptoms that it provides.

The assumption behind the behavioral learning theory is that alcoholics drink because alcohol ingestion is followed by a reduction in anxiety, stress and tension. To change this response, either the situation that induces the psychological stress must be altered or the individual's response to the stress must be changed. This theory is now questioned because of contradictory evidence regarding alcohol's role as a tension reducer.

A number of behavior theorists, including Bandura, recognize that factors other than tension reduction, such as social reinforcement (peer approval), imitative learning (family drinking styles) and specific situational cues (bars, cocktail parties), may play a significant role in the development of alcoholism. Careful attention is therefore given to the specifics of each individual case.

David J. Armor, Michael Polich and Harriet B. Stambul, *Alcoholism and Treatment* (New York: John Wiley and Sons, 1978), pp. 22–24.

Albert Bandura, *Principles of Behavior Modification* (New York: Holt, Rinehart and Winston, 1969), passim.

Belgium   Although alcohol retains an important place in the social life of Belgians, the country experiences only limited alcohol abuse problems. One reason is the national preference for beer over all other alcoholic beverages: fully 70% of all alcohol consumed is taken in the form of beer, followed by smaller amounts of wine and very small amounts of distilled spirits. The established drinking pattern also plays a part in limiting alcohol abuse. Alcohol is seldom drunk before meals, and there is rarely heavy drinking during special family and social occasions. The Flemish northern population and the French southern population, both predominantly Roman Catholic, display a generally controlled acceptance of alcohol. One useful indicator of the national attitude toward alcohol is the law that permits sale of distilled spirits in grocery stores but only in quantities larger than 2 liters, which are not conducive to the casual drinking associated with smaller, cheaper and more portable quantities.

Per capita consumption of alcohol is a relatively low 138 liters per year, virtually all of it in the form of beer. For the population over 15 years of age the per capita consumption of ABSOLUTE ALCOHOL is 13.2 liters per year. This figure, however, represents a 13% increase between 1960 and

1970 and progressive increases since that year. Daily consumption of alcohol is highest among university students and military personnel, 69% of those two portions of the population drink alcoholic beverages daily, but only an insignificant proportion exceed 3 glasses of beer or 2 glasses of wine per day. In recent years Belgium, like most countries, has documented a trend toward a greater acceptance of drinking by women and a higher incidence of alcohol-related problems.

Using the JELLINEK formulation, authorities in Belgium calculated that the number of alcoholics in the country in 1980 was about 1% of the total population of 10 million. Treatment programs for alcoholism are concentrated in a few psychiatric hospitals. The mortality rate attributed to alcoholism is 2.3 males and 0.6 females per 100,000 population. The rate of mortality from liver cirrhosis doubled between 1956 and 1976, but despite the rise this disease still accounts for less than 1% of hospital deaths. One-third of the country's auto accidents and one-half of its occupational accidents are attributed to alcohol. Legal regulations on alcohol consumption include a 1939 law against public drunkenness and a 1968 drunk driving law, which was modified in 1975 to lower the permissible level of alcohol in the blood to 0.8 grams of ethanol per 1000 grams of blood.

The agencies charged with addressing alcohol abuse in Belgium are the National Committee for Study and Prevention of Alcoholism and Other Drug Addictions, the National Federation of Consulting Bureaux and Institutions for the Care of Alcoholics and Other Drug Addicts and the Volksbond ("People United") Against the Abuse of Alcohol. All are private bodies working in close cooperation with each other. The National Committee, established in 1949, concentrates on statistical records; the National Federation, established in 1972, on hospital care; and the Volksbond, established in 1972, on secondary school preven-

tion programs. In 1980 formation of a new National Committee on Alcohol and Other Drugs was announced. The committee will help coordinate funding and redistribute activities among the three existing agencies.

bender   A drinking spree or bout, as in "on a bender" (on a drunken spree).

Benedictine   Benedictine, an amber-colored French liquer, was first manufactured by the monks of the Benedictine Order at the Abbey Fecamp in Normandy. It contains approximately 43% alcohol by volume and has a somewhat sweet taste. Like other liquers, it is meant to be sipped in a relaxed manner as a digestif. Although the exact recipe is a carefully guarded secret, Benedictine includes among its ingredients at least 30 different aromatic plants, honey, sugar, fruit peels and brandy (generally Cognac). At one time it also contained China tea.

Benedictine is said to have been invented during the early 16th century (possibly 1510) by Dom Bernardo Vincelli, one of the monks at the Abbey Fecamp. The monks at Fecamp continued to manufacture Benedictine until 1793, when the abbey was destroyed in the French Revolution. The recipe was preserved among the monastic documents entrusted to the *procureur fiscal* ("civil administrator"). Over 70 years later one of the *procureur*'s descendants, Alexandre le Grand, established a distillery on the same grounds where the abbey had been. Benedictine is still manufactured there today, although it is no longer associated with the religious order.

Beta alcoholism   The second of five categories of alcoholism defined by JELLINEK. Victims eventually develop such medical complications as ALCOHOLIC POLYNEUROPATHY or CIRRHOSIS, but Beta alcoholism is not associated with either physical or psychological dependence on alcohol and WITHDRAWAL symtoms do not emerge. This type of alcoholism may result from the customs of a certain social group in conjunction with poor nutritional habits.

Beta alcoholism can develop into GAMMA ALCOHOLISM, but this is less likely to occur than in the case of ALPHA ALCOHOLISM.

biological models   See PHYSIOLOGI-CAL ETIOLOGICAL MODELS.

black Americans   Blacks are the largest ethnic minority in the United States, but as with other minorities, there is a scarcity of data on drinking problems among them. Frederick D. Harper, professor in the Department of Psychoeducational Studies at Howard University, reported that a 1976 analysis of literature on alcoholism found fewer than 15 articles which focused on black alcoholics as the major research group. Studies have tended to examine only lower-class black males, from which generalizations have been made about the entire black population.

Alcoholism rates for black males are not greatly different than those for white males. Surveys in the 1960s showed 38% of black men were abstainers compared with 31% of white men and 19% of black men were heavy drinkers compared with 22% of white men. Of black women 51% were abstainers compared with 39% of white women, but the proportion of heavy drinkers among black women exceeded that among white women—11% to 4%. These results suggest that the majority of black women drink heavily or not at all *(Third Special Report to the U.S. Congress on Alcohol and Health).*

Alcoholism is a serious problem in the black community, particularly in urban areas, where CIRRHOSIS mortality rates are unusually high. In seven major cities (Baltimore, Chicago, Detroit, Los Angeles, New York, Philadelphia and Washington, D.C.) deaths from cirrhosis among black males aged 25 to 34 are 10 times as high as among white males of the same age group. For all

ages the cirrhosis mortality rate for blacks is nearly twice that for whites *(Fourth Special Report to the U.S. Congress).* In the 35-year period from 1940 to 1974 cirrhosis rates increased rapidly, from 5.8 per 100,000 to 20.4 per 100,000.

Blacks are more susceptible to CANCER of the upper digestive tract and they suffer from a significantly higher rate of hypertension, further complicated by drinking, than do other groups (see HEART).

Alcohol also plays an important role in influencing a large proportion of crimes in urban and rural black communities. Blacks have a significantly higher incidence of alcohol-related homicide than whites.

Some theorists, such as Harper, suggest that black drinking problems may have begun when black slaves were sometimes encouraged to drink on weekends in order to pacify them and keep them from escaping. Drinking was a way for slaves to forget temporarily about the drudgery endured in the fields. Today a pattern of weekend drinking still exists in black communities, so much so that many liquor stores in black areas open on Friday and close on Monday.

Racism and economic frustration no doubt cause many blacks to drink. In ghettos, where blacks are separated and alienated from the rest of society, alcohol may help dull the senses against intolerable living conditions and a sense of powerlessness.

Another contributing factor, as Harper points out, is the location of liquor stores in residential areas of black neighborhoods, in contrast to many white communities, where liquor stores are located in commercially zoned business areas. Thus, with the easy availability of liquor, drinking becomes a major source of recreation and social activity. Status is achieved by drinking certain types of liquor and by buying rounds of drinks for friends. For example, black Americans buy 30% of the nation's scotch, which ranks high on their list of status liquors (Pettigrew, cited in Hornick).

In comparison with white adolescents,

adolescent blacks reported a higher abstention rate and a lower heavier-drinking rate—about one-third that of whites the same age. As social, familial and economic pressures increase with age, so do drinking problems. Black alcoholic adults are often younger than white alcoholic adults and often experience alcohol-related illness at a younger age.

There are significantly higher rates of both nondrinkers and heavy drinkers among black women than among white women. Ironically both may be due to lower expectations that result in a fatalistic attitude toward life. A conservative or fundamentalist upbringing and the necessities of coping with an unusually difficult environment may account for the high abstention rates among black women, who focus on a "happier hereafter" rather than on the frustrations of daily living. On the other hand the same stresses that cause some to abstain may drive other black women to despair and to drink heavily. For example, domestic and economic stresses, particularly for the numerous black women who head households, may be too much to cope with.

The rate of alcoholism among minority women has been increasing. A study by the Metropolitan Life Insurance Company showed that between 1964 and 1974 alcohol-related deaths rose 36% among white women and 71% among nonwhite women, most of whom were black (Sandmaier). This figure may be due in part to the fact that minority women are less likely to receive treatment, and so may literally drink themselves to death. In 1976 only 17% of the patients in black treatment programs were women, indicating the stigma still attached to female alcoholism.

Blacks are underrepresented in most treatment programs, partly because the problem of alcoholism has not yet been recognized and accepted in the black community. There is a kind of general DENIAL of the problem and more tolerance of drunks than in white communities. This tolerance

is indicated by the much greater dependence black skid row alcoholics have on the black community than their white counterparts have on their community. A lack of culture-specific treatment programs and failure to study the needs of blacks in treatment further undermines the hope of success of treatment for alcohol problems in the black community. Alcoholics Anonymous is often perceived by blacks as white and middle class, although there are some primarily black AA groups. Many blacks are unable to pay for alcoholism treatment and are less likely to have insurance coverage for such treatment. There is also a lack of knowledge about free social services. However, Melvin Porche, Sr., director of the Total Community Action Alcoholism Program in New Orleans, reports that black alcoholics admitted to hospitals and clinics show stronger motivation and cooperation in treatment than do white alcoholics.

John R. DeLuca, ed., *Fourth Special Report to the U.S. Congress on Alcohol and Health* (Rockville, Md.: National Institute on Alcohol Abuse and Alcoholism, 1981), passim.

Frederick D. Harper, "Research and Treatment with Black Alcoholics," *Alcohol Health and Research World* 4, no. 4 (Summer 1980):10–16.

Edith Lynn Hornick, *The Drinking Woman* (New York: Association Press, 1977), passim.

Ernest P. Noble, ed., *Third Special Report to the U.S. Congress on Alcohol and Health* (Rockville, Md.: National Institute on Alcohol Abuse and Alcoholism, 1978), pp. 61–62.

Melvin Porche, Sr., "Report to the 29th Annual Forum of the NCA" (a summary), *U.S. Journal of Drug and Alcohol Dependencies* 5, no. 4 (May 1981):10.

Marian Sandmaier, *The Invisible Alcoholics* (New York: McGraw-Hill Book Company, 1980), passim.

blackout   A temporary loss of memory during and following a period of drinking. Blackout is not a state of unconsciousness; it is rather a condition in which the alcoholic is able to walk and talk but later cannot remember anything. Blackout is a common early warning sign of alcoholism, and as the illness progresses, blackouts may become more frequent and last for longer periods of time. The amount of alcohol needed to produce a blackout is often unpredictable—the ingestion of a relatively small amount may sometimes produce a blackout, while at other times a very large quantity may be necessary to produce the same effect in the same individual. It is not known why some alcoholics are susceptible to blackouts and others are not or have only mild blackouts. The reason why an individual may have a blackout on one occasion and not another is also unknown. Several factors have been associated with blackouts, including drinking large amounts rapidly (gulping), a history of frequent head injuries, fatigue, and concurrent ingestion of hypnotics, tranquilizers or sedatives with alcohol. MARIJUANA WITH ALCOHOL may have a synergistic effect that results in memory loss. Some blackouts are psychologically rather than chemically induced: the individual cannot bear to remember his or her behavior and so represses all memory of a drinking episode. These are not equivalent to true alcoholic blackouts, however, as repressed memories are often retrievable under the influence of hypnosis or such drugs as sodium pentothal. In the case of true alcoholic blackout, no information can be retrieved.

Those who have had one blackout are likely to have subsequent ones. The highest incidence of blackouts occurs in heavy drinkers who have a considerable CRAVING for and a high TOLERANCE to alcohol and who are solitary, gulping drinkers. Blackouts can last for short periods of time or for days. Neither the drinker nor those around him or her are usually aware of the memory loss, which can be explained by an inability to transfer short-term memories to long-

term storage sites. The drinker is able to perform because immediate memory is retained and retrieval of information from long-term memory banks is only partially disturbed.

It is not known what causes blackout. It may be that the processing and storage of new information is disturbed when high concentrations of alcohol come in contact with brain cells involved in the transfer process.

Sidney Cohen, "Blackouts," *Drug Abuse and Alcoholism Newsletter* 10, no. 2 (February 1981).

blood alcohol concentration (or content) (BAC)   An individual's degree of intoxication can be measured by the concentration of alcohol in the bloodstream. When a blood sample is tested for alcohol, the findings are reported in the form of blood alcohol concentration (BAC), also called blood alcohol level (BAL), which measures, in percentages, the weight of the alcohol in a fixed volume of blood. In certain countries, including the United States, BAC for 7 parts of alcohol per 10,000 parts of blood, for example, is expressed as .07%. In Canada and some other nations the equivalent would be 70 milligrams per 100 milliliters of blood, expressed as 70 mg%. In Sweden it would be recorded as 0.7 promille. Each system records the same percentage of alcohol.

While medical facilities and alcohol treatment centers use BACs as guides for immediate treatment of a presumably inebriated patient, BAC tests are most often given to motorists suspected of DRIVING WHILE INTOXICATED. In Idaho and Utah any driver with a BAC over .08% is considered legally intoxicated. In other areas of the United States, including the District of Columbia, the figure is .10% (many critics consider this level abnormally high and permissive). In Canada the limit is 80 mg%; in Sweden 0.5 promille is evidence of second-

Calculation of Estimated Blood Alcohol Concentration (BAC)

Body Weight: Calculations are for people with a *normal* body weight for their height, free of drugs or other affecting medication and neither unusually thin nor obese.

Drink Equivalents: 1 drink equals:
1½ ounces of rum, rye, scotch, brandy, gin, vodka etc.
1 12-oz bottle of normal-strength beer
3 ounces of fortified wine
5 ounces of table wine

Using the chart: Find the appropriate figure using the proper chart (male or female), body weight and number of drinks consumed. Then subtract the time factor (see Time Factor Table below) from the figure on the chart to obtain the approximate BAC. For example, for a 150-lb man who has had 4 drinks in two hours, take the figure .116 (from the chart for males) and subtract .030 (from the Time Factor Table) to obtain a BAC of .086%.

Time Factor Table

Hours since first drink

	1	2	3	4	5	6
Subtract from BAC	.015	.030	.045	.060	.075	.090

Males

Ideal Body Weight (lbs)	Number of Drinks									
	1	2	3	4	5	6	7	8	9	10
100	.043	.087	.130	.174	.217	.261	.304	.348	.391	.435
125	.034	.069	.103	.139	.173	.209	.242	.278	.312	.346
150	.029	.058	.087	.116	.145	.174	.203	.232	.261	.290
175	.025	.050	.075	.100	.125	.150	.175	.200	.225	.250
200	.022	.043	.065	.087	.108	.130	.152	.174	.195	.217
225	.019	.039	.058	.078	.097	.117	.136	.156	.175	.195
250	.017	.035	.052	.070	.087	.105	.122	.139	.156	.173

Females

Ideal Body Weight (lbs)	Number of Drinks									
	1	2	3	4	5	6	7	8	9	10
100	.050	.101	.152	.203	.253	.304	.355	.406	.456	.507
125	.040	.080	.120	.162	.202	.244	.282	.324	.364	.404
150	.034	.068	.101	.135	.169	.203	.237	.271	.304	.338
175	.029	.058	.087	.117	.146	.175	.204	.233	.262	.292
200	.026	.050	.076	.101	.126	.152	.177	.203	.227	.253
225	.022	.045	.068	.091	.113	.136	.159	.182	.204	.227
250	.020	.041	.061	.082	.101	.122	.142	.162	.182	.202

degree drunken driving and 1.5 promille of first degree, a very serious offense.

BAC varies according to a number of factors:

1. *Sex.* Pound for pound of body weight, the increase in BAC per drink is less for men than for women, because men generally have more muscle than women. Women have a larger percentage of fatty tissue, which has a smaller blood supply than muscle tissue. Consequently, given persons of equal weight, the ingestion of equal

amounts of alcohol will result in higher blood concentrations in women than in men.

2. *Weight.* In general the larger (and heavier) a person is, the greater the blood supply is and, thus, the more alcohol can be accommodated. But as noted above, in men and women of equal weight, fatty tissue is a major determinant of BAC levels. The same is true for overweight people. Since their excess weight is stored in the form of fat, their blood supply is not increased in proportion to the additional weight. Therefore a fat person of 170 pounds will have a higher BAC from a given amount of alcohol than a lean person of the same weight.

3. *Time of consumption.* On the average, unless consumption is limited to less than one full drink an hour, BAC will continue to rise. The body will slowly excrete the alcohol as follows: oxidization by the liver, 95%; breath, 2%; urine, 2%; perspiration, 1%.

4. *Food consumption.* A "full" stomach will retard the absorption of alcohol but much less so than is commonly believed. Furthermore the effect of food on BAC varies according to the individual.

5. *Quantity.* Two to four 1½-oz. shots of 86-proof liquor or an equivalent amount of wine or beer approaches the danger limit for drivers (see tables).

BAC may be determined by testing a person's urine or breath as well as his or her blood. Urine tests are difficult to administer and are rarely used. Blood tests are both difficult to perform and often unsatisfactory, since the analysis frequently cannot be made for up to two hours after the suspect is apprehended. However, through the use of batmobiles, mobile blood laboratories, the results of blood tests can often be given within minutes. Despite past legal difficulties and problems of accuracy, breath analyzers are in common use, particularly for preliminary, on-the-spot analysis.

blood alcohol level (BAL) See BLOOD ALCOHOL CONCENTRATION.

blood sugar Consumption of alcohol can affect blood sugar levels. The effects vary depending upon the body's physical state when alcohol is consumed. If carbohydrate stores in the LIVER are adequate, ETHANOL appears to bring about a rise in blood glucose levels (hyperglycemia). If carbohydrate reserves are low, as when the body is fasting, the opposite effect, low blood sugar (hypoglycemia), occurs. This condition is apparently due to the interference of alcohol with the normal conversion of carbohydrates into sugar. Alcohol may also indirectly stimulate the hormone insulin, which works to lower blood sugar. An adequate supply of blood sugar from a meal or a snack is generally protection against the effects of low blood sugar produced by the consumption of alcohol. However, when alcohol and sugar are taken together, such as in a gin and tonic, the combination may increase stimulation of insulin production and thereby produce a hypoglycemic effect.

Alcoholics are often hypoglycemic, possibly because the impairment of liver function, caused by heavy drinking, may interfere with the ability to metabolize glucose; alcoholics who have stopped drinking often experience a craving for sweets. Inadequate food intake also contributes to hypoglycemia (see NUTRITION). Low blood sugar may be a cause of the HANGOVER effect. (See also DIABETES.)

bock beer A seasonal beer whose name derives from the German *Einbecker Bier* (literally, beer from Einbeck), shortened in the dialect of Bavaria, where it originated, to *Bockbier*. Bock beer, sometimes simply called bock, is brewed in winter from the residue collected from vats before they are cleaned for another year's brewing. Stronger and sweeter in taste than most lagers, of which it is a variety, true bock beer is dark and has a life of about six weeks. The day on which the product is first ready for consumption, Bock Beer Day, is traditionally associated with the coming of spring.

boom towns   In communities that either spring up almost overnight or become prosperous suddenly because of some new industry or the discovery of a valuable resource, the incidence of alcohol and drug abuse usually jumps markedly or, in new communities, establishes itself at a level well above the norm for other communities of similar size. In studies done in the United States during the mid- and late-1970s, the pattern was repeated in community after community, with the increase in alcohol abuse considerably higher than the rise in drug abuse (overwhelmingly marijuana).

The characteristics of these boom towns are very similar. There is an influx of young, often blue-collar males (single or without their wives) into an area where the social fabric is strained by economic and population changes. Wages and prices are high and amenities, including recreational facilities, are scarce or non existent. Drinking is the only major social activity and is done in bars. Prostitution often flourishes. Treatment for alcohol-related problems generally rises but the pattern is erratic and hard to measure. Alcohol-related arrests show a marked increase, particularly those for DRIVING WHILE INTOXICATED. (See also DEPRESSED COMMUNITIES.)

booze   (Formerly spelled "boose" but pronounced "booze," from early Germanic sources via the early modern Dutch *buisen* and Middle English *bousen*.) The word "booze" has always been a slang term for drinking excessively, usually to get drunk quickly. As a verb it means to guzzle; to drink to excess. As a noun it is the alcoholic beverage that one "boozes," often whiskey, such as that made around 1840 by a Philadelphia distiller named E. G. Booze. Both the verb and the noun predate Mr. Booze by many centuries. From booze come "boozing it up," "boozer," "boozy" and other such terms.

booze fighter   One for whom BOOZE has become a habit, a compulsion or an addiction and who is determined to "fight" the habit. The term implies an ongoing, and therefore unsuccessful, battle with a continuous stream of good intentions and broken resolutions. It is sometimes used synonymously with BOOZE HOUND.

booze hound   A heavy drinker; one whose life is greatly influenced by, even dedicated to, the consumption of alcoholic beverages. (See also BOOZE FIGHTER.)

bootlegging   A possible derivation of the term "bootlegging," referring to traffic in illegal whiskey, dates back to the post-Revolutionary period, when the government first started imposing taxes on whiskey. Distillers were required to buy tax stamps and display them on their whiskey barrels. To avoid the tax, some distillers had their deliverymen remove the stamps from the barrels after the whiskey was delivered and return them in their bootlegs for use on the next shipment.

In 1880 Kansas incorporated prohibition into its constitution, "bootlegging"—apparently the practice of carrying flasks of whiskey concealed in boot tops—gained widespread popularity. Later other areas of the country established similar laws, resulting in an increase in bootlegging from wet communities to dry ones. During PROHIBITION (1920–1933) bootlegging became a major racket as well as a familiar term across the nation. In the early days of Prohibition a great deal of liquor was smuggled into the United States across the Canadian and Mexican borders and from ships anchored off the coast. As the Coast Guard increased its campaign against those smuggling liquor into the country from ships, bootleggers began to rely more on industrial alcohol, which they washed of noxious chemicals, diluted with water and sometimes flavored with a small amount of real liquor. Liquor was also obtained from government-supervised warehouses, where it was being held for medical use or for export. Bootleggers delivered the liquor to speakeasies, which were mostly controlled by gangsters, although the small-scale bootlegger was usually not a gangster. Bootlegging continued after Prohibition and is still a problem today.

Although bootlegging is generally associated with the United States, other nations have had similar problems. During World War I the Russian government banned the sale of vodka as a war measure. After the war the Communist regime continued the prohibition, but by 1925 bootlegging was so widespread that the government rescinded the ban on vodka.

Alice Fleming, *Alcohol: The Delightful Poison* (New York: Dell Publishing Co., 1975), p. 34.
"Bootlegging." *Encyclopedia Britannica* (USA: William Benton, 1972).

Bordeaux   See RED WINE.

bottom fermentation   Fermentation of a hop wort with a yeast that sinks as sediment in the course of brewing lager beer. Beer yeasts are selected strains of bacterial enzymes that flocculate, or separate themselves from the brewing beer, so that they may be drawn off at the end of the process. This process, in conjunction with the different blend of cereal grains employed, accounts for the lighter flavor of lager beers in comparison with that of ales which are brewed by a process called TOP FERMENTATION. Bottom fermentation is typically carried out at temperatures between 38° and 48°F. It ordinarily takes between seven and 11 days for the yeast to convert the soluble sugar of the grains into the desired level of alcohol content.

bourbon   A spirit distilled from a fermented mash of grain that is at least 51% corn (Indian maize). Bourbon is the most distinctly American of all whiskeys. Particularly regional in origin and history, it continues to be produced almost exclusively in north-central Kentucky.

Of the three principal types of American whiskey—rye, corn whiskey and bourbon—both rye and corn whiskey predate bourbon, which to some extent must be considered a compromise between these earlier spirits. Bourbon is distilled in a process identical to that used to produce RYE WHISKEY, but the mash from which it is distilled contains a high proportion of corn to which other grains, such as rye, have been added. In fact, according to one apocryphal story, bourbon originated when the rye whiskey distillers of Kentucky were faced with a crop failure of their preferred grain.

Most histories date the origin of bourbon as 1789 and the originator as Elijah Craig, a Baptist minister in the village of Georgetown in Bourbon County, then a part of Virginia. The harsh taste of the early bourbons was in keeping with the frontier life style of that region, which was settled from Virginia through the Cumberland Gap after the American Revolution, but it also made bourbon a poor competitor with rye and rum elsewhere in the early United States. Until the Civil War bourbon production remained at a level of about 1,000 barrels per year, most of which came from family distilleries catering to local markets. After the Civil War, however, the highly publicized exposure of a "whiskey ring" with connections to President Ulysses S. Grant's administration brought about sudden government regulation of the bourbon trade. Such regulation tended to reduce the distinct qualities of the various individual brands of bourbon, but it also modernized production of the whiskey and increased its availability in mass markets.

Today production of bourbon begins with the cleaning and milling of the basic corn grain. After the kernels are crushed, the corn is soaked, traditionally in limestone water, and additional grains, such as rye and malted barley, are added. In the "sweet-mash" method an unusually high proportion of malted barley is added to encourage fermentation. In the "sour-mash" method fermentation is encouraged by adding a "slop" of residue from a previous distillation. In both methods the grain mash is then poured into open-topped fermenting vats and yeast is added. Once fermentation has produced enough alcohol to qualify the mash as "distiller's beer," distillation is begun. Originally carried out in pot stills, distillation of bourbons is now almost exclusively done in patent stills. Because of the content of the grain mash, distilled bourbon is considered a "heavy" whiskey and requires two or three years more aging than Scotch whiskey or Irish whiskey.

Most commercially sold bourbon is blended before bottling, a process that involves mixing a single distillate with at least one other distillate and sometimes with flavorless or "neutral," spirits. Less commonly, bourbon is sold as "bottled in bond," a designation that indicates a "straight" bourbon produced by a single distillation.

Bowery   A street and section in lower Manhattan, New York City that was once notorious for its cheap theatres, dance halls, drinking gardens etc. Today the Bowery is an impoverished area populated in large part by derelicts, although it has been partially rehabilitated. The Bowery contains a large SKID ROW area and its inhabitants are the source of the term "Bowery bum."

brain   Alcoholism was first linked to brain damage over 100 years ago, when three patients were described as suffering from delirium, visual problems, imbalance in walking and muscle tremors. Their condition came to be known as WERNICKE'S ENCEPHALOPATHY and there have been hundreds of thousands of such cases since then. In 1887 another form of brain damage was linked to alcoholism—KORSAKOFF'S PSYCHOSIS, characterized by disorientation, memory failure and a tendency to recite imagined occurrences.

Today there is a substantial amount of evidence indicating that prolonged heavy consumption of alcoholic beverages has a negative effect on the brain (and not all forms of brain damage are as extreme as Wernicke's encephalopathy). CAT scanner X rays of heavy drinkers who are not noticeably ill have shown brain atrophy (loss of brain cells). O. A. Parsons concluded in 1977 that in any given sample of alcoholics from 50% to 100% have brain atrophy. Tests have shown deficits in cognition and perception in alcoholics similar to those in patients with brain damage that is not related to alcohol. More research is needed to determine the relationship between alcohol consumption, brain atrophy and psychological performance. However, there seems to be a continuum of alcohol effects on the brain, ranging from little or no effect in light social drinkers to moderate or severe impairment in late-stage alcoholics. Evidence suggests that some brain damage may be partly reversible in abstinent alcoholics.

Medical researchers at the University of California at Irvine have found that in addition to causing atrophy of the brain, excessive drinking led to brainstem abnormalities in 40% of the alcoholic patients they studied. The brainstem connects the brain to the spinal cord and controls such vital functions as respiration, heart rate and blood pressure. Abnormalities of these functions appear to have a strong link to alcohol abuse and are most prevalent in older patients who have already shown neurological complications resulting from extended alcohol use. A correlation between brainstem abnormalities and cerebral atrophy has been found.

How Alcohol Affects the Brain

Alcohol inhibits the brain's ability to use oxygen and reduces its capacity to utilize glucose. Nerve cell transmission and the transport of ions in and out of brain cells are affected. Insufficient oxygen in the brain may cause the brain cells to die, and excessive alcohol intake can result in permanently impaired brain function, although several studies show that partial reversal of atrophy and impairment can occur in abstinent alcoholics. For very moderate drinkers there is no clear evidence that alcohol harms the brain. Nutritional deficiencies associated with alcoholism may also play a role in brain damage (see NUTRITION).

RNA and protein synthesis in the brain both play important roles in learning and memory. Studies by Drs. Sujata Tewari and Ernest Noble of the University of California at Irvine have shown that alcohol interferes with the manufacture of RNA and protein in the brains of mice. This effect may be partly responsible for alcoholic BLACKOUT.

The ACETALDEHYDE produced when alcohol is metabolized (see METABOLISM) may also affect the brain, and investigators have suggested that acetaldehyde may be responsible for the DEPENDENCY which characterizes alcohol addiction. The mechanisms of this effect are still unclear. (See also CENTRAL NERVOUS SYSTEM.)

Lawrence K. Altman, "Alcohol-Linked Brain Damage Is Subtle, but Deadly," *New York Times,* December 22, 1981.

"Brainstem Abnormalities in 40% of Alcoholic Patients," *U.S. Journal of Drug and Alcohol Dependence* 5, no. 5 (June 1981):14.

John R. DeLuca, ed., *Fourth Special Report to the U.S. Congress on Alcohol and Health* (Rockville, Md.: National Institute on Alcohol Abuse and Alcoholism, 1981), pp. 52–57.

Ernest P. Noble, ed., *Third Special Report to the U.S. Congress on Alcohol and Health* (Rockville, Md.: National Institute on Alcohol Abuse and Alcoholism, 1978), pp. 93–107.

brain damage   See BRAIN.

brandy   An alcoholic beverage distilled from the fermented juice of grapes (i.e., wine) or other fruits. The term "brandy" without further qualification usually refers to grape brandy. When fruits other than grapes are used, the name of the fruit precedes the term "brandy" (e.g., apricot brandy, cherry brandy, orange brandy or apple brandy, particularly the French CALVADOS and the American APPLEJACK). Many of these fruits go through a "wine stage" similar to that of the grape, and several are actually made into wines (e.g., apple wine, elderberry wine).

Sometimes the term "brandy" is extended to include what the French call *marc* (pronounced *mar*) and the Italians refer to as *grappa*. *Marc* and *grappa* are inexpensive brandies made from the stems, pips and skins of grapes after the juice has been pressed from them to make wine.

Brandies are produced all over the world. The chief producers are France and the United States, but other important sources include Greece, Spain, Portugal, Italy, Peru and South Africa. The name, therefore, is often also qualified by the country or region where it is produced (e.g., French brandy, California brandy). The best known brandy is COGNAC, which is named after the town of Cognac in southwestern France. Another popular French brandy is ARMAGNAC, also named for the region that produces it.

Brandy is thought to be the oldest of the

distilled alcoholic beverages; its production can be traced back to the 13th century. The art of distillation itself was originated in the eastern world. It was first introduced to the Italians, who produced *acqua di vite* or *arzente*. From Italy the technique traveled to France, where its product was called EAU DE VIE, and then to Spain. By the end of the 17th century the production of brandy had spread throughout Europe.

It is not known when the name "brandy" was first applied to distilled wine. However, it was originally a compound term: brandywine, brandewine or brandwine, which came from the Dutch *brantewijn* (from *branden* to burn + *wijn* wine).

The first step in the production of grape brandy is to press the grapes in the usual way to make wine. The wine is then stored in casks until it is distilled into brandy. It takes approximately 10 casks of wine to produce one cask of brandy.

In the distillation process the wine is placed in pots constructed to retain the impurities, or CONGENERS, which give brandy its characteristic flavor and aroma. The congeners in brandy include normal propyl alcohol, normal butyl alcohol, amyl alcohol, hexyl alcohol, ethyl acetate and oenanthic ether, which provides one of the main taste characteristics that distinguishes brandy from other distilled liquors, such as whiskey or rum.

When first distilled, brandy is a colorless liquid with a very high alcoholic content. The exact percentage of alcohol at this stage of production varies among the different brandies. California brandy, for example, is approximately 102 proof, while Cognac is between 140 and 150 proof.

Before being bottled, brandy is aged in wooden casks for at least three years. As it ages, it mellows and acquires a yellow color that grows darker the longer the brandy remains in the casks. However, depth of color is not an accurate indicator of age, for producers often artificially color brandy with caramel. Brandy also loses some of its al-

coholic content in the aging process, and, frequently, through the addition of distilled water. Bottled Cognac, for example, is between 68 and 80 proof.

Brandy is usually drunk by itself as an after-dinner drink. It is also sometimes used in mixed drinks, such as cocktails, punches and so-called dessert drinks, and as a flavoring in coffee and foods.

brewing   A process that combines cereal grains, water, hops and yeasts to produce beer or ale.

Records of early brewing processes for creating "barley water" appear on a Mesopotamian clay tablet from 4000 B.C. and on a wooden model of a brewery in Thebes from 2000 B.C. The Egyptians developed the most extensive primitive brewing techniques, which were later adopted by the Greeks and ultimately brought to western Europe by the Romans. Early European brewing was based principally in monasteries and homes until the 16th century, when significant commercial breweries emerged. Gradually there evolved a process of brewing that has remained essential to the production of all commercial beers—lager, ale, stout, porter.

The first stage in the process is the preparation of a cereal mash. The principal grain used is barley, which is malted by milling it, soaking it until it germinates and they drying it. Most beers also contain a blend of other cereal grains, which are soaked separately and then mixed with the malted barley in mash tuns. There the grain content is cooked in water, a process that liquefies the starches present and converts them into soluble sugars, chiefly maltose and dextrin, which are essential to fermentation. The result, once filtered, is a liquid called wort.

In the next stage hops, the ripened cones found on the female hop vine, are combined with the wort in a brew kettle, traditionally a copper one, and boiled for several hours. Technically the term "brewing" refers to just this stage of beer production, but the term is commonly used to describe the entire process. The brew is then strained through a hop separator and the result is known as hop wort.

The third stage is fermentation, a process carried out in a fermenting tank and initiated by adding yeast enzymes to the sugar-rich hop wort. The yeast employed must produce sufficient fermentation to create the desired alcohol content and it must also flocculate, or separate itself from the beer, to enable its removal at the end of the process. Two types of brewing yeast have these properties. The first type rises in the beer during fermentation; the product of this process, known as TOP FERMENTATION, is ale. The second type sinks in the beer during fermentation; the result of this process, called BOTTOM FERMENTATION, is lager. In both cases, fermentation is carried out at temperatures in the range of 40° to 60° F and requires anywhere from five to 11 days to complete. Also during both processes gases emitted by the beer are collected and returned to the liquid for carbonation. "Krausened" beers are entirely carbonated by naturally active yeasts, but most beers are carbonated, at least in part, by the introduction of carbon dioxide.

The final stages of the process are aging and packaging. All beers are kept in chilled aging tanks for the last stages of fermentation. Once aged, beer is filtered to remove most of its yeast content and placed in barrels or in smaller consumer containers, such as cans or bottles. If barreled, usually in aluminum kegs, beer requires no further processing and has a short storage life. To extend their shelf life, bottled and canned beers are usually pasteurized to destroy the remaining yeast enzymes and prevent further fermentation.

Burgundy   See RED WINE.

business   See EMPLOYEE ASSISTANCE PROGRAMS.

butyl alcohol   A colorless liquid made by the fermentation of glucose, butyl alcohol is used as a solvent. It should not be confused with ETHANOL, the principal chemical in alcoholic beverages. (See INTRODUCTION TO ALCOHOL, p.XVI.)

C

caffeine   Because it is a stimulant, caffeine has been thought to counteract the effects of alcohol, but it is not a sobering agent. Both antagonistic and additive interactions between alcohol and caffeine have been reported, but generally the effects are quite small. When alcohol is acting to reduce inhibition of behavior, caffeine may increase this effect; when alcohol is acting as a depressant, caffeine may act antagonistically. It does not speed up the elimination of alcohol and may provide a false sense of security to those who drink excessively in the belief that they can always sober up quickly with coffee or another source of caffeine.

Since it constricts the blood vessels, caffeine may provide some relief for the headache experienced during a hangover, which is related to overdilation of the blood vessels caused by the consumption of alcohol.

Heavy coffee consumption is often associated with heavy alcohol use and smoking.

calorie   A unit of measure used to express the heat- or energy-producing value of food when it is metabolized in the body. On an average, ABSOLUTE ALCOHOL contains about 150 to 200 calories per ounce. These are so-called empty calories, which may, in some circumstances, provide quick energy but will not serve the body's nutritional needs.

The calories contained in alcohol cannot be stored, so the body burns them before it burns food calories, which are stored and used as fat. Therefore for someone interested in losing weight it is important to reduce alcohol consumption. Continued consumption of a high level of alcohol while cutting down on food may lead to malnutrition.

Calvados   A famous French apple brandy from the Normandy region of the same name. The production of alcohol from apples was first developed by the Vikings who settled in Normandy over a thousand years ago.

Calvados is distilled from apple cider or, sometimes, apple pulp and aged in oak casks for six years. It is bottled at around 80 proof and has a distinct applelike flavor.

Campari   An alcoholic beverage made in Milan, Italy, Campari belongs to the class of drinks known as BITTERS. It is 48 proof, reddish in color and has a somewhat bitter flavor. In Italy, Campari is one of the most popular APERITIFS. It is drunk either neat with soda as a chaser or mixed in cocktails.

Canada   As is most other developed Western countries, attitudes toward alcohol consumption in Canada are undergoing a process of liberalization. Drinking is becoming increasingly common among youths and women, groups that in the past did not generally drink; the proportion of abstainers may have dropped as much as 50% between 1950 and 1980; and holiday sales of liquor indicate a greater popularity of alcoholic beverages at social celebrations. The general pattern of drinking in Canada is one of increased consumption on weekends and holidays throughout the year. Only about one-sixth of the country's alcohol consump-

tion takes place in public places, but the overwhelming amount of drinking in private places has resulted in a higher level of consumption because of the absence of inhibitions associated with public drinking. The proportions of alcoholic beverages consumed are approximately 50% beer, 40% distilled spirits and 10% wine, with the proportions of distilled spirits and wines rising sharply in recent years.

Controls on the sale and consumption of alcoholic beverages are a matter of provincial rather than federal authority in Canada, and statistics on consumption are also gathered on the provincial level. The highest annual rates of per capita consumption are found in the western provinces of British Columbia and Alberta (2.97 gallons of ABSOLUTE ALCOHOL and 2.83 gallons of absolute alcohol respectively in 1979). These are also the provinces experiencing the most population growth, due to their mineral wealth, and alcohol consumption in them most likely stems from the conjunction of their frontier character with their sudden economic wealth. The lowest annual rates of consumption per capita are in the Maritime Provinces of New Brunswick and Nova Scotia (1.80 gallons of absolute alcohol and 2.29 gallons of absolute alcohol respectively in 1979).

Computed on the national level, per capita consumption rose 34% between 1966 and 1974 and then declined slightly between 1975 and 1979. During this period of slight per capita decline, however, per capita expenditure on alcoholic beverages continued to rise because of increased prices. Statistics for the fiscal year ending in 1979 revealed a national consumption of 2.36 billion liters of alcohol at a cost of $4.37 billion,[1] or about 100 liters of alcohol at a cost of $185 per person.

---

[1]All dollar figures are Canadian. Because of the fluctuations in the value of both Canadian and U.S. currencies, it is difficult to give precise U.S. dollar equivalents. Between 1975 and 1979 the rate of exchange went from C$.99 = US$1.00 to C$1.16 = US$1.00.

Between 1975 and 1979 Canada's total sales of alcoholic beverages by value rose 46%, from $2.9 billion in 1975 to the aforementioned $4.37 billion in 1979. Wine, which is consumed in limited proportions, accounted for the largest rise in sales, from $350 million in 1975 to $686 million in 1979, an increase of 96%. During the same period sales of distilled spirits rose from $1.4 billion in 1975 to $2 billion in 1979, or 38%, and sales of beer increased from $1.1 billion in 1975 to $1.6 billion in 1979, or 42%. The total population growth rate during the same period was only about 6%.

While there are no estimates of the national rate of alcoholism, Ontario, Canada's most populous province, conducted a survey in 1976 to determine the rate of alcoholism among its inhabitants based on consumption and mortality from alcohol-related health problems. According to the survey, the alcoholic population in 1976 was 225,000, or 2.7% of the province's total population.

Alcohol is thought to be the cause of 40% of all fatal auto accidents in Canada, and an equal proportion of all murders has been attributed to alcohol abuse, by either the victim or the perpetrator of the crime. Again, Ontario's surveys are the only representative data available for computing the additional costs of alcohol abuse in the country. In 1972 the rate of mortality from liver cirrhosis in Ontario was 21.5 per 100,000 population over 25 years of age— 75% of these cases were believed to be alcohol related. This rate represented an increase of 300% over the rate in 1950. In 1971 the same province estimated that its expenditures directly attributable to alcohol abuse included well over $100 million for health care, over $50 million for protection of public order, and over $10 million for children's aid. In the same year revenue loss resulting from absenteeism and reduced productivity related to alcohol was put at $124 million.

The agencies responsible for combating

Annual Per Capita Consumption of Absolute Alcohol, by Province (1979)

Province	Gallons
British Columbia	2.97
Alberta	2.83
Ontario	2.56
Manitoba	2.53
Newfoundland	2.34
Prince Edward Island	2.34
Quebec	2.33
Saskatchewan	2.30
Nova Scotia	2.29
New Brunswick	1.80

alcohol abuse are the federal and provincial ministries of health, whose jurisdictions in this respect overlap. Most provinces maintain research foundations, alcohol and drug abuse programs, health facilities for alcoholics and drug addicts, and education programs for both the general and school-age populations. At the same time, however, there is a lack of formal policies aimed at reducing alcohol abuse and few efforts to encourage alterations of environments considered conducive to alcohol abuse.

Canada has acknowledged a need for comprehensive training programs, which are presently limited to the training provided by medical schools and various foundations concerned with the problem. Many

Sales of Alcoholic Beverages in Millions of Dollars, by Province (1975, 1977, 1979)

Province	1975	1977	1979
Ontario	1,090	1,325	1,549
Quebec	669	837	999
British Columbia	388	471	586
Alberta	268	357	454
Manitoba	137	171	182
Saskatchewan	121	151	173
Nova Scotia	112	135	156
New Brunswick	80	99	115
Newfoundland	77	97	110
Prince Edward Island	16	20	23

of the most successful efforts to address the problem of alcoholism in Canada remain wholly voluntary and charitable, including the work of Alcoholics Anonymous and the Salvation Army in individual provinces.

Canadian whisky   An alcoholic beverage produced in Canada by distilling a fermented mash of barley, rye and corn. The distilled alcohol is subjected to secondary extraction and rectification processes that leave it with a very low level of heavy CONGENERS. For that reason it is known as the lightest of all whiskies. Individual Canadian whiskies are aged for four, eight or 12 years and then blended with others before final filtering and bottling. They are sold at 86.6 proof.

The origins of Canadian whisky are not known, but it is assumed that distillation of grains in Canada was begun by Irish and Scottish settlers around the end of the 18th century. Although the whisky was no doubt prized by pioneers, particularly during the harsh Canadian winters, effective temperance movements controlled its distribution throughout the 19th century. There were also several provincial prohibitions on alcohol distillation in Canada, and consequently the Canadian whisky industry developed much later than its American counterpart.

A law banning the distillation of alcohol in Canada was being drafted when Prohibition was enacted in the United States with the passage of the Volstead Act in 1919. Bolstered by the sudden lack of competition from America, distillers in Canada prevailed on the government to abandon its plans for instituting prohibition there. Canadian whisky subsequently became enormously popular in the United States as the cheapest safe alternative to "bathtub gin" and other illegal distillates, and the Canadian liquor industry boomed. When Prohibition ended in the United States in 1933, Canadian distillers were able to extend their syndicates across the border before

producers of domestic brands of whiskey could establish themselves.

cancer   Excessive alcohol consumption is known to increase the risk of cancer at various sites in the body. Relative to the rest of the population, alcoholics and heavy drinkers show a high incidence of mortality from cancer of the mouth, pharynx, larynx, esophagus, liver and lung as well as excessive mortality from other causes. In the United States cancer associated with alcohol accounts for 6.1% to 27.9% of the total incidence of all cancer. Alcohol itself has not been shown to act as an independent carcinogen, but it is thought to act as a "co-carcinogen," a substance that promotes cancer in conjunction with a carcinogen. Studies indicate that alcohol and cigarettes together act synergistically to increase carcinogenic potential, particularly in the mouth and throat. So far it has been difficult to separate the effects of drinking from the effects of smoking because most heavy drinkers are also heavy smokers. Smokers risk developing cancer of the mouth and throat and smokers who also drink heavily run an even greater risk of developing such cancers. It has been estimated that when drinking and smoking are combined, the risk of developing cancer of the mouth and throat is 15 times greater than normal, i.e., the risk among the nondrinking and nonsmoking population.

There are a number of theories about why alcohol increases the incidence of cancer. The diets of alcoholics are often poorly balanced and nutritionally inadequate (see NUTRITION). Cancers of the mouth, esophagus and pharynx have been linked to deficiencies of VITAMINS AND MINERALS. Consumption of alcohol may also weaken the body's entire immune defense system, leaving it vulnerable to other cancer-causing agents. Alcohol is known to damage cellular tissue, especially the MITOCHONDRIA, the source of cellular energy. In addition alcohol has an effect on the cell membrane—possibly increasing the ability of carcinogens to affect the cells themselves. All alcoholic beverages consumed by man contain chemicals other than ETHANOL, and these may be carcinogenic, or these plus alcohol may act in SYNERGY to produce cancer.

CONGENERS, pharmacologically active molecules other than ethanol present in alcoholic beverages, may also play a role in the development of cancer. Known carcinogens have been found in many alcoholic beverages. Beer, for example, has been found to contain asbestos fibers from the filters used in its manufacture. Different beers, liquors and wines have varying quantities of contaminants that are by-products of distillation.

Cancer of the Mouth, Tongue, Pharynx and Larynx

Alcohol consumption, usually in combination with smoking, increases the risk of developing most cancers of the upper respiratory and digestive tracts. The mechanisms of the combined action of alcohol and tobacco are complex and vary from site to site. One theory is that tobacco carcinogens have easier access to the mucous membranes if the cells have been saturated in alcohol, with its solvent effects. Another theory is that alcohol and tobacco each independently exert a direct effect on the mucous membranes. Tobacco may contribute to cancer of the roof of the mouth, the nasopharynx (which connects with the nostrils), the larynx and the lung, where it directly contacts the mucous membranes. Alcohol may play more of a role in cancer of the floor of the mouth, the lower pharynx and the esophagus, where contact is most direct.

Esophagus

The cancer-causing role of alcohol among smokers was found to be even greater in cases of cancer of the esophagus than in those of cancer of the mouth and larynx. There is an increased risk of esophageal cancer among all drinkers, although it is apparently greater for whiskey drinkers than for wine or beer drinkers. Between 60% and 80% of patients who develop cancer of the esophagus have a history of alcohol abuse. Alcohol may destroy the chemical barriers in the esophagus, exposing susceptible cells to carcinogens. A study done in France in 1977 showed that the risk of esophageal cancer is 44 times greater for heavy users of both alcohol and tobacco than for abstainers from both drugs, compared with 18 times greater for heavy users of alcohol and five times greater for heavy users of tobacco.

Liver

Primary liver cancer (hepatoma) is very often accompanied by and probably preceded by CIRRHOSIS. In a series of studies, cited in the *Third Special Report to the U.S. Congress on Alcohol and Health,* on the association of primary liver cancer and cirrhosis, 64% to 90% of the victims had suffered from both conditions. There are possibly two stages involved in liver cancer: liver damage due to alcoholism, followed by intervention of a secondary agent setting off the actual malignancy.

There are several risks for alcoholic patients who have cancer, including the development of WITHDRAWAL as a postoperative complication. Such patients have poorer chances of survival and greater chances of developing another primary tumor than other patients with the same type of cancer.

More research on the exact relationship between alcohol and cancer is needed. Cell study tests are currently being conducted to detect precancerous cells at sites associated with alcohol consumption.

American Association for Cancer Research, "Alcohol and Cancer Workshop," *Cancer Research* 39, no. 7 (July 1979).

carbohydrate   Alcohol affects carbohydrate metabolism and may increase or decrease blood sugar depending on the state of nutrition in the body. It appears that when hepatic (liver) carbohydrate stores are adequate, ethanol induces hyperglycemia, whereas when they are low, hypoglycemia results (see BLOOD SUGAR). Although it contains calories, alcohol has no nutritional value.

Beer is very high in carbohydrates as well as calories, and wine contains some carbohydrates. Most distilled liquors, such as gin and whiskey, have almost no carbohydrates. This lack of carbohydrates in hard liquor has become the basis for some fad diets, such as "the drinking man's diet." However, hard liquor has a lot of "empty calories" that must be metabolized before food calories, such as those in carbohydrates, which are then stored as fat. Therefore if someone drinks large amounts of alcohol and eats, he or she is likely to gain rather than lose weight.

cardiac arrhythmia   See HEART.

Catholicism   See RELIGION.

causes of alcoholism   See ETIOLOGY.

central nervous system (CNS)   The part of the nervous system made up of the brain, the spinal cord and the nerves originating from it. Sensory impulses are transmitted to the CNS and motor impulses pass out of it. When alcohol acts on the CNS, intoxication occurs, affecting emotional and sensory functions, judgment, memory and learning ability. While sight and hearing are not significantly changed, smell and taste are dulled, and the ability to withstand pain increases as BLOOD ALCOHOL CONCENTRATION rises. Alcohol slows reaction time, especially at blood alcohol levels above .10%, and disturbs motor control. With increased intoxication there are disturbances

of speech and gait. At very high concentrations, alcohol in the blood suppresses the respiratory and cardiac centers in the lower brain, which can lead to shock and then death.

The way in which alcohol acts on the CNS tissue is not completely understood. The most prominent theory is that alcohol has the ability to interfere with the transfer of ions across the nerve cell membranes, reducing transmission of nerve impulses from one nerve cell to the next. It is known that alcohol inhibits the production and propagation of electrical impulses in nerves and disrupts nerve cell membranes.

Alcohol has a depressant effect on the CNS, slowing down the action of the nerves. At first alcohol may seem to have a stimulating effect, because the depression of certain functions of the cerebral cortex caused by alcohol consumption may reduce the inhibitory effects they have on some lower centers. Different parts of the brain appear to be affected by alcohol at different rates. Restlessness, excitement and agitation may all occur during the early part of intoxication. This early-release phenomenon must be distinguished from the hyperexcitability state that occurs as the blood alcohol content begins to drop (see WITHDRAWAL, SEDATIVE).

The long-term effects of alcohol on the central nervous system include TOLERANCE and DEPENDENCY, which show an adaptational process occurring in the brain tissue. When an individual develops a tolerance for alcohol, increasingly larger amounts are required to produce the same effect. After tolerance is established, the alcoholic develops a need for the drug in order to function.

There are a number of disorders of the CNS associated with heavy consumption of alcohol. Some of these, such as impaired judgment, increasing "highs" and "lows" in an individual with normally stable moods, diminished concentration and attention span and poor memory, are reversible if the patient abstains from alcohol, although the recovery process may take several months. These problems can occur in well-nourished individuals and increase in severity with age.

There are several more serious diseases of the CNS caused by excessive consumption of alcohol. After sustained heavy drinking alcoholics eventually develop irreversible brain tissue damage. Deficiencies in NUTRITION probably contribute to this process. Alcohol affects protein and nucleic-acid synthesis in the brain, which may be related to disturbances in learning and memory exhibited by alcoholics and to mental deficiences and malformation in children with FETAL ALCOHOL SYNDROME. Another disease of the CNS, ALCOHOLIC POLYNEUROPATHY affects first and most severely the lower portions of the legs. ALCOHOL AMBLYOPIA, a relatively infrequent disease that involves a blurring of vision which may be followed by optic nerve degeneration, results from nutritional complications associated with alcoholism. WERNICKE'S ENCEPHALOPATHY, a disorder characterized by ocular abnormalities, uncoordination and mental confusion, is related to thiamine deficiency (see VITAMINS AND MINERALS) and can lead to KORSAKOFF'S PSYCHOSIS, which is distinguished by a severe impairment of memory and learning. Alcoholics also suffer from structural changes in the BRAIN, some of which are due to head injuries incurred while intoxicated and others, such as cerebellar degeneration and cerebral atrophy, are of unknown origin.

central pontine myelinolysis   A rare disease of unknown origin that occurs in a group of brain nerve fibers known as the pons. It is most often found in long-time alcoholics suffering from malnutrition. Difficult to diagnose, the principal symptoms are a progressive weakness in the muscles extending from the lowest part of the brain to the spinal cord, an inability to swallow and an absence of the gag reflex. As the disease progresses, the patient becomes drowsy and, finally, comatose.

champagne   See SPARKLING WINE.

chaser   A mild liquid, such as water or beer, taken after a drink of strong liquor. The term and perhaps the custom derive from the French *chasser*. In France a *chasse-cafe* is a liqueur used to "chase" coffee. It is served as a digestif after a meal. The chaser has something of a soothing effect after a jolt of hard liquor, but its major use is to provide a contrast—a distinct, opposite sensation—just as the *chasse-cafe* contrasts with coffee.

child abuse   There are an estimated 1 million cases of child abuse and neglect each year, of which at least 200,000 are assaults (National Center on Child Abuse and Neglect). It has been suggested that alcohol may play a role in as many as one-third of all reported cases of child abuse *(Fourth Special Report to the U.S. Congress on Alcohol and Health)*. However, there has been a great deal of controversy about how strong the link between child abuse and alcoholism really is. To date little research has been done in this area, and the results so far have not been consistent. In a 1981 review of all English-language studies linking alcohol misuse with child abuse, Terri C. Orme and John Rimmer of the University of Washington found that there was not adequate evidence to support an association between the two. In fact the percentage of alcoholics and misusers of alcohol in the general population appears to be almost identical to the percentage of alcoholics among child abusers. Margaret Hindman of the National Clearinghouse for Alcohol Information suggests that alcoholism may be more clearly associated with child neglect, both physical and emotional, than with actual abuse.

In 1978 the National Center on Child Abuse and Neglect funded three projects in the area of specialized treatment for families with both substance abuse (including alcohol) and child maltreatment problems. These projects, which ended in March 1982, have yet to be evaluated, but since the families selected for the projects already showed a correlation between the two problem areas, it will not be possible to apply the results to the general population.

While the exact connection between child abuse and alcoholism is not known, there are certain characteristics common to both. One of the most striking is the repetitive cycle from generation to generation of both alcoholism and family violence. Lt. Cdr. Daniel W. Behling of the Naval Regional Medical Center in Long Beach, Calif. and others have reported a "generational" pattern of family violence and alcoholism. Behling found that 63% of abused children had at least one grandparent who was alcoholic or abused alcohol (Sanchez-Dirks). Abuse in the form of incest may also be related to alcoholism. One counselor estimated that half of the women she saw at a treatment center for alcoholics and drug addicts were or had been involved in an incestuous relationship with either a father or a brother (Youcha). Most had alcoholic fathers and those with alcoholic mothers became their replacements in bed. Alcohol dependence plays a role in nearly one-third of all reported cases of father-daughter incest, according to a study by researchers involved in the National Study on Child Neglect and Abuse Reporting in Denver, Colo.

While alcoholics may not personally abuse their children, they may abuse their spouses, who in turn may abuse the children. Alcoholics also may be in a state of withdrawal when they are not drinking, so that their level of irritability is very low. While alcohol misuse may not be a causal factor in child abuse, it can be said that in a family in which child abuse exists, alcohol misuse may aggravate the problem.

Few services aimed at abused children and battered wives focus on the possibility of alcohol involvement. In cases of severe abuse, the usual course of action used to be to remove the children to foster homes and jail the parents. More recently attempts have been made to rehabilitate the parent as well as protect the child. Joseph Mayer and Rebecca Black found that alcoholics in treatment for their drinking problems were likely to recognize their potential for inflicting physical abuse and were thereby often able to avoid it (Hindman). There is a growing awareness of the need to treat all members of the family in cases of family violence. (See also SPOUSE ABUSE.)

Margaret H. Hindman, "Family Violence: An Overview," *Alcohol Health and Research World* 4, no. 1 (Fall 1979):2–11.

V. Julian and C. Mohr, *Father-Daughter Incest—Profile of the Offender* (Denver: National Study on Child Neglect and Abuse Reporting, 1980).

Joseph Mayer and Rebecca Black, "The Relationship between Alcoholism and Child Abuse and Neglect," paper presented at the 7th Annual Medical Scientific Session of the National Council on Alcoholism Forum, Washington, D.C., 1976.

Terri C. Orme and John Rimmer, "Alcoholism and Child Abuse: A Review," *Journal of Studies on Alcohol* 42, no. 3 (March 1981):273–287.

Ruth Sanchez-Dirks, "Reflections on Family Violence," *Alcohol Health and Research World* 4, no. 1 (Fall 1979):12–16.

Geraldine Youcha, *A Dangerous Pleasure* (New York: Hawthorn Books, 1978), passim.

children of alcoholics   Recently attention has been focused on the children of alcoholics. There are many negative effects associated with having an alcoholic parent; perhaps the most unfortunate is an increased liklihood that the child will become an alcoholic. Studies have shown that the best prediction of a child's drinking habits is the drinking pattern of his or her parents. Mothers seem to have more influence than fathers (Youcha). Daughters of alcoholics become alcoholic 20% to 50% of the time (Youcha). If they escape becoming alcoholics, they are likely to marry an alcoholic— half of the Al-Anon members (spouses of alcoholics) in a West coast city had an alcoholic parent.

Children of alcoholics generally do not completely understand the problem and are confused about their own responsibility for their parents' behavior. The alcoholic parent often shifts between being overly affectionate to neglectful or abusive. Children cannot understand this treatment in terms of their own behavior and become frightened and anxious. The alcoholic parent is often unavailable to the children because of drinking, and the spouse is unavailable because of his or her concerns about the alcoholic. The children may be used by one parent in maneuvers against the other, or they may blame themselves for their parents' drinking.

Some children may seem to cope with their parents' drinking and not really suffer because of it. However, as Claudia Black, family program coordinater for Raleigh Hills Hospitals in Irvine, Calif., points out, the children of alcoholics run a high risk of developing a variety of problems, and even those who appear to handle the situation well are affected by parental alcoholism. The ways in which such children have learned to adjust may eventually be the source of problems later in life. A child who takes the responsible role, attempting to care for his parents, his siblings and himself, may be unable to depend on others in later life and will always need to feel in control of a situation. A child who adjusts to a drinking parent's mood changes and to the various commotions occurring in the family may later continue to allow himself to be manipulated by others and lose his or her self-esteem. A child who always tries to smooth over conflicts and help others in the family feel at ease may later fear and deny his or her own feelings of anger and be constantly trying to please others. The roles that seemed positive in childhood may have negative consequences in adulthood.

Because even the responsible, independent children are likely to develop problems later in life, it is important that the whole family be involved in treatment. In the past, children who have been neglected by alcoholic parents have often been sent to foster homes. Today it is recognized that this approach is not always the answer. A child who is sent away may feel increased guilt, possibly believing that he or she has failed completely. Furthermore a mother who fears that her child will be taken away is less likely to enter into treatment.

Family life does not immediately get better after an alcoholic parent stops drinking. A child may meet a parent's sobriety with resentment or hostility, having grown accustomed to living without rules and doing what he or she pleases. The child may also be upset that the parent can no longer be used as the scapegoat for misbehavior. A family needs time to adjust to the new situation.

ALCOHOLICS ANONYMOUS sponsors ALATEEN, a group designed primarily to help the children of alcoholics.

Claudia Black, "Innocent Bystanders at Risk: The Children of Alcoholics," *Alcoholism* 1, no. 3 (January–February 1981):22–25.
Geraldine Youcha, *A Dangerous Pleasure* (New York: Hawthorn Books, 1978), passim.

chronic   A term used to describe a disease or condition that continues for a long time and is characterized by slowly progressing symptoms, as distinguished from an ACUTE disease or condition.

chronic alcohol intoxication   A state of intoxication maintained by repeated consumption of alcohol before or just after previously taken alcohol has been metabolized. The term is sometimes also used generally to refer to ALCOHOLISM, although of course many alcoholics are not continually intoxicated.

chronic alcoholic   See CHRONIC ALCOHOLISM.

chronic alcoholism   A redundant term since alcoholism is itself a chronic disorder. The term "chronic alcoholism" is sometimes used to refer to alcoholism without complications or to a long lasting alcoholic disorder, in order to distinguish it from more severe phases of the disease. (See ACUTE ALCOHOLISM.)

chug-a-lug   A slang term meaning to drink a glassful of a beverage in one gulp or in a series of uninterrupted swallows. The practice is somewhat popular among students, who have "chug-a-lug" contests, usually with beer.

Chug-a-lugging is a drinking fad, along with a number of other similar practices, such as "one-a-minute," in which a drinker consumes a shot of beer a minute for an hour. These contests and styles of drinking are generally part of a tradition in which virility and social acceptance are equated with the ability to consume large amounts of alcohol. Aside from producing rapid intoxication, these contests can be quite dangerous and may result in coma or death, particularly when hard liquor is consumed.

Church of England Temperance Society   The largest British temperance society, it was founded in 1862 and reconstituted in 1873 with the dual goal of promoting total abstinence and general anti-intemperance.

The society supported measures of reform, rather than prohibition, and, in particular, reduction of licences to sell alcohol and popular control of the alcohol traffic. It had an extensive publication department, educational courses, missions and homes for inebriants. The society's comparative moderation contrasted with the extreme stance of many other temperance societies. In 1909 total membership was 636,233, including 485,888 members of the juvenile division. The numerical strength of several temperance societies at this time was provided by juvenile contingents.

cigarettes   See SMOKING.

cirrhosis   (From the Greek *kirrhos* orange-colored—the color of a cirrhotic liver.) The U.S. Department of Health and Human Services defines cirrhosis as "a chronic inflammatory disease of the liver in which functioning liver cells are replaced by scar tissue." It involves a disruption of the liver structure by fibrous tissue and nodule formation, which results in impaired liver function.

Cirrhosis is the result of the normal reaction of the liver to injury, whatever the cause. The vast majority of cases, particularly in the United States, are secondary to chronic alcohol abuse. Usually it takes from five to seven years of steady drinking to develop cirrhosis. Each time alcohol is abused, the liver is injured only mildly, but continuous abuse has a cumulative effect over the years. The liver cells are slowly replaced by fibrous scar tissue, resulting in irreparable damage and leaving a smaller and smaller fraction of the liver to carry on the organ's normal functions (including the detoxification of alcohol).

Although the majority of cirrhotic deaths are related to alcoholism, no more than approximately 10% of alcoholics develop cirrhosis, so there is reason to believe that genetic and other factors, particularly NUTRITION, play an important role in the contraction of or immunity from cirrhosis.

Malnutrition, from which many alcoholics suffer, can increase the severity and degree of alcoholic fatty liver development. However, studies have shown that even with

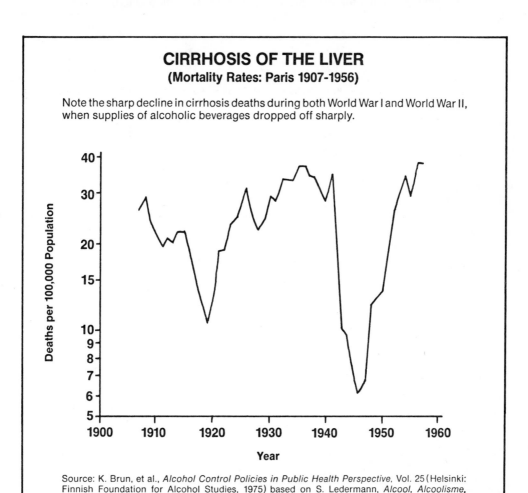

CIRRHOSIS OF THE LIVER
(Mortality Rates: Paris 1907-1956)

Note the sharp decline in cirrhosis deaths during both World War I and World War II, when supplies of alcoholic beverages dropped off sharply.

Source: K. Brun, et al., *Alcohol Control Policies in Public Health Perspective*, Vol. 25 (Helsinki: Finnish Foundation for Alcohol Studies, 1975) based on S. Ledermann, *Alcool, Alcoolisme, Alcoolisation: Mortalite, Morbidite, Accidents du Travail*, Paris (1964).

an adequate diet, high alcohol consumption damages the liver. In one such study, despite receiving a high-protein, nutritionally adequate diet, baboons developed severe liver damage as a result of forced heavy ingestion of alcohol over a prolonged period.

Different racial groups are affected differently—American JEWS tend to have a lower-than-average incidence of cirrhosis, whereas among AMERICAN INDIANS the rate is considerably higher. And according to the *Fourth Special Report to the U.S. Congress on Alcohol and Health,* cirrhosis mortality is nearly twice as high for blacks as for whites, the rate for urban black males aged 25 to 34 is 10 times as high as that for white males in the same age group.

Women seem more susceptible to developing cirrhosis than men. The amount of drinking required to produce cirrhosis in women is considerably less than in men. This finding has not been fully explained, although it may be due in part to the fact that women have a greater proportion of body fat, which takes up alcohol less readily and gives women a smaller distribution volume for a given body size. A report in the *British Medical Journal* stated that the epidemiologic pattern of cirrhosis is changing from a disease of middle-aged and elderly

Mortality From Cirrhosis of the Liver in 26 Countries with Complete Data for Period 1955–1959 and for 1971 and 1974, Rate per 100,000 Population, by Sex

Country	Males Period 1955–59 Rate[1]	Position	Year 1971 Rate[1]	Position	Year 1974 Rate[1]	Position	Females Period 1955–59 Rate[1]	Position	Year 1971 Rate[1]	Position	Year 1974 Rate[1]	Position
AMERICA												
Canada	8.80	14	14.24	13	16.0	13	5.19	15	7.73	14	7.3	13
Chile	49.22	1	71.87	1	39.0	5	23.73	1	28.56	1	15.4	6
United States	15.42	10	22.52	8	21.2	10	8.25	10	11.65	7	10.6	9
Venezuela	24.44	5	21.92	10	9.1	17	15.24	4	10.59	8	4.3	20
ASIA												
Israel	6.68	16	8.20	18	7.5	19	5.26	14	6.31	16	4.9	18
Japan	18.37	9	22.36	9	19.7	11	12.63	5	10.52	9	7.3	12
EUROPE												
Austria	25.13	4	43.26	5	49.3	1	9.92	8	14.26	6	17.9	4
Belgium	9.96	13	13.09	14	17.8	12	5.87	13	8.18	12	11.2	8
Czechoslovakia	10.25	12	21.53	11	* 24.6	7	7.47	11	8.84	11	9.7*	10
Denmark	6.04	17	10.03	16	12.5	15	9.88	9	8.07	13	8.4	11
Finland	5.25	19	6.19	19	8.3	18	3.67	22	3.38	21	2.8	24
France	38.27	3	48.04	3	47.6	2	18.23	3	20.06	3	18.6	2
Germany, W.	19.35	8	32.09	6	37.8	6	10.62	6	14.41	5	17.0	5
Hungary	11.01	11	16.66	12	21.3	9	7.32	12	9.63	10	11.3	7
Ireland	2.76	25	2.90	26	4.8	24	1.82	26	2.21	26	2.6	26
Italy	24.17	6	14.73	4	46.4	3	10.17	7	15.90	4	18.1	3
Netherlands	4.66	20	5.47	21	5.7	22	4.07	18	3.75	19	3.4	22
Norway	3.69	23	4.43	22	5.5	23	3.88	20	2.89	23	2.7	25
Portugal	40.03	2	50.64	2	44.7	4	20.08	2	24.94	2	19.9	1
Sweden	5.42	18	10.28	15	15.1	14	4.13	17	5.46	17	6.0	15
Switzerland	22.00	7	24.29	7	23.0	8	5.07	16	6.86	15	6.9	14
United Kingdom												
England and Wales	2.70	26	3.05	25	3.8	26	2.19	25	2.66	25	3.4	23
Northern Ireland	3.01	24	3.50	24	4.2	25	3.15	23	2.88	24	4.5	19
Scotland	4.51	21	4.37	23	7.2	20	3.77	21	3.52	20	5.4	16
OCEANIA												
Australia	7.05	15	8.82	17	11.6	16	3.96	19	4.44	18	4.9	17 e
New Zealand	4.22	22	5.58	20	7.2	21	2.62	24	3.12	22	3.7	21

[1]Rate per 100,000 population, standardized by the direct method; standard population Switzerland 1971.

*1973.

Figures for 1955–1959 and 1971: WHO (1976).

Figures for 1974: WHO (1977).

men to a disease whose victims are predominantly women; In Britain four times as many women were admitted to hospitals for cirrhosis in 1977 as in 1970. The rise in cirrhosis cases among women is a major indicator of increased alcohol consumption by this group.

Cirrhosis is the final stage of liver injury in alcoholics. Heavy drinking over a period of years can produce a FATTY LIVER, which, as the name indicates, is characterized by a buildup of increased amounts of fat on the liver. However, if the patient abstains from alcohol, the abnormal accumulation of fat will disappear (see LIVER). If drinking continues, fatty liver, in most people, will evolve into more severe liver diseases, such as ALCOHOLIC HEPATITIS and irreversible cirrhosis. Exactly why the liver may lose its ability to adapt to alcohol has not been clearly established. Symptoms of cirrhosis usually become apparent after a person reaches 30 and more severe problems appear after 40.

There are many types of cirrhosis, but one type—portal cirrhosis—is predominant and most frequently affects alcoholics. Portal cirrhosis is named for the portal vein, a large vein that transports blood from the stomach and spleen to the liver, where it is dispersed into the capillaries. This type of cirrhosis is also known as Laennec's, nutritional or alcoholic cirrhosis. Portal cirrhosis is characterized by small diffuse nodules and, usually in the alcoholic, extensive fatty infiltration of the liver. Frequently there are also signs of considerable inflammation. Because of the size of the nodules, this type of cirrhosis has recently been classified by some as micronodular cirrhosis.

The onset of cirrhosis is associated with such nonspecific complaints as weakness and fatigability. As the disease progresses, some of the associated effects may include:

1. Jaundice, because bilirubin pigment (a reddish-yellow pigment) can no longer be removed by the liver;

2. Fluid accumulation in the legs (edema) or in the abdomen (ascites), because the liver cannot make enough albumin, which normally holds this fluid in the body's vessels;
3. Uncontrolled bleeding due to a decrease in clotting factors in the blood; and
4. Increased sensitivity to drugs because the liver cannot inactivate them.

No successful therapeutic treatment has been developed for cirrhosis. Long-term survival of patients with portal cirrhosis is markedly improved by abstinence from alcohol. In a recent study the five-year survival rate after diagnosis of portal cirrhosis was 63% for abstainers compared with 40.5% for those who continued to drink.

Research conducted in 1981 by a team under the direction of Yedy Israel and funded by the Addiction Research Foundation in Toronto may lead to significant progress in the understanding of cirrhosis. The researchers found that prolonged heavy drinking causes liver cells to swell, which in turn can block the flow of blood in the organ. They feel that the relative health of the liver is indicated by the size of its cells and the condition of the blood vessels and not by the presence or absence of cirrhosis. Backing up this theory are figures which show that about 10% of the alcoholics seen by the researchers had completely normal liver function and yet had full-grown cirrhosis, yet alcoholics who are free of cirrhosis can die of portal hypertension or hepatic coma (caused by swollen liver cells that squeeze the fine blood vessels and block the flow of blood). Since the swelling of the liver cells is reversible with abstinence—while cirrhosis is not—the finding of the research team indicates some hope for cirrhotic patients.

There are many varieties of cirrhosis that are less common than portal cirrhosis. One kind that may also affect alcoholics is called postnecrotic cirrhosis, which follows liver damage caused by toxic or viral hepatitis. The difference between portal cirrhosis and postnecrotic cirrhosis is that in the latter the nodules are larger and more widely spaced. Because of the larger nodules, postnecrotic cirrhosis is sometimes classified as macronodular cirrhosis.

Among the types of cirrhosis not related to alcoholism are several that affect children and two types of biliary cirrhosis: primary biliary, a rare form of unknown etiology affecting chiefly middle-aged women, and secondary biliary resulting from obstruction or infection of the bile ducts.

"Cirrhosis in Women Is Up," *The Journal,* Toronto, 10, no. 6 (June 1, 1981):6.

Charles S. Lieber, "The Metabolism of Alcohol," *Scientific American* 234, no. 3 (March 1976):25–33.

———, L. M. DeCarli and E. Rubin, "Sequential Production of Fatty Liver, Hepatitis, and Cirrhosis in Subhuman Primates Fed with Adequate Diets," *Proceedings of the National Academy of Sciences* 72, no. 2 (February 1975):437–441.

"Liver Ailments—Part I: Cirrhosis," *The Harvard Medical School Health Letter* 6, no. 3 (January 1981).

Pat Ohlendorf, "Key to Liver Dysfunction Spotted?" *The Journal,* Toronto, 10, no. 3 (March 1, 1981):1–2.

co-alcoholic   See PARA-ALCOHOLIC.

codeine with alcohol   A dangerous combination the possible effects of which include respiratory arrest and depression of brain activity. The same effects can result from combinations of alcohol with other narcotic analgesics, such as morphine, Demerol and methadone. (See also DRUGS.)

coffee   See CAFFEINE.

Cognac   Under French law, the name "Cognac" may be given only to BRANDY produced in an officially defined region in and around Cognac, a town in the Charente *department* of southwestern France. The

Cognac region is divided into seven subregions according to the quality of the brandy produced in each. A Cognac is usually a blend of two or more Cognacs from the different subregions. Blends with the highest proportion of Cognac produced in the Grande Champagne subregion are thought to be the best. The differences in quality are due to differences in the soil in which the grapes used in the production are grown.

Cognac undergoes a double-distillation process known as the *methode charentaise.* The product of the first distillation is called *brouillis,* which is a liquid between 50 and 60 proof. The *brouillis* is then returned to the still for a second distillation, the product of which is raw Cognac, or *bonne chauffe,* whose proof is between 140 and 150.

The *bonne chauffe* is placed in specially made oaken casks to age. Standard Cognacs are normally aged from five to 20 years; the finest may be aged for as long as 50 or even 100 years. As it ages, Cognac loses some of its alcoholic content, which may be further reduced through the addition of distilled water. Most bottled Cognac is between 68 and 80 proof.

Like other brandies Cognac is usually sipped by itself as an after-dinner drink.

cold turkey   The act of being taken off a drug suddenly and completely, without preparation (see WITHDRAWAL).

compulsion   A term used by psychologists usually to refer to a psychological force that makes an individual act against his or her own will. In that sense compulsion does not cover the type of behavior described in WITHDRAWAL, whereby the need to drink arises from physical sources. The term "compulsion" is often used interchangeably with CRAVING.

congeners   The organic alcohols and salts formed in the manufacture of alcoholic beverages are called congeners. They provide the distinctive flavor and pungency of various beverages. Different liquors have different congener contents; vodkas contain the least and bourbons and brandies the most.

Congeners have been suspected of contributing to the HANGOVER effect, but because of the small amounts used, their role is thought to be unimportant. They may compete with ethanol for its metabolizing enzyme, alcohol dehydrogenase, resulting in the buildup of unmetabolized alcohols in the body and a toxic effect (see METABOLISM). However, pure ethanol has been shown to be the major cause of hangovers.

Congeners may play some part in the development of CANCER, but how much is not known. A study published in 1979 showed that the risk of cancer of the esophagus was more pronounced in alcoholics who drank apple brandy, which has a high congener content, and less apparent in those who drank beer and wine (Tuyns et al.).

A. J. Tuyns, G. Pequinot and J. S. Abbatucci, "Oesophageal Cancer and Alcohol Consumption," *International Journal of Cancer* 23 (1979):443–447.

consumption   There are two principal ways of estimating consumption: apparent consumption, which is derived from official reports of states, tax records and, in some cases, reports of sales by the alcoholic beverage industry; and self-reported consumption, which is derived from responses to surveys of individuals.

In the United States from 1934 to 1978 apparent consumption of beer, wine and distilled spirits increased, with the rate of increase varying for given periods and types of beverages. During the 1960s there was a rapid rise in apparent consumption, as the relatively stable rate of 2 gallons of 100% ethanol (ABSOLUTE ALCOHOL) per person per year of the 1950s grew to 2.5 gallons by 1970, a 25% increase in apparent consumption during one decade. In the 1970s the rate of growth in apparent consumption slowed to 8%.

Apparent consumption in the United States now averages about 1 ounce of 100% ethanol (approximately 2 drinks) per day for each person 14 years of age and older. Since approximately one-third of the United States adult population reports abstaining (Clark and Midanik), daily average consumption for those who drink is higher, 1.5 ounces of 100% ethanol (3 drinks). This average is still somewhat misleading because a small proportion of adults drink far more than the average and the majority drink less. It has been estimated that more than 16 million adults 18 years and older (approximately 11% of the adult population) consume about half of all beverages sold in the United States (Malin et al.).

Americans drink more beer than either wine or distilled spirits. Per capita consumption for the population aged 14 and over equals nearly 30 gallons of beer each year.

Nevada is the leading state in per capita apparent consumption, just behind Washington, D.C., although both have substantial nonresident sales which may inflate values. For the period of 1970 to 1978 most Southern states showed large percentage increases in per capita consumption, although their average per capita apparent consumption is still lower than that of many states in other regions. The largest growths in consumption were in Tennessee (44%), Alabama (42%) and Mississippi (35%). Increases of more than 20% were also recorded in half of the Western states.

In 1979 approximately one-third of the adults surveyed reported abstaining from drinking, one-third reported lighter drinking (0.01–0.21 ounces of 100% ethanol per day), and one-third reported either moderate (0.22–0.99 ounces of 100% ethanol per day) or heavier (1 or more ounces of 100% ethanol per day) drinking. Twenty-five percent of males and 40% of females reported abstaining. In the heavier drinking category males (14%) outnumbered females (4%).

Table 1
Alcoholic Beverage Consumption in the United States
Absolute Alcohol for Each Beverage, Per Capita of Total Population, in U.S. Gallons

Year	Spirits Bev.	Spirits Abs. Alc.	Wine Bev.	Wine Abs. Alc.	Cider Bev.	Cider Abs. Alc.	Beer Bev.	Beer Abs. Alc.	Total Abs. Alc.
1710	2.0	.9	.1	<.05	18.	1.8	-	-	2.7
1770	3.7	1.7	.1	<.05	18.	1.8	-	-	3.5
1785	3.0	1.4	.3	.1	18.	1.8	-	-	3.3
1790	2.7	1.2	.3	.1	18.	1.8		-	3.1
1795	3.1	1.4	.3	.1	18.	1.8		-	3.3
1800	3.8	1.7	.3	.1	17.	1.7	-	-	3.5
1805	4.3	1.9	.3	.1	16.	1.6	-	-	3.6
1810	4.6	2.1	.2	<.05	16.	1.6	.7	<.05	3.7
1815	4.4	2.0	.2	<.05	16.	1.6	-	-	3.6
1820	4.7	2.1	.2	<.05	15.	1.5	-	-	3.6
1825	5.0	2.2	.2	<.05	15.	1.5	-	-	3.7
1830	5.2	2.3	.3	1.	15.	1.5	-	-	3.9
1835	4.2	1.9	.3	.1	8.5	.8	-	-	2.8
1840	3.1	1.4	.3	.1	2.	.2	1.3	.1	1.8
1845	2.1	.9	.2	<.05	-	-	1.4	.1	1.0
1850	2.1	.9	.2	<.05	-	-	1.6	.1	1.0
1855	2.2	1.0	.2	<.05	-	-	2.7	.1	1.1
1860	2.3	1.0	.3	1.	-	-	3.8	.2	1.3
1865	2.1	.9	.3	.1	-	-	3.5	.2	1.2
1870	1.9	.9	.3	.1	-	-	5.2	.3	1.3
1875	1.7	.8	.5	.1	-	-	6.2	.3	1.2
1880	1.5	.7	.6	.1	-	-	6.9	.3	1.1
1885	1.4	.6	.5	.1	-	-	11.4	.6	1.3
1890	1.4	.6	.4	.1	-	-	13.3	.7	1.4
1895	1.2	.5	.4	.1	-	-	15.2	.8	1.4
1900	1.2	.5	.4	.1	-	-	15.5	.8	1.4
1905	1.3	.6	.5	.1	-	-	17.3	.9	1.6
1910	1.4	.6	.6	.1	-	-	19.8	1.0	1.7
1915	1.2	.5	.5	.1	-	-	20.2	1.0	1.6
1920	1.4	.6	-	-	-	-	-	-	.6
1925	1.4	.6	-	-	-	-	-	-	.6
1930	1.4	.6	-	-	-	-	-	-	.6
1935	1.1	.5	.3	.1	-	-	10.9	.5	1.1
1940	1.0	.4	.7	.1	-	-	12.9	.6	1.1
1945	1.1	.5	.8	.1	-	-	17.9	.8	1.4
1950	1.1	.5	.8	.1	-	-	17.6	.8	1.4
1955	1.1	.5	.9	.2	-	-	16.2	.7	1.4
1960	1.3	.6	.9	.2	-	-	15.2	.7	1.5
1965	1.5	.7	.9	.2	-	-	16.0	.7	1.6
1970	1.8	.8	1.3	.2	-	-	18.4	.8	1.8
1975	1.8	.8	1.6	.2	-	-	21.4	1.0	2.0

Note: Different versions of Tables I and 2 appeared in W. J. Rorabaugh, "Estimated U.S. Alcoholic Beverage Consumption, 1790–1860," *Journal of Studies on Alcohol* 37 (1976) 360–361.

Source: W. J. Rorabaugh, *The Alcoholic Republic: An American Tradition.* (New York: Oxford University Press, 1979).

Table 2
Alcoholic Beverage Consumption in the United States
Absolute Alcohol for Each Beverage, per Capita of Drinking-age (15+) Population, in
U.S. Gallons

Year	Spirits Bev.	Spirits Abs. Alc.	Wine Bev.	Wine Abs. Alc.	Cider Bev.	Cider Abs. Alc.	Beer Bev.	Beer Abs. Alc.	Total Abs. Alc.
1710	3.8	1.7	.2	<.05	34.	3.4	-	-	5.1
1770	7.0	3.2	.2	<.05	34.	3.4	-	-	6.6
1785	5.7	2.6	.6	.1	34.	3.4	-	-	6.1
1790	5.1	2.3	.6	.1	34.	3.4	-	-	5.8
1795	5.9	2.7	.6	.1	34.	3.4	-	-	6.2
1800	7.2	3.3	.6	.1	32.	3.2	-	-	6.6
1805	8.2	3.7	.6	.1	30.	3.0	-	-	6.8
1810	8.7	3.9	.4	.1	30.	3.0	1.3	.1	7.1
1815	8.3	3.7	.4	.1	30.	3.0	-	-	6.8
1820	8.7	3.9	.4	.1	28.	2.8	-	-	6.8
1825	9.2	4.1	.4	.1	28.	2.8	-	-	7.0
1830	9.5	4.3	.5	.1	27.	2.7	-	-	7.1
1835	7.6	3.4	.5	.1	15.	1.5	-	-	5.0
1840	5.5	2.5	.5	.1	4.	.4	2.3	.1	3.1
1845	3.7	1.6	.3	.1	-	-	2.4	.1	1.8
1850	3.6	1.6	.3	.1	-	-	2.7	.1	1.8
1855	3.7	1.7	.3	.1	-	-	4.6	.2	2.0
1860	3.9	1.7	.5	.1	-	-	6.4	.3	2.1
1865	3.5	1.6	.5	.1	-	-	5.8	.3	2.0
1870	3.1	1.4	.5	.1	-	-	8.6	.4	1.9
1875	2.8	1.2	.8	.1	-	-	10.1	.5	1.8
1880	2.4	1.1	1.0	.2	-	-	11.1	.6	1.9
1885	2.2	1.0	.8	.1	-	-	18.0	.9	2.0
1890	2.2	1.0	.6	.1	-	-	20.6	1.0	2.1
1895	1.8	.8	.6	.1	-	-	23.4	1.2	2.1
1900	1.8	.8	.6	.1	-	-	23.6	1.2	2.1
1905	1.9	.9	.7	.1	-	-	25.9	1.3	2.3
1910	2.1	.9	.9	.2	-	-	29.2	1.5	2.6
1915	1.8	.8	.7	.1	-	-	29.7	1.5	2.4
1920	2.1	.9	-	-	-	-	-	-	.9
1925	2.0	.9	-	-	-	-	-	-	.9
1930	2.0	.9	-	-	-	-	-	-	.9
1935	1.5	.7	.4	.1	-	-	15.0	.7	1.5
1940	1.3	.6	.9	.2	-	-	17.2	.8	1.6
1945	1.5	.7	1.1	.2	-	-	24.2	1.1	2.0
1950	1.5	.7	1.1	.2	-	-	24.1	1.1	2.0
1955	1.6	.7	1.3	.2	-	-	22.8	1.0	1.9
1960	1.9	.8	1.3	.2	-	-	22.1	1.0	2.0
1965	2.1	1.0	1.3	.2	-	-	22.8	1.0	2.2
1970	2.5	1.1	1.8	.3	-	-	25.7	1.2	2.5
1975	2.4	1.1	2.2	.3	-	-	28.8	1.3	2.7

Table 3
Estimated Patterns of American Adult Drinking Practices
(1977)

Type of Drinker	Total Population (Millions)	Percent	Male Population (Millions)	Percent	Female Population (Millions)	Percent	Ounces of 100% Ethanol Consumed in 1 Day	Example[1]
ALL PERSONS 18+	152.6	100	72.9	100	79.7	100	—	—
Abstainer	53.4	35	19.7	27	34.3	43	0	Drinks less than once a year or never
Lighter	46.8	32	20.4	28	29.5	37	0.01–0.21	1 drink/year up to 3 drinks/week or 12 drinks/month
Moderate	33.6	22	19.7	27	12.8	16	0.22–0.99	4 to 13 drinks/week or 13 to 58 drinks/month
Heavier	16.8	11	13.1	18	3.2	4	1.0 or more	2 or more drinks/day or 14 or more drinks/week

[1]A drink is the equivalent of one 12-oz can of beer, one 4-oz glass of wine or one 1-oz shot of distilled spirits, each of which contains approximately ½ ounce of ethanol.

Source: National Clearinghouse for Alcohol Information (U.S.).

The percentages of male and female drinkers showed a decrease with age except for a rise in the proportion of female drinkers from ages 18 to 20 and ages 21 to 34. Heavier drinking appeared to peak at ages 21 to 34 for males and ages 35 to 49 for females and thereafter to decrease for both sexes. A comparison of the 1979 figures with those in Table 3 for 1977 reveals a decrease in the proportion of abstainers and increases in the proportion of drinkers in the lighter category and male drinkers in the heavier category.

Per capita consumption of alcohol is lower in the United States than in many countries. In 1976 the World Health Organization ranked the United States 22nd out of 26 countries surveyed, with a per capita consumption of 8.1 liters of 100% ethanol (see Table 4). The same year the consumption level in France was more than twice as high—16.5 liters—and the United

Kingdom had a per capita consumption of 8.4 liters.

There has been a debate in recent years over the relationship between the general level of alcohol consumption in a population and the percentage of heavy drinkers. This issue is still unresolved and while some countries have shown increases in hospital admission rates for patients with a diagnosis of alcoholism or alcoholic psychosis where there have been increases in per capita consumption, there has so far been little evidence of a decrease in rates with decreased consumption.

W. B. Clark and L. Midanik, "Alcohol Use and Alcohol Problems among U.S. Adults," *Alcohol Consumption and Related Problems*, Alcohol and Health Monograph no. 1 (Rockville, Md.: National Institute on Alcohol Abuse and Alcoholism, in press).

John R. DeLuca, ed., *Fourth Special Report to the U.S. Congress on Alcohol and Health,*

Table 4
Per Capita Consumption of Alcoholic Beverages as Liters of 100% Ethanol in 26
Countries, Total Population, 1950, 1960, 1970 and 1976, with Total and Average Annual
Percentage Changes

Country*	Per Capita Consumption: Liters 100% Ethanol				Percentage Change			
					Total		Average Annual	
	1950	1960	1970	1976	1950–1976	1950–1976	1960–1970	1970–1976
France	17.2	17.3	15.6	16.5	− 4	+ 0.05	− 1	+ 1
Portugal	-	10.9	11.7[b]	14.1	+ 29[a]	-	− 0.6[e]	+ 3.4
Spain	-	8.5	10.7	14.0	+ 65[a]	-	+ 3	+ 5
Luxembourg	6.8	8.3	10.1	13.4	+ 97	+ 2	+ 2	+ 5
Italy	9.2	12.2	13.7	12.7	+ 38	+ 3	+ 1	− 1
Germany, W.	2.9	6.9	10.4	12.5	+331	+14	+ 5	+ 4
Austria	5.0	8.7	12.0	11.2	+124	+ 7	+ 4	− 1
Hungary	4.8	6.2	9.1	10.7	+123	+ 3	+ 5	+ 3
Switzerland	7.9	9.8	10.5	10.3	+ 30	+ 2	+ 0.7	− 0.3
Belgium	6.3	6.4	8.9	10.2	+ 62	+ 0.2	+ 4	+ 2
Australia	6.1	6.5	8.2	9.6	+ 57	+ 0.7	+ 3	+ 3
New Zealand	5.4	6.5	7.5	9.3	+ 72	+ 2	+ 2	+ 4
Czechoslovakia	4.0	5.5	8.4	9.2	+130	+ 4	+ 5	+ 2
Denmark	3.6	4.2	6.8	9.2	+156	+ 2	+ 6	+ 6
Yugoslavia	-	4.7	7.5	8.9[c]	+ 89[d]	-	+ 6	+ 4[f]
Ireland	3.3	3.4	5.4	8.7	+164	+ 0.3	+ 6	+10
Canada	4.4	4.8	6.6	8.6	+ 95	+ 0.9	+ 4	+ 5
United Kingdom	4.9	5.1	6.4	8.4	+ 71	+ 0.4	+ 3	+ 5
Netherlands	2.1	2.6	5.5	8.3	+295	+ 2	+11	+ 8
Germany, E.	1.2	4.6	6.1	8.3	+592	+28	+ 3	+ 6
Poland	3.0	3.8	5.2	8.2	+173	+ 3	+ 4	+10
USA	5.0	4.8	6.3	8.1	+ 62	− 0.4	+ 3	+ 5
Finland	1.7	1.8	4.3	6.4	+276	+ 0.6	+14	+ 8
Sweden	3.6	3.7	5.7	5.9	+ 64	+ 0.3	+ 5	+ 0.6
Norway	2.2	2.5	3.6	4.3	+ 95	+ 1	+ 4	+ 3
Peru	1.2	1.7	2.4	3.1	+158	+ 4	+ 4	+ 5

*Classed by order of 1976 (1975) consumption.

[a]1960–1976   [b]1972   [c]1975   [d]1960–1975   [e]1960–1972   [f]1970–1975

Sources of data: for years 1950, 1960, 1970—Finnish Foundation for Alcohol Studies and WHO (1977); for 1976—Produktschap voor Gedistilleerde Dranken (1977).

Adjusted estimates: For a few countries the total per capita consumption did not include a figure for spirits and an estimated amount has been added based on the average consumption level for spirits over the next five-year period. The amounts included (as liters of 100% ethanol) are as follows: Peru, 1950: 0.81; Portugal, 1960: 0.51; Spain, 1960:2.01.

Table 5
Alcohol Consumption in 25 Countries, 1960, 1970, and 1976 Per Capita, 15 Years and Older, in Liters of 100% Ethanol

Country*	Per Capita Consumption: liters 100% Ethanol			Percentage Change		
				Total	Average Annual	
	1960	1970	1976	1960–1976	1960–1970	1970–1976
France	27.32	23.98	21.3	− 12	− 1	− 2
Portugal	15.32	15.72	19.4	+ 3	+ 0.2	+ 4
Spain	11.89	16.89	19.3	+ 42	+ 4	+ 2
Luxembourg	13.75	16.21	16.8	+ 18	+ 2	+ 0.6
Italy	19.05	20.73	16.8	+ 9	+ 1	− 3
Germany, W.	10.15	16.04	15.8	+ 58	+ 6	− 0.2
Austria	10.85	13.29	. 14.6	+ 23	+ 2	+ 2
New Zealand	9.49	11.02	13.7	+ 16	+ 2	+ 4
Hungary	9.15	12.95	13.4	+ 42	+ 4	+ 0.6
Australia	9.45	11.68	13.3	+ 24	+ 2	+ 1
Switzerland	12.58	14.52	13.2	+ 15	+ 2	− 2
Belgium	11.71	13.21	13.2	+ 13	+ 1	0
Ireland	4.90	7.27	12.6	+ 48	+ 5	+12
Yugoslavia	6.79	10.36	12.0	+ 53	+ 5	+ 3
Czechoslovakia	10.38	14.55	11.9	+ 40	+ 4	− 3
Denmark	6.11	9.70	11.8	+ 59	+ 6	+ 4
Canada	7.85	9.58	11.7	+ 22	+ 2	+ 4
Netherlands	3.82	7.81	11.1	+104	+10	+ 7
United Kingdom	6.80	8.32	11.0	+ 22	+ 2	+ 5
Poland	6.16	7.52	10.8	+ 22	+ 2	+ 7
USA	7.83	9.74	10.7	+ 24	+ 2	+ 2
Germany, E.	7.29	10.47	10.5	+ 44	+ 4	0
Finland	3.87	6.33	8.1	+ 64	+ 6	+ 5
Sweden	5.86	7.94	7.4	+ 36	+ 4	− 1
Norway	3.56	4.37	5.6	+ 23	+ 2	+ 5

*Classed by order of 1976 consumption.

Sources: de Lint, (1975); Produktschap voor Gedistilleerde Dranken (1977); population statistics: International Labor Organization (1977); United Nations (1977).

(Rockville, Md.: National Institute on Alcohol Abuse and Alcoholism, 1981), pp. 15–27.

H. Malin et al. "An Epidemiologic Perspective on Alcohol Use and Abuse in the United States," *Alcohol Consumption and Related Problems,* Alcohol and Health Monograph no. 1 (Rockville, Md.: National Institute on Alcohol Abuse and Alcoholism, in press).

Joy Moser, *Prevention of Alcohol-Related Problems* (Toronto: World Health Organization, 1980), pp. 50–53.

controlled drinking   Drinking within a socially acceptable context, well short of intoxication, by a person who deliberately sets a limit on the number of drinks he or she will take and stops drinking when that limit is reached. The concept, as applied to alcoholics, runs directly contrary to the traditional belief that complete ABSTINENCE is the only course to recovery.

Among those who have suggested that alcoholics may resume drinking—as long as it is controlled drinking—are David J. Armor, J. Michael Polich and Harriet B. Stambul, the authors of the RAND REPORTS. They feel that certain types of patients might successfully exercise controlled drinking under proper circumstances. According to their findings, patients with a relatively short history of problem drinking have a greater likelihood of success with controlled drinking than those with a long history of alcoholism. Those able to control their drinking showed fewer alcoholic symptoms than those who could not, and they were often younger and had generally lower consumption rates than those who were not able to exercise control. The authors point out that today therapists have a wider range of treatment possibilities and can gear the treatment to suit the patient rather than impose a uniform program of abstinence upon all.

Opponents have responded, many quite vehemently, that the studies are faulty. They insist, citing past experience, that the time span of the study was too short and that most, if not all, of the controlled drinkers will eventually begin again to drink alcoholically. They also question whether many of the controlled drinkers in the sample were really alcoholics, pointing out such aspects of the sample as "youth," "short history of problem drinking" and "lower consumption rates." Furthermore they argue that controlled drinking places abnormal pressures on those whose most basic problem is LOSS OF CONTROL. But most importantly opponents see controlled drinking as a tempting illusion presented with scientific authority. They argue that even if some controlled drinking is possible by some al-

coholics, the possibility will be most tempting to those least able to cope with it. Supporters of the Rand Reports counter that objective scientific study, with its possible future benefits, should not be suppressed simply because there are some who would distort or misuse it. See BEHAVIOR MODIFICATION.

controlled substance   A pyschoactive drug, such as a narcotic, which is strictly controlled by law. Stringent requirements govern the prescribing and dispensing of these substances as well as their manufacture, storage and transport, and an exact inventory of the quantities on hand and dispensed must be maintained at all times.

Although alcoholic beverages are sometimes said to be "controlled," they are not; they are regulated. Most countries and states have laws governing the sale and purchase of alcoholic beverages, but from manufacture through retail sales there is no strict enforcement and the supplier is not held accountable for every ounce of the substance. (For an overview of the articles on regulation of the manufacture and sale of alcoholic beverages, see REGULATION.)

convulsions   When alcoholics who are physically dependent on alcohol do not drink, they go through WITHDRAWAL. This process can be relatively mild, but in severe cases convulsions may occur. These can begin as early as 12 hours after the start of ABSTINENCE, but they more often appear during the second or third day after an alcoholic stops drinking. The number of seizures and their duration vary from individual to individual. (See also DELIRIUM TREMENS.)

cordial   (From the Latin *cor* heart.) Broadly defined, a cordial is any medicine, food or beverage that is believed to steady or stimulate the heart. In the case of alcoholic beverages, "cordial" is simply another name for LIQUEUR. These beverages are made by adding the flavor of fruits, herbs, roots, flowers or juices to an alcohol base. In addition they are sweetened and, in most cases, colored. Most cordials are between 40 and 80 proof. They are sold under the name of their particular flavor preceding the word "cordial" (for example, blackberry cordial, clove cordial, mint cordial).

corn whiskey   A spirit distilled from a fermented mash that is at least 80% corn (Indian maize). Along with rye and bourbon, corn whiskey is a distinctively American spirit. Until the early part of the 19th century, it rivaled the other two types in popularity, but since then a preference for less harsh whiskeys has made it commercially unfeasible. Corn whiskey is a colorless spirit that is bottled without aging. For this reason it has an extremely raw taste, similar to that of neutral grain spirits.

Costa Rica   The smallest and one of the least populated countries in Central America, Costa Rica has for some time supported one of the more advanced antialcohol programs in the hemisphere. A state committee on alcoholism has existed since 1954, when alcoholism was declared a disease by presidential decree in order to facilitate treatment in public health centers. Since 1973 there has been a complete ban on consumption of alcoholic beverages in government buildings, and legal penalties for alcohol-related offenses are severe. Alcoholism orientation programs for teachers are given annually.

Seventy-two percent of the population is considered abstinent, and although total alcohol consumption in the country remains low, some alcohol abuse is reported among this relatively small drinking population. The preferred beverages are gin, dark rum and *aguardiente,* a distilled alcohol common in Hispanic countries; all are potent, with an average ethanol content of 35.5%.

Per Capita Consumption of Absolute Alcohol in Liters (1977)

Beverage	Total Pop.	Pop. 15 Yrs and Older
Distilled Spirits	1.74	2.91
Beer	0.93	1.56
Wine	0.06	0.11
Total	2.73	4.58

The government maintains a monopoly on distilled alcohol production; beer and wine production is in private hands. A significant supplement to the amount of spirits legally produced is the substantial amount of illegal alcohol distilled from fermented sugar cane in rural areas. One report estimated annual consumption of this *guaro contrabando* at 4 million liters, and in an isolated area one in three houses were found to be engaged in the production of this illegal liquor.

Production of Alcoholic Beverages in Thousand Liters

Year	Beer	Wine	Distilled Spirits
1973	26,833	75	7,332
1974	32,856	86	7,332
1975	35,140	97	7,490
1976	48,130	180	7,782
1977	48,125	229	8,072

The government estimates that there are nearly 100,000 "abnormal drinkers" in Costa Rica, or about one out of every 20 persons. An unusual aspect of the drinking patterns of the country is the fact that a third of the known problem drinkers are female. The incidence of alcoholism is higher in rural than in urban areas, and the highest incidence of heavy drinking is among males who began to drink between ages 15 and 19 and have experienced unemployment.

It is estimated that the population spends about $100 per capita on alcohol; the total figure represents 6% of the national revenue. In 1974 the rate of deaths from cirrhosis was 58 per 100,000 population, half of which was among females; the total number remained about the same in 1976, but the proportion of female deaths from cirrhosis was higher. There has also been a dramatic increase in road accidents related to alcohol: there were 17.3 such accidents per 1,000 population in 1961 and 26.2 per 1,000 in 1965. During the 1960s hospital admissions for alcoholism averaged up to 80 per 100,000 inhabitants. Diagnosis patterns changed in that decade; for example, the rate of 7.3 per 100,000 for alcoholic psychoses in 1961 rose to 53.3 per 100,000 in 1969.

If figures for alcohol-related mental health, psychoneurosis and personality disorder problems are included, alcohol accounts for 32% of all medical admissions in the country. The government also provides outpatient clinics for alcoholics; 13,424 persons received assistance of this sort in 1976 and 19,914 in 1978.

Treatment of alcoholism in Costa Rica comes under the authority of the National Institute on Alcoholism and the Center for Studies on Alcoholism, which are attached to the country's Ministry of Health and operate in cooperation with the Ministry of Public Education. Enforced treatment of alcoholism is made possible by a 1970 addition to the penal code that defines the alcoholic as a patient in need of protection and rehabilitation. The Social Security Institution guarantees financial assistance to alcoholics and their families. Costa Rica's alcoholism prevention measures include mass media campaigns, primary school education sessions, and special training programs for teachers, nurses, police and social workers. These programs and others are currently being expanded, and all are monitored by the National Institute on Alcoholism.

cough medicine   Most cough medicines on the market today, even those designed for children, contain a fairly high percentage of alcohol. Those intended for nighttime use have about 25% alcohol, around 15% less than found in most hard liquor—whiskey, gin, vodka—and more than twice the amount in wine, which is normally about 12%.

Alcohol Content of Some Common Cough Medicines

Brand	% of Alcohol
ChlorTrimeton Allergy Syrup	7.0
Comtrex Nighttime	25.0
Pertussin Cough Syrup for Children	8.0
Robitussin Cough Formula	3.5
Vick's Formula 44D	10.0
Vick's Nyquil Cold Medicine	25.0

Alcoholics using cough medicines containing alcohol may develop a CRAVING for more of the medicine, and those taking ANTABUSE could have a reaction to the alcohol in the preparation. As with other seemingly harmless products containing alcohol, there is also a potential for abuse of cough medicines.

craving   The term "craving" is often used in explanations of alcoholism, but thus far it has not been well defined. There appear to be two types of craving: one physiological, otherwise referred to as physical dependence (see DEPENDENCY), and one psychological. The physical craving occurs in persons who have been drinking over a long period of time, and is manifested by the symptoms of WITHDRAWAL from alcohol. The craving in this case may arise out of a need for relief from the distress of withdrawal rather than from an actual desire for alcohol. The second kind of craving is thought to account for the initial abuse of alcohol and for relapses after the start of abstinence. During a period of abstinence there is a buildup of psychological tension, which provokes a desire for alcohol as a means of relief.

One major question is whether the craving in alcoholics is for the alcohol itself or for its intoxicating effects.

crime   The full extent to which alcohol is responsible for crime is not known, but alcohol use and its subsequent effects have been related to formation of criminal intent, aggravation of the criminal event through excess violence and influence of the outcome of a completed crime *(Fourth Special Report to the U.S. Congress on Alcohol and Health)*.

A number of theories have attempted to explain the role of alcohol in criminal and violent behavior. Alcohol may release inhibitions or intensify certain mental states. If anger is released or increased, it may enhance the likelihood of aggression and violence. The relationship between the physiological effects of alcohol and aggressive behavior has not yet been clearly established. Some violent behavior may be explained by a seizure-like reaction to alcohol called PATHOLOGICAL INTOXICATION. The effect of combining alcohol with other DRUGS may result in increased violent behavior (see SYNERGY).

The proportion of alcoholics and problem drinkers with criminal records is far higher than the national average *(Fourth Special Report)*. It is not clear, however, whether drinking alcohol leads to criminal behavior or whether involvement in criminal behavior (and perhaps incarceration) leads to drinking. Statistics on the involvement of alcohol in different types of crime vary widely. Studies have reported alcohol involvement in 13% to 50% of rape offenders and 6% to 31% of rape victims. Alcohol involvement also varies with different types of rape; for example, alcohol has been more related to rapes committed by two

men rather than by one man or a group. In assault cases evidence of alcohol use has been reported in 24% to 72% of offenders and 4% to 79% of victims. Studies on homicide have found that from 28% to 86% of the offenders and 14% to 87% of the victims used alcohol (Aarens et al.). (For alcohol-related crimes, see DRIVING WHILE INTOXICATED, PUBLIC DRUNKENNESS. See also SPOUSE ABUSE, CHILD ABUSE.)

M. Aarens et al., *Alcohol, Casualties, and Crime,* final report C.18 (Berkeley, Calif.: Social Research Group, School of Public Health, 1977), passim.

John R. DeLuca, ed., *Fourth Special Report to the U.S. Congress on Alcohol and Health,* (Rockville, Md.: National Institute on Alcohol Abuse and Alcoholism, 1981), pp. 83–84.

Joy Moser, *Prevention of Alcohol-Related Problems* (Toronto:World Health Organization, 1980), pp. 46–47.

cross-addiction   A term used to describe a mutual or interchangeable addiction between drugs within the same group. A person addicted to alcohol, which belongs to a group of drugs known as sedatives, will have some degree of addiction to all other sedatives. Therefore an alcoholic could prevent withdrawal symptoms by taking sufficient quantities of another SEDATIVE, such as Librium, and someone addicted to Librium could stem withdrawal by taking alcohol. However, for someone addicted to a sedative no drug from another group, such as a narcotic, would be effective. (See also CROSS-TOLERANCE.)

cross-dependence   A term used to describe a mutual or interchangeable dependence between drugs within the same group, such as sedatives. For example, alcohol and Librium, both sedatives, are cross-dependent.

cross-tolerance   A condition that occurs in alcoholics or heavy drinkers whose TOLERANCE for alcohol produces an equivalent tolerance for other SEDATIVE drugs. Alcoholics, for instance, are more difficult to anesthetize with ether than are nonalcoholics. Cross-tolerance may be caused either by an increased ability to metabolize another drug (metabolic tolerance) or by changes in the tissues of the central nervous system (CNS) that make the system less responsive to another drug (cellular tolerance). Both increased metabolic ability and changes in CNS tissue result from prolonged heavy ingestion of alcohol.

cultural etiological theories   Several studies, while recognizing the importance of physiological and psychological factors, have shown that alcoholism is related more to ethnic and social background (McCord et al.; Calahan, Cisin and Crossley). Cultural etiological theories, also known as SOCIOCULTURAL ETIOLOGICAL THEORIES, suggest that individual attitudes toward alcohol and alcoholism to a large extent reflect the attitudes of the culture as a whole toward those subjects; customs and codes of behavior regulating drinking practices, environmental support for drinking and level of "appropriate" intoxication are largely determined by cultural setting. For example, the low rates of alcoholism among Jews and Moslems can be traced to cultural proscriptions against the use or abuse of alcohol, whereas the extremely high rate of alcoholism among the Irish may be attributed to cultural support for excessive consumption of alcohol.

D. Calahan, I. H. Cisin and H. M. Crossley, *American Drinking Practices: A National Survey of Behavior and Attitudes,* Rutgers Center of Alcohol Studies Monograph, no. 6, 1969.
W. McCord, J. McCord and J. Goodman, *Origins of Alcoholism* (Stanford: Stanford University Press, 1960), passim.

cultural stress etiological theories   Some theorists feel that the incidence of alcoholism in a society may be re-

lated to the degree of stress produced by the culture. In 1946 R. F. Bales suggested that if the use of alcohol is accepted under the societal norms, then it will be used to reduce the anxiety and tension produced by that society. Bales listed three major factors affecting the rate of alcoholism in a given society: the degree of stress and inner tension produced by the culture; the attitudes toward drinking held by the culture; and the opportunity for alternative means of satisfaction and coping with anxiety. In 1943, after studying the relation between social stress and alcohol consumption in primitive societies, D. Horton found that where alcohol use was sanctioned, there was a correlation between a high degree of anxiety and a high level of consumption.

David J. Armor, J. Michael Polich and Harriet B. Stambul, *Alcoholism and Treatment* (New York: John Wiley and Sons, 1978), passim.
R. F. Bales, "Cultural Differences in Rates of Alcoholism," *Quarterly Journal of Studies on Alcohol* 6 (1946):480–499.
D. Horton, "The Functions of Alcohol in Primitive Societies: A Cross-Cultural Study," *Quarterly Journal of Studies on Alcohol* 4 (1943):199–320.

D

de-alcoholized beverage   A beverage from which most of the alcohol has been removed *after* it has been made into a full-strength alcoholic beverage. Since the alcohol content of de-alcoholized beverages is less than 0.5%, they are not classified as alcoholic beverages for purposes of taxation or for regulation of sale and consumption. There are two principal types of de-alcoholized beverages: malt beverages (formerly known as NEAR BEER) and wines—red, white and sparkling.

Although many alcoholics drink de-alcoholized beverages, there are conflicting opinions on the advisability of this practice. To some in the field the substitution of a nonaddictive beverage is a harmless, even beneficial way for an alcoholic to fill the void left by the elimination of alcohol. But many others view the consumption of substitute "beer" and "wine" as reinforcing old drinking patterns and possibly leading to the resumption of drinking.

debauch   A drinking spree or bout that usually includes excessive sexual activity.

delirium tremens   The D.T.'s. One of the most dramatic and serious conditions associated with alcoholism, delirium tremens is the last and severest stage of WITHDRAWAL, beginning two to three days after abstinence following a long period of heavy drinking. Symptoms of this form of alcoholic psychosis may include vivid and frequently terrifying auditory, visual and tactile hallucinations (alcoholic hallucinosis), profound confusion, disorientation, severe agitation and restlessness, insomnia, fever and abnormally rapid heartbeat. Since there is a 10% mortality rate associated with this stage of withdrawal, it is considered a medical emergency and the patient should be hospitalized. Sedation may be required, but extreme caution should be used to avoid oversedation, for a drug dosage that would suppress all tremors would also seriously depress the patient's respiration. The D.T.'s can last for three to four days. With proper care recovery is usually complete, although a few patients do not recover and remain in a psychotic state. There have been reported cases of delirium tremens occurring after operations, trauma and severe illness in patients who claimed to have abstained from alcohol for several months. More research is needed to determine the exact nature of the condition and the circumstances under which it occurs.

Delta alcoholism   The fourth of five categories of alcoholism defined by JELLINEK. Delta alcoholism, like GAMMA ALCOHOLISM, is characterized by an acquired tissue tolerance for alcohol, adaptive cell METABOLISM and WITHDRAWAL symptoms. However, instead of the LOSS OF CONTROL found in Gamma alcoholism, there is an INABILITY TO ABSTAIN. The Delta alcoholic cannot stop drinking for even a few days without showing some withdrawal symptoms; he can, however, control the amount of intake on any given occasion. His consumption of alcohol, though large, is steady over a long period of time and less "explosive" than that of a person with Gamma alcoholism. Delta alcoholism is the predominant form of alcoholism in FRANCE and some other countries with a significant wine consumption.

dementia   "A syndrome of progressive, irreversible cerebral insufficiency caused by organic factors and characterized by predominant cognitive functional loss" (*Merck Manual,* 10th ed.). One of the many possible causes of dementia is alcoholism. The early symptoms, which vary greatly from patient to patient, include a slow disintegration of personality and intellect. Judgment and insight as well as speech and motor activity are affected. There is an impairment of memory, which becomes progressively worse. Personal habits deteriorate, and in the later stages of the illness the patient requires total nursing care.

denatured alcohol   ETHANOL made unfit for drinking by the addition of a substance such as METHANOL.

denial   This term describes one of the alcoholic's most characteristic psychological defense mechanisms: a refusal to admit the existence of a drinking problem. Denial is one of the main methods alcoholics use to deal with life. They deny their emotional problems and their dependence on alcohol, declaring that they do not have a problem or that they only drink "a little." When confronted with his intoxicated state, the alcoholic is likely to respond that he can stop any time he wishes. One of the first aspects of denial is concealment of the amount of alcohol consumed. This posture distinguishes the alcoholic from the social drinker. Considering society's negative attitude toward alcoholics, denial is understandable; it is hard for any individual to admit publicly that he is an alcoholic when there is such a stigma attached to the problem.

Spouses, relatives and friends will often deny an alcoholic's problem to protect him from friends and neighbors; employers will ignore an uneven work record or fire an alcoholic rather than discuss his drinking problem; physicians will prescribe tranquilizers rather than confront an alcoholic patient with his drinking problem.

In treatment, denial should be dealt with quickly, since otherwise severe physical and psychological damage is likely to occur over time. The recognition of denial allows the alcoholic to be more aware of his problem and his role in its creation.

Denmark   There is a liberal attitude toward alcohol consumption in Denmark and the country experiences few problems with alcohol abuse. The national drinking pattern is one of frequent but temperate consumption of alcoholic beverages, mostly beer. The majority of consumption takes place in the home; initial drinking by adolescents is usually done in the presence of adults; and there is little increase in the rhythm of drinking on weekends or holidays. Alcoholic beverages, including distilled spirits, are sold in virtually all retail food outlets. There has been little variation in these patterns for years, although authorities now note some increase in preference for distilled spirits over beers.

In 1977 per capita consumption of alcoholic beverages, computed as ABSOLUTE AL-COHOL, was 9.0 liters for the total population and 11.5 liters for the population over 14 years of age; both figures increased approximately 50% between 1967 and 1977. The total consumption in 1977, again computed as absolute alcohol, was 28,400 liters of beer; 7,900 liters of wine; and 9,200 liters of distilled spirits. From 1967 to 1977 the consumption of both wine and distilled spirits rose twice as fast as that of beer.

Denmark computes the health costs of alcohol consumption according to the 1967 manual of the World Health Organization. Based on WHO guidelines, the country reported a mortality rate from alcohol abuse of 6.7 per 100,000 population in 1977. That year the mortality rate from liver cirrhoses was 9.4 per 100,000 population, and alcohol was considered a factor in 40% of all admissions to psychiatric hospitals, although in most of these cases alcoholism was a secondary diagnosis. There were more than 16,000 arrests for alcohol-impaired driving, including repeat offenses, in 1977. Authorities consider that statistic a useful indicator of the number of problem drinkers in the country.

The Danish government believes that regulation of alcohol consumption is suitable only if agreeable to the majority of the population. For this reason it limits controls on consumption to taxation of alcoholic beverages and licensing of public drinking places. Further action is left to private health and charitable organizations. There is a National Commission on Alcohol and Narcotics, but its purpose is primarily an advisory one. All public responsibility for prevention and treatment of alcohol-related problems remains in the hands of county-level government. The only government spokesmen for antialcohol causes are appointees with limited advisory status within existing government agencies, such as the Ministry of Education.

dentistry   Dentists should be aware of the possible existence of alcoholism in their patients and the special precautions that must be taken if anesthesia is to be used on such patients.

Dentists can recognize alcoholism in patients who otherwise appear normal through attention to certain details. A routine dental exam will frequently disclose general deficiencies in oral hygiene; there has often been long-term neglect of the teeth, as evidenced by coated tongue, heavy plaque formation, and deposits of calculus. Alcoholics have a rate of permanent tooth loss three times that of the general population. They are more likely to come in for treatment of an emergency, such as a severe toothache, than for a routine checkup. Many alcoholics are heavy smokers and the combination of alcohol and tobacco has a synergistic effect that has been associated with an increased susceptibility to cancer of the head and neck. Alcoholics often have enlarged, but otherwise asymptomatic, parotid glands (the largest salivary glands). Wounds heal more slowly in alcoholics, as alcohol and, to a lesser degree, the congeners in alcoholic beverages interfere with the proper formation and deposition of collagen. Dentists should be on the lookout for such warning signs so that they can aid the patient in getting proper treatment for alcoholism.

Alcoholism may also complicate dental surgery. If such surgery for a known or suspected alcoholic is elective, he or she should be completely detoxified before the operation because the stress of surgery may precipitate WITHDRAWAL. Care must be taken in the use of anesthetics, since both CROSS-TOLERANCE and synergistic effects can result from alcohol-anesthetic combinations (see SYNERGY). Chronic alcoholics are more resistant to the effects of anesthesia, and cross-tolerance with both chloroform and ether has long been observed. If the patient has alcohol in his or her system while undergoing surgery, the initial phase of anesthesia will be followed by a synergistic interaction that produces a deeper and pos-

sibly more dangerous narcosis and an increase in sleeping time. After surgery, healing may take longer than normal and there is an increased incidence of infection among alcoholics. During DELIRIUM TREMENS any dental surgical procedure should be avoided if possible.

"Alcohol-Drug Interactions," *Anesthesia Progress* (September-October 1979) 26 (5): 129–132.
Charles E. Becker, "Review of Pharmacologic and Toxicologic Effects of Alcohol," *Journal of the American Dental Association* 99 (September 1979): 494–500.
Marc A. Shuckit, "Overview of Alcoholism," *Journal of the American Dental Association* 99 (September 1979): 489–493.

dependency   A person who is an alcoholic has developed a dependency on alcohol. This dependency has two aspects: physical, as exhibited by the WITHDRAWAL symptoms, such as severe anxiety, tremors, and nausea, that occur when drinking stops; and psychological, as exhibited by the "need to have a drink" in order to function or to relieve stress. Some individuals develop a dependency rapidly and others gradually, over a few years. (See also ADDICTION.)

depressant   See SEDATIVE.

depressed communities   Communities that show a decline in economic growth and/or population also tend to experience an increase in alcohol and drug abuse, although less so than BOOM TOWNS. A study of depressed towns during the mid- and late-1970s showed that, as in the case of boom towns, the growth of alcohol abuse was higher than that of drug abuse.

Unlike boom towns depressed communities are usually stable and long-established areas whose economy and population have declined over a period of time. Since young people generally leave such areas in search of employment, the population is older and therefore itself well established. Increases in drug abuse are usually low; alcohol abuse is higher and tends to reflect a variety of factors, such as individual (rather than mass) reaction, ethnic and religious makeup of the community and the social classes affected. Arrests for DRIVING WHILE INTOXICATED are erratically (but often substantially) higher while treatment for alcoholism declines or falls off sharply. Although there is less money to spend, and presumably less to spend on alcohol, liquor provides a ready sedative for problems. In addition drinking is often much cheaper than other forms of recreation and can be indulged in at any time of the day or night.

National Institute of Drug Abuse, *Drug and Alcohol Abuse in Booming and Depressed Communities*, DHEW publication no. (ADM) 80-960, 1980.

depression   One of the disorders often associated with alcoholism is depression which may be a reason for drinking or a result of heavy use of alcohol that could possibly be alleviated by abstinence. Since alcohol can enhance pleasant feelings and raise optimism and self-confidence for a short time, someone with a pre-existing depression may be sensitized to its pleasurable effects. However, the EUPHORIA experienced is quickly followed by a return to the state of depression, and prolonged ingestion nearly always leads to a deterioration of mood. The state of depression following alcohol use may be even less tolerable than that the one preceding it. Studies have shown that alcoholics become more depressed and hostile after drinking and that drinking, instead of raising their self-esteem, makes them feel even more worthless than before. Postdrinking depression may lead to suicide attempts. A study conducted at Duke University Medical Center showed that 26 of 29 people who had attempted suicide were intoxicated at the time of their attempt. Doctors sometimes prescribe tranquilizers in an attempt to calm the patient, but these simply add to the effects of alcohol and worsen the depression (see SEDATIVE.)

John Langone, *Bombed, Buzzed, Smashed, or . . . Sober* (Boston: Little, Brown and Company, 1976), pp. 67, 106, 107.

deprivation   One of the major psychological theories of alcoholism posits that alcoholism is the result of disturbance and deprivation in early infantile experience. According to this theory, the alcoholic is deprived of a significant emotional relationship during the early years of his or her life. Because of the lack of a warm relationship with a mother figure in infancy, usually as a result of death or emotional or physical absence, he or she becomes fixated in the oral stage of development (see ORAL FIXATION). The object loss early in life causes the alcoholic to have primitive, excessive and insatiable demands. Interpersonal relationships fail and long-suppressed feelings of loss and rejection in infancy are reawakened. There is so much pain from this experience that an intense rage develops, and rather than destroy another, the alcoholic turns his or her anger inward and consumes it with alcohol.

detoxification   (From the Latin *de* reversing or undoing + *toxicum* poison.) Also known as detoxication, detoxification is a treatment process by which a patient addicted to a drug is withdrawn from that drug under supervision. The symptoms that occur during this WITHDRAWAL reflect the type of drug involved, the length of use and the kind of services provided during withdrawal. After detoxification the patient is able to abstain from the drug without severe physical discomfort and is no longer *physically* dependent upon it.

Decisions concerning where and how a patient should be detoxified depend on a number of factors. The severity of the withdrawal symptoms is a primary consideration; those with severe symptoms require close medical supervision and management, usually in a hospital. Patients who have alcohol- or nonalcohol-related complications, such as cardiac disease or hypertension, also generally require hospitalization. However, those with mild or moderate withdrawal symptoms and no complications may not need the care of a hospital and may be able to go through the detoxification process in a more social setting. As alternatives to hospitalization, some states provide nonhospital social setting detoxification centers and others have nonhospital medical detoxification centers.

There has been some interest recently in the possibility of limited use of ambulatory detoxification for carefully screened patients. Under this program the patient would return daily to a clinic for medication and counseling. Family and friends are encouraged to participate in the program.

Detoxification is generally accomplished during a short confinement (five to 10 days) in a general hospital. Hospitalization has several advantages: it removes the alcoholic from his or her drinking environment, emphasizes the disease nature of the condition, protects the patient from the sometimes fatal effects of withdrawal and gives him or her an opportunity to commence REHABILITATION. In a hospital an alcoholic patient is usually given an appropriate sedative to control withdrawal symptoms.

According to the clinical state of the patient, chlordiazepoxide (Librium) or a similar drug may be prescribed on a three-hour basis. Generally 50 to 100 milligrams are administered upon admission and tapered doses are given thereafter. An attempt is made to keep the patient alert but not tremulous. All medications are discontinued before discharge. The patient generally receives instruction about alcoholism from a physician as well as a plan for further rehabilitation, such as ALCOHOLICS ANONYMOUS, psychiatric examination, ANTABUSE therapy or GROUP THERAPY. Frequently the patient is discharged from the hospital to an alcohol rehabilitation center. Some such centers have their own detoxification facilities.

diabetes   There has been some controversy about whether or not diabetics should be allowed to have alcoholic beverages in their diets. Proper diet is of primary importance in achieving control of hyperglycemia (high blood sugar), the principal manifestation of diabetes mellitus. While the effects of alcohol vary from individual to individual and depend on kind, dosage and whether taken in the fasting or fed state, small amounts of alcohol consumed close to or with a meal generally produce little change in the blood sugar levels of diabetics whose disease is under control. However, excessive alcohol consumption can cause many problems if taken in a fasting state or if sweet dessert wines, port or liqueurs are consumed. These beverages contain high amounts of sugar (up to 50%). Diabetics should consult their physicians about the advisability of including alcohol in their diets.

On the simplest level, alcohol can disrupt diet control, provide extra calories and stimulate the appetite. Alcohol should not contribute more than 6% of the total calories consumed per day by a diabetic (see CALORIE). For a 70-kg (154-lb) man this standard amounts to approximately 160 kcal (kilogram calories) per day, or two 4-oz glasses of dry wine. Alcohol is considered a "fat exchange," or a food with the nutritive equivalent of fat, in the "food-exchange" terminology used in diabetic diets. To compute the alcohol calories in one serving of a beverage, the following formula can be used:

$0.8 \times$ proof $\times$ ounces per serving = kcal.
Example: A 2-oz serving of 80-proof whiskey equals 128 kcal. 0.8×80 (proof) $\times 2$ (ounces) = 128 kcal.

When the alcohol content is expressed as

a percentage, such as in wines and beers, double the percentage and apply the same formula.

0.8 × double the % of alcohol listed on the bottle × ounces per serving = kcal from alcohol.
Example: A 4-oz serving of wine containing 14% alcohol equals 89.6 kcal. 0.8 × 28 (double the % of alcohol) × 4 (ounces) = 89.6 kcal.

Any carbohydrate kcal (in beer, wine, mixers) should be added to the alcohol kcal for total kcal (see table under CARBO-HYDRATE).

If alcohol is taken in a fasting state, it can precipitate hypoglycemia (low blood sugar). Alcohol consumed in this state can enhance the blood sugar-lowering action of insulin and interfere with the body's ability to produce its own glucose. Insulin-dependent diabetics in a fasting state are especially susceptible to hypoglycemia. Because the symptoms are similar to those of intoxication, a hypoglycemic reaction may not be recognized, and necessary treatment may therefore be delayed. If alcohol is consumed, it is essential that it be taken with food or shortly before or after a meal. Alcohol ingestion raises the level of triglyceride (a type of fat) in the blood. Excessive levels of this fat, known as hypertriglyceridemia, are believed to be a major cause of atherosclerosis. Hypertriglyceridemia is more common in diabetics than in nondiabetics, and anyone with high triglyceride levels should be discouraged from drinking.

Alcohol can cause a reaction in diabetics using oral glucose-lowering agents that are sulfonyl derivatives (Orinase, Diabinese). Possible symptoms include dizziness, flushing and nausea.

The sugar content of wine varies a great deal. Information about sugar content can be obtained by writing to the quality control laboratories of wineries. An alternative is to use the reducing sugar tablets, which measure the percentage of glucose and fructose

(Clinitest) to determine sugar concentration. Since wine contains sugars other than glucose, tests that measure only glucose (Tes-Tape, Diastix, Clinistix) should not be used.

Janet McDonald, "Alcohol and Diabetes," *Diabetes Care* 3, no. 5 (September–October 1980): 629–637.
——,"Whiskey or Water?" *Diabetes Forecast,* November–December 1980, pp. 17–20, 42.

digestion   In small quantities alcohol may aid digestion. Its mild anesthetic effect overcomes the "dry mouth" associated with stress and allows freer salivation, which in turn triggers motility, the gentle motion that empties the stomach and is considered beneficial to digestion. Wine in particular is thought to be good for this purpose because the type of acid in wine is close to that in the gastric juices.

While one or two glasses of wine may stimulate digestion, heavier doses can result in an irritated stomach wall, an increased concentration of alcohol and a stomach too anesthetized to move.

dipsomania   (From the Greek *dipsa* thirst + *mania* madness.) A term, generally in disuse in North America, that refers to an uncontrollable CRAVING for alcohol, often of a periodic nature (see EPSILON ALCOHOLISM). Dipsomania is also improperly used as a synonym for persistent drunkenness or alcoholism. The slang word "dipso" means drunkard.

disease concept   The disease concept provides the basis for many of the current approaches to the treatment of ALCOHOLISM. There is a misconception that the disease concept is of recent origin, perhaps because only recently has it gained widespread acceptance. Actually the concept has a long and controversial history. Mark Keller of the Rutgers Center of Alcohol Studies points out that as early as the first century the Roman philosopher Seneca distinguished between "a man who is drunk" and one who "has no control over himself . . . who is accustomed to get drunk, and is a slave to the habit." The 18th century American physician Benjamin Rush said of drunkenness that it "resembles certain hereditary, family and contagious diseases." The idea of alcoholism as a disease was accepted in the 19th century by a large part of the medical community. In 1952 JELLINEK distinguished alcohol addiction as a specific diagnostic category and elaborated a developmental course of the addiction process. While his theoretical progression of the major symptoms has been seriously questioned, most authorities still affirm the major elements of the disease concept. Both the American Medical Association and the World Health Organization regard alcoholism as a specific disease entity.

Perhaps the major advantage of the disease concept is that it shifts the emphasis from the idea of alcoholism as a moral issue requiring punitive measures to the notion that an alcoholic is the victim of an illness that requires medical and psychological treatment. The stigma is thereby lifted from the patient and some of his guilt is relieved, guilt that is often a stimulus to further drinking. The disease concept emphasizes social support rather than punishment of the alcoholic. Making alcoholism a medical category has permitted some of the personal economic costs to be handled by IN-SURANCE, disability payments and workmen's compensation.

Some arguments against the disease model are that it overemphasizes the medical aspects, leading to the (probably erroneous) assumption that alcoholism is essentially a singular entity, like tuberculosis, and ignores the fact that it may be a symptom of a number of quite separate problems. Some doctors feel that for alcoholism to be classified as a disease there must be some manifest abnormality of the anatomic structure. But this requirement would eliminate all behavioral disorders from the classification of disease.

It is also thought that the disease model takes inadequate account of the sociocultural factors which may play a causal role, and fosters irresponsibility in the patient, allowing him or her to be passive. Another danger with this model is that alcoholism may be considered an all-or-nothing disease entity, with no degrees in between.

Proponents of the disease model generally agree that while it may not be completely adequate in dealing with a complex disorder with many causal factors, it seems to provide the most sound basis for an approach to alcoholism.

David J. Armor, J. Michael Polich and Harriet B. Stambul, *Alcoholism and Treatment* (New York: John Wiley and Sons, 1978), pp. 9–11.
Mark Keller, "The Disease Concept of Alcoholism Revisited," reprint from *Journal of Studies on Alcohol* 37, no. 11 (November 1976): 1694–1717.

diseases   There are several diseases caused by extended heavy use of alcohol and others in which alcohol abuse may play a role.

In the first category are a number of diseases of the LIVER, such as ALCOHOLIC LIVER DISEASE, CIRRHOSIS, FATTY LIVER and ALCOHOLIC HEPATITIS. Heavy alcohol use can damage the BRAIN and the CENTRAL NERVOUS SYSTEM, resulting in such disorders as DELIRIUM TREMENS, KORSAFOFF'S SYNDROME, WERNICKE'S ENCEPHALOPATHY and ALCOHOLIC POLYNEUROPATHY as well as less common diseases, including MARCHIAFAVA-BIGNAMI DISEASE and CENTRAL PONTINE MYELINOLYSIS. Other diseases caused by excessive alcohol consumption include FETAL ALCOHOL SYNDROME, ALCOHOL AMBLYOPIA, ALCOHOLIC MYOPATHY, HEMOCHROMATOSIS, RHINOPHYMA and ACNE ROSACEA.

Excessive use of alcohol may be a contributing factor in such diseases as CANCER and DIABETES, and in some diseases of the HEART, STOMACH and PANCREAS. It may also be harmful to the fetus during PREGNANCY.

distillation   The process of separating or purifying liquids by boiling them, collecting the vapors emitted and recondensing the vapors into liquid form. Distillation is used for a variety of purposes, ranging from oil refining to desalinization of seawater. It takes place naturally in the cycle by which groundwater evaporates into clouds and then recondenses to fall as rainwater.

In the production of alcoholic beverages, distillation involves heating a fermented mash, collecting the alcohol content that vaporizes before the water (because it has a lower boiling point) and then collecting the recondensed alcohol as a distillate.

Distillation of alcoholic beverages is generally considered to have been a discovery of Arab cultures, although they never fully refined the technique because of Moslem strictures against consumption of alcohol. Classical Greek and Roman societies used distillation processes to purify water but apparently never distilled their wines into spirits to any great extent. It was not until after 1000 A.D. that distillation of alcohols became common in Europe, with the first spirits probably being crude brandies distilled from wines in Italy. The procedure also has a long history in Ireland, where the fermented material was a mash of grains rather than wine.

The early motivation for distillation may have been economic: producers of wines or beers could reduce the cost of transport if they shifted to smaller quantities of more potent alcoholic beverages, and distilled spirits are also more stable than wines or beers. Inevitably, however, a new preference for the more potent beverages developed, and continental Europe's early *aqua fortis* ("strong water") and Ireland's *uisce beathadh* ("water of life") were prized for their superior powers as intoxicants before their recorded histories began in the early 16th century.

Today distillation of potable spirits begins with the production of a fermented mash. Grains are the most common material employed, and they are generally malted, or germinated, to make soluble sugars. Once yeast is introduced, these sugars convert into alcohols, creating a fermented "wash," or "wort," from which the alcohol content can be distilled. Two types of apparatus are used for distillation: the traditional pot still or the newer and more efficient patent still, sometimes called the continuous still. In either case the alcohol distillate is the base from which any number of potable spirits can be produced by various flavoring, dilution and aging processes.

DNA   Deoxyribonucleic acid; with RNA, one of the two main types of nucleic acid, an organic substance found in the chromosomes of all living cells. DNA plays an important role in the storage and replication of hereditary information and in protein synthesis.

doctor   Slang for a person who sells liquor at higher prices when bars and liquor stores are closed. The term is also used, as a verb, to refer to the addition of alcohol to a drink, often without the drinker's knowledge.

dram   (From the weight of the ancient Greek coin the drachma. In modern fluid measurement, 1 dram = ⅛ ounce.) Although a dram is too small a portion to have ever been used seriously as a measurement of liquor, it was a common measure of medicine (1 teaspoon = 1 ⅛ drams), with which it was first associated, and liquor has often been euphemistically referred to as "medicine." "Taking a dram" (like "having a wee nip") is a way of playing down the amount of alcohol consumed. Usually a dram, like a SHOT (which is what the word "dram" most often means today), is downed in a single gulp. As early as the 17th century, "dram-drinking" and "dramming" were terms usually reserved for habitual drinking to the point of mild intoxication. (See also DRAM SHOP LAW.)

dram shop law   A law which provides that a person, usually a tavern keeper, who supplies alcoholic beverages to another person who then becomes intoxicated is responsible for damages done by that other person, as a result or consequence of his intoxification, to the person or property of others and even to himself.

drinker   A person who consumes alcoholic beverages, as opposed to someone who abstains. In popular usage the term "drinker" is also used to refer to an alcoholic or drunk.

drinking   Consuming alcoholic beverages; not abstaining.

drive reduction   See HORMONES, MALE SEX.

driving-and-drinking   See DRIVING WHILE INTOXICATED.

driving under the influence (DUI)
See DRIVING WHILE INTOXICATED.

driving while intoxicated (DWI)
There are approximately 118 million drivers in the United States and 95 million drinkers. Each year about 46,700 people die on U.S. highways—over half of these fatalities are alcohol related. Each year motor vehicle accidents involving alcohol result in more than $1 billion in property damage, insurance costs and medical services, inju-

ries to more than a half million people and several hundred thousand arrests. In 1976 federal, state and local government agencies spent an estimated $100 million for activities aimed at reducing the amount of drunken driving or the level of risk involved.

Studies have shown that alcohol causes degeneration of driving skills, including reaction time, coordination, attention, visual awareness and judgment. In an average person some degree of impairment can usually be demonstrated at a BLOOD ALCOHOL CONCENTRATION (BAC) of 0.05%; above 0.08% the risk of an accident rises appreciably; and beyond 0.10% there is a definite increase in risk for all drivers. At a BAC of 0.15% the risk is 10 times higher than normal and 0.20% it is 20 times greater.

Studies conducted in California in the early 1970s showed that 53% of drivers killed in accidents had BACs over 0.09%. In Wisconsin two out of three drivers killed had been drinking and three out of five had BACs over 0.10%. Apparently excessive consumption of alcohol also diminishes a driver's ability to avoid the mistakes of others on the road. In a study by Drs. A. Waller and M. W. Perrine of the University of Vermont, 18% of fatally injured drivers not at fault were found to have BAC levels above 0.10% (2% of the population on the road at the time but not involved in accidents were found to have BACs above 0.10%). Of those at fault 50% had BACs at or above the 0.10% level.

Statistics have shown that up to 29% of passengers involved in fatal accidents had BAC levels in the legally impaired range. And it has been estimated that in up to 83% of pedestrian fatalities, either the driver or the pedestrian was intoxicated. Studies by the National Highway Safety Administration showed that more than one-third of all fatally injured pedestrians had BACs of 0.10% or more. The majority of alcohol-related accidents occur at night, and a larger proportion of men than women are involved, perhaps partly because of different drinking patterns (women tend more to drink at home).

The biggest menace on the highway is the PROBLEM DRINKER who has previous arrests for offenses involving alcohol. Studies indicate that persons with severe drinking problems are disproportionately involved in all kinds of crashes. Nationally problem drinkers, who make up 7% of the driving population, are invorved in 33% (18,000 annually) of all fatal crashes. In 1975 there were 45,853 traffic deaths, an estimated 22,926 of which may have been alcohol related, including as many as 10,546 that may have been associated with alcoholism. Of alcoholics who drive 24% to 40% have at least one traffic crash on their driving records.

About half of all fatally injured drinking drivers are less than 30 years old, and from 40% to 60% of all fatal crashes involving young drivers are alcohol related. Young people are inexperienced in both drinking and driving and, therefore, at a particularly high risk of being involved in a traffic accident. In addition they are more likely to combine alcohol with other drugs and the simultaneous presence of alcohol and some other drug (or drugs) in the system may have a greater effect on driving than that produced by either alcohol or another drug alone (see SYNERGY).

All 50 states have laws against driving under the influence of alcohol (DUI) and impose various penalties for the offense. In most states the determination of whether or not someone is intoxicated is based on blood alcohol concentration, as measured by a breath tester, urinalysis or direct analysis of the blood. The Breathalyzer, used frequently today, is a chemical photometric device that determines BAC by testing a sample of breath from deep inside the lungs. In many states there is an implied consent law that requires a motorist to submit to a BAC test or face fines or suspension of his or her driving privileges.

In the majority of states a BAC level of 0.10% is considered evidence of intoxication. In Idaho and Utah the level is 0.08% and a few states have two levels: 0.10%, with less severe penalties, and 0.15%, with harsher penalties. Most countries have similar legal limits, and a few, such as the USSR and other Communist-block countries, completely prohibit alcohol consumption before and while driving.

Penalties for drunken driving also vary from place to place. The Scandinavian Countries have the strictest laws in the world, some calling for automatic imprisonment and loss of driver's license. Although early studies of these laws found no significant changes in the number or rate of fatal motor vehicle crashes after they went ino effect, the laws have not yet been adequately evaluated and are still under study. It has generally been found that strict penalties in themselves do little to prevent drunken driving unless they are enforced and perceived to be enforced. Surveys have shown that severe laws which are highly publicized work well at first, but if drivers learn that the actual level of arrests and convictions is very low, within a few months the laws have little deterrent effect.

There are many problems related to enforcing drinking-and-driving laws. Only motorists who give evidence of erratic or illegal driving or who become involved in a crash are likely to be apprehended for driving under the influence or while intoxicated. And after an intoxicated motorist is stopped, there are several loopholes through which he or she can escape. A recent study showed that experienced police failed to recognize approximately 40% of the drivers who were over the 0.10% BAC level (Kletta). Roadside breath tests, while not always accurate, improve the probability of detecting drinking drivers. However, even under an implied consent law, drivers can refuse to take the test. And in Connecticut, for example, no one has been convicted of refusing to take the test for at least 10 years (Condon). Furthermore revocation of a driver's license often fails to prevent a person from driving. A California study showed that three out of four drivers who had their licenses revoked received traffic citations during periods when they were supposedly prohibited from driving (Coppin). The lowering of the drinking age in some states from 21 to 18 may also increase the number of fatalities caused by drunken driving. A study by the Insurance Institute conducted in a number of Midwestern states and a Canadian province showed an approximately 5% increase in the number of 15- to 20-year-old drivers involved in fatal crashes.

It is generally believed that to reduce traffic fatalities and accidents the amount of drinking-and-driving must be reduced. A higher risk of arrest through the use of targeting patrols by day, time and location, breath tests that are easier to administer both legally and physically, simplification of the process for making a DWI arrest and increased motivation for police to make such arrests may help to deter the drinking driver. On the other hand, increasing the severity of penalties might result in fewer arrests, fewer convictions and more plea bargaining as well as lengthier trials and appeals that could cost the taxpayer more. Public education may help reduce the amount of drinking-and-driving, although so far there is no strong evidence that this is the case. Improving the safety of cars and highways might help cut the number of fatalities, although such measures will not solve the problem.

Some states require individuals arrested for driving while intoxicated to attend a drinking driver program. More extensive programs may be needed for drivers recognized to be problem drinkers. In many places there are citizens action groups that work not only to educate drivers but to put pressure on law enforcement agencies to enforce driving laws strictly. Federal efforts have been increased with the establishment, in 1982, of a commission on drunk driving by President Reagan.

Tom Condon, "Weak Law Keeps Drunken Drivers on Road," *Hartford Courant,* April 6, 1980, p. 29.

R.S. Coppin and G. Van Oldenbeek, *Driving under Suspension and Revocation,* California Department of Motor Vehicles, Division of Administration, Research and Statistics Section report 18 (1965).

John R. DeLuca, ed., *Fourth Special Report to the U.S. Congress on Alcohol and Health* (Rockville, Md.: National Institute on Alcohol Abuse and Alcoholism, 1981), pp. 81, 82, 131, 132, 157, 158.

Paul Ditzel, *Alcohol and Driving,* Automobile Club of Southern California, n.d.

Insurance Institute for Highway Safety, *To Prevent Harm* (Washington, D.C., 1978), passim.

H. Kletta, "On the Possibilities for the Police to Detect Low Blood Alcohol Concentrations," *Alcohol and Highway Safety,* Swedish Government Committee Report, SOU (1970): 61.

Joy Moser, *Prevention of Alcohol-Related Problems* (Toronto: World Health Organization, 1980), pp. 211–218.

Robert B. Voas, *Vehicle Violence: An American Tragedy,* National Council on Alcoholism, 1971.

drunk and disorderly   See PUBLIC DRUNKENNESS.

drug addiction   See ADDICTION.

drug interaction   See DRUGS. See also SYNERGY.

drugs   Chemical substances used to diagnose, treat or prevent disease or other abnormal conditions, to relieve pain or to alter the state of body or mind. Alcohol is classified as a drug. Pharmacologically it is a member of a group of compounds generally known as sedatives that act as depressants on the central nervous system (see SEDATIVE). These compounds include barbiturates, "minor tranquilizers," such as Valium, and general anesthetic agents, such as ether. The patterns of misuse of alcohol are similar to those of other drugs.

In the past 30 years the use and abuse of alcohol and other drugs—prescription, illicit and over the counter—have increased greatly. Combining alcohol with drugs has become increasingly popular, often resulting in dual or multiple addiction. A survey conducted by ALCOHOLICS ANONYMOUS (AA) in 1977 showed that a high percentage of alcoholics coming into AA were addicted to alcohol and one or more psychoactive prescription drugs. This was especially true of young women: 55% of all women under 30 in the survey reported that they were addicted to prescription tranquilizers as well as alcohol. That figure was more than three times the percentage of all AA members—18%—who admitted being addicted to other drugs besides alcohol. Drinkers are also several times more likely to use psychoactive substances for nonmedical reasons than are nondrinkers.

Another major problem with combined drug and alcohol use is the danger that arises from the interaction of the two within the body. The *Third Special Report to the U.S. Congress on Alcohol and Health* defined an interaction between alcohol and a drug as "any alteration in the pharmacologic properties of either due to the presence of the other." The report classified three different types by interactions:

1. Antagonistic, in which the effects of one or both drugs are blocked or reduced;
2. Additive, in which the effect is the sum of the effects of each;
3. Supra-additive (synergistic or potentiating), in which the effects of the two drugs in combination is greater than it would be if the effects were additive.

The supra-additive effect is the most dangerous, because when combined, even safe levels of both alcohol and drugs can at times prove fatal (see SYNERGY). For example, when alcohol and another drug are present in the system, the alcohol competes for the enzymes that would normally be used to metabolize the drug. The drug then accumulates in the body and has a greater impact than it would normally have. This effect most commonly occurs when alcohol is combined with barbiturates, which, like alcohol, are central nervous system depressants. Although not quite as dangerous, the antagonistic effect can be hazardous when the therapeutic effects of one drug are reduced by the presence of alcohol.

Drugs also have a half-life, which is the amount of time it takes for the body to remove half of the drug from the system. For drugs with a half-life of 24 hours or more, such as Valium, half of the first dose may still be in the body when the next is taken. After several days the buildup in the body can be fairly large, and the result of taking a drink at this point can be devastating.

The chart on p. 94 shows the interaction between alcohol and various other drugs.

drunk   Slang for a person who is intoxicated or under the influence of alcohol; also an alcoholic. The state of being intoxicated (see INTOXICATION). A drinking spree is sometimes referred to as a drunk.

drunk driving   See DRIVING WHILE INTOXICATED.

dry   A person who is against drinking or the sale of liquor, a prohibitionist; opposed to WET. When applied to an alcoholic, it means abstinent. The term is also used, particularly in ALCOHOLICS ANONYMOUS, to describe someone who is marginally sober and abstinent but who may relapse at any time. Such a person is also called a "dry drunk." (See also SOBRIETY.)

dry drunk   One who has stopped drinking but who still craves alcohol. The term, particularly as used by ALCOHOLICS ANONYMOUS, refers to a person who has not achieved real SOBRIETY but exists in a sort of "white-knuckled sobriety," gritting his teeth and trying hard not to drink. Such sobriety is seen as a temporary condition, with

Alcohol-Drug Interactions

Drug	Possible effects
AMPHETAMINES: Benzedrine, Dexadrine, Rialtin etc.	Excessive rise in blood pressure with alcoholic beverages containing the chemical tyramine, e.g., Chianti wine; possible antagonism of central nervous system (CNS) depressant effects of alcohol but no improvement of impaired motor coordination; may result in false sense of security; at high levels of both, possible gastrointestinal upset.
ANALGESICS, NARCOTIC: Darvon, Demerol, Dilaudid etc.	Reduction in function of the CNS; may lead to loss of effective breathing function (respiratory arrest); may be fatal.
ANALGESICS, NON-NARCOTIC: Aspirin, APC, Pabalate etc.	Increased stomach irritation and/or internal bleeding.
ANESTHETICS, General: ANTABUSE (disulfiram)	Additive CNS depressant effects in acute stage of intoxication; in alcoholics possible high tolerance, requiring large dosage. Blocks oxidation of alcohol at acetaldehyde stage; results in nausea, dizziness, flushing, vomiting. (See also ANTABUSE.)
ANTIALCOHOL PREPARATIONS (excluding Antabuse): Calcium Carbonate	Reaction resulting in nausea, vomiting, headache, increased blood pressure and possible erratic heartbeat; may be fatal.
ANTIANGINAL PREPARATIONS: Nitrates, Nitrites	Possible excessive lowering in blood pressure resulting in fainting, dizziness or lightheadedness.
ANTIBIOTICS	May reduce therapeutic effects; may produce acetaldehyde toxicity similar to that caused by Antabuse.
ANTICOAGULANTS: Coumadin, Dicumarol, Panwarfin, Sintrom etc.	Possible increased anticoagulant effects, which may lead to hemorrhage.
ANTICONVULSANTS: Dilantin, Diphenyl, EKKO etc.	Decrease of drug's ability to stop convulsions.
ANTIDEPRESSANTS: Elavil, Sinequan, Tofranil, Vivacti etc.	Increased CNS depression, reduced motor skills; high blood pressure crisis in combination with Chianti wine; reduced motor skills.
ANTIDIABETIC DRUGS: Chloronase, Diabinese, Insulin, Orinase etc.	With insulin, may induce severe hypoglycemia; with the others, may cause a reaction producing such symptoms as dizziness, flushing and nausea.
ANTIHISTAMINES: ChlorTrimeton, Dramamine, Norflex etc.; most cold remedies; Actified Coricidin	Increased sedative effects.
ANTIHYPERTENSIVE AGENTS: Aldomet, Esidrix, Serpasil etc.	Increase in blood pressure-lowering effects with possibility of dizziness. Some agents also cause increased CNS depressant effects.
ANTI-INFECTIVE AGENTS: Chloromycetin, Flagyl etc.	Possible Antabuse effects.
ASPIRIN SUBSTITUTES (containing acetaminophen): Datril, Tylenol	Alcohol appears to enhance the liver-damaging effects of aspirin substitutes.

Alcohol-Drug Interactions

Drug	Possible effects
BARBITURATES: Amytal, Butisol, Nembutal, Seconal etc.	Increased CNS depression with possible coma and respiratory arrest. Chronic alcohol consumption can produce a cross-tolerance to sedative effects but not to respiratory depressive effects. May be fatal.
BROMIDES	Confusion; delirium; increased intoxication
CAFFEINE	False sense of security; no improvement of impaired motor coordination
CANNABIS: Marijuana, hashish	Greater impairment of motor and mental skills than with either drug alone.
DIURETICS: Diuril, Lasix, Hydromox etc.	Increase in blood pressure-lowering effects; possible dizziness when standing.
MORPHINE AND OTHER OPIATE DERIVATIVES: heroin, methadone etc.	Possible potentiation of alcohol's depressant effect; frequently results in death. Chronic use of alcohol may sensitize an individual to the effects of opiates and vice versa. (A large proportion of heroin addicts and methadone maintenance patients are heavy users of alcohol.)
NARCOTICS: (See also ANALGESICS, NARCOTIC)	Excessive sedation.
PENICILLIN	Alcohol enhances the degradation of penicillin and large amounts of alcohol interfere with the amount of penicillin available for absorption.
SEDATIVE-HYPNOTICS: Doriden, Nembutal Quaalude etc.	Increased CNS depression with possible coma or respiratory arrest; may be fatal.
TRANQUILIZERS, MAJOR: Tindal, Mellaril, Thorazine etc.	Increased CNS depression; possible severe impairment of voluntary movements. Combination can cause loss of effective breathing function and may be fatal.
TRANQUILIZERS, MINOR	Increased CNS depression, especially during first few weeks of drug use; decreased alertness and judgment.
VITAMINS	Prevention of vitamins from entering blood stream, which is reversible once drinking is stopped.

(See also CAFFEINE, CODEINE WITH ALCOHOL, MARIJUANA WITH ALCOHOL, METHADONE WITH ALCOHOL, NICOTINE.)

an inevitable return to drinking unless help is accepted. The term "dry drunk" is also used to describe an experience in which the alcoholic participates without consuming any alcohol, in a social and emotional occasion (usually in a drinking environment) that he or she associates with excessive drinking. If the psychological impact and aftermath of an experience have many of the aspects and symptoms of a drunken spree, it is called a dry drunk. The term is also used to describe a person who shows symptoms of intoxication although having had nothing to drink.

DUI   Driving under the influence. See DRIVING WHILE INTOXICATED.

Dutch gin   See GIN.

DWI   See DRIVING WHILE INTOXICATED.

dysphoria   A feeling of malaise or nonspecific illness or general discomfort that often accompanies a HANGOVER or WITHDRAWAL.

E

---

eau de vie   (French, "water of life.") Any spirit distilled from wine, especially BRANDY.

ebriate   (From Latin *ebriare* to intoxicate.) To intoxicate, inebriate.

ebriety   (From Latin *ebrius* intoxicated.) See INEBRIETY.

economic impact   The economic costs of alcohol abuse result both from a decrease in normal production levels and from increased spending for such items as health and social services and police and fire protection. Based on an analysis of six major categories, R.E. Berry, Jr. and his associates estimated that alcoholism and alcohol misuse cost the United States almost $43 billion in 1975.

Some researchers have asserted that this amount is inflated and that none of the costs in the six categories may be attributed unconditionally to alcohol misuse (McGuire). Others have claimed that the figures are conservative and that the omission of several groups, including males older than 59 and younger than 21, SKID ROW alcoholics

and women in all age brackets, results in a serious understatement (Schifrin et al.).

Cost of Alcoholism and Alcohol Misuse in the United States (1975)

	($ Billions)
Lost production	19.64
Health and medical services	12.74
Motor vehicle accidents	5.14
Violent crime	2.86
Social responses	1.94
Fire losses	0.43
Total	42.75

R. E. Berry, Jr. et al., *The Economic Costs of Alcohol Abuse and Alcoholism—1975,* Final Report to National Institute on Alcohol Abuse and Alcoholism, contract no. ADM 281-76-0016 (Boston: Policy Analysis, August 1977).

John R. DeLuca, ed., *Fourth Special Report to the U.S. Congress on Alcohol and Health,* (Rockville, Md.: National Institute on Alcohol Abuse and Alcoholism, 1981), p. 93.

T.G. McGuire, "Measuring the Costs of Alcohol Abuse," in *An Assessment of Statistics on Alcohol-Related Problems,* prepared for The Distilled Spirits Council of the United States (New York: Columbia University School of Public Health, 1980).

L. G. Schifrin, C. E. Hartsog and D. H. Brand, "Costs of Alcoholism and Alcohol Abuse and Their Reaction to Alcohol Research," in *Alcoholism and Related Problems: Opportunities for Research* (Washington, D.C.: Institute of Medicine of the National Academy of Sciences, 1980).

Eighteenth Amendment   Under the Eighteenth Amendment, which banned the manufacture, transportation and sale of intoxicating beverages, PROHIBITION officially began on January 17, 1920. The VOLSTEAD ACT provided the mechanism for its enforcement. It was repealed in 1932 by the TWENTY-FIRST AMENDMENT.

elderly   In the United States and other countries alcohol abuse among the elderly is a serious and growing problem. The number of alcoholics over the age of 60 in the United States is now estimated at 3 million and there may be twice as many by the year 2000, when the size of the elderly population will have greatly increased. Alcohol abuse is the foremost form of substance abuse among the elderly, but alcohol-related problems, including alcoholism, are often ignored for a number of reasons. One is that DENIAL of an alcohol problem is greater in the elderly and is more likely to be encouraged by relatives and friends, for instance, who feel that alcohol is one of the few pleasures left in old age. Alcoholism and alcohol abuse are also difficult to diagnose in the elderly because their manifestations may be perceived as the result of frailty, senility or just the unsteadiness of old age. The symptoms exhibited by alcoholics are very similar to those of nonalcoholics suffering deterioration of cerebral function because of advanced age.

As a result of more effective treatment, such as proper NUTRITION and antibiotics, more people with histories of alcoholism now survive into old age than in the past. Many elderly people, however, become addicted to alcohol after retirement as a result of loneliness, boredom and feelings of being unneeded. Stressful situations, such as bereavement, separation from children and physical deterioration, multiply in old age. The elderly who begin abusing alcohol late in life generally have fewer deep-seated psychological problems and are more amenable to counseling than those who become alcoholics at a younger age. Alcoholism is higher among elderly men than among elderly women and highest among widowers and the divorced.

Alcohol has a somewhat different effect on the elderly than on the rest of the adult population. Older people generally consume less alcohol, although they are more likely to drink every day, possibly because the slower metabolism associated with aging may induce WITHDRAWAL symptoms in those who have become dependent on alcohol, thus increasing the frequency of alcohol intake. Furthermore the ratio of body fat to body water increases with age, and as alcohol is almost completely soluble in water but not in fat, the same amount of alcohol intake per body weight consumed by older people results in higher concentrations in the blood and brain.

There are several problems related to treatment of alcoholism and alcohol abuse among the elderly. Social agencies for the aged are usually poorly equipped to treat alcohol problems and many alcohol treatment centers are geared to a younger patient population. In addition to staying in the body longer, alcohol as well as other drugs tend to have a more prolonged and toxic effect on elderly people. Alcohol can also mask pain and other warning signs of illness and disease and interfere with the therapeutic effects of prescription DRUGS, which older people frequently must take. The possible existence of cardiovascular difficulties in the aged person often restricts or prevents the use of such alcohol antagonist drugs as ANTABUSE and TEMPOSIL in the treatment of alcoholism.

An elderly alcoholic is more likely to stay in therapy longer and generally show a better response to rehabilitation than a younger alcoholic. The problem of alcohol abuse among the elderly must be recognized and given the attention it deserves.

electric shock   See AVERSION THERAPY. Electric shock is also sometimes used to treat depression associated with alcoholism.

emetine   A nausea-inducing drug used in AVERSION THERAPY.

employee assistance programs (EAPs)   Also known as occupational alcoholism programs, employee assistance programs were begun in the 1930s and 1940s, first by DuPont and Kodak and later by a small number of progressive companies. Between 1950 and 1973 the number of EAPs increased from about 50 to 500 and in the past eight years the figure has grown to more than 4,400 programs in the private sector and more than 600 in the public. A 1972 survey of the Fortune 500 companies and 250 financial, insurance and utility organizations found that 25% of these companies had such programs; seven years later another survey revealed that the proportion had risen to 57%. And that percentage is even higher today.

According to Dr. Dale A. Masi, director of employee and counseling services for the U.S. Department of Health and Human Services, the highest rate of recovery from alcoholism is found in the office or factory rather than the clinic or hospital program. According to the U.S. National Council on Alcoholism the average alcoholic will allow his or her family ties to disintegrate five years before he or she loses a job. The rate of recovery for EAP referrals is between 50% and 85%.

The National Institute on Alcohol Abuse and Alcoholism has estimated that 50% of people with job performance problems suffer from alcoholism. Because it is a progressive disease, alcoholism frequently takes as long as 10 to 15 years to reach its middle stages. At this point the worker is often occupying a position of responsibility. The Stanford Research Institute has calculated that by treating workers with a drinking problem, industry saves about $6,000 per alcoholic employee each year.

Among the sources that provide programs for alcoholic employees are voluntary associations, labor unions and organizations for employees in both the public and private sectors. A variety of counseling services are offered but the basic orientation of most programs is alcoholism identification and intervention. The work place provides structures for effective early intervention and confrontation. Poor job performance is the best indicator of a possible drinking problem. The rationale underlying the modern approach to employee alcoholism is that any alcoholic, even one in the early stages of the disease, will tend to exhibit a pattern of deteriorating job performance that can be observed by an alert individual (Dunkin). A return to adequate job performance should be regarded as the criterion for judging whether or not treatment has been a success.

There are 107 million workers in the United States, 15% of the work force (excluding the military) is in the public sector. Few public sector programs existed before 1972, but gradually, partly because of legislation, they have been increasing. Today, while less than one-half of all U.S. government installations report having alcoholism counseling services, those that do have such services employ over 80% of all federal personnel.

While many organizations are well served by EAPs, the majority of workers still do not have access to such programs for problems of substance abuse (alcohol and other drugs), according to James Lawrence, acting deputy director of the National Institute on Alcohol Abuse and Alcoholism. This is especially true for employees of small- and medium-sized businesses. There is also a strong need for programs to help women and minorities. In Canada, for example, women make up about one-third of the alcoholic population, but according to Louise Nadeau, director of the University of Montreal's training program in addiction, only about 5% of them are referred for treatment through assistance programs (Birenbaum). Women have a double problem on the job: drinking is part of the process of becoming accepted by male coworkers, but women also have to deal with men's ambivalence about competing with them (as well as their own identity conflicts).

Another group of hard-to-reach employees are those holding senior or high-income positions. Such employees often work in an isolated or insulated environment, frequently change job location, work with minimal supervision, or are responsible to multiple supervisors and have a flexible work schedule. Supervisors often cover up problems they see in senior personnel, and those in senior positions may feel that EAPs are only for lower-level employees. The key to reaching these individuals is to involve them in the development of the programs, in the advisory and policy-making processes and in educational awareness programs. When this is not possible, the best approach is through peers and colleagues.

Rhonda Birenbaum, "EAPs Failing Female Alcoholics" (report of a speech given by Louise Nadeau, director of the University of Montreal's training program in addiction, to the 4th Biennial Canadian Conference on Alcohol and Addiction Problems in the Workplace, Ottawa), *The Journal* 10, no. 12 (Dec. 1, 1981): 3.

John R. DeLuca, ed., *Fourth Special Report to the U.S. Congress on Alcohol and Health* (Rockville, Md.: National Institute on Alcohol Abuse and Alcoholism, 1981), pp. 124–130.

William Dunkin, "The EAP Movement, Past and Present," *Alcoholism* 1, no. 4 (March–April): 27–28.

"EAPs Neglect Execs, Shift Workers" (report of a speech given by John Harder, director of the Canadian Forces Addiction Rehabilitation Centre, Kingston Ontario, to the 4th Biennial Canadian Conference on Alcohol and Addiction Problems in the Workplace, Ottawa), *The Journal* 10, no. 12 (Dec. 1, 1981): 12.

Alan Massam, "EAPs Have Highest Alcoholism Recovery Rates" (report of a speech given by Dale A. Masi, director of employee and counseling services, for the U.S. Department of Health and Human Services, to the World Conference on Alcoholism, London), *The Journal* 11, no. 1 (Jan. 1, 1982): 12.

Richard Roth, "The EAP Works," *Alcoholism* 1, no. 4. (March–April): 23–27.

enabling   A term that refers to attempts to protect an alcoholic from the consequences of his or her drinking. Although these attempts are generally aimed at helping the alcoholic, they allow his and her alcoholism to continue unchecked. Any member of society can be an enabler—family members and friends can provide reassurance and sympathy; an employer may find ways of keeping an alcoholic on the job; doctors and counselors may be protective of the alcoholic or blind to his or her problem; law enforcement officials may choose not to penalize alcohol-related incidents. These methods "enable" an alcoholic to continue in an uncontrolled drinking pattern by shielding him or her from the consequences.

An awareness of the negative effects of enabling by the enabler could eventually help the alcoholic. If forced to suffer the negative consequences of his or her behavior, the alcoholic may eventually develop more motivation to change. (See also PARA-ALCOHOLIC.)

endocrine etiological theories   A physiological approach to the cause of alcoholism, endocrine etiological theories hypothesize that dysfunction of the endocrine system leads to the development of alcoholism. A pituitary-adrenocortical deficiency resulting in hypoglycemia is believed to cause symptoms that stimulate drinking. Alcohol temporarily relieves the hypoglycemia by elevating blood sugar, but ultimately it intensifies the hypoglycemic condition, causing dependence on increased amounts of alcohol. To date there has been no strong evidence to support this view. (See also PHYSIOLOGICAL ETIOLOGICAL MODELS.)

epidemiology   (From the Greek *epidemios* among the people; *epi* in + *demos* people + *logy* discourse.) The medical study of the occurrence and prevalence of disease. The term "epidemiology" is often applied to the study of a disease that affects large numbers of people in a community.

Epsilon alcoholism   The fifth of five categories of alcoholism defined by JELLINEK, Epsilon alcoholism refers to periodic alcoholism. Less is known about the causes of Epsilon than about any of the other categories.

esophagus   Relative to the rest of the population, alcoholics and heavy drinkers show a high incidence of esophageal CANCER.

ethanol   The principal chemical in distilled spirits, wine and beer, ethanol is a highly soluble, colorless, inflammable liquid produced by the reaction of fermenting sugar with yeast spores. It can also be made in small amounts in the human intestines when dietary sugars are fermented, but it is then detoxified by a liver enzyme called alcohol dehydrogenase. (See also DENATURED ALCOHOL; INTRODUCTION TO ALCOHOL, p. XVI.)

ethyl alcohol   See ETHANOL.

etiological theories of alcoholism   Because of the complex nature of alcoholism, there are numerous theories on its cause. To date much is still unknown regarding the etiology of alcoholism, and no theory alone can completely explain the syndrome. The current theories generally can be divided into three main categories, each of which encompasses a number of different approaches to alcoholism. These are discussed in more detail under separate headings.

One main category is PHYSIOLOGICAL MODELS OF ETIOLOGY. Theories in this category postulate that individuals are predisposed to develop alcoholism because of some organic defect. They include GENETOTROPHIC ETIOLOGICAL THEORIES, ENDOCRINE ETIOLOGICAL THEORIES and genetic theories (see GENETICS).

A second main category is PSYCHOLOGICAL MODELS OF ETIOLOGY. Most psychological theories are based on the assumption that some flaw in the personality structure leads to the development of alcoholism. Among these is the theory, originally advanced by Freud, of ORAL FIXATION. BEHAVIORAL LEARNING THEORIES are another psychological model.

A third category of theories on the causes of alcoholism is SOCIOCULTURAL ETIOLOGICAL THEORIES, also known as CULTURAL ETIOLOGICAL THEORIES. These theories postulate relationships between various factors in society, such as ethnic and cultural differences, and the incidence of alcohol use. Also in this category are CULTURAL STRESS ETIOLOGICAL THEORIES.

In addition, there is a category known as MORAL ETIOLOGICAL THEORY, which holds that alcoholism is either a moral fault or a sin of the alcoholic. Once almost universally embraced in Western countries, this theory is now most commonly held by fundamentalist religious organizations.

etiology   (From the Greek *aitia* cause + *logos* discourse.) The science of causes, especially the investigation of the causes and origins of disease.

euphoria   After consuming alcoholic beverages, a drinker may feel elated and without worries or fears. For an alcoholic, however, the euphoric effect may be reduced because of his or her TOLERANCE for alcohol. While the desire to re-experience the euphoric effect may start a new drinker on the road to alcoholism, there is some debate as to whether alcoholics will continue to drink because they have not experienced the desired and expected euphoria they once did or because they have. It is agreed that the alcoholic expects this euphoria.

F

familial etiological theories   A sociocultural approach to the etiology of alcoholism, these theories place emphasis on the role of the family in providing models and social learning experiences for children. Children will tend to follow the parental mode of coping with problems of depression, feelings of inadequacy and rejection. Studies of the family backgrounds of alcoholics have shown an unusually high incidence of familial alcoholism. While this finding may suggest a genetic interpretation, the pattern of drinking and the range of circumstances in which such drinking occurs is usually the same for both parents and offspring, giving weight to a social learning component.

The family plays an important role in the development of personality and behavior. In various studies it was found that the prevalence of alcoholism among parents of alcoholics was two to 10 times that among parents of nonalcoholics. Among siblings of alcoholics there was a prevalence of two to 14 times that among siblings of nonalcoholics. (See also SOCIOCULTURAL ETIOLOGICAL THEORIES.)

David J. Amor, J. Michael Polich and Harriet B. Stambul, *Alcoholism and Treatment* (New York: John Wiley and Sons, 1978), pp. 25–26.
James G. Rankin, *Core Knowledge in the Drug Field (8 Etiology)* (Toronto: Addiction Research Foundation, 1978), p. 27.

family problems   See FAMILIAL ETIOLOGICAL THEORIES. See also SPOUSE ABUSE, CHILD ABUSE, CHILDREN OF ALCOHOLICS, ORAL FIXATION.

fatty liver   A type of liver damage characterized by an accumulation of fat in the liver. Alcohol upsets the normal METABOLISM of fat in the liver, resulting in an accumulation of fatty acids, and changes in the liver can occur after a few days of heavy drinking. The underlying cause of fatty liver is not well understood, but the primary cause may be damage to the liver MITOCHONDRIA, which break down chemical bonds in the complex molecules of nutrients during oxidation, causing an impairment of the oxidation of fatty acids and resulting in fatty acid accumulation. When alcohol is consumed with a high-fat diet, the fatty acids that accumulate are derived primarily from the diet; when alcohol is consumed with a low-fat diet, the fatty acids are synthesized within the liver. A low-fat diet is nevertheless preferable to a high-fat diet (see NUTRITION).

Fatty liver is a common occurrence among alcoholics: in one liver biopsy study of chronic alcoholics, 90% had fatty liver. In recent years the incidence of fatty liver has been increasing both in the United States and Europe. Patients with fatty liver may be quite asymptomatic, and an uncomplicated fatty liver is generally considered to be a relatively mild condition and fully reversible. However, in a number of autopsies performed on alcoholics, particularly younger alcoholics, the only finding was a massive fatty liver.

fetal alcohol syndrome (FAS)   The dangers of excessive drinking during pregnancy have been long recognized. The ancient Greeks noted that alcohol abuse by pregnant women often resulted in harmful effects to their unborn children. During the so-called gin epidemic in London during the 1700s the connection between alcohol abuse and birth defects was made again. However, it is only recently, in 1973, that an apparent clinical entity, the fetal alcohol syndrome, was identified by Kenneth L. Jones and David W. Smith of the University of Washington in Seattle, who utilized studies done a few years earlier by Christie Ulleland, also of the University of Washington. Alcohol-related birth defects are the third leading cause of congenital mental disorder, ranking behind Down's Syndrome and Spina Bifida. Of the three disorders only alcohol-related defects are preventable.

Children with fetal alcohol syndrome, born to mothers who have used alcohol excessively during pregnancy, exhibit a complex of characteristics, including growth deficiencies, physical malformations and mental retardation. FAS is not based on one single feature observable in all cases but on a constellation of abnormalities. It may be more appropriate to refer to fetal alcohol syndrome as fetal alcohol *effects*.

Certain features are commonly found in cases of FAS. Most victims fail to reach normal length, both before and after birth. At age one, children with FAS are, on the average, only 65% of normal length. They are also below normal weight, tend to remain thin and small as they get older and have unusually small head circumference. Most have elongated folds in their eyelids, causing eye slits. Other physical abnormalities that occur frequently include low nasal bridge, short nose, indistinct philtrum (the vertical groove between the nose and mouth), narrow upper lip, small chin and flat midface. About 30% of children with FAS have heart defects.

The effects of FAS on the central nervous system include retarded mental and motor development, tremulousness, hyperactivity and poor attention span. The average IQ of children with FAS is around 68. Varying degrees of mental deficiency are the most common signs of fetal damage among the children of maternal alcoholics. Such children show no improvement with time, even when placed in supportive atmospheres.

How Alcohol Affects the Fetus

When a pregnant woman drinks, alcohol passes freely across the placental barrier into the baby's bloodstream in concentrations at least as high as those in the mother (see BLOOD ALCOHOL CONCENTRATION). The system of the fetus, however, is not as equipped to handle the effects of alcohol as is the mother's system. The undeveloped liver of the unborn baby burns up alcohol at less than half the rate of the adult liver, so that alcohol remains in the fetal system longer than in the adult system. At low concentrations and for short durations, alcohol is a rapidly metabolized source of energy. At higher concentrations and for longer durations it is a toxic agent.

Deficiencies of MINERALS AND VITAMINS resulting from maternal drinking may also be harmful to the fetus. Alcoholic women commonly suffer from insufficient amounts of calcium, magnesium and zinc, all of which play an important role in fetal development. Low zinc content in certain infant diets has resulted in limited growth. Deficiencies of vitamins, such as folic acid and thiamine, also common in alcoholics, may play a role in fetal malformations and central nervous system lesions. Research in this area is still in its early stages.

Sudden WITHDRAWAL from alcohol by the mother during pregnancy may subject the fetus to major metabolic and physiologic disturbances. However, withdrawal under controlled conditions with progressively reduced doses of alcohol will probably be better for the fetus than continued drinking. Controlled withdrawal can result in rebound growth in the infant, compensating for an earlier disruption.

Heavy drinking is often associated with heavy SMOKING, which can also have harmful effects on the development of the fetus. Smoking mothers generally have a higher percentage of low-birth-weight infants. In 1976 French investigators reported stillbirth rates (also associated with maternal drinking) of 9.9 per 1,000 for light drinkers, 25.5 per 1,000 for heavy drinkers and 50.5 per 1,000 for women who both drank and smoked heavily.

How Much Alcohol Is Safe?

Although most documented cases of FAS have been children of women whose drinking meets the criteria of alcoholism, it is not yet known exactly how much alcohol is harmful to the fetus. Many states and organizations, such as the National Institute on Alcohol Abuse and Alcoholism and the American Medical Association Panel on Alcoholism, recommend complete abstinence from alcohol during pregnancy. They warn that since the effects of even a small amount of alcohol are still unknown and safe levels of intake have not yet been established, the wisest course is to abstain completely. Other organizations, such as the March of Dimes, do not emphasize complete abstinence because they feel that such a prohibition may unnecessarily frighten women whose custom is to have a drink or two in the evening during pregnancy. These organizations point out that the incidence of FAS is relatively low and that millions of social drinkers have healthy babies. They feel it is better to raise the consciousness of drinkers by alerting them to the dangers than to counsel perfection. Those who do not counsel complete abstinence suggest there is a risk to the fetus if the alcohol intake of the potential mother is 3 ounces of ABSOLUTE ALCOHOL or more per day. Unless complicated by some other factor, such as smoking, there are rarely any adverse effects in the offspring of drinkers whose normal daily consumption falls below that level. This does not mean, however, that drinks can be "saved up" by not drinking during the week and then making up for it in a single evening. As has been noted above, the fetus achieves the same blood alcohol concentration (BAC) as the mother, and a large amount of alcohol can be extremely harmful and, over a period of time,

may be an even more serious consideration than volume consumption. There is some evidence that the systems under development at the time maximum BAC is reached are most likely to reveal malformations later.

Babies of mothers who drink excessively may exhibit a range of symptoms from mild physical and behavioral defects to fully developed FAS. Until more is known about exactly what level of alcohol intake is safe, most agencies and organizations continue to recommend either caution or abstinence.(See also PREGNANCY.)

Judy Dobbie and Philippa Bell, *Fetal Alcohol Syndrome* (Addiction Research Foundation of Ontario, 1978).

Ernest P. Noble, ed., *Third Special Report to the U.S. Congress on Alcohol and Health* (Rockville, Md.: National Institute on Alcohol Abuse and Alcoholism, 1978), pp. 171–193.

Henry L. Rosett, "Clinical Pharmacology of the Fetal Alcohol Syndrome," in *Biochemistry and Pharmacology of Ethanol,* vol. 2, ed. Edward Majchrowicz and Ernest P. Noble (Plenum Press: New York, 1979), pp. 485–509.

Marian Sandmaier, *Alcohol and Your Unborn Baby* (Rockville, Md.: National Institute on Alcohol Abuse and Alcoholism, 1978), passim.

A. P. Streissguth, S. Landesman-Dwyer, D. C. Martin and D. W. Smith, "Teratogenic Effects of Alcohol in Humans and Laboratory Animals," *Science* 209 (July 18, 1980): 353–361.

Finland   The per capita consumption of alcohol in Finland seems insignificant in comparison with that of most other European nations, but for a variety of reasons specific to this country it has nevertheless been a cause for concern. This concern led in 1959 to the consolidation of studies on alcohol consumption issues, previously handled by various temperance societies, within a national Foundation for Alcohol Studies, a branch of the State Alcohol Monopoly, which regulates liquor sales throughout the country.

The agency discovered that in 1970 Finland had about 30,000 alcoholics, as defined by the JELLINEK method. Moreover there was a 2.2% increase in alcohol consumption between 1968 and 1974. During these years hospital admissions for alcohol-related problems showed a similar increase. Although 30% of the people are considered "almost abstemient" and 20% are total abstainers, the remaining 50% manifest a pattern of intermittent but excessive consumption. More than half of the alcoholic beverages consumed are strong liquors, usually a distilled vodka called *viina,* rather than beer or wine. A tradition of illegal distilling for home use perseveres in most rural areas; estimates suggest that perhaps 10% of the alcohol consumed in Finland is distilled illegally. Since the country abolished its experiment with total prohibition following a referendum in 1931, legalized distribution has been controlled solely by the State Alcohol Monopoly, which maintains restricted distribution centers in cities but has eliminated them entirely in rural areas. To some extent these measures have unintentionally encouraged the national pattern of occasional but heavy drinking that prevails today.

The Finnish Foundation for Alcohol Studies has estimated the national average consumption at a regular Saturday night sitting to be 60 centiliters of liquor, and the frequency of drinking occasions leading to intoxication was calculated to be 1.5 times greater in 1976 than in 1969. Each year there are about 140,000 arrests for drunkenness, a statistic that omits drunkenness incidence in rural areas, where arrests are uncommon. This arrest rate is five times higher than that in neighboring Sweden. The hospital admission rate for alcoholism was 529.3 per 100,000 in population in 1975, and for alcoholism and alcohol-related problems that year it totaled 786.5 per 100,000. Statistics on alcohol poisoning, recorded by the government since 1802, are particularly high because of the traditional acceptance of illegally distilled liquor. The highest statistic ever recorded for alcohol poisoning, 2.2 per 100,000 population, occurred during the national prohibition from 1921 to 1925, when methyl alcohol was in large demand.

A special area of concern is the territory of Lapland, in the northern part of the country. Deprived of liquor stores by the State Alcohol Monopoly, the Lapps, heavy drinkers, travel great distances to purchase liquor legally or drink dangerous varieties of home-brewed alcohol. Many alcoholics among the Lapps are also known to drink industrial and medicinal alcohol products. One problem confronting those who travel to legal liquor stores is that the trip takes, on the average, a full day. These trips are themselves occasions for ritualistic and excessive drinking. Experiments have been conducted to test the effect of local liquor distribution on the Lapps' drinking habits. In these experiments legal alcohol replaced illegal brews in large proportions, but the overall problem of excessive drinking and drunkenness remained virtually unchanged.

Beginning in 1962 care of alcoholics in Finland has been regulated by a special "Act Governing the Treatment of Misusers of Intoxicants." However, the Finnish government has provided institutions for the care of alcoholics since 1937. In addition to hospitals these include outpatient clinics managed by the National Board of Social Welfare and, in eight large cities, voluntary admission A-clinics maintained since 1955 by an independent government foundation. There are also a variety of homes for skid row alcoholics, nursing homes for chronic abusers of alcohol and half-way houses for young alcoholics. The Finnish Temperance Movement privately funds several programs for the treatment of alcoholism.

Given the acknowledged failure of its experiment with total prohibition, the primary task facing this country of sporadic but excessive drinkers is to encourage moderation, perhaps by finding a way to shift consumption habits away from strong liquors toward beers and wines. At the same time, the country is aware of the danger of changing its citizens from occasional to habitual consumers of alcoholic beverages. Its emphasis at present is on increased governmental supervision of public drinking places, such as licensed restaurants, where drinking habits and cultural alcohol trends are most likely to be formed.

E. J. Immonen, "New Trends in the Alcohol Problem in Finland," *Social Psychiatry* 4, no. 4 (1969): 173–176.
Kari Poikolainen, "Increase in Alcohol-Related Hospitalizations in Finland 1969–1975," *British Journal of Addiction* 75 (1980): 281–291.

formaldehyde   Formaldehyde is a colorless pungent gas formed in the oxidation of methyl alcohol, which is produced naturally in the body in small amounts. Formaldehyde is even more toxic than the ACETALDEHYDE produced by the METABOLISM of ethyl alcohol, but normally the LIVER has ample capacity to break down both formaldehyde and acetaldehyde into nontoxic units. However, if the liver is flooded with ethyl alcohol, as occurs when someone has had a great deal to drink, the liver works first to metabolize the ethyl alcohol, at a rate 16 times faster than it breaks down the methyl alcohol. Therefore methyl alcohol builds up as the liver acts on the excess ethyl alcohol. When the methyl alcohol is finally metabolized, a considerable amount of formaldehyde is produced. This may be responsible for WITHDRAWAL symptoms and may also be at least partially responsible for the HANGOVER effect, which has been shown to begin as soon as all ethanol has been metabolized.

fortified wine   Wine to which another alcoholic substance, usually grape brandy, has been added during the vinification process. This addition not only increases the alcohol content of the wine—making it from 16% to 23% alcohol—but changes its flavor and character by interfering with the normal fermentation process. The principal fortified wines are PORT, SHERRY, MARSALA, MADEIRA and VERMOUTH.

France   Throughout the history of France, alcohol, especially wine, has played a very important role culturally, socially and financially. The French have a liberal attitude toward the use of alcohol and abstinence is unusual. Any concern over consumption is more likely to focus upon a reduction of drinking to moderate levels than upon complete abstinence. The French view alcohol as a natural part of their daily diet. Nonalcoholic drinks are often considered too sweet to be consumed with meals or to quench thirst, and in cafes wine is much cheaper than fruit juice or soft drinks. One Frenchmen in 10 derives his income directly or indirectly from the alcoholic beverage industry, and one in five French parliamentarians represents the industry.

France is a large-scale producer of alcoholic beverages, particularly wine. While there are controls on production, to date the amount of wine produced has far exceeded demand, even though exportation increased 500% from 1969 to 1979. There is some illicit brewing, principally of rums and aperitifs, both in homes and in larger operations.

The French have one of the highest rates of alcohol consumption in the world, although the rate has declined since the beginning of the century. Per capita consumption of alcohol in 1976 for the French population over 15 years of age was 21.3 liters. In 1978 the French consumed 16 liters of alcohol per person (all ages), double the per capita rate in the United States. As might be expected, wine is the most popular beverage, and although wine consumption is decreasing, France continues to have the highest level of any country after Italy. The drop in wine drinking has been accompanied by an increase in the sales of beer and hard liquor. And although overall consumption of ABSOLUTE ALCOHOL is decreasing, alcoholic beverages still represent more than 80% of the total of all drinks consumed; the French drink eight times as much alcohol as fruit juices. With the trend toward beer and hard liquor has come a change in drinking styles, as such beverages are usually drunk quickly and in public places while wine is traditionally drunk more slowly and primarily at home.

It is estimated that out of a population of approximately 53 million, 2 million people are alcoholics and an additional 3 million to 5 million are problem drinkers. The drinking of red wine is estimated to account for 70% of all alcoholism cases in France. Almost one-third of all hospital beds are occupied by people suffering from an alcohol-related ailment. Forty percent of the patients in psychiatric hospitals suffer from an illness related to alcohol. According to Dr. Jean Bernard, a cancer specialist and president of a group of specialists named by the government to study alcoholism, each year an estimated 70,000 French people die of alcohol-induced ailments. Although some other estimates of the mortality rate are much lower, the figures are still quite disturbing.

Alcohol consumption, after cardiovascular diseases and cancer, is the leading cause of death in France. In 1978 there were approximately 30.2 deaths per 100,000 people from cirrhosis and 6.6 deaths per 100,000 from alcoholism and alcoholic psychoses. Most cancers of the mouth and digestive tract are attributable to alcohol abuse. Experts estimate that 50% of the country's murders, 25% of its suicides and 75% of Parisian delinquency are related to drinking; 15% to 20% of accidents at work and 33% to 40% of all automobile and motorcycle accidents are also attributed to alcohol consumption. In addition two-thirds of the 450,000 mentally handicapped children in France have been born to alcoholics.

In 1977 the estimated overall cost of alcoholism in France was 20 billion francs (about $4.26 billion); taxes on the sale of alcoholic beverages in the same year yielded an estimated 6.5 billion francs (about $1.38 billion), less than one-third of the amount the government paid out in social costs.

Because of a growing awareness of the problem, the French government, under Valery Giscard d'Estang, announced a drive against alcoholism in December 1980. The campaign represented a new political backing for a cause that has traditionally been unpopular. Politically alcohol abuse has never been a "noble subject," partly because of the enormous power of the wine and spirits industry. A committee was set up under Dr. Bernard to study the problem of alcoholism and determine what could be done to reduce it. Aiming to cut alcohol consumption by 20% in five years, the government passed 35 measures in the program to combat alcoholism, including higher taxes on alcohol, stricter application of breath tests for motorists, prohibition of store sales to minors and a publicity campaign.

The program aims to reduce the amount of alcohol intake rather than achieve the unrealistic goal of total abstinence. Some proposals by the committee include forbidding advertisements for alcoholic drinks, making access to alcohol less easy, doubling exportation of wine, producing products that have a lower percentage of alcohol, developing new incitements to drink nonalcoholic beverages, promoting a new policy for wine consumption ("Drink less but drink better") and raising the price of alcohol.

Friends For Sobriety (FFS)   A recovery support group, Friends For Sobriety was organized by five recovering alcoholics in March 1980 to help persons addicted to mood-altering chemicals, including alcohol.

FFS offers an alternative, nontheistic recovery program in the belief that most people cannot endure a crisis of religious conscience and the crisis of confronting their alcoholism, for example, at the same time. Groups meet for one hour three times a week to hold open discussion structured around a *Nine-Step Recovery Booklet.* Emphasis is on both the emotional needs of the recovering individual and the necessity of assuming personal responsibility for one's behavior. FFS is not in competition with other recovery or support programs and encourages members to attend such programs as needed for maintaining their sobriety. The group's headquarters are located in Paradise Valley, Ariz.

fructose   A sugar that occurs naturally in fruits and honey, fructose may help to speed up the metabolic rate at which ethanol is metabolized, but the degree of acceleration of metabolism is thought to be relatively small. The mechanism by which the rate of elimination is increased is unknown. Although adding fructose to the diet may somewhat reduce the HANGOVER effect, it is not generally a practical sobering agent.

G

Gamma alcoholism   The third of five categories of alcoholism defined by JELLINEK. "*Gamma alcoholism* means that species of alcoholism in which (1) acquired increased tissue tolerance to alcohol, (2) adaptive cell metabolism, (3) withdrawal symptoms and 'craving,' i.e., physical dependence, and (4) loss of control are involved." There is a progression from psychological DEPENDENCE to physical AD-

DICTION. This type of alcoholism causes the most damage both to the interpersonal relationships of the individual and to his or her health. Gamma alcoholism is apparently the dominating form of alcoholism in the United States and is the type recognized by ALCOHOLICS ANONYMOUS. (See also LOSS OF CONTROL, METABOLISM, WITHDRAWAL.)

gastrointestinal tract   The organs from the mouth to the rectum associated with digestion (otherwise known as the GI tract). Alcohol passes through the mouth to the stomach, where about 20% of it is absorbed. The rest is absorbed in the upper small intestine. The presence of food in the stomach decreases the rate of alcohol absorption.

Alcohol is eliminated from the body chiefly through METABOLISM in the liver. Less than 10% of the amount consumed is lost through the kidneys, lungs and skin. Consumption of alcohol produces a number of deleterious effects on the gastrointestinal tract, depending on the quantity ingested and the susceptibility of the individual. (For the effects of alcohol on the various parts of the GI tract, see STOMACH, LIVER, PANCREAS.)

In addition to the damaging effects of chronic alcohol ingestion on the GI tract itself, alcohol impairs the absorption of certain VITAMINS AND MINERALS and interferes with the nutritional process, adversely affecting the well-being of the entire body (see NUTRITION).

gay alcoholics   See HOMOSEXUALS.

genetic models of etiology   See GENETICS.

genetics   The precise role played by genetic factors in the etiology of alcoholism remains unknown. There is evidence that alcoholism is to some extent genetically determined. The incidence of alcoholism is high in families and the lifetime risk of alcoholism developing in the sons of severely impaired alcoholic men ranges from 30% to 50%.

Genetic theories of alcoholism are based primarily on studies of twins and of adoptions. Studies of twins show that the identical twin of an alcoholic will be alcoholic in 60% of the cases, whereas in fraternal twins the rate is only approximately 30%. Studies of adoptions show a high rate of alcoholism in children of alcoholic parents who were adopted shortly after birth and reared separately. The largest study of this type was done in Denmark on children who had been separated from their alcoholic parents after reaching six weeks of age and reared in adoptive homes. They were compared with a control group of children who were similar except that they had no family history of alcoholism. When they were studied later, at the mean age of 30, 20% of the children of alcoholic parents and 5% of the control group were alcoholic. From this particular study it appears that hereditary aspects of alcoholism may appear with the same degree of variability as similar hereditary aspects of diabetes.

While alcoholism may to some extent be determined genetically, inheritance alone is not an adequate explanation. Many cases of alcoholism cannot be explained by inheritance, and even when genetics seem important, other factors—social, psychological and biological—play a role in influencing its course.

There is still lack of agreement regarding the nature of the inherited mechanism that would predispose some to alcoholism. Some suggest the possibility that it is a disturbance in brain chemistry.

D. W. Goodwin, *Is Alcoholism Hereditary?* (New York: Oxford University Press, 1976).
Marc A. Shuckit, "Overview of Alcoholism," *Journal of the American Dental Association* 99 (September 1979): 489–493.

genetotropic etiological theory   A theory, first advanced by R. J. Williams, which suggests that alcoholism is related to a genetically determined biochemical defect—the desire to drink is an inner urge mediated by nervous structures, perhaps in the hypothalamus of the brain. These nervous structures, according to Williams' theory, are deranged by alcohol and malnutrition. Williams believes that satisfaction of all nutritional needs will end the desire for alcohol. Although his methods and studies have been criticized, it is acknowledged that NUTRITION may well play some role in the etiology of alcoholism.

Germany (West)   West Germany reports one of the highest levels of consumption of ABSOLUTE ALCOHOL in the world. This is not surprising in view of the fact that almost all meals and social occasions are complemented with beer, wine and other alcoholic beverages. According to a 1974 report, the annual level of consumption of absolute alcohol was approximately 14.8 liters per person aged 15 and over. However, although this level is very high, it is still far below those of Portugal (23.4 liters per person) and France (22.4 liters per person) for the same study period.

From 1975 until 1978 West Germany reported a slight decline in the consumption of pure alcohol. Although the drop in consumption was only .3 liters, from 12.4 liters to 12.01 liters, per capita, it was significant because until 1975 the level had been rising steadily.

A report by the Institut fur Demoskopie Allensbach attributed the drop in consumption to the public's increased awareness of the problem of alcohol abuse. This awareness has been brought about in part by the Anti-Alcohol Campaign of the Bundesfamilienministerium (the federal ministry for families) begun in 1975. In a survey conducted by the ministry in 1979, 56% of the approximately 2,000 questioned were concerned about the high consumption of alcohol. This figure represents a significant increase over the 31% who expressed concern in an inquiry made five years earlier. In addition 67% recommended a strict ban on allowing children to have alcohol, while only 52% recommended such a prohibition five years before.

The problem of alcohol abuse in West Germany is not limited to any particular age category, social group or sex. It is indicative of a general problem of the society that such large numbers of people are seeking their satisfaction through alcohol. Many of the factors contributing to alcohol abuse in West Germany are the same as in numerous other countries: broken homes, unsuccessful marriages, lack of fulfillment in personal life and work and feelings of inability to cope with reality. In a 1974 report on alcoholism among women in the *Stuttgarter Nachtrichten,* Annelies Griebler and Ladislaus Kuthy pointed out that the effects of World War II should not be overlooked for the generation whose formative years coincided with the war period. According to Griesler and Kuthy, after the war West Germans in this category found themselves faced with starvation and the responsibility of cleaning up debris. In addition they had grown up in a dictatorship, in which a highly structured social order was imposed, and were suddenly responsible for looking after themselves in the democracy created following the war.

The following information concerning types of programs for alcoholics is based on reports from Frankfurt and Hamburg. Many of the programs, however, are available in towns and cities throughout the country. These programs fall into three general categories: self-help groups, advice bureaus *(Beratungsstellen)* and treatment centers.

Among the best known of the self-help groups is Anonymen Alkoholiker (ALCOHOLICS ANONYMOUS). Modeled after the American organization of the same name, Anonymen Alkoholiker has approximately 800 groups throughout West Germany. In Frankfurt there are several programs for the families of alcoholics. Among these are the Al-Anon Familiengruppen and the Elternkreise des Jugenberatung und Jugendhilfe, a program for the parents of young alcoholics. In many towns an organization known as the Freundeskreise ("Circle of Friends") provides assistance to the families of alcoholics. None of the aforementioned programs are affiliated with any religious or political groups.

Self-help groups with a religious affiliation include the Protestant Blaue Kreuz ("Blue Cross"), the Catholic Kreuzbund ("League of the Cross") and the Jewish Guttempler ("Good Templar").

Advice bureaus are numerous throughout West Germany. They are usually located in health services, churches, clubs and other organizations. Frankfurt lists among its advice bureaus the Sozialpadagogischen Dienst der Stadt ("Social-Educational Service of the City"), the Beratungsstellen von Evangelischen Regionalverband ("Advisory Board of the Protestant Regional Alliance") and, for young people, the Vereins Arbeits- und Erziehungshilfe ("Society for Work and Educational Assistance").

In Hamburg an organization known as Das Kreisgesundheitgesamt Homberg ("The Collected Health Circle of Hamburg") has developed a program in which a doctor, a social worker and a self-help group work together with individual alcoholics.

In the mid-1970s the first centralized center for the intoxicated opened in Hamburg. The center was designed primarily to provide a place where individuals whom the police suspected of being drunk could sober up overnight. Such a center was felt to be necessary because of reported incidences of persons dying in police "coolers" because they were in need of medical attention. At the Hamburg center a doctor examines each person brought in by the police. Those in need of medical care are taken to a hospital and those who are merely drunk are kept in the center overnight at their own expense.

Among the other West German cities considering opening such treatment centers are Stuttgart, Frankfurt, Dusseldorf and Cologne.

GI tract   See GASTROINTESTINAL TRACT.

gin   An alcoholic beverage made from distilled fermented grains (chiefly rye but also corn, barley and oats) and flavored with juniper berries. Most gin is colorless and its proof usually falls between 80 and 94.

The name "gin" is an anglicized and abbreviated form of *jenever* (sometimes spelled *genever* or *geneva*), one of the terms that the Dutch used for gin. The Dutch term is an altered form of the French *genievre*, meaning juniper.

The word "gin" has been used in a number of popular expressions, particularly during the 20th century. Among the best known is the card game GIN RUMMY. At the turn of the century the expression "ginned up," meaning "drunk," came into use. Ginned up was shortened to "ginned" in the 1920s. During the same period cheap saloons, bars and nightclubs were sometimes referred to as "gin mills," an expression that is still used. Cirrhosis of the liver has sometimes been referred to as "gin drinker's liver."

Gin was first invented in the Netherlands during the 17th century by Dr. Franciscus Sylvius, also known as Franciscus de la Boe (1614–1672), a professor of medicine at Leyden University. Dr. Sylvius was attempting to find a prophylactic against certain tropical diseases by distilling spirits in the presence of juniper berries. His aim was to prepare a specific with known diuretic properties.

Since the origins of gin were medicinal, it was at first available only in apothecary shops. As its popularity increased, many apothecary shops set up their own distilleries. By the end of the 18th century, the Dutch were producing approximately 14 million gallons of gin each year, of which around 10 million were exported.

The taste for gin was brought to England in the 17th century by soldiers returning from wars on the Continent. It was officially introduced there by William of Orange, who reigned from 1686 to 1702. He thought that gin would be an acceptable substitute for French brandy, since at that time the English considered the French their enemies.

Gin rapidly acquired popularity in England. Within 40 years of its introduction there, annual production rose from a half million to 20 million gallons. Gin's popularity in the early years of the 18th century has been attributed in part to the fact that it was more refined than the spirits made by English distillers from beer and wine lees (dregs). Perhaps a more important reason was its low cost. Both William of Orange and his successor, Queen Anne, who reigned from 1702 until 1714, raised the duties and taxes on imported goods and lowered the excise on home products. In addition, during their reigns, anyone who applied to the excise bureau was allowed to set up a distillery, making it very easy to manufacture gin.

For many of the poor in England during the 18th century, there was almost no alternative alcoholic drink to gin. It was given the nickname "mother's ruin" because so many women could be seen lying in the streets drunk on gin. Gin was also sometimes referred to as "Dutch courage," a term still used for bravery (or perhaps foolhardiness) inspired by alcohol.

Today most countries that distill spirits produce gin. Its chief manufacturers are the Netherlands, Britain and the United States. Despite the many local variations, there are basically only two types of gin: Dutch gin, referred to variously as Geneva, Genever,

Schiedam or Hollands; and London dry gin, which is distilled in both Britain and the United States. Another type of gin, so-called Plymouth gin, is manufactured only in Plymouth, England. Now Plymouth gin and London dry gin are about the same, but at one time the gin made in Plymouth was midway between London dry gin, which is only lightly flavored with juniper berries, and Dutch gin, which is more heavily flavored with juniper. In addition, Dutch gin and London dry gin are manufactured by different distillation processes using different ingredients.

Dutch gin is doubly distilled. First a low-proof spirit is distilled from a fermented mash consisting of approximately two-thirds rye meal. This low-proof spirit is then rectified and flavored with juniper berries, salt and other agents. The resultant spirits are then redistilled, producing a gin between 94 and 98 proof.

Dutch gins are not aged, which accounts for their lack of color, and have a strong, malty aroma, which makes them unsuitable for mixing in cocktails. Consequently they are usually chilled and drunk straight.

In contrast to Dutch gin, which is first distilled from a low-proof spirit, manufacturers of English and American gin begin by rectifying a high-proof (about 190) grain whiskey to a completely pure and flavor-free spirit. The spirit is then distilled off at approximately 160 proof, which is further decreased to around 114.2 by adding water. This product is placed in a pot still with various flavoring agents and redistilled. The resultant gin is reduced to either 80, 86 or 94 proof. Although gin is usually bottled immediately, some types produced in the United States are aged, giving them a pale golden color.

In addition to juniper berries, English and American gins usually contain other botanicals in varying proportions, including orris, angelica and licorice roots; bitter almonds, caraway, coriander, cardamom, anise and fennel seeds; and calamus, cassis bark, lemon peels, and sweet and bitter orange peels. The kinds and proportions of these flavorings account for the differences between the various brands of gin.

English and American gins have a dry, astringent taste, which makes them less likely to be drunk straight. In varying proportions they are combined with dry vermouth to make martinis. They are also mixed with tonic water, and with water and angostura bitters. Some ordinary gins are given a fruit flavor, such as orange, lemon or pineapple. Old Tom gin is slightly sweetened.

Sloe gin is not gin in the usual sense but a liqueur made by steeping sloe berries—small bluish-black plums with a sour, astringent taste—in gin.

grog   A mixture of rum and water. In 1740 a British admiral, Edward Vernon (1684–1757), concerned that his men were becoming habitually intoxicated on their daily RUM RATION, ordered the rum to be diluted with water. The resulting mixture was named for the admiral's sobriquet, "Old Grog," which he earned for his habit of braving inclement weather in a coat made of a wool-silk-mohair combination known as grogham. Vernon's practice was soon widely imitated, and some captains found a way to line their pockets by watering the grog further. Sailors, unhappy with "half and half grog," were incensed by the even weaker "seven-water grog." From the term "grog" are derived "groggy," "groggily," "grogginess," "grogged" and "grog-fight" (drinking party).

George Washington's brother, Lawrence, served under Adm. Vernon and the Washingtons' Virginia estate, Mount Vernon, was named after him.

grog blossom   (From GROG.) A pimple or reddishness of the nose often attributed to excessive drinking over a prolonged period (see RHINOPHYMA).

group therapy   Collective therapeutic treatment often led by a psychiatrist or psychologist. Groups are usually kept small, less than a dozen persons, to allow for the maximum amount of participation from each member. Under the direction of the leader, who acts as a moderator, individual members bring up recent or long-standing problems for discussion by the group. Ideally the individual benefits by opening his problems to the scrutiny of others and by being forced to analyze his behavior and come to grips with it. The group benefits from the communality of shared problems and by participating vicariously in the resolution of the problems of others that may be similar to their own. The communal and cathartic effect of group therapy differs from that of "meetings" of such groups as ALCOHOLICS ANONYMOUS, which are larger, feature speakers and must consider topics of interest to a broader range of people. In such meetings there generally is no time for the same intimate, intensive exploration of problems as afforded by group therapy. (See also PSYCHODRAMA.)

H

habituation   Accommodation or adaptation to a stimulus or to an interfering response. The term is often used to refer to the process of forming a habit and as a synonym for TOLERANCE. Since it is frequently unclear which meaning is intended, it is preferable to use one of the other more specific terms, such as tolerance or ADDICTION.

halfway house   Also known as intermediate care facilities, these residences, developed mainly during the 1970s, are used as transition points for alcoholics moving from inpatient care to normal life. They were conceived as a result of the failure of larger, impersonal institutions to provide the needed support for this transition.

Halfway houses are primarily for the homeless alcoholic who does not need medical care but rather support and protection while he or she gradually finds a place in the community. They are generally staffed by nonprofessionals, although professionals are available for needed medical care. The setting provides residents with adequate food and shelter and a therapeutic environment that facilitates the maintenance of sobriety. Following discharge alcoholics may return to the house for evening meetings and social support. Halfway houses may be publicly or privately funded and the residents are usually expected to contribute what they can.

The halfway house movement developed with the belief that to be effective the houses should have only a small number of residents, impose few rules and maintain an informal "homelike" atmosphere. Today, however, many of these houses have grown to the size of large institutions, which, according to one study, limits their effectiveness (Rubington).

E. Rubington, "Halfway Houses and Treatment Outcomes: A Relationship between Institutional Atmosphere and Therapeutic Effectiveness," *Journal of Studies on Alcohol* 40, no. 5 (1979):419–427.

hangover   (In this sense "hang" means "linger," from the Gothic *hahan* via the Anglo-Saxon *hangian*.) Hangover is an Americanism introduced in the early 20th century. The use of the word "hang" to describe the unpleasant aftereffects of excessive drinking is similar to that in "just *hanging* around," in the sense of aimlessly lingering.

A hangover generally follows intoxication by eight to 12 hours. Some common effects are a splitting headache and sensitivity to movement, bright light and loud sounds. Other symptoms may include nausea and vomiting, dizziness, sweating, loss of appetite and dry mouth. These are accompanied by general malaise or tiredness and, often, anxiety or depression or both.

The causes of hangover are not completely understood, but there are probably a number of factors involved. For most drinkers the stress of intoxication has been worsened by other contributing elements, such as heavy smoking, lack of sleep and feelings of guilt resulting from uninhibited behavior. The changes that are expected in the body following a stress reaction are seen in the signs of hangover. Another factor that may be at work is a state of lowered BLOOD SUGAR, or hypoglycemia. Blood glucose levels are at their lowest during the height of a hangover, and many symptoms of a hangover are similar to those of hypoglycemia.

When alcohol is consumed, its degradation in the liver causes an accumulation of organic acids and ketones in the blood, known as ketoacidosis (see METABOLISM). The degree of ketoacidosis corresponds fairly well to the intensity of the hangover and may be partially responsible for its onset. Water balance is also altered when alcohol is consumed. Increased urinary excretion, sweating, vomiting and diarrhea can lead to dehydration, which appears as dry mouth and thirst. On the other hand a drop in BLOOD ALCOHOL CONCENTRATION, can stimulate an antidiuretic hormone, so that hyperhydration can also develop during a hangover. CONGENERS, the organic alcohols and salts other than ethanol that are formed when alcoholic beverages are manufactured, have been thought to play a role in the hangover effect, but it has been well demonstrated that pure ethanol can by itself produce a hangover. Therefore the role of congeners in causing hangovers is probably small. The irritation produced by alcohol on the STOMACH lining may be a cause of the nausea and vomiting that can occur during a hangover.

It has not been proved that the amount of alcohol consumed is related to the appearance and severity of a hangover, although this is generally thought to be the case. The hangover experience varies from individual to individual. Some consider the hangover syndrome a symptom of early WITHDRAWAL. According to this theory, a certain DEPENDENCY has been established by overdrinking, and the body is reacting because it has a need for more alcohol. The fact that resumption of drinking ("the hair of the dog that bit you,") will reverse or alleviate some hangover symptoms is evidence in support of this concept.

The traditional use of a small amount of alcohol to correct the metabolic rebound brought on by a hangover may be justified as long as it does not lead to another round of overindulgence. To correct acidosis, water balance disturbance and low blood sugar, fruit juice, such as orange juice, may be of help. Aspirin may be taken for a headache, but sedatives and tranquilizers are not indicated. Rest and time correct other unpleasant effects.

Sidney Cohen, "Hangover," *Drug Abuse and Alcoholism Newsletter* 9, no. 8 (October 1980).

heart   There are a number of alcohol-related diseases of the heart that can adversely affect blood pressure, heart muscle contractility and heart rhythm. On the other hand alcohol may play a somewhat beneficial role in the prevention of coronary artery disease.

Hypertension (High Blood Pressure)

At least six studies have reported a significant association between high alcohol consumption and high blood pressure. A study of 84,000 people conducted by Klatsky and Associates of the Kaiser-Permanente Program found that blood pressures were significantly higher in those subjects who consumed three or more drinks daily. This relationship was statistically independent of age, sex, race, smoking, coffee use and overweight. The risk of hypertension was increased by a factor of between two and three in frequent and/or heavy drinkers.

Alcohol use and hypertension may be linked through a common association with an unidentified third factor, such as stress, or other psychosocial factors. What seems more likely is that an average of three or more drinks per day may have a direct causal effect on the elevation of blood pressure. The proof has yet to be obtained and there is a need for further study to establish or refute a causal relationship between alcohol and hypertension.

· Alcoholic Cardiomyopathy

Heavy alcohol consumption is the specific cause of alcoholic cardiomyopathy, a disease of the heart muscle associated with the development of coronary artery disease. In victims of alcoholic cardiomyopathy, which can occur in those who drink excessively over a long period of time regardless of the level of nutrition, the heart appears large and flabby, although the arteries and valves look normal. In such cases the tissue of the heart is remarkably similar to tissue seen in livers damaged by alcohol (see AL-COHOLIC LIVER DISEASE). Exactly how the heart muscle is affected is unknown. A study by A. I. Cederbaum and E. Rubin in 1975 and other studies have shown that AC-ETALDEHYDE, the first metabolite of ethanol (see METABOLISM), damages the mitochondria of the heart muscle and may play a key role in the development of alcoholic cardiomyopathy.

While the evidence is not definite, it probably takes about 10 years of high alcohol intake to cause serious damage to the heart. If the damage is detected in time and if the patient stops drinking alcohol completely, there is a fairly good chance of recovery. If severe heart failure has occurred, however, the outlook is usually poor.

There appears to be great individual variation in susceptibility to alcoholic cardiomyopathy. It usually appears in men 25 to 50 years of age. Common early symptoms are difficult or labored breathing, swelling of feet and ankles, fatigue, and palpitations or chest pain. If excessive alcohol consumption continues, the disease often progresses to heart failure.

A very rare version of cardiomyopathy, known as beri-beri heart disease, is seen only in alcoholics who are extremely malnourished and is thought to be due to a thiamine deficiency (see NUTRITION).

Cardiac Arrhythmia

An irregularity in heartbeat, cardiac arrhythmia can occur both in patients with alcohol-related disease and in other individuals during alcoholic intoxication. The most common form in patients with a previous history of heart disease has come to be known as the "holiday heart syndrome." Cardiac arrhythmia is seen in individuals who show up in emergency rooms between Sunday and Tuesday or around holidays associated with high alcohol ingestion. They generally report palpitations, sharp left chest pain or "passing out" spells. Both the direct effects of alcohol on the heart muscle and the effects of either alcohol or acetaldehyde on the heart's conduction system are the likely causes of arrhythmia. The best treatment generally is a few days abstinence.

Coronary Heart Disease

Coronary heart disease results from atherosclerosis, which is characterized by the localized accumulation of lipids on the inner lining of the large- and medium-sized arteries serving the heart. Several studies, including one by Charles Hennekens and associates in 1973–74, have shown that the consumption of alcohol in small amounts (up to 2 ounces of ABSOLUTE ALCOHOL per day) decreases the risk of coronary heart disease, although higher levels of consumption show no decrease or an increase in risk.

The mechanism behind this effect is not entirely clear, but apparently alcohol increases the HDL (high-density lipoprotein) cholesterol in the blood and lowers the LDL (low-density lipoprotein) level. HDLs seem to block the internalization of LDLs, which build up in the arteries and are associated with the mechanism by which the cells are filled with fat droplets. HDLs, on the other hand, seem to be moved out of the body and to remove cholesterol from deposits in the arteries. Therefore the higher the percentage of HDLs in the blood the better. The exact relation between alcohol and HDL is not known. Many other factors, such as physical exercise, affect HDL levels, and more study is needed to determine exactly what role alcohol plays.

G. E. Burch, "Alcoholic Cardiomyopathy," *Comprehensive Therapy* 3, no. 8 (August 1977):10–15.

A. I. Cederbaum and E. Rubin, "Molecular Injury to Mitochondria Produced by Ethanol and Acetaldehyde," *Federation Proceedings* 34, no. 11 (1975):2045–2051.

"Drinkers and the 'Holiday Heart' Syndrome," *Medical World News,* Dec. 27, 1976, p. 19.

Elizabeth Rasche Gonzales, "Unresolved Issue: Do Drinkers Have Less Coronary Heart Disease?" *Journal of the American Medical Association* 242, no. 25 (Dec. 21, 1979):2745–2746.

Charles Hennekens et al., "Effects of Beer, Wine, and Liquor in Coronary Deaths," *Journal of the American Medical Association* 242, no. 18 (Nov. 2, 1979):1973–1974.

Lawrence E. Ramsay, "Alcohol Use and Hypertension," *Practical Cardiology* 5, no. 11 (November 1979):27–32.

heavy drinker   A person who drinks beyond the normal limits of moderation as defined by the society in which he or she lives. Often a heavy drinker is in danger of or well on his or her way to becoming an ALCOHOLIC. Many heavy drinkers, however, do not become alcoholic, although the figure is probably much higher than those revealed in the available studies since numerous alcoholic heavy drinkers have never been diagnosed as such. Some heavy drinkers escape most of the criteria for a PROBLEM DRINKER, but most cannot escape the cumulative effects of alcohol upon the human body, which are due to consumption at a given time or over a period of time rather than to addiction. For statistical purposes a heavy drinker has been defined (by Eagleville Hospital in Pennsylvania for the National Institute on Drug Abuse in 1979) as an individual with a consumption level "averaging above 3.82 ounces of 90-proof whiskey daily." This level amounts to an average daily consumption of 1.72 ounces of ABSOLUTE ALCOHOL. (SEE ANSTIE'S LAW.)

hemochromatosis   A little understood and relatively uncommon disorder that involves excessive deposition of iron within the body tissues and terminates after many years of widespread tissue damage. Victims often suffer from liver disease, diabetes and a bronze pigmentation of the skin.

The cause of hemochromatosis is not known, but one theory is that it may not be a single disease entity but rather a type of CIRRHOSIS in which two conditions occur simultaneously—an excess buildup of ingested iron and liver disease caused by alcohol consumption or malnutrition. At Boston City Hospital hemochromatosis was found to be most prevalent in patients who were heavy and chronic users of wine, which contains large amounts of iron.

hepatitis   See ALCOHOLIC HEPATITIS.

hepatoma   Also known as hepatocarcinoma, hepatoma is a cellular cancer of the liver, often associated with CIRRHOSIS (see CANCER).

heredity   It is recognized that alcoholism is common in certain families, suggesting that at least a tendency toward the disease might be inherited. Studies of families of twins and of adoptees conducted to determine whether genetics or environment is the cause of a predisposition to alcohol suggest that a genetic factor may be present in some alcoholic individuals, but there is no conclusive evidence to support this theory. Most of these studies, however, were mostly done without controls and the evidence has been contradictory.

Inherited traits may also help ward off alcoholism by causing unusual discomfort when alcohol is consumed, possibly through excessive production of ACETALDEHYDE in the metabolic process. This seems to be the case with some Orientals, for instance, who have a low rate of alcoholism and a high level of acetaldehyde.

While it is generally accepted that genetic factors may play a role in alcoholism, it is also usually agreed that factors other than genetic ones are primarily responsible for its development, even in families where it is a frequent problem.

high   *Slang* for being under the influence of alcohol or a drug, especially marijuana. The term "high" usually refers to a state of pleasurable intoxication, not to the point of unconsciousness. The "high" associated with alcohol, often expressed in uninhibited behavior bordering on or lapsing into the irresponsible, is an ironic effect of the SEDATIVE nature of the drug. The "high" phase of the effect is actually the result of the sedating of those areas of the brain that guard against abnormal behavior by producing inhibitions. The high from alcohol is thus the opposite of a high from such stimulants as amphetamines or cocaine.

high blood pressure   (hypertension)
A number of studies have linked heavy alcohol consumption with high blood pressure (see HEART).

highway safety   See DRIVING WHILE INTOXICATED.

Hispanics   There are nearly 25 million Hispanics in the United States today, and by the end of the 1980s they are projected to surpass the black population as the nation's largest minority. The Hispanic population is not uniform but composed of many subgroups; Mexican Americans form the largest subgroup, followed by Puerto Ricans, Cubans, Central Americans, South Americans and those of Spanish ancestry.

Alcoholism is the leading public health problem among the Hispanic population in the United States. It is estimated that the rate of alcoholism among Hispanics is two to three times the national average and that the alcoholism mortality rate is nearly five times higher for Hispanics than for the general population. In Los Angeles over half the deaths of Hispanic males between the ages of 30 and 60 are from disorders of the LIVER. In 1970 H. Edmandson found in studies of autopsies performed at the University of Southern California-Los Angeles County Medical Center that among Mexican-American men CIRRHOSIS of the liver accounted for 52% of all deaths compared with 24% of the deaths among Anglo men. Studies have reported that Hispanics have higher arrest rates for public drunkenness and drunk driving than the national average (although this may be due in part to overpolicing). Accidents while driving under the influence are reported to be higher among Hispanics than among the general population. A study in 1977 revealed that one-half of the adult population in Puerto Rico drove after drinking, reflecting a general lack of concern about traffic safety (Kaye).

According to self-reported statistics, there is a lower percentage of drinkers and a higher percentage of abstainers among Hispanic youth than among Anglo youth; yet Hispanic adults have higher rates of alcohol use and abuse than their Anglo counterparts. Some of the major causes cited for this paradox are the poverty, inadequate health care and discrimination suffered by Hispanics. In addition there are problems of acculturation and language difficulties. Hispanics who try to meet Anglo economic goals and fail often feel deprived and alienated. And factors within Hispanic culture may promote alcoholism. For example, the concept of machismo calls for men to drink frequently and in quantity but, at the same time, to hold their liquor and maintain their dignity. A drinking problem is not readily recognized or admitted because it is seen as a weakness that reflects poorly on machismo. Family pride and support, which also play important roles in Hispanic culture, can foster DENIAL of a drinking problem. Pride may prevent family members from admitting the existence of such a problem. If the alcoholic becomes hard to handle, on the other hand, the family may reject him or her completely, further hindering treatment. Female Hispanic alcoholics are much more often rejected and stigmatized than their male counterparts and are frequently the victims of verbal or physical abuse from their families.

Hispanics are less likely to seek treatment voluntarily than are non-Hispanics. They view alcoholism as a moral weakness, not as an illness, and are less familiar with treatment resources than the rest of the population. Only around 45% of Hispanics know about ALCOHOLICS ANONYMOUS and they often have difficulty approaching the organization because of a lack of facility with English or fear of discriminatory treatment, an indifferent environment or, in the case of illegal aliens, discovery. There are some Spanish-speaking AA groups, but more culturally specific treatment services staffed with bilingual personnel are needed. There is also a need for additional research on the Hispanic alcohol problem, which, like the drinking problem of many other minorities, has generally been overlooked.

John R. DeLuca, ed., *Fourth Special Report to the U.S. Congress on Alcohol and Health* (Rockville, Md.: National Institute on Alcohol Abuse and Alcoholism, 1981), pp. 86–87.

H. Edmandson, "Mexican-American Alcoholism and Deaths at LAC-USC Medical Center," testimony before the Subcommittee on Alcoholism of the California Senate Health and Welfare Committee (Feb. 17, 1975).

S. Kaye, "The Problem Drinker and Traffic Fatalities in Puerto Rico—1976," *Boletin Associacion Medica de Puerto Rico* 69, no. 11 (1977):346–371.

Antonio Melus, "Culture and Language in the Treatment of Alcoholism: The Hispanic Perspective," *Alcohol Health and Research World* 4, no. 4 (Summer 1980):19–20.

Ernest P. Noble, ed., *Third Special Report to the U.S. Congress on Alcohol and Health* (Rockville, Md.: National Institute on Alcohol Abuse and Alcoholism, 1978), pp. 58–61.

Richard Roth and David Fernandez, "Historic Accord between Hispanic Alcoholism Community and NIAAA," *Alcoholism* 1, no. 2 (November–December 1980):20–22.

holiday heart syndrome   An irregularity in the heartbeat that may occur after a period of high alcohol ingestion. (See *Cardiac Arrhythmia* under HEART).

homicide   See CRIME.

homosexuals   It has been conservatively estimated that one out of every four homosexuals in the United States is an alcoholic (Stephens), compared with approximately one out of every 10 in the general population. A 1975 study found that approximately one-third of the total homosexual population of Los Angeles County abused alcohol on a regular basis.

The social structure of the homosexual community encourages drinking. A large part of a homosexual person's social time is spent at bars or at parties where alcohol is available. According to one estimate, homosexuals frequent bars an average of 19 times a month and drink an average of six drinks per visit (Fifield). The homosexual alcoholic, typically in his or her mid-30s, has been drinking in bars for at least 10 years. This exposure may produce a gradual increase in alcohol TOLERANCE resulting in alcoholism, although the subject may not drink excessively at first.

Other factors contributing to alcoholism stem from the stigma attached to homosexuality. Male and female homosexuals may perceive themselves as being outside of society and thus not required to follow certain societal norms. Some homosexuals who have difficulty dealing with their sexuality use alcohol to cope with this problem. The "coming out" process, whereby a person publicly acknowledges his or her homosexuality, often takes place in an environment where alcohol is prevalent and so a pattern of drinking develops as an important aspect of the homosexual identity. Ego defenses that homosexuals sometimes use to protect themselves against a hostile society may also block awareness of a growing dependency on alcohol.

Marian Sandmaier reports that lesbians are more likely to have a problem with alcohol than homosexual men. One study found that 35% of lesbians had problems with alcohol at some point in their lives compared with 28% of homosexual men and only 5% of heterosexual women. Lesbians suffer from the stigmas attached to homosexuals and to WOMEN who drink.

The majority of treatment centers are not geared to the specific problems of homosexual alcoholics. Many have a negative attitude toward homosexuals, and some centers may even refuse to treat them or try to cure their homosexuality rather than their alcoholism. Few staff members in treatment programs are homosexual themselves. As a result the success ratio for homosexual alcoholics in existing programs is much lower than that for the general population.

There is a need for recovery programs oriented toward homosexuals and for education on the problem in the various homosexual communities. Alcoholics Anonymous has a few homosexual groups in urban areas. In Boston the Homophile Alcohol Treatment Service (HATS), funded in part by the Massachusetts Division of Alcoholism, helps homosexuals with alcohol problems. The National Association of Gay Alcoholism Professionals publishes a newsletter and works to improve treatment for alcoholic clients.

Lilene Fifield, "Introductory Address to the National Council on Alcoholism Forum Session on Alcohol Abuse in the Gay Community," *National Institute on Alcohol Abuse and Alcoholism (NIAAA) Information and Feature Service,* no. 75 (Sept. 3, 1980).

Marian Sandmaier, *The Invisible Alcoholics* (New York: McGraw-Hill Book Company, 1980), pp. 179–183.

Bryan Stephens, "Alcoholism: The Dark Side of Gay," *The Magazine* 6, no. 3 (Fall 1980).

hooch   (Short form of *Hoochinoo,* a variation of *Hutsnuwu,* the name of an Alaskan Tlingit tribe. The name was applied to a liquor secretly produced by the tribe.) Slang for whiskey or liquor, especially inferior homemade or cheap whiskey or surreptitiously obtained whiskey. The term "hooch" became common during Prohibition, when it was used to refer to bootlegged whiskey of unknown origin. Today it is seldom used.

hops   Cones formed on the female *Humulus lupulus* vine. The cones are green with a surface of broad scales and a base that includes twin blossoms. When ripe, they are dried and used as an essential ingredient in the production of virtually all beers. It is the hop that produces the distinctively bitter, or "hoppy," flavor of beer, and the proportion of hops used in brewing is an important factor in creating distinct varieties of beer. First cultivated in Bavaria for use in beer, hops have been successfully transplanted to other areas for the same purpose. The shoots of the vine are also sometimes eaten as a vegetable and are especially popular in Belgium.

hormones, male sex   Numerous studies have demonstrated that alcohol lowers testosterone levels in males of all species, including man. Many male alcoholics show signs of sexual impotence, loss of libido and symptoms of hypogonadism (diminished function of the sex glands), including breast enlargement, loss of facial hair and testicular atrophy, as a result of lower testosterone levels.

The lower levels may be due to either of two direct causes: increased breakdown of testosterone or reduced synthesis.

Breakdown of Testosterone

It appears that alcohol increases the synthesis of LIVER enzymes called 5-alpha-reductases, which are responsible for the degradation of testosterone by converting it to dehydrotestosterone. There is also evidence that administration of alcohol over a long period of time causes estrogen levels to rise, and this increase correlates with an increase in the level of a liver enzyme called hepatic aromatase, which is involved in the conversion of androgens (male sex hormones) to estrogens (female sex hormones). It has also been shown that there is an increased rate of conversion of testosterone to its respective estrogen. The signs of "feminization" in male chronic alcoholics are probably due to a simultaneous reduction in androgens and an increase in estrogens.

Reduced Testosterone Synthesis

In addition, there is evidence to indicate that alcohol administered acutely or chronically depresses testosterone synthesis in the testes. The levels of testosterone are lowest three to five hours after a high level of alcohol consumption and become normal or higher than normal six to eight hours later, when BLOOD ALCOHOL CONCENTRATION is very low. Apparently the effect of alcohol is biphasic—low doses increase testosterone levels and high doses depress them.

Most researchers have found that heavy use of alcohol over a long period of time has a strong toxic effect on the testes. Serum testosterone levels are low in chronic alco-

holics and it appears that repeated and persistent alcohol use eventually causes irreversible damage to the structural and biochemical composition of the testes. Several recent studies have shown that the toxic agent may be ACETALDEHYDE, the metabolic product of ethanol, rather than ethanol.

John R. DeLuca, ed., *Fourth Special Report to the U.S. Congress on Alcohol and Health* (Rockville, Md.: National Institute on Alcohol Abuse and Alcoholism, 1981), pp. 50–52.

hyperglycemia   Unusually high blood sugar level (see BLOOD SUGAR, DIABETES).

hypertension (high blood pressure).   Heavy alcohol consumption has been linked with high blood pressure in a number of studies (see HEART).

hypoglycemia   Low blood sugar; a condition sometimes seen in alcoholics (see BLOOD SUGAR).

I

---

impairment   (From the Latin *in* intensive + *pejorare* to make worse.) Damage to an individual or impaired functioning as a result of the use of alcohol. Impairment must be measured on an individual basis, because there are people who drink large amounts of alcohol with few problems while others are strongly affected by small amounts. The term "impairment" is used to describe both short- and long-term effects. For a person on a drinking bout, for example, impairment may mean difficulty in walking and/or talking, confusion, and drowsiness or unconsciousness. Impairment is also used to determine whether or not a person is an alcoholic, since alcoholism can rarely be measured in terms of comsumption alone.

David J. Armor, J. Michael Polich and Harriet B. Stambul of the Rand Corporation list 12 signs of behavioral impairment that indicate a diagnosis of alcoholism:

1. Tremors (shakes)
2. Alcoholic blackouts (loss of memory)
3. Missing meals due to drinking
4. Drinking on awakening
5. Being drunk
6. Missing work days due to drinking
7. Difficulty in sleeping
8. Quarreling with others while drinking
9. Drinking on the job
10. Continuous drinking
11. Drinking alone
12. Time between drinking sessions

If alcohol is interfering with an individual's ability to function in society, then he or she is suffering from alcohol impairment.

David J. Armor, J. Michael Polich and Harriet B. Stambul, *Alcoholism and Treatment* (New York: John Wiley and Sons, 1978) p. 89.

inability to abstain   A term used to describe someone who is unable to abstain from drinking for even a day or two, although he or she can control the amount consumed on any given occasion. This inability is characteristic of DELTA ALCOHOLISM.

India   On the Indian subcontinent in general and in the nation of India in particular, drug and alcohol problems, while long standing, have been seen as less pervasive than in many developed nations. Part of the disparity is due to religious and cultural restraints, but it also stems from the fact that these problems are secondary to the national concern about overpopulation, extreme poverty and the constant threat of starvation.

In a 1977 report, *Drug Abuse in India,* issued by the National Committee on Drug Abuse, an attempt was made to present the meager and scattered data available in a coherent manner and to lay the foundation for future research and treatment of the problem. Some of the terms, particularly those used to define the parameters of study, differ somewhat from those used in other countries. The report notes that "the expression 'drug abuse' has a much wider connotation and includes, not only 'drug addiction' but also other forms such as experimental or occasional use, or even a type of regular use which has no appreciable harmful effects on the individual and society . . . these other forms of drug abuse cannot be isolated from drug addiction and it is these that now form the major problem rather than drug addiction as such."

Alcohol and tobacco are included as drugs, and their use and abuse are not always clearly differentiated from the use and abuse of other drugs. "Abusers" are divided into two categories: "experimental user—for less than a month to about once a week" and "regular user—several times a week and daily." By most Western standards these categories, especially "experimental use," are descriptive of alcohol "use" rather than "abuse."

Compared with other nations, India has a low rate of alcohol use—somewhere in the low range of a scale from 0.2% to 1.9% of the general population; in contrast, the rate of alcohol use in the United States ranges from 5.9% to 6.23%. Translated into actual numbers of problem drinkers, however, these low percentages are greatly magnified—from 1.4 million to 13.3 million problem drinkers, compared with 12.6 to 13.3 million in the United States. Considering the money and facilities available for treatment programs, the figures represent an enormous burden.

Of the few studies available on alcohol use in India, one of the most comprehensive was made in 1977 in the nine largest vil-

Table 1
Alcohol Use in the Punjab
(1977)

Category	% of Nonusers	% of Past Users	% of Experimental Users	% of Regular Users	% of Addicts
Male	33.5	8.1	52.7	5.6	3.92
Female	98.3	0.2	1.3	0.2	0.06
Both sexes	61.1	4.8	30.8	3.3	2.28

Sample: male 2,064; female 1,536.

lages of the Sangrur District of the Punjab. But even this study was not entirely representative, since the Punjab population has traditionally been above average in literacy and affluence. The study showed that 30% of those over age 10 had "ever used" a drug, 28.8% were currently using a drug and 7.37% were using alcohol. (See Table 1 for a breakdown of users by type and sex.) Alcohol and drug abuse in India are conditioned by the caste system, which is still prevalent in India despite some recent partly successful efforts to abolish it; religion; and the relative affluence of the individual. There is no single pattern of a substance use and abuse but a number of patterns, even within the various religions. Christianity permits use of alcohol but some Christians abstain; Islamism forbids drinking, yet some Moslems drink. While Sikhism prohibits smoking, some Sikhs smoke.

Among Hindus the use of alcohol and drugs varies from caste to caste. Brahmins, the highest caste, are not permitted alcohol but may use bhang or ganja. Another high caste, the Kayasthas, who are generally associated with writing and clerical work, are leading users of alcohol and other drugs.

The traditional rule of thumb that in India the rich use drugs to induce euphoria and the poor use alcohol to kill pain has been modified under the impact of Western culture. Alcohol has become chic, a status symbol of upward mobility. Moreover the two traditional patterns can be altered by specific pressures and circumstances; among the very poor mothers often narcotize their infants with opium so that they can go to work. Table 2 gives a brief summary of recent available information on alcohol addiction in India.

For a variety of reasons the Indian gov-

Table 2
Alcohol Addiction in India

Location	Sample	Date	Percent of Total Population Addicted*
Pondicherry	general	1964	0.36
Vellore	general	1972	0.20
Agra	general	1972	1.35
Lucknow	urban	1973	1.86
West Bengal	rural	1976	1.90
Punjab	rural	1977	2.28**

Note: Data are based on limited studies in particular areas.

*Addiction is defined as having an "expressed craving for the drug."

**By sex: male 3.92%; female 0.06%.

Table 3
Alcohol Use Among Indian Students
(1976)

Center*	Total Sample	%	Male Sample	%	Female Sample	%
Bombay	4,151	15.1	2,334	20.6	1,817	8.5
Madras	3,580	9.5	2,157	13.8	1,423	2.9
Delhi	3,991	12.2	2,000	21.7	1,991	2.6
Jaipur	4,081	9.8	3,092	12.1	989	1.5
Hyderabad	1,097	9.0	539	15.4	558	2.8
Varanasi	3,852	10.4	3,391	11.6	461	1.7

*Universities were chosen as follows: metropolitan—Bombay, Madras, Delhi; nonmetropolian—Jaipur, Hyderabad; and "an odd representative [Varanasi], mainly as a residential university."

ernment is focusing a substantial portion of its study of alcohol and drug problems on the student population. Students are readily available to the centers conducting the research; they are intellectually easier to communicate with than the general population; and above all, they are among the first to reflect change and the impact of new ideas and mores.

In India, as Table 3 shows, the consumption of alcoholic beverages is substantially higher among all segments of the student population than among the population as a whole. However, consumption is much lower than that among students in many other countries; the national rate of alcohol use among Indian students is 11%, compared with 90% among the student population in the United States. Moreover the combined use of alcohol and another drug by students is both higher than that found in the general population and on the increase. In the sample used in Table 3, 6.5% were users of "tobacco/alcohol or both + a drug."

As of 1977, there were no centers in India devoted exclusively to the treatment of alcoholism and drug addiction. Limited inpatient facilities, however, are available at mental hospitals and psychiatric departments of general hospitals. Furthermore the government feels that "it is not desirable to provide specific and separate treatment facilities for drug addicts."

The principal treatment methods for alcoholism emphasize the use of antagonistic drugs, such as disulfiram (ANTABUSE), in an outpatient program.

inebriate   An alcoholic.

inebriety   Excessive drinking or ALCOHOLISM.

infancy   In addition to the serious danger of being exposed to excessive amounts of alcohol (see FETAL ALCOHOL SYNDROME), an infant is also at risk if the mother drinks excessively after giving birth. Breast-fed infants may be exposed to alcohol in their mother's milk. Alcohol enters the breast milk at the same level it enters the mother's bloodstream. Ingesting breast milk that contains alcohol may cause an effect in the infant known as the pseudo-Cushing syndrome, which is characterized by high levels of the hormone cortisol and of glucose in the blood as well as obesity, purple striations on the abdomen, easy bruising and a "moon" face. The long-term effects are unknown. It has also been shown that alcohol inhibits the milk-ejection reflex and may cause a reduction in the milk supplied to the nursing infant. (See also CHILD ABUSE.)

input-output model for treatment   The input-output model is a method proposed by David J. Armor, T. Michael Polich and Harriet B. Stambul, authors of the RAND REPORTS, to help facilitate matching an alcoholic client with the proper treatment. Input is divided into client inputs and treatment inputs. Client inputs are the characteristics of the client at the onset of treatment that might be relevant in determining what treatment is best for him or her. Treatment inputs concern the type and amount of treatment available at a particular treatment center. A successful outcome depends on the appropriateness of the treatment selected for the type of client.

instability and crisis etiological theory   One of a number of SOCIOCULTURAL ETIOLOGICAL THEORIES, the instability and crisis etiological theory posits that social factors which produce heavy stress on the individual may bring about the onset of alcoholism. During crisis periods when significant changes have occurred in an individual's life, he or she may turn to alcohol to alleviate the stress. WOMEN are especially likely to become alcoholic as a result of a particular event, such as the death of a spouse, a divorce or the departure of children from home. Heavy consumption of alcohol, however, exacerbates the social picture, and a cyclical relationship develops in which a stressful event leads to heavy drinking that in turn causes more stress and more drinking.

insurance   The World Health Organization formally recognized alcoholism as a disease in 1951 and the American Medi-

An input-output model for treatment evaluation

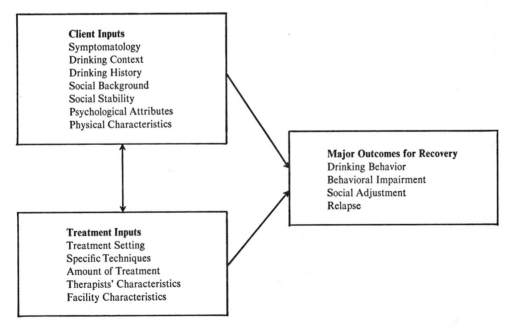

cal Association followed suit in 1956. Before this time and for several years thereafter, large amounts of insurance money were spent to cover treatment for the complications and secondary manifestations of alcoholism, such as liver dysfunction or accidents involving alcohol abuse, but the primary disorder of alcoholism went undiagnosed and untreated. Gradually a few companies began to provide coverage for treatment of alcoholism. In 1964 Kemper Insurance Companies and Wausau became the first and they were followed by other companies, such as Capital Blue Cross in 1969. Today many companies provide some form of coverage for alcoholism, but a number of issues related to insurance coverage of alcoholism have yet to be solved, and policies are gradually changing as more is learned about the field.

One of the problems with insurance coverage for alcoholism is that systems for reimbursement tend to be related to traditional physician and hospital care. Alternative modes of treatment, such as outpatient services, residential programs and halfway houses, have generally not been included in basic health insurance coverage. Alternative programs are often less expensive and less disruptive to employed individuals and may be as effective as hospital treatment. The National Institute on Alcohol Abuse and Alcoholism estimated that the cost of treatment per client per year was $740 for an outpatient treatment program, $4,730 for an intermediate long-term alcoholism treatment service, $20,780 for hospital detoxification and $13,730 for hospital alcoholism treatment.

Insurance companies might well benefit from extending coverage to outpatient facilities, and some have started to do so. In 1973 Kemper began providing group health coverage for both outpatient and inpatient treatment in qualifying nonhospital alcoholism centers. Since then other companies have provided coverage for outpatient treatment, but such coverage is still the excep-

tion. And while, by December 1979, 24 states had enacted legislation concerning health insurance coverage for alcoholism—some mandating coverage for alcoholism, some requiring specified health insurers to make defined coverage available for the treatment of alcoholism at the policyholder's option—fewer than half of the statutes mentioned outpatient treatment.

Insurance companies must be able to determine what is appropriate, cost-effective treatment, and it is more difficult to evaluate nontraditional treatment modes. Some programs are now accredited by the Joint Commission on Accreditation of Hospitals and some are accredited by various states. Corporate occupational program directors can also evaluate local treatment programs.

Coverage for alcoholism treatment is not available to most disadvantaged members of minority groups in the country. Affluent people often pay for treatment of alcoholism without health insurance coverage, frequently in very expensive settings, and this is one of the reasons there has been no significant motivation to develop an insurance plan with broad coverage. Many minority group members do not belong to a group insurance plan and cannot afford an individual comprehensive policy.

Women alcoholics, many of whom have a DUAL ADDICTION, need longer for detoxification. The limit on coverage for detoxification services, however, is often a matter of days, which may not be adequate to treat dual addiction. More than half of all company insurance policies cover only the individual and not the family, although the family is often involved in an alcoholic's problem.

Data seem to indicate that treatment of an alcoholic and his or her family will decrease subsequent health care costs. There should be a growing movement by insurers to encourage their clients to use occupational alcoholism programs and other treatment so as to prevent the progression of the disease and its costly effects.

Gary Graham, "Occupational Programs and Their Relation to Health Insurance Coverage for Alcoholism," *Alcohol Health and Research World* 5, no. 4 (Summer 1981): 31–34.

Sandra S. Sternberger and Helen Drew, "Women, Health Insurance and Alcoholism," op. cit.:37–38.

Charles D. Watts, "Health Insurance Coverage for Underserved Populations," op. cit.:35–36.

William G. Williams, "Nature and Benefit Packages in Health Insurance Coverage for Alcoholism Treatment," op. cit.:5–11.

intemperance   Habitual or excessive drinking or drunkenness.

intervention   A term used to describe the action taken by a person who confronts an alcoholic with his problem in order to interrupt the progress toward permanent disability or death that may result if alcoholism is allowed to progress uninterrupted. Effective intervention can be achieved by someone who plays a significant role in the alcoholic's life, usually a member of the immediate family, a close friend or an employer. Even more effective is confrontation of the alcoholic by two or more persons genuinely concerned about his welfare. The subject must be sober and clearheaded and the best time is during a crisis, when his defenses are apt to be lowered. The alcoholic is then presented with factual data about his behavior and the costs of his addiction to himself and to those around him. It is important during a time of crisis to take advantage of the situation in a calm, rational manner. The alcoholic should be told that his behavior caused the crisis and the responsibility is his. When forced to face the consequences of his actions, he may become more depressed and seem to be regressing. Such a reaction, however, is a step toward his realization that he needs treatment. Those confronting the alcoholic should be prepared to help him find suitable treatment.

It is not enough for the alcoholic to make promises to do better; despite his good intentions the situation is generally not within his control. He must be made to accept professional help that will enable him to establish new patterns of behavior.

Alcoholism: A Treatable Disease (Minneapolis: The Johnson Institute, 1972).

intoxication   (From Latin *in* + *toxicum* poison.) An abnormal state produced by ingesting alcohol (or another drug) that can range from exhilaration to stupor. Degree and experience of intoxication vary from individual to individual. Recent studies have indicated that intoxication may have as much or more to do with psychological processes as with physical processes. Psychologists G. Alan Marlatt and Damaris J. Rohsenow of the University of Wisconsin used a "balanced placebo" experiment to determine the physical effects of drinking alcohol as distinguished from the expected or imagined effects on someone who *thinks* he is drinking alcohol. Marlatt and Rohsenow divided subjects into four groups: one expecting alcohol and receiving alcohol, one expecting alcohol and receiving tonic, one expecting tonic and receiving alcohol, and one expecting tonic and receiving tonic. The groups were then observed with focus on social behavior, aggression and sexual arousal.

The study showed that men who mistakenly believed they had been drinking alcohol became less anxious in social situations. On the other hand, WOMEN in the same group became more anxious, possibly because their drinking experience and expectancies were different from those of the men.

Alcoholics were found to experience the same craving after taking one or two placebo drinks as they did after drinking real alcohol, but they reported little or no craving when they were given drinks containing alcohol that they believed were non-alcoholic.

Men became more aggressive when they drank tonic that they believed contained vodka and relatively less aggressive when they drank vodka believing they were getting only tonic. Men tended to become more sexually aroused when they believed they were drinking alcohol but actually were drinking only tonic. Women reported feeling more aroused when they believed they had been drinking alcohol, but a measure of vaginal blood flow showed that physically they were becoming less aroused.

The authors of this study reported that more than 25 other published experiments using the balanced placebo design had also found the "expectancy effect" in the use of alcohol. These studies suggest that people have strong beliefs about what alcohol does, and react accordingly. They indicate that women whose experiences with alcohol and expectancies about its effects differ from those of men will not react to alcohol in the same way as men. In most states a person with a BLOOD ALCOHOL CONCENTRATION of .10% is considered intoxicated. While the level of intoxication varies from individual to individual, depending on such factors as the amount of food in the stomach, body weight and individual tolerance, most people with a BAC of 0.15% are definitely intoxicated. Their voluntary motor action is affected, they are unable to walk properly and they have lost some control over their emotions. At a BAC of 0.20%, which can be achieved by drinking about 10 ounces of distilled spirits in a few hours, there is generally severe impairment, and behavior is loud and incoherent and emotionally confused. At 0.30% the deeper areas of the brain are affected and the drinker becomes stuporous, and at 0.40% he or she becomes unconscious. Death can occur between 0.40% and 0.70%, but this is rare because most drinkers have lapsed into unconsciousness at these levels.

John Langone, *Bombed, Buzzed, Smashed, or . . . Sober* (Boston: Little, Brown and Company, 1976), pp. 78–80.

Alan G. Marlatt and Damaris J. Rohsenow, "The Think-Drink Effect," *Psychology Today* 15, no. 12 (December 1981):60–69, 93.

Ireland   It is a common belief that the Irish are prone to alcohol-related problems. The thought of Ireland is likely to conjure up images of beer drinking in public houses, Irish whiskey and the boisterous celebration of St. Patrick's Day. Surprisingly, however, by international standards alcohol consumption in Ireland (adjusted for population) is quite low, beneath that in the United States. In 1974, for example, the Irish consumed 9.9 quarts (9.4 liters) of AB-SOLUTE ALCOHOL for every person aged 15 and over; for the same age group per capita consumption in the United States in 1975 was 11.1 quarts (10.5 liters) and in France in 1972 23.7 quarts (22.4 liters) per person. However, it must be noted that Ireland has a high percentage of nondrinkers (43% of the over-15 population in 1974, but the rate has been declining annually at 2.9%). Thus the average is maintained by heavier consumption on the part of the drinking population.

Alcohol consumption in Ireland is on the rise, particularly among women and those between the ages of 18 and 24, and the percentage of abstainers, still relatively high (25% of the women and 10% of the men), is falling. Between 1950 and 1979 alcohol consumption per person over 14 years rose by 113%. And the Irish themselves regard alcoholism as an increasing problem.

Although the Irish have a relatively low rate of alcohol consumption, because of a high excise tax, they spend a larger proportion of their income—12%—on alcoholic beverages than that recorded in any other country today. Their closest competitors, the Finns and the British, spend about 7% of their income on drinking.

The Exchequer (treasury) is heavily dependent on the excise taxation of alcohol as a source of revenue. In 1975 it contributed

**Estimates of the Components of Growth of Alcohol
Consumption Per Person Aged 15 and Over**

	Consumption per Person Aged 15 and over (liters/ year)	Estimated Proportion of Drinkers in Population Aged 15 and over (%)	Estimated Consumption per Drinker (liters/year)
1968	6.45	48	13.5
1974	9.27	57	16.3
Annual average growth rates, 1968–74	6.2%	2.9%	3.2%

11.72% of all tax revenue. A rough estimate of the total cost of alcohol abuse, to the Irish government, including the cost of road accidents, health care, social services, lower production because of absences, unemployment benefits etc., was £60 million ($ 29.4 million). However, the tax yield from the sale and production of alcohol was £119 million ($58.3 million).

Although drinking is relatively expensive in Ireland, cost does not seem to hinder those who drink. Evidence suggests that the expenditure on drink rises at least in proportion to income, and higher alcohol prices result in higher expenditures on drink rather than decreased consumption.

Most drinking in Ireland is done in public houses rather than at home, a contributing factor to the proportion of traffic accidents caused by alcohol, around 50%, which is close to the percentage in the United States. Premises where alcoholic beverages are sold must be licensed by the state and the number allowed is related to the population of an area and the existing distribution of already licensed premises.

As more of the population drinks, drinking patterns are changing. There has been a more rapid growth in the consumption of distilled spirits and wine than of beer. Exports of spirits have accelerated in recent years and beer is an important source of net foreign exchange earnings.

The number of admissions to mental hospitals for the treatment of alcoholism increased by more than 300% from 1965 to 1977, although the alcohol consumption rate rose by 70% during this time. The top socioeconomic group has one of the highest hospital admission rates for alcoholism, but the average length of stay is much shorter than that for, say, unskilled manual laborers. This is probably because professional people are more likely to seek medical treatment for heavy drinking than others although their intake of alcohol may not be exceptionally high.

The rate of prosecution for drunken driving has risen enormously in Ireland, partly as a result of more stringent laws and the introduction of a BLOOD ALCOHOL CONCENTRATION test in 1971. The number of arrests for this offense rose from 4,000 in 1961 to over 10,000 in 1977. However, it is not simply a case of more drivers being apprehended; there are more drunk drivers on the road. Both the total number and the percentage of the driving population have risen.

The Irish are searching for effective ways to control alcohol abuse but have not yet found satisfactory solutions. The cost of alcohol is already extremely high and raising it does not seem to prevent people from purchasing alcohol. Restrictive social measures often impinge on the rights of drinkers who do not abuse alcohol, and resistance to these measures may result in increased abuse. One area that might warrant more attention is heavier penalization for drunk drivers and for those whose alcoholism causes absence from work. However, as Ireland has changed from a nation where drinking was polarized (e.g., heavy drinkers vs. abstainers) to one where there is increased social drinking, alcoholism problems have become more complex.

Brendan M. Walsh, *Drinking in Ireland* (Dublin: The Economic and Social Research Institute, 1980).

Irish Americans   Ethnic background and generational status are both important determinants of drinking patterns in the United States. It has been reported that Irish Americans have a rate of problem drinking two or three times as high as that of other ethnic groups. The Irish in general do not strongly disapprove of drunkenness, and a drunken man is frequently looked upon with amusement rather than pity or disgust. Intoxication is often deliberately sought. Drink is accepted as fulfilling a functional need of relieving stress, and it is not used in a ritualistic way, as with some ethnic groups. Irish Americans are likely to drink in public bars, to drink beer and to drink with members of their own sex. According to a recent study by the National Opinion Research Center, forty percent of Irish Americans reported there was a drinking problem in their homes when they were children.

Morris E. Chafetz and Harold W. Demone, Jr., *Alcoholism and Society* (New York: Oxford University Press, 1962), pp. 76–80.
Barry Glassner, "Differences in Ethnic Drinking Habits," *Alcoholism* 1, no. 4 (March/April 1981): 19–21.
John Langone, *Bombed, Buzzed, Smashed, or . . . Sober* (Boston: Little, Brown and Company, 1976), pp. 47–49.

Irish whiskey   A distilled spirit made from mixed grains. The production of Irish whiskey differs from that of Scotch whiskey in three ways: the grain mixture fermented contains a lower proportion of malted barley, the malted barley used is cured with charcoal rather than peat and the fermented mash is triple distilled. The result is a drier and more subtle spirit than most varieties of Scotch whiskey.

The Irish were in all likelihood the first people of the British Isles to distill grain spirits, although the precise date is unknown. Some legends attribute the importation of distilling techniques to missionary monks from Europe who arrived after St. Patrick sometime between 500 A.D. and 600 A.D.. By about 1200 the Irish were known for their *uisce beathadh* ("water of life") more than anything except perhaps their Catholicism. The English word "whiskey" is an Anglicization of the Gaelic *uisce*.

Irish whiskey remained a notorious cottage industry through Elizabethan times despite English efforts to regulate and tax the trade. Even today, in response to high taxes on whiskey levied by the government of Ireland, home distilling remains a right insisted upon by the Irish in defiance of the authorities. The most common illegal distillate is *poteen,* a spirit that is colorless and raw to the taste because of a lack of aging. *Poteen* is currently available throughout the rural districts of Ireland, and it is often offered to visitors instead of licensed distillates as a gesture of greater ceremony.

In 1608, on the bank of the River Bush, Sir Thomas Phillips established the first distillery in Ireland chartered by the English crown. Bushmills, as the distillery was called, has remained the trade name of the leading whiskey of Northern Ireland. Despite this charter distilling continued to be largely a cottage industry, producing an erratic product heavy with congeners. In the 18th century efforts to evade British regulations took the form of a division of labor: "sugar bakers" assumed charge of fermenting the grain mash, an entirely legal activity at the time, and they then exchanged the mash with independent distillers for a quantity of the finished spirit. Realizing that measures to control the trade had failed, the British decided to charter a number of Irish distilleries. Between 1779 and 1829 virtually all the major Irish whiskey distillers other than Bushmills came into existence: John Jameson in 1780, John Power in 1791, Daly in 1807, Murphy Brothers in 1825 and Tullamore in 1829. The national industry underwent a major transformation during the 1960s, when most distillers merged to form the Irish Distillers Limited, a conglomerate that manufactures separate brand names and distinct distillates at a central location.

Irish whiskey is distilled from a grain mixture that is low in malted barley and peat-drying cured over charcoal to avoid giving it the heavy flavor of Scotch whisky produced by peat-drying the grains. Traditional Irish whiskeys are distilled in pot stills that are larger than those used to make Scotch. Most are triple distilled, a drawn-out process that reduces the quantity produced, strengthens it and brings it to an unusually high degree of rectification. Aging is generally done in casks that have previously held sherry or other whiskeys and continues for a minimum of three years. Most exported Irish whiskey is between 10 and 12 years old. As in the case of Scotch whiskey, the product is usually blended with any number of whiskeys from other distillations to broaden its appeal in the marketplace and to ensure consistency of taste.

isopropyl alcohol   Also known as isopropanol and 2-propanol, isopropyl alcohol is a colorless liquid that can be mixed with water. Poisonous if taken internally, it is a major component of rubbing alcohol and has replaced ethanol for many uses because it is cheaper and has similar solvent properties.

Israel   Israelis are known to have a relatively low incidence of alcoholism, but the Israeli government now recognizes that there is a problem of alcohol use within the country. Although by no means epidemio-logical, the incidence of alcoholism in Israel is high enough to have attracted the attention of the Ministry of Labour and Social Affairs and the Ministry of Social Welfare. Their investigations have isolated factors that tend to encourage alcoholism despite the cultural restraints inhibiting the disease among the Jewish people.

When Israel was established in 1948, only about 650,000 Jews lived within its borders. Today that figure is well over 3 million. The people who immigrated to Israel during these years came from about 80 different countries, and they brought with them as many different attitudes toward alcohol consumption as there were countries of origin. The traditional image of abstemious consumption of alcohol is for the most part derived from the habits of European Jews. This portion of the population brought with it virtually no habits of alcohol abuse, largely because drinking had been socially inhibited to avoid confrontations with the non-Jewish segments among which it had formerly lived.

Those Jews who immigrated from Asia and North Africa, however, brought with them a relatively casual attitude toward alcohol consumption because they had come from predominantly Islamic countries, which had prohibitions on the use of alcohol; in the past they therefore had less need to separate themselves from a non-Jewish population who drank and less fear of confrontations with antagonists as a result of alcohol abuse. Moreover once these Asian and North African immigrants entered Israel, they were forced to relinquish vestiges of their patriarchal culture, alter their traditional family structure and accept a lower position in the scale of classes than they had formerly enjoyed. The trauma of this integration into what was for these immigrants a secularized Israeli culture caused some of them to degenerate from moderate to excessive drinkers. Today this group of Asian and North African immigrants accounts for more than half of the alcoholics in Israel.

Statistics on drunk driving offenses, drinking among youth and the incidence of alcoholism among women all suggest that alcohol abuse is worsening in Israel. In 1980 it was estimated that there were 6,000 alcoholics in the country. The figure represented the end result of years of neglect of the problem, an increasing acceptance of European social and dietary habits and a gradual loss of the special sense of mission associated with the early years of the state of Israel. Of the 6,000, 55.3% were immigrants from Asia and North Africa; 80% of the alcoholics born in Israel were descended from the same group of immigrants.

Most known alcoholics, that is, those who have received some treatment, in the country are married men with an average of four children, a finding which has led authorities to speculate that in Israel the family unit is the primary motivation for an alcoholic to seek professional treatment. There were no treatment facilities for alcoholics in Israel until 1974, when small experimental programs began operation, and today there are no legal means of forcing alcoholics to accept treatment. The existing treatment facilities are voluntary and reach only a small portion of the alcoholic population, e.g., 1,200 in 1979. The Ministry of Social Welfare has now established a policy to compensate in part for the absence of adequate facilities and compulsory hospitalization for alcoholics. It stresses above all the rehabilitative influence of the family, alternative group sessions with nonfamily members and limited clinical abstinence in psychiatric wards for those who request such treatment.

Italian Americans   Italian Americans have strong attitudes against drunkenness, apply little social pressure to participate in drinking and usually consume alcohol with meals. Wine is a staple in the diet of Italian Americans and most have their first drink between six and 10 years of age. First-generation Italian Americans drink frequently but have few alcohol-related problems; later generations have higher rates of heavy drinking, and they consume more distilled spirits than Italians in Italy and first-generation Italians. When there is drunkenness, it generally occurs at festive occasions where a group is present, including members of both sexes (as opposed to Irish-American drunkenness, which may be a regular occurrence and is not connected solely with festivity). As Italians become more Americanized, they may begin to lose the protective Italian drinking traditions and develop more drinking problems, but the rate of alcoholism among them is still significantly low compared with that of other groups, such as Irish Americans, Hispanics and blacks.

Morris E. Chafetz and Harold W. Demone, Jr., *Alcoholism and Society* (New York: Oxford University Press, 1962), pp. 80–84.
John Langone, *Bombed, Buzzed, Smashed, or . . . Sober* (Boston: Little, Brown and Company, 1976), pp. 47–49.

J

jackroller   SKID ROW slang for a thief, usually one who robs drunks.

Japan   There is a deeply ingrained acceptance of social consumption of alcoholic beverages in Japan that has led to a national pattern of infrequent but heavy drinking on special occasions. There is some actual encouragement of drunkenness during festive celebrations, and expensive distilled spirits are favored as gifts to hosts of social functions. One recent survey showed that 52% of the Japanese polled considered alcohol a part of their lives, and 35% of those polled considered abstinence harmful to social life. These patterns have a lengthy history, for although the majority of Japanese are nominally adherents to Buddhism or the native Shintoism, these religions have long been secularized in respect to prohibitions on alcohol consumption. Recent increases in the level of drinking, especially among women and youth, have resulted from wider advertisement of alcoholic beverages and a general trend toward westernization since World War II that has weakened the traditional hierarchical society.

Surveys in 1976 reported that 85% of the male population and 52% of the female population in Japan were drinkers. Habitual heavy drinking, however, was limited to 4% of the male population and 1.6% of the female population. The rate of drinking was heaviest among males between the ages of 40 and 49 years; 90% of this group drank, and 43% of it drank daily. Per capita consumption was 5.4 liters of ABSOLUTE ALCOHOL per year for the entire population and 7.1 liters of absolute alcohol per year for the population over 15 years of age.

The preferred beverage in Japan is sake, a fermented rice wine usually sold in varieties that average 16% absolute alcohol. In 1978 the available alcoholic beverages, measured as absolute alcohol, included sake, 243,000 liters; beer, 173,000 liters; whiskey 139,000 liters. The amount of illegal fermented or distilled beverages produced in the country is negligible. Most of the whiskey and beer in Japan is made by large corporations or imported, but sake is produced by smaller, more local companies. The manufacture and sale of alcoholic beverages in Japan employ 5% of the work force and account for 4% of the country's total revenues.

Alcohol-related health problems in Japan are recorded according to definitions established by the government. Authorities estimate, on the basis of limited surveys, that 2.5% of the total population may be considered alcoholics. The national rate of hospitalization for a primary diagnosis related to alcohol abuse was 12.8 per 100,000 population in 1977. The same year the rate of mortality from liver cirrhosis was 13.8 per 100,000 population; the number of male deaths from this disease was three times that of female deaths. In 1977 alcoholism, alcoholic psychoses and alcoholic cirrhosis patients occupied 3.6% of the nation's hospital beds and alcohol was involved in 12% of all traffic fatalities, up from 9% in 1973.

The economic cost of alcohol abuse in Japan is calculated to be 260 billion yen (about $1.3 billion) per year. The major factors in this loss, in order of importance, are premature death, absenteeism and medical care.

Additions to Japan's legal controls on alcohol abuse include a 1961 law that stiffened penalties for public drunkenness and a 1970 law that set permissible blood alcohol levels for drivers to 0.25 grams of ethanol per 1,000 grams of blood.

The Liaison Conference for Alcoholic Problems, an organization funded by the Ministry of Health and Welfare, coordinates alcoholism prevention and treatment programs, including the efforts of the Japanese Medical Society on Alcohol Studies and the All Nippon Sobriety Society, Japan's version of Alcoholics Anonymous. Significant contributions are also made by the Christian Women's Temperance Association and the Salvation Army. As yet, there are no school programs for the prevention of alcoholism, no investigations of the effect of alcohol on family life in Japan and no national limitations on advertisement of alcoholic beverages.

Jellinek, E. M. (1890–1963)

Jellinek was the author of *The Disease Concept of Alcoholism,* an influential study of alcoholism, and founder of the Center of Alcohol Studies and Summer School of Alcohol Studies, formerly at Yale University and now at Rutgers University. He was also a cofounder of the National Council on Alcoholism and was the World Health Organization Consultant on Alcoholism.

In *The Disease Concept of Alcoholism* Jellinek distinguished between five categories of alcoholism, which he referred to as ALPHA ALCOHOLISM, BETA ALCOHOLISM, DELTA ALCOHOLISM, EPSILON ALCOHOLISM and GAMMA ALCOHOLISM.

Jews   Research has indicated that Jews have lower rates of alcoholism than other ethnic groups; a study by the National Opinion Research Center found that only 4% of Jews reported a drinking problem in their homes. Although Jews have largely avoided alcoholism for over 2,500 years, it is false to believe that they are somehow immune to alcoholism.

The vast majority of Jews drink on a fairly regular basis; only 5% are abstainers. Drinking is first introduced to children in a family context, which has been shown to be a strong force in determining later drinking habits. Alcoholic beverages are used in positive settings, including religious rituals and mixed social gatherings, rather than as a means of coping with stress. When a baby is circumsized, he is given a few drops of wine and wine is drunk at bar mitzvahs and weddings. Consumption of wine is a part of the Sabbath ceremony and all family members partake. Sobriety is a factor in Jewish identity and intoxication is generally not tolerated.

One study revealed that of all Jewish men, the most orthodox drank most frequently but also had the lowest incidences of intoxication (Snyder). Furthermore the study showed that in general the more orthodox the participant, the lower the incidence of intoxication. However, there are orthodox Jewish rabbis who are alcoholics, and religious disaffiliation is not necessarily an indication of a drinking problem. Rates of alcoholism are low among Reform Jews as well as Orthodox Jews, but there appears to be a correlation between a move away from orthodoxy and an increase in the incidence of alcoholism. Identification with Judaism generally seems to act as a protective factor against alcoholism and an aid in recovery from alcoholism when it develops.

In a 1975 study researchers W. Schmidt and R. E. Popham found four types of coping mechanism used by Jews to deal with their alcoholism: (1) denial—"Since I'm a Jew I can't be an alcoholic"; (2) disaffiliation—"Since I'm an alcoholic I can't be much of a Jew"; (3) rationalization—"I drink to excess but so do most Jews"; and (4) acceptance—"I drink excessively and I am Jewish."

Difficulties in treating Jews who are alcoholic stem from a generalized DENIAL of the problem by the Jewish community and a lack of tolerance, which make subjects feel isolated from their community and may worsen their situation. In addition ALCOHOLICS ANONYMOUS meetings are often held in churches, where Jews may feel uncomfortable. Increased awareness by the Jewish community of the problem of alcoholism is needed to eliminate denial. More AA meetings in synagogues might also help treatment.

Sheila Blume, Dee Dropkin and Lloyd Sokolow, "The Jewish Alcoholic: A Descriptive Study," *Alcohol Health and Research World* 4, no. 4 (Summer 1980):21–26.

Morris Chafetz and Harold W. Demone, Jr., *Alcoholism and Society* (New York: Oxford University Press, 1962), pp. 84–88.

Barry Glassner, "Irish Bars and Jewish Living Rooms: Differences in Ethnic Drinking Habits," *Alcoholism* 1, no. 4 (March-April 1981):19–21.

W. Schmidt and R. E. Popham, "Impressions of Jewish Alcoholics," *Quarterly Journal of Studies on Alcohol* 37 (1976):931–934.

C. R. Snyder, *Alcohol and the Jews: A Cultural Study of Drinking and Sobriety,* Yale Center of Alcohol Studies monograph no. 1 (New Haven, 1958).

job safety   See ACCIDENTS, EMPLOYEE ASSISTANCE PROGRAMS.

Judaism   See RELIGION, JEWS.

K

katzenjammers   Slang for DELIRIUM TREMENS.

Kenya   The drinking patterns in Kenya, an independent member of the British Commonwealth since 1963, parallel those of other equatorial African nations. Approximately 90% of the population is composed of African ethnic groups living in rural areas, where alcoholic beverages are often home brews and drinking occasions are related to cultural activities among the various tribal societies. Imported liquors and bottled beers are sold through licensed retail stores, but there is widespread and unregulated consumption of *busaa,* a fermented beverage made from maize flour and sugar honey, and *chang'aa,* a beverage similar to gin distilled from a variety of fermented brews. Consumption of such alcoholic beverages is an integral part of social celebrations, settlements of disputes, agrarian festivals and hunting expeditions. Assistance from distant neighbors in construction and repair of rural farms and homes is usually rewarded with alcoholic beverages, and in certain places consumption of alcohol has become a part of sacrificial rites within communities.

In Nairobi and Mombasa there is a greater availability of imported wines and liquors, such as brandy, whiskey and gin, and the number of public bars has risen in recent years. Drinking of imported alcoholic beverages, as in other developing nations, is most common among educated people and is considered a mark of high social status. As Kenyan society becomes more modernized, licensed drinking premises have tended to replace the communal gatherings to which drinking was once limited and cultural restraints on drinking have been relaxed.

There is growing concern in Kenya about the spread of alcoholism resulting from this process of modernization. Figures on consumption are unreliable because of the amount of noncommercial alcoholic beverage production, but it is known that the principal Kenyan brewery increased its profits 33% between 1978 and 1979 and plans future expansion. Limited surveys have reported an especially dangerous increase in alcoholism among women, with a consequent deterioration of family life. It is difficult to collect statistics because of increased migration within the country, which has further loosened social inhibitions on drinking as a result of the loss of traditional environments. Crime related to alcohol abuse has become common, and in 1978, 1,500 people died in traffic accidents, most of which involved alcohol. Heavy costs to the country in lowered productivity have been attributed to the susceptibility of economically depressed peoples to drunkenness and the availability of inexpensive home-brewed alcoholic beverages.

At present Kenya has no governmental commission on alcohol abuse and no legislation to promote prevention. Public education on alcoholism is limited to the activities of independent professors of medicine and sociology and the efforts of Catholic missionaries in the country.

Korsakoff's psychosis (syndrome, disease)   Named after Sergei Korsakoff (1854–1900), a Russian psychiatrist who founded the Moscow school of psychiatry and was the first to identify this form of psychosis in 1897. (The disease was officially named Korsakoff's psychosis at the 12th International Medical Congress in Moscow in 1897.)

Korsakoff's psychosis is primarily a mental disorder characterized by confusion, memory failure and a tendency to recite imaginary occurrences. Other symptoms include disorientation in time, emotional apathy and loss of insight, which prevents the patient from becoming aware of the disability. Patients are often moderately cheerful and noncomprehending. The disease usually affects only those who have been drinking steadily for years, although it has been known to appear in nonalcoholics suffering from severe nutritional deficiencies. Thiamine deficiency is suspected to be partly responsible. Treatment consists of nutritional supplements (see VITAMINS AND MINERALS), but Korsakoff's psychosis is usually irreversible. It is often preceded by WERNICKE'S ENCEPHALOPATHY and given the single designation Wernicke-Korsakoff syndrome.

L

lager   A light, foamy BEER brewed by means of BOTTOM FERMENTATION. The procedure utilizes a yeast that sinks to the bottom of the brewing vat and bubbles up through the liquid. The name "lager" is derived from the German *Lagern,* meaning "to rest," in reference to the yeast. Lager beer is usually aged several months in a cool place to clear it of sediment.

Lager beer was first brewed in Bavaria, and the process has remained the principal brewing method for German beers. Since that time it has also become the dominant process used by the American brewing industry. The first known lager brewery was started in Philadelphia some time prior to 1840. It initially served the German-American population of that city, but lager beers quickly became popular across the country and were the basis of the major American brewing industries established in Milwaukee and St. Louis. In the United States the influence of German lager beer has completely eclipsed that of English ALE.

labor   See EMPLOYEE ASSISTANCE PROGRAMS.

laudanum   Formerly any of various preparations of opium, laudanum is now a TINCTURE, or alcoholic solution, of opium. Before it was known to be addictive, it was used to treat a variety of disorders. Laudanum was first compounded by Paracelsus in the 16th century and used medicinally through the 19th century.

L-Dopa   Currently used in treating the crippling effects of Parkinson's disease, L-Dopa is under investigation as a possible counteractant to the effects of alcoholism. Researchers interested in developing AMETHYSTIC, or sobering, agents have been studying drugs that might reverse the acute effects of alcohol intoxication and thus stop or relieve the depression of CENTRAL NERVOUS SYSTEM function caused by consumption of alcohol. A study of nonalcoholic volunteers by Ronald L. Alkana and Ernest P. Noble investigated the potential of L-Dopa for reversing the effects of moderate doses of alcohol (0.8 grams of alcohol per kilogram of body weight). Treatment with L-Dopa significantly reduced alcohol's effects on coordination, maintenance of attention and brain functions as recorded on electroencephalograms. Use of the drug for treating alcohol-related problems is still very much in the experimental stage.

Ronald L. Alkana and Ernest P. Noble, "Amethystic Agents: Reversal of Acute Ethanol Intoxication in Humans," in *Biochemistry and Pharmacology of Ethanol,* vol. 2, ed. Edward Majchrowicz and Ernest P. Noble (New York: Plenum Press, 1979).

Ernest P. Noble, ed., *Third Special Report to the U.S. Congress on Alcohol and Health* (Rockville, Md.: National Institute on Alcohol Abuse and Alcoholism, 1978), p. 100.

legal aspects of alcohol abuse   Until recently the approach to alcohol abusers was to consider them or their behavior a criminal justice matter and to imprison them for PUBLIC DRUNKENNESS. This approach was not very successful; abusers often were repeatedly arrested with no improvement in their condition. Prior to 1971 the alcoholic population was estimated to account for one-third of all arrests excluding traffic violations.

In the last 15 years the criminal justice philosophy has been replaced by an approach that defines the problem in medical terms and calls for treatment and rehabilitation rather than incarceration. In 1971 the Uniform Alcoholism and Intoxication Treatment Act was adopted by the National Conference of Commissioners on Uniform State Laws. This act declares that alcoholics and intoxicated persons may not be subjected to criminal prosecution because of their consumption of alcoholic beverages but should instead be provided with appropriate treatment.

The major piece of social legislation dealing with problems of alcohol abuse and alcoholism is the Comprehensive Alcohol Abuse and Alcoholism Prevention, Treatment, and Rehabilitation Act of 1970, also known as the Hughes Act. This act created the NATIONAL INSTITUTE ON ALCOHOL ABUSE AND ALCOHOLISM (NIAAA) and was amended in 1973 to establish the Alcohol, Drug Abuse, and Mental Health Administration, of which NIAAA became a part.

Each state has its own particular set of laws concerning the legal drinking age, purchase and sale of alcoholic beverages, business hours for establishments that sell liquor etc. (See ALCOHOLIC BEVERAGE CONTROL LAWS.) States also determine their own regulations regarding DRIVING WHILE INTOXICATED.

National Institute on Alcohol Abuse and Alcoholism *Federal Activites on Alcohol Abuse and Alcoholism: FY 1977 Final Report* (Silver Spring, Md.: Marco Systems, 1978), pp. 4–6.

lesbians   See HOMOSEXUALS. See also WOMEN.

lethal dose   It is difficult to die from an overdose of alcohol, as people usually lose consciousness before they are able to drink themselves to death. For death to result, more than a quart of whiskey or its equivalent must be drunk in a short time. Cases of death have occurred during drinking contests.

At a BLOOD ALCOHOL CONCENTRATION of 0.4% a drinker usually becomes unconscious. Deep coma sets in at 0.5% and at 0.6% death may result from suppression of the nerve centers that control the heartbeat and breathing (see CENTRAL NERVOUS SYSTEM).

liqueur   An alcoholic beverage, usually from 35 to 60 proof, produced by combining a distilled spirit with strong flavorings and, in most cases, a sweetener. In the United States liqueurs are sometimes known as cordials, and in the United States and elsewhere they are often referred to as fruit brandies.

Today's liqueurs have in all likelihood evolved from the flavored wines popular in earlier times when fermentation processes were erratic and vintages sometimes scarcely potable. Liqueurs that were based on distilled spirits rather than on wines probably originated in Italy during the 15th century, and their present name derives from the Italian *liquori,* corrupted by later French usage. Benedictine, a liqueur that is still produced today, may have been made as early as 1510 in a monastery in Fecamp, France. Early liqueurs were produced exclusively by monasteries for their reputed medicinal powers. Monks in the Middle Ages were experienced herbalists, and it is likely that they switched from a wine base to a distilled spirit base in the hope of increasing the potency of their remedies.

The distilled spirit base of a liqueur and the flavoring additive are combined by one of two methods. The first is percolation, in which alcohol vapors are circulated through flavoring herbs, spices or fruit and then recondensed by cooling. The second is infusion, in which the flavoring additives are simply soaked in a distilled spirit and fil- tered out once the flavor has been absorbed. In either case the flavored distillate is gen- erally rectified for greater strength, sweet- ened, artificially colored and aged before being bottled for distribution.

Liqueurs are produced from virtually every combination of spirit and flavoring imaginable, and the precise ingredients and proportions in any given liqueur are usually a matter of long tradition and professional secrecy. The spirit bases vary according to country of origin, with France and Italy being known for grape brandy liqueurs, Scotland and Ireland for whiskey liqueurs, and many other countries for a variety of grain and potato spirit liqueurs. The flavor- ings used are even more varied, although the majority are natural produce, such as fruit and fruit rinds, herbs, spices, roots and even flowers used in combination with each other. The most common liqueurs are those flavored principally with oranges, strawber- ries, almonds or honey, all marketed under a number of different brand names.

liquor   The Latin term for liquidity in general. In its earliest English usages, the term "liquor" was used to refer to any mixed liquid, such as "meat liquor," or to any measured solution of a solid in liquid. It was only in the 17th century that the term came to be closely associated with spe- cifically alcoholic beverages. Its most com- mon usage today is in reference to those al- coholic beverages created by diluting a distilled spirit with water.

liver   The largest and most metaboli- cally complex organ, the liver has among its functions circulation, excretion, immunol- ogy and detoxification. Seventy-five percent of the blood carried to the liver comes from the intestinal tract through the portal cir- culatory system. The liver is therefore the first recipient of digested material, includ- ing alcohol, absorbed from this tract. It also receives blood from the hepatic artery that carries alcohol and other substances from the general circulatory system.

Unlike fats and carbohydrates, alcohol is not effectively oxidized in the tissues. Ninety percent of the alcohol in the system is rapidly absorbed from the gastrointes- tinal tract and must be oxidized in the liver. As a result the liver, more than any other organ, bears the brunt of alcohol's deleteri- ous effects. While alcohol is detoxified in the liver by oxidation (see METABOLISM), both alcohol and its metabolic products, es- pecially ACETALDEHYDE, can scar the liver and break down liver tissue. Because the liver has many functions, such as conversion of vitamins and foods into usable forms needed by other organs and tissues, produc- tion of enzymes and antibodies, and storage and release of sugar, damage to it adversely affects other parts of the body. (For diseases of the liver, see ALCOHOLIC LIVER DISEASE, ALCOHOLIC HEPATITIS, CIRRHOSIS, FATTY LIVER.)

London Dry Gin   See GIN.

loss of control   A major symptom of alcoholism, loss of control is an inability on the part of an alcoholic to choose consis- tently between drinking and not drinking. There are two types of loss of control: an inability to stop drinking once drinking has begun and an inability to refrain from start- ing to drink. Loss of control does not mean that every time an alcoholic takes a drink he or she will be unable to stop before get- ting drunk. The symptom appears only spo- radically. However, at certain times, the al- coholic, compelled by some unknown stimulus, is powerless to decide not to drink. The stimulus may be outside of the alco- holic's conscious awareness, and after a while alcohol itself may become the stimulus.

The unpredictable nature of this symp- tom has been used to bolster the concept of absolute ABSTINENCE for alcoholics, since there can be no loss of control if an alcoholic refrains from alcohol completely. There have been studies examining the possibility of CONTROLLED DRINKING for some alcoholics under certain conditions.

M

macronodular cirrhosis   A contemporary classification of a type of cirrhosis that is similar to postnecrotic cirrhosis (see CIRRHOSIS).

Madeira   The name given to any of several fortified wines made on Madeira, a Portuguese-owned island located in the Atlantic Ocean about 400 miles off the northwestern coast of Africa.

There are four basic types of Madeira: Malmsey, a very sweet dark brown wine that is usually drunk as a dessert wine; Bual (or Boal), a golden-brown wine that is only slightly less sweet than Malmsey and also drunk as a dessert wine; Verdelho, a golden wine that is less sweet than either Malmsey or Bual and drunk either with dessert or as an aperitif; and Sercial, a pale gold wine that is the driest of the four and is generally drunk as an aperitif. In addition to these four types there is a blend of different Sercial wines called Rainwater Madeira. The alcohol content of Madeira wines usually falls between approximately 18.5% and 19.5% by volume.

The wines made on Madeira are fortified with brandy, which is added during the fermentation process. The brandy serves to slow down and gradually halt fermentation. The longer the wine is allowed to ferment before the brandy is added, the drier it will be.

After fermentation is completed, the wine is subjected to a special heating process unique to the production of the Madeira wines. The fermented wine is placed in a heated chamber called an *estufa,* where its temperature is gradually raised to 140°F. It is held at this temperature for six weeks and then gradually reduced to normal. The process is intended to simulate the effects of a slow sea voyage through the tropics. Madeira wine has been subjected to this procedure since the 18th century, when it was discovered that such a voyage had actually improved the flavor of the wine.

Mallory-Weiss syndrome   A condition caused by frequent vomiting that results in laceration of the gastroesophageal junction and, in turn, massive hemorrhage. Many victims of the syndrome are alcoholics, as the local toxic and irritating effects of alcohol may result in frequent morning nausea and vomiting. The syndrome, however, is not restricted to alcoholics, and the bleeding may accompany any condition associated with frequent vomiting. Prognosis is excellent once the bleeding has been stopped, although surgery is usually necessary to stop the bleeding.

malt   A grain, almost invariably barley, steeped in water until it germinates, or "malts," and produces the soluble sugar maltose. It is then spread and dried to produce pure malt. Pure malt is a highly nutritive ingredient of certain nonalcoholic beverages and many cereal foods, but it has traditionally been used in brewing or distilling processes. In fact it is one of the oldest ingredients of alcoholic beverages, dating back to the ancient Egyptians, who used it to produce beer. Malted barley is found in nearly all lager, ale, stout, porter and bock beers. It is also mixed with other ingredients to make most types of whiskey. Some nearly 100% malt whiskey is produced in Scotland, but it is rarely consumed in this form.

The drying process for malt is especially

cially important, and several different methods of turning the malt during drying have been developed. In the traditional method drying is accomplished on a malting floor large enough to scatter the grain, which is turned with hand shovels to disperse the heat generated by germination and to speed the drying process. In the more modern Saladin technique the grain is strewn along troughs and turned by mechanical blades. Some malters employ a procedure known as the drum method, in which the grain is poured into barrels that can be rotated and ventilated with cool air.

Whatever method is used, malting is a very delicate process that continues for up to two weeks until the germinated sprout has reached the desired length.

malt beverage   A beerlike beverage made from MALT. Most malt beverages are about the same as NEAR BEER. Popular during Prohibition, they began to reappear in the 1970s as a refreshment for those who enjoyed the taste of beer but who did not want the effects of the alcohol in beer. For this reason malt beverages have enjoyed some popularity among alcoholics who no longer consume alcohol. (see also DE-ALCOHOLIZED BEVERAGE.)

malt liquor   An alcoholic beverage similar to BEER but with a higher alcohol content (6.5% to 7.0%).

Marchiafava-Bignami disease   This disease was first detected in Italy in 1903 by two pathologists, Ettore Marchiafava (1847–1935) and Amico Bignami (1862–1929), among heavy drinkers of wine. It mainly afflicts middle-aged alcoholic males, although only a few cases have been reported. The disease can take several months to develop. Symptoms include agitation, confusion, hallucinations, memory disturbances and disorientation. The exact causes of this disease are unknown, but it has been seen in conjunction with WERNICKE'S ENCEPHALOPATHY and ALCOHOL AMBLYOPIA and may be due to malnutrition.

marijuana with alcohol   A pattern of multiple drug use is common among those who use marijuana and other cannabinoids. The National Commission on Marijuana and Drug Abuse found that alcohol and tobacco were the two other substances most commonly used by regular marijuana smokers. Today alcohol seems to be replacing marijuana as the drug of choice among the young (under 21). (See also DRUGS.)

Massachusetts Society for the Suppression of Intemperance   One of the earliest temperance societies in America, founded in Andover in 1813. It was organized by a number of Calvinist ministers and included other prominent community members. They published a number of antialcohol tracts and spread their message around the country.

Mauritius   An island nation in the Indian Ocean east of Madagascar, Mauritius has a population of just over 1 million, including a sizable proportion of Europeans and Indians—28%. Significant proportions of the native population belong to Hindu or Moslem religious sects. Since most of these sects observe a prohibition on alcohol, an estimated 60% of the Mauritian people are considered total abstainers. Nevertheless a segment of the population consumes large quantities of alcohol, the production of which is entirely in private hands. Consumption in 1976 totaled over 11 million liters of beer and nearly 37 million liters of distilled spirits, primarily rum. On the basis of these figures and the estimated number of abstainers, authorities calculate that 15% of the population must be considered "heavy drinkers." Statistics also suggest that drinking is gaining greater acceptance among the Mauritian people as urbanization and modernization ease traditional religious and communal restrictions on drinking.

Economic and legislative controls on drinking habits are considered impractical in Mauritius because of the country's developing and presently precarious fiscal situation. Consequently inexpensive liquors are readily available, and the drinking of cheap rum, production of which doubled between 1972 and 1976, has become widespread. Officials also note that after-hours sales of alcoholic beverages are common because penalties, while strict, are rarely enforced. Excessive consumption of alcohol is especially prevalent among the nation's poorer classes. The average family, existing on less than $27 per month, spends an estimated 2% of its income on alcohol, and the proportion of income expended on alcohol rises with the amount of money available.

Reliable statistics on the extent of the country's alcoholism problem have not been compiled, and the limited number of health care facilities in Mauritius render preliminary figures inadequate. In 1977 only 325 cases of alcoholism and 11 cases of delirium tremens were recorded in the country's hospitals. A year later 255 cases of alcoholism and 32 cases of alcoholic psychosis were reported. In these two years, however, the number of first admissions to hospitals for alcoholism rose from 85 to 140. There were 224 cases of cirrhosis of the liver reported in 1977, and traffic accidents nearly doubled between 1971 and 1975, but the role of alcohol in these statistics has not yet been estimated. The rate of job absenteeism on Mondays and following public holidays is significant, and 5% to 10% of all job dismissals may be related to alcohol.

All efforts at prevention of alcoholism are voluntary and operate without state support. The government's Ministry of Youth and Ministry of Social Security have expressed interest in antialcohol and public education programs, but at present most prevention programs are run by local committees in communities near the capital of Port Louis. Mauritius has no restrictions on advertising of alcoholic beverages. The only controls on the production and distribution of alcohol are contained in the 1974 Excise Act.

mead   A beverage made of fermented honey, water and spices. Although it is often incorrectly identified as a kind of beer, mead is essentially a honey wine. It is considered to have been among the earliest alcoholic beverages developed by man, along with fermented fruit juice (wine) and fermented grains (beer). Little is known about the history of mead, but it has been especially associated with Anglo-Saxon and Teutonic cultures of the early Middle Ages. The name "mead" has also been used to refer to numerous other beverages, some not in any way related to honey and some nonalcoholic.

medication   Alcohol is a basic ingredient in many liquid medications (see COUGH MEDICINE.) Historically alcohol alone was used as a medicine; before the introduction of antibiotics, physicians prescribed small doses of whiskey for infants suffering from pneumonia. Today it is dispensed in some chronic disease wards as a sedative.

memory   Alcoholics and nonalcoholics alike commonly report an experience of impaired memory function after consumption of a large quantity of alcohol. While the effects of alcohol on memory have been studied, they are difficult to measure objectively because of such factors as the uniqueness of each person's memory and the difficulty of obtaining controls in studies; for example, there is no way to determine if a recovered alcoholic would have a better memory if he or she had never had a drink or how much better that memory would be.

Investigation of the relationship between alcohol and memory has centered on two areas. The first concern is to determine the impact on memory produced by the state of intoxication: how does the memory function during intoxication? The second aspect is to ascertain the long-term effects of chronic alcohol use on memory: are there different degrees of impairment for different levels of consumption? what aspects of memory are affected? is any of the damage reversible?

Among the factors that must be assessed when investigating the effects of intoxication are the dose size; the kind of memory impaired—recent or remote or both; the impact of rising or falling BLOOD ALCOHOL CONCENTRATION, if any; the effect on storage of information or the ability to recall information previously stored (retrieval); and the sex of the participant. When studying the impact of alcohol on memory over a long period of time, the duration of alcoholism as well as the age and sex of the subject must be considered.

Effects of Alcohol on Memory During a Period of Intoxication

Dose Size

For some kinds of memory function it appears that a greater amount of alcohol consumed in a sitting causes a correspondingly impairment of memory. Researchers Ben Morgan Jones and Marilyn K. Jones tested two groups, one of which was given a high dose of alcohol and the other a low dose, for immediate and short-term memory. To test immediate memory, subjects were given six lists of 12 words each and tested for immediate memory after each list. To test short-term memory the subjects were given five minutes to recall words from all six lists in any order. It was found that on the short-term memory test a high dose of alcohol (1.04 grams of ethanol per kilogram of body weight) caused a significantly greater level of impairment than a low dose (0.52 grams per kilogram). On the test of immediate memory, however, there were no

significant differences in the amount of impairment caused by high and low doses.

Rising or Falling Blood Alcohol Concentration

When someone has a drink, his or her blood alcohol concentration rises to a peak and then gradually falls off. A number of studies have found that the direction of the blood alcohol concentration (BAC), i.e., rising or falling, affects both behavior and psychology. Generally memory performance is more impaired by a rising BAC than by a falling BAC given the same amount of alcohol in the bloodstream. Jones and Jones studied the effects of rising and falling BACs on immediate and short-term memory (using the same tests described under dose size). They found that immediate memory experienced significantly greater impairment when BAC was rising than when it was falling. However, impairment of short-term memory, which on the whole was greater than that of immediate memory, appeared unrelated to either the rise or fall of the blood alcohol concentration.

Storage and Retrieval

When the mind receives information, it must first store it in the memory. Later, in order to use such information, the trace that has been stored must be searched for and found, a process known as retrieval. It is possible to have information stored in the memory that is not available for immediate retrieval; this is demonstrated by the "tip of the tongue" phenomenon—someone is sure he or she knows a fact but, at the moment, is unable to recall it. When an individual is able to remember something learned previously, it is assumed that first the information was consolidated in the storage process and that later it was searched for and retrieved. In the case of an individual who cannot recall information previously learned, researchers studying the affects of alcohol on memory must determine whether the storage or the retrieval phase of memory has been affected. Most researchers today agree that alcohol impairs the storage of information and not its retrieval. This conclusion is supported by the work of Isabel M. Birnbaun and Elizabeth S. Parker, who found that information previously learned in the sober state could be retrieved equally well under sober and intoxicated conditions. Furthermore the finding that immediate recall of events is less impaired than subsequent delayed retrieval of those events indicates that in an intoxicated state the formation of a permanent trace of an event (storage) is somehow disrupted.

Sex Difference

Jones and Jones report that males and females given equal doses of alcohol adjusted for body weight perform equally well on immediate memory tests, but that females experienced greater impairment than males on memory tests which required a delayed response. The researchers are continuing their study of this area.

Long-Term Affects of Alcohol Use

Many alcoholics, when they finally submit to treatment, complain of memory disturbances. It is known that prolonged overuse of alcohol affects the BRAIN. If alcoholism has reached the stage of diagnosable organic brain syndrome, memory disturbance is typically present; it is often one of the primary symptoms leading to such a diagnosis. The most notable example of such a state is KORSAKOFF'S PSYCHOSIS. In some alcoholics with this condition immediate memory of information is relatively unimpaired, but the same information appears to be inaccessible after even short periods of delay. Alcoholics with a history of 10 or more years of heavy drinking perform significantly worse on abstracting tasks than those with a history of less than 10 years of such drinking. Age appears to exacerbate the loss of memory by alcoholics—

those around age 50 perform considerably worse than those around 40 even when the duration of alcoholism is the same. Both age and alcoholism can result in failure of the cognitive system to process information in sufficient depth or with sufficient elaboration.

Jones and Jones found that drinking habits and age have an additive effect in female social drinkers. Alcohol had a significantly greater impact on the short-term memory scores of middle-aged women than on those of young women and on the scores of female moderate drinkers than on those of female light drinkers. These findings suggest that social drinking may lead to certain types of cognitive impairment which increase as a woman ages and as she drinks more alcohol.

For the alcoholic without severe brain damage there is often marked improvement of memory function after three or more weeks of abstinence, although this improvement does not generally reach the extent of non-drinking controls.

Blackout

Perhaps the most dramatic disturbance in memory function associated with alcoholism is BLACKOUT, a loss of memory by an individual for events during a period when he or she was completely conscious. About two-thirds of chronic alcoholics frequently experience blackouts while drinking; these generally occur midway or late in the course of alcoholism and rarely after the ingestion of moderate amounts of alcohol (Goodwin).

State Dependency

In some cases it has been reported that information learned in one state—either sober or intoxicated—is recalled better in that state than in the other state. This phenomenon is known as state dependency. State-dependent retrieval is demonstrated most readily using moderate doses of alcohol—high doses often produce severe retention deficits and low doses are not sufficient either to greatly inhibit or facilitate the memory process. State dependency has been under investigation only since the mid-1960s. There have been several reports of alcohol-related state dependency, but to date the findings are not consistent.

Isabel M. Birnbaum and Elizabeth S. Parker, "Acute Effects of Alcohol on Storage and Retrieval," *Alcohol and Human Memory,* ed. Isabel M. Birnbaum and Elizabeth S. Parker (New Jersey: Lawrence Erlbaum Associates, 1977), pp. 99–108.

Donald W. Goodwin "The Alcoholic Blackout and How to Prevent It," op. cit., pp. 177–183.

Ben Morgan Jones and Marilyn K. Jones, "Alcohol and Memory Impairment in Male and Female Social Drinkers," op. cit., pp. 127–138.

Ernest P. Noble, ed., *Third Special Report to the U.S. Congress on Alcohol and Health* (Rockville, Md.: National Institute on Alcohol Abuse and Alcoholism, 1978), p. 212.

Oscar A. Parsons and George P. Prigatano, "Memory Functioning in Alcoholics," op. cit., pp. 185–194.

metabolism   Once ingested, alcohol is absorbed into the bloodstream from the stomach, duodenum and gastrointestinal tract by a process of passive diffusion. It is then carried in the blood through the circulatory system from the digestive organs to the LIVER. The rest is excreted through sweat, saliva and breath. Unlike fat and most carbohydrates, which can be metabolized by almost all tissues, more than 90% of the alcohol absorbed into the body is metabolized in the liver, a process that accounts for many of the damaging effects alcohol can have on that organ.

The primary pathway of metabolism of ethyl alcohol (C_2H_5OH) consists of a series of reactions. The first reaction is catalyzed by the enzyme alcohol dehydrogenase, which removes two hydrogen atoms from each molecule of ethyl alcohol to form ACETALDEHYDE (CH_3CHO). Acetaldehyde is even more toxic to the body than ethyl alcohol before the enzyme catalysis, but it is quickly oxidized to form acetic acid (CH_3COOH), which is eventually converted to carbon dioxide (CO_2) and water (H_2O). (See formula below.)

A number of the metabolic effects of alcohol on the body are linked to the products of oxidation. One consequence of heavy alcohol consumption is a metabolic derangement called alcoholic ketoacidosis—the production of excess blood acidity. The excessive breakdown of fatty acids causes a buildup of the intermediate acidic products of the breakdown, which normally would be burned to carbon dioxide. These intermediate compounds back up into the bloodstream, increase blood acidity and produce toxic effects. Susceptibility to alcoholic ketoacidosis varies from individual to individual. It appears to be more prevalent in women than in men.

Another effect of alcohol is that the excess hydrogen given off in the first reaction upsets the liver cell's chemical balance. The cell must get rid of the excess hydrogen, and one way in which it does this involves the

---

METABOLISM OF ETHANOL

ETHANOL	ACETALDEHYDE	ACETIC ACID	

$$
\begin{array}{cccc}
\text{H} \quad \text{H} & \text{H} & \text{H} & \\
| \quad | & | & | & \\
\text{H—C—C—OH} \rightarrow & \text{H—C—C—O} \rightarrow & \text{H—C—C—O} \rightarrow & CO_2 + H_2O \\
| \quad | & | \quad | & | \quad | & \\
\text{H} \quad \text{H} & \text{H} \quad \text{H} & \text{H} \quad \text{OH} &
\end{array}
$$

formation of lipids (fats). The hydrogen is used in the synthesis of the precursors of the lipids that accumulate and result in alcoholic FATTY LIVER. In addition the liver uses the excess hydrogen from the alcohol as a fuel instead of fat that would normally be metabolized, again causing an accumulation of lipids leading to fatty liver.

The excess acetaldehyde produced in the reactions may have direct toxic effects on the liver. Acetaldehyde also affects the heart and other muscles and, possibly, the brain. Some researchers suggest that acetaldehyde may play a part in the development of DEPENDENCY.

A secondary metabolic pathway occurs at high levels of alcohol consumption. This pathway utilizes the microsomal system of structures within the cells, which also works to metabolize certain drugs. As a result alcohol competes with other drugs normally metabolized by this system, thereby delaying their metabolism and increasing their effect (see SYNERGY).

A figure frequently cited for the rate at which alcohol can be metabolized is 7 grams, or about ¾ of an ounce, of alcohol per hour for a man weighing 70 kilograms or 150 pounds (see BLOOD ALCOHOL CONCENTRATION). However, this rate can vary as much as ±50%. There is a widespread belief (if little hard evidence) that heavy drinkers can develop an increased metabolic rate and that in time the rate of metabolism for an alcoholic without liver disease may become double the average (see TOLERANCE). Nevertheless the rate of alcohol metabolism is decreased in those with liver disease (see LIVER, ALCOHOLIC LIVER DISEASE).

Charles S. Lieber, "The Metabolism of Alcohol," *Scientific American* 234, no. 3 (March 1976):25–33.

methadone with alcohol   It is a common but false belief that there is an absence of alcoholism among heroin addicts. People who consume large quantities of either alcohol or heroin have a tendency to use other drugs, and investigators have found a considerable amount of crossover between the use of these agents. Increasing evidence suggests a relationship between alcohol and opiate dependency and there may be a specific interaction between the two drugs. Studies reported by Dr. Barry Stimmel of the Mount Sinai School of Medicine in New York suggest that alcohol is the drug initially and most frequently abused before heroin is first used and before addiction occurs. In addition, when heroin or other opiates are not available, alcohol is the drug most often sought as a substitute to relieve symptoms of anxiety and discomfort brought on by withdrawal.

Methadone is an opium derivative that blocks the euphoric effects of heroin. In maintenance programs it is administered in controlled doses that allow the addict to function normally. Such programs are thought to help prevent the criminal activity through which addicts get money to buy heroin.

Figures on the prevalence of alcoholism among methadone-maintained addicts vary. For example, it has been estimated that 40% of such patients consume excessive amounts of alcohol and 5% are severe alcoholics (Bihari), but other estimates of the proportion of methadone patients who drink excessively have ranged from 12% to 40%. These rates, however, are no greater and may be even less than those for similar socioeconomic populations of nonaddicts. Alcoholism does not develop as a result of methadone maintenance. However, for persons on methadone maintenance the medical consequences of consuming large quantities of alcohol are considerable. The majority of heroin addicts have had an episode of viral hepatitis, and if such a pre-existing liver condition is aggravated by alcohol abuse, a rapid progression to FATTY LIVER or CIRRHOSIS may occur. In addition there is the danger of a significant increase in the depressant effects of alcohol when combined with methadone (see SYNERGY). Mortality rates are much higher for methadone patients who are also alcoholics than for those patients who are not alcoholics.

Alcoholism interferes with the rehabilitative process and may be responsible for the termination of methadone therapy. A methadone client suffering from alcoholism is likely to become aggressive and refuse to follow clinic rules. This refusal, and the complexities of his CROSS-ADDICTION, may lead to improper detoxification and premature discharge from the program.

Withdrawal from methadone does not necessarily alleviate alcoholism and, in fact, may have the opposite effect, especially if rehabiliatation has not progressed to a sufficient degree. After completion of detoxification, alcoholism appears to be the single most important obstacle preventing an individual from functioning well in society.

It is difficult, if not impossible, to refer alcoholic methadone patients for treatment because most alcoholism programs will not accept methadone-maintained patients. Therefore methadone programs must be geared toward recognizing alcoholism and treating it. Both psychological and biological tests can help identify the problem drinker as well as the potential problem drinker. Treatment should be geared to the individual's needs and the highest success has been achieved with patients who were offered a number of different treatment modes.

B. Bihari, "Alcoholism and Methadone Maintenance," *American Journal of Drug and Alcohol Abuse* 1 (1974): 79–89.
Barry Stimmel, "Methadone Maintenance and Alcohol Use," in *Drug and Alcohol Abuse: Implications for Treatment* (Rockville, Md.: National Institute on Drug Abuse, 1981).

methanol   Also known as methyl alcohol or wood alcohol, methanol is a colorless flammable liquid that can be mixed with water in all proportions. It is a fatal poison and, in small doses, may cause blindness. Because it is poisonous, it is sometimes used as a denaturant (see DENATURED ALCOHOL) for ethanol, making the latter unfit to drink. Methanol is often called wood alcohol because it was once produced chiefly as a by-product of the distillation of wood; today it is produced synthetically.

Many people have died from unknowingly drinking wood alcohol in bootleg whiskey or moonshine; others have died after knowingly consuming it because it is an alcohol and may initially have intoxicating effects.

methyl alcohol   See METHANOL.

micronodular cirrhosis   A contemporary classification of a type of cirrhosis that is similar to portal cirrhosis (see CIRRHOSIS).

minerals   See VITAMINS AND MINERALS.

Minnesota Multiphasic Personality Inventory   A test used in many studies to help define the alcoholic personality. It is scored on scales arranged in diagnostic categories—e.g., hysteria, depression etc. In general, studies indicate that alcoholics score high on the "psychopathic deviant" scale. This trait, however, is also found among other groups, such as criminals and heroin addicts, and does not appear to be unique to alcoholics. There is some question about how useful this test is for distinguishing a separate alcoholic personality.

mitochondria   The part of the cell that supplies the organism with energy by breaking down the chemical bonds in the molecules of complex nutrients.

mixed cirrhosis   Any combination of MICRONODULAR and MACRONODULAR CIRRHOSIS (see CIRRHOSIS).

mixing drinks   Contrary to popular belief, mixing, or changing, alcoholic beverages in the course of a drinking session does not in itself cause a HANGOVER. It is rather the alcohol content and concentration of the drinks consumed that are to blame. In addition the CONGENERS in the various beverages may intensify the hangover.

In some cases the order in which drinks are mixed produces a different effect. If beer, for instance, is taken before whiskey, the first alcohol entering the bloodstream (in the form of beer) has already been diluted and is therefore less potent. Beer takes up volume in the stomach, which slows the absorption of whiskey, diluting it and delaying its effects.

If whiskey is followed by beer, the effect is a concentrated rush of alcohol to the bloodstream, with the alcohol in the whiskey reinforced by the alcohol in the beer. This combination, known as a boilermaker, is more dangerous to the drinker and results in more rapid intoxication.

moderate drinking   Occasional drinking or a regular habit of drinking small amounts of alcohol, perhaps a drink or two; a level and frequency of drinking consistent with the pattern in the community and resulting in no pathological behavior or consequences. According to statistics published in the *Second Report to the U.S. Congress on Alcohol and Health* (1974), moderate drinkers, as a group, live longer than ex-drinkers, heavy drinkers or abstainers. (See ANSTIE'S LAW.)

moderation   See MODERATE DRINKING.

moonshine   Moonshine is the name given to corn whiskey that is not aged to any extent. It has the clear color and raw taste of pure alcohol, and its other name, "white lightning," is well merited. Moonshine dates back to the days when the government first started imposing taxes on whiskey — 1791. Distillers and private whiskey makers sought to avoid paying government taxes by producing whiskey secretly. They set up stills in out-of-the-way places and usually worked at night by moonlight. This illegal production became known as moonshining and the product was called moonshine.

Moonshining is still common in Tennessee, Kentucky, North Carolina and other parts of the rural South. Moonshine is said to be the preferred drink of some Americans and is now legally available in some areas. However, illegal manufacture continues. Some experts believe that even today between 10% and 20% of all whiskey consumed in the United States is illegally produced (Wilkinson). A major incentive for moonshining is the opportunity to make an extra profit by not paying customs and/or excise taxes. If the government increases taxes on legally produced liquor substantially to recoup the lost tax revenues, the public may rebel and encourage moonshiners.

John A. Ewing and Beatrice A. Rouse, "Drinks, Drinkers and Drinking" in *Drinking,* ed. Rouse and Ewing (Chicago: Nelson-Hall, 1978), pp. 12–13.

Rupert Wilkinson, *The Prevention of Drinking Problems* (New York: Oxford University Press, 1970), pp. 56–57.

morning drinking   A warning sign indicating the possibility of alcoholism.

mortality   Clinical research has shown that alcoholics and people admitted for treatment of alcohol problems have a higher mortality rate than that of the general population. The mortality rate for men with alcohol problems is two to six times higher than average for men.

There are two major causes of alcohol-related mortality. Alcohol is directly responsible for a number of DISEASES result-

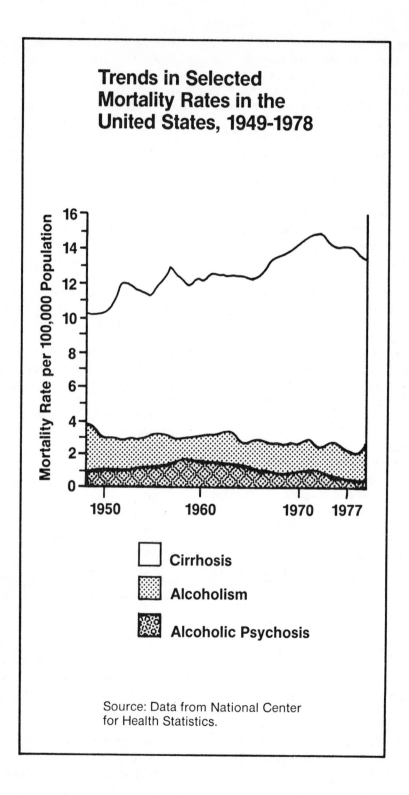

**Trends in Selected
Mortality Rates in the
United States, 1949-1978**

Cirrhosis

Alcoholism

Alcoholic Psychosis

Source: Data from National Center
for Health Statistics.

Death Rate from Alcohol-Related Diseases (and Diseases Affected by Alcohol Abuse) Per 100,000 Population in the United States (1900–1970)

Year	Hepa-titis	Malig-nant neo-plasms[1]	Diabe-tes mel-litus	Major cardio-vas-cular-renal diseases	Gas-tritis, duo-denitis, enteri-tis, and colitis[2]	Cirrho-sis of liver	Motor vehicle acci-dents[3]	Acci-dental falls	All other acci-dents[4]	Suicide
1970 ..	0.5	162.8	18.9	496.0	0.6	15.5	26.9	8.3	21.2	11.6
1969 ..	.5	160.0	19.1	501.7	.9	14.8	27.6	8.8	21.2	11.1
1968 ..	.4	159.4	19.2	512.1	.3	14.6	27.5	9.3	20.7	10.7
1967 ..	.4	157.2	17.7	511.5	3.8	14.1	26.7	10.2	20.2	10.8
1966 ..	.4	155.1	17.7	521.4	3.9	13.6	27.1	10.2	20.7	10.9
1965 ..	.4	153.5	17.1	516.4	4.1	12.8	25.4	10.3	20.1	11.1
1964 ..	.4	151.3	16.9	514.3	4.3	12.1	24.5	9.9	19.8	10.8
1963 ..	.5	151.3	17.2	527.3	4.4	11.9	23.1	10.2	20.1	11.0
1962 ..	.5	149.9	16.8	521.2	4.4	11.7	22.0	10.5	19.8	10.9
1961 ..	.5	149.4	16.4	511.4	4.3	11.3	20.8	10.2	19.4	10.4
1960[5]	.5	149.2	16.7	521.8	4.4	11.3	21.3	10.6	20.4	10.6
1959[6]	.5	147.3	15.9	515.9	4.4	10.9	21.5	10.6	20.1	10.6
1958 ..	.5	146.8	15.9	523.5	4.5	10.8	21.3	10.5	20.4	10.7
1957 ..	.5	148.6	16.0	523.4	4.7	11.3	22.7	12.1	21.1	9.8
1956 ..	.5	147.8	15.7	510.5	4.5	10.7	23.7	12.1	20.9	10.0
1955 ..	.5	146.5	15.5	506.0	4.7	10.2	23.4	12.3	21.2	10.2
1954 ..	.5	145.6	15.6	495.1	4.9	10.1	22.1	12.3	21.5	10.1
1953 ..	.5	144.7	16.3	514.8	5.4	10.4	24.0	13.0	23.1	10.1
1952 ..	.5	143.3	16.4	511.9	5.6	10.2	24.3	13.5	24.0	10.0
1951 ..	.4	140.5	16.3	513.2	5.2	9.8	24.1	13.9	24.5	10.4
1950 ..	.4	139.8	16.2	510.8	5.1	9.2	23.1	13.8	23.7	11.4
1949 ..	.4	138.8	16.9	502.1	6.7	9.2	21.3	15.0	24.3	11.4
1948 ..	....	134.9	26.4	488.0	6.0	11.3	22.1	16.6	28.2	11.2
1947 ..	....	132.3	26.2	491.0	5.6	10.4	22.8	16.7	29.7	11.5
1946 ..	....	130.0	24.8	476.8	5.8	9.6	23.9	16.1	29.8	11.5
1945 ..	....	134.0	26.5	508.2	8.7	9.5	21.2	17.7	33.2	11.2
1944 ..	....	128.8	26.3	500.5	9.9	8.6	18.3	17.0	36.0	10.0
1943 ..	....	124.3	27.1	510.8	9.6	9.3	17.7	18.0	37.7	10.2
1942 ..	....	122.0	25.4	479.5	8.8	9.4	21.1	16.6	33.5	12.0
1941 ..	....	120.1	25.4	475.3	10.5	8.9	30.0	16.7	29.2	12.8
1940 ..	....	120.3	26.6	485.7	10.3	8.6	26.2	17.2	29.8	14.4
1939 ..	....	117.5	25.5	466.3	11.6	8.3	24.7	17.5	28.1	14.1
1938 ..	....	114.9	23.9	456.8	14.3	8.3	25.1	19.5	27.2	15.3
1937 ..	....	112.4	23.7	454.6	14.7	8.5	30.8	20.4	30.0	15.0
1936 ..	....	111.4	23.7	461.1	16.4	8.3	29.7	20.8	34.9	14.3
1935 ..	....	108.2	22.3	431.2	14.1	7.9	28.6	19.2	30.1	14.3
1934 ..	....	106.4	22.2	430.0	18.4	7.7	28.6	18.8	32.0	14.9
1933 ..	....	102.3	21.4	413.6	17.3	7.4	25.0	15.1	31.8	15.9
1932 ..	....	102.3	22.0	418.2	16.1	7.2	23.6	14.8	32.4	17.4
1931 ..	....	99.0	20.4	407.1	20.5	7.4	27.1	14.6	36.1	16.8
1930 ..	....	97.4	19.1	414.4	26.0	7.2	26.7	14.7	38.4	15.6
1929 ..	....	95.8	18.8	418.9	23.3	7.2	25.5	14.5	39.7	13.9
1928 ..	....	95.7	19.0	419.1	26.4	7.5	23.2	14.1	40.8	13.5
1927 ..	....	95.2	17.4	398.3	27.1	7.4	21.6	14.0	41.5	13.2
1926 ..	....	94.6	17.9	410.6	32.9	7.2	19.9	14.0	43.3	12.6
1925 ..	....	92.0	16.8	391.5	38.6	7.2	16.8	13.4	46.3	12.0
1924 ..	....	90.4	16.4	383.4	33.7	7.3	15.3	13.1	45.4	11.9
1923 ..	....	88.4	17.7	380.8	39.1	7.1	14.6	12.8	46.9	11.5
1922 ..	....	86.2	18.3	366.6	38.9	7.4	12.4	12.1	43.8	11.7
1921 ..	....	85.5	16.7	351.2	50.7	7.3	11.3	11.4	44.1	12.4
1920	....	83.4	16.1	364.9	53.7	7.1	10.3	11.8	47.9	10.2

Death Rate from Alcohol-Related Diseases (and Diseases Affected by Alcohol Abuse) Per 100,000 Population in the United States (1900–1970) (*continued*)

Year	Hepa-titis	Malig-nant neo-plasms[1]	Diabe-tes mel-litus	Major cardio-vas-cular-renal diseases	Gas-tritis, duo-denitis, enteri-tis, and colitis[2]	Cirrho-sis of liver	Motor vehicle acci-dents[3]	Acci-dental falls	All other acci-dents[4]	Suicide
1919 ..	....	81.0	15.0	348.6	55.2	7.9	9.3	11.3	50.5	11.5
1918 ..	....	80.8	16.1	387.0	72.2	9.6	9.3	12.7	59.5	12.3
1917 ..	....	80.8	16.9	396.4	75.2	10.9	8.6	14.8	62.6	13.0
1916 ..	....	81.0	16.9	389.4	75.5	11.8	7.1	15.1	59.4	13.7
1915 ..	....	80.7	17.6	383.5	67.5	12.1	5.8	14.8	52.9	16.2
1914 ..	....	78.7	16.2	374.5	75.1	12.5	4.2	15.0	57.5	16.1
1913 ..	....	78.5	15.4	370.6	86.7	12.9	3.8	15.4	64.5	15.4
1912 ..	....	77.0	15.1	375.7	79.6	13.1	2.8	15.4	62.6	15.6
1911 ..	....	74.2	15.1	366.5	86.8	13.6	2.1	15.0	66.5	16.0
1910 ..	....	76.2	15.3	371.9	115.4	13.3	1.8	15.4	67.0	15.3
1909 ..	....	74.0	14.1	362.0	101.8	13.4	1.2	....	77.5	16.0
1908 ..	....	71.5	13.8	356.7	112.5	13.5	.8	....	82.1	16.8
1907 ..	....	71.4	14.2	389.8	115.0	14.8	.7	....	94.1	14.5
1906 ..	....	69.3	13.4	364.3	123.6	14.1	.4	....	94.0	12.8
1905 ..	....	73.4	14.1	384.0	118.4	14.0	....	....	81.3	13.5
1904 ..	....	71.5	14.2	388.8	111.5	13.9	....	....	85.4	12.2
1903 ..	....	70.0	12.7	364.4	100.3	13.5	....	....	81.4	11.3
1902 ..	....	66.3	11.7	349.8	104.9	13.0	....	....	72.5	10.3
1901 ..	....	66.4	11.6	347.7	118.5	13.1	....	....	83.8	10.4
1900 ..	....	· 64.0	11.0	345.2	142.7	12.5	....	....	72.3	10.2

[1]Includes neoplasms of lymphatic and hematopoietic tissues.

[2]All years, excludes diarrhea of newborn; 1900–20, includes ulcer of duodenum.

[3]1906–25, excludes automobile collisions with trains and streetcars and motorcycle accidents.

[4]1900–21, includes legal executions; 1900–08, food poisoning; and 1900–05, motor vehicle accidents.

[5]Includes Alaska.

[6]Denotes first year for which figures include Alaska and Hawaii.

Source: U.S. Bureau of the Census, *Historical Statistics of the United States: Colonial Times to 1970* (Washington, D.C., 1975).

ing in death; it is indirectly involved in deaths from ACCIDENTS and from aberrant behavior, such as SUICIDE and CRIME.

An increase in the CONSUMPTION level usually results in an increase in the number of individuals with diseases related to alcohol abuse and, consequently, an increase in mortality. This conclusion has been demonstrated by dramatic drops in deaths from cirrhosis during times of war or prohibition, when alcohol was not available.

Ernest P. Noble, ed., *Third Special Report to the U.S. Congress on Alcohol and Health,* (Rockville, Md.: National Institute on Alcohol Abuse and Alcoholism, 1978), pp. 17–20.

Mothers Against Drunk Driving (MADD)

A community action group organized to fight drunken driving, the organization was begun by Candy Lightner in 1979 after her daughter was killed by a drunk driver who had had five drunk driving arrests since 1976. MADD seeks to change the climate of acceptance and tolerance of the drunk driver and to change the response of the legal system toward drunk driving. It also serves as an advocate

Estimated Excess Male Deaths in 1975 Due to Frequent Heavy Drinking, by Major Cause

Cause of Death:	Relative Mortality Rate of Heavy Drinkers	Percentage of Excess Deaths	Number of Excess Deaths
All causes	2.13	100.00	31,269
Cancer of the upper digestive and respiratory organs	5.15	4.12	1,288
Cancer of the lung	2.11	4.03	1,260
Cancer of other digestive organs	1.00	0.00	0
Cancer of reproductive organs	2.64	1.74	544
Other cancers	0.36	−5.08	(1,588)
Alcoholism	24.63	8.08	2,527
Vascular lesions of the central nervous system	1.32	2.21	691
Arteriosclerotic and degenerative heart disease	1.90	31.22	9,762
Pneumonia	3.44	4.89	1,529
Cirrhosis of the liver	12.71	15.99	5,000
Stomach and duodenal ulcer	3.67	2.60	813
Accidental falls	5.77	3.80	1,188
Accidental poisoning	14.71	4.76	1,488
Accidents caused by fire	9.70	2.98	932
Motor vehicle accidents	1.45	1.34	419
Other accidents	1.65	1.71	535
Suicide	6.17	10.91	3,411
Other causes	1.30	4.70	1,470

Sources: Relative mortality rates and percentage of excess deaths are derived from data in W. Schmidt and J. deLint, "The Mortality of Alcoholic People," *Alcohol Health and Research World*, DHEW Publication No. (NIH) 74–652 (Washington, D.C.: U.S. Government Printing Office, 1973), pp. 16–20.

for those who have been victimized by drunk drivers. Its headquarters is in Fair Oaks, Calif.

mouthwash   Many mouthwashes contain a high percentage of alcohol, as high as 26.9% (Listerine); most hard liquor—gin, vodka, whiskey—is about 40% alcohol, and wine generally contains about 12% alcohol.

While mouthwash containing alcohol has potential for abuse, the main danger posed by such products is that an alcoholic using one of them legitimately may develop a CRAVING for more. Also those who are taking ANTABUSE may have a reaction to the alcohol.

Mouthwashes with High Alcohol Content

Brand	% of alcohol
Cepacol	14.0
Listerine	26.9
Scope	18.5
Signal	15.5

muscle, noncardiac   See ALCOHOLIC MUSCLE DISEASE.

N

National Institute on Alcohol Abuse and Alcoholism (NIAAA) The NIAAA (established in 1971) predates the Alcohol, Drug Abuse, and Mental Health Administration (ADAMHA), of which it is a component institute. It is charged with providing

> leadership, policies, and goals for the Federal effort in the prevention, control, and treatment of alcohol abuse and alcoholism and the rehabilitation of affected individuals. In carrying out these responsibilities the Institute conducts and supports research on the biological, psychological, sociological, and epidemiological aspects of alcohol abuse and alcoholism; supports the training of professional and paraprofessional personnel in prevention, treatment, and control of alcoholism; conducts and supports research on the development and improvement of alcoholism services delivery, administration, and financing, and supports alcoholism services programs and projects, including facilities construction as appropriate; collaborates with and provides technical assistance to State authorities and Regional offices, and supports State and community efforts in planning, establishing, maintaining, coordinating and evaluating more effective alcohol abuse and alcoholism programs; collaborates with, provides assistance to, and encourages other Federal agencies, national, foreign, State, and local organizations, hospitals, and voluntary groups to facilitate and expand programs for the prevention of alcohol abuse and alcoholism, and for the care, treatment, and rehabilitation of alcoholic persons; develops, implements, and administers an alcoholism detection, referral, and treatment program for Federal civilian employees within the Public Health Service; carries out administrative and financial management, policy development, planning and evaluation,

and public information functions which are required to implement such programs.

(United States Government Manual, 1979–1980.)

As part of its information program, the NIAAA has published four special reports to the U.S. Congress on alcohol and health:

The *First Special Report to the U.S. Congress on Alcohol and Health* (1971) "broadly described historical and contemporary alcohol uses and abuses, the causes of alcoholism, and treatment methods. Effects of alcohol on the nervous system, and the legal status of intoxication and alcoholism were discussed in detail."

The *Second Special Report to the U.S. Congress on Alcohol and Health* (1974) "focused on the advances in knowledge gained in the interim between the two reports and supplemented the first volume with discussions of health consequences and of alcohol use among adults, young people, and the elderly."

The *Third Special Report to the U.S. Congress on Alcohol and Health* (1978) "incorporates the most significant findings of recent research in the field of alcoholism. The findings are described in extensive detail in the *Technical Report in Support of the Third Special Report*." It includes references as well as additional data and discussion.

The *Fourth Special Report to the U.S. Congress on Alcohol and Health* (1981) "is concerned largely with new information that has been developed since publication of the *Third Report*" and "is an attempt to update information ... [but] is not intended to serve as a comprehensive historical review of the literature."

The NIAAA has also funded various research projects in the field. Perhaps the best known, and most controversial, is an ongoing study, conducted by the Rand Corporation, designed "to assess the nature of treatment outcomes." The findings of this

study have been published in the RAND RE-
PORT and RAND REPORT II.

National Institute on Drug Abuse
(NIDA)
NIDA is a component insti-
tute (established in 1972) of the Alcohol,
Drug Abuse, and Mental Health Administration (ADAMHA), which is charged
with providing "leadership, policies, and
goals for the Federal effort in the prevention, control, and treatment of narcotic addiction and drug abuse, and the rehabilitation of affected individuals." *(United States
Government Manual, 1979–1980.)* Its man-
date is much the same as that of the NA-
TIONAL INSTITUTE ON ALCOHOL ABUSE AND
ALCOHOLISM.

National Prohibition Act
See VOL-
STEAD ACT.

National Temperance League
A
British TEMPERANCE organization.

near beer   Beer with an alcoholic content of less than 0.5%. Near beer is not considered an alcoholic beverage either for purposes of taxation or for the regulation of
sale or consumption. During PROHIBITION
much near beer was manufactured and
sold, but because of its weakness or poor
quality or both, it was generally ridiculed
even by those who drank it. When Prohibi-
bition ended, near beer all but disappeared
until the 1970s, when it surfaced under a
new and less objectionable name: MALT BEV-
ERAGE. (See also DE-ALCOHOLIZED BE-
VERAGE.)

Netherlands, The   Alcohol has an
important place in the life style of most
Dutch citizens. Proportionately, drinkers in
the country make up 93% of the male population and 82% of the female population.
Even more striking is the fact that only 3%
of the population recommends abstinence

from alcoholic beverages and that an overwhelming majority approve of drinking by
adolescents when they reach the legal age
of 16 years. One reason why alcohol use is
so widely accepted is because there is little
obvious evidence of alcohol abuse in the
Netherlands. More than two-thirds of the
nation's total consumption takes place in
the home, where familial restrictions are an
effective control. Although some consumption of alcohol is widespread, less than one-
quarter of the population drinks daily.
Nevertheless increases in problems associated with alcohol prompted a governmental
inquiry in 1975 that was intended to lay the
groundwork for the country's first official
policy on alcohol.

There is no appreciable production of illegal alcoholic beverages in the Netherlands. Of commercial alcoholic beverages
beer is preferred by a vast majority of the
country's drinkers. Computed as ABSOLUTE
ALCOHOL, the per capita amount of alcoholic beverages available for the entire population in 1977 was 83.9 liters of beer, 11.7
liters of wine and 2.9 liters of distilled spirits. Per capita consumption of alcoholic beverages, computed as absolute alcohol, by
the population over 15 years of age in 1977
was 111.8 liters of beer, 15.5 liters of wine
and 3.85 liters of distilled spirits. The number of "heavy drinkers," defined as those
who drink more than 6 glasses of beer at a
sitting, is only slightly higher in the 19 to
24-year-old bracket than in all other age
groups.

Hospital admissions for alcohol-related
problems numbered 2,357 in 1975, up from
1,724 in 1973. The 1975 figures included
236 cases of delirium tremens and 291 cases
of other alcohol psychoses. The rate of mortality from liver cirrhosis in 1976 was 18.4
males and 7.6 females per 100,000 population. A problem of greater national concern
is abuse of other drugs aggravated by
alcohol.

Until an official body is created to over-
see the government's as yet undetermined

policy, efforts aimed at the prevention and treatment of alcohol-related problems in the Netherlands will remain in the hands of various private agencies. The principal agencies are the National Commission against Alcoholism, a temperance organization, and *Federatie van Instellingen voor Alcohol an Drugs,* the national service group created to assist treatment facilities operated by a variety of community organizations. There are indications that a number of additional programs are forthcoming from nationalized industries, law enforcement groups and medical associations.

New Zealand   Alcoholism is recognized as one of New Zealand's major public health problems, and since the late 1970s the government has become more actively involved in passing legislation aimed at preventing alcohol abuse. The pattern of drinking in New Zealand is one of excessive consumption, usually of beer, in homes and clubs. Fully half the country's alcohol consumption takes place in such private residences and facilities, which are not liable to normal legislative restrictions. A problem related to this high proportion of alcohol consumption in private places is that of adolescent access to alcohol, which is facilitated by a lack of necessary supervision. New Zealand's Alcohol Liquor Advisory Council, created in 1976, cites ignorance of the dangers of excessive consumption among the important factors contributing to the country's drinking problems. The council also notes that prices of alcohol have not risen as quickly as other items in the general consumer price index, making the cost of liquor too low to act as a curb on the country's acknowledged drinking problem.

Surveys have estimated that there are 50,000 "chronic alcoholics" among New Zealand's population of just over 3 million, or about one alcoholic per 60 citizens. These surveys distinguish between "chronic alcoholics" and "excessive drinkers," who are

Per Capita Consumption of Alcoholic Beverages in Liters per Year

Year	Beer	Wine	Distilled Spirits
1940	51	0.9	1.2
1950	85	2.1	2.2
1960	100	2.1	2.4
1970	117	5.6	2.5
1977	131	10.3	4.7

Source: New Zealand Department of Statistics.

estimated to number another 200,000. Per capita consumption, which the government considers proportionate to social and medical problems related to alcohol, has been rising for some time; from 1965 to 1975 annual per capita consumption of ABSOLUTE ALCOHOL in New Zealand rose from 5.8 to 8.4 liters. From 1970 to 1977 per capita consumption of distilled spirits rose from 2.5 to 4.7 liters per year, accompanied by sharp increases in consumption of beer. Given this trend, it is not surprising that in its 1977 statement on budget policy the government expressed concern over the public expenditures for medical care, hospitalization, crime, police, social welfare and accident compensation related to alcohol. The next year saw the nation's first recorded drop in the total amount of alcoholic beverages sold: from 405.4 million liters of beer in 1977, for example, to 366.5 million liters

Per Capita Consumption of Absolute Alcohol in Liters per Year

Year	Beer	Wine	Distilled Spirits	Total
1955	4.0	0.3	1.2	5.4
1965	4.2	0.4	1.2	5.8
1975	5.4	1.2	1.8	8.4
1976	5.2	1.4	2.0	8.5
1977	5.3	1.5	2.0	8.8

Source: New Zealand Alcoholic Liquor Advisory Council.

in 1978. Similar decreases were recorded in sales of table wines, fortified wines and distilled spirits.

The social costs of alcoholism in New Zealand are indicated by the fact that 45% of all fatal traffic accidents in 1977 were related to alcohol abuse. In addition alcohol-related problems are the second leading diagnosis among the country's psychiatric hospital admissions, with a slightly lower number of cases than depressive neurosis. As in other countries, most of these alcohol-related cases are readmissions.

Hospital admissions related to alcoholism are a poor indication of the country's drinking problems, however, because of the country's acknowledged need for new clinics, too heavy reliance on untrained volunteers to cope with alcoholism and lack of even a single supervised detoxification unit. The only existing efforts to control alcoholism in New Zealand are indirect preventative measures that target the potential rather than the existing problem drinker. These include recent revision of regulations on the sale and public consumption of alcohol, stricter enforcement of drunk driving laws and new restrictions on advertisement of alcoholic beverages.

NIAAA   See NATIONAL INSTITUTE ON ALCOHOL ABUSE AND ALCOHOLISM.

nicotine   See SMOKING.

NIDA   See NATIONAL INSTITUTE ON DRUG ABUSE.

Nigeria   The most populous country in Africa, Nigeria has lately experienced a period of relative economic well-being, based on oil and natural gas production, that brought with it an increase in the manufacture and consumption of alcoholic beverages, particularly beer. An already well-established permissive attitude toward consumption of alcoholic beverages has resulted in greater alcohol abuse. Drinking

and even drunkenness are generally tolerated, and both social and familial gatherings are now considered incomplete without alcohol. Representatives of the older tribal society, such as traditional "healers," now commonly incorporate alcohol into their functions. The general pattern is one of heavy consumption, with the unusual feature of virtually indistinguishable drinking habits among both adolescents and adults. Consumption is high during both traditional festivals and nontraditional holidays; the heaviest consumption of all is commonly on nontraditional occasions among skilled laborers, such as factory workers. This rising consumption of alcoholic beverages has completely outpaced any governmental efforts or mechanisms to control alcohol-related problems.

The preferred alcoholic beverage in Nigeria is beer, including various kinds of stout. There are eight breweries in the country, five of which are controlled by the government and the other three by private concerns. The availability of beer has varied with the fortunes of the country's governments and military regimes, which have affected importation. Imports of beer rose from 1.3 million liters in 1970 to 132 million liters in 1976 and then fell to 62.6 million liters in 1977, when an almost equal amount of distilled spirits, about 66 million liters, was imported. There are no prohibitions on home brewing and distilling in Nigeria, and enormous quantities of palm wine are fermented from local trees across the country. This beverage is also distilled into native gin in large quantities. Thus availability of alcoholic beverages is so widespread that it is difficult to measure precisely.

The Nigerian government has acknowledged alcoholism as a major medical problem, but the country has no mechanism for documenting the extent of it. Not a single death was officially attributed to alcoholism in 1977 despite obvious evidence to the contrary. Limited hospital facilities and a general reluctance to contact those that exist render statistics on alcohol-related clinical admissions completely inadequate; for example, two such admissions were recorded in 1977. Similarly the country maintains no police records on traffic fatalities or incidents of public disorders related to alcohol. Most sources, however, completely agree on the widespread and increasing prevalence of alcoholic psychosis, delirium tremens, and gastric and malnutrition problems related to alcohol.

Despite its acknowledgment as a medical problem in Nigeria, alcoholism has been given a low priority because of the country's other problems, and there is no specific government agency established to address alcohol abuse. Furthermore there are no controls on advertising of alcoholic beverages, no restrictions on hours of sale or sale to minors and no maximum BLOOD ALCOHOL CONCENTRATION level for drivers. The Ministry of Health's efforts to combat Nigeria's worsening alcohol problems are limited to "moral instruction," as are the efforts of such voluntary organizations as the Christian Youth Fellowships. It appears that this situation is unlikely to change in the near future.

nonaddictive alcoholic   See NON-ADDICTIVE PATHOLOGICAL DRINKER.

nonaddictive pathological drinker Someone who drinks excessively as a way of handling unconscious problems and who is in some way impaired by this drinking but who does not have the same overwhelming need or compulsion or LOSS OF CONTROL characteristic of alcohol ADDICTION.

Norway   As reported by Norway's Central Bureau of Statistics, the country's per capita consumption of ABSOLUTE ALCOHOL in 1977 was 5.74 liters for the population aged 15 and over. Although the level of consumption in Norway is substantially

lower than in many other European countries, such as FRANCE and WEST GERMANY, the amount of alcohol consumed has nevertheless been increasing each year. Indeed, according to a 1979 report in *News of Norway,* the consumption level rose by approximately 156% between 1955 and 1979. In addition, during the same 24-year period, the average age of the heaviest drinkers decreased from just under 40 to between 18 and 20.

Marguerite Ingels, in an article entitled "Alcohol: A Cause for Concern," reported that the increased use of alcohol in Norway has had a number of effects. Among them are a marked rise in the number of alcohol-related deaths and traffic accidents, in admissions to hospitals and psychiatric clinics and crimes committed while under the influence of alcohol. In 1977 the number of work days lost due to alcohol abuse is estimated to have cost Norway 2 billion kroner (about $3.9 million). Other effects of alcohol abuse on industry include inefficiency, accidents and lower productivity.

According to Ingels, poverty and unemployment can no longer be considered the main underlying causes of alcohol abuse, because at present few Norwegians can be said to live below the poverty line. However, Ingels offers no other explanations for Norway's rising consumption of alcohol.

Norway has one of the most stringent approaches to drunk driving in the world. Police conduct spot tests on motorists regularly, and drivers have come to expect them about once a month. Any driver found with a BLOOD ALCOHOL CONCENTRATION of 0.05% or more is required to serve a minimum prison sentence of three weeks. In addition a judge may extend the sentence and impose a fine at his discretion in certain cases the judge may substitute a fine for the prison term. Any person convicted of drunk driving will also have his license suspended for at least a year and sometimes permanently.

Insurance regulations in Norway penalize drunk driving too. If a person causes an accident while drunk, he receives no compensation. Furthermore no insurance is paid to his estate if the accident is fatal.

Norway's severe penalties for drunk driving have been effective in curtailing accidents and discouraging people from driving under the influence of alcohol. Detailed studies, financed by the government, from 1970 through 1972 found that only 2.8% of all drivers stopped had any measurable blood alcohol concentration.

One way in which the Norwegian government has attempted to control the rise in alcohol consumption is through advertising. In 1975 the *Storting* (Parliament) passed a bill banning the advertising of alcoholic beverages in the print media, which became effective immediately. Another part of the same bill concerning other forms of alcohol advertising, such as neon signs, was supposed to go into effect at a later date.

In 1980 the Norwegian government proposed over 30 measures to reduce the consumption of alcohol by providing information, altering licensing and pricing policies and creating a greater awareness of the alcohol problem. The measures proposed included a ban on wine making in the home, a complete ban on strong beers (5.5% alcohol content), a lowering of the alcohol content in mild beers (from 4.7% to 3.5%), and stricter control of all these areas by police, customs officers and licensing authorities.

According to available information, it seems that almost all cases involving alcohol abuse are handled by Temperance Committees. Under the Act concerning Temperance Committees and the Treatment of Alcohol Addicts passed in 1932, a Temperance Committee was set up in almost every municipality. In municipalities where there is no temperance committee, a Social Welfare Board serves the same purpose.

The Temperance Committees have four main functions: to take care of persons who abuse alcohol, where necessary making de-

cisions about their possible committal to hospitals or sanatoria; to give advice and assistance to the families of alcohol abusers; to promote education and information concerning the use and abuse of alcohol in schools and other areas of life; and to submit proposals and recommendations to municipal authorities for implementing committee programs.

With respect to the individual alcohol abuser, a Temperance Committee may act either at the request of someone functioning on behalf of the abuser or on its own initiative. According to a 1978 report compiled by the Central Bureau of Statistics, the possible courses of action open to Temperance Committees are counseling, ANTABUSE treatment, selection of a person to support a discharged alcoholic patient, suggestion that an alcoholic join a temperance society and imposition of restrictions on the way an alcoholic spends his wages.

The bureau's statistical report lists the following types of institutions where treatment may be obtained.

1. detoxification stations
2. sections for medical treatment
3. A-clinics
4. sanatoria
5. supervision homes
6. protection homes
7. psychiatric clinics and hospitals

These institutions may be owned either by the central government or by private concerns licensed by the government.

There is very little information available concerning the specific nature of treatment for alcoholics offered at various institutions in Norway. The traditional institutions for the care of alcoholics are sanatoria. In 1973 there were 20 sanatoria, to which 2,911 patients were admitted. The sanatoria are financed by the Health Insurance Fund which covers 100% of the operational costs.

A-clinics are generally run by private organizations. Patients are admitted on the same basis as in ordinary hospitals. These

A-clinics are financed according to the regulations of the Hospital Act.

Many patients discharged from sanatoria and A-clinics are placed in supervision homes. In such homes patients live and receive treatment while working. Supervision homes that are connected with A-clinics are also financed under the Hospital Act. Those that are not attached to A-clinics are financed in part by the National Insurance Fund and in part by either a municipality, if it referred the patient, or by the patient himself.

Protection homes are for those patients who have been judged not capable of being rehabilitated to working life. The financing of these homes is somewhat similar to that of the supervision homes which are not attached to A-clinics.

nutrition   Unlike other drugs, alcohol has a high caloric value. A gram of alcohol provides 7.1 calories, compared with 4 calories provided by a gram of carbohydrates and 9 calories provided by a gram of fat. Twenty ounces, slightly more than one pint, of an 86-proof beverage contains about 1,500 calories, or from one-half to two-thirds of a person's normal daily caloric requirement. While a small dose of alcohol may stimulate the appetite, a larger intake often diminishes appetite. Alcoholics are likely to devote more time and energy to drinking than eating, and since alcohol contains no proteins, vitamins or minerals, an individual who consumes large quantities of it in place of other food is likely to receive insufficient amounts of the essential nutrients. The calories in alcohol may provide energy but cannot be stored for future use. They also do not aid in building body tissue, as do carbohydrates, fats and proteins. As a result alcoholics often suffer from malnutrition in addition to the directly damaging effects of alcohol itself.

Heavy consumption of alcohol causes inflammation of the stomach, pancreas and intestine, which can impair the digestion of food and the absorption of nutrients into the blood, increasing malnutrition. Alcohol inhibits the transport of nutrients to the GASTROINTESTINAL TRACT and adversely affects nutrient absorption even when a balanced diet is maintained. Alcoholics exhibit poor absorption of a number of essential nutrients, including vitamins B_1 and B_{12}. Malnutrition can in turn cause a sluggish intestine.

Alcohol may also interfere with the activation of vitamins by the liver cells (see VITAMINS AND MINERALS), often resulting in deficiency diseases. Vitamin deficiencies, such as zinc or thiamine deficiency, common in alcoholics, may contribute to a decreased desire for food. Malnutrition can play a role in the LIVER damage associated with alcoholism, although a heavy drinker who is well nourished can also develop liver disease. A low fat diet, however, may have some effect in the prevention of a FATTY LIVER. A study conducted by Charles S. Leiber and N. Spritz showed that for a given alcohol intake there was more abnormal fat formation on the liver with a diet of normal fat content than with a diet low in fat (see ALCOHOLIC LIVER DISEASE). There is some evidence that the development of CANCER may also be influenced by the direct consequences of alcoholism resulting from malnutrition. Deficiencies of various vitamins and minerals associated with alcoholism may play a role in carcinogenesis.

Some researchers have theorized that vitamin deficiencies play a role in the initial development of alcoholism. So far, however, there is little proof of this theory, and most nutritional deficiencies in alcoholics appear to be a result of the disease rather than the cause.

Nutrition also plays an important role in the rate that alcohol is absorbed into the body tissues and blood (see BLOOD ALCOHOL CONCENTRATION). Two factors are involved: the quantity and the type of food in the stomach. Alcohol is absorbed rapidly from an empty stomach and more slowly from a full stomach. A high-carbohydrate meal has been shown to reduce alcohol absorption more than a high-fat or high-protein meal. In addition different alcoholic beverages are absorbed at different rates, perhaps because of ingredients other than alcohol.

In the treatment of alcoholism, nutrition plays an important role. For treatment of cirrhosis and other liver diseases, a high-protein diet and massive amounts of B vitamins are prescribed. Regularly scheduled meals, especially breakfast, are important for an alcoholic because the lowering of blood sugar at any time of day increases the desire for alcohol. An alcoholic who is properly nourished may find it easier to abstain from alcohol, although good nutrition in itself is not a cure for alcoholism.

Beer and wine contain some carbohydrates and vitamins, but distilled spirits have none. (See Table 43, Appendix 1.) Drinkers often fail to account for the high caloric value of all alcoholic beverages.

Daphne A. Roe, *Alcohol and the Diet* (Westport, Conn.: AVI Publishing Company, 1979), passim.

O

oral fixation   A psychoanalytic theory on the cause of alcoholism. According to this theory, trauma affects the infant in the earliest stage of psychosexual development, a time when his sole means of achieving security and release from tension is through stimulation of the oral cavity. During this stage the child feels ominpotent and through his mouth he is given sustenance and expresses there his love and hate. However, as a result of an absent or uncaring mother, the infant is deprived of a warm relationship with a mother figure and subse-

quently continues to seek gratification of his primary emotional hunger. There is fixation at this oral stage of development and an unconscious desire for warmth and nurturance that cannot be satisfied in normal interpersonal relationships. As the infant seeks through ingestion to fill his emptiness so does the alcoholic. Alcohol is a liquid nourishment that generates a sensation of warmth and satisfaction. The alcoholic's feelings of anger and rage at his parents, who failed him, coupled with an intense fear of losing them and a need to obtain some sort of gratification cause him to redirect his rage from his parents (or later other people who cannot meet his excessive needs) to himself, and so he consumes his rage in alcohol.

David J. Armor, J. Michael Polich and Harriet B. Stambul, *Alcoholism and Treatment* (New York: John Wiley and Sons, 1978), p. 17.
Morris E. Chafetz and Harold W. Demone, Jr., *Alcoholism and Society* (New York: Oxford University Press, 1962), pp. 21–25, 220–223.

Order of Good Templars   The first international TEMPERANCE organization, the Order of Good Templars, began in 1851 in Utica, N.Y. Started by a society of abstainers, it spread throughout the United States and Canada, and in 1868 it was introduced into Britain. Some years later the organization emerged in Scandinavian and other countries. The first international conference was held in 1885 in Antwerp, Belgium.

Oxford Group   Originally called The First Century Christian Fellowship, the Oxford Group was founded in 1908 by Frank Buchman. Its popularity under the name the "Oxford Group"—from Buchman's preaching among the students at Oxford—peaked in the late 1920s and early 1930s. It was a nondenominational, theologically conservative, evangelical attempt to recapture the spirit of what its members understood to be primitive Christianity.

Bill Wilson, founder of ALCOHOLICS ANONYMOUS, became familiar with the Oxford Group while he was still drinking. He included a number of its principles, such as self-survey, confession, restitution and giving of oneself in service to others, in the philosophy of AA.

P

pancreas   A flat glandular organ situated below and behind the stomach and connected to the small intestine at the duodenum (where the stomach ends and the small intestine begins). The pancreas secretes a clear fluid, called pancreatic juice, that contains three important digestive enzymes which complete the digestion of proteins, carbohydrates and fats. It also secretes two hormones—insulin and glucagon—that regulate the level of glucose in the blood. Failure of the insulin-secreting cells to function properly results in DIABETES.

The association between alcoholism and pancreatic disease is well established. Alcoholics often experience acute pancreatitis after heavy drinking bouts, and the incidence of alcoholism in patients with pancreatitis is high. In alcoholics pancreatitis is usually preceded by episodes of abdominal pain following heavy drinking, although in some cases no preceding pain occurs.

Pancreatitis may be caused by a dual effect produced by consumption of alcohol, which simultaneously stimulates pancreatic secretion and obstructs pancreatic outflow. The increased pressure on the ducts of the pancreas results in pancreatic tissue swelling, and, in severe cases, cell death. The exact mechanism behind these effects is still unknown.

Pancreatitis is classified as either chronic or acute. In patients with acute pancreatitis, pancreatic functioning returns to normal and symptoms disappear when the causes are removed. In those with chronic pancreatitis, or chronic relapsing, functional and anatomic changes remain even if the causes are removed. Protein plugs obstruct the smaller ducts of the pancreas and result in distal dilation of the ducts. Scarring occurs initially at the site of the plug and then spreads. Chronic pancreatitis is associated with a number of symptoms, including abdominal pain, nausea, vomiting, diabetes mellitus and digestive disturbances. In milder cases abstinence from alcohol and a low-fat diet may be all the treatment required. Malnutrition may also play a role in the development of pancreatitis (see NUTRITION).

pancreatitis   Inflammation of the PANCREAS.

para-alcoholic   Often referred to as a co-alcoholic, a para-alcoholic is anyone who has an ongoing close relationship with an alcoholic, such as a spouse, a parent, a brother or sister or even an employer.

It is recognized today that the persons directly involved with an alcoholic can be victims of the disease and its damaging effects. When the relationship is examined, the para-alcoholic will often find that his or her needs are being served in some way by being involved in such a potentially destructive relationship.

DENIAL of a drinking problem plays a large role in alcoholism, and the para-alcoholic is almost as likely to deny the problem as the alcoholic. Rev. Joseph Kellerman, former director of the Charlotte (N.C.) Council on Alcoholism, reports that on an average the family of an alcoholic does not admit that he or she is an alcoholic until the illness has been critical for seven years.

Once this fact has been admitted, the family generally waits another two years before seeking help. Such denial is usually to the detriment of the alcoholic, who is best served by receiving treatment as soon as possible.

Frequently the para-alcoholic will attempt to assign blame. Wives often feel at fault if their husbands drink too much. They blame themselves and feel they have failed as wives. Husbands of alcoholics may also blame themselves, but more often they tend to blame their drinking wives and the wives accept this blame. (Men are also more likely to desert their alcoholic spouses than are women.) Casting blame obscures the fact that alcoholism is a disease. The para-alcoholic may also attempt to protect the alcoholic from the consequences of his or her drinking, but this generally encourages the alcoholic to continue drinking.

Both the alcoholic and the para-alcoholic need treatment. The para-alcoholic must learn his or her own role in the perpetuation of the alcoholism and the ways in which it has served him or her. Geraldine Youcha points out that the woman who marries an alcoholic often may show striking similarities to women who drink too much. Both tend to have had a parent who was an alcoholic and both generally think very little of themselves.

Should the alcoholic become sober, the para-alcoholic may continue to have problems. Sometimes the para-alcoholic has an investment in keeping the alcoholic in a dependent role and finds it hard to change a familiar pattern. When the alcoholic changes, the para-alcoholic may lose some control over the household and may feel replaced and unappreciated. The outside world will forget what a rough time he or she has had keeping the family together, and there will no longer be a scapegoat for all family problems. In addition the alcoholic's time is often taken up by treatment.

Organizations such as AL-ANON are equipped to deal with the problems of the para-alcoholic. (See also ENABLING.)

Joseph Kellerman, "The Souse's Spouse: Victim or Villain?" *Alcoholism* 1, no. 3 (January/February 1981):26–29.
Geraldine Youcha, *A Dangerous Pleasure* (New York: Hawthorn Books, 1978), passim.

paregoric   A solution, first prepared in the 18th century, of opium, camphor and alcohol. Paregoric has been commonly used as a constituent of many cough medicines and also, because of its constipating effects, as an antidiarrhetic.

Like any substance containing substantial amounts of alcohol, paregoric is subject to abuse orally. In addition it is sometimes taken by injection for the effects of the opium, which, because of the blood-clotting potential of the camphor, may result in death.

pathological drinker   Someone who drinks excessively as a means of handling unconscious problems; an alcoholic or problem drinker.

pathological intoxication   Also known as alcohol idiosyncratic intoxication, pathological intoxication is an infrequent condition that has as a primary characteristic a strong behavioral change, usually in the form of explosive rage or aggressiveness, following the ingestion of a small amount of alcohol. The amount may be as little as one drink or it may be more, but it is not a quantity sufficient to produce intoxication. The resultant behavior is a radical change from the person's normal behavior. Confusion and disorganization of thought are evident, and speech can be incoherent or delusional. The episode ends in deep sleep, with no memory of the event upon awakening.

Pathological intoxication appears to be due to the hypersensitivity of a few people to small, nonintoxicating amounts of alcohol. It may occur in brain-damaged individuals or those with tissue or behavioral intolerance. Although difficult to diagnose, the condition represents a distinct diagnostic entity.

Sidney Cohen, "Pathological Intoxication," *Drug Abuse and Alcoholism Newsletter,* Vista Hill Foundation, 10, no. 5 (June 1981).

pathological reaction to alcohol
See PATHOLOGICAL INTOXICATION.

periodic alcoholism   A form of alcoholism characterized by bouts of excessive drinking with intervals of abstinence or moderate drinking. Periodic alcoholism is also known as EPSILON ALCOHOLISM.

periodic drinking   See PERIODIC ALCOHOLISM

peripheral neuritis   See ALCOHOLIC POLYNEUROPATHY.

Pernod   An anise-flavored aperitif named after Henri-Louis Pernod, the first manufacturer of ABSINTHE. Pernod was initially produced as a substitute for absinthe when the latter was banned for health reasons because it contained wormwood.

When diluted with water, Pernod takes on a cloudy appearance. In comparison with absinthe, it is lower in alcoholic content (45% compared with 60% to 80%) and contains no wormwood.

personality trait theories   One category in a group of PSYCHOLOGICAL MODELS OF ETIOLOGY used to explain alcoholism. Personality trait theories have concentrated on finding a specific set of characteristics that would be associated with the development of alcoholism. However, most studies have generally failed to identify any set of personality traits that clearly distinguish alcoholics from other deviant groups or from persons judged to be normal.

Studies done on alcoholics have revealed a certain grouping of personality traits, including low stress tolerance, dependency, negative self-image, and feelings of isolation and depression. However, it has not been possible to determine from these studies whether these traits preceded alcoholic behavior or were a consequence of it.

David J. Armor, J. Michael Polich and Harriet B. Stambul, *Alcoholism and Treatment* (New York: John Wiley and Sons, 1978), p. 21.

physiological models of etiology
Theories in this category postulate that some individuals are predisposed to develop alcoholism because of an organic defect: an underlying biological malfunction results in a craving for alcohol that in turn leads to alcoholism. Models in this group include GENETOTROPHIC ETIOLOGICAL THEORIES, ENDOCRINE ETIOLOGICAL THEORIES and genetic theories (See GENETICS).

It is difficult to measure physiological differences between alcoholics and nonalcoholics because researchers must use those who are already alcoholic for their studies. The results of testing may therefore be due to the consequences of alcohol abuse rather than to physiological differences antecedent to this abuse. To date there is no clear evidence about what role physiological variables play in alcoholism. (See also PSYCHOLOGICAL MODELS OF ETIOLOGY, SOCIOCULTURAL MODELS OF ETIOLOGY.)

pilsner beer   Now generally used as a generic name for any light lager beer, the term originally was applied only to a product brewed in Pilsen (Plzen), in what is now Czechoslovakia.

Pilsner beer originated during the Middle Ages, when Slavic peoples developed an especially light beer because of a lack of barley, which forced them to combine a high proportion of wheat with the malted barley in the cereal mash from which they brewed their beer. At the time private brewing rights were an especially sensitive issue in Bohemia, which is today western Czechoslovakia. Attempts to restrict private trade in beer resulted in the brief Parsons War of the 14th century, a struggle by monasteries to protect their brewing rights.

Modern pilsner beer dates from the 19th century, when, in response to similar restrictions, families in Pilsen joined together to form a cooperative brewery. That venture lasted until World War II ended its ability to export and brought about its collapse. Today the only true pilsner beer is brewed under the brand name "Pilsner Urquell," but because of its long and distinguished reputation other brewers have adopted the label "pilsner" to describe their finest beers.

Plymouth gin   See GIN.

Poland   Very little information is available concerning alcohol abuse in Poland. Most of the following information is drawn from a 1981 report in *The New York Times;* the source of the report, however, was not named. According to this report, the consumption of alcohol in Poland has been increasing for the last several decades. Today the Polish people consume seven times as much alcohol as they did before World War II and three times as much as they did a decade ago. The consumption level in 1981 was 14 pints per capita.

Of the approximately 35 million people in Poland, an estimated 2 million are termed "excessive drinkers." Another estimated 700,000 alcoholics require constant medical attention. Over the years the age level of alcoholics has been decreasing: the majority today are between the ages of 21 and 24. Furthermore the number of teenage alcoholics is rising.

In 1977 it was estimated that the expenditure for alcoholic beverages comprised 30% of Poland's total expenditure for food and drink, and the proportion of personal income used for alcohol also appeared to be high. However, it is difficult to make comparisons with a communist system of national accounting because of undervaluation of expenditures and services.

Until recently Poland had no comprehensive program designed to combat alcoholism. However, stemming in part from attacks by leaders of the independent labor movement, the government has now begun a campaign against alcohol abuse. Some of the campaign's proposals include limiting sales outlets, printing health warnings on the labels of bottles and readjusting prices to make high-proof alcoholic beverages more expensive.

Despite the severity of its alcohol problem, Poland has made little effort to provide treatment. No mention is made of any self-help groups similar to ALCOHOLICS ANONYMOUS. A recent report by the Polish Academy of Sciences mentions that there are approximately 428 "clinics" in Poland. These clinics, however, are open for only a few hours each week, most are not staffed with full-time doctors and it is not known what specific forms of treatment are given. Treatment is also available at hospitals but it is often very difficult to obtain because of long waiting lists.

port   A fortified wine (18% to 20% alcohol) traditionally associated with the town of Oporto on the upper Douro river in Portugal. It is now produced in the United States, Australia and South Africa as a varietal wine.

Fermentation of port wine grapes begins when they are pressed and the grape sugars and juice combine. The process is then halted at an early stage, and brandy is added to the mixture of grape juice and wine. The mixture is then aged by one of two methods: in bottles or in casks.

When the quality of the grape harvest is exceptional, the grapes are reserved for a vintage port. In this case the mixture of grape juice, wine and brandy is kept for one year and then refortified and bottled. Vintage port is aged in bottles for 15 to 20 years in order to produce the desired strength and flavor. Further aging is considered a mark of distinction, and vintage ports survive in the bottle for more than 40 years before separating and deteriorating.

When the quality of the harvest is less exceptional, the grapes are used to make tawny port, the only variety produced outside of Portugal. Tawny port is the product of a blend of grapes from several years aged in wooden casks for periods shorter than those for vintage port. After 12 years of aging the wine is considered tawny port, but it is commonly bottled earlier and sold as ruby port. These wines usually survive less than five years in the bottle.

Port from Oporto is usually bottled and sold in Britain, where a taste for it developed when wars with France halted importation of French wines. There are a number of different blends and types, including a white port. It is often drunk like wine, but because of its alcoholic strength it is also commonly mixed with lemon or tonic water and poured over ice.

portal cirrhosis   Also known as Laennec's, nutritional or alcoholic CIRRHOSIS, portal cirrhosis is the most common form of cirrhosis among alcoholics.

porter   A dark and sweet ALE that is in effect a combination of ale and stout, although more carbonated than stout. Porter is supposed to have originated in response to the demands of 18th century market porters in London for a "half and half" potion of ale and stout. Now generally referred to as "dark ale," "porter" remains the designation of stouts in Ireland that are more carbonated than those intended for bottling and exportation.

postintoxicated state   A term with no specific meaning that is used to refer to the agitated state immediately following a drinking bout, to a HANGOVER or to the symptoms attributed to WITHDRAWAL.

postnecrotic cirrhosis   A form of CIRRHOSIS that follows hepatitis or other inflammations of the liver. It may occur in alcoholics.

pot still   A primitive form of still used especially in the DISTILLATION of Irish grain whiskey and Scotch malt whisky. The heat of the fire is applied directly to the pot containing the wash.

potentiation   A condition that occurs when the net effect of two drugs in combination is greater than the effect of each drug added together (see SYNERGY).

pregnancy   Some women may use alcohol to deal with the stresses of pregnancy, such as fatigue, swelling, fear of labor and concerns about motherhood. Furthermore changes in their bodies may be disorienting and cause women to dislike themselves. Heavy drinking can be dangerous to the fetus. When a pregnant woman takes a drink, the alcohol crosses the placenta and reaches the bloodstream of the fetus in about the same concentrations as in the mother. In a sense, when the mother drinks the baby drinks too. The most severe form of damage caused by prolonged heavy drinking is known as FETAL ALCOHOL SYNDROME, but even moderate, social drinking has been linked to weight and behavioral defects in newborns. A study, published in *The Lancet,* a British medical journal, of 32,000 women in California showed that pregnant women who had 3 drinks a day were three times as likely to miscarrry as those who did not drink at all or who averaged less than 1 drink a day.

No absolutely safe drinking limit has yet been established for pregnant women, but the highest danger seems to increase with the dosage. There is no compelling evidence of significant harm in consuming 2 drinks or less. However, as heavy alcohol consumption is known to be a cause of mental retardation, moderation is advised.

problem drinker   A person who experiences personal, social and/or professional problems whenever he or she drinks. The problems may take various forms, such as frequent excessive drinking or infrequent excessive drinking usually resulting in extreme drunkenness, accidents, bizarre or antisocial behavior etc. Often the distinction between problem drinking and ALCO-HOLISM is a matter of degree or depends on the number of symptoms exhibited. Problem drinkers are almost always heavy drinkers (see HEAVY DRINKER), but there are exceptions.

problem   drinking   See   PROBLEM DRINKER.

progression   While the disease of alcoholism follows no single course in every individual affected, a number of the same symptoms are often observed. Alcoholism progresses through several stages of varying length, depending on the individual.

During the onset of alcoholism it may be difficult to distinguish the alcoholic from the heavy drinker. However, the alcoholic has a stronger emotional response to alcohol and often, from the very first drink, attaches an unusual amount of significance to it. One sign of alcoholism may be that alcohol has become a requirement for pleasure or enjoyment rather than an accompaniment to it. Alcohol becomes the highlight of social activities and is soon used for other reasons, such as to cope with stress or anxiety. In time the alcoholic becomes severely intoxicated with increasing frequency and usually is annoyed with those commenting on his intake or behavior.

In the second stage the alcoholic begins to hide his drinking; to drink faster; and to start drinking earlier in the day. Along with a growing preoccupation with alcohol comes a strong feeling of guilt, leading him to become defensive about his drinking and hostile when it is alluded to by others. The alcoholic may try to gain control of the problem by rationing intake, changing brands or trying to prove he can "take it or leave it." He may use other drugs as a substitute for alcohol in an attempt to attain abstinence.

As the illness progresses, BLACKOUT becomes common. Irresponsible behavior and excessive emotion are often observed at this time and the alcoholic may make great plans for the future in an attempt to restore his image in the eyes of others.

Next the alcoholic experiences LOSS OF CONTROL over drinking. He plans his life around alcohol in order to maintain a high intake, commonly leaving work and dropping old friends who show concern about his behavior. Supplementation of alcohol with other drugs frequently increases. Social, mental and occupational disintegration commonly occur as the alcoholic seeks more and more isolation. Eventually physical complications of the disease often begin to dominate the psychological and social aspects. Finally the alcoholic "reaches bottom," at which point he may either seek help or drop out of normal life entirely. Ultimately the alcoholic may drink himself to death.

American Medical Association, *Manual on Alcoholism* (1977), pp. 34–36.

proof   A measure of the amount of AB-SOLUTE ALCOHOL in a distilled spirit. As early as the 15th century, drinkers demanded "proof" that a liquor was fit (i.e., had a high enough alcohol content) for human consumption. To this end various tests were devised. Oil was floated on liquor; if it sank, that was "proof" of the spirit's strength. If a liquor-soaked cloth could be

A Comparison of Common British and American Proofs

British Proof	American Proof	Absolute Alcohol (Percent)
100.0	114.2	57.1
87.6	100.0	50.0
76.0	86.8	43.4
70.0	80.0	40.0

easily and satisfactorily ignited, that was "proof." If a mixture of liquor and gunpowder burned smoothly with a blue flame, it was exactly on the mark; if it blew up, it was over "proof."

John Clarke in 1725 and Bartholomew Sikes in 1803 pioneered modern measurements of proof in Britain with the use of hydrometers. The height at which the hydrometer floated in the liquor determined the proof.

The British and the Americans use different systems for measuring proof. The British system is based upon a comparison of equal volumes of water and liquor at 51°F. If the liquor weighs 12/13th as much as the water, it is 100° proof. In Britain liquor bottled for home consumption has a lower proof and a slightly lower alcohol content than that intended for export. For example, Scotch whisky meant for the domestic market is bottled at 70 proof (40% alcohol), but that exported to the United States is 86.8 proof (43.4% alcohol) under the American system. British proof is lower than American proof for spirits of equal strength.

The American system is based upon the percentage of absolute alcohol in the liquor at 60°F. The proof measurement is double the percentage of alcohol: 100 proof = 50% alcohol.

psychodrama   A form of GROUP THERAPY in which individuals act out their problems before a group under the direction of a therapist. Usually a member with a problem portrays himself while a different member takes the role (father, wife, boss) of another person associated with the member and his problem. The two (or more) "performers" then act out their roles. Sometimes roles will be reversed, with the member acting out a role other than his own. The purpose of psychodrama is to heighten the member's awareness of his problem through performance, giving it an immediacy that simple discussion lacks.

psychological models of etiology A category of theories, with sociocultural theories and physiological theories, on the etiology of alcoholism. Most psychological theories are based on the assumption that some element in the personality structure leads to the development of alcoholism. There has been a search for an "alcoholic personality" that would have a built-in vulnerability to the development of alcoholism. However, most studies have failed to find any specific personality traits that clearly differentiate alcoholics from either normal people or those with problems. There is evidence that once drinking patterns have been established, alcoholics display certain common traits. These include low stress tolerance, dependency, negative self-image, and feelings of insecurity and depression. Since most studies have been made on populations of alcoholics, however, it is not clear whether these traits precede alcoholism or are a result of it.

There are several different psychological models of etiology. Under the psychodynamic model alcoholism results from unconscious tendencies that are expressed in excessive consumption of alcohol. A major theory, developed by Freud, posits that alcoholism is related to a traumatic experience in early childhood caused by a poor parent-child relationship. The loss or absence of the object of love, usually the mother, in the oral stage creates demands in the alcoholic that are insatiable. As a result his interpersonal relations eventually fail and are interpreted by him as rejection.

A consequent loss of self-esteem develops and there is an enormous rage stemming from the original rejection by the parent figure. He turns a desire to destroy that figure upon himself and consumes his rage in alcohol (see ORAL FIXATION). Another theory holds that alcoholics suffer from strong feelings of inferiority and powerlessness but are inhibited from expressing their hostility or aggression. Alcohol, which provides improved feelings of self-esteem and confidence, allows them to feel competent and to express their impulses.

It has also been postulated that alcoholics experience unusually strong conflicts between dependency needs and a desire for autonomy. Drinking allows dependency through sociability and dependence on alcohol, and at the same time it gives rise to feelings of independence and strength.

Behavioral models propose that alcoholism is a conditioned behavioral response which can be helped through modification of stimuli and reinforcement in the environment (see BEHAVIORAL LEARNING THEORY).

David J. Armor, J. Michael Polich and Harriet B. Stambul, *Alcoholism and Treatment* (New York: John Wiley and Sons, 1978), pp. 17–29.

Morris E. Chafetz and Harold W. Demone, Jr., *Alcoholism and Society* (New York: Oxford University Press, 1962), pp. 19–29, 39–56.

public drunkenness   The public inebriate is the most visible alcoholic and therefore has symbolic importance for all alcoholics. Public·intoxication has been regarded as a legal matter ever since the English Parliament prescribed punishment in 1606 for that "loathesome and odious sin of drunkenness" that is "the root and foundation of many other sins" (Kurtz and Regier). This approach was brought to America and remained the general rule for three centuries. Around 1910 the merit of treating alcoholics as criminals was questioned, and attempts were made to develop alternative facilities. These attempts failed and

local police departments continued to be responsible for public inebriates. Several other attempts were made through the years to provide treatment for public inebriates but without success. By 1965 arrests for public drunkenness numbered more than 1.5 million annually, accounting for approximately 40% of all nontraffic arrests (FBI). In the 1960s alcoholism gradually came to be regarded as a disease and in the early 1970s the Uniform Alcoholism and Intoxication Act was established, which provided the states with "a legal framework within which to approach alcoholism and public intoxication from a health standpoint." The Declaration Policy of the Uniform Act states, "It is the policy of this State that alcoholics and intoxicated persons may not be subjected to criminal prosecution because of their consumption of alcoholic beverages but rather should be afforded a continuum of treatment in order that they may lead normal lives as productive members of society" (National Conference of Commissioners on Uniform State Laws). To date this act, which decriminalizes public drunkenness, has been adopted by 31 states and the District of Columbia.

While the Uniform Act has worked to reduce the number of alcoholics incarcerated for drunkenness, it has not been sufficient to eliminate the public inebriate problem. The act has helped to destigmatize alcoholism and to increase access to treatment, but it has not brought chronic public inebriates into treatment voluntarily or kept them in treatment. One reason is that not enough funds have been appropriated to develop the needed resources for treatment. Skid row programs in particular are often given low priority, and public inebriates are frequently written off by treatment programs as unlikely to recover.

John R. DeLuca, ed., *Fourth Special Report to the U.S. Congress on Alcohol and Health* (Rockville, Md.: National Institute on Alcohol Abuse and Alcoholism, 1981), pp. 155–156.

N. R. Kurtz and M. Regier, "The Uniform Alcoholism and Intoxication Treatment Act: The Compromising Process of Social Policy Formulation," *Journal of Studies on Alcohol* 36, no. 11 (1975):1421–1441.

National Conference of Commissioners on Uniform State Laws, *Uniform Alcoholism and Intoxication Treatment Act* (Washington, D.C.: U.S. Government Printing Office, 1973).

National Institute on Alcohol Abuse and Alcoholism (NIAAA) Information and Feature Service, *Client Funds Contribute to Public Inebriate Program* (July 18, 1980).

———. *Public Inebriate Conference Addresses Range of Issues,* August 28, 1981, p. 3.

Ernest P. Noble, ed., *Third Special Report to the U.S. Congress on Alcohol and Health* (Rockville, Md.: National Institute on Alcohol Abuse and Alcoholism, 1978), pp. 329–330.

U.S. Federal Bureau of Investigation, *Uniform Crime Reports for the United States, 1965* (Washington, D.C.: U.S. Government Printing Office, 1965).

Puerto Rico   The U.S. island commonwealth now has the world's highest per capita consumption of ethanol in the form of distilled spirits, and consumption of distilled spirits continues to rise while that of beer and wine has been falling. The Puerto Rican Department of Addiction Services has attributed this trend to several factors, including a deeply ingrained tradition of drinking in Puerto Rico and a general tolerance of drunkenness as well as the dramatic change affecting all spheres of life since Puerto Rico became a U.S. territory following the Spanish-American War in 1898. Various kinds of alienation associated with drinking have been traced to the Spanish-speaking population's constitutional link with the English-speaking U.S. authorities. The social problems affecting most of the population are also considered a contributing factor. About 58% of the population lives in densely populated urban areas, and unemployment is high—18.8% of the work force in 1977–78. The per capita income in 1978 was $2,678, leaving 60% of the population below the official U.S. poverty level, and 18.6% of this income was spent on alcohol.

Finally, the most popular alcoholic beverage in Puerto Rico is rum, consumption of which rose in 1978–79. The national preference for this strong and highly intoxicating drink over all other alcoholic beverages is perhaps the most important factor in Puerto Rico's widespread alcohol abuse problem.

The largest consumers of alcohol in Puerto Rico are classified as "heavy drinkers," rather than alcoholics, by the Department of Addiction Services. Three out of every 10 drinkers fall into the heavy drinker category, defined as an individual who consumes 4 drinks or more at least one or two times a week. Statistics show that these heavy drinkers tend to be males between the ages of 20 and 49. The age at which this group begins to drink has been constantly declining.

The Assistant Secretariate for Alcoholism Treatment in Puerto Rico served 7,818 clients in 1979–80, 36% of whom had been referred to it after being apprehended for drunken driving. Of these clients 187 entered detoxification programs at a total cost to the government of $156,100, and the rest enrolled in various orientation, consultation and conference programs at a total cost of $2,038,645.

There were 10,087 arrests for drunkenness in 1979–80, 92% of which were for drunk driving. The commonwealth's six deaths per 100,000 miles traveled by car is twice the rate for the continental U.S. Of drivers and pedestrians killed 59.4% and 55.6% respectively were found to have a BLOOD ALCOHOL CONCENTRATION over the legal limit.

To help deal with the toll of these alcohol-related problems, the Department of Addiction Services was established in 1973 to coordinate efforts aimed at treatment, rehabilitation and prevention of alcohol and drug abuse. Its present program has taken the form of a Plan for Integral Development, adopted by the legislature in 1979. The plan emphasizes a community approach to treatment of alcoholism and preventative education. Presently there are Municipal Alcohol Centers in San Juan, Bayamon and Carolina. Public education sessions of various kinds were attended by 2,059 students, 983 parents and 89 teachers in 1979–80 and were supplemented with public television and radio broadcasts about the dangers of alcohol abuse.

R

Rand Report   In June 1976 the Rand Corporation of Santa Monica, Calif. issued a highly controversial report on alcoholism. The report was sponsored and subsidized by the National Institute on Alcohol Abuse and Alcoholism (NIAAA), which contracted with the Rand Corporation, an independent, nonprofit research organization, to participate in an analysis of its comprehensive alcoholism treatment program begun in 1971, to codify and examine the results and to release the findings. The Rand Corporation published its report under the title *Alcoholism and Treatment.*[1]

Conclusions and Considerations of the Rand Report

The major conclusions and considerations of the Rand Report were as follows:

Treatment

Clients who underwent treatment had a slightly higher rate of remission than those who had a single contact with a treatment center, with some slight additional advantage as the amount of treatment increased. ("Single contact" and "untreated" are used synonymously throughout the report.)

Remission rates

1. Untreated clients; "natural" remission: 50%
2. Untreated clients with AA attendance: almost 70%
3. Treated clients: 70%

The remission results for treated clients varied little from one treatment program to another.

The report contained a new "definition of remission that includes both abstention and 'normal' drinking. Normal drinking means consumption in moderate quantities commonly found in the general nonalcoholic population, provided no serious signs of impairment are present."

Relapse analysis

1. " ... relapse rates for normal drinkers are no higher than those for long-term abstainers. ...."
2. " ... [the study] suggests the possibility that for some alcoholics moderate drinking is not necessarily a prelude to full relapse. ...."

Other Conclusions

1. The study was unable to find a pattern upon which to conclude that one program was best for one type of client and another was best for another client.

---

[1]The Rand Report, *Alcoholism and Treatment,* was republished in 1978 by John Wiley and Sons, Inc. The reissue included an important new section: "Appendix B. Reaction to the Rand Report on 'Alcoholism and Treatment,'" which contained documents and analyses by supporters and detractors of the original report. The appendix was prepared by the authors of the original report.

2. It was found that "recovery from alcohol dependency may depend upon
mechanisms quite unrelated to the
factors that led to excessive drinking
in the first place."

Future Considerations

1. Total abstinence is not the only goal
of treatment *if* future research con-
firms the initial conclusions of the
survey.
2. If the survey's initial conclusions are
confirmed, research is needed to determine which alcoholics can return
to normal drinking.
3. If the theory that the results of most
programs are uniform is true, not
only as applied to an individual's
drinking but other behavior patterns
as well, less expensive methods of
treatment can be used.

Throughout the report, the authors
pointed out the limitations of their sample:
that the size of the sample was small and
the time frame of the study was limited;
that the conclusions about behavior were
based on observation and not on controlled,
experimental data; and that future behavior
would not necessarily conform to the data
in the survey.

Critics' Conclusions

Critics of the report seized upon the limitations noted by the authors. What the authors viewed as a careful delineation of the
limitations of their survey was seen by its
detractors as factors that made the report
not merely worthless but actively harmful.
They claimed the facts did not support the
conclusions and that the result was a "legit-
imized" report which deluded alcoholics
into believing that they could resume drinking, with disastrous results. A summary of
some of their objections follows:

Size of Sample

Critics of the report challenged its use of
"on the basis of over 1000 subjects . . ." and
countered that the Rand sample was "(actually a subsample of only 161 former patients, not randomly selected and from only
8 out of 45 government alcoholism treatment centers) with about 74% of all interviews at 4 sites (a large proportion over the
phone by opinion interviewers who had 2-
weeks training)."

Time Period

Noting "the time period for the Rand
study *was 18 months after entering treatment*" [emphasis theirs], critics pointed out
that Drs. D. L. Davies and John A. Ewing
had examined the possibilities of alcoholics
resuming social drinking in independent
studies over substantially longer periods
and had rejected them.

Makeup of Sample

Critics have questioned whether all the
clients in the Rand sample were in fact
alcoholics.

The Ongoing Controversy

In January 1980 a second Rand Report,
*The Course of Alcoholism: Four Years
After Treatment,* was published. In this new
study (actually a continuation of the previous one) many of the conclusions of the
original report were modified, although it
was not, as some of the original report's
critics claimed, a "retraction." The authors
suggested a greater complexity of the issues
involved than originally reported and characterized the report as another phase of a
continuing program of study by the Rand
Corporation. (See also RAND REPORT II.)

Rand Report II   Critics of the first
RAND REPORT pointed out two major defects: the study's follow-up period of six
months was too short (a substantial number

of clients were still in treatment) and only about one-quarter of all clients in the study responded to the six-month follow-up interviews. As a result the National Institute on Alcohol Abuse and Alcoholism (NIAAA) drew up a series of contracts for follow-up studies of sample clients involved in the first Rand study. The subjects were to be interviewed at 18 months and then again four years after entry into treatment. The second report was completed by the same three doctors who worked on the first report: J. Michael Polich, David J. Armor and Harriet B. Stambul. The four-year study of alcoholism, which cost about $500,000, was the most extensive and comprehensive of its kind to date.

The findings of the study were published in January 1980 in a 361-page report entitled *The Course of Alcoholism: Four Years After Treatment.* This second report received much less criticism and press coverage than the first Rand Report, and the picture that emerged from it was less optimistic than that of the earlier report. While the first report concluded "clients of NIAAA treatment centers show substantial improvement on a number of outcome indices," the second stated that "although there is a frequent improvement there is also frequent relapse and much instability."

The second Rand Report nevertheless confirmed the earlier finding that some alcoholics are able to return to social drinking. But for most, the study showed, total abstinence seemed to be the surest method of maintaining remission. The second report substantiated the need for a more flexible definition of "recovering from alcoholism," but it significantly refined the earlier report's conclusions.

Rand Report II found that there were at least two different types of alcoholics and that what worked best for one type might not work as well for the other. In general the second report showed that alcoholics who were under 40 years old and who had

shown relatively few symptoms of alcohol dependence within the month previous to treatment were less likely to relapse into alcoholism if they resumed social drinking. Those under 40 who attempted total abstinence were more likely to relapse. For alcoholics over 40 with strong symptoms of alcohol dependence, total abstinence offered the best prognosis. (Dependence symptoms included tremors and shakes, morning drinking, blackouts, missed meals because of drinking, loss of control while drinking, and continuous drinking for 12 hours or more.)

In other words, for younger unmarried alcoholics who are often under social pressures to drink, the attempts to maintain abstinence may be more stressful than nonproblem, social drinking; older married alcoholics are more likely to be encouraged by their spouses to remain abstinent and less likely to relapse than if they attempted controlled drinking.

Remission Rates

Four years after entering treatment at one of eight centers around the country, 46% of the approximately 900 men studied were found to be "in remission" from the symptoms of alcoholism, with 28% abstaining and 18% drinking socially. Among those engaged in social drinking, half consumed more than 4 drinks a day and half drank less than that.

The study showed that alcoholics who entered treatment programs were highly unstable in their ability to refrain indefinitely from problem drinking. Many relapsed several times during the four years, and most entered other treatment programs from time to time. Only 28% of the respondents were free of alcoholism problems both at 18 months and at four years after they first entered treatment and only 15% were in continuous remission for the entire four years. (Of the latter 7.5% maintained abstinence for the entire four-year study period and 7% maintained low amounts of consumption or a mixture of abstinence and low consumption without adverse consequences or symptoms.) Fifty-four percent were having drinking problems four years after they first started treatment. Nevertheless there was some improvement, since upon admission to treatment at least 90% were drinking with serious problems.

Alcoholic men who regularly attended AA meetings had the highest rate of long-term abstinence: 57%. However, while regular attendance at AA sessions offered the best chance for recovery from alcoholism, those who attended the sessions were just as likely to have relapsed as those who had not attended. Alcoholics who regularly went to AA were not more likely than others to be free of serious alcohol problems later. (Permanent abstinence is fairly infrequent, even for regular AA members.) Those who attended AA irregularly or sometime in the past were even more likely to have relapsed at four years than those who had never been to the organization's meetings.

Alcoholics who abstained for less than six months had the worst prognosis; these "short-term" abstainers had a much higher rate of relapse and many more alcohol-related deaths than either long-term abstainers or social drinkers.

The authors of the second Rand Report emphasized again that the study "does not recommend a particular treatment approach and does not recommend that any alcoholic resume drinking." It does, however, raise questions about the nature and treatment of alcoholism.

rational emotive therapy (RET)
Sometimes used to treat alcoholics undergoing REHABILITATION, rational emotive therapy (RET) is an educational, rather than psychodynamic or medical, model of psychotherapy. RET, developed by Albert Ellis and Robert A. Harper, asserts that people have choice in their lives, that most of their conditioning consists of self-conditioning

and that the therapist serves to help them see a range of alternatives to their behavior. RET stresses a semantic approach to understanding; change in semantic usage is stressed so as to concomitantly change thinking, emotions and behavior. The therapy shows people how they behave self-defeatingly and how they can get themselves to change. Both individual and small-group therapy as well as large workshops and lectures are used.

reality therapy   Developed by a psychiatrist, Dr. William Glasser, who has worked extensively in corrections and education, reality therapy is based on the theory that behavior is generated by what happens in the mind rather than what happens in the real world. Individuals attempt to control the world outside through use of a control system made up of millions of perceptions, including perceptions of what is ideal. A gap between the perceived world and the ideal world is called a "perceptual error" and is sensed through comparison. Actions are adjusted so that the perception from the real world eventually corresponds with the mind's idealization. Alcohol, according to Glasser, blots out perceptual error and destroys the comparing system that shows the difference between what a person wants and what he or she gets. In reality therapy alcoholics are taught alternative solutions to drinking and learn to fulfill their needs through ALCOHOLICS ANONYMOUS or other forms of REHABILITATION.

Anita Diamant, "Reality Therapy," *U.S. Journal of Drug and Alcohol Dependence* 5, no. 9 (November 1981): 13.

recovery   Defining recovery from alcoholism is not a simple matter, since there is no clear-cut definition of alcoholism. It is difficult to say that an alcoholic who no longer drinks has recovered because at some future date he quite possibly may resume alcoholic drinking or he may be suffering from some other alcohol-related impairment. Some definition of recovery, however, is desirable in order to distinguish alcoholics who are still drinking excessively from those who are managing to deal with their problem.

Recovery is defined differently by different groups; for those who espouse the philosophy of ALCOHOLICS ANONYMOUS or who are strong believers in the ADDICTION model of alcoholism, only complete abstinence for a long period constitutes recovery. Other schools of thought, however, hold that once the psychological causes of alcoholism are removed and reconditioning has been achieved, the alcoholic can return to non-alcoholic, social drinking.

The best definition of recovery appears to be a stable REMISSION of symptoms over a period of time. This means that for a relatively long period the patient has exhibited no alcoholic drinking behavior; emphasis is on the drinking rather than on the social condition of the patient, although there are those who use social criteria to judge whether or not an alcoholic has recovered.

Recovery seems to be a distinct stage in the course of alcoholism and is not strongly related to the social and psychological factors that may cause alcoholism in the first place. A great deal of the recovery process appears to depend on the individual, who must recognize the costs of his alcoholism, allow a breakdown of the defenses that prolong his alcoholism (see DENIAL) and commit himself to change.

David J. Armor, J. Michael Polich and Harriet B. Stambul, *Alcoholism and Treatment* (New York: John Wiley and Sons, 1978).

red wine   Red wine is produced by fermenting grape juice with the grape skins and a certain quantity of grape stems. It is the presence of the skins, in particular, that gives red wines their color, for the juice of virtually all grapes is colorless. Unlike red wines, white wines are produced by fermenting grape juice without the grape skins, and rose wines are usually produced by fermenting grape juice that has had limited contact with grape skins. The alcohol content of red wines ranges from 10% to 14%.

Once grapes intended for red wines have been gathered, they are crushed and loaded into fermenting tanks with the skins and, according to the tannin content desired, some amount of stems from the vine. This wine "must" is then mixed with less than one part per thousand of an antiseptic, usually sulfur dioxide, to eliminate all but the alcohol-tolerant natural yeasts in the grapes. Other active yeast cultures are sometimes added at this stage to assist fermentation.

In the fermentation process the sugars in the grapes are converted into alcohol and carbonic gas by the yeasts. The skins and the stems are forced to the surface of the fermenting must by the gas (some red wine vinters use a grill to keep this "cap" submerged in the fermenting vat for greater flavor and color). Fermentation of red wines lasts anywhere from two days to two weeks, with wines that are intended for long aging being fermented the longest. When the grape juice has attained the desired level of alcohol content and has extracted the desired level of tannin from the skins and stems, the solids are separated and the process follows the same steps used in the production of white and rose wines (see WINE).

Most experts agree that the finest red wines in the world are those bottled in the Bordeaux district of France. Located in the southeastern part of the country, this area is officially about 90 miles from north to south and about 60 miles from east to west. The soil is an especially favorable one for growing grapes, consisting of a sandy topsoil and a clay subsoil, and it is drained by the Garonne and Dordogne rivers that meet to form the Gironde, a term sometimes considered synonymous with Bordeaux. The principal subdivisions of the region include

Medoc, Saint-Emilion and Pomerol, which produce red wines exclusively, and Graves, which produces both red and white wines. Second only to Bordeaux is Burgundy, located in eastern France, which holds the distinction of being the oldest wine-producing region in the country. It is hillier than Bordeaux, and the finest vineyards in Burgundy are those located midway up the slopes of the hills. The most famous vineyards in the region are those of the Cote d'Or, a range of low hills to the southwest of Dijon. Among the notable Cote d'Or red wines is Beaujolais, a fruity red wine usually drunk young. It is sometimes sold after incomplete fermentation as a seasonal wine known as *beaujolais nouveau.*

Besides French wines the famous European red wines are mostly Italian. These include the northern Piedmont wines, such as Barbaresco, Barbera and Barolo; the Tuscany wines from central Italy known as Chianti; and wines from the Lago di Garda region, such as Bardolino and Valpolicella. Other leading European red wines include the Riojas from Spain, the Dao red wines from Portugal and the Tokay wines from Hungary.

rehabilitation   After DETOXIFICATION a patient is physically free of alcohol dependence, but his or her behavior patterns and needs have not been changed. Therefore some sort of follow-up treatment is usually necessary to enable the patient to function soberly in society without relapsing into alcoholism. Patients may be encouraged to go to ALCOHOLICS ANONYMOUS meetings, to individual or group therapy or to both. Some enter special rehabilitation centers for a certain length of time in order to establish ways of living without alcohol.

The same facilities may provide detoxification and rehabilitation services, but generally these services are offered in different places. Detoxification usually takes place in a hospital setting and lasts about a week. Rehabilitation is normally accomplished in a special environment, where patients dress in their everyday clothes (as opposed to hospital clothing) and keep regular hours. The duration of rehabilitation in private treatment centers varies, but usually the stay is longer than for detoxification, often up to four weeks. Many private treatment centers are located in nonhospital settings, often in rural areas or other pleasant surroundings. Some, however, are in general hospitals.

Modes of treatment also vary, but almost all emphasize the value of Alcoholics Anonymous and AL-ANON. Alcoholism is treated as a disease, patient responsibility is stressed and abstinence is a primary aim. During rehabilitation patients receive a good deal of instruction about alcoholism and living without alcohol. Most programs encourage family involvement and aftercare following the inpatient stay, either through therapy, AA or both.

In a private rehabilitation treatment center the patient is surrounded by an enormous support system. He is also removed from the pressures of daily life and the presence of alcohol and is surrounded by people who understand the problem. This environment may help him to restructure his life, but because it is so sheltered a return to normal living may be difficult. There, with the availability of liquor stores and bars and daily pressures of work and social life, he may soon return to drinking. Or the opposite may occur: the alcoholic may feel that he is cured and free of alcohol problems and therefore can return to drinking normally, the so-called "flight into health," which generally leads to a relapse. This is one reason why aftercare is stressed and why it is important to involve the family.

relapse   A return to uncontrolled drinking by an alcoholic in a stage of recovery. Recovery may mean complete abstinence or the ability of an alcoholic to drink moderately without LOSS OF CONTROL. Alcoholism is a disorder characterized by a tendency to relapse.

Relapse seems related to a number of factors, including personality, environmental influences, physiology, social attitudes and the availability of alcohol. Social pressures during treatment that tempt the alcoholic to break abstinence are particularly important. Individual problems or even positive achievement may lead to relapse. An alcoholic may begin to feel confident after he has made progress in treatment, and attempt to tackle a difficult situation that he is not ready to handle, causing him to return to drinking. Or he may relapse because of depression or frustration. But an alcoholic generally is not considered to be completely recovered until he is able to maintain continued sobriety without relapse.

religion   The attitudes of different religious groups toward the use of alcoholic beverages vary widely. A number of religious groups regard drinking alcohol as immoral or sinful; total abstinence is the accepted norm in these groups. Other religions permit members to use alcohol socially, as well as in such ceremonies as Holy Communion, which may involve the drinking of wine. All the major religions frown on drunkenness. The views on alcoholism of most of the major religions in the United States follow:

Roman Catholics

The Roman Catholic Church permits the use of alcoholic beverages by all except those who are diagnosed as alcoholic. Use is considered to be appropriate on holidays and during celebrations. Alcoholism is considered a disease involving the physical, mental and spiritual qualities of man. The church recommends INTERVENTION and treatment followed by membership in ALCOHOLICS ANONYMOUS.

A national study of American drinking practices conducted in 1969 by the Rutgers Center for Alcohol Studies found relatively high proportions of drinkers and heavy drinkers among Catholics. Those who attended church more often were more likely to report infrequent drinking and consumed less per occasion. The incidence of alcohol-

ism among Catholics appears to be determined by ethnic background; both Irish Americans and Italian Americans are primarily Catholic but Irish Americans have a higher rate of drinking problems while Italian Americans have a lower rate.

Greek Orthodox

The Greek Orthodox Archdiocese permits the use of alcoholic beverages and finds them traditionally appropriate following a wedding or baptism. Occasional overindulgence of alcoholic beverages is tolerated but not condoned. Alcoholism is considered an illness to be understood and treated.

Jews

Judaism permits the use of any alcoholic beverage that conforms to the laws of kashruth. The only prohibition against drinking is during fast days, when consumption of food is not allowed. There are several religious ceremonies that require the use of wine, including the Passover seder and certain rites of passage. People who do not consume alcoholic beverages may substitute grape juice on occasions when wine is required. There is one holiday during the year when excessive intake of alcohol is sanctioned: Purim.

JEWS have the lowest percentage of abstainers of any of the major American religions. They also have a very high proportion of light drinkers and the lowest proportion of heavy drinkers. The rate of alcoholism among Jews is very low.

Protestants

The Protestant position on the use of alcohol varies from sect to sect. Many sects that preached abstinence at one time have switched to an emphasis on moderation. In the aforementioned survey liberal Protestants demonstrated a drinking pattern somewhat similar to that of Catholics, although there were fewer heavy drinkers. Conservative Protestants had a large proportion of abstainers and a low proportion of heavy drinkers.

Methodists

The Methodist Church is the largest American church proscribing the use of alcohol. In a 1980 position paper, the United Methodist Church stated: "We affirm our long-standing support of abstinence from alcohol as a faithful witness to God's liberating and redeeming love for persons. . . . The drug dependent person is an individual of infinite human worth in need of treatment and rehabilitation and misuse should be viewed as a symptom of underlying disorders for which remedies should be sought." An increasing number of younger Methodists, however, are using alcohol, sometimes in an extreme manner, possibly indicating that the ideal of abstinence implies conversely that any drinking is equivalent to drunkenness.

Baptists

The American Baptist Association forbids the use of alcoholic beverages and considers alcoholism a sin rather than a disease, a "violation of God's will and word toward man." The Christian Life Commission of the Southern Baptist Convention also holds that use of alcohol is immoral but it advocates the demonstration of "love, patience, and forgiveness of God in dealing with alcoholics."

Presbyterians

In 1970 the General Assembly of the Presbyterian Church noted the obligation of persons to make responsible decisions regarding the use of alcoholic beverages, the danger of excessive drinking and the responsibility to seek constructive solutions for social problems related to the use of alcoholic beverages.

Mormons

The Mormons recommend strongly against the use of alcohol. Only 21% of Mormon males who attend church weekly consume alcohol.

Jehovah's Witnesses

Jehovah's Witnesses allow the use of alcohol, since according to their teachings, God's word does not require total abstinence. Wine is a symbol of happiness in the Bible; therefore it is not forbidden to mankind. However, the Witnesses caution strongly against alcohol dependence and abuse.

Friends United Meeting (Quakers)

The position of the Friends toward the use of alcohol is based on the belief that the human body is the temple of the Lord and that to mar it is to dishonor Him. Any pleasurable or exhilarating effects produced by intoxicants are temporary and tend to react injuriously on both mind and body. Total abstinence is advocated and the entire liquor traffic is considered detrimental to human welfare.

Seventh-Day Adventists

Seventh-Day Adventists forbid the use of alcohol. Temperance is considered to be a way of life and is equated with self-control through Jesus Christ.

Morris E. Chafetz and Harold W. Demone, Jr., *Alcoholism and Society* (New York: Oxford University Press, 1962), pp. 84–99.
John Langone, *Bombed, Buzzed, Smashed, or . . . Sober* (Boston: Little, Brown and Company, 1976), pp. 48–49.
Unpublished correspondence with spokesmen of various denominations (1982).

remission   Remission is defined as "a temporary and incomplete subsidence of the force or violence of a disease or of pain," according to *Webster's Second International*. In the field of alcoholism the term "remission" is often used instead of "recovery," since it is extremely difficult to say when someone is completely recovered from alcoholism (see RECOVERY). Remission is generally measured in terms of drinking behavior rather than social behavior.

There are two conflicting schools of

thought on what constitutes remission. One school, including ALCOHOLICS ANONYMOUS, believes that remission exists only when an alcoholic is in a state of complete abstinence. Another school, which includes the authors of the RAND REPORT, expands the definition of remission to cover an alcoholic who is able to maintain a course of "normal drinking," defined as a daily consumption of less than 3 ounces of ABSOLUTE ALCOHOL, no tremors and no serious symptoms related to drinking, such as frequent episodes of blackouts, absences from work or drunkenness. Both abstainers and those who drink at normal levels without showing signs of alcoholism are considered to be in remission.

rhinophyma   (New Latin, from Greek *rhinos* nose + *phyma* swelling.) A skin condition of the nose characterized by swelling, redness and, often, broken capillaries. It is sometimes, but not always, caused by heavy drinking over a prolonged period. W. C. Fields was a well-known victim of rhinophyma; in his case it was called by its popular name—"whiskey nose."

RNA   Ribonucleic acid. One of the two main types of nucleic acid (the other is DNA), RNA is an organic substance found in the chromosomes of all living cells. RNA plays an important part in the storage and replication of hereditary information and in protein synthesis.

rose wine   Having an alcohol content from 12% to 15%, rose wine is produced by fermenting grape juice that has had limited contact with grape skins. Since the juice of virtually all grapes is colorless, the difference in color between red and white wines stems from the fact that the former is fermented in a "must" that includes grape skins and the latter is fermented in a "must" of pure grape juice.

Once grapes intended for rose wines have been gathered, they are crushed to extract their juice, which is allowed to mix with the grape skins for a period of 12 to 36 hours. Then the solids are separated and the process continues through steps similar to those used to produce red or white wines (see WINE). Today some inexpensive rose wines are produced in bulk by simply adding a tasteless red coloring, called cochineal, to finished white wines. The product is a wine that resembles true rose in color but lacks the flavoring tannins extracted from the grape skins in the traditional process.

The most prized rose wines come from the Anjou, Bordeaux and Tavel wine districts of France. The south Tyrol region of Italy is also noted for its rose wines, and both Portugal and Spain produce roses in virtually all of their wine districts. A number of rose wines made in California are considered comparable to the European varieties. Inexpensive rose wines are produced in nearly all wine-producing countries, often by means of artificial coloring, as a way to dispose of marginal wines.

rubbing alcohol   A nondrinkable solution made with isopropyl alcohol rather than ethyl alcohol, or ethanol. Rubbing alcohol is used externally for medicinal purposes. It has a bad taste and is poisonous.

rum   An alcoholic beverage made from the distillation of fermented products of sugar cane. Most frequently rum is produced by distilling molasses, but it is also sometimes made from the juice of sugar cane.

It is thought that the term "rum" has its origins in the British word "rumbullion" (meaning tumult or uproar), or possibly "rumbustion" (meaning rum). When rum was first manufactured in the West Indies during the early 17th century, it was referred to as "kill devil" and, later, "rumbullion." By 1667 "rumbullion" had been abbreviated to "rum."

Rum is often thought of as the drink of romantics and adventurers. In the 18th century, British sailors used rum as the base of their daily GROG, which consisted of rum, water and lemon juice. Rum was also the alcoholic beverage consumed in the largest quantities by the American colonists just before the Revolutionary War. It has been estimated that at that time the colonists, women and children included, drank 3¾ gallons of rum per person per year (Tannahill).

Throughout the 17th and 18th centuries until the time of the Revolution, rum was the key item of trade in what was dubbed the New England Rum Triangle, a trade route between New England, Africa and the West Indies. In this trade route rum manufactured in New England was shipped to Africa, where it was exchanged for slaves. The slaves in turn were taken to the West Indies, where they were traded for the molasses needed to make rum. This trade route was a major source of revenue for New England shipowners. Their business as well as that of the rum manufacturers thus suffered greatly during the Revolutionary War, when molasses supplies were cut off from Cuba and the West Indies. At the time that the American rum business began to suffer, the newly emerging American WHISKEY business began to flourish, since it did not depend upon foreign trade for its essential ingredients. The rum business never fully recovered, and whiskey gradually replaced rum as the most popular alcoholic beverage in the United States (see RYE, BOURBON).

In the 19th century, rum acquired a rather low reputation in the United States. Its name became a synonym for intoxicating beverages in general, and a hard drinker was referred to as a "rum sucker" (in the 1850s) and a "rummy" or "rummie" (in the 1860s). In addition cheap saloons were sometimes called "rum holes" (1830s). During the 20th century, "rumdum" (1920s) and "rumbag" (1940s) became slang expressions for a drunkard. The popular card game GIN RUMMY made references to both gin and rum.

Although rum is produced in most countries where sugar cane is grown, the chief producers on an international scale are the islands in the West Indies, of which the more important sources are Barbados, Jamaica, Trinidad, Cuba, Puerto Rico, Haiti and the Virgin Islands. Other important producers of rum are Indonesia, Australia, South Africa, Germany and the United States.

Basically there are two kinds of rum: white rum, which is usually dry and light-bodied; and dark rum, a richer, more full-bodied product that ranges in color from amber to mahogany. The best known white rums are made in Puerto Rico, Cuba and the Virgin Islands, and the best known dark or heavier rums are made in Jamaica, Barbados and Guyana (formerly British Guiana). In the United States, white rum is preferred, but in other northern countries, such as Britain and Germany, heavier rums are favored.

The many variations within the two basic types of rum are the result of differences in the quality of the ingredients used and in the methods of fermentation, distillation and aging. The two most common fermentation techniques are the Demerara (the name of a river and an early name for Georgetown in Guyana) method and the Jamaican method. In the Demerara method, which takes approximately 48 hours, the molasses or sugar cane is prepared into a liquid known as wash, to which sulfuric acid and ammonium sulfate are added to encourage fermentation of the alcohol yeasts. In the Jamaican method, neither sulfuric acid nor ammonium sulfate are added to the alcohol yeasts in the wash to hasten fermentation. As a result fermentation by this method takes 10 to 12 days.

Distillation may take place in either a pot still or a continuous still. If a pot still is used, two distillations are required, as the product of the first distillation is too weak for consumption. Distillation in a continuous still is more economical and the product can be brought to any strength with only one distillation.

All rum is colorless when first distilled.

Many rums, especially those sold in the United States, are not aged or aged for only a year. These rums are often colored by the addition of artificial caramel coloring. The better rums are aged in oak casks for three to 20 years, during which time they acquire some of their color, but even these more expensive rums are subjected to artificial coloring. The proof of rum ranges from 80 to 150.

In the United States, rum is most often used in mixed drinks, especially those made with fruit juices, although it is occasionally drunk straight. It is also employed as a flavoring agent in meat marinade, dessert sauces and ice cream.

Reay Tannahill, *Food in History* (New York: Stein and Day, 1973).

rum fits   Convulsive seizures associated with WITHDRAWAL from alcohol, rum fits appear to develop in a minority of alcoholics (13%, according to two studies). The seizures are of the grand mal type, in which the patient loses consciousness. They often occur in clusters, although the number can vary from one to several repeated attacks. The seizures may start as early as 12 hours after abstinence but usually develop during the second or third day. Once the period of seizure activity has passed, the patient is free of convulsions until another cycle of drinking occurs. Rum fits may be followed by the last stage of withdrawal: DELIRIUM TREMENS.

rye whiskey   A spirit distilled from a grain mash that contains at least 51% rye. The production of rye, along with that of bourbon and corn whiskeys, is an American adaptation of European distilling practices. Today most Canadian whisky is also produced from a grain mixture like that used to make American rye.

Rye was probably the first grain whiskey distilled in America. Its beginnings date from the arrival of Irish and Scottish immigrants in colonial Pennsylvania. Because

of the difficulty involved in transporting grain to market, distillation of grain into whiskey became economically advantageous. Nevertheless during colonial times rye was slow to challenge rum in popularity. During the American Revolution rum distillers were forced to shut down for lack of foreign sugar cane supplies, and rye distillers, who required only domestic products, came into prominence.

As a result of abundant grain supplies the popularity of rye whiskey rose steadily during the 1790s and quickly attracted the interest of the new government as a source of revenue. In 1791 the first whiskey tax was levied. A segment of the population, however, firmly believed that having won independence from Britain, they had a right to distill whiskey. The result of this conflict was the Whiskey Rebellion of 1794, in which distillers based in western Pennsylvania refused to pay the new tax. President George Washington was forced to dispatch a military contingent to confront the distillers in Pittsburgh, but the distillers dispersed and their leader, David Bradford, fled the state. Thus rye whiskey was the provocation of one of the first domestic political crises in American history and the means by which the new government demonstrated its federal authority.

Rye remained the leading spirit in the United States through the Civil War years. Its principal domestic competitor, after the decline of rum, was corn whiskey, a raw tasting, colorless spirit that was sold without aging. Rye's appeal was advanced during the early 19th century, when distillers began to age the product in charred barrels. This process moderated the alcoholic taste of rye and gave it an amber color. After the Civil War bourbon began to rise in popularity. Distilled like rye but from a greater proportion of corn grains, bourbon was originally a compromise between harsh corn whiskey and smoother but more expensive rye.

Rye distillers usually buy malted barley

from specialized manufacturers rather than malt their own, as in Scotland and Ireland. The grain mixture, predominantly rye filled out with barleys, corns and oats, is cooked into a mash called "slurry," either by atmospheric cooking in an open vat, pressure cooking or a continuous cooking method that utilizes steam. Once cooked, the slurry is cooled and poured into fermentation tanks, which traditionally have been made of wood but today are usually stainless steel. Yeast is then added, and fermentation produces the "distiller's beer" from which the spirit can be distilled, generally in large patent stills. The rectified spirit is then barreled in charred white oak. Rye is almost always blended, a process that involves combining the products of several distillations, for consistency of flavor and appeal to a broad market.

S

sake   A "rice wine" fermented from a mixture of rice and malted barley. Sake is not a true wine because a raw material other than grapes is used, but since the fermented beverage is colorless or amber in color and slightly sweet, it resembles a wine in both appearance and taste.

Sake, which has an alcohol content of about 17%, is the traditional alcoholic beverage of Japan and probably originated as an outgrowth of the brewery fermentation of beers there. It is generally served in ceramic cups and often heated.

saloon   (From French *salon* drawing room, lounge; Italian *salone* room.) Generally speaking, a saloon is a place to which the public may go for any specified purpose, such as billiards, boxing or other recreation. In the United States the term "saloon" is used generally to refer to a shop where in-

toxicating beverages are sold and drunk, usually without meals. In this usage, saloon and BAR are synonymous.

In Britain the expression "saloon bar" is used to refer to the best of the bars in an ordinary public house. Bar in this sense simply means the counter over which drinks are sold.

schnapps   (German *Schnaps* spirits, brandy, gin, liquor.) A broad term that may refer to any distilled alcoholic beverage. Often the beverages called schnapps resemble Holland GIN. They are usually a colorless grain distillate and have a fiery taste. Schnapps is particularly associated with Sweden, Norway, Denmark, the Netherlands and northern Germany, each of which produces its own variety. In Scandinavia the term "schnapps" is sometimes used to mean AQUAVIT.

Alternate spellings of schnapps include *schnaps* (Denmark) and *snaps* (Sweden).

Scotch whisky   A spirit distilled in Scotland from a fermented mash of cereal grains. Scotch whisky is considered by many to be the finest in the world. Unlike American, Canadian or Irish whiskeys, true Scotch whisky is usually identified by the region where it is produced. There are four principal regional varieties: Highland malts, Lowland malts, Campbeltowns and Islays. They all differ subtly because of their various water sources, grain contents, methods of malting and distillation processes.

Although the precise origins are obscure, methods of distilling grain whiskies probably came to Scotland directly from Europe, rather than from Europe through Ireland, as many believe. This must have taken place during the early Middle Ages, although there is no written record of whisky in Scotland until the Scottish Exchequer Rolls of 1494. By that time the liquor was already accepted as a legal unit for business transactions.

The Scottish Parliament, then independent of England, first attempted to tax whisky as a source of public revenue in 1644. The trade proved impossible to control, and illicit distillation became a matter of fierce local pride. Increasing English intervention in Scotland brought further attempts to tax the whisky trade, which eventually led to riots in Edinburgh in 1713. England's control over Scotland became complete with its victory at the Battle of Culloden in 1746, giving the English control over the Scottish Highlands and the especially prized malt whiskies produced there. In 1823 the Duke of Gordon proposed legalization of local distillation and taxation of the trade at a new lower rate. Once in effect, this program slowly eroded the illegal whisky trade. In 1860 the first organized exportation of Scotch whisky to England began, and since that time whisky has become one of Scotland's most valuable exports.

There are two principal types of Scotch whisky: pot-still and patent-still, distinguished by the methods used to produce them. Pot-still malt whiskies are the most traditional sort. The only grain employed in their manufacture is barley that has been malted over peat, making them smokier in taste than the Irish malt whiskeys, which are cured over charcoal. Pot-still Scotch whiskies are nevertheless extremely heavy in taste and usually blended with the lighter, patent-still types. Only a small amount of pot-still Scotch whisky, intended for a limited but affluent market of aficionados, is bottled. Most commercial Scotch whiskies are produced by patent stills and employ a mixture of grains that includes only a portion of malted barley. The different grain content and distillation process of patent-still Scotch yields a lighter and clearer product, which for a time was challenged by some as not deserving of the designation "Scotch" or "Scotch whisky." Both pot-still and patent-still distillates are matured in casks made of either new wood

or woods previously used to age sherry or whisky. Virtually all Scotch whiskies commercially available are blends of several types and distillations; only those called "self-whiskies" are the yield of a single distillation.

sedative   Any of a number of substances, including alcohol, that acts as an irregular depressant of the central nervous system (CNS). A depressant is a substance that diminishes or stops normal body function. Sedatives are irregular because they do not depress all parts of the CNS at once but work first on the cerebrum and cerebellum, second on the spinal cord and finally on the vital centers. Sedatives (or soporifics) include liquid substances, such as alcohol; solid drugs, such as barbiturates; and gases, such as ether and chloroform. All these belong to a group of compounds that produces similar pharmacological behavior. All sedatives are potentially addicting compounds with associated severe withdrawal syndromes. However, for physical dependence to develop, the daily intake of each drug must exceed a certain threshold level. Sedatives are probably the most widely abused drugs in Western nations.

When alcohol or other sedatives enter the system, they first work on the brain to depress psychomotor activity, thereby relieving anxiety and tension. For approximately two to three hours the blood alcohol (or sedative) level rises and a sedative, or calming, effect is produced. Then, however, the level of alcohol or sedative in the blood begins to fall and the psychomotor activity level increases. This second effect usually lasts for about 12 hours after consumption of a large drink. Thus the sedative effect is always followed by an agitating effect, which often leaves the subject more tense than before he or she began drinking. This is one reason why people who have been drinking often crave another drink and also why a drink can relieve some of the agitating effects of a hangover. The agitation is multiplied with each pill or drink, and at high levels of consumption the individual may become tremulous, have hallucinations or—at severer levels, when unable to get another drink—experience DELIRIUM TREMENS (WITHDRAWAL).

Aside from alcohol the most commonly used (and abused) sedatives are barbiturates and the so-called minor tranquilizers, such as Librium and Valium, which were at first believed to be safer than barbiturates but subsequently found to produce similar patterns of addiction and withdrawal.

The most commonly abused barbiturates are short acting agents, such as pentobarbital (Nembutal), secobarbital (Seconal) and amobarbital (Amytal). The first barbiturate (barbital) was made available for medical use in 1903, followed by a second (phenobarbital) in 1912. By 1914 German medical literature already contained a description of barbiturate withdrawal syndrome.

Today Valium is the most widely prescribed drug in North America. Dependence on Valium can develop even at prescribed doses. After 10 to 14 weeks larger doses may be required to maintain a patient's feeling of well being. After four to six months abrupt cessation may result in physical withdrawal symtoms. Discomforts, such as tremors, agitation, stomach cramps and sweating, can occur for two to four weeks.

Perhaps the most dangerous effect of barbiturates and other sedatives occurs when they are used in combination with alcohol, which multiplies the potency and dangers of each drug (see SYNERGY). In humans a level of 100 milligrams of ethanol per 100 milliliters of blood combined with a level of 0.5 milligrams of barbiturate per 500 milliters of blood has proved fatal. This compares to lethal blood levels of alcohol alone of 100 to 800 milligrams per 100 milliters and of phenobarbital alone of 10 to 29 milligrams per 100 milliters.

Alcoholics with a high tolerance to alcohol have a similar tolerance to other sedatives (see CROSS-TOLERANCE). It takes a large amount of ether to induce surgical anesthesia in an alcoholic. In addition CROSS-ADDICTION occurs in alcoholics, for one sedative drug can be replaced with another that produces approximately the same effects. The rate increase in the number of people, especially young women, addicted to both Valium and alcohol is alarming, especially in view of the low threshold level for fatalities when these substances are combined. Nevertheless some doctors continue to prescribe sedatives to patients with emotional problems, often without bothering to inquire about their drinking habits. Complaints of anxiety, nervousness and insomnia may in fact reflect the early stages of alcoholism, and treatment with sedatives only exacerbates the problems of an alcoholic. As late as 1978 the October issue of the Federal Drug Administration's *Consumer* said that such minor tranquilizers as Valium "are of value in treating such conditions as alcoholism and epilepsy...." (See also DRUGS.)

Minimal (or Threshold) Doses of Some Generalized Depressant Drugs Required for Establishment of Physical Dependence

Drug	Threshold Dose (mg/day)
pentobarbital (Nembutal)	400
secobarbital (Seconal)	400
ethchlorvynol (Placidyl)	2,000*
ethinamate (Valmid)	13,000*
glutethimide (Doriden)	2,500*
methyprylon (Noludar)	2,400*
chlordiazepoxide (Librium)	300
diazepam (Valium)	100
meprobamate (Miltown, Equinal)	1,600–2,400

*The true threshold dose may be lower; the value given is merely the lowest thus far reported to have produced physical dependence.

P. M. Broughton, G. Higgins and J. R. P. O'Brien, "Acute Barbiturate Poisoning," *The Lancet* 270 (1956):180–184.

Stanley E. Gitlow, "A Pharmacological Approach to Alcoholism," *A. A. Grapevine,* October 1968.

R. C. Gupta and J. Kofold, "Toxicological Statistics for Barbiturates, Other Sedatives and Tranquillizers in Ontario: a 10-year Survey," *Canadian Medical Association Journal* 94 (1966):863–865.

Frederick G. Hofmann, *A Handbook on Drug and Alcohol Abuse: The Biomedical Aspects* (New York: Oxford University Press, 1975).

Frank A. Seixas "Alcohol and Its Drug Interactions," *Annals of Internal Medicine* 83, no. 1 (July 1975):86–92.

sedativism   Addiction to one of the sedatives, which includes alcohol. The term "sedativism" is also used to describe dual or multiple addiction to sedatives. (See also SEDATIVE, CROSS-ADDICTION.)

self-esteem   See PSYCHOLOGICAL MODELS OF ETIOLOGY.

sensitivity   The term sensitivity is sometimes used to explain why an individual may be prone to alcoholism. However, it is generally used without being well defined and may refer to TOLERANCE or to an inability to abstain from drinking. There is usually a more precise alternate term.

Serenity Prayer   A prayer used by members of ALCOHOLICS ANONYMOUS in times of stress or anxiety. It is used to open AA meetings and is often analyzed in group discussions. The full text is as follows: "God grant me the serenity to accept the things I cannot change, the courage to change the things I can, and the wisdom to know the difference."

The prayer is based on one delivered by the Protestant theologian Reinhold Neibuhr (1892–1971) at a church near Heath, Mass. in the summer of 1934. Since then it has been widely quoted. It reads: "O God, give us serenity to accept what cannot be changed, courage to change what should be changed, and the wisdom to distinguish the one from the other."

sex   Small doses of alcohol may relax people and help remove inhibitions, thereby allowing freer expression of sexual inclinations. In this respect alcohol can be considered an indirect aphrodisiac, anesthetizing the control centers of the brain. Alcohol is also used as an excuse by some individuals for engaging in normally forbidden sexual activity without taking responsibility for their actions.

While small doses of alcohol may enhance sexual relations, after a number of drinks men may be unable to complete the sex act. (See also HORMONES, MALE SEX; WOMEN.)

sherry   A fortified wine varying in color from amber to dark brown, sherry is the product of fermented palomino grapes to which spirits distilled from other wines have been added. Historically Spanish sherry has been extremely popular in Britain since the 15th century, and the present name is an Anglicization of Jerez, or Jerez de La Frontera, a town in southern Spain where the wine was first produced. The name is now a generic designation, applied to specific wines made around the world, but purists insist that true sherry is still produced only in Jerez, Sanlucar de Barrameda and Puerto de Santa Maria, all just west of Gibraltar.

Palomino grapes for sherry production are allowed to stand for one day after harvesting to increase their acidity before crushing. After pressing, gypsum is added to the grape juice to increase acidity, and because of the technique it takes longer to ferment sherry than to ferment most other wines—about three months. After "racking" (when the clear liquid is siphoned off from the dregs), the fermented grape juice secretes a sediment known as *flor,* a fungus

---

TYPICAL EFFECTS OF ALCOHOL ON SEXUAL FUNCTIONING

ACUTE

1. May increase sexual desire, if taken in small quantities.
2. In larger quantities, sedates the cerebral cortex, reducing inhibitions, but also impeding translation of external sexual information for the hypothalamus.
3. Interferes with transfer of sexual functioning messages from the brain to other parts of the central nervous system and sex organs.
4. Relaxes necessary muscle tension.
5. In males, may impede or prevent erection; in females, may interfere with or prevent lubrication.
6. Reduces serum testosterone level.
7. Prevents orgasm.
8. Reduces sexual desire.
9. Produces sedation to the point of sleep.
10. In males, can aid in development of psychological impotence.

CHRONIC

1. Any of the above, occurring on a repeated basis, can become chronic and permanent.
2. Liver damage—reduces serum sex hormone levels.
3. Brain damage—prevents sexual messages from being transmitted and/or interpreted.
4. In males, may produce testicular atrophy.
5. In males, may produce permanent impotence.

Source: "Sexual Dysfunction and the Alcoholic," *Focus on Alcohol and Drug Issues, July–August 1981.*

---

that is considered essential to the character of sherry wines.

Once filtered, sherries are fortified by the addition of Spanish brandies, or the distilled spirits of other wines, to give them an alcohol content between 15% and 20%. They are then aged in wood for up to two years. After this initial aging period all sherries are blended in a *bodega* containing casks of different local varieties and vintages. Blended sherry is often shipped from Spain to Britain for final processing and bottling.

Sherry comes in two varieties, dry *(fino)* and sweet *(oloroso)*. The first sort, dry in taste and light in color, includes the varieties called Manzanilla and amontillado. The second sort, artificially sweetened and darker in color, includes the varieties called amorosa and "cream" sherry. Dry sherry is usually drunk as an aperitif, and *oloroso* is generally consumed as a dessert wine or a substitute for port. Marginal sherries are commonly used as cooking wines.

shot   A single drink of liquor usually consumed in one gulp. A shot glass or jigger generally holds 1½ ounces of liquor. When used as an adjective, shot can mean drunk or afflicted with a hangover.

skid row   The term "skid row" originated in Seattle, Wash. The city's first sawmill was built in 1852 in the Pioneer Square district near Puget Sound. The logs were dragged into the mill over a set of tracks, or skids, and the road along which they were dragged became known as Skid Road (which later was shortened to Skid Row). As Seattle grew, the Pioneer Square area became dilapidated and the term took on the meaning it has today: a hangout for alcoholics and vagrants.

One false stereotype of alcoholics is that they are mostly skid row bums, sleeping in doorways without a home or job. In reality only about 3% to 5% of alcoholics are true skid row types and many skid row bums are not alcoholics.

sleep   While a small amount of alcohol taken before going to bed may help relieve tension and thus induce sleep, a large quantity is likely to have the opposite effect. Alcohol blocks REM (rapid eye movement) sleep, or dreaming sleep, which is necessary for complete rest. Alcohol anesthetizes the control centers that regulate sleep and dreaming.

A team of investigators at the University of Florida College of Medicine found that drinking results in lower levels of oxygen in the blood and periods when breathing is arrested for 10 seconds or more. This condition is called sleep apnea, and while it is usually harmless in healthy people, it could prove fatal for those with serious pulmonary or cardiac conditions.

"Drinkers' Sleep Disturbed, Not helped, by Nightcap," *The Journal* 11, no. 1 (Toronto, Jan. 1, 1982):7.

sloe gin   See GIN.

small intestine   See GASTROINTESTINAL TRACT.

smoking   People who drink heavily also tend to smoke heavily, and most alcoholics are heavy smokers. One study showed that more than 90% of male and female alcoholics were smokers. Another study found that 60% of all alcoholics smokes more than one pack of cigarettes a day and 30% smoked more than two packs (Bates).

There is a high incidence of pulmonary disease among alcoholics. It has been noted that in patients with severe alcoholism, chronic lung disorders, such as lung abscess, bronchitis and emphysema, are the most common problems other than liver disease (Pollard). Numerous studies have established the strong association between alcohol and tobacco consumption and cancers of the head and neck (see CANCER). It has been suggested that alcohol acts as a solvent and dissolves the tars in tobacco smoke, making them more available to the body tissues, particularly those in the head, neck and esophagus. Alcohol may alter the intracellular metabolism of the epithelial cells at cancer sites, resulting in an enhanced metabolic activation of tobacco-associated carcinogens. There is an apparent SYNERGY between alcohol and tobacco consumption that increases the risk of developing cancers of the upper alimentary tract and upper respiratory tract. According to some researchers, the risk of developing cancer of the mouth and throat among those who both smoke and drink is 15 times greater than the risk among those who neither smoke nor drink.

Heavy drinking appears to increase the urge to smoke, and therefore a high level of cigarette smoking may in some ways be attributable to the use of alcohol. Cigarette burns between the fingers are frequently exhibited by drunks who "nod off" while smoking.

R. C. Bates, "Pathologies Associated with Alcoholism," *Quarterly Journal of Studies on Alcohol* 27 (1966):110.

C. S. Lieber, et al., "Alcohol-Related Diseases and Carcinogenesis," *Cancer Research* 39, no. 7 (July 1979):2863–2885.

A. B. Lowenfels, M. Mohman and K. Shibutani, "Surgical Consequences of Alcoholism." *Surgery, Gynecology and Obstetrics* 131 (July 1970):129–138.

G. D. McCoy and E. L. Wynder, "Etiological and Preventive Implications in Alcohol Carcinogenesis," *Cancer Research* 39 (July 1979):2844–2850.

H. M. Pollard, W. A. Gracie, and J. C. Sisson, "Extrahepatic Complications Associated with Cirrhosis of the Liver," *Journal of the American Medical Association* 169 (1959):318.

sober   Not under the influence of alcohol. The term is also used to describe an alcoholic who is no longer drinking. A person with a BLOOD ALCOHOL CONCENTRATION (BAC) of 0.05% or less is considered legally sober. However, someone with a BAC of 0.05% is not necessarily as sober as someone who has had nothing to drink.

sobering pill   See L-DOPA, AMETHYSTIC.

sobering up   Detoxification after drinking. To date no way of speeding up the detoxification process (other than by kidney dialysis) has been found. Coffee or a cold shower may wake up someone who is drunk, but he or she will still be drunk. It usually takes an hour for a 150-lb person to metabolize three-quarters of an ounce of absolute alcohol (see METABOLISM).

sobriety   Among alcoholics, and particularly among members of ALCOHOLICS ANONYMOUS, sobriety has a precise meaning. It refers to a state of abstinence in which the alcoholic is comfortable and secure, either free of a desire to drink or able to cope with such urges. The patient usually accepts outside help and support, including formal rehabilitation and therapy programs. AA insists upon the support systems of group fellowship and regular attendance at meetings as necessary to continuing sobriety.

The words SOBER and sobriety have been part of all languages as long as drunk and drunkenness, but in the view of AA and others, the definition has been narrowed and made more precise. In this context sobriety does not mean a state characterized by moderation in drinking or one short of intoxication—it means total abstinence. AA, among others, is firm in its belief that an alcoholic can attain sobriety only through total abstinence and that he can never resume "normal" drinking or CONTROLLED DRINKING. If he resumes drinking,

in AA's view, that first drink will trigger a chain of events which will lead, perhaps not immediately but certainly eventually, to a return to active alcoholic behavior.

In this belief they have followed the lead of the TEMPERANCE societies, without embracing the moral and religious tenets of that earlier movement. However, just as the temperance movement changed the meaning of the word "temperance" from moderation to prohibition, AA has changed the meaning of the word "sober" from unaffected by liquor to absolutely free of liquor.

In AA sobriety begins after the alcoholic has taken his last drink, admitted that he is "powerless over alcohol" and begun to live a sober life. Length of sobriety, as counted in years, months and even days, looms large as a measure of the alcoholic's success in coping with his enemy—alcohol. Alcoholics joining the AA program are often urged to make "ninety meetings in ninety days," which translates into one meeting a day every day for three months. Thereafter the number of meetings to attend is up to the individual, although the recommended number continues to be high indefinitely. Many AA groups call special attention to attendance achievements at their regular meetings and award "ninety day" pins. Anniversaries—a year's sobriety, two years' and so on—are faithfully remembered and celebrated. Length of sobriety is thus a major concern in the lives of AA members, and while the groups are informally democratic, longtime sobriety confers a measure of seniority. Thus a woman of 40 with 20 years of sobriety has more of the authority of an "elder" than a man of 60 with only two years of sobriety.

While length of sobriety is used as a major reinforcement factor in AA, fears over the "interminability" of sobriety are an ever present danger. The prospect of "never having another drink as long as I live" can be depressing, even terrifying, and can lead to disaster. To counter this danger, AA focuses on short-term sobriety. "One day at a time" is the slogan used to help face down immediate desires to drink. The idea is too concentrate on remaining sober today without worrying about tomorrow. The same procedure is followed tomorrow and so on. Fears, doubts and anxieties must not be projected into the future. On the other hand, grandiose dreams and expectations of remaining sober are also considered dangerous. Sobriety is grounded in today and in a realistic assessment of today's pitfalls and opportunities.

One measure of sobriety is quality. There is "good" sobriety and "poor" sobriety. Good sobriety consists of staying sober, attending meetings and functions and participating in the activities of the group, and enjoying your sobriety and the fellowship of those like you. If you do these things, particularly if you make an effort to do them properly and systematically, you are said to be "following your program" and the prognosis is good.

Poor sobriety is ignoring or fighting some, if not all, of the aspects of the program. This attitude may stem from a basic subconscious DENIAL of alcoholism, an inability to accept help or face up to reality of the situation. These are seen as symptoms of conflict and turmoil that may lead the alcoholic back to drinking. Another form of poor sobriety is "white-knuckled" sobriety, which means that the alcoholic stays sober through grim determination. He lives in constant fear of a relapse and thinks incessantly of drinking, often with the feared result.

The term "dry drunk" is often applied to those with poor sobriety. The dry drunk has "dried out" and is no longer drinking but that is the only step he has taken. The implication is that the "dry" drunk will soon be "wet," or active, again.

social class   In the United States different social classes have different attitudes toward drinking. It has been found that as education and income rise there is a rise in the number of drinkers and the frequency of drinking (with the exception of young males). Those in the upper socioeconomic groups do not regard drinking as a moral problem, as is often the case with members of the lower socioeconomic groups, and upper-class groups generally have more permissive attitudes toward drinking. There are more abstainers in the lower class; according to statistics in the first RAND REPORT *(Alcoholism and Treatment)* 52% of the population in the lower social class were abstainers, compared with 34% in the middle class, and 21% in the upper class. However, poor males under 25 are perhaps the most likely to encounter trouble with the police or society because of drinking.

As education and income rise, there is less difference between the drinking patterns of men and WOMEN. Drinking settings also differ according to class, with upper-class groups doing more drinking in cocktail party settings and lower-class groups engaging in more pub drinking. Alcoholics in the upper socioeconomic class appear less in official statistics because their style of drinking is less visible and is covered up by the stability of their jobs, marriages and residences. They are more likely to be protected by others close to them, who help to hide their alcoholism from their peers (see PARA-ALCOHOLIC).

Social class also may play a role in treatment. The authors of the first Rand Report found that lower-class patients drop out of therapy more quickly than patients from the middle and upper class.

David J. Armor, J. Michael Polich and Harriet B. Stambul, *Alcoholism and Treatment* (New York: John Wiley and Sons, 1978), pp. 61–77.

social drinking   Social drinking usually refers to moderate drinking on social occasions. Alcohol stimulates sociability and relaxes inhibitions among people in groups. The term "social drinking" is also used to refer to drinking in a way accepted by a certain cultural group. Sometimes an individual participates in social drinking as a result of social pressures, at a cocktail party, for example, where one is urged to have a drink or to have another.

sociocultural models of etiology
The many theories about what causes alcoholism can generally be divided into three major groups: physiological, psychological and sociocultural. Sociocultural etiological theories postulate relationships between various factors in society and the incidence of alcohol use. For example, ethnic and cultural differences in the use of alcohol suggest that society plays an important role in the development of alcoholism. Different cultures have different attitudes toward alcohol, set different standards for what constitutes appropriate use of intoxicants, and provide greater or lesser environmental support for drinking. Jews, Mormons and Moslems have very low rates of alcoholism, and the French have a very high rate. This disparity may be due to cultural proscriptions against alcohol in the case of the first three groups, and cultural support for high consumption of alcohol in the case of the last group.

Stress factors in a culture may also contribute to alcoholism. Individuals may react to a crisis situation generated by external events with an increase in consumption of alcohol. WOMEN in particular are likely to begin heavy drinking in response to a traumatic event. There is a cyclical relationship between social instability and alcoholism: heavy consumption in reaction to social stress in turn increases the deterioration of the social environment.

Family patterns are another social factor that plays a role in alcoholism. An unusually high incidence of familial alcoholism has been found in the backgrounds of alcoholics. While the part played by GENETICS cannot be ignored, there no doubt is also a strong social learning factor involved in the development of alcoholism.

Sociocultural etiological theories of alcoholism receive wide support among experts in the field today. However, they are generally considered in conjunction with physiological and psychological theories, since none of these alone can completely explain the causes of alcoholism.

solitary drinking   Drinking alone is generally considered to be a sign of a drinking problem. Those who often take a drink alone after work or before bed or who drink a beer or two while mowing the lawn are not usually classified as solitary drinkers. Drinking to excess is characteristic of solitary problem drinkers, since there are no social activities to divert them from almost continuous drinking. Then, too, many solitary drinkers choose to be alone as a way of escaping from other problems. These problems lead the solitary drinker into a cycle in which the seclusion, the drinking and the initial problems all feed on each other and contribute to a worsening of the original situation.

Often solitary drinking is distinguished from BAR DRINKING, and the activities of many alcoholics tend to fall largely within one of these two categories. While individual behavior may vary from time to time, distinctions have been made between those who seek out public places to do their drinking and those who drink at home. It has been suggested, although more documentation is needed, that those who are more outwardly gregarious in their drinking habits are more likely to seek out and be more comfortable in highly supportive and organized groups, such as ALCOHOLICS ANONYMOUS, when attempting to resolve their drinking problems.

sour mash   A particular grain mixture used to prepare the mash, or "wash," from which bourbon is distilled. The grain content of bourbon is at least 51% corn (Indian maize), with the remainder being made up of rye and malted barley. In sour mash bourbon this grain content is mixed with a residue from a previous distillation in order to encourage fermentation. The residue, called "slop," is acidic in taste and smell, and these characteristics, rather than the taste of the finished bourbon, give sour mash whiskey its nam‿. The chief alternative to sour mash as an aid to fermentation is SWEET MASH, in which a high proportion of malted barley is blended with the corn and rye grains.

Spanish Americans   See HISPANICS.

sparkling wine   Wine that has been subjected to a second fermentation to make it effervescent and heavily carbonated. Champagne is the best known sparkling wine. It is now produced in all wine-growing countries and not just in the Champagne region of France. While Champagne is a white sparkling wine, there are also many red sparkling wines and rose, or "pink," sparkling wines. The alcohol content of sparkling wines is about 12% to 12.5%.

Wine has been produced in the Champagne district since the third century A.D., but sparkling wine is a relatively recent invention of the region. By most accounts, it originated in the 1690s and, according to tradition, was the work of Dom Perignon, a monk in the Haut Villers Abbey. He is also credited with the first use of cork stoppers, without which carbonation of effervescent wines in bottles would not be possible.

The discovery of sparkling wine most likely happened when a wine in the later stages of fermentation was bottled and stoppered with a cork. The effect of the carbonic gas produced by the continuing fermentation and retained in the bottle by a close-fitting cork would then have been obvious once the wine was opened. After it became desirable to produce such effervescent wines, the precise technique became a closely guarded secret. Sparkling wines did not gain popularity until the end of the 18th

century. Since that time they have often been imitated in various fashions, which have included simply pumping a STILL WINE full of gas.

The traditional method of producing sparkling wines is to subject a chosen wine to a second fermentation in the bottle. In this case the chosen wine, called the cuvee, is bottled in especially thick glass, combined with controlled amounts of yeast and sugar and stoppered with a cork that is held in place by a wire wrapping. The wine is then aged for a period between one and three years. With a minimum loss of pressure the sediment produced by fermentation must be removed before shipment to market. For this reason the bottles are temporarily stored upside down, allowing the sediment to collect on the cork. The pressure in the bottle is reduced for a time by chilling it to about 25° F. Then, in a step called *degorgement,* the cork is pulled, the frozen yeast sediment is removed, the bottle is topped off with a clarified wine and sugar solution and a new cork is inserted.

Because of the costs involved in bottle fermentation, many sparkling wines today are produced by subjecting the cuvee to a second fermentation in large closed stainless steel tanks. Once fermentation has reached the desired level, the wine can be filtered in bulk, mixed with the clarified wine and sugar solution and then bottled. This method, called *cuve close,* is considered inferior to bottle fermentation because of the different contact of the wine with the yeast in the second fermentation.

The finest sparkling wine is of course French Champagne, a term that refers to a region recently broken into titular districts called Marne, Heute-Marne, Aube and Ardennes. Spain, however, produces a greater quantity of sparkling wines than France, many of which are red or rose. The Panades district in northeastern Spain is especially noted for its sparkling wines, and some argue that the sparkling wines produced at Cordorniu by the *cuve close* method of second fermentation actually predate all French sparkling wines. Portugal is also known for sparkling wines bottled in the southern Dao district, and in Germany such wines are bottled under the Perlwein and Sekt designations. Sparkling wines are also produced in most of the wine-producing areas of the United States, with New York state being the leader.

spirit still   The second and smaller of the two stills employed in some double-distillation processes. The first and larger still, known as a WASH STILL, produces a weak and impure distillate, called "low wine," that is usually strengthened and purified by further rectification in the spirit still. Passed once or repeatedly through the spirit still, the distillate is then collected in a final receiver vessel.

spirits   Originally the term "spirit" or "spirits" meant the essence of any substances. Now it is commonly used to refer to the alcoholic essence of a fermented substance from which it has been extracted. In a more general sense the term "spirits" is also a synonym for alcoholic beverages, as distinguished from the many varieties of chemical alcohols and denatured ethanols, which are nonpotable.

The alcohol content of all potable spirits is ethanol, a clear and colorless distillate. The variations in potable spirits are produced by impurities retained from the fermented mash, by flavorings added after distillation and by containers used for aging. The purest are the so-called natural spirits, which are flavorless and high in ethanol content.

The distinguishing feature of most common spirits is provided by the content of the fermented mash from which they are distilled. Gin and whiskey are spirits distilled from grains, brandy is a spirit distilled from wine, rum is a spirit distilled from sugar cane or molasses and vodka is a spirit tra-

ditionally distilled from potatoes. A variety of other fermented substances, such as agave or dates, are distilled throughout the world to produce less well-known potable spirits.

spouse abuse   Family violence in the United States is a significant and often ignored problem. American society tolerates a high level of violence in general and is usually unwilling to interfere in people's private lives. A national survey found that there were over 6 million incidents of serious physical abuse in families each year (Straus 1977). Although a large percentage of this violence is directed toward children, there is also an extremely high number of incidents of spouse abuse. The number of spousal assaults each year in the United States has been estimated at 1.7 million. According to the FBI's *Uniform Crime Reports,* 25% of all murders are intrafamilial and half of these are spouse killings (Hindman). Both men and women may be the aggressors, although wives are more often seriously injured, because of their physical disadvantage. Women, however, are just as likely to kill their spouses as are men, often citing as motivation the abuse they received from their husbands.

Spouse abuse is also related to CHILD ABUSE. A man who beats his wife may also beat his children; the abused wife may take out her anger and resentment on the children. A chain reaction may start with each member in turn and in his or her own way provoking or imposing violence. Quarrels arise when one partner complains about the other's behavior, leading to violence by the second partner, leading to more complaints. M. A. Stuart and C. S. de Blois in 1978 found that at one psychiatric clinic 65% of mothers who had abused their sons had been abused by their husbands.

A clear connection has been shown between alcoholism and all kinds of family violence. According to one estimate, up to

80% of all cases of family violence involve drinking, either before, during or after the incident (Flanzer). Moderate and problem drinkers are more frequently involved in such incidents than light drinkers.

Alcohol breaks down inhibitions, often resulting in violent behavior between husbands and wives. However, most research supports the conclusion that alcohol abuse does not itself cause family violence, but rather that the use of alcohol may provide an excuse to be violent. Intoxication may be perceived by the abuser as a time when normal rules for behavior do not apply.

Alcoholism and family abuse have many characteristics in common. Some consider family violence to be a disease, just as alcoholism is considered a disease. Both allow the subject to gain temporarily some form of mastery over his or her world, both resolve conflicts and both temporarily mask depression. Similarities have been found in the characters of spouse abusers and alcoholics, members of each group often are dependent, impulsive, frustrated and depressed and have low self-esteem (Sanchez-Dirks). Both violence and alcoholism seem to provide coping mechanisms for abusers and alcoholics. More research is needed to uncover the particular circumstances leading to these traits. Children of alcoholics also show many of the same character patterns.

Violence and drinking may be connected in several different ways. Perhaps the most common pattern is an eruption of violence that happens only when alcohol is consumed—either the abuser drinks and then hits, or the victim drinks until he or she becomes a target for abuse. The drinker, however, may drink to avoid hitting someone or, in some instances, hit someone instead of taking a drink. Violence occurs in a more subtle form when a heavy drinker neglects or disturbs his or her family to such an extent that it causes severe damage. Such neglect may also cause so much pressure in the family that it eventually erupts into violence. In addition quarrels that begin over a spouse's drinking can result in physical abuse.

Because there is a high acceptance of violence in American society and victims often hide the fact that they have been abused because of fear of reprisal or lack of understanding by the community, treatment of the dual problem of alcoholism and spouse abuse can be difficult. Women often do not report the beatings they receive because of their own sense of helplessness and despair. They may believe that they have failed their marriage and are incompetent as wives and mothers. Instead of seeing alcoholism or their husbands' violence as the problem, they feel that they have gotten what they deserved and are powerless to change things. Both alcoholism and family violence are often part of a repetitive cycle from generation to generation. Abusers and alcoholics have learned to hit and drink in order to resolve their problems and reassert control. Children from abusive families learn these coping patterns from the same individuals who teach them to love. Thus loving and hitting become linked in their minds. It is therefore important to involve the whole family in treatment.

A problem in treatment of alcohol-related abuse is that the programs designed to deal with battered victims frequently are not capable of addressing alcohol problems, and often alcoholic counselors do not know much about the mechanics of family violence. The two problems tend to be treated separately, although in reality they are closely linked. It is important to look for alcohol problems when dealing with family violence, for while treating an alcoholism problem will not necessarily stop the violence, it will make it easier to work on.

Jerry Flanzer, "The Vicious Circle of Alcoholism and Family Violence," *Alcoholism* 1, no. 3 (January/February 1981):30–32.

Margaret H. Hindman, "Family Violence," *Alcohol Health and Research World* 4, no. 1 (Fall 1979).

U.S. Department of Justice, FBI, "Crime in the U.S." *Uniform Crime Report* (1975).

Ruth Sanchez-Dirks, "Reflections on Family Violence," *Alcohol Health and Research World* 4, no. 1 (Fall 1979).

M. A. Stewart and C. S. de Blois, "Is Alcoholism Related to Physical Abuse of Wives and Children?" (paper presented at the National Council on Alcoholism Annual Meeting, St. Louis, 1978).

M. A. Straus, "A Sociological Perspective in the Prevention and Treatment of Wifebeating," *Battered Women,* ed. M. Roy (New York: Van Nostrand Reinhold, 1977).

spree   A drinking bout; an episode of prolonged excessive drinking.

spree drinking   Drinking characterized by periods of sobriety lasting weeks or months and drinking binges that continue for days or weeks. This type of periodic drinking is more common in the United States than in a country like FRANCE, where there is a higher percentage of steady drinkers.

While a spree drinker may not consume more alcohol over the space of a year than a steady moderate drinker, he or she is at more of a health risk. For expectant mothers particularly, a drinking spree presents a grave danger to the fetus (see FETAL ALCOHOL SYNDROME). JELLINEK categorized this type of drinking as EPSILON ALCOHOLISM.

Sri Lanka   Some medical authorities in Sri Lanka, formerly known as Ceylon, argue that alcoholism is the single most important health and social problem facing the country. Heavy drinking is concentrated among a small segment of the population, but a pattern of excessive consumption appears to be spreading as the country becomes more urban and less rigorous in the observance of Buddhist and Hindu strictures on drinking.

In 1977 total consumption of legally produced alcoholic beverages, measured as ABSOLUTE ALCOHOL, in Sri Lanka was nearly 11 million liters. Of these legal liquors the preferred beverages were arrack, a spirit made from rice or coconut milk with an alcohol content of 35%, and toddy, a beverage made from molasses and various beers with an alcohol content of 6% to 8%. In addition various wines, brandies, whiskeys and gins are imported. However, illegally produced alcoholic beverages are estimated to equal half the amount of legal alcohol available, and production of these home brews, which have an alcohol content ranging from 20% to 60%, has doubled in recent years. Consumption of most legal alcoholic beverages has decreased since 1974, but the drop is thought to be entirely the result of increased availability of illicit liquor. As is true throughout the world, illegal liquor in Sri Lanka is often based on methylated spirits, contains hazardous amounts of distillation by-products and has gained wide acceptance because it sells at a cheaper price than licensed, taxed liquors.

Quantities of Alcoholic Beverages Legally Produced

Year	Arrack (1,000 liters)	Toddy (1,000 liters)	Beers (1,000 liters)
1973	27,406	13,440	7,906
1974	30,855	13,059	6,460
1975	29,203	10,773	5,244
1976	26,848	9,496	7,114
1977	28,178	8,025	8,629

Statistics on per capita consumption indicate the presence of a large proportion of abstainers and, consequently, a small proportion of heavy drinkers. These figures, however, do not take into account illegal alcoholic beverages, and there is ample evidence to suggest a greater alcoholism problem than official estimates acknowledge. Consumption of home-brewed alcohol is especially high among the lower classes,

Total Consumption and Per Capita Consumption of Legal Alcoholic Beverages, as Absolute Alcohol

Year	Total Consumption of Absolute Alcohol (1,000 liters)	Per Capita Consumption of Absolute Alcohol (1,000 liters)
1974	12,020	0.89
1975	11,189	0.82
1976	10,411	0.74
1977	10,882	0.78

whose members are unlikely ever to seek professional help. Alcohol has had no traditional place in the country's social or ceremonial occasions, but in recent times drinking has become common at such events. Weekend drinking in urban areas and drinking at agrarian celebrations in rural areas are also rising.

There has been an increase in physical complications, sometimes resulting in coma or death, associated with drinking illegal alcoholic beverages. Because of the lack of special hospital facilities for the treatment of alcoholism in Sri Lanka, statistics on the incidence of alcoholism are unavailable, but it is known that the incidence is higher in the capital city of Colombo than in other areas of the country.

The sole authority charged with alcoholism prevention policies in Sri Lanka is the Department of Excise. This agency, assisted by the police, concentrates entirely on licensing of public drinking places and taxation of legally produced liquors. Neither of these efforts have much impact because of the number of private drinking clubs in the country and the easy availability of illegal alcoholic beverages. There are at present no public education programs regarding the dangers of alcohol abuse, and the Department of Health has no alcoholism-related activities.

steam beer A bottom-fermented lager beer distinguished by a bitter, "hoppy" flavor similar to that of ales. Steam beer is fermented at higher than normal temperatures and naturally carbon-ated. It is named for the fact that during its unique fermentation process the fermentation vat builds up pressure like a steam engine.

Steam beer is the only kind of beer entirely indigenous to the United States. It originated in San Francisco in the mid-19th century, when the Gold Rush brought a sudden population explosion to the area. Lacking ice for the chilling required in normal fermentation, California brew masters were forced to experiment with fermentation at higher temperatures, and in the process they discovered a beer especially prized for its flavor by the working class in San Francisco. Steam beers were hurt by the shift in American taste to lighter, paler lager beers and the status that was attached to them around the turn of the century. The final blow to the industry came from Prohibition, and today steam beer is brewed and bottled by only one company, Anchor, in San Francisco.

Steam beer is brewed exclusively from barley malt, unlike most lager beers, which use other cereal grains. It also has a far higher hop content, about four times the average of other beers. After a bottom-fermentation yeast is added to the hop wort, fermentation of steam beer takes place at temperatures between 65° and 75° F, as opposed to the 40° to 60° F range for most lagers, and the fermentation tank is usually an exceptionally shallow one. Carbonation is entirely accomplished by "krausening"— the introduction of carbolic acid from a newly fermented and active wort—rather than by injection of artificially produced carbon dioxide. The result is a distinctive but rather fragile beer, one subject to clouding when excessively chilled and often drunk at warmer than usual temperatures for that reason.

still   An apparatus used to distill alcohol from a fermented mash. In its simplest form a still consists of a vessel in which to heat the fermented mash, a collector in which to catch the alcohol vapor then given off, an exterior tube in which to cool and, thus, recondense the alcohol vapor and a receiving vessel in which to collect the liquid distillate.

The pot still is the oldest, the most traditional and the simplest type currently in use. It produces intermittent batches of distillate according to the process described above. In the years before legalization of private distilling, the pot still was prized because it was small and easily dismantled for hiding and was extremely portable. The product of the pot still, however, was and remains erratic—subject to unintentional variations in temperatures—and relatively impure. This "low wine" distillate is weak in strength and heavy in taste unless further rectified by costly secondary distillations. However, the pot still remains the favorite of those who want the strong character and variable qualities of a single distiller's product. Most pot-still products, especially Scotch whiskies, enter the commercial marketplace only after being blended with other, lighter distillates.

The patent still, or continuous still, is the type most used today. It was invented in 1831 by Aeneas Coffey, an Irish exciseman, and has remained essential to commercially efficient distillation. The key advantage offered by the patent still is the fact that it combines twin distillation columns for semi-independent double distillations that can operate without halt. Although the product lacks the strong character of pot-still distillates, it can be mass produced. Patent-still spirits are generally blended with small amounts of pot-still spirits to create a product that is distinctive and yet light enough to appeal to a broad market.

still wine   A noncarbonated wine. Still wine refers to any wine except SPARKLING WINE, which is heavily carbonated and not "still" when poured in a glass.

stomach   The ingestion of alcohol has been widely associated with inflammation of the stomach, especially its mucous membrane. The actual mechanism of damage has not been conclusively established, but it is generally accepted that alcohol stimulates secretion of stomach acid. Solutions of less than 10% ethanol stimulate the gastric glands to produce acid and ingestion of higher concentrations of alcohol produces gastric irritation and reduces appetite. In addition alcohol delays the emptying time of the stomach. These factors in combination may cause a hyperacidic condition that in time could lead to stomach disorder. The most frequent are nausea, vomiting and diarrhea.

Irritation of the mucous membrane is common after a period of prolonged drinking. In most cases this subsides after alcohol consumption ceases, but prolonged and excessive use of alcohol may result in more serious erosion of the stomach membrane, ranging from inflammation to ulceration and hemmorrhage. Excessive drinking is frequently associated with heavy smoking and together these abuses may have an additive or synergistic effect causing chronic inflammation of the stomach (see SYNERGY).

stout   A very dark and especially sweet variety of ale that was traditionally common in England but is now almost exclusively associated with Ireland. The grain content of stout has a far higher proportion of malted barley than that of other ales, and the maltose, a soluble sugar produced by malting, gives stout its distinctive taste and color. Stout is top fermented and processed in ways that are otherwise indistinguishable from those used in making ale.

substance abuse   A general term used to describe ABUSE of alcohol and other drugs, including tobacco and caffeine.

Sudan   The largest country in Africa, Sudan has a population of about 17 million. The Moslem religion, embraced by 85% of the population, is the single greatest restraint on drinking in the country, for the Koran prohibits consumption of alcoholic beverages and no Moslem in Sudan is permitted to hold a license for a drinking establishment or liquor store. As a result of the Koran's prohibition, there is virtually no drinking among the female Moslem population, but among the male Moslem population drinking has been rising lately, indicating this religious ban may be losing its effect. Fifteen percent of the Sudanese population consists of Christians and persons belonging to no recognized sect, on whom the religious law against drinking has no effect.

The predominant legally produced liquors in Sudan are beer and sherry, and demand for both exceeds supply. Because of limited production and distribution problems restricting the availability of these beverages, there is widespread unregulated production—and consumption—of two illegal alcoholic beverages: *marisa,* a fermented sorghum, and *aragi,* a liquor distilled from either date or sorghum mashes. *Marisa,* which has alcohol content ranging from 1.8% to 5.1%, is common throughout the country. The date variety of *aragi,* with an alcohol content as high as 49%, is especially common in the northern districts of the country; the *aragi* distilled from sorghum has a lower alcohol content. Consumption of illegally produced aragi is an especially serious health problem in Sudan because this beverage often contains toxic by-products resulting from crude distillation processes.

Studies of drinking patterns in Sudan suggest that the drinking population is small and that excessive drinking is occasional. One survey of Khartoum province found that the rate of alcoholism among the male population was 1.8%, that less than half the male population drank and that of these drinkers only about 13% drank to excess. (Drinking to excess in this context meant taking a drink daily, for most drinkers surveyed drank only once or twice each month.) These statistics are thought to be above the national average because they included the country's largest urban population. Consequently the rate of alcoholism for the entire country is estimated to be somewhere below 1.8%.

Even this limited drinking, however, has a significant effect on the nation. Most excessive drinkers in Sudan suffer from symptoms of liver cirrhosis aggravated by endemic diseases, a high percentage of social drinkers suffer physical complications from illegally distilled alcohols, and as a result one-quarter of the hospital admissions in the entire country are either directly or indirectly related to alcohol abuse. In addition 86% of the country's automobile accidents and 75% of its job absenteeism are alcohol related. In the city of Khartoum 87% of the alcoholics are known to have had fathers who drank, and the divorce rate in that city is six times higher for alcoholics than for nondrinkers.

The only efforts to combat alcohol abuse in Sudan are nongovernmental, and it is generally agreed that what legal penalties exist for alcohol-related crimes are rarely enforced. The nation's general policy toward alcohol abuse is to encourage abstinence on religious rather than social grounds. Religious groups have begun to contribute to antialcohol campaigns, particularly in the country's most heavily populated areas to the north. These organizations, however, remain the sole source of preventative measures.

sugar See BLOOD SUGAR, FRUCTOSE.

suicide Alcoholics are at a particularly high risk of committing suicide. Although estimates of the level of risk vary, at least one study reported it to be 30 times greater than the risk of suicide among the general population (Medhus).

Alcoholics who commit suicide have attempted to kill themselves more often than nonalcoholics who commit suicide, and alcoholic suicide attempters more closely resemble actual suicides than do nonalcoholic attempters. These findings suggest that alcoholics who try to kill themselves form a significant part of the population that eventually succeeds in committing suicide. Studies have shown that between 15% and 64% of suicide attempters and up to 80% of suicides were drinking at the time of the event. Use of other DRUGS with alcohol is probably responsible for a substantial proportion of accidental deaths as well as suicides.

In the general population women have a higher attempted suicide rate than men but men have a higher completed suicide rate than women. Among alcoholic women the number of suicide attempts clearly exceeds that among the female population as a whole, and recent data indicate that the rate of completed suicides among female alcoholics is 23 times the general population rate (Adelstein).

A. Adelstein, "Alcoholism and Mortality," *Population Trends* 7 (1977).
John R. DeLuca, ed., *Fourth Special Report to the U.S. Congress on Alcohol and Health,* (Rockville, Md.: National Institute on Alcohol Abuse and Alcoholism, 1981), p. 84.
A. Medhus, "Mortality among Female Alcoholics," *Scandinavian Journal of Social Medicine* 3 (1975):111–115.

supra-additive effect See SYNERGY.

surgery When operating on alcoholics, surgeons must be aware of a number of factors. The depressive effects of general anesthesia and those of alcohol on acutely intoxicated patients are synergistic (see SYNERGY). Chronic alcoholics may have a CROSS-TOLERANCE to general anesthesia, requiring greater amounts to induce sleep. They may also undergo a prolonged second stage of anesthesia after the administration of inhalation anesthetics. In addition there is the possibility of myocardial depression and altered blood volume in alcoholics, which increases the risk of anesthesia.

Often alcoholics who are apparently healthy have damaged liver function, which may seriously affect the postoperative course. Even in the absence of severe liver damage, increased bleeding frequently complicates operations on alcoholic patients, who have been found to have a decreased number of platelets, which aid in clotting of the blood.

Delirium tremens is another serious potential complication for the alcoholic patient. Patients who drink the equivalent of 1 or more pints of whiskey per day or who have a previous history of delirium tremens are likely to develop this condition after the operation. Delirium tremens usually starts within 48 to 72 hours after cessation of drinking, a period when it is wise to avoid operating on known heavy drinkers.

Albert B. Lowenfels, Michael Rohman and Kinichi Shibutani, "Surgical Consequences of Alcoholism," *Surgery, Gynecology, and Obstetrics* 131 (July 1970):129–138.

susceptibility Certain individuals may show a strong readiness to turn to alcohol in times of stress, and such people who cannot cope in any other way are said to be more "susceptible" to alcohol. "Susceptibility," however, is a vague term that does little to clarify or explain alcoholism and is generally best avoided.

sweet mash   A grain mixture used in preparation of the mash, or "wash," from which bourbon is distilled. The grain content of bourbon is at least 51% corn (Indian maize), with the remainder made up of rye and malted barley. In sweet mash bourbon there is an unusually high proportion of malted barley, which is rich in maltose, a soluble sugar that enhances fermentation by combining with yeast to produce alcohol. The chief alternative to sweet mash is SOUR MASH, in which a residue from a previous distillation is added as an aid to fermentation in the grain wash of bourbon.

Switzerland   Long known for its progressive attitude toward alcoholism and alcohol-related problems, Switzerland opened its first treatment center for alcoholics in Zurich before 1900. The Swiss temperance movement is one of the oldest in Europe.

Increased concern about alcoholism often results in increased awareness of the extent of the problem, and this may be the case in Switzerland. The country's per capita consumption of 11.23 liters of ABSOLUTE ALCOHOL in 1973 ranked it seventh among countries from which reliable statistics were available. In 1976 there were 33,930 admissions to various clinics and hospitals for alcohol-related medical problems, a figure that authorities estimate represents about a quarter of the alcoholic population. Continuing concern and government sponsorship of a variety of antialcoholism programs, however, has resulted in a decrease in per capita consumption since 1973. More specifically the decrease can be attributed to public education programs, increased taxes on alcoholic beverages and a general economic recession that restricted purchasing power for most of the population.

In the early 19th century the most prevalent drinking pattern was consumption of potato schnapps, a distilled alcohol that was produced in abundance because of surplus potato crops. When the Swiss Federal State was established in 1848, an indirect effect of its new constitution was increased availability of cheap potato schnapps because of liberalized trade controls. To change that situation the government in 1885 introduced a constitutional amendment that imposed heavy taxes on potato schnapps, restricted sales of the liquor and created a state monopoly on its production. The result was a shift in agricultural production to fruit and a consequent rise in distillation of various cider and fruit schnapps. In 1930 these products were also brought under the state alcohol monopoly and made subject to similar sales taxes and restrictions.

Today the revenues of the state alcohol monopoly are distributed equally among the federal and canton, or provincial, authorities. The cantons are required to devote 10% of their share to programs aimed at combating alcoholism; in 1972 this amounted to 12.5 million Swiss francs, or about $3.3 million.

As a result of this unusually broad government involvement in alcohol affairs, a great deal of information about the extent of Switzerland's alcoholism problems has been available. In 1972 alcohol abuse accounted for 1.2 million hospital days across the country, and that year the cost of alcoholism in production and labor losses was estimated to be 1.5 million Swiss francs (about $400,000). Of all industrial accidents in Switzerland in 1973, 19.4% were considered alcohol-related, as was 9% of the country's crime. An isolated study in 1977 in Basel, the country's third largest city, revealed that a third of its 16- to 20-year-old population reported getting drunk occasionally or frequently. Authorities have indicated that 80% of those drafted into the Swiss military admit to steady drinking before the age of 20.

Between 1963 and 1965, 41% of all automobile license suspensions were related to alcohol offenses. In response to this problem the country instituted a BLOOD ALCOHOL CONCENTRATION (BAC) limit of 0.08% on drivers. By 1976 the percentage of all driving license suspensions related to alcohol offenses had risen to 44%. Similarly, traffic fatalities related to alcohol use rose from 14% in 1970 to almost 20% in 1976. As a result the government has been considering a proposal to lower the BAC limit to 0.05%.

Automobile Deaths and Injuries Related to Alcohol

Year	Automobile Fatalities	Percent Related to Alcohol	Automobile Injuries	Percent Related to Alcohol
1972	1,722	15.7	37,108	7.3
1974	1,372	17.1	31,749	7.6
1975	1,245	19.2	29,951	8.0
1976	1,188	19.7	28,778	11.6
1977	1,302	20.7	31,206	12.3

Source: Swiss Institute for the Prevention of Alcoholism.

Estimates on the number of alcoholics in Switzerland vary because of the number of presumed alcoholics who refuse state aid and the different standards employed to define their condition. However, 31,958 Swiss citizens were admitted to one or another of the state's various inpatient and outpatient clinics and hospitals in 1970, the last year such statistics were recorded. In 1975 authorities estimated that there were approximately 116,000 clearly defined cases of alcoholism among the male population over 20 years of age.

Cases of Liver Cirrhosis Caused by Alcoholism

Years	Men	Women	Total	Number per 100,000 Population
1951–55	409	79	488	10.0
1956–60	467	79	546	10.5
1961–65	583	92	675	11.7
1966–70	638	105	743	12.1
1971–75	614	139	753	11.8

Source: Swiss Institute for the Prevention of Alcoholism.

Treatment of alcoholism in Switzerland is difficult to describe because the government stresses a broad-based scientific, educational and economic initiative to reduce alcohol consumption over the more traditional public health model. This program has to some extent been inhibited by the structure of the federal constitution, which grants some autonomy to individual cantons.

There are three agencies addressing the problem of alcoholism: the Federal Commission Against Alcoholism formed in 1947; the Swiss National Science Foundation, created in 1952, which has devoted a significant proportion of its energies to the country's alcohol abuse problem; and the Swiss Office for the Prevention of Alcoholism. Now working in cooperation to emphasize the social causes of alcoholism, these agencies have the avowed purpose of creating "an intact alcohol legislation which is above all always aimed at the greatest possible efficiency on behalf of public welfare."

symptomatic alcoholism   Alcoholism that is secondary to another medical problem, such as psychoneurosis, psychosis or mental deficiency.

symptomatic drinking   Excessive drinking that is used as a way of handling tensions or unconscious problems or drinking that is a symptom of some mental disorder other than alcoholism.

synergistic effect   See SYNERGY.

synergy   Also known as potentiation. When two or more drugs are taken together, the joint action increases the normal effect of each. A classic case involves the use of alcohol in combination with barbiturates. A small amount of alcohol combined with a very small dose of barbiturates produces a synergistic effect, or an effect that is much greater than the individual effects of alcohol and barbiturates added together.

The synergistic process begins in the liver, which metabolizes ingested materials. When two drugs are taken together, the enzyme system that processes them is overwhelmed. The two drugs, alcohol and barbiturates, for example, compete for the same enzymes, which do not have the capacity to metabolize both drugs at the same time. Alcohol is always processed first, allowing the second drug, barbiturates in this case, to accumulate in the blood. While the second drug is not being metabolized, it has an exaggerated effect on the body and mind. The delayed metabolization of the second drug can result in a tripling or quadrupling of its potency when it enters the central nervous system. Because of this phenomenon, an amount of a drug that might normally be safe can have devastating effects if taken with a drug that acts synergistically with it. (See also DRUGS.)

T

tank   (From "drunk tank.") Slang for a cell or jail where drunks are kept to sober up. The term is also used to refer to a drunk.

teetotal   (From "tee-total", a local British intensive for "total.") Total abstinence.

teetotaler   One who teetotals (see TEETOTAL).

temperance   While the word "temperance" has usually been synonymous with moderation, in the 1800s it took on the narrower meaning of abstinence. Although as early as 1785 Dr. Benjamin Rush presented a strong scientific argument on the dangers of alcohol and the need for temperance,

Americans were more receptive to moral pleas. The first temperance organization in the United States was founded in 1789 by some residents of Litchfield, Conn. who pledged never to drink. Similar groups began to operate on a local scale. The first national organization, the American Temperance Society, was formed in 1826. The movement was supported by Presbyterian and Methodist churches and drew its largest following in rural areas. By 1830 there were more than 1,000 temperance societies in existence and these organizations gained strength in rural communities between 1830 and 1860.

Temperance leaders used two techniques to persuade people to abstain: they advocated religious faith as a means for people to ease the anxieties that might lead them to drink and they portrayed liquor as the agent of the devil and, therefore, a source of these anxieties. During this time a number of states adopted antialcohol measures ranging from licensing to complete prohibition. These measures lacked the support of the general nonrural populations and many were rapidly repealed. The earlier temperance groups (1825–40) were concerned with the plight of drunkards and many tried to help them to sobriety. After 1830, however, the societies began to stress that the drunk was a moral sinner who could stop drinking if he so desired. The goal of the groups changed from helping the drunkard to removing the cause of his problem—alcohol. The idea of universal prohibition became prominent and all who drank were attacked as moral degenerates. The early temperance movement was very powerful among rural populations and those with strong religious backgrounds.

The Civil War divided the early and late temperance movements. After the war the notion of temperance grew increasingly popular. More churches became directly involved in the movement. Catholics formed the Total Abstention Union in 1872, and the WOMAN'S CHRISTIAN TEMPERANCE

UNION was founded in 1874. Eventually the movement shifted from moral attacks toward legislative measures, particularly PROHIBITION. On December 18, 1917 Congress submitted the Eighteenth Amendment to the states for ratification and on January 16, 1920 Prohibition went into effect.

Richard W. Howland and Joe W. Howland, "200 Years of Drinking in the United States: Evolution of the Disease Concept," in *Drinking,* ed. John A. Ewing and Beatrice A. Rouse (Chicago: Nelson-Hall, 1979), pp. 39–60.

W. J. Rorabaugh, *The Alcoholic Republic* (New York: Oxford University Press, 1979), pp. 187–222.

Temposil   The compound calcium carbamide, Temposil is used to produce an ANTABUSE effect in alcoholics participating in recovery programs. It differs fron Antabuse in that its effect lasts only 12 to 24 hours whereas that of Antabuse can extend four to five days before the danger of a reaction passes. Temposil. is administered in alcohol treatment programs in Canada and Japan but has not been approved for use in the United States.

tequila   A spirit distilled from a pulque, or fermented mash, of some species of agave plant, usually maguey. Its name derives from the district in the Mexican state of Jalisco where it originated. Tequila is sometimes referred to as mescal.

The national alcoholic beverage of Mexico, tequila dates from the Spanish exploration of that country in the 15th and 16th centuries. Its production undoubtedly began when the Spanish, who already possessed knowledge of distillation, adapted distillation processes to the local vegetation most suitable for fermentation because of its natural sugar content. The maguey agave they employed is also known as blue agave. Now, because its principal use is distillation, it is sometimes called the tequilana plant.

Tequila is a strong spirit, ranging from 86 to 100 proof, traditionally drunk straight, preceded by a taste of salt and followed by a taste of lemon or lime. Since being mass marketed in recent times, it is now also used in cocktails.

terminator characteristics   Many patients in outpatient facilities for the treatment of alcoholism drop out of such programs soon after admission. E. J. Larkin reviewed the literature on treatment termination, including literature not specifically related to alcoholism, and compiled a summary of terminator characteristics. He found that patients who terminated treatment were more restless, nomadic, impulsive and rigid in their attitudes and less dependable and less inhibited by anxiety than patients who remained in treatment. They were also less willing to reveal personal feelings or express ideas spontaneously. Aside from personality characteristics, lower economic class patients were more likely to terminate psychotherapy prematurely than patients from higher economic classes.

E. J. Larkin, *The Treatment of Alcoholism* (Toronto: Addiction Research Foundation, 1974), pp. 31–36.

Thailand   Thailand, like many other countries in Southeast Asia, has been subjected to severe military conflicts and a general undermining of cultural stability by foreign influences. The effects of these factors are especially apparent in the rise in alcohol consumption among the Thai people. The population is 90% Buddhist, 4% Islamic and 2% Confucian. Although these religions have traditional strictures against alcohol consumption, alcohol-related job absenteeism produces daily expressions of concern from the business community.

While in the past the country had little need for strict licensing of drinking places, the current situation appears to justify some control of drinking environments. One-third of the alcoholism cases in urban areas, such as Bangkok, where such establishments have proliferated, are estimated to be female employees of the various pubs, clubs and cafes that serve a clientele of national military officers. Importation of beer and whiskey remains relatively low, but there is an increasing daily use of such bootleg products as "Mekong whiskey" in both rural and urban areas.

The Thais have a tradition of limited alcohol consumption with evening meals. Authorities have noted, however, a recent general trend toward consumption of alcohol with other meals, including, in rural areas, breakfast, and a new pattern of continued drinking into the night in public places. Illegally distilled liquors comprise the primary alcoholic drinks for most of the population; during a typical drinking occasion various alcoholic beverages are mixed. The increasing acceptance of alcohol as a social beverage has reached all levels of Thai society, from the military officers' clubs, stocked with imported brandy, to the rural villages, where rice whiskey is distilled.

The cost of alcoholism to Thailand is difficult to estimate due to a lack of data. The government's overriding concern at present is control of narcotic drugs. Only one hospital in the country is equipped to test the blood alcohol concentrations of traffic fatalities. Between 1970 and 1972 the hospital found that 40% of the traffic mortalities it tested could be related to alcohol. In another limited survey the nation's major medical school estimated that half the deaths from car injuries were related to alcohol.

Statistics on the prevalence of physical complications caused by alcohol abuse have not been compiled since the 1950s, and data on mortality from cirrhosis of the liver are unreliable because of the prevalence of viral and nutritional problems. Nevertheless informal surveys have clearly linked alcohol abuse with economic and psychological crises in the wives of alcoholics.

Prevention of alcohol-related problems in Thailand is delegated to the Department of Treasury, with responsibility for educational programs left to the Ministry of Public Health. In February 1975 the International Congress on Alcohol and Drug Dependency met in Bangkok, and one year later the country established a Drug Education and Prevention Office. Each of the 72 provinces has its own Provincial Health Authority and mobile teams to treat health problems of all sorts in rural areas. There are 30 centers specifically designed for the treatment of alcohol and drug problems in Thailand.

tight   A slang term used to describe someone who is intoxicated, more so than someone who is HIGH.

tobacco   See SMOKING.

Tokay   (In Hungarian, Tokaji.) A famous Hungarian wine named after Tokay, a village in northeast Hungary near the Carpathian mountains.

There are three basic types of Tokay wine: Tokay Essencia, Tokay Aszu and Tokay Szamorodini. With the exception of some types of Tokay Szamorodini, Tokay wines are very sweet and thus generally used as dessert wines. The distinctive flavor of Tokay wines comes from *aszu* berries, which are grapes that have been allowed to remain on the vine until late autumn, when they have shriveled and their juice has become very concentrated with sugar. The particular type of Tokay is determined by the amount of *aszu* berries used in making the wine.

Tokay Essencia is made entirely from

aszu berries and is so rare that it is not marketed but used as private stock. Tokay Aszu is made from a carefully measured blend of normally ripened grapes and *aszu* berries. *Aszu* berries are added in amounts that vary from 1 to 6 *puttonys*, a *puttony* holding approximately 30 pounds of grapes. Tokay Aszu varies in taste from rather dry to extremely sweet, depending on the number of *puttonys* added. It is golden or amber in color and around 7 or 8 proof.

The term "Szamorodini" means "as it is grown," and it indicates that in making Tokay Szamorodini no special attention is given to the *aszu* berries. Whatever *aszu* berries get into the vats are pressed with the other grapes. If the result is a very dry wine, it is drunk as an aperitif rather than as a dessert wine.

tolerance   The variation in the effect on different individuals of a specific amount of alcohol. After a few drinks an inexperienced drinker may become intoxicated rapidly, while an experienced drinker can consume the same amount with little visible effect. The degree of intoxication exhibited at a given BLOOD ALCOHOL CONCENTRATION varies widely among individuals.

The most significant factor in tolerance to alcohol is related to the adaptation of the CENTRAL NERVOUS SYSTEM to alcohol. Long-term alcoholics display higher than average adaptation of the CNS to alcohol, which enables them to tolerate larger doses of all sedatives. They also have an increased ability to metabolize alcohol, but this is rapidly lost when drinking stops. One study showed that metabolic tolerance could be lost after three weeks of abstinence even in those who had been severe alcoholics for five years or more.

Some alcoholics have reported losing their high tolerance to alcohol suddenly; in such cases a relatively small amount of alcohol would have an unexpectedly strong effect. This effect may be due to impaired ME-TABOLISM or to the increased sensitivity of an organically damaged brain to alcohol.

While alcoholics may have a higher tolerance for alcohol than social drinkers or abstainers, the size of a lethal dose is probably not much greater than for others.

top fermentation   Fermentation of a hop wort with a yeast that rises to the surface of the liquid in the course of brewing beer. Top fermentation is the process used in brewing ales, whereas BOTTOM FERMENTATION is used to brew lager beers. Beer yeasts are selected strains of bacterial enzymes that flocculate, or separate themselves from the brewing beer, so that they may be drawn off at the end of the process. Top fermentation, in conjunction with the blend of different cereal grains employed, accounts for the heavier flavor of ales in comparison with that of lagers. Typically top fermentation is carried out at temperatures between 50° and 70° F, and it ordinarily takes between five and six days to produce the desired level of alcohol content.

tranquilizer   See SEDATIVE.

treatment   Treatment of alcoholism may begin with INTERVENTION, when a concerned party steps in to alert the alcoholic about his or her problem. The next step for the alcoholic is DETOXIFICATION, where he or she is sobered up and treated for any alcohol-related DISEASES. After detoxification some type of REHABILITATION is usually required for successful treatment. The alcoholic may enter ALCOHOLICS ANONYMOUS or GROUP THERAPY or undergo BEHAVIOR MODIFICATION. In addition he or she may be taught proper NUTRITION.

Twenty-First Amendment   This amendment repealed the EIGHTEENTH AMENDMENT and returned to the states the right to make their own liquor laws. Michigan was the first state to ratify the Twenty-

First Amendment and Utah was the 36th, completing the ratification process. On December 5, 1933 it became part of the Constitution and ended Prohibition.

U

Ulster Temperance Society   One of the earliest temperance organizations in Europe, it was founded in Northern Ireland in 1829. Thereafter, the organized temperance movement began to make effective progress.

uncontrolled drinking   A rather vague term generally used to refer to behavior that deliberately transgresses the social rules related to drinking. (JELLINEK suggested the use of the term "undisciplined drinking" to describe such behavior.) This behavior is not the same as LOSS OF CONTROL, which deprives the drinker of free choice.

under the influence of alcohol   When used in the general sense, this term refers to a mild disturbance of function caused by alcohol consumption. In many parts of the United States the condition is defined by the law in terms of specific concentrations of alcohol in the blood. The BLOOD ALCOHOL CONCENTRATION of someone who is considered to be "under the influence of alcohol" is generally lower than that of someone classified as legally intoxicated. (See also DRIVING WHILE INTOXICATED.)

undisciplined drinking   See UNCONTROLLED DRINKING.

Union of Soviet Socialist Republics (USSR)   There is ample evidence, mostly from indirect sources, that alcoholism is one of the primary social problems facing the USSR today. The Soviet government, however, has ceased to publish statistics on the problem and even suppressed what statistical evidence existed in early published reports. The government is known to have initiated several antialcohol drives, and the lack of official published reports on the subject probably derives more from the government's characteristic concern about its international image than from willful disregard of the problem. The government position is further complicated by the fact that while concerned about the extent of the national alcohol abuse problem, it relies on alcoholic beverage taxes for approximately 12% of all state revenues.

The leading authority in the West on alcohol consumption in the USSR is Dr. Vladimir G. Treml, a Russian-born economist on the faculty of Duke University. He has been assisted in his research by the Project on Alcoholism and Alcohol Abuse in the USSR and Eastern Europe, which is conducted by the Russian Research Center of Harvard University. Given the lack of official information on the subject, data on alcohol use in the Soviet Union are compiled by examining available economic, legal, and medical data as well as technical and commercial reports and handbooks of regional statistics. Researchers have gained additional information by visits to the Soviet Union and by interviews with Soviet immigrants to the United States and other Western countries.

The results of this research suggest that the USSR has the highest per capita consumption of distilled alcohol in the world and ranks lower in per capita consumption of all alcoholic beverages only because of its lower consumption rates for beer and wine. In 1972, for example, the Soviets consumed 828 million liters of legally produced distilled spirits and 754 million liters of wine and beer, or 4.63 liters of ABSOLUTE ALCO-

HOL per capita for the drinking-age population.

Even these high figures belie the national consumption rate because over 25% of the nation's alcohol supply comes from illegal sources. Primary among these is *samogon,* a moonshine vodka that is often distilled to more than 100 proof. One interesting aspect of this moonshine industry is that it apparently has no long tradition in the rural areas in which it is most common. There is little mention of illegal home brews in Russian literature prior to 1914. In that year, however, Czar Nicholas II instituted a national prohibition of alcoholic beverages in preparation for World War I. Although this prohibition was repealed by the Bolshevik government in 1923, the blackmarket trade in moonshine had become firmly established. Since that time *samogon* has consistently sold at half the price of legal alcohol, and a 1972 limit of 90 proof on legally distilled alcohols has since given the home brew the additional attraction of greater potency. It has been estimated that over 250,000 Soviets are full-time moonshiners, a trade that pays them up to six times the national average income.

The problems associated with this high rate of alcohol consumption are difficult to assess because of government reluctance to acknowledge it, but programs have been initiated in the Soviet Union to cope with the social costs of alcohol abuse. Studies have established links between alcoholism and infant mortality, heart disease, industrial accidents and automobile fatalities. By the late 1960s the average Soviet family spent an estimated 13% of its income on alcohol, and feminist documents from the USSR have charged the male population with a pattern of widespread drunkenness that forces women to endure food queues and other hardships of daily life. Reports suggest that 90% of Soviet alcoholics are male. Isolated studies have also begun to suggest the social costs of widespread alcoholism in the USSR. For example, 39% of the suicides in Leningrad in one year were alcoholics, and of those, 36% committed suicide while drunk.

Information on types of treatment for alcoholism in the USSR is not available, but the means used by the Soviet government to discourage excessive consumption of alcohol are known. Measures have been taken throughout the country to restrict the number of places where alcohol can be legally consumed and the hours of legal consumption, and sentences for violations have been toughened. Efforts to reduce the proportion of distilled alcohols in relation to beverages with less alcohol content during the 1970s resulted in decreased production of legal vodka and increased production of beer and wine. Education programs have sought to create a public association between alcohol consumption by pregnant women and birth defects in their children. Perhaps the harshest and most characteristic governmental step to combat alcoholism, one reflective of official Soviet ambivalence about the problem, was the 1972 decision to deprive those stricken by diseases resulting from alcoholism of some public medical benefits.

United Kingdom   In 1980 Secretary of Health and Social Services Patrick Jenkins described alcohol abuse in the United Kingdom as "an epidemic." Lately there has been a great deal of concern expressed about alcoholism in the United Kingdom, a country where the government actively intervened to shift drinking patterns away from gin toward beer in the late 19th century. In this century, however, a pub society has evolved and drinking in public places has become the primary form of entertainment outside the home. While beer has remained the most popular alcoholic beverage in the United Kingdom, consumption of this relatively diluted alcohol has reached dangerous proportions. Average consumption per adult in 1980 was 6 pints of distilled spirits, 15 pints of wine, and 270 pints of beer. Between 1972 and 1978, per capita consumption of beer rose 3.9%, the fourth highest per capita increase among Western European nations. In 1978 income spent on beer in the United Kingdom represented 4.5% of household expenses, the highest proportion of any Western European country.

The alarming rise of alcohol abuse in the United Kingdom is partly the result of economic factors that have increased the availability of alcohol. The cost of alcoholic beverages has risen, but not as fast as that of other items in the economy. In 1960 it took the average worker 23 minutes to earn the price of a pint of beer; by 1980 the figure had fallen to 12 minutes. The price of a bottle of whisky required 6 hours of labor in 1960 but only 2 hours in 1980. During this 20 year-period there were increases in consumption of alcohol, convictions for drunkenness, convictions for drunk driving and premature deaths related to alcohol. Deaths from cirrhosis of the liver in the United Kingdom doubled between 1960 and 1980.

Drinking patterns within the United Kingdom vary considerably, with a far higher incidence of alcohol abuse in Scotland and Northern Ireland than in England and Wales. Not only is average consump-

Deaths from Liver Cirrhosis in the United Kingdom

Year	Male	Female	Total
1970	741	651	1,392
1971	806	764	1,570
1972	858	804	1,662
1973	943	861	1,804
1974	901	853	1,754
1975	920	915	1,835
1976	1,038	852	1,890
1977	991	829	1,820
1978	1,023	903	1,926

Source: Office of Population Censuses and Surveys.

tion higher in Scotland and Northern Ireland, but there are more heavy drinking days and concentrated drinking occasions. Two reasons cited for the greater rate of alcohol abuse in these lands are the poorer economy of each and a lack of public education about the dangers of alcoholism. Surveys have shown that a mythical association between drinking and health survives in the harsh climate of Scotland, in particular, but not in southern England. Deaths from cirrhosis of the liver per capita are twice as high in Scotland as in England.

The British government has estimated that 700,000 citizens personally suffer from alcohol-related problems. According to the Department of Health and Social Services, taking into account the impact of alcoholism on family and friends, one in 25 persons in England and Wales are affected by alcohol abuse. In Scotland and Northern Ireland the figure is one in 10.

The rate of hospital admissions for alcoholism rose 8% to 10% annually from 1970 to 1976, and this upward trend has continued. In 1978 hospital admissions for alcoholism totaled 14,820. Convictions for drunkenness increased from 54,483 in 1950 to 119,817 in 1978. The economic cost of alcohol abuse in 1979 was estimated to be 14.8 million days of labor lost, or about £500 million (about $1.11 billion). If health service, police and prison costs were included, the expense to the nation was an estimated £650 million (about $1.44 billion).

Convictions for drunken driving in the United Kingdom have more than tripled since 1968, the year after police first introduced the Breathalyser test. During the year this test was introduced, the number of drunken driving convictions dropped to 20,000, a 10-year low. Since then, however, the threat of Breathalyser tests has diminished considerably; in 1979, for example, 75,000 drunk driving offenses were recorded. The British government has been considering a proposal to lower the legal BLOOD ALCOHOL CONCENTRATION for drivers from 80 milligrams to 50 milligrams of ethanol per 100 milliliters of blood.

Within the United Kingdom both legislative controls on alcohol and treatment for alcohol-related problems are handled by the individual divisions. In Scotland alcohol problems fall under the authority of the Scottish Health Education Unit and the Scottish Council on Alcoholism. In Northern Ireland the sole autonomous agency handling alcohol problems is the Council on Alcohol-Related Problems. In England and Wales the Department of Health and Social Security acts in cooperation with the national Council on Alcoholism, which is primarily concerned with preventative education, and with the Advisory Committee on Alcoholism, which deals mainly with clinical facilities. These agencies attempt to reverse or, at least, to slow drinking trends in the United Kingdom by means of public education, promotion of stricter laws governing alcohol-related legal offenses, and revision of licensing and taxing laws affecting alcohol consumption. Legislative efforts along these lines, however, have met opposition from the public, the liquor industry and the British Exchequer. The public opposes any form of prohibitive taxation of alcohol. The industry resists efforts to restrain a trade that employed 700,000 people and exported £800 million (about $1.63 billion) worth of goods in 1978. The Exchequer is concerned about losing some of the £2,500 million (about $4.55 billion) generated each year by alcohol taxes, a figure that represents 10% of all tax revenues in the United Kingdom.

Treatment of alcohol-related problems is handled mostly by volunteer organizations, assisted by the Department of Health and Social Security and by substantial grants from the liquor industry.

The government's recent concern that the country's alcohol problems have indeed reached epidemic proportions is reflected in several white papers. Current reassessment of its responsibility to control alcohol problems among its citizens promises to result in a significant reorganization of governmental efforts to control alcohol abuse in the future.

United States   There is in the United States an unusually acute awareness of the dangers of alcohol abuse. Many believe this awareness is a direct result of the country's role in developing early theories about the "disease concept" of alcoholism and its experience with the most sweeping prohibition of alcoholic beverages among western countries. Most states have operated antialcohol programs since the 1950s, and the federal government has been involved in similar efforts to reduce abuse of alcohol since the 1960s. Many surveys have found that an overwhelming majority of Americans consider alcohol a harmful influence on their lives and alcoholism as a social and medical problem of major proportions.

At the same time, however, availability and consumption of alcohol in the United States rose during the 1950s and 1960s at a rate surpassing that of population growth. Americans have deeply ingrained associations between alcohol and release from familial and occupational pressures and a heavy use of alcohol is seen as an "escape" from these and other tensions. Thus, among many American adults there is an apparent divergence between avowed beliefs about alcohol and actual use of alcohol. Some observers have theorized that overt public campaigns against teenage drinking and drug use are in part a manifestation of adult Americans' position in regard to alcohol; such campaigns are, in this view, an oblique response to addiction problems that leave the habits of most adult drinkers untouched.

Domestic production accounts for an unusually high proportion of the alcoholic beverages available in the United States. Domestic products comprise 99% of the beer, 86% of the wine and 73% of the distilled spirits consumed in the United States. The availability of all three types of alcoholic beverages rose dramatically between 1960 and 1970: in that period there was a net increase in distributed liters of beer of 42%, of wine of 63% and of spirits of 59%. At the same time the number of operating breweries, vinters, and distilleries as well as the number of workers they employed declined steadily because of shifts to mass production. In 1980 the number of retail liquor stores in the United States totaled 16,556, which was 1,000 more than the previous year's total and more than double the number of such retail outlets as hardware stores or shoe stores.

Per capita consumption of alcoholic beverages in the United States has also increased in recent decades. Between 1950 and 1970, among the population over 15 years of age, per capita consumption of ABSOLUTE ALCOHOL in the form of beer rose 12%, in the form of wine 26% and in the form of distilled spirits 49%. During the same period the proportion of the population who described themselves as "abstainers" or "infrequent drinkers" fell 5%, from 47% to 42%. The highest proportion of regular drinkers (88%) is found among middle- and upper-income males between the ages of 12 and 39 years. The proportion of expenditures on alcohol relative to total expenditures has declined from 4.1% in 1950 to 3.0% in 1960 to 2.8% in 1970. During these years the amount of dollars Americans spent on alcoholic beverages rose steadily, but the proportion of their budget it represented was offset by increases in income.

Annual Per Capita Consumption of Liters of Absolute Alcohol in the United States

Year	Total Population	Population Over 15 Yrs.
1950	5.60	7.72
1960	5.29	7.83
1970	6.85	9.88

Per Capita Consumption of Liters of Absolute Alcohol in the United States, by Beverage (1970)

Beverage	Total Population	Population Over 15 Yrs.
Beer	3.17	4.43
Wine	0.79	1.10
Spirits	2.90	4.35
Total	6.86	9.88

The health costs of alcohol consumption in the United States as tabulated in 1970, included over 31,000 deaths attributed to liver cirrhosis, over 4,000 deaths attributed to alcoholism and over 600 deaths attributed to alcoholic psychosis. Statistics from 1976 indicated that 1.7 hospital admissions in that year were for alcohol-related problems, a rate of 800 per 100,000 of total admissions.

Between 1965 and 1975 arrests for alcohol-related abuses declined in some categories. Drunkenness arrests fell from 30% of total arrests in 1965 to 15% of total arrests in 1975, and disorderly conduct arrests dropped from 12% of total arrests to 8% of total arrests during the same period. These figures reflect a general trend toward decriminalization of such offenses, however, rather than a decline in excessive drinking. In the same decade arrests for drunk driving, for example, rose from 5% of total arrests to 11% of the total. In 1975, 13% of all child abusers were intoxicated at the time of their offense, and estimated alcohol-related productivity losses in that year amounted to $42 billion.

Prevention of alcohol abuse in the United States is the goal of various federal programs that generally operate in conjunction with similar efforts by state and local governments. The principal federal body charged with combating alcohol-related problems is the National Institute on Alcohol Abuse and Alcoholism (NIAAA) which was established in 1970. In addition to its own programs, this body operates the National Clearinghouse for Alcohol Information. The U.S. Department of Transportation has actively worked to reduce alcohol-related driving fatalities since the 1960s, and the Department of Education is responsible for school antialcohol programs.

user   Anyone who drinks alcoholic beverages, as opposed to ABSTAINER.

V

Venezuela   Thanks to its vast oil resources, Venezuela experienced enormous economic growth during the 1970s, which resulted in a major increase in the availability of alcoholic beverages. Wine and beer production doubled in that decade, and the production of distilled spirits rose 500% between 1970 and 1976. Substantial increases were also reported in the importation of spirits, most of them entering the country through the duty-free port of Margarita. Available information suggests that the illegal production of alcoholic beverages also grew despite this glut of regulated alcoholic beverages. The primary illegal drinks are *cocuy,* a distillate of cactus agave similar to Mexican tequila, and *guarapo fuerte,* a meadlike drink fermented from molasses. Almost 2,000 illegal stills were seized in 1975 alone.

It is acknowledged that virtually the entire adult male population of Venezuela consumes alcoholic beverages, that there is a general acceptance of heavy drinking throughout the country and that on festival occasions there is considerable pressure to drink. It has been estimated that 20% of the female population consumes alcohol and that the rate of women drinkers is far

higher in urban centers such as Caracas. All social occasions involve drinking, and the country's many religious and secular festivals are considered a major factor contributing to alcohol abuse.

No official estimates of the incidence of alcoholism in Venezuela exist. However, there is ample evidence from traffic and criminal statistics to suggest the extent of the problem. Alcohol is considered a factor in 50% of all traffic fatalities, which were the leading cause of death in the country in 1978. Public drunkenness offenses represented 30% of all arrests in 1978. Estimates from the Ministry of Justice indicate that up to half the criminal activity in the country is related to alcohol abuse. Furthermore arrests rose more than 10% per year during the influx of large quantities of alcoholic beverages in the 1970s. There have been regular increases in alcohol-related problems, including higher rates of job accidents on Mondays and higher homicide rates during festival occasions. Considerable evidence suggests that families who exist near the poverty level are frequently deprived of their basic subsistence because of income spent on alcohol.

Despite these statistics there is a lack of governmental policies for prevention or treatment of alcohol problems in Venezuela and a general failure to enforce what legal restrictions on drinking and drunkenness exist. The primary agencies concerned with such problems are the Ministry of Health and the Ministry of Mental Health, both of which announced plans and surveys that have yet to take the form of effective programs.

vermouth   A popular aperitif with a base of either red or white wine. During its manufacture vermouth is flavored with as many as 40 aromatic herbs, fortified with spirits, pasteurized, refrigerated and thoroughly filtered. In the United States and many other places, it is used mainly as an ingredient in cocktails. The lighter dry vermouth, known as French vermouth, frequently is combined with gin to make a martini. Italian vermouth, which is sweeter, is often served on the rocks. Vermouth contains up to 19% alcohol (38 proof).

violence   See CRIME.

vitamins and minerals   Vitamin and mineral deficiencies may occur in alcoholics with or without an adequate food supply. According to an expert in the field, Dr. Esteban Mezey, "Alcoholism is probably the principal cause of vitamin and protein deficiencies among civilized people with adequate food supplies."

Nutritional deficiencies found in alcoholics can be attributed to a number of factors. One is malnutrition, commonly found in alcoholics with poor eating habits (see NUTRITION). A second factor is impairment of the absorption and storage of ingested vitamins caused by consumption of ethanol. Most vitamins are stored in the liver, but alcoholics with liver damage frequently lack the capacity to store them. Third is a diminished ability to convert vitamins into metabolically active cofactors, preventing the body from using vitamins properly. Fourth is an increased need for some minerals required by the enzymes that are used to metabolize excessive amounts of ingested ethanol and to repair tissue damaged by ethanol. Zinc, for example, is needed for a number of enzymes. Excessive amounts of alcohol also affect mineral metabolism and cause excessive excretion of minerals in the urine.

Chronic alcoholism is most frequently associated with deficiencies of thiamine, vitamin B_{12} and folic acid. The minerals most commonly affected by excessive use of alcohol are magnesium, calcium and zinc.

Vitamins

Thiamine

There is a direct connection between thiamine deficiency and alcoholism. Thia-
mine deficiency results from impaired absorption (from 40% to 60% of the body's ability to absorb thiamine is impaired by alcohol), decreased dietary intake and acute liver injury. Because a damaged liver lowers the body's response to administered thiamine, alcoholic patients need increasing amounts of thiamine in order to make certain enzymes react properly. Thiamine deficiency can cause beriberi, a condition associated with disease of the HEART muscle. It also appears to play a major role in WERNICKE'S ENCEPHALOPATHY.

Vitamin B_{12}

Vitamin B_{12} is necessary for cell replication. High alcohol consumption causes impairment of vitamin B_{12} absorption, even with adequate intake of nutrients. Increased amounts of this vitamin are needed for metabolism of a high quantity of alcohol and for repair of tissue damage.

Folic Acid

Deficiencies of folic acid have been found in alcoholics, especially those with liver disease. Lack of folic acid, which is used in cell replication, may lead to impairment of DNA and protein synthesis.

Minerals

Magnesium

An element involved in energy production of cells, magnesium plays an important role in the work of the central nervous system (CNS) and in the action of many body enzymes. During periods of alcohol ingestion there is a depletion of magnesium through urinary excretion. Because of magnesium's influence on the CNS this diminution may account in part for the irritability experienced after a period of drinking. Symptoms of WITHDRAWAL are similar to those of magnesium deficiency. Deficiencies of magnesium may play a role in cardiac arrhythmia (see HEART) and interfere with the body's response to thiamine.

Calcium

Acute ethanol consumption increases urinary excretion of calcium, particularly during withdrawal. Lack of calcium may be involved in alcoholic cardiomyopathy (see HEART). Osteoprosis, a degeneration of bone tissue associated with calcium deficiency, is frequently found in alcoholics.

Zinc

Many enzymes associated with DNA synthesis and RNA metabolism require zinc. Zinc is important to the growth and repair of the liver. Alcoholics are often deficient in zinc, generally because of poor dietary habits. Zinc deficiency has been related to anorexia, which leads to further malnutrition.

Esteban Mezey "Effects of Alcohol on the Gastrointestinal System," in *Practice of Medicine*, 10 vols. (Hagerstown, Md.: Harper and Row, Harper Medical, 1970) 7:1–9.

Gary and Steve Null, *Alcohol and Nutrition* (New York: Pyramid Publications, 1977).

vodka   (Russian, a little water, diminutive of *voda* water.) Vodka is the traditional alcoholic beverage of Russia, Poland and the Baltic states. In Russian the term is sometimes used to refer to any kind of distilled alcoholic beverage, which is not incompatible with the fact that vodka may be distilled from a wide variety of agricultural products. The substances from which vodka is most often distilled are rye, corn, barley, wheat, potatoes, and less frequently, sugar beets. In its history, however, vodka has been produced from whatever material was abundant and cheap at any given time. The base from which vodka is made is not especially important because it is first distilled at or above 190 proof, which is almost pure alcohol.

Vodka was first produced in Russia during the 14th century, and up until World War II, its production and consumption were limited almost exclusively to Russia, Poland and the Baltic states. After the war the production and consumption of vodka spread to other countries, particularly the United States but also Austria, Britain, the Netherlands, Finland, Denmark and Israel, where a kosher vodka has been produced.

The basic method currently used to make vodka was first developed in Russia and Poland; producers of vodka in other countries follow this basic method but have added their own variations. Today the distilling operation is usually dispensed with. Producers begin by buying distilled spirits that have already been highly rectified, or purified. These spirits are further rectified by filtration through beds of vegetable charcoal. The resultant liquid is at least 190 proof, which is reduced to a marketable strength by the addition of distilled water. Unlike other distilled alcoholic beverages, such as brandy or whiskey, vodka is not aged. Russian vodka is usually bottled at about 80 proof, and Polish vodka at around 90 proof. According to U.S. government regulations, vodka must be bottled at not less than 80 proof and not more than 110 proof.

In the United States federal regulations describe vodka as "neutral spirits . . . without distinctive character, aroma or taste." However, although vodka is usually colorless, contrary to popular opinion, it is not without odor or taste. Like any alcoholic beverage, it has both a taste and a smell. The absolute alcohol in vodka gives a mild burning sensation, or "sting," accompanied by an astringent taste. The CONGENERS present, depending on the particular type of vodka, can also contribute to the taste. The smell of vodka on the breath (or through the pores), while not so pronounced as that of whiskey, rum or, to a lesser extent, gin, is still detectable in close quarters, even when the vodka has been diluted by the addition of fruit juice, tonic or other mixers. While it does not change the basic taste of orange juice or tomato juice, for example, vodka's presence is clearly detectable in cocktails made with fruit juice or other mixers.

Some varieties of vodka have additional coloring or flavoring added to them. One Polish vodka, for instance, is flavored with buffalo grass, which gives it a yellowish color and a somewhat bitter taste. Certain other foreign vodkas are colored brown (from walnut shells), blue and even lavender.

In the Soviet Union vodka is popular as an aperitif. It is gulped from a small glass and followed by hors d'oeuvres, such as caviar, herring and anchovies. In the United States vodka is often added to orange juice and tomato juice to make the drinks known respectively as a screwdriver and a Bloody Mary. It is also sometimes used as a substitute for gin in mixed drinks. For example, it may be substituted for gin with tonic water or mixed with vermouth, in place of gin, to make a vodka martini.

Volstead Act   The National Prohibition Act, popularly known as the Volstead Act, provided for the enforcement of wartime PROHIBITION and constitutional prohibition as established by the EIGHTEENTH AMENDMENT to the U.S. Constitution.

The bill, introduced in the House of Representatives on May 17, 1919, was quickly adopted by both the House and Senate but was vetoed by President Woodrow Wilson on the ground that since the emergency of war had long since passed, the section authorizing wartime prohibition was unnecessary. Wilson's veto was overruled by the House on October 27 and by the Senate on the next day.

The Volstead Act consisted of three titles: Title I provided for the enforcement of wartime prohibition; Title II banned intoxicating beverages; and Title III contained technical provisions for users of industrial alcohol.

Title II comprised the general provisions for the enforcement of constitutional prohibition. The text of this title follows:

Title II. Prohibition of Intoxicating Beverages.

Sec. I . . . (1) the word "liquor" or the phrase "intoxicating liquor" shall be construed to include alcohol, brandy, whiskey, rum, gin, beer, ale, porter, and wine, and in addition thereto any spirituous, vinous, malt, or fermented liquor, liquids, and compounds, whether medicated, proprietary, patented, or not, and by whatever name called, containing one-half of 1 per centum or more of alcohol by volume which are fit for use for beverage purposes. . . .

Sec. 2. The Commissioner of Internal Revenue, his assistants, agents, and inspectors shall investigate and report violations of this act to the United States Attorney for the district in which committed. . . .

Sec. 3. No person shall on or after the date when the Eighteenth Amendment to the Constitution of the United States goes into effect, manufacture, sell, barter, transport, import, export, deliver, furnish or possess any intoxicating liquor except as authorized in this act, and all the provisions of this act shall be liberally construed to the end that the use of intoxicating liquor as a beverage may be prevented.

Liquor for non-beverage purposes and wine for sacramental purposes may be manufactured, purchased, sold, bartered, transported, imported, exported, delivered, furnished, and possessed, but only herein provided. . . .

Sec. 4. The articles enumerated in this section shall not, after having been manufactured and prepared for the market, be subject to the provisions of this act if they correspond with the following descriptions and limitations, namely: (a) Denatured alcohol or denatured rum produced and used as provided by laws and regulations now or hereafter in force. (b) Medicinal preparations manufactured in accordance with formulas prescribed by the United States Pharmacopoeia, National Formulary, or the American Institute of Homeopathy that are unfit for use for beverage purposes. (c) Patented, patent, and proprietary medicines that are unfit for use for beverage purposes. (d) Toilet, medicinal, and antiseptic preparations and solutions that are unfit for use for beverage purposes. (e) Flavoring extracts and syrups that are unfit for use as a beverage, or for intoxicating purposes. (f) Vinegar and preserved sweet cider. A person who manufactures any of the articles mentioned in this section may purchase and possess liquor for that purpose, but he shall secure permits to manufacture such articles and to purchase such liquor, give the bonds, keep the records, and make the reports specified in this act and as directed by the Commissioner. No such manufacturer shall sell, use, or dispose of any liquor otherwise than as an ingredient of the articles authorized to be manufactured therefrom. No more alcohol shall be used in the manufacture of any extract, syrup, or the articles named in paragraph b, c, and d of this section, which may be used for beverage purposes, than the quantity necessary for extraction or solution of the elements contained therein and for the preservation of the article.

Sec. 6. No one shall manufacture, sell, purchase, transport, or prescribe any liquor without first obtaining a permit from the Commissioner so to do, except that a person may, without a permit, purchase and use liquor for medicinal purposes when prescribed by a physician as herein provided, and except that any person who in the opinion of the Commissioner is conducting a bona fide hospital or sanatorium engaged in the treatment of persons suffering from alcoholism, may, under such rules, regulations, and conditions as the Commissioner shall prescribe, purchase, and use, in accordance with the methods in use in such institution, liquor, to be administered to the pa-

tients of such institution under the direction of a duly qualified physician employed by such institution.... Nothing in this title shall be held to apply to the manufacture, sale, transportation, importation, possession, or distribution of wine for sacramental purposes, or like religious rites....

Sec. 7. No one but a physician holding a permit to prescribe liquor shall issue any prescription for liquor....

Sec. 11. All manufacturers and wholesale or retail druggists shall keep as a part of the records required of them a copy of all permits to purchase on which a sale of any liquor is made....

Sec. 17. It shall be unlawful to advertise anywhere, or by any means or method, liquor, or the manufacture, sale, keeping for sale, or furnishing of the same, or where, how, from whom, or at what price the same may be obtained. No one shall permit any sign or billboard containing such advertisement to remain upon one's premises. But nothing herein shall prohibit manufacturers and wholesale druggists holding permits to sell liquor from furnishing price lists, with description of liquor for sale, to persons permitted to purchase liquor, or from advertising alcohol in business publications, or trade journals circulating generally among manufacturers of lawful alcoholic perfumes, toilet preparations, flavoring extracts, medicinal preparations, and like articles....

Sec. 20. Any person who shall be injured in person, property, means of support, or otherwise by any intoxicated person, or by reason of the intoxication of any person, whether resulting in his death or not, shall have a right of action against any person who shall, by unlawfully selling to or unlawfully assisting in procuring liquor for such intoxicated person, have caused or contributed to such intoxication, and in any such action such person shall have a right to recover actual and exemplary damages. In case of the death of either party, the action or the right of action given by this section shall survive to or against his or her executor or administrator, and the amount so recovered by either wife or child shall be his or her sole and separate property. Such action may be brought in any court of competent jurisdiction. In any case where parents shall be entitled to such damages, either the father or the mother may sue alone therefor, but recovery by one of the parties shall be a bar to suit brought by the other.

Sec. 21. Any room, house, building, boat, vehicle, structure, or place where intoxicating liquor is manufactured, sold, kept, or bartered in violation of this title, and all intoxicating liquor and property kept and used in maintaining the same, is hereby declared to be a common nuisance, and any person who maintains such a common nuisance shall be guilty of a misdemeanor and upon conviction thereof shall be fined not more than $1,000, or be imprisoned for not more than one year, or both. . . .

Sec. 26. When the Commissioner, his assistants, inspectors, or any officer of the law shall discover any person in the act of transporting in violation of the law, intoxicating liquors in any wagon, buggy, automobile, water or air craft, or other vehicle, it shall be his duty to seize any and all intoxicating liquors found therein being transported contrary to law. . . .

Sec. 29. Any person who manufactures or sells liquor in violation of this title shall for a first offense be fined not more than $1,000, or imprisoned not exceeding six months, and for a second or subsequent offense shall be fined not less than $200 nor more than $2,000, and be imprisoned not less than one month nor more than five years. . . .

Sec. 33. After February 1, 1920, the possession of liquors by any person not legally permitted under this title to possess liquor shall be prima facie evidence that such liquor is kept for the purpose of being sold, bartered, exchanged, given away, furnished, or otherwise disposed of in violation of the provision of this title. . . .

W

wagon, on the   A phrase meaning temporary abstinence from alcoholic beverages. The term was probably first used by the American Army during the 19th century to refer to the water wagon taken by soldiers on extended trips, on which, presumably, they had no access to liquor.

wash still   The first and largest of the two stills employed in some double-distillation processes. The wash still produces a weak and impure distillate, known as "low wine," that is usually strengthened and purified by further rectification in a small and secondary SPIRIT STILL.

water of life   Any of several distilled spirits, the term "water of life" originally was used to refer to an elixir, probably not alcoholic, that would confer immortality or even perpetual youth on the drinker. The obsessive quest of mankind for such an elixir was probably best exemplified by Ponce de Leon's search for the Fountain of Youth. As early as Roman times, the term was associated with particularly strong forms of drink that would produce in the user a temporary feeling of blissful immortality. There was the added implication that life without this water was not worth living.

The Latin term was aqua vitae ("water of life"), which was translated into the Irish Gaelic *uisce beathadh* and the Scotch Gaelic *uisge beatha* and later anglicized to WHISKEY. It also became the Scandinavian AQUAVIT and the French EAU DE VIE.

Webb-Kenyon Law   Adopted by Congress in 1913, this law was designed to allow the dry states to exercise sovereignty over alcohol-related affairs within their borders. The law gave each state the right to make its own laws concerning mail-order shipments of liquor. It was approved by a large majority in both houses, vetoed by President William Howard Taft, and passed over his veto.

Wernicke's encephalopathy (syndrome, disease)   Named after Carl Wernicke (1848–1905), a German neurologist who first described this condition, Wernicke's syndrome is characterized by an acute confusional state, loss of balance and disorders of the eye nerves and is often accompanied by ALCOHOLIC POLYNEUROPATHY and a high risk of congestive heart failure.

Wernicke's encephalopathy is associated with thiamine deficiency (see VITAMINS AND MINERALS) and usually affects only those persons who have been heavy drinkers for years. Although victims of the disease require hospitalization, and with the administration of thiamine, treatment is often successful if the condition is caught in its early stages. If not, it may progress into KORSAKOFF'S PSYCHOSIS, which has a much lower rate of cure. The signs of Wernicke's encephalopathy may coexist with those of Korsakoff's psychosis, and the two are sometimes linked together under the single designation Wernicke-Korsakoff syndrome.

whiskey (or whisky)   A potable alcoholic beverage distilled from the mash of fermented grains, such as rye, wheat, corn, oats and barley, in various combinations. The name is derived from the Irish Gaelic *uisce beathadh* and the Scottish Gaelic *uisge beatha,* meaning "water of life," shortened to *uisce* and then to the current pronunciation and spelling. "Whiskey" (plural "whiskeys") is the preferred spelling in Ireland and the United States, and "whisky" (plural "whiskies") is the preferred spelling in Scotland and Canada. None of these countries produce a whiskey or whisky that remotely resembles the original beverage, a raw alcohol flavored with

saffron, nutmeg and other spices to make it palatable. However, the whiskeys or whiskies they make are distinct, although the Canadian and American varieties may be considered together.

There are two types of Scotch whisky: pot still and patent still. Pot-still whiskies are made from malted barley only, and patent-still whiskies are made from a variety of cereal gains, including malted barley. Pot-still whiskies are the heaviest "malt" whiskies and are traditionally distinguished by their place of origin: the Highlands, the Lowlands, the Campbeltowns and the Islays. The distinct flavor created in each region is the result of the type of barley used, the method of curing, or "malting," the distillation process and the aging technique. Patent-still products are the lighter "grain" whiskies, which are generally less expensive and have a wider appeal than the pot-still types. In the production of patent-still whiskies the grain mixture is varied and the barley is cured without the traditional peat-drying, or turf-drying, process. These whiskies have lower levels of congeners because the rectification process used to make them takes longer than that employed to produce pot-still whiskies. Traditionalists sometimes object to the classification of these patent-still beverages as true Scotch whisky.

For the past 100 years most Scotch whiskies have been blended for greater market appeal. This process has led to a more consistent and generally more palatable beverage at the cost of the local distinctions favored by traditionalists. All Scotch whisky is aged for a minimum of three years, although a period of at least 12 years is favored. Aging for the most part takes place in wood casks of two sorts: "plain wood," seasoned oak that has never come in contact with another liquor; or "sherry wood," oak seasoned with that liquor and, in some cases, brandy or Madeira.

Irish whiskeys are also produced by the pot-still and patent-still techniques. However, unmalted grain and a different distilling process are used in their production. Irish pot-still whiskeys are made from a mash of less than 50% malted barley supplemented by such grains as rye, wheat and oats. Irish patent-still whiskeys are made the same way as the Scotch varieties until the distillation stage: all Irish whiskeys are distilled three times whereas Scotch whiskies are distilled twice. The result is a lower level of congeners and, therefore, a "cleaner" and "sweeter" beverage. Irish whiskeys are aged at least seven years, but longer aging periods are preferred.

The American and Canadian varieties of whiskey are bourbon, produced principally in the United States, and rye, generally associated with Canada. The primary difference is that rye is blended from a mash in which rye predominates and bourbon is blended from a mash in which corn predominates. Both the distinctions in mash content and the aging of rye and bourbon in charred wood casks give the liquors a heavier body and a stronger taste than either Scotch whiskies or Irish whiskeys. The American and Canadian varieties are considered to have roughly twice the quantity of congeners and by-products as the Scotch and Irish varieties.

Many more countries than these four produce flavored neutral grain spirits that can be considered whiskey, but the products inevitably derive from and fall within one of the four principal categories discussed.

whiskey nose   See RHINOPHYMA.

white wine   An almost colorless wine produced by fermenting grape juice without the grape skins or stems, which give red and rose wines their color. Red wines are produced by fermenting grape juice with grape skins and stems, and rose wines are made by fermenting grape juice that has usually been allowed to soak for a period in grape skins. The alcohol content of white wines is about the same as that of red wines, ranging from 10% to 14%.

Once grapes intended for white wines have been gathered, they are crushed in an extractor or wine press to drain off their juice. The juice is then allowed to settle for a period of up to two days and decanted to ensure a product that is as clear as possible. The making of white wines differs from that of red wines in two other ways: a slightly higher proportion of antiseptic, usually sulfur dioxide, is used to eliminate all but the alcohol-tolerant natural yeasts, and additional active yeast cultures are added to assist fermentation.

White wines are usually fermented at low temperatures, ranging from 50° to 60°F. Fermentation is usually allowed to proceed until virtually all of the soluble sugars in the grape juice have been converted into alcohol and carbonic gas by the yeasts. The yeasts and sediments created by fermentation are then removed from the alcoholic grape juice, and the process continues through the same steps used in making red or rose wines (see WINE).

The most valued white wines currently produced are those from the French wine-growing regions. The white wines of the Bordeaux region are produced in Graves, south of the city of Bordeaux, and Sauterne, known for its sweeter, dessert wines. The most renowned white wine of the Burgundy region is Montrachet, produced in the southern areas of the Cote d'Or, but the most commonly known is Chablis, which has become a generic name for white wines made outside of France.

Other notable white wines include the Orvieto, Frascati and Soave varieties produced in Italy, and the Rhine and Moselle wines of Germany, where far more white than red wines are made. Portugal's Dao wine district is known for white wines produced from the grapes of its mountain vineyards, and Hungary, which makes twice as much white wine as red wine, is known for Riesling grape white wines produced near Balaton Lake. Austria, Switzerland, Czechoslovakia and Yugoslavia also produce significant quantities of white wine, as does the United States, where far more white wine than red wine is consumed.

wine   (From the Latin *vinum* wine.) The fermented juice of grapes. The fermented juices of other fruits are only designated as wines when qualified by their basic raw material: i.e., "rice wine," "apple wine," "plum wine," etc. In addition to this etymological distinction grape juice is chemically distinct from other fruit juices by the presence of tartar, or potassium bitartrate, and natural yeasts that will produce fermentation without addition of active cultures.

The history of wine making, or viticulture, began before the first Egyptian dynasty, around 4000 B.C., according to the first known hieroglyphic records on the subject, which were found in funereal carvings. Most historians agree that wine making postdates fermentation of grains for beer and honey for mead, both in Egypt and elsewhere. The discovery of the fermentative properties of grape juice in all likelihood occurred accidently. The length of time required for grape vines to mature would have restricted their cultivation to settled rather than nomadic societies, suggesting that viticulture was probably a development of the later stages of early agrarian civilizations.

Because climate and soil conditions limited the yield of vineyards, wine was less a staple of Egyptian life than beer. Before 1000 B.C. viticulture was introduced in Greece, where the combination of better conditions for grape cultivation and a relatively advanced knowledge of botany brought wine, or *oinos,* a new prominence. Greek literature contains many tracts on the art of wine making, and Greek society was the first to ritualize and institutionalize wine drinking. Other Greek contributions to practical viticulture were the introduction of efficient pressing devices, flavoring methods and aging vessels. The Greeks invaria-

bly drank their wine mixed with water, suggesting that these beverages were somewhat lacking in palatability, but wine making was nevertheless an important part of their culture spread during the Greek age of exploration and conquest.

The Romans further advanced viticulture after it was introduced in Rome immediately prior to the advent of Christianity. They were the first to coat the insides of the *amphorae,* ("aging vessels") to prevent evaporation, and because of this superior aging technique they were the first to develop an appreciation of individual vintages. One of the earliest vintages to be stored for its special value was Opimian wine, fermented in individual seasons during the late second century B.C. and named for the reigning first consul. Like the Greeks before them, the Romans spread viticulture during their own period of conquest and expansion. Their introduction of wine grape vineyards in Spain was so successful that by the first century A.D. the Roman republic introduced trade controls on Spanish wine to protect the domestic wine industry. Wine making became common in the Rhone and Moselle valleys following the Gallic Wars, and the beginnings of the French and German wine industries also date from the Roman occupation.

In the Dark Ages, following the collapse of the Roman Empire, viticulture declined, but in medieval times a slow rediscovery of wine making re-emerged because of the demand for sacramental wines that accompanied the spread of Christianity. Fermentation practices during this time were often based on incomplete classical texts, with the result that important improvisations were introduced in France and Germany. Lacking ceramic vessels, for example, wine makers substituted wooden casks which are now considered essential for controlled aging of wines. Presented with other problems, they devised fortified wines, dwarf grape vines, "plastering" (a method of producing good wine from thin grape juice) and a number of other variations that have become essential steps in modernized wine making.

Production of wine begins with the cultivation of grapes, generally varieties of *Vinum vinifera*. Since fermentation processes are relatively uniform, the particular character of any distinct wine or vintage depends primarily on the choice of the grape variety, the composition of the soil and the weather during the growing season. The goal is to harvest a grape with a particular sugar content, generally between 18% and 24%, before the crop begins to deteriorate in early fall. Once harvested, grapes are crushed to release their juice, a step now accomplished by means of either roller crushers or rotary paddle crushers. In the production of WHITE WINE the skins are then separated from the juice; in the making of ROSE WINE the skins are generally allowed to soak in the juice for a day or two before separation; and in the manufacture of RED WINE the skins are allowed to remain in the juice. After an antiseptic, usually sulfur dioxide, has been introduced to kill all but the alcohol-tolerant natural yeasts in the grape juice, fermentation begins naturally, although it is sometimes assisted by the introduction of active yeast cultures. After fermentation, which can last anywhere from two days to two weeks, the alcoholic juice is subjected to "racking," a process that removes suspended yeasts and various sedimentary deposits. Further purification is achieved by filtration and "fining," in which substances are added to assist the separation of wine from deposits. All wines are then aged in wood for at least one year and often far longer before being bottled, and aging continues in the bottle. The amount of aging that will produce the wine's finest quality depends on both its variety and the character of its vintage.

withdrawal   A syndrome that develops in some physically dependent users of alcohol after abstinence or a sharp reduction of intake. The effects of withdrawal from alcohol closely resemble the effects of abstinence from other generalized depressant drugs. Both the nature and the intensity of the withdrawal syndrome usually depend on the length and degree of chronic intoxication before abstinence. The abruptness of the cessation of drinking and individual susceptibility also play a role. There are different degrees of withdrawal, from the kind associated with a severe hangover to the terrifying hallucinations (alcoholic hallucinosis) accompanying DELIRIUM TREMENS.

The first symptoms of withdrawal appear within a few hours after the discontinuation of drinking. The BLOOD ALCOHOL CONCENTRATION may still be as high as 100 milligrams of ethanol per 100 milliliters of blood or even higher. Usually the first signs to develop are weakness and tremulousness, possibly accompanied by anxiety, headache, nausea and abdominal cramps. The patient is restless and agitated and has a craving for alcohol or a sedative drug. In time the tremors become more marked and the patient may begin to "see" or "hear" things.

For an alcoholic with only a mild degree of physical dependence, the withdrawal syndrome may not extend beyond the duration of these symptoms, which disappear within a few days. However, some alcoholics experience a second stage, marked by convulsive seizures known as RUM FITS. These seizures may begin as early as 12 hours after abstinence, but more often they appear during the second or third day. The number of seizures varies depending on the individual.

The third stage of withdrawal involves alcoholic hallucinosis and delirium tremens, in which auditory, visual and tactile hallucinations occur, commonly with loss of insight. This period often lasts three to four days, during which the patient is in a severe state of agitation, is often completely disoriented and sleeps little, if at all. The delusions are almost always terrifying to patients and may produce violent behavior in them. Yet it is difficult to prescribe a safe dose of a depressant drug to calm the patient sufficiently. There is a 10% mortality rate associated with the third stage of withdrawal. After the patient passes through this stage, recovery is usually complete, although a small percentage of alcoholics remain chronically incapacitated in a psychotic state. The entire withdrawal process usually lasts from five to seven days.

One explanation of alcohol withdrawal symptoms focuses on the manufacture and detoxification of small amounts of various alcohols in the body. These alcohols include ethanol, which is the kind used in alcoholic beverages, and methanol, which is the main component in wood alcohol. Usually both are detoxified in the liver (see METABOLISM), with acetaldehyde produced from ethanol and formaldehyde produced from methanol. Because the liver enzymes involved in oxidation have a preference for ethanol, they break it down 16 times more rapidly than methanol. When ethanol is consumed, the liver, which has the capacity to handle all the alcohols that the body produces, becomes occupied with detoxifying it and consequently the amount of methanol builds up. After all the ethanol has been disposed of, the liver enzymes begin to work on the methanol, producing a large amount of formaldehyde, which is very toxic to the body. This greatly increased production of formaldehyde may be responsible for withdrawal symptoms.

Proper treatment can eliminate some of the worst aspects of withdrawal. A gradual tapering off of the use of alcohol is known to be safer than abrupt deprivation. It has been found that convulsions can often be avoided by the substitution of a drug that is cross-dependent with alcohol (see CROSS-DEPENDENCY); the minimal dosage that will alleviate the symptoms should be given. It is unlikely that dependence on a substitute drug will develop, since the drug is administered on a short-term basis and in small, decreasing dosages.

Samuel Kaim, "The Acute Withdrawal Syndrome," *Alcoholism* 1, no. 5 (May–June, 1981): 43.

Woman's Christian Temperance Union (WCTU)   Founded in Cleveland in 1874, this union grew out of a women's crusade to shut down saloons and promote morality, and gradually developed into a national organization. In 1883 the organization was carried to other countries, increasing its total membership to a half million. By 1907 the WCTU had branches in every state in the nation, with an aggregate national membership of 350,000.

The WCTU was a strong voice during the Prohibition era, and it gradually became concerned with other problems of society, particularly when Frances Willard became its president. The members spoke out on women's rights, civil reform and the general morals of society.

Although the WCTU lost members and influence during the Depression and thereafter, it still exists today, claiming a national membership of 250,000 as of 1972.

women   Although statistics show that nearly one-third of all alcoholics in the United States are women (Sandmaier), alcoholism has traditionally been considered a male problem. Women's drinking, especially excessive drinking, has been and still is less acceptable than men's. The consumption of large amounts of alcohol can be interpreted as a sign of masculinity for a man; for a woman it is inappropriate, nonfeminine behavior. The same person who laughs at a drunk man may find a drunk woman disgusting. Women have been expected to maintain social and moral values that men have not been held to, and it is assumed that the morals of a woman who drinks heavily are questionable. While female drinking has grown to be more publicly acceptable, a woman drinking alone in public is still regarded in quite different terms than a man drinking alone. As a result women have hidden their drinking more than men have and women with drinking problems have received little attention. Dr. Marc Shuckit noted that between 1929 and 1970 there were only 29 English-language studies on women alcoholics.

According to Dr. Morris Chafetz:

Women account for the largest increase in the drinking problem in recent years and the figures are rising rapidly. The concealment of women's drinking has long misled researchers on the true dimensions of alcoholism among women. Only in recent years have changing social attitudes toward women spurred efforts to research the magnitude of the problem more thoroughly. It is very likely that greater condemnation, fear of being a social outcast, and feelings of guilt contribute both to the concealment of drinking and its telescoped development in women.

The increased attention given to alcohol abuse among women has resulted in the discovery of a rise in the percentage of women drinkers and a decrease in the age at which women begin to use alcohol. According to a Gallup poll, between 1939 and 1981 the proportion of women drinkers in the United States jumped 21%, from 45% to 66% of the female population, while the overall increase in the proportion of male drinkers was only 5%, from 70% to 75% of the male population. And this trend seems to be accelerating. Between 1974 and 1981 the proportion of women drinkers increased 5%; the proportion of male drinkers dropped from 77% in 1974 to 75% in 1981. By the year 2000, many experts predict, women will account for half of all drinkers in the United States.

As the percentage of women drinkers has risen, so too has the number of women alcoholics. The proportion of women in ALCOHOLICS ANONYMOUS rose from 22% in 1968 to 29% in 1977, and women comprised 32% of the new members joining AA between 1974 and 1977. This increase is probably due to more female alcoholics seeking help (as it is somewhat easier for women to acknowledge that they drink today than it has been) and to an overall increase in the number of alcoholics.

Women begin to use alcohol at an earlier age now than they did in the past and there has been a dramatic increase in alcohol consumption by adolescent girls. Studies conducted in San Mateo County, Calif. showed that drinking by teenage girls more than tripled from 1968, when 15% reported some alcohol use, to 1975, when 54% admitted they drank.

History

Women throughout history have been consumers as well as, at times, producers of alcohol. Babylonian women around 5000 B.C. brewed beer and ran wine shops. To honor Bacchus, the god of wine and fertility, the ancient Greeks held drunken rites for women only. Nevertheless the double standard toward men's drinking and women's drinking began early. In ancient Rome a man could kill his wife if he smelled wine on her breath, because drinking was thought to lead women to adultery. In the literature of the Middle Ages women's drinking is rarely discussed, but it is known that alcohol was given to women for medicinal purposes. And during the Renaissance women were allowed to drink fairly openly. In London's gin epidemic, between 1700 and 1750, women's drinking was impossible to ignore (see GIN). Women were blamed for their drinking and especially for its effects on their children (see FETAL ALCOHOL SYNDROME). In colonial America women often ran taverns and were allowed to enjoy alcohol at parties. Drunkenness, however, was not accepted and offenders were subject to punishment by being whipped publicly or forced to wear the letter "D". During the

1800s some women began to oppose the use of alcohol and out of this grew the TEMPERANCE movement, which included such groups as the WOMAN'S CHRISTIAN TEMPERANCE UNION. The movement eventually led to PROHIBITION in the early 20th century. (Most historians feel that without women's involvement this social movement would never have gotten underway.) Women in this movement felt that liquor led men to financial ruin, disruption of family life and physical harm, which they inflicted both on themselves and their wives and children. In addition Victorian culture promoted the idea that women should be morally above reproach, and the use of alcohol did not fit in with this concept.

One ironic aspect of the temperance movement was that many of the women who campaigned vehemently against the use of alcohol were at the same time consuming large amounts of patent medicines, which often contained up to 50% opiates or alcohol.

In the 1920s women began drinking more openly, and during Prohibition some made money from bootlegging. Today women's drinking is taken for granted, but female drunkenness is still frowned upon. The stigma attached to female alcoholism continues to prevent many women from seeking help.

Female Alcoholic Population

Women with drinking problems can be found in every age category, social class, race and ethnic group. While the sterotype of the alcoholic woman is the bored suburban housewife, married women with jobs have higher rates of problem drinking than either housewives or single working women. Unemployed women looking for jobs have the highest rate of problem drinking.

When the rates are compared on the basis of marital status, the highest rate of alcohol-related problems is among divorced and separated women, higher than that among divorced and separated males. Single women are next; married women and widows have the lowest rates.

Poor women are more likely to have alcohol problems than affluent women (the same holds true for men) and rural women are more likely to have them than those living in cities (the opposite is true for men). Alcoholism makes women vulnerable to extreme economic deprivation and to forced separation from their families, because men are often unwilling to support women who can no longer care for them and their children.

Housewives

Some women are not happy being housewives but feel guilty about wanting a life beyond the home. Others have enjoyed being at home, but when their children leave or their spouse dies or a divorce occurs, they may be left with few economic resources—no job—and few interests outside the family. They are often overwhelmed by feelings of insecurity and loneliness, which can create an emotional crisis that leads to drinking.

Women have been expected to derive their sense of self-worth primarily through their relationships with men rather than through achievements and activities of their own. If something happens to this relationship, they may have little to fall back on.

Working Women

The stress faced by women on the job is greater than that confronting working men, as indicated by the fact that employed women are almost as likely to have drinking problems as unemployed women, whereas employed men are only about half as likely to have problems as unemployed men (Sandmaier). The reason the rate is so high among working women may not be because women's liberation is causing an increase in alcoholism, but because women are not really liberated yet. Women must work harder than their male counterparts to prove that they are competent, and there is pressure to act like a man and, hence, to drink like a man. A job can also produce additional conflicts about moving away from the traditional roles of wife and mother. On the other hand employed women who are also wives and mothers are overburdened because they must both work and take care of the home. And, of course, an unsatisfactory job situation can contribute to drinking problems. Divorced or separated women often have financial difficulties and the responsibilities of child care, and loneliness is frequently a problem for them.

Minority Women

Minority women with drinking problems have not received much attention. In 1980 there existed not a single study devoted entirely to the alcohol problems of nonwhite women (Sandmaier). Nevertheless a study conducted by Metropolitan Life which compared mortality rates for white and minority women showed that between 1964 and 1974 alcohol-related deaths among white women rose 36% and among nonwhite women 71%.

Minority women face oppression both because of their race and their sex. They have higher unemployment rates than either white women or minority men and are far more likely to head families subsisting below the official poverty level. Because of strong cultural taboos against drinking or, alternately, because of a more compassionate view of drinking by the community, the minority woman is less likely to seek or receive treatment.

Lesbians

Alcoholism is a particularly severe problem for both male and female homosexuals and the percentage of homosexuals with alcohol problems is much higher than found in the general population. According to a variety of estimates, one out of four homosexuals is an alcoholic as opposed to one out of 10 in the general population.

Lesbians are even more likely to have alcohol problems than homosexual men. A study in 1970 found that 35% of all lesbians had severe drinking problems, compared with 28% of homosexual men and only 5% of heterosexual women (Sandmaier). This high rate has been attributed to the effects of an environment that is openly hostile to lesbians and forces isolation upon them. One of the few places where lesbians are socially accepted is the gay bar, which reinforces their isolation in an atmosphere of alcohol. Outside of the homosexual environment, their sexual preference must usually be kept secret for fear of being fired from their jobs or, in some cases, losing custody of their children. Lesbian alcoholics have even experienced discrimination in applying for treatment.

Women on Skid Row

Because SKID ROW women have been isolated and generally ignored by society until recently, their problems are only now being studied. It is known that they are usually poorer than their male counterparts and end up on skid row at an earlier age. Many of these "shopping bag ladies" wandering the streets of major cities are alcoholics. About two-thirds of them drink alone, as opposed to one-quarter of the male derelicts. Little in the way of shelter or treatment has been offered to these women, and even when such services are provided, most of these women have no place to return to other than the streets.

Causes

The causes and consequences of alcoholism are now acknowledged to be different for women than for men; in earlier studies women were considered to be a subgroup of men.

There is no single cause of alcoholism for either men or women. Alcoholics of both sexes often suffer an unusual amount of stress and deprivation in their lives. It has been theorized that men drink because of dependency needs or to create an illusion of power over others. Neither of these seem to be true for women. Studies show women drink primarily to relieve loneliness, inferiority feelings and conflicts about their sex role regardless of their life style. Nearly all alcoholic women express doubts about their adequacy as women. Those who subscribe to the traditionally "feminine" modes of behavior are forced to deny any supposedly "masculine" traits, and the women who consciously reject the feminine role may be punished by society and feel they are not proper women. Drinking helps them to forget the conflicts imposed by the narrow social role assigned to them.

Edith Gomberg of the University of Michigan has described a number of ways in which women's drinking differs from men's. Women begin to drink and experience their first intoxication later than do men. Female drinking bouts are shorter than male drinking bouts. Women more often use alcohol to reduce stress on the job, but men lose their jobs more frequently because of drinking. Women are more inclined to perceive their alcoholism as getting worse.

Women are very likely to have had an alcoholic father or other important male relative who was an alcoholic (Gomberg). Unlike men, whose alcoholism generally progresses slowly, the symptoms of alcoholism appear rapidly in women. A period of 15 years or more leading up to severe alcoholism in men is telescoped into a few years in women. Women are more prone to begin drinking after experiencing a severe crisis, such as divorce, death or separation. Periods of depression prior to the onset of problem drinking occur far more frequently in women than in men (this is not surprising since in the United States twice as many women as men suffer from depression). Such depression may be the result of the restricted and self-denying roles women must often play.

Women drink alone more often than men, probably in large part because society frowns on women going to bars alone. Male alcoholics are publicly more visible and, as a result, are sent to treatment more often than women. A woman must deal with the consequences of her drinking within a circle of family and friends who are likely to try to hide or ignore the problem because it is so shameful, and therefore their "protection" actually interferes with proper treatment. When drinking becomes out of control, however, men are much more likely to leave their alcoholic spouses than are women. The alcoholic woman is considered a failure as a wife and mother as well as an "unnatural" woman. Excessive use of alcohol is seen as overstepping the bounds of the feminine role. Although excessive drinking among women has always been linked to promiscuity and neglect of the home, evidence to support these assumptions is limited and contradictory. Furthermore women alcoholics generally show more concern for their children than do male alcoholics.

Women with alcohol problems are much more likely to use prescribed drugs, particularly tranquilizers, than are men. The alcoholic woman often does not want her doctor to know about her drinking and thus exhibits the symptoms for which tranquilizers are normally prescribed: anxiety, tension, depression and so on. Use of tranquilizers, however, can lead to dual addiction (see SEDATIVE, CROSS-ADDICTION) and it can be harder to break a dual addiction than an addiction to alcohol alone. A 1977 survey of more than 15,000 AA members showed that 29% of the women but only 15% of the men were addicted to drugs other than alcohol. Of new AA members 30 years and younger 55% of the women were cross-addicted compared with 36% of the men (Sandmaier). Taking alcohol with certain psychoactive drugs is also dangerous because of the synergistic effect of the combination (see SYNERGY). A drug and alcohol taken together have a much more powerful effect than would be expected from either alone and the chances of an overdose are greatly increased. The availability of drugs also increases the temptation to commit suicide, a real concern since alcoholic women are more suicidal than alcoholic men.

Physical Effects

Physically alcohol has different effects on women than on men. Women show higher BLOOD ALCOHOL CONCENTRATION levels, adjusted for weight, than men for equivalent doses of alcohol. This disparity stems from the fact that women have more fatty tissue and men have more muscle tissue. Muscle tissue contains more water than fatty tissue, and as alcohol is distributed through the body in proportion to the water content of the body tissue, the alcohol tends to be more diluted in men's bodies than in women's. This process is ignored by many researchers who base their definition of alcoholism on the quantity of alcohol consumed and use the same figure for both sexes, also ignoring the fact that women weigh much less than men. In addition since sex hormone levels are apparently related to blood alcohol concentrations, and to consequent behavioral effects—the same amount of alcohol will produce higher blood alcohol concentrations during premenstrual phases than at other times.

Gynecological and obstetrical problems are relatively high among alcoholic women. They have a comparatively larger number of infertility problems, miscarriages and hysterectomies. However, these problems may sometimes precipitate the onset of alcoholism rather than be the result of it. Because of the high incidence of alcoholism in the families of alcoholic women, it is thought that a genetic component may be a contributing factor. Although it has been documented that excessive use of alcohol can damage a fetus (see FETAL ALCOHOL SYNDROME), it must be remembered that many alcoholic women are also heavy smokers and are on inadequate diets during pregnancy.

Women appear to be more susceptible than men to alcoholic CIRRHOSIS, and it has been hypothesized that there is an interaction between menopausal hormonal status and the susceptibility of the liver to the toxic effects of alcohol.

Treatment

The first professional an alcoholic woman is likely to see is her doctor. But, doctors often prescribe pills instead of confronting alcoholism. If a woman looks for a treatment program, she may have difficulty finding one that has room for her, since many programs are for men only and coed programs allocate an average of only 10% to 30% of their beds for women (Sandmaier). When alcohol treatment programs are not readily available, women are sometimes sent to mental institutions, where they are treated as insane. Programs that admit women may respond to them in exactly the way they do to men, despite the fact that women have different reasons for drinking. And child care is rarely provided by alcoholism programs.

Follow-up support may be more important for alcoholic women than for alcoholic men, since women are less likely to receive support from their families (if they have not already lost them). Yet few alcohol treatment programs provide any sustained follow-up service, and as a result a large percentage of the women who complete treatment do not recover. Another problem is the stigma attached to female alcoholics, which may make it difficult for these women to find jobs.

More attention is now being paid to women alcoholics and some therapy and support groups are designed specifically for them. These groups may make it easier for women to talk freely about issues such as sexuality and family relationships. There are now several hundred all-women's AA groups across the country. A new network designed specifically for alcoholic women, Women for Sobriety (WFS), has approximately 200 groups in the 50 states. Founded in 1975 by Jean Kirkpatrick, a sociologist who had been an alcoholic for 28 years, WFS is geared toward dealing with the different emotional needs of women which are often neglected by AA. The WFS program is secular and offers 13 steps as guidelines in the affirmation of the value of each woman. Anonymity is left up to the individual. Many women are members of both WFS and AA.

Stella B. Blume, "Diagnosis, Casefinding, and Treatment of Alcohol Problems in Women," *Alcohol Health and Research World 2*, no. 3 (Fall 1978): 10–22.
Ed Vasanti Burtle, *Women Who Drink* (Springfield, Ill.: Charles C. Thomas, 1979).
Health Communications, *An Emerging Issue: The Female Alcoholic* (Hollywood, Fla.: 1977).
Edith Lynn Hornik, *The Drinking Woman* (New York: Association Press, 1977).
Marian Sandmaier, *The Invisible Alcoholics: Women and Alcohol Abuse in America* (New York: McGraw-Hill, 1980).
Geraline Youcha, *A Dangerous Pleasure* (New York: Hawthorn Books, 1978), passim.

wood alcohol   See METHANOL.

Y

---

youths   If an individual is ever going to be a drinker, he or she usually starts before graduating from high school. While state laws prohibit the sale or serving of alcoholic beverages to minors, surveys show that most teenagers drink, generally beginning at age 13 or 14. Alcohol is the most widely used drug among American teenagers. According to a nationwide survey conducted in 1978 for the National Institute on Alcohol Abuse and Alcoholism, 87% of senior high school students reported that they had tried alcohol at least once; over 20% reported drinking at least once a week (Rachal et al.).

Adolescent drinking cannot be judged by the same standards as adult drinking. Alcohol-related diseases, classical symptoms of alcohol dependence and many other adverse consequences of drinking that develop in adult alcoholics show up infrequently in adolescent drinkers. However, problem drinking affects a substantial proportion of adolescents. Analysis of a 1974 national survey by the National Institute on Alcohol Abuse and Alcoholism (NIAAA) of more than 10,000 students in grades seven through twelve revealed that nearly 19% were problem drinkers—23% of the boys and 15% of the girls. Problem drinking was defined as either getting drunk at least six times in the past year or experiencing negative consequences from drinking on two or more occasions in at least three of five specified areas in the past year, or both. The five areas were: (1) getting into trouble with teachers or the principal; (2) getting into difficulties with friends; (3) driving when having had "a good bit" to drink; (4) being criticized by someone the student was dating; and (5) getting into trouble with the police. Adolescents have only recently developed many adult skills and these skills can be easily disrupted by lower quantities of alcohol than those necessary to produce similar effects in adults. For example, it has been established that adolescents become involved in fatal automobile crashes at significantly lower blood alcohol concentrations than those found in adults involved in such accidents (see BLOOD ALCOHOL CONCENTRATIONS).

Many teenagers look upon drinking as a mature, adult form of behavior. They wish to be admitted to the adult world and their drinking reflects this desire. While drinking can be a form of rebelliousness for some teenagers, for many it is a normal adaptive behavior. Most adolescents who drink during their high school years do not later become delinquent or drunkards. Sensible, moderate drinking may help prepare adolescents for their role in adult society, where social drinking is the norm.

Both parental attitudes and peer pressure influence youthful drinking. Most studies of the effects of parental drinking on youths indicate that children of parents who drink usually drink too and children of parents who abstain are likely to abstain. Peers may pressure adolescents to drink at a stage when their sense of individual identity is still weak and the need to be accepted by a group is very strong. Adolescents may drink with peers in order to relax and be comfortable as much as from the pressure to conform to the dictates of the group.

Consumption

The frequency of adolescent drinking according to the NIAAA survey was not as big a problem as the quantity consumed on a given occasion. Only 1.8% of the 10th to 12th graders surveyed reported being daily drinkers. The mean number of drinks consumed on each occasion, however, rose to a total number of 6 drinks for males and more than 4 drinks for females, and then declined with age. Frequency of drinking increased with age into early adulthood. The percentage of teenage drinkers also rose steadily with age until 18, when it was approximately the same as that of the adult population. About two-thirds of the 18-year-olds surveyed drank at least occasionally and approximately two-thirds of the females and three-fourths of the males reported some use of alcohol in the month prior to questioning.

Drinking among teenagers in the United States and the proportion of drinkers in the teenage population increased considerably until 1965, when they leveled off. During the late 1970s alcohol use among teenagers rose modestly.

Although among 10th to 12th graders in the NIAAA survey the proportion of male problem drinkers (20.9%) was higher than that of female problem drinkers (8.9%), drinking among young women has increased rapidly since World War II and is gradually approaching that among young men. Today more girls are drinking and drinking more heavily than in the past, and they are more likely to use hard liquor. In a 1974 study of alcohol use among secondary school students in two Massachusetts communities few differences were found between girls and boys in grades seven and eight; the differences that appeared were largely confined to the reported use of and intoxication on beer. In grades nine to 12, however, girls exceeded boys in both use of and intoxication on wine and hard liquor (Carrigan).

Drinking-and-Driving

From 1960 to 1978 the overall death rate in the United States dropped 20%, but for young people 15 to 24 years old it rose 11%. Much of this increase was attributable to deaths from automobile accidents. In 1978 drivers under age 20 were involved in 11,500 crashes with at least one fatality per crash. That year there were 5.6 million reported traffic accidents of all kinds caused by drivers aged 15 to 20 years old.

From 40% to 60% of traffic fatalities among young people are alcohol related, and traffic accidents are the leading cause of death in the 15- to 24-year-old age group. Much adolescent drinking takes place away from home, in or around cars and prior to driving and teenagers are inexperienced at both drinking and driving.

Treatment

Treatment of youthful alcoholics and problem drinkers is a relatively new area, as is research on its effectiveness. It appears that the rate of successful treatment for adolescents is the same or higher than that for older alcoholics and problem drinkers. A number of different methods are being put into practice today to reduce the incidence of alcohol problems among teenagers. These range from alcohol education programs to more general health promotion projects. Most seek to help adolescents understand the risks associated with drinking rather than reduce the supply of alcoholic beverages. Parents can help by educating themselves about the signs of alcohol problems so that they can recognize them in their children. Many states have developed programs that focus on prevention of both drug and alcohol problems.

Jerald G. Bachman, Lloyd D. Johnston and Patrick M. O'Malley, "Smoking, Drinking, and Drug Use among American High School Students: Correlates and Trends, 1975–1979," *American Journal of Public Health* 71, no. 1 (January 1981): 59–69.

Zoe Henderson Carrigan, "Research Issues: Women and Alcohol Abuse," *Alcohol Health and Research World* 2, no. 3 (Fall 78): 2–9.

John R. DeLuca, ed., *Fourth Special Report to the U.S. Congress on Alcohol and Health,* (Rockville, Md.: National Institute on Alcohol Abuse and Alcoholism, 1981), passim.

Ernest P. Noble, ed., "Alcohol Use and Abuse among Youth," *Third Special Report to the U.S. Congress on Alcohol and Health,* Technical Support Document (Washington, D.C.: U.S. Government Printing Office, 1978), pp. 1–9.

J. V. Rachal et al., "Alcohol Use Among Adolescents," *Alcohol Consumption and Related Problems,* National Institute on Alcohol Abuse and Alcoholism, Alcohol and Health Monograph no. 1 (Rockville, Md.: in press).

Alvin Silverstein and Virginia Silverstein, *Alcoholism* (New York: J. B. Lippincott Company, 1975), passim.

Millree Williams and Jill Vejnoska, "Alcohol and Youth: State Prevention Approaches," *Alcohol Health and Research World* 6, no. 1 (Fall 1981): 2–13.

APPENDICES

Appendix 1 Tables and Figures

Appendix 2 Sources of Information

Appendix 1
Tables and Figures

Tables and figures have been grouped in this appendix so that they can be consulted conveniently without disrupting the main text.

The following abbreviations are used in several tables and figures:

1. NDATUS—National Drug and Alcoholism Treatment Utilization Survey
2. NIAAA—National Institute on Alcohol Abuse and Alcoholism
3. SAPIS—State Alcoholism Profile System

CONTENTS

Table 1

Age Limit for Purchase and Consumption of Alcoholic Beverages (International)

Region* Country	Purchase to Carry Away	Consumption on Premises	Enter Licensed Premises	References**
Americas				
Brazil		18		1977 response
Canada	18 (in 4 provinces) 19 (in 6 provinces + in territories)			1979 response
Mexico	18	18	18	1977 response
Peru		Minors not served		1977 response
Venezuela		18		1977 response
Europe				
Austria	16			
Belgium		20	It is prohibited for persons under 16 years to enter dancing places where alcohol is served unless accompanied by an adult in charge	Law of 1939 on repression of inebriety Law on moral preservation of young people 1960 (1977 response)
Bulgaria	18 (except beer)	16		Bratanov (1968)
Czechoslovakia			15 (after 8 p.m, only if accompanied by an adult)	
Finland	18	18–19 (may consume bevs. < 17% ethanol), 20 (bevs. ≧ 17% ethanol)		1977 response
France	14 (fermented bevs.) 16 (spirits)	14–16 (may consume fermented bevs. if accompanied by an adult) 18 (spirits), 16–18 (may consume fermented bevs.)	16 (unless accompanied by an adult in charge, aged over 18)	Code des Debits de Boissons et des Mesures contre l'Alcoolisme

233

Table 1 (continued)

Age Limit for Purchase and Consumption of Alcoholic Beverages (International)

Region* Country	Purchase to Carry Away	Consumption on Premises	Enter Licensed Premises	References**
Germany, W.	16	16 (beer, wine) 18 (spirits)	16 (unless accompanied by an adult and some other exceptions)	Law for protection of youth in public (1951–57)
Iceland	21			Jellinek (1963)
Ireland	15 15–18; unless: the container is stoppered, sealed and contains at least 1 reputed pint	18	14	1977 response
Italy	16			1977 response
Netherlands	16 (beer, wine)	16 (bevs. with ≥ 18% ethanol)		National Council of Women 1976
Poland	18 (bevs. with ≥ 4.5% ethanol)	18 (bevs. with ≥ 4.5% ethanol)		Anti-Alcoholism Act 1959
Romania		16		1977 response
Spain	16	16	18 (nightclubs)	
Sweden	20	18, 16 (beer)		
Switzerland		16 (in some cantons, under 16 if accompanied by an adult)	16 (in some cantons, under 16 if accompanied by an adult)	1977 response
United Kingdom				
—England & Wales	18	18, 16 (beer and cider with meals)	14	1978 response
—Scotland	18	18, 16 (beer, porter, cider and perry with meals)	14	1977 response
USSR	18	Vodka may not be served to people under 18.		
Yugoslavia		15		1972 response

Region / Country				Source
Eastern Mediterranean				
Tunisia			20	1977 response
South-East Asia				
India			No consumption in some states; 18 or 21 in other states	1977 response
Indonesia			16	1977 response
Sri Lanka	18		18	1977 response
Thailand	18		18	1978 response
Western Pacific				
Australia	18		18	1977 response
Fiji	18		18	WHO, 1976
Japan	20	18	20 (liquor)	WHO, 1976
New Zealand	20		20 (18, if accompanied by an adult)	1977 response
Papua New Guinea	18			WHO, 1976
Philippines	21			WHO, 1976
Tonga	21			WHO, 1976
Western Samoa	21			WHO, 1976
Cook Islands	18			WHO, 1976
Gilbert Islands	18			WHO, 1976
Guam	18			WHO, 1976
Hong Kong	18			WHO, 1976
Samoa, American	18			WHO, 1976
Solomon Islands	18			WHO, 1976

Source: Joy Moser, *Prevention of Alcohol-Related Problems* (Toronto: Alcoholism and Drug Addiction Research Foundation, 1980), pp. 119–121.

*The WHO member states are divided into six regional areas: Africa, Americas, Eastern Mediterranean, Europe, South-East Asia and Western Pacific.

**1977/78/79 response: information received in response to request relating to current WHO project
1972 response: report prepared for WHO Inter-Regional Seminar for National Programmes on Problems of Alcohol and Drug Dependence, 1972
1971 response: report prepared for WHO Inter-Regional Training Course for National Programmes on Problems of Alcohol and Drug Dependence
bevs. = beverages

Table 2
Age Limit for Purchase and Consumption of Alcoholic Beverages
(United States)

18 For All Alcoholic Beverages	19 For All Alcoholic Beverages	20 For All Alcoholic Beverages	21 For All Alcoholic Beverages (Unless otherwise noted)
Hawaii	Alabama	Delaware	Arkansas
Louisiana	Alaska	Maine	California
Texas	Arizona	Massachusetts	Colorado—B, 3.2
Vermont	Connecticut	Nebraska	Illinois
West Virginia	Florida	New Hampshire	Indiana
Wisconsin	Georgia	Rhode Island	Kansas—3.2
Washington, D.C.	Idaho		Kentucky
Puerto Rico	Iowa		Maryland—WB, 3.2
Virgin Islands	Minnesota		Michigan
Guam	Montana		Mississippi—B, 3.2
American Samoa	New Jersey		Missouri
Trust Territory (Pacific Islands)	New York		Nevada
Northern Marianas	Tennessee		New Mexico
	Wyoming		North Carolina—WB, 3.2
			North Dakota
			Ohio—3.2
			Oklahoma—3.2
			Oregon
			Pennsylvania
			South Carolina—WB, 3.2
			South Dakota—3.2
			Utah
			Virginia—B, 3.2
			Washington

Source: State Alcoholism Profile System (SAPIS).

B: For these states, the legal drinking age for beer is 18.

3.2: These states permit the drinking of beer containing 3.2% alcohol at age 18.

WB: For these states, the legal drinking age for both wine and beer is 18.

Map 1

LEGAL DRINKING AGE (United States)

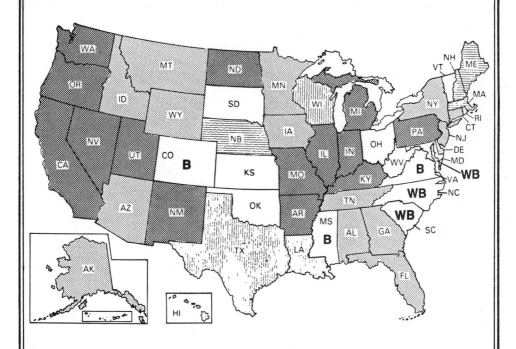

	FOR ALL ALCOHOLIC BEVERAGES: 18 years old.
	FOR ALL ALCOHOLIC BEVERAGES: 19 years old.
	FOR ALL ALCOHOLIC BEVERAGES: 20 years old.
	FOR ALL ALCOHOLIC BEVERAGES EXCEPT 3.2 BEER: 21 years old. FOR BEER CONTAINING 3.2% ALCOHOL: 18 years old.
	FOR ALL ALCOHOLIC BEVERAGES: 21 years old.
WB	FOR DISTILLED SPIRITS: 21 years old. FOR WINE AND BEER: 18 years old.
B	FOR DISTILLED SPIRITS AND WINE: 21 years old. FOR BEER: 18 years old.

Table 3
Alcohol Education
(State Fiscal Year 1980—Dates Vary from State to State)

State	State Mandates Alcohol Education	Designated Lead Agency	State Funds Obligated (in $1,000)
Alabama	Yes	State Alcoholism Authority	220
Alaska	Yes	State Alcoholism Authority	600
Arizona	No	State Alcoholism Authority	126
Arkansas	No	State Alcoholism Authority	0
California	Yes	Department of Education	0
Colorado	No	None	0
Connecticut	Yes	SAA/Department of Education	0
Delaware	Yes	Department of Public Instruction	0
Florida	Yes	State Alcoholism Authority	0
Georgia	No	State Alcoholism Authority	123
Hawaii	No	State Alcoholism Authority	29
Idaho	Yes	State Alcoholism Authority	179
Illinois	No	State Alcoholism Authority	0
Indiana	Yes	SAA/Board of Health	0
Iowa	Yes	Department of Public Instruction	40
Kansas	No	State Alcoholism Authority	100
Kentucky	Yes	Department of Education	0
Louisiana	Yes	State Alcoholism Authority	--
Maine	Yes	State Alcoholism Authority	0
Maryland	Yes	Department of Education	70
Massachusetts	Yes	SAA/Department of Education	402
Michigan	Yes	State Alcoholism Authority	1,010
Minnesota	Yes	Department of Education	317
Mississippi	Yes	Department of Education	0
Missouri	No	Department of Education	0
Montana	No	State Alcoholism Authority	0
Nebraska	Yes	State Alcoholism Authority	0
Nevada	Yes	SAA/Department of Education	19
New Hampshire	Yes	State Alcoholism Authority	57
New Jersey	Yes	State Alcoholism Authority	200
New Mexico	No	State Alcoholism Authority	82
New York	Yes	Department of Education	0
North Carolina	Yes	Department of Public Instruction	0
North Dakota	No	State Alcoholism Authority	--
Ohio	Yes	Department of Education	483
Oklahoma	Yes	Dept of Educ/Dept of Health	79
Oregon	Yes	State Alcoholism Authority	83
Pennsylvania	No	Governors Council	--
Rhode Island	Yes	Department of Education/SAA	7
South Carolina	Yes	State Alcoholism Authority	53

Table 3 (continued)
Alcohol Education
(State Fiscal Year 1980—Dates Vary from State to State)

State	State Mandates Alcohol Education	Designated Lead Agency	State Funds Obligated (in $1,000)
South Dakota	Yes	Department of Education	--
Tennessee	No	State Alcoholism Authority	0
Texas	Yes	State Alcoholism Authority	106
Utah	Yes	SAA/Department of Education	90
Vermont	Yes	State Alcoholism Authority	5
Virginia	Yes	Department of Higher Education	0
Washington	No	State Alcoholism Authority	553
West Virginia	No	None	0
Wisconsin	Yes	SAA/Department of Public Instruction	862
Wyoming	No	State Alcoholism Authority	0
Washington, D.C.	No	Alc and Drug Abuse Services Admin	35
Puerto Rico	Yes	State Alcoholism Authority	253
National Value	Yes—35		6,183
Number of States Reporting	52		
Virgin Islands	No	State Alcoholism Authority	0
Guam	No	State Alcoholism Authority	3
American Samoa	No	State Alcoholism Authority	0
T.T. Pacific Islands	No	State Alcoholism Authority	0
N. Mariana Islands	No	None	0

Source: State Alcoholism Profile System (SAPIS), *National Status Report* (Rockville, Md., National Institute on Alcohol Abuse and Alcoholism [NIAAA], May 1981), pp. 146–147.

General Table Notes

The last five island territories are not included in calculations of summary statistics.

Two dashes (--) indicate that data are not available.

The sum or row amounts may not equal the total due to rounding.

Notes for Table 3

The data in the table indicate whether or not the state mandates provision of alcohol education in the public schools and the designated lead agency for alcohol education within the state government. The final column indicates the total amount of state funds obligated by the SAA during state fiscal year 1980. Data are reported by state.

Table 4
Special Emphasis Alcohol Programs
(State Fiscal Year 1980—Dates Vary from State to State)

State	WOMEN'S ALCOHOLISM PREVENTION ESTABLISH-MENTS Number	WOMEN'S ALCOHOLISM TREATMENT ESTABLISH-MENTS Number	YOUTH ALCOHOLISM PREVENTION ESTABLISH-MENTS Number	YOUTH ALCOHOLISM TREATMENT ESTABLISH-MENTS Number
Alabama	0	4	0	0
Alaska	--	--	--	--
Arizona	6	29	0	11
Arkansas	0	6	10	0
California	5	21	4	4
Colorado	1	3	18	3
Connecticut	0	5	15	0
Delaware	1	0	4	0
Florida	2	16	6	5
Georgia	60	61	60	61
Hawaii	1	3	3	3
Idaho	2	2	0	1
Illinois	4	21	14	15
Indiana	4	28	23	21
Iowa	0	2	16	3
Kansas	5	2	18	1
Kentucky	0	3	0	0
Louisiana	--	32	--	23
Maine	3	6	12	2
Maryland	33	63	7	25
Massachusetts	8	8	8	7
Michigan	--	23	8	--
Minnesota	12	28	26	45
Mississippi	15	37	15	15
Missouri	0	126	17	91
Montana	0	25	0	3
Nebraska	0	4	9	3
Nevada	11	35	9	15
New Hampshire	0	2	0	1
New Jersey	31	92	20	14
New Mexico	0	0	0	0
New York	39	25	44	34
North Carolina	0	31	0	25
North Dakota	0	15	0	15
Ohio	0	9	7	2
Oklahoma	5	30	10	80
Oregon	0	9	5	3
Pennsylvania	--	62	--	36

Table 4 (continued)
Special Emphasis Alcohol Programs
(State Fiscal Year 1980—Dates Vary from State to State)

State	WOMEN'S ALCOHOLISM PREVENTION ESTABLISH- MENTS	WOMEN'S ALCOHOLISM TREATMENT ESTABLISH- MENTS	YOUTH ALCOHOLISM PREVENTION ESTABLISH- MENTS	YOUTH ALCOHOLISM TREATMENT ESTABLISH- MENTS
	Number	Number	Number	Number
Rhode Island	0	1	0	1
South Carolina	1	1	24	25
South Dakota	0	0	0	0
Tennessee	0	21	4	12
Texas	0	31	8	7
Utah	3	74	22	73
Vermont	0	5	12	3
Virginia	58	12	108	17
Washington	0	8	0	12
West Virginia	7	0	14	0
Wisconsin	49	34	91	37
Wyoming	6	27	12	13
Washington, D.C.	4	8	4	7
Puerto Rico	14	0	14	0
National Total	390	1,090	701	774
Number of States Reporting	48	51	49	50
Virgin Islands	1	2	1	1
Guam	1	2	0	0
American Samoa	1	1	1	1
T.T. Pacific Islands	0	0	0	0
N. Mariana Islands	0	0	0	0

General Table Notes

The last five island territories are not included in calculations of summary statistics.

Two dashes (--) indicate that data are not available.

The sum or row amounts may not equal the total due to rounding.

Notes for Table 4

The data in the table indicate the number of alcohol prevention and treatment establishments that have programs targeted for youth, women or the elderly. The criterion for a "youth," "women's" or "elderly" alcoholism program is either (1) the total admissions to an establishment are at least 50% youth, women or the elderly, respectively, or (2) the establishment has specially trained staff and programs to deal with the needs of youth, women or the elderly. For the purpose of this table, youth is defined as age 18 and under. Elderly is defined as age 65 and older.

The data are obtained from the individual states and are current as of the end of their fiscal years.

Table 4 (continued)
Special Emphasis Alcohol Programs
(State Fiscal Year 1980—Dates Vary from State to State)

State	ELDERLY ALCOHOLISM PREVENTION ESTABLISHMENTS Number	ELDERLY ALCOHOLISM TREATMENT ESTABLISHMENTS Number	FETAL ALCOHOL SYNDROME PREVENTION PROJECTS Number
Alabama	0	0	13
Alaska	--	--	0
Arizona	0	10	3
Arkansas	0	0	2
California	0	2	8
Colorado	0	0	1
Connecticut	1	0	0
Delaware	0	0	0
Florida	1	2	1
Georgia	20	60	1
Hawaii	0	0	0
Idaho	2	0	0
Illinois	2	0	2
Indiana	1	0	1
Iowa	0	0	0
Kansas	0	0	3
Kentucky	0	0	1
Louisiana	--	23	1
Maine	0	0	0
Maryland	0	24	0
Massachusetts	8	1	0
Michigan	5	--	12
Minnesota	1	12	3
Mississippi	15	15	0
Missouri	0	21	22
Montana	0	1	0
Nebraska	0	0	0
Nevada	0	26	2
New Hampshire	0	0	2
New Jersey	18	15	12
New Mexico	0	0	3
New York	14	9	1
North Carolina	0	14	0
North Dakota	0	15	0
Ohio	0	0	1
Oklahoma	3	54	5
Oregon	0	0	0
Pennsylvania	0	0	0
Rhode Island	0	0	1
South Carolina	0	0	1

Table 4 (continued)
Special Emphasis Alcohol Programs
(State Fiscal Year 1980—Dates Vary from State to State)

State	ELDERLY ALCOHOLISM PREVENTION ESTABLISHMENTS Number	ELDERLY ALCOHOLISM TREATMENT ESTABLISHMENTS Number	FETAL ALCOHOL SYNDROME PREVENTION PROJECTS Number
South Dakota	0	0	0
Tennessee	0	0	0
Texas	0	3	1
Utah	10	73	3
Vermont	0	0	0
Virginia	8	3	14
Washington	0	1	1
West Virginia	4	0	6
Wisconsin	41	9	80
Wyoming	3	4	0
Washington, D.C.	0	6	0
Puerto Rico	0	0	0
National Total	157	403	207
Number of States Reporting	50	50	52
Virgin Islands	0	1	0
Guam	0	0	0
American Samoa	1	1	2
T.T. Pacific Islands	0	0	0
N. Mariana Islands	0	0	0

Source: SAPIS, *National Status Report,* pp. 160–163.

General Table Notes

The last five island territories are not included in calculations of summary statistics.

Two dashes (--) indicate that data are not available.

The sum or row amounts may not equal the total due to rounding.

Notes for Table 4

The data in the table indicate the number of alcohol prevention and treatment establishments that have programs targeted for youth, women or the elderly. The criterion for a "youth," "women's" or "elderly" alcoholism program is either (1) the total admissions to an establishment are at least 50% youth, women or elderly, respectively, or (2) the establishment has specially trained staff and programs to deal with the needs of youth, women or the elderly. For the purpose of this table, youth is defined as age 18 and under. Elderly is defined as age 65 and older.

The data are obtained from the individual states and are current as of the end of their fiscal years.

Table 5
Alcoholism Funding Received by Treatment Units
(Funding in Effect September 30, 1980)

State	NIAAA Amount (in $1,000)	OTHER FEDERAL Amount (in $1,000)	THIRD-PARTY REIMBURSE- MENTS Amount (in $1,000)	CLIENT FEES Amount (in $1,000)
Alabama	1,681	1,609	2,643	569
Alaska	147	476	41	57
Arizona	1,896	4,098	3,584	993
Arkansas	1,550	1,840	1,562	85
California	8,345	13,206	32,476	25,406
Colorado	1,326	1,452	4,471	1,672
Connecticut	937	556	6,578	1,353
Delaware	286	0	4	21
Florida	3,794	2,809	6,809	8,712
Georgia	1,550	3,909	3,322	1,278
Hawaii	516	198	653	96
Idaho	739	428	660	308
Illinois	851	5,027	13,723	1,676
Indiana	758	3,293	6,936	1,143
Iowa	415	1,668	3,194	414
Kansas	627	2,887	7,983	1,717
Kentucky	1,770	1,355	3,439	494
Louisiana	1,182	256	441	105
Maine	1,092	579	2,032	688
Maryland	133	912	5,222	1,789
Massachusetts	2,054	4,827	20,329	1,930
Michigan	2,050	1,923	15,066	4,575
Minnesota	528	2,537	26,840	6,624
Mississippi	1,307	1,525	1,132	108
Missouri	850	729	9,257	883
Montana	440	783	1,289	347
Nebraska	298	1,488	2,597	1,209
Nevada	702	260	182	158
New Hampshire	69	500	3,500	387
New Jersey	1,734	1,929	7,125	1,359
New Mexico	1,419	716	2,032	226
New York	5,893	2,634	29,545	4,839
North Carolina	2,115	1,192	4,508	2,329
North Dakota	331	187	3,591	935
Ohio	1,550	780	25,146	1,945
Oklahoma	792	2,339	2,180	872
Oregon	1,223	1,905	3,433	1,492
Pennsylvania	2,357	2,006	20,000	2,907
Rhode Island	857	55	1,439	201
South Carolina	820	857	912	398

Table 5 (continued)
Alcoholism Funding Received by Treatment Units
(Funding in Effect September 30, 1980)

State	NIAAA Amount (in $1,000)	OTHER FEDERAL Amount (in $1,000)	THIRD-PARTY REIMBURSE-MENTS Amount (in $1,000)	CLIENT FEES Amount (in $1,000)
South Dakota	402	1,936	340	315
Tennessee	822	3,491	5,792	1,019
Texas	2,858	6,556	7,169	2,406
Utah	744	541	1,376	729
Vermont	1,020	206	386	176
Virginia	1,578	3,989	6,061	1,508
Washington	1,338	2,150	8,941	2,454
West Virginia	752	1,552	537	193
Wisconsin	1,462	1,809	17,649	2,437
Wyoming	293	516	40	221
Washington, D.C.	107	3,213	2,609	255
Puerto Rico	2,090	470	12	0
National Total	70,450	102,159	336,788	94,013
Number of States Included	52	52	52	52
Virgin Islands	118	0	0	0
Guam	30	19	0	2
American Samoa	10	0	0	0
T.T. Pacific Islands	39	0	0	0
N. Mariana Islands	--	--	--	--

General Table Notes

The last five island territories are not included in calculations of summary statistics.

Two dashes (--) indicate that data are not available.

The sum or row amounts may not equal the total due to rounding.

Notes for Table 5

The data in the table are the amount of funds (in $1,000) reported as received by alcoholism treatment units in each state by the source of that funding. Data are abstracted from the results of the 1980 National Drug and Alcoholism Treatment Utilization Survey (NDATUS).

Table 5 (continued)
Alcoholism Funding Received by Treatment Units
(Funding in Effect September 30, 1980)

State	PRIVATE Amount (in $1,000)	STATE Amount (in $1,000)	LOCAL Amount (in $1,000)	TOTAL REPORTED FUNDS Amount (in $1,000)
Alabama	264	1,527	304	8,668
Alaska	68	2,122	2,437	5,398
Arizona	357	3,632	951	15,865
Arkansas	174	857	70	6,146
California	2,157	15,319	22,412	123,255
Colorado	408	5,810	2,082	17,503
Connecticut	1,140	8,704	169	19,664
Delaware	40	744	0	1,099
Florida	733	6,833	3,722	33,648
Georgia	220	8,001	665	19,013
Hawaii	90	424	3	1,991
Idaho	74	1,089	43	3,458
Illinois	1,472	10,617	2,918	36,449
Indiana	330	4,076	622	17,192
Iowa	74	2,433	1,721	9,965
Kansas	173	2,948	637	17,163
Kentucky	461	829	58	8,457
Louisiana	230	2,914	1,128	6,257
Maine	19	1,013	39	5,472
Maryland	100	4,856	1,233	14,265
Massachusetts	694	7,026	887	37,757
Michigan	1,280	7,616	1,231	33,814
Minnesota	1,473	5,847	7,813	51,702
Mississippi	7	2,015	151	6,245
Missouri	173	3,360	502	15,845
Montana	94	1,668	1,470	6,238
Nebraska	179	973	340	7,586
Nevada	79	212	38	1,665
New Hampshire	29	303	15	4,805
New Jersey	443	1,344	2,785	16,771
New Mexico	81	4,479	205	9,177
New York	708	17,864	8,800	71,213
North Carolina	621	11,721	4,618	27,411
North Dakota	49	241	66	5,415
Ohio	1,377	6,411	3,152	40,502
Oklahoma	925	3,268	108	10,774
Oregon	280	3,764	2,759	15,481
Pennsylvania	627	4,283	2,733	35,286
Rhode Island	57	2,324	47	4,991
South Carolina	64	2,307	689	6,124

Table 5 (continued)
Alcoholism Funding Received by Treatment Units
(Funding in Effect September 30, 1980)

State	PRIVATE Amount (in $1,000)	STATE Amount (in $1,000)	LOCAL Amount (in $1,000)	TOTAL REPORTED FUNDS Amount (in $1,000)
South Dakota	42	357	227	3,640
Tennessee	313	2,128	371	14,102
Texas	1,378	6,070	1,963	28,475
Utah	359	668	662	5,146
Vermont	40	712	32	2,600
Virginia	245	3,443	6,398	23,526
Washington	1,260	4,619	1,310	22,156
West Virginia	150	1,019	81	4,362
Wisconsin	318	12,662	3,527	41,000
Wyoming	15	1,284	202	2,582
Washington, D.C.	16	0	2,366	8,756
Puerto Rico	98	1,310	206	4,186
National Total	22,058	206,046	96,968	940,261
Number of States Included	52	52	52	52
Virgin Islands	0	0	0	118
Guam	0	94	0	145
American Samoa	0	0	0	10
T.T. Pacific Islands	0	0	0	39
N. Mariana Islands	--	--	--	--

Source: SAPIS, *National Status Report,* pp. 34–37.

General Table Notes

The last five island territories are not included in calculations of summary statistics.

Two dashes (--) indicate that data are not available.

The sum or row amounts may not equal the total due to rounding.

Notes for Table 5

The data in the table are the amount of funds (in $1,000) reported as received by alcoholism treatment units in each state by the source of that funding. Data are abstracted from the results of the 1980 NDATUS.

Table 6
State Funding for Specific Alcohol Prevention Activities
(State Fiscal Year 1980—Dates Vary from State to State)

State	FETAL ALCOHOL SYNDROME Amount (in $1,000)	YOUTH ALCOHOL PREVENTION Amount (in $1,000)	WOMEN ALCOHOL PREVENTION Amount (in $1,000)
Alabama	0	0	0
Alaska	0	600	0
Arizona	--	--	--
Arkansas	0	0	0
California	--	--	--
Colorado	0	0	0
Connecticut	0	35	0
Delaware	0	0	0
Florida	0	--	0
Georgia	30	0	13
Hawaii	0	14	10
Idaho	20	139	20
Illinois	0	0	0
Indiana	0	0	0
Iowa	0	100	0
Kansas	10	203	8
Kentucky	--	--	--
Louisiana	0	0	0
Maine	0	0	0
Maryland	0	0	0
Massachusetts	0	0	0
Michigan	--	810	--
Minnesota	0	1,872	0
Mississippi	0	0	0
Missouri	0	0	0
Montana	0	0	0
Nebraska	0	0	1
Nevada	0	0	0
New Hampshire	0	2	0
New Jersey	10	196	36
New Mexico	0	0	0
New York	0	--	--
North Carolina	0	0	0
North Dakota	0	0	0
Ohio	1	47	0
Oklahoma	2	40	5
Oregon	0	74	0
Pennsylvania	0	--	--
Rhode Island	0	0	0
South Carolina	0	0	0

Table 6 (continued)
State Funding for Specific Alcohol Prevention Activities
(State Fiscal Year 1980—Dates Vary from State to State)

State	FETAL ALCOHOL SYNDROME Amount (in $1,000)	YOUTH ALCOHOL PREVENTION Amount (in $1,000)	WOMEN ALCOHOL PREVENTION Amount (in $1,000)
South Dakota	0	0	1
Tennessee	0	51	0
Texas	0	6	0
Utah	0	64	0
Vermont	0	0	0
Virginia	7	0	10
Washington	0	5	0
West Virginia	0	0	0
Wisconsin	4	264	51
Wyoming	0	0	0
Washington, D.C.	0	0	0
Puerto Rico	0	126	86
National Total	84	4,648	241
Number of States Reporting	48	46	46
Virgin Islands	0	0	0
Guam	0	3	0
American Samoa	0	0	0
T.T. Pacific Islands	0	--	0
N. Marina Islands	0	0	0

Source: SAPIS, *National Status Report,* pp. 164–165.

General Table Notes

The last five island territories are not included in calculations of summary statistics.

Two dashes (--) indicate that data are not available.

The sum or row amounts may not equal the total due to rounding.

Notes for Table 6

This table presents the funds obligated by the states for alcohol prevention activities in each of the specified areas. These data reflect funding during the state's fiscal year. For the purpose of this table, youth is defined as age 18 and under.

Table 7
Amount and Percentage of Funding for Each Funding Source Reported by Alcoholism Treatment Units
National Drug and Alcoholism Treatment Utilization Survey (NDATUS)
September 30, 1980

Funding Source	FUNDING	
	Thousands of Dollars	Percent
NIAAA[1]		
NIAAA contracts or grants	45,751	4.9
NIAAA formula funds	21,944	2.3
NIAAA Uniform Act funds	2,954	0.3
TOTAL	70,649	7.5
Other federal[2]	102,177	10.9
Third-Party		
State or local government fees for service	37,574	4.0
Title XX Program	35,356	3.8
Public welfare	12,501	1.3
Public health insurance	67,395	7.2
Private health insurance	183,957	19.6
TOTAL	336,783	35.8
Private donations	22,058	2.4
Client fees	94,015	10.0
State government	206,139	21.9
Local government	96,969	10.3
Other	11,782	1.3
TOTAL	940,572	100.0

Source: National Institute on Alcohol Abuse and Alcoholism, (NIAAA), *National Drug and Alcoholism Treatment Utilization Survey (NDATUS)* (Rockville, Md., June 1981), p. 24.

Note: This table is based on the 4,311 alcoholism treatment units that reported funding information to NDATUS.

[1]National Institute on Alcohol Abuse and Alcoholism (NIAAA) funds were underreported, since it is known from other sources that over $30 million of Formula Grant funds were expended on treatment and over $50 million were expended on contracts and grants.

[2]Other federal represents all non-NIAAA federal funding.

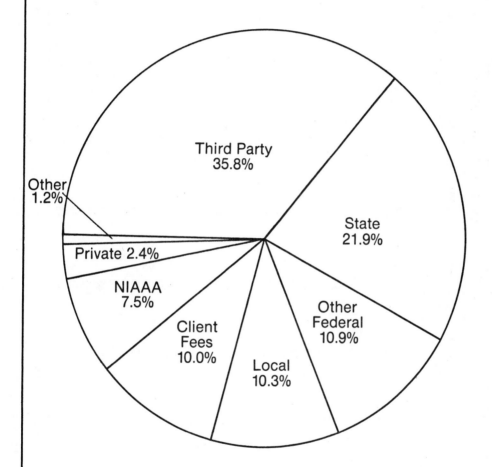

Figure 1

Proportion of Total Funding Contributed by Each Major Funding Source

Third Party 35.8%

Other 1.2%

Private 2.4%

NIAAA 7.5%

Client Fees 10.0%

Local 10.3%

Other Federal 10.9%

State 21.9%

Based on total reported funding of $940,572,177.

Source: NIAAA, *Drug & Alcoholism Treatment Survey,* p. 25.

Table 8
Number of Alcoholism Treatment Units Supported by Percentage of Funding and Funding Source
National Drug and Alcoholism Treatment Utilization Survey (NDATUS)
September 30, 1980

Funding Source[1]	PERCENTAGE OF FUNDING							Total No. of Clients in Units
	.01–19.99	20–39.99	40–49.99	50–59.99	60–79.99	80–100	TOTAL	
NIAAA contracts or grants	122	114	61	69	87	175	628	56,143
NIAAA Formula Funds	411	165	47	24	50	90	787	62,944
NIAAA Uniform Act funds	36	11	4	3	5	10	69	3,812
TOTAL NIAAA	445	253	114	98	153	288	1,351	112,126
Bureau of Prisons	45	3	1	1	—	9	59	2,272
Veterans Administration	28	2	1	—	—	79	110	13,695
LEAA	52	19	1	1	5	3	81	6,652
Indian Health Service	26	7	3	11	8	42	97	5,805
NIMH	75	50	22	19	22	11	199	11,385
Administrative Office of U.S. Courts	11	4	—	—	—	2	17	983
CETA	378	78	27	12	4	6	505	36,979
Other federal funds	102	24	9	11	7	58	211	24,782
TOTAL NON-NIAAA FEDERAL FUNDS	566	181	57	41	59	223	1,127	86,678
State/local government fees for service	234	98	40	29	64	84	549	32,862
Title XX Program	265	175	60	45	84	50	679	38,881
Public welfare	357	58	17	8	13	10	463	17,607
Public health insurance	542	100	23	11	26	24	726	61,434
Private health insurance	553	98	41	49	115	95	951	67,997
TOTAL THIRD-PARTY FUNDING[2]	839	349	133	146	265	422	2,154	135,895
State government	402	528	251	228	369	551	2,329	164,410
Local government	790	348	112	88	103	172	1,613	126,097
Private donations	754	133	33	23	20	47	1,010	57,124
Client fees	1,975	352	75	42	42	171	2,657	186,958
Other	312	42	12	8	5	15	394	28,829

Source: NIAAA, *Drug & Alcoholism Treatment Survey*, p. 26.

Note: This table includes both alcoholism treatment only units and combined treatment units.

[1] Units receiving funds from more than one source are included in the totals for each of the sources.

[2] Units receiving funds from any of the following sources: state/local government fees for service, Title XX Program, public welfare, public health insurance

Table 9
Global and Continental Production of Wine, Beer and Distilled Alcoholic Beverages, 1960 and 1972, in Millions of Liters

	1960	1972	Number of Countries Included	Percentage of Continental Population Covered 1972
Wine				
Africa	2,268.2	1,604.2	12	42.5
America, Central	17.5	37.6	4	68.8
America, North	726.7	1,263.0	2	99.0
America, South	2,403.0	3,004.8	8	79.0
Asia	72.3	173.1	20	12.7
Europe	17,845.8	19,556.6	24	78.5
Oceania	140.6	327.5	3	91.3
USSR	777.0	2,930.0	1	100.0
WORLD	24,251.0	28,896.7	74	40.2
Beer				
Africa	737.8	2,121.2	37	95.4
America, Central	1,177.3	2,022.3	14	89.9
America, North	12,242.6	18,259.3	2	99.0
America, South	2,313.7	3,014.0	12	99.1
Asia	1,270.5	4,527.5	29	53.8
Europe	19,207.8	31,891.4	26	99.1
Oceania	1,302.1	2,037.5	4	81.8
USSR	2,497.9	4,686.1	1	100.0
WORLD	40,749.8	68,559.3	125	72.8
Distilled Alcoholic Beverages 100%				
Africa	29.0	48.5	20	61.0
America, Central	59.1	103.4	13	85.8
America, North	421.7	430.4	2	99.0
America, South	137.4	217.8	9	92.4
Asia	239.6	361.6	26	26.6
Europe	736.3	1,454.2	24	98.6
Oceania	14.5	13.9	3	91.3
USSR	—	—	0	0
WORLD	1,636.6	2,629.8	97	47.0

Source: Joy Moser, *Prevention of Alcohol-Related Problems* (Toronto: Alcoholism and Drug Addiction Research Foundation, 1980), p. 52.

Table 10
Total Number of Alcoholism Treatment Units by Type of Service
(State Fiscal Year 1980—Dates Vary from State to State)

State	DETOXIFI-CATION, MEDICAL MODEL Number	DETOXIFI-CATION, SOCIAL SETTING Number	REHABILI-TATION MODEL Number	CUSTODIAL/ DOMICILIARY MODEL Number
Alabama	18	10	15	0
Alaska	3	2	6	7
Arizona	9	26	53	0
Arkansas	4	2	1	10
California	59	85	303	--
Colorado	2	16	32	0
Connecticut	23	0	34	3
Delaware	2	0	1	1
Florida	22	7	47	4
Georgia	12	0	7	0
Hawaii	0	0	7	0
Idaho	0	9	11	0
Illinois	84	23	37	30
Indiana	13	37	40	20
Iowa	14	2	32	0
Kansas	8	8	19	18
Kentucky	3	16	10	0
Louisiana	20	10	11	5
Maine	6	0	6	2
Maryland	16	2	47	2
Massachusetts	22	0	47	0
Michigan	246	16	45	0
Minnesota	10	22	91	12
Mississippi	5	23	23	18
Missouri	16	3	43	3
Montana	5	11	18	0
Nebraska	3	3	10	15
Nevada	2	2	9	3
New Hampshire	3	0	2	1
New Jersey	2	11	38	9
New Mexico	7	9	15	1
New York	35	26	46	0
North Carolina	21	14	45	15
North Dakota	1	4	6	2
Ohio	42	0	31	15
Oklahoma	38	16	0	31
Oregon	0	17	29	1
Pennsylvania	23	17	79	0

Table 10 (continued)
Total Number of Alcoholism Treatment Units by Type of Service
(State Fiscal Year 1980—Dates Vary from State to State)

State	DETOXIFI-CATION, MEDICAL MODEL Number	DETOXIFI-CATION, SOCIAL SETTING Number	REHABILI-TATION MODEL Number	CUSTODIAL/ DOMICILIARY MODEL Number
Rhode Island	1	1	0	5
South Carolina	11	2	28	1
South Dakota	1	4	11	10
Tennessee	14	2	30	0
Texas	26	25	77	4
Utah	12	2	28	3
Vermont	0	2	4	2
Virginia	2	3	11	0
Washington	20	0	25	17
West Virginia	2	0	8	0
Wisconsin	106	9	78	12
Wyoming	27	4	8	0
Washington, D.C.	6	22	2	2
Puerto Rico	1	0	4	0
National Total	1,028	525	1,610	284
Number of States Reporting	52	52	52	51
Virgin Islands	0	0	0	0
Guam	0	0	1	0
American Samoa	0	0	0	0
T.T. Pacific Islands	0	0	0	0
N. Mariana Islands	0	0	0	0

General Table Notes

The last five island territories are not included in calculations of summary statistics.

Two dashes (--) indicate that data are not available.

The sum or row amounts may not equal the total due to rounding.

Notes for Table 10

This table presents the number of alcoholism treatment units providing each type of treatment service. Units that provide more than one type of treatment service are entered under all applicable categories. The total refers to the number of treatment units in each reporting state and may not be equal to the sum of the individual table cells.

Data reflect treatment service units in operation at the end of each state's fiscal year.

Table 10 (continued)
Total Number of Alcoholism Treatment Units by Type of Service
(State Fiscal Year 1980—Dates Vary from State to State)

State	AMBULATORY MEDICAL DETOXIFICATION Number	LIMITED CARE, INCLUDING DAY CARE Number	OUTPATIENT SERVICES Number	TOTAL Number
Alabama	0	0	83	126
Alaska	0	0	30	48
Arizona	1	17	98	204
Arkansas	0	0	7	26
California	--	--	225	672
Colorado	0	0	64	114
Connecticut	0	1	44	106
Delaware	0	0	9	13
Florida	0	3	59	142
Georgia	36	8	58	121
Hawaii	0	1	4	12
Idaho	0	0	11	23
Illinois	0	0	138	312
Indiana	7	38	128	283
Iowa	0	0	32	80
Kansas	0	0	43	96
Kentucky	1	1	15	68
Louisiana	1	3	7	57
Maine	1	1	32	48
Maryland	0	7	57	131
Massachusetts	0	4	75	148
Michigan	0	0	254	561
Minnesota	0	0	66	201
Mississippi	0	15	17	101
Missouri	0	6	49	120
Montana	0	0	29	41
Nebraska	0	2	58	91
Nevada	0	1	27	44
New Hampshire	0	0	17	23
New Jersey	0	11	35	95
New Mexico	0	3	31	66
New York	0	17	73	197
North Carolina	11	7	79	192
North Dakota	0	1	9	23
Ohio	0	0	138	226
Oklahoma	3	21	111	220
Oregon	1	0	69	117
Pennsylvania	1	8	215	343
Rhode Island	1	0	10	14
South Carolina	0	0	61	103

Table 10 (continued)
Total Number of Alcoholism Treatment Units by Type of Service
(State Fiscal Year 1980—Dates Vary from State to State)

State	AMBULATORY MEDICAL DETOXIFICATION Number	LIMITED CARE, INCLUDING DAY CARE Number	OUTPATIENT SERVICES Number	TOTAL Number
South Dakota	0	0	26	52
Tennessee	0	0	44	66
Texas	0	3	53	188
Utah	0	11	52	108
Vermont	0	0	27	35
Virginia	0	0	22	38
Washington	1	0	59	122
West Virginia	2	3	14	29
Wisconsin	0	9	101	315
Wyoming	0	4	33	76
Washington, D.C.	2	2	18	54
Puerto Rico	9	5	9	28
National Total	78	213	3,025	6,719
Number of States Reporting	51	51	52	52
Virgin Islands	0	2	2	2
Guam	0	0	1	2
American Samoa	0	1	1	2
T.T. Pacific Islands	0	0	0	0
N. Mariana Islands	0	0	1	1

Source: SAPIS, *National Status Report,* pp. 40–43.

General Table Notes

The last five island territories are not included in calculations of summary statistics.

Two dashes (--) indicate that data are not available.

The sum or row amounts may not equal the total due to rounding.

Notes for Table 10

This table presents the number of alcoholism treatment units providing each type of treatment service. Units that provide more than one type of treatment service are entered under all applicable categories. The total refers to the number of treatment units in each reporting state and may not be equal to the sum of the individual table cells.

Data reflect treatment service units in operation at the end of each state's fiscal year.

Table 11
Physical Environment of Units Providing Alcoholism Treatment Only
(As Opposed to Combined Alcoholism and Drug Abuse Treatment)
(As of September 30, 1980)

State	COMMUNITY MENTAL HEALTH CENTER* Number	MENTAL/ PSYCHIATRIC HOSPITAL Number	GENERAL HOSPITAL, INCLUDING VETERANS ADMINISTRATION HOSPITAL Number	OTHER SPECIALIZED HOSPITAL Number
Alabama	7	0	2	0
Alaska	1	0	0	0
Arizona	4	0	4	0
Arkansas	4	1	1	0
California	17	7	45	16
Colorado	14	3	6	1
Connecticut	3	3	18	0
Delaware	0	3	0	0
Florida	26	2	6	1
Georgia	3	4	2	1
Hawaii	0	1	0	0
Idaho	0	0	0	1
Illinois	46	6	19	0
Indiana	3	5	5	1
Iowa	2	1	9	0
Kansas	1	2	6	1
Kentucky	20	1	1	0
Louisiana	2	2	2	0
Maine	6	0	4	0
Maryland	12	3	9	1
Massachusetts	10	3	18	10
Michigan	10	1	24	2
Minnesota	9	4	12	1
Mississippi	2	1	3	0
Missouri	6	1	6	0
Montana	4	0	6	0
Nebraska	16	0	5	0
Nevada	0	1	1	0
New Hampshire	1	1	2	1
New Jersey	5	1	8	3
New Mexico	4	2	1	3
New York	25	19	43	2
North Carolina	52	5	1	2
North Dakota	0	0	1	0
Ohio	7	3	20	3
Oklahoma	1	1	4	1
Oregon	14	0	2	1
Pennsylvania	13	1	18	0

Table 11 (continued)
Physical Environment of Units Providing Alcoholism Treatment Only
(As Opposed to Combined Alcoholism and Drug Abuse Treatment)
(As of September 30, 1980)

State	COMMUNITY MENTAL HEALTH CENTER* Number	MENTAL/ PSYCHIATRIC HOSPITAL Number	GENERAL HOSPITAL, INCLUDING VETERANS ADMINISTRATION HOSPITAL Number	OTHER SPECIALIZED HOSPITAL Number
Rhode Island	1	1	1	0
South Carolina	1	0	2	0
South Dakota	2	0	4	0
Tennessee	1	0	5	0
Texas	19	7	9	3
Utah	1	0	1	0
Vermont	2	0	0	0
Virginia	4	3	9	0
Washington	3	0	7	1
West Virginia	0	1	2	0
Wisconsin	1	0	6	2
Wyoming	0	0	0	0
Washington, D.C.	4	1	2	0
Puerto Rico	0	0	1	1
National Total	389	101	363	59
Number of States Included	52	52	52	52
Virgin Islands	0	0	0	0
Guam	0	0	0	0
American Samoa	1	0	0	0
T.T. Pacific Islands	0	0	0	0
N. Mariana Islands	--	--	--	--

General Table Notes

The last five island territories are not included in calculations of summary statistics.

Two dashes (--) indicate that data are not available.

The sum or row amounts may not equal the total due to rounding.

Notes for Table 11

The data in the table are the number of alcoholism treatment units within each state that can be categorized by each of the physical environments listed. Units included in this table provide treatment for clients with alcohol-related problems but do not provide treatment for clients with drug abuse problems. Data are taken from the 1980 NDATUS.

*CMHCs are defined here as institutions operating under P.L. 94-63 or state or local legislation modeled on that act.

Table 11 (continued)
Physical Environment of Units Providing Alcoholism Treatment Only
(As Opposed to Combined Alcoholism and Drug Abuse Treatment)
(As of September 30, 1980)

State	CORRECTIONAL FACILITIES Number	FREESTANDING FACILITIES Number	OTHER UNITS Number	TOTAL UNITS Number
Alabama	0	30	2	41
Alaska	0	8	5	14
Arizona	0	26	6	40
Arkansas	0	24	2	32
California	2	313	57	457
Colorado	0	52	9	85
Connecticut	0	38	4	66
Delaware	0	4	2	9
Florida	1	61	3	100
Georgia	0	6	1	17
Hawaii	0	7	3	11
Idaho	0	12	0	13
Illinois	0	41	4	116
Indiana	0	15	5	34
Iowa	0	10	6	28
Kansas	0	25	0	35
Kentucky	0	23	1	46
Louisiana	0	3	2	11
Maine	0	15	2	27
Maryland	0	35	9	69
Massachusetts	1	89	8	139
Michigan	0	83	15	135
Minnesota	3	71	18	118
Mississippi	0	15	7	28
Missouri	1	19	4	37
Montana	0	31	10	51
Nebraska	0	18	9	48
Nevada	0	8	2	12
New Hampshire	0	2	0	7
New Jersey	1	40	3	61
New Mexico	0	19	6	35
New York	1	110	14	214
North Carolina	1	42	5	108
North Dakota	0	2	1	4
Ohio	0	67	30	130
Oklahoma	0	28	2	37
Oregon	0	38	8	63
Pennsylvania	1	37	2	72
Rhode Island	0	16	0	19
South Carolina	0	8	0	11

Table 11 (continued)
Physical Environment of Units Providing Alcoholism Treatment Only
(As Opposed to Combined Alcoholism and Drug Abuse Treatment)
(As of September 30, 1980)

State	CORRECTIONAL FACILITIES Number	FREESTANDING FACILITIES Number	OTHER UNITS Number	TOTAL UNITS Number
South Dakota	0	10	3	19
Tennessee	0	9	2	17
Texas	1	68	4	111
Utah	1	14	2	19
Vermont	0	10	14	26
Virginia	0	31	8	55
Washington	1	63	19	94
West Virginia	0	4	0	7
Wisconsin	0	33	2	44
Wyoming	0	4	1	5
Washington, D.C.	0	10	4	21
Puerto Rico	0	14	1	17
National Total	15	1,761	327	3,015
Number of States Included	52	52	52	52
Virgin Islands	0	0	0	0
Guam	0	0	0	0
American Samoa	0	0	0	1
T.T. Pacific Islands	0	0	0	0
N. Mariana Islands	--	--	--	--

Source: SAPIS, *National Status Report,* pp. 54–57.

General Table Notes

The last five island territories are not included in calculations of summary statistics.

Two dashes (--) indicate that data are not available.

The sum or row amounts may not equal the total due to rounding.

Notes for Table 11

The data in the table are the number of alcoholism treatment units within each state that can be categorized by each of the physical environments listed. Units included in this table provide treatment for clients with alcohol-related problems but do not provide treatment for clients with drug abuse problems. Data are taken from the 1980 NDATUS.

*CMHCs are defined here as institutions operating under P.L. 94-63 or state or local legislation modeled on that act.

Table 12
Physical Environment of Units Providing Combined Alcoholism and Drug Abuse
Treatment
(As of September 30, 1980)

State	COMMUNITY MENTAL HEALTH CENTER* Number	MENTAL/ PSYCHIATRIC HOSPITAL Number	GENERAL HOSPITAL, INCLUDING VETERANS ADMINISTRATION HOSPITAL Number	OTHER SPECIALIZED HOSPITAL Number
Alabama	8	2	0	0
Alaska	1	0	0	0
Arizona	24	0	2	1
Arkansas	26	0	0	0
California	8	1	8	1
Colorado	5	1	0	0
Connecticut	1	2	1	2
Delaware	0	1	0	0
Florida	6	1	0	0
Georgia	19	8	1	0
Hawaii	1	0	0	0
Idaho	0	0	0	0
Illinois	11	0	0	0
Indiana	33	1	3	0
Iowa	1	3	6	0
Kansas	9	2	2	0
Kentucky	87	0	1	2
Louisiana	13	1	5	0
Maine	6	0	0	0
Maryland	4	0	1	0
Massachusetts	0	0	2	0
Michigan	5	0	5	1
Minnesota	4	1	8	0
Mississippi	40	1	1	0
Missouri	13	3	1	0
Montana	0	0	0	0
Nebraska	1	0	0	0
Nevada	0	0	0	0
New Hampshire	7	1	0	0
New Jersey	1	0	1	0
New Mexico	9	0	0	0
New York	3	0	3	0
North Carolina	18	1	0	0
North Dakota	5	1	3	1
Ohio	7	1	4	0
Oklahoma	23	2	1	0
Oregon	11	1	0	0
Pennsylvania	18	3	11	0

Table 12 (continued)
Physical Environment of Units Providing Combined Alcoholism and Drug Abuse Treatment
(As of September 30, 1980)

State	COMMUNITY MENTAL HEALTH CENTER* Number	MENTAL/ PSYCHIATRIC HOSPITAL Number	GENERAL HOSPITAL, INCLUDING VETERANS ADMINISTRATION HOSPITAL Number	OTHER SPECIALIZED HOSPITAL Number
Rhode Island	1	0	0	0
South Carolina	5	1	0	0
South Dakota	4	0	1	1
Tennessee	32	6	3	0
Texas	14	3	3	0
Utah	13	1	2	0
Vermont	7	0	0	1
Virginia	9	1	0	0
Washington	5	0	0	0
West Virginia	14	1	0	0
Wisconsin	33	4	10	3
Wyoming	9	1	1	0
Washington, D.C.	2	0	0	0
Puerto Rico	0	0	0	0
National Total	576	56	90	13
Number of States Included	52	52	52	52
Virgin Islands	0	0	0	0
Guam	1	0	0	0
American Samoa	0	0	0	0
T.T. Pacific Islands	0	0	0	0
N. Mariana Islands	--	--	--	--

General Table Notes

The last five island territories are not included in calculations of summary statistics.

Two dashes (--) indicate that data are not available.

The sum or row amounts may not equal the total due to rounding.

Notes for Table 12

The data in the table are the number of combined alcoholism and drug abuse treatment units within each state that can be categorized by each of the physical environments listed. Units included in this table provide treatment for all substance-abuse clients, whether alcohol or drugs are involved. Data are taken from the 1980 NDATUS.

*CMHCs are defined here as institutions operating under P.L. 94-63 or state or local legislation modeled on that act.

Table 12 (continued)
Physical Environment of Units Providing Combined Alcoholism and Drug Abuse Treatment
(As of September 30, 1980)

State	CORRECTIONAL FACILITIES Number	FREESTANDING FACILITIES Number	OTHER UNITS Number	TOTAL UNITS Number
Alabama	0	2	0	12
Alaska	0	0	0	1
Arizona	0	15	5	47
Arkansas	0	0	0	26
California	0	39	2	59
Colorado	3	6	3	18
Connecticut	8	11	0	25
Delaware	0	3	0	4
Florida	0	9	1	17
Georgia	0	13	1	42
Hawaii	0	7	1	9
Idaho	0	3	6	9
Illinois	0	6	1	18
Indiana	6	9	1	53
Iowa	1	13	4	28
Kansas	2	11	1	27
Kentucky	1	8	0	99
Louisiana	0	17	7	43
Maine	0	0	0	6
Maryland	2	7	6	20
Massachusetts	0	6	0	8
Michigan	3	36	10	60
Minnesota	2	22	7	44
Mississippi	5	2	11	60
Missouri	1	12	2	32
Montana	3	4	1	8
Nebraska	0	1	0	2
Nevada	0	5	3	8
New Hampshire	0	1	1	10
New Jersey	0	3	0	5
New Mexico	0	1	2	12
New York	1	9	1	17
North Carolina	0	4	0	23
North Dakota	0	2	2	14
Ohio	0	11	5	28
Oklahoma	1	6	3	36
Oregon	0	3	0	15
Pennsylvania	2	76	7	117
Rhode Island	1	2	0	4
South Carolina	0	28	8	42

Table 12 (continued)
Physical Environment of Units Providing Combined Alcoholism and Drug Abuse Treatment
(As of September 30, 1980)

State	CORRECTIONAL FACILITIES Number	FREESTANDING FACILITIES Number	OTHER UNITS Number	TOTAL UNITS Number
South Dakota	0	3	2	11
Tennessee	0	5	3	49
Texas	2	15	1	38
Utah	0	10	1	27
Vermont	0	0	2	10
Virginia	1	10	3	24
Washington	3	6	0	14
West Virginia	0	0	0	15
Wisconsin	3	48	8	109
Wyoming	0	5	0	16
Washington, D.C.	0	3	0	5
Puerto Rico	12	8	0	20
National Total	63	526	122	1,446
Number of States Included	52	52	52	52
Virgin Islands	0	2	0	2
Guam	0	1	0	2
American Samoa	0	0	0	0
T.T. Pacific Islands	0	1	0	1
N. Mariana Islands	--	--	--	--

Source: SAPIS, *National Status Report,* pp. 58–61.

General Table Notes

The last five island territories are not incuded in calculations of summary statistics.

Two dashes (--) indicate that data are not available.

The sum or row amounts may not equal the total due to rounding.

Notes for Table 12

The data in the table are the number of combined alcoholism and drug abuse treatment units within each state that can be categorized by each of the physical environments listed. Units included in this table provide treatment for all substance-abuse clients, whether alcohol or drugs are involved. Data are taken from the 1980 NDATUS.

*CMHCs are defined here as institutions operating under P.L. 94-63 or state or local legislation modeled on that act

Table 13
Utilization Rates of Alcoholism Treatment Capacities by Type of Care
(As of September 30, 1980)

State	DETOXIFICATION, MEDICAL MODEL		DETOXIFICATION, SOCIAL SETTING		REHABILITATION MODEL		CUSTODIAL/ DOMICILIARY MODEL	
	Utilization Rate	(Rank)	Utilization Rate	(Rank)	Utilization Rate	(Rank)	Utilization Rate	(Rank)
Alabama	65	34	92	7	80	36	88	15
Alaska	68	29	0	--	95	2	100	2
Arizona	58	41	190	1	77	43	89	12
Arkansas	73	20	65	35	74	46	78	22
California	73	20	83	9	88	12	72	32
Colorado	79	9	69	28	78	41	87	16
Connecticut	66	32	63	31	68	51	78	22
Delaware	60	39	0	--	91	4	0	--
Florida	70	24	77	19	84	25	77	25
Georgia	74	17	47	37	94	3	100	2
Hawaii	25	51	0	--	70	50	0	--
Idaho	50	45	46	38	79	39	16	44
Illinois	73	20	63	31	86	18	74	29
Indiana	75	13	71	25	75	45	91	8
Iowa	59	40	81	14	90	5	100	2
Kansas	56	42	72	23	84	25	89	12
Kentucky	63	36	71	25	85	23	71	33
Louisiana	91	1	0	--	74	46	142	1
Maine	56	42	0	--	89	9	91	8
Maryland	63	36	83	9	88	12	0	--
Massachusetts	91	1	82	13	90	5	77	25
Michigan	26	50	74	21	81	31	68	35

266

State							
Minnesota	80	7	75	20	84	25	87	16
Mississippi	50	45	104	4	82	28	90	11
Missouri	75	13	46	38	79	39	75	27
Montana	36	49	78	17	72	49	46	42
Nebraska	84	5	37	42	82	28	74	29
Nevada	75	13	87	8	90	5	0	--
New Hampshire	90	3	0	--	73	48	100	2
New Jersey	74	17	69	28	89	9	91	8
New Mexico	67	30	43	40	80	36	0	--
New York	70	24	61	34	88	12	75	27
North Carolina	50	45	59	35	77	43	69	34
North Dakota	67	30	74	21	81	31	0	--
Ohio	69	27	81	14	86	18	63	36
Oklahoma	66	32	80	16	81	31	78	22
Oregon	84	5	83	9	85	23	94	7
Pennsylvania	75	13	78	17	78	41	60	38
Rhode Island	55	44	70	27	90	5	100	2
South Carolina	78	11	40	41	87	16	89	12
South Dakota	73	20	117	3	89	9	63	36
Tennessee	62	38	83	9	82	28	87	16
Texas	64	35	62	33	88	12	36	43
Utah	89	4	150	2	102	1	73	31
Vermont	0	--	59	35	81	31	0	--
Virginia	77	12	93	6	80	36	50	41
Washington	74	17	19	43	86	18	80	20
West Virginia	70	24	0	--	87	16	80	20
Wisconsin	79	9	72	23	86	18	87	16
Wyoming	42	48	100	5	81	31	53	40

Table 13 (continued)
Utilization Rates of Alcoholism Treatment Capacities by Type of Care
(As of September 30, 1980)

State	DETOXIFICATION, MEDICAL MODEL		DETOXIFICATION, SOCIAL SETTING		REHABILITATION MODEL		CUSTODIAL/ DOMICILIARY MODEL	
	Utilization Rate	(Rank)	Utilization Rate	(Rank)	Utilization Rate	(Rank)	Utilization Rate	(Rank)
Washington, D.C.	69	27	0		86		55	
Puerto Rico	80	7	0		58		0	
National Value	67		74		84		74	
Number of States Included	52		52		52		52	
Virgin Islands	0		0		0		0	
Guam	0		0		67		0	
American Samoa	33		0		0		0	
T.T. Pacific Islands	100		0		0		0	
N. Mariana Islands	--		--		--		--	

General Table Notes

The last five island territories are not included in calculations of summary statistics.

Two dashes (--) indicate that data are not available.

The sum or row amounts may not equal the total due to rounding.

Notes for Table 13

This table presents the utilization rates (expressed as percentages) by state for alcoholism treatment capacities in each of the specified categories of care. Utilization is defined as the actual number of clients in treatment as of September 30, 1980 divided by the total capacity of the units. Data are obtained from the 1980 NDATUS. It should be noted that such factors as local climate and funding cycles may affect the degree to which these September 30 data are representative of a state's average yearly utilization.

Table 13 (continued)
Utilization Rates of Alcoholism Treatment Capacities by Type of Care
(As of September 30, 1980)

State	AMBULATORY MEDICAL DETOXIFICATION		LIMITED CARE INCLUDING DAY CARE		OUTPATIENT SERVICES		TOTAL	
	Utilization Rate	(Rank)	Utilization Rate	(Rank)	Utilization Rate	(Rank)	Utilization Rate	(Rank)
Alabama	100	3	50	25	83	36	83	30
Alaska	44	16	13	40	82	38	78	43
Arizona	0	--	50	25	76	49	79	41
Arkansas	0	--	82	9	96	6	91	9
California	60	13	0	--	78	45	78	43
Colorado	0	--	8	41	83	36	81	37
Connecticut	57	14	50	25	87	19	81	37
Delaware	0	--	0	--	88	16	86	18
Florida	69	11	67	16	87	19	85	21
Georgia	68	12	87	5	78	45	79	41
Hawaii	0	--	17	38	77	47	70	52
Idaho	0	--	0	--	84	34	82	34
Illinois	0	--	65	20	81	40	81	37
Indiana	5	25	43	31	92	13	88	13
Iowa	0	--	0	--	82	38	82	34
Kansas	7	24	0	--	79	43	78	43
Kentucky	0	--	85	7	91	13	88	13
Louisiana	0	--	53	24	85	29	84	25
Maine	0	--	0	--	88	16	88	13
Maryland	0	--	0	--	96	6	94	6
Massachusetts	22	21	86	6	95	8	93	7
Michigan	40	18	79	12	81	40	77	47

Table 13 (continued)
Utilization Rates of Alcoholism Treatment Capacities by Type of Care
(As of September 30, 1980)

State	AMBULATORY MEDICAL DETOXIFICATION		LIMITED CARE INCLUDING DAY CARE		OUTPATIENT SERVICES		TOTAL	
	Utilization Rate	(Rank)	Utilization Rate	(Rank)	Utilization Rate	(Rank)	Utilization Rate	(Rank)
Minnesota	0	--	14	39	85	29	84	25
Mississippi	80	9	80	10	93	10	90	9
Missouri	100	3	64	22	85	29	83	30
Montana	0	--	20	37	88	16	83	30
Nebraska	86	8	71	13	79	43	80	40
Nevada	0	--	0	--	94	9	93	7
New Hampshire	0	--	67	16	91	13	90	10
New Jersey	0	--	66	19	85	29	83	30
New Mexico	0	--	25	34	93	10	89	12
New York	95	7	100	2	87	19	87	16
North Carolina	80	9	67	16	85	29	82	34
North Dakota	110	2	132	1	77	47	78	43
Ohio	0	--	65	20	86	26	85	21
Oklahoma	420	1	44	30	74	51	75	50
Oregon	44	16	85	7	87	19	87	16
Pennsylvania	38	19	70	15	86	26	84	25
Rhode Island	0	--	0	--	99	2	96	2
South Carolina	98	6	45	28	86	26	85	21
South Dakota	0	--	0	--	76	49	76	48
Tennessee	27	20	45	28	87	19	85	21
Texas	0	--	25	34	91	13	86	18

Utah	--	0	2	42	97	4	95	4
Vermont	--	0	30	32	87	19	86	18
Virginia	--	0	80	10	97	4	95	4
Washington	--	0	25	34	71	52	72	51
West Virginia	23	9	30	32	87	19	84	25
Wisconsin	--	0	97	4	84	34	84	25
Wyoming	22	17	59	23	81	40	76	48
Washington, D.C.	3	100	100	2	99	2	96	2
Puerto Rico	14	57	71	13	108	1	104	1
National Value		72	80		85		83	
Number of States Included		52	52		52		52	
Virgin Islands		0	20		53		48	
Guam		0	0		28		35	
American Samoa		0	0		0		17	
T.T. Pacific Islands		0	0		100		100	
N. Mariana Islands		1–	1–		--		--	

Source: SAPIS, *National Status Report*, pp. 70–73.

General Table Notes

The last five island territories are not included in calculations of summary statistics.

Two dashes (--) indicate that data are not available.

The sum or row amounts may not equal the total due to rounding.

Notes for Table 13

This table presents the utlization rates (expressed as percentages) by state for alcoholism treatment capacities in each of the specified categories of care. Utilization is defined as the actual number of clients in treatment as of September 30, 1980 divided by the total capacity of the units. Data are obtained from the 1980 NDATUS. It should be noted that such factors as local climate and funding cycles may affect the degree to which these September 30 data are representative of a state's average yearly utilization.

Table 14
Alcohol Treatment Capacities by Type of Facility*
(As of September 30, 1980)

State	HOSPITAL Capacity	QUARTERWAY HOUSE Capacity	HALFWAY HOUSE/ RECOVERY HOME Capacity	OTHER RESIDENTIAL FACILITY Capacity
Alabama	185	163	308	92
Alaska	4	14	45	88
Arizona	1,319	48	380	219
Arkansas	588	5	638	342
California	5,826	20	6,222	9,899
Colorado	736	36	485	548
Connecticut	1,605	10	343	406
Delaware	16	36	32	27
Florida	698	164	1,221	854
Georgia	615	15	201	322
Hawaii	20	0	105	59
Idaho	34	66	163	316
Illinois	1,225	40	379	1,077
Indiana	1,411	76	232	312
Iowa	409	0	120	100
Kansas	699	0	267	390
Kentucky	71	22	346	402
Louisiana	502	0	19	24
Maine	296	0	45	153
Maryland	1,688	116	501	239
Massachusetts	2,549	20	1,222	297
Michigan	2,676	90	593	520
Minnesota	1,791	7	753	922
Mississippi	389	21	281	0
Missouri	1,187	0	290	227
Montana	289	19	178	192
Nebraska	411	69	173	27
Nevada	38	0	19	52
New Hampshire	108	0	12	68
New Jersey	986	73	93	734
New Mexico	137	48	103	186
New York	4,085	264	519	2,272
North Carolina	1,163	71	768	534
North Dakota	406	0	0	96
Ohio	1,467	182	471	398
Oklahoma	683	0	392	476
Oregon	233	0	333	591
Pennsylvania	731	7	241	1,064
Rhode Island	100	0	240	65
South Carolina	173	0	146	248

Table 14 (continued)
Alcohol Treatment Capacities by Type of Facility*
(As of September 30, 1980)

State	HOSPITAL Capacity	QUARTERWAY HOUSE Capacity	HALFWAY HOUSE/ RECOVERY HOME Capacity	OTHER RESIDENTIAL FACILITY Capacity
South Dakota	145	0	521	60
Tennessee	807	0	180	297
Texas	2,611	154	1,308	1,335
Utah	151	6	218	133
Vermont	0	20	41	72
Virginia	1,429	0	189	355
Washington	632	0	384	598
West Virginia	167	0	26	0
Wisconsin	1,359	22	755	271
Wyoming	70	55	146	126
Washington, D.C.	416	42	142	72
Puerto Rico	30	0	190	104
National Total	45,366	2,001	22,979	28,261
Number of States Included	52	52	52	52
Virgin Islands	0	0	0	0
Guam	0	0	0	11
American Samoa	6	0	0	0
T.T. Pacific Islands	3	0	0	0
N. Mariana Islands	--	--	--	--

General Table Notes

The last five island territories are not included in calculations of summary statistics.

Two dashes (--) indicate that data are not available.

The sum or row amounts may not equal the total due to rounding.

Notes for Table 14

This table presents the total alcoholism treatment capacity reported by each type of facility for the 1980 NDATUS, categorized by type of facility. These data reflect the capacity for treatment as of September 30, 1980. It should be noted that such factors as funding cycles may affect whether or not these September 30 data are representative of a state's average yearly capacity.

*In comparing these capacities with Tables 11 and 12 (Physical Environment of Units), it should be noted that the terms "hospital" and "correctional facility" may present some problems. For example, a unit classified in Table 11 or 12 as a freestanding unit might provide outpatient services and, in addition, provide services on a regular basis to inmates housed in correctional facilities. Similarly, a hospital program might report capacity under "outpatient."

Table 14 (continued)
Alcohol Treatment Capacities by Type of Facility*
(As of September 30, 1980)

State	OUTPATIENT FACILITY Capacity	CORRECTIONAL FACILITY Capacity	TOTAL Capacity
Alabama	2,171	0	2,919
Alaska	1,050	0	1,201
Arizona	4,745	0	6,711
Arkansas	2,082	0	3,655
California	47,396	77	69,440
Colorado	8,660	145	10,610
Connecticut	2,443	120	4,927
Delaware	426	0	537
Florida	7,578	40	10,555
Georgia	7,297	0	8,450
Hawaii	215	0	399
Idaho	1,546	0	2,125
Illinois	7,256	20	9,997
Indiana	4,885	98	7,014
Iowa	2,132	0	2,761
Kansas	1,988	51	3,395
Kentucky	3,820	175	4,836
Louisiana	4,309	0	4,854
Maine	2,444	94	3,032
Maryland	5,698	91	8,333
Massachusetts	7,775	450	12,313
Michigan	11,561	70	15,510
Minnesota	4,630	211	8,314
Mississippi	1,702	132	2,525
Missouri	3,294	0	4,998
Montana	1,441	30	2,149
Nebraska	2,601	0	3,281
Nevada	637	0	746
New Hampshire	641	0	829
New Jersey	2,707	150	4,743
New Mexico	2,409	0	2,883
New York	18,696	25	25,861
North Carolina	6,968	295	9,799
North Dakota	1,582	0	2,084
Ohio	7,401	0	9,919
Oklahoma	4,568	8	6,127
Oregon	7,114	0	8,271
Pennsylvania	7,017	189	9,249
Rhode Island	1,478	2	1,885
South Carolina	3,652	30	4,249

Table 14 (continued)
Alcohol Treatment Capacities by Type of Facility*
(As of September 30, 1980)

State	OUTPATIENT FACILITY Capacity	CORRECTIONAL FACILITY Capacity	TOTAL Capacity
South Dakota	1,869	0	2,595
Tennessee	3,903	0	5,187
Texas	4,409	3,714	13,531
Utah	1,320	50	1,878
Vermont	1,397	30	1,560
Virginia	7,335	2	9,310
Washington	7,938	200	9,752
West Virginia	1,566	5	1,764
Wisconsin	9,400	6	11,813
Wyoming	880	0	1,277
Washington, D.C.	1,606	60	2,338
Puerto Rico	4,920	357	5,601
National Total	262,558	6,927	368,092
Number of States Included	52	52	52
Virgin Islands	65	0	65
Guam	20	0	31
American Samoa	0	0	6
T.T. Pacific Islands	24	0	27
N. Mariana Islands	--	--	--

Source: SAPIS, *National Status Report*, pp. 74–77.

General Table Notes

The last five island territories are not included in calculations of summary statistics.

Two dashes (--) indicate that data are not available.

The sum or row amounts may not equal the total due to rounding.

Notes for Table 14

This table presents the total alcoholism treatment capacity reported by each type of facility for the 1980 NDATUS, categorized by type of facility. These data reflect the capacity for treatment as of September 30, 1980. It should be noted that such factors as funding cycles may affect whether or not these September 30 data are representative of a state's average yearly capacity.

*In comparing these capacities with Tables 11 and 12 (Physical Environment of Units), it should be noted that the usage of the terms "hospital" and "correctional facility" may present some problems. For example, a unit classified in Table 11 or 12 as a freestanding unit might provide outpatient services and, in addition, provide services on a regular basis to inmates housed in correctional facilities. Similarly, a hospital program might report capacity under "outpatient."

Table 15
Utilization Rates of Alcoholism Treatment Capacities by Type of Facility
(As of September 30, 1980)

State	HOSPITAL		QUARTERWAY HOUSE		HALFWAY HOUSE/ RECOVERY HOME		OTHER RESIDENTIAL FACILITY	
	Utilization Rate	(Rank)	Utilization Rate	(Rank)	Utilization Rate	(Rank)	Utilization Rate	(Rank)
Alabama	74	37	90	12	90	13	42	48
Alaska	75	36	71	24	91	10	94	2
Arizona	74	37	100	2	133	2	84	10
Arkansas	121	1	100	2	63	46	66	38
California	77	32	55	28	85	23	84	10
Colorado	64	46	75	22	83	27	64	40
Connecticut	79	30	100	2	58	49	74	28
Delaware	56	48	97	9	84	24	63	41
Florida	87	13	78	20	74	41	76	22
Georgia	80	27	40	33	91	10	65	39
Hawaii	25	51	0	--	70	44	63	41
Idaho	88	11	44	32	60	48	72	33
Illinois	90	7	100	2	75	38	77	19
Indiana	85	17	79	19	78	33	79	16
Iowa	84	20	0	--	90	13	71	34
Kansas	80	27	0	--	91	10	75	24
Kentucky	80	27	223	1	73	42	75	24
Louisiana	81	24	0	--	142	1	58	44
Maine	83	22	0	--	100	3	74	28
Maryland	99	4	96	10	92	8	84	10
Massachusetts	110	2	80	18	92	8	86	7
Michigan	52	49	62	26	87	16	89	4

Minnesota	85	17	100	2	84	24	77	19
Mississippi	76	34	62	26	77	34	0	–
Missouri	87	13	0	–	67	45	71	34
Montana	47	50	74	23	93	6	73	32
Nebraska	81	24	86	15	81	29	37	50
Nevada	87	13	0	–	89	15	85	9
New Hampshire	85	17	0	–	100	3	88	5
New Jersey	86	16	64	25	95	5	77	19
New Mexico	77	32	52	30	50	50	80	15
New York	89	9	90	12	87	16	75	24
North Carolina	68	44	54	29	76	36	63	41
North Dakota	68	44	0	–	0	–	86	7
Ohio	83	22	82	17	86	20	75	24
Oklahoma	63	47	0	–	71	43	74	28
Oregon	79	30	0	–	79	32	90	3
Pennsylvania	72	41	100	2	80	31	76	22
Rhode Island	99	4	0	–	86	20	55	46
South Carolina	76	34	0	–	87	16	78	17
South Dakota	89	9	0	–	75	38	42	48
Tennessee	106	3	0	–	86	20	74	28
Texas	72	41	96	10	82	28	70	36
Utah	88	11	100	2	75	38	78	17
Vermont	0	–	90	12	61	47	82	13
Virginia	74	37	0	–	81	29	87	6
Washington	84	20	0	–	87	16	58	44
West Virginia	71	43	0	–	77	34	0	–
Wisconsin	90	7	86	15	84	24	82	13
Wyoming	74	37	78	20	76	36	45	47
Washington, D.C.	81	24	52	30	93	6	67	37
Puerto Rico	97	6	0	–	37	51	95	1

Table 15 (continued)

Utilization Rates of Alcoholism Treatment Capacities by Type of Facility

(As of September 30, 1980)

State	HOSPITAL		QUARTERWAY HOUSE		HALFWAY HOUSE/ RECOVERY HOME		OTHER RESIDENTIAL FACILITY	
	Utilization Rate	(Rank)	Utilization Rate	(Rank)	Utilization Rate	(Rank)	Utilization Rate	(Rank)
National Value	82		82		83		78	
Number of States Included	52		52		52		52	
Virgin Islands	0		0		0		0	
Guam	0		0		0		82	
American Samoa	17		0		0		0	
T.T. Pacific Islands	100		0		0		0	
N. Mariana Islands	--		--		--		--	

General Table Notes

The last five island territories are not incuded in calculations of summary statistics.

Two dashes (--) indicate that data are not available.

The sum or row amounts may not equal the total due to rounding.

Notes for Table 15

This table presents the utilization rates of alcoholism treatment capacities (expressed as percentages) for each state by the location of alcoholism treatment units. Utilization rates are calculated by dividing the actual number of clients reported in treatment on September 30, 1980 by the total capacity reported. The data are abstracted from the 1980 NDATUS. It should be noted that such factors as local climate and funding cycles may affect the degree to which these September 30 figures are representative of a state's average yearly utilization.

Table 15 (continued)
Utilization Rates of Alcoholism Treatment Capacities by Type of Facility
(As of September 30, 1980)

State	OUTPATIENT FACILITY		CORRECTIONAL FACILITY		TOTAL	
	Utilization Rate	(Rank)	Utilization Rate	(Rank)	Utilization Rate	(Rank)
Alabama	83	36	0	--	83	30
Alaska	77	45	0	--	78	43
Arizona	76	50	0	--	79	41
Arkansas	95	5	0	--	91	9
California	77	45	55	31	78	43
Colorado	84	33	92	15	81	37
Connecticut	88	16	58	28	81	37
Delaware	88	16	0	--	86	18
Florida	88	16	100	5	85	21
Georgia	79	44	0	--	79	41
Hawaii	77	45	0	--	70	52
Idaho	88	16	0	--	82	34
Illinois	80	40	150	3	81	37
Indiana	90	11	88	16	88	13
Iowa	82	37	0	--	82	34
Kansas	76	50	61	26	78	43
Kentucky	90	11	81	17	88	13
Louisiana	85	30	0	--	84	25
Maine	89	14	95	11	88	13
Maryland	94	6	57	30	94	6
Massachusetts	88	16	74	21	93	7
Michigan	82	37	93	12	77	47
Minnesota	86	25	64	24	84	25
Mississippi	94	6	100	5	90	10
Missouri	85	30	0	--	83	30
Montana	90	11	80	19	83	30
Nebraska	80	40	0	--	80	40
Nevada	94	6	0	--	93	7
New Hampshire	91	10	0	--	90	10
New Jersey	84	33	81	17	83	30
New Mexico	92	9	0	--	89	12
New York	88	16	68	23	87	16
North Carolina	85	30	99	9	82	34
North Dakota	80	40	0	--	78	43
Ohio	86	25	0	--	85	21
Oklahoma	77	45	63	25	75	50
Oregon	87	22	0	--	87	16
Pennsylvania	86	25	76	20	84	25
Rhode Island	99	3	100	5	96	2
South Carolina	86	25	93	12	85	21

Table 15 (continued)
Utilization Rates of Alcoholism Treatment Capacities by Type of Facility
(As of September 30, 1980)

State	OUTPATIENT FACILITY		CORRECTIONAL FACILITY		TOTAL	
	Utilization Rate	(Rank)	Utilization Rate	(Rank)	Utilization Rate	(Rank)
South Dakota	77	45	0	--	76	48
Tennessee	82	37	0	--	85	21
Texas	89	14	99	9	86	18
Utah	101	2	110	4	95	4
Vermont	87	22	93	12	86	18
Virginia	99	3	100	5	95	4
Washington	71	52	74	21	72	51
West Virginia	86	25	60	27	84	25
Wisconsin	84	33	167	2	84	25
Wyoming	80	40	0	--	76	48
Washington, D.C.	87	22	510	1	96	2
Puerto Rico	110	1	58	28	104	1
National Value	84		93		83	
Number of States Included	52		52		52	
Virgin Islands	48		0		48	
Guam	10		0		35	
American Samoa	0		0		17	
T.T. Pacific Islands	100		0		100	
N. Mariana Islands	--		--		--	

Source: SAPIS, *National Status Report,* pp. 78–81.

General Table Notes

The last five island territories are not included in calculations of summary statistics.

Two dashes (--) indicate that data are not available.

The sum or row amounts may not equal the total due to rounding.

Notes for Table 15

This table presents the utilization rates of alcoholism treatment capacities (expressed as percentages) for each state by the location of alcoholism treatment units. Utilization rates are calculated by dividing the actual number of clients reported in treatment on September 30, 1980 by the total capacity reported. The data are abstracted from the 1980 NDATUS. It should be noted that such factors as local climate and funding cycles may affect the degree to which these September 30 figures are representative of a state's average yearly utilization.

Table 16

Estimated Frequency by First-Listed Diagnosis of Hospital Discharges That Also Include an Alcohol-Related Diagnosis, Short-Stay Hospitals (1975)

First-Listed Discharge Diagnosis (ICDA Code)[1]	Number of First-Listed Discharge Diagnoses Accompanied by an Alcohol-Related Diagnosis[2]	Total Number of First-Listed Discharge	Percentage of All Discharges with Any Alcohol-Related Diagnosis[2]
ALCOHOLISM (303)[3]	423,910	423,91）	—
CIRRHOSIS OF LIVER (571)[3]	106,010	106,010	—
ALCOHOLIC PSYCHOSIS (291)[3]	17,930	17,930	—
Neuroses (300)	26,340	421,220	6.3
Symptomatic heart disease (427)	14,350	499,880	2.9
Chronic ischemic heart disease (412)	14,250	1,193,330	1.2
Gastritis and duodenitis (535)	12,590	288,630	4.4
Diseases of pancreas (577)	12,380	92,510	13.4
Diabetes mellitus (250)	11,260	532,810	2.1
Other diseases of intestines and peritoneum (569)	10,570	183,370	5.8
Other diseases of liver (573)	9,390	41,720	22.5
Other diseases of respiratory system (519)	8,370	296,250	2.8
Pneumonia, unspecified (486)	6,440	299,970	2.1
Varicose veins of other sites (456)	5,660	21,210	26.7
Adverse effect of other and unspecified drugs (977)	5,550	87,550	6.3
Cholelithiasis (574)	5,390	467,790	1.2
Other and unspecified laceration of head (873)	5,200	99,560	5.6
Schizophrenia (295)	4,570	165,370	2.8
Injury, other and unspecified (996)	4,330	194,270	2.2
Personality disorders (301)	3,670	38,190	9.6
Other conditions (all other codes)	198,010	31,343,360	0.6
TOTAL	910,040	36,814,840	2.5

Source: *Fourth Special Report to the U.S. Congress on Alcohol and Health* (Rockville, Md.: National Institute on Alcohol Abuse and Alcoholism, 1981), p. 45.

[1]Eight Revision International Classification of Diseases, adapted 1965 (ICDA-8).

[2]The phrase "alcohol-related diagnosis" is defined in this table as a diagnosis of any one of the following ICDA-8 codes: 291 or 303 or 571.

[3]The first three diagnoses (capitalized) are defined in this table as alcohol-related and therefore the value in the third column would be 100% by definition.

Figure 2

Distribution of Treatment Capacity by Facility Location and Type of Care in Alcoholism Only and Combined Treatment Units

National Drug and Alcoholism Treatment Utilization Survey (NDATUS) September 30, 1980

OUTPATIENT FACILITIES
(Capacity 262,119)

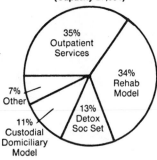

98%
Outpatient Services

2%
Other

HOSPITALS
(Capacity 45,231)

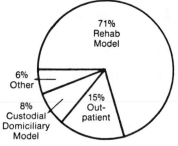

46%
Outpatient Services

5%
Other

29%
Rehab Model

Detox
Med Model
20%

OTHER RESIDENTIAL FACILITIES
(Capacity 27,691)

35%
Outpatient Services

34%
Rehab Model

7%
Other

13%
Detox
Soc Set

11%
Custodial
Domiciliary
Model

HALFWAY HOUSES/RECOVERY HOMES
(Capacity 22,749)

71%
Rehab Model

6%
Other

15%
Out-
patient

8%
Custodial
Domiciliary
Model

CORRECTIONAL FACILITIES
(Capacity 6,903)

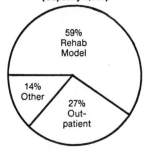

59%
Rehab
Model

14%
Other

27%
Out-
patient

QUARTERWAY HOUSES
(Capacity 1,696)

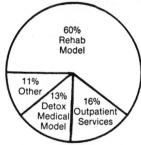

60%
Rehab
Model

11%
Other

13%
Detox
Medical
Model

16%
Outpatient
Services

Source: NIAAA, *Drug & Alcoholism Treatment Survey*, p. 8.

Table 17
Ownership Characteristics of All Alcoholism Only and Combined Treatment Units
National Drug and Alcoholism Treatment Utilization Survey (NDATUS)
September 30, 1980

Ownership	ALCOHOLISM ONLY		COMBINED		TOTAL	
	Number	(%)	Number	(%)	Number	(%)
Total Profit	192	6.4	56	3.9	248	5.6
Individual	33	1.1	5	.3	38	.9
Partnership	28	.9	9	.6	37	.8
Corporation	131	4.3	42	2.9	173	3.9
Total Nonprofit	2,069	68.6	890	61.4	2,959	66.3
Church related	122	4.0	40	2.8	162	3.6
Nonprofit	1,777	58.9	798	55.1	2,575	57.7
Other nonprofit	170	5.6	52	3.6	222	5.0
Total State/Local Gov't	616	20.4	446	30.8	1,062	23.8
State gov't	163	5.4	184	12.7	347	7.8
County gov't	285	9.4	192	13.3	477	10.7
City gov't	66	2.2	9	.6	75	1.7
City-county gov't	32	1.1	11	.8	43	1.0
Hospital district	12	.4	6	.4	18	.4
Other substate gov't	58	1.9	44	3.0	102	2.3
Total Federal Gov't	139	4.6	57	3.9	196	4.4
U.S. Public Health Service	14	.5	2	.1	16	.4
Armed Forces	10	.3	41	2.8	51	1.1
Veterans Administration	90	3.0	1	.1	91	2.0
BOP			8	.6	8	.2
Other federal agencies	25	.8	5	.3	30	.7
TOTAL	3,016	100.0	1,449	100.0	4,465	100.0

Source: NIAAA, *Drug & Alcoholism Treatment Survey,* p. 18.

Table 18
Physical Environments of Alcoholism Only and Combined Treatment Units
National Drug and Alcoholism Treatment Utilization Survey (NDATUS)
September 30, 1980

Facility	ALCOHOLISM ONLY		COMBINED		TOTAL	
	Number	(%)	Number	(%)	Number	(%)
Community mental health center	390	12.9	577	39.9	967	21.7
Mental/psychiatric hospital	101	3.4	56	3.9	157	3.5
General hospital (including VA hospital)	362	12.0	88	6.1	450	10.1
Other specialized hospital	59	2.0	13	.9	72	1.6
Correctional facility	15	.5	63	4.4	78	1.8
Freestanding facility	1,762	58.4	529	36.5	2,291	51.3
Other	326	10.8	122	8.4	448	1ʳ 9
TOTAL	3,015	100.0	1,448	100.0	4,463	100.0

Source: NIAAA, *Drug & Alcoholism Treatment Survey,* p. 21.

Note: Because two units were not classified by physical environment, the total figure differs from other tables in this section.

Table 19
Distribution of Full-Time and Part-Time Paid and Volunteer Staff by Staff Category for All Units Providing Alcoholism and Drug Abuse Treatment

National Drug and Alcoholism Treatment Utilization Survey (NDATUS)
September 30, 1980

Staff Category	FULL-TIME EMPLOYEES				PART-TIME EMPLOYEES					
	PAID		VOLUNTEER		PAID			VOLUNTEER		
	Number	Percent	Number	Percent	Number	Number of Full-Time Equivalent[1] (FTE)	Percent Distribution of FTE	Number	Number of Full-Time Equivalent[1] (FTE)	Percent Distribution of FTE
Psychiatrists	92	0.7			604	119.5	6.4	22	2.2	0.7
Other physicians	91	0.7			410	81.0	4.3	28	3.7	1.1
Psychologists—doctoral level	158	1.2			353	76.1	4.1	18	1.3	0.4
Psychologists—master's level	420	3.2			300	75.2	4.0	20	3.4	1.0
Nurse practitioners or physician's assistants	46	0.4			26	8.8	0.5	2	0.1	0.1
Registered nurses	870	6.7	1	0.4	504	184.8	9.9	20	3.8	1.1
Licensed practical and vocational nurses	534	4.1	1	0.4	162	75.1	4.0	7	1.4	0.4
Social workers, MSW	677	5.2	2	0.9	371	100.7	5.4	19	3.3	1.0
Counselors—bachelor's level and above—counseling degree	2,346	18.1	2	0.9	595	195.2	10.5	212	30.3	9.2
Counselors—other	2,115	16.3	39	17.1	398	156.9	8.4	313	45.5	13.8
Vocational recreational therapists	193	1.5			101	30.8	1.7	56	25.8	7.8

Table 19 (continued)

Distribution of Full-Time and Part-Time Paid and Volunteer Staff by Staff Category for All Units Providing Alcoholism and Drug Abuse Treatment

National Drug and Alcoholism Treatment Utilization Survey (NDATUS)
September 30, 1980

| | FULL-TIME EMPLOYEES | | | | PART-TIME EMPLOYEES | | | | | |
| | PAID | | VOLUNTEER | | PAID | | | VOLUNTEER | | |
Staff Category	Number	Percent	Number	Percent	Number	Number of Full-Time Equivalent[1] (FTE)	Percent Distribution of FTE	Number	Number of Full-Time Equivalent[1] (FTE)	Percent Distribution of FTE
Other direct-care staff	1,570	12.1	26	11.4	447	175.1	9.4	633	70.6	21.3
Total direct-care staff	9,112	70.3	71	31.1	4,271	1,279.8	68.5	1,350	191.9	58.0
Administrative staff	1,949	15.0	12	5.3	903	237.6	12.7	58	10.4	3.1
Other support staff	1,780	13.7	60	26.3	991	294.9	15.8	346	57.1	17.3
Student trainees	123	0.9	85	37.3	153	55.2	3.0	277	71.3	21.6
TOTAL	12,964	100.0	228	100.0	6,318	1,867.6	100.0	2,031	330.8	100.0

Source: NIAAA, *Drug & Alcoholism Treatment Survey*, p. 67.

Note: This table is based on the 1,449 units providing both alcoholism and drug abuse treatment that responded to NDATUS.

[1] Full-time equivalent is calculated in the following manner: $\dfrac{\text{number of hours worked per week}}{\text{35 hours per week}}$

Table 20
Client/Staff Ratios[1] for Single Type of Care Units Providing Alcoholism Treatment Only
National Drug and Alcoholism Treatment Utilization Survey (NDATUS)
September 30, 1980

Staff Category	Detox. Medical Model	Detox. Social Setting	Rehab. Model	Custodial/ Domiciliary Model	Ambulatory Medical Detox.	Limited Care (Including Day Care)	Outpatient Services
Psychiatrists	23.6	91.9	57.4	214.5	154.5	235.8	413.2
Other physicians	21.8	34.2	62.2	172.0	1,691.7	130.8	473.6
Psychologists—doctoral level	27.6	127.0	54.1	48.9	294.2	318.9	206.8
Psychologists—master's level	18.6	28.6	30.9	24.9	1,086.0	12.0	128.7
Nurse practitioners or physician's assistants	11.0	15.7	34.2	92.6		11.6	220.2
Registered nurses	4.0	12.3	10.2	31.0	116.3	55.4	193.3
Licensed practical and vocational nurses	7.1	7.4	13.1	15.4	47.7	73.8	135.1
Social workers, MSW	18.0	16.6	26.4	68.5	123.5	52.1	102.4
Counselors—bachelor's level and above—counseling degree	11.3	7.8	18.7	12.4	103.8	27.5	66.9
Counselors—other	8.1	4.2	8.5	11.3	50.7	25.9	56.7
Vocational, recreational therapists	18.9	19.4	32.4	35.5	841.2	87.0	166.1
Other direct-care staff	2.5	3.1	8.3	12.3	619.0	24.9	94.4
Total paid direct-care staff	7.0	6.1	14.0	20.2	119.8	48.8	90.6
Administrative staff	9.3	9.2	15.7	17.0	134.4	37.8	80.4
Other support staff	6.5	7.5	10.3	11.7	52.6	104.3	94.6
Student trainees	6.6	6.1	19.5	14.6	41.0	38.6	139.8
TOTAL	7.1	6.6	13.6	17.7	104.3	49.2	90.0

Source: NIAAA, *Drug & Alcoholism Treatment Survey*, p. 68.

[1]Client to staff ratio is defined as the number of clients in units with the position divided by the number of paid full-time employee (FTE) staff in the position.

Table 21
Permissible Blood Alcohol Content (BAC) for Drivers, Permissible Testing and Penalization

Region Country	BAC %₀₀: G Ethanol Per 1,000 G Blood	Permissible Testing	Penalization	References
Americas				
Argentina		Capacity of driving measured by tests	Fine or detention 15–20 days	DF*
Brazil			Prohibited to drive under the influence of alcohol; penalties: loss of driving license	ISPA**
Canada	0.8	Breath testing permissible in all provinces	Detention 6 months (1st offense and/or fine $50–$2,000), 2 weeks to 1 year (2nd offense), 3 months to 2 years (each subsequent offense) Suspension of license in some provinces	Criminal Code of Canada, Section 234
Colombia			Any degree of alcohol intoxication is an aggravating circumstance in case of accident.	Road Traffic Code (1977 response)
Costa Rica			Penal responsibility for car accidents occurring during state of intoxication	1972 response
USA:				
Idaho, Utah Most States 4 States	0.8 1.0 1.5	Laws vary according to state		National Highway Traffic Safety Adm., Dept. of Transport

Europe

Europe				
Austria	0.8	A positive breath test is not sufficient; should be confirmed by evident symptoms of inebriety. In certain cases the road police may carry out clinical examination, in serious cases including blood test.		Regulations on Road Traffic, 1960; DF
Belgium	0.8	Breath test may be taken at random; blood sample taken of people showing signs of inebriety involved in road accidents.	Courts nearly always convict at 1.5, seldom below.	Law of 1975 Law of 1967 DF Havard, 1975
Bulgaria	0.0			Road Traffic Code 1964
Czechoslovakia	0.0	Blood test and medical examination may be imposed; limit for analytical error 0.3.	Penalty may include transfer from sector of work.	DF Havard, 1975
Denmark	0.6	Blood test may be imposed; police screening; breath test.	Detention, suspension of driving license. Courts nearly always convict at 1.0, often at 0.8.	ISPA DF 1977 response Havard, 1975
Finland	road: 0.5 rail: 0.5 air: 0.0 water: 1.5	Psychological tests, blood and urine sample	Road traffic: 0.5–1.5: fine or maximum of 3 months detention; 1.5 or more: maximum of 2 years detention or at least "60 day-fines" (worked out on income)	1977 response ("per mille limit act," passed by Parliament, 1976), DF
France	0.8 >1.2: major offense	Systematic road control of drivers on request of Public Prosecutor (initially at publicized times and places); breath testing alone when new apparatus officially approved	0.8–1.2 g: fine 400–1,000 F plus possible detention 10 days to 1 month; above 1.2 g: fine 500–5,000 F plus possible detention 1 month to 1 year; above 1.2	Law of 12 July 1978: cited in Alcool ou Santé, 1978

289

Table 21 (continued)
Permissible Blood Alcohol Content (BAC) for Drivers, Permissible Testing and Penalization

Region Country	BAC ‰: G Ethanol Per 1,000 G Blood	Permissible Testing	Penalization	References
			g plus homicide, involuntary injury or recidivism: cancelation of driving license (also possible in other cases—alternatively temporary withdrawal). Delay for new application up to 3 years after medical and psychotechnical examination.	
Germany, E.	0.0	Blood test may be imposed: assumption of impairment, under certain conditions, at 0.8 and severe impairment at 1.4	Detention, conditional sentences, fines, suspension of driving license	Baatz, 1969
Germany, W.	0.8	If breath test positive, medical examination and blood and urine samples are compulsory.	Detention, fines, suspension of driving licenses (for a minimum of six months for first offenses)	Law, 1973
Greece	0.5	Blood test may be imposed.		ISPA DF
Hungary	0.0		Fine; over 0.8, more severe penalties—fine or one-year detention	DF
Iceland	0.5	There are rules for blood tests.		ISPA DF

				1977/78 response
Ireland	1.25	Screening breath test if alcohol suspected; if positive, blood test (subject's option to give urine specimen)	Loss of license for minimum of 1 year, plus fine up to £100 and/or imprisonment up to 6 months	
Italy	Not fixed; jurisprudence: 1.5–2.3		Temporary or definitive suspension of driving license, fines, detention up to six months	DF
Luxembourg	0.8	Medical examination is compulsory; blood and urine sample may only be taken with the driver's consent.	Above 0.8: fine 200–500 F and/or detention 1–7 days; above 1.2: fine 501–10,000 F and/or detention 8 days to 3 years; driving license may be suspended and the vehicle confiscated 2.	
Monaco	Not fixed		Penalties possible	ISPA
Netherlands	0.5	Random controls carried out (compulsory to assist)	Detention up to 3 months	Law on Road Traffic, 1972 (amended 1973), effective 1974
Norway	0.5	Breath tests carried out; if positive, medical examination, including blood test	Detention of at least 21 days. Driving license may be suspended for at least one year	Law of 1936, amended 1959, 1962 & 1965
Poland	0.3		Over 0.5, +0.2 for error: fine or detention for maximum of 3 months, suspension of license; in case of drunken driving leading to death or severe injury 1–10 years detention.	DF

Table 21 (continued)
Permissible Blood Alcohol Content (BAC) for Drivers, Permissible Testing and Penalization

Region Country	BAC ‰: G Ethanol Per 1,000 G Blood	Permissible Testing	Penalization	References
Portugal	Not fixed	Medical examination may be carried out.	Penalties possible: detention, fine, suspension of driving license, definitive for "alcoholics"	DF
Rumania	0.0			ISPA
Spain	0.8	Breath tests carried out; if positive, blood test	Fines above 0.8	DF Decree of 1973
Sweden	0.5 >1.5 (major offense)	Police allowed to take breath tests at traffic control points; positive tests followed by blood tests	0.5–1.5: at least 10-day fines, or a maximum of 6 months detention; 1.5: maximum detention of 1 year or no less than 25-day fines; temporary withdrawal of license in both cases	Law of 1941, amended 1951 & 1957 (1972 response) Havard, 1975
Switzerland	0.8 <0.8, if driving impaired. 0.5 under discussion	Police may carry out random breath tests, and blood sample may be imposed.	Detention for maximum of 6 months or fine; loss of driving license for at least two months (unlimited for incorrigible drunken drivers)	1977 response Decision by Federal Supreme Court, 1964
Turkey	0.0		Prohibited to drive under the influence of alcohol:	DF

Country	BAC limit			
USSR	0.0		fine or detention + suspension of driving license	DF
United Kingdom England & Wales	0.8	Screening breath tests allowed. Medical examination, including blood test, may be asked for by police or driver.	Suspension of driving license for 1 year (2nd time, 3 years); if consequences of unsober driving, penal sanction	Road Safety Act, 1967
Northern Ireland Scotland	0.8		More severe offense if BAC exceeds 1.25	Road Traffic Act, 1968
Yugoslavia	0.5	Medical judgment may suffice.		ISPA
Southeast Asia				
India	Not fixed	Legislation provides for breath tests if police officer considers reasonable cause.	Legal sanctions against drunken driving: cancelation of driving license for certain time; up to 6 months detention for first offense; up to 2 years for subsequent offense within 2 years, or fines	1977 response Motor Vehicles Amendment Act, 1977
Sri Lanka	Not fixed	Bill before Parliament seeks to empower police to administer breath tests. Ceylon Transport Board administers breath tests to bus drivers.	Dismissal if test positive	1978 response

Table 21 (continued)

Permissible Blood Alcohol Content (BAC) for Drivers, Permissible Testing and Penalization

Region Country	BAC ‰: G Ethanol Per 1,000 G Blood	Permissible Testing	Penalization	References
Western Pacific				
Australia		Breathalyzer legislation was introduced in Victoria in 1960s and random breath testing is currently operating. In South Australia, according to law of 1973, blood sample is required from all persons over 14 taken to hospital within 8 hours of road accident; similar legislation was enacted in Victoria in 1974.		Law of 1971
Victoria	0.5			Hetzel (1976)
Other states	0.8			Johnston (1976)
Tasmania	0.0 (first-year drivers)			1979 response
Japan	0.5		Loss of driving license; maximum of 2 years detention or fine of 50,000 yen	Law of 1972 DF
New Zealand	1.0		Police may take the car keys from a person considered unfit to drive.	Transport Act, 1962

Source: Joy Moser, *Prevention of Alcohol-Related Problems*, pp. 223–228.

*DF = France, Secrétariat général du Gouvernement, Documentation Française, 1977.

**ISPA = Institut Suisse de Prophylaxie de l'Alcoolisme (1977).

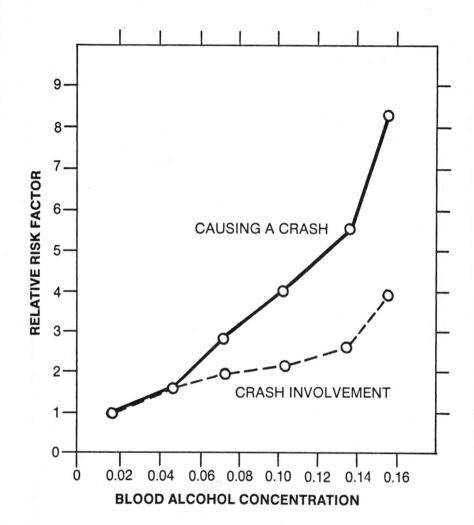

Figure 3

Relative Probability*That a Driver Causes and Is Involved in a Crash as a Function of BAC Level

Source: Marc Aarens, Tracy Cameron, Judy Roizen, Ron Roizen, Robin Room, Dan Schneberk and Deborah Wingard, *Alcohol Casualties and Crime,* special report prepared for National Institute on Alcohol Abuse and Alcoholism under Contract No. ADM 281-76-0027 (Berkeley: Social Research Group, University of California, 1977) reprinted in Ernest P. Noble, ed., *Third Special Report to the U.S. Congress on Alcohol and Health* (Rockville, Md.: NIAAA, 1978), p. 238.

*Relative to the probability that a driver with a BAC of less than 0.03% is in or causes a crash.

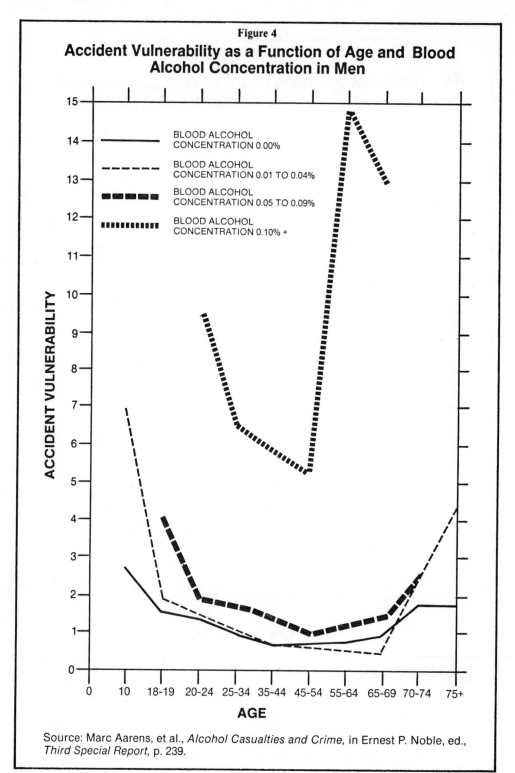

Figure 4

Accident Vulnerability as a Function of Age and Blood Alcohol Concentration in Men

Source: Marc Aarens, et al., *Alcohol Casualties and Crime,* in Ernest P. Noble, ed., *Third Special Report*, p. 239.

Table 22
Race/Ethnicity of Alcoholism Clients in Treatment on September 30, 1980

State	AMERICAN INDIAN OR ALASKAN NATIVE Number	ASIAN OR PACIFIC ISLANDER Number	BLACK, NOT OF HISPANIC ORIGIN Number	HISPANIC Number	WHITE, NOT OF HISPANIC ORIGIN Number	TOTAL CLIENTS* Number
Alabama	0	0	815	5	1,591	2,411
Alaska	529	1	3	5	403	941
Arizona	1,939	8	160	760	2,450	5,317
Arkansas	13	4	806	9	2,504	3,336
California	1,533	420	4,772	12,336	30,510	54,482
Colorado	334	6	446	2,465	5,114	8,626
Connecticut	7	9	616	278	2,804	4,000
Delaware	0	0	103	2	356	461
Florida	96	6	1,418	501	6,977	8,998
Georgia	5	11	1,901	44	4,504	6,656
Hawaii	14	116	4	6	141	281
Idaho	225	1	18	80	1,414	1,738
Illinois	64	3	1,296	370	6,125	8,115
Indiana	10	5	874	68	5,212	6,169
Iowa	53	0	43	29	2,149	2,274
Kansas	101	1	221	75	2,237	2,635
Kentucky	10	5	561	28	3,640	4,244
Louisiana	9	2	1,467	45	2,515	4,089
Maine	167	1	25	3	2,462	2,658
Maryland	126	9	2,666	109	4,829	7,867
Massachusetts	82	6	1,077	415	9,687	11,422
Michigan	167	6	1,820	287	9,712	11,992
Minnesota	525	1	215	126	6,108	6,975
Mississippi	158	1	642	5	1,454	2,260
Missouri	15	1	881	60	3,057	4,173

297

Table 22 (continued)

Race/Ethnicity of Alcoholism Clients in Treatment on September 30, 1980

State	AMERICAN INDIAN OR ALASKAN NATIVE	ASIAN OR PACIFIC ISLANDER	BLACK, NOT OF HISPANIC ORIGIN	HISPANIC	WHITE, NOT OF HISPANIC ORIGIN	TOTAL CLIENTS*
	Number	Number	Number	Number	Number	Number
Montana	435	1	1	10	1,331	1,778
Nebraska	122	6	111	91	2,281	2,611
Nevada	191	0	10	21	323	693
New Hampshire	1	0	4	5	635	745
New Jersey	2	4	898	255	2,786	3,945
New Mexico	1,077	1	56	905	514	2,553
New York	139	10	6,455	3,000	12,149	22,404
North Carolina	156	3	2,220	16	5,343	7,990
North Dakota	132	1	7	9	1,473	1,622
Ohio	17	3	1,129	58	6,956	8,419
Oklahoma	1,119	4	439	28	2,983	4,573
Oregon	618	24	257	317	5,505	7,185
Pennsylvania	9	3	1,617	382	5,731	7,742
Rhode Island	3	0	172	20	1,612	1,807
South Carolina	18	0	1,142	25	2,444	3,629
South Dakota	719	0	12	5	1,247	1,983
Tennessee	3	0	809	2	3,612	4,426
Texas	124	27	2,291	2,709	6,367	11,617
Utah	236	13	58	273	1,212	1,792
Vermont	24	0	7	15	1,294	1,340

Virginia	9	16	1,994	89	6,363	8,804
Washington	458	38	431	230	5,488	6,980
West Virginia	0	0	131	1	1,349	1,481
Wisconsin	427	4	635	222	8,691	9,979
Wyoming	96	0	26	81	762	965
Washington, D.C.	2	2	1,782	115	323	2,244
Puerto Rico	0	0	0	5,829	6	5,835
National Total	12,319	783	45,544	32,824	206,735	307,262
Number of States Included	52	52	52	52	52	52
Virgin Islands	0	0	26	0	5	31
Guam	0	10	0	0	1	11
American Samoa	0	1	0	0	0	1
T.T. Pacific Islands	0	26	0	0	1	27
N. Mariana Islands	--	--	--	--	--	--

Source: SAPIS, *National Status Report*, pp. 84–85.

General Table Notes

The last five island territories are not included in calculations of summary statistics.

Two dashes (--) indicate that data are not available.

The sum or row amounts may not equal the total due to rounding.

Notes for Table 22

The data in the table are the number of alcoholism clients in each racial/ethnic category reported to be in treatment on September 30, 1980. Data are taken from the 1980 NDATUS. While it might be desirable from an analytic standpoint to examine these data in terms of total U.S. population of each target group, census estimates at that level of detail are not sufficiently valid to permit such an analysis. In addition, the rates of alcohol abuse and alcoholism for these racial/ethnic categories are not known with sufficient accuracy, either nationally or on a state-by-state basis, to make any comparisons meaningful.

*Note that race/ethnicity identification was not reported for 9,057 of the total 307,262 clients reported to be in treatment.

Table 23
Sex of Alcoholism Clients in Treatment on September 30, 1980

State	MALE CLIENTS Number	FEMALE CLIENTS Number	TOTAL CLIENTS* Number
Alabama	1,848	563	2,411
Alaska	718	223	941
Arizona	3,447	1,494	5,317
Arkansas	2,841	495	3,336
California	37,757	9,417	54,482
Colorado	5,972	1,361	8,626
Connecticut	2,393	1,343	4,000
Delaware	396	65	461
Florida	6,547	2,451	8,998
Georgia	4,948	1,555	6,656
Hawaii	211	70	281
Idaho	1,428	310	1,738
Illinois	5,675	2,224	8,115
Indiana	4,910	1,259	6,169
Iowa	1,839	347	2,274
Kansas	1,783	852	2,635
Kentucky	3,704	540	4,244
Louisiana	3,115	923	4,089
Maine	1,897	761	2,658
Maryland	6,243	1,549	7,867
Massachusetts	8,273	3,013	11,422
Michigan	8,665	3,327	11,992
Minnesota	4,899	2,076	6,975
Mississippi	1,711	549	2,260
Missouri	2,996	866	4,173
Montana	1,137	641	1,778
Nebraska	1,919	692	2,611
Nevada	502	191	693
New Hampshire	486	259	745
New Jersey	2,926	1,019	3,945
New Mexico	1,963	590	2,553
New York	15,939	5,167	22,404
North Carolina	6,237	1,525	7,990
North Dakota	901	521	1,622
Ohio	5,698	1,633	8,419
Oklahoma	3,495	943	4,573
Oregon	5,263	1,458	7,185
Pennsylvania	5,731	2,011	7,742
Rhode Island	1,131	676	1,807
South Carolina	3,020	609	3,629
South Dakota	1,418	565	1,983
Tennessee	3,609	817	4,426

Table 23 (continued)
Sex of Alcoholism Clients in Treatment on September 30, 1980

State	MALE CLIENTS Number	FEMALE CLIENTS Number	TOTAL CLIENTS* Number
Texas	9,855	1,199	11,617
Utah	1,363	429	1,792
Vermont	1,017	323	1,340
Virginia	6,929	1,542	8,804
Washington	5,696	1,284	6,980
West Virginia	1,150	331	1,481
Wisconsin	7,082	2,897	9,979
Wyoming	716	249	965
Washington, D.C.	1,728	269	2,244
Puerto Rico	5,580	255	5,835
National Total	226,717	65,728	307,262
Number of States Included	52	52	52
Virgin Islands	29	2	31
Guam	5	6	11
American Samoa	1	0	1
T.T. Pacific Islands	24	3	27
N. Mariana Islands	--	--	--

Source: SAPIS, *National Status Report,* pp. 86–87.

General Table Notes

The last five island territories are not included in calculations of summary statistics.

Two dashes (--) indicate that data are not available.

The sum or row amounts may not equal the total due to rounding.

Notes for Table 23

The data in the table are the number of male alcoholism clients and female alcoholism clients reported to be in treatment on September 30, 1980. Data are taken from the 1980 NDATUS. While it might be desirable to examine these data in terms of the total population of males and females in the U.S., the rates of alcohol abuse and alcoholism for males and females have not been estimated with sufficient accuracy to make comparisons meaningful.

*Note that sex was not reported for 14,817 of the total 307,262 clients reported to be in treatment.

Table 24
Age of Alcoholism Clients in Treatment on September 30, 1980

State	CLIENTS 18 AND UNDER Number	CLIENTS 19–20 Number	CLIENTS 21–44 Number	CLIENTS 45–59 Number
Alabama	64	112	1,417	676
Alaska	34	108	655	106
Arizona	289	575	2,632	1,068
Arkansas	142	261	1,822	774
California	1,840	2,767	26,592	13,129
Colorado	262	516	4,818	1,393
Connecticut	236	294	1,906	1,000
Delaware	34	36	262	99
Florida	245	·581	4,606	2,519
Georgia	108	293	3,490	1,990
Hawaii	42	14	165	51
Idaho	86	202	997	362
Illinois	436	409	4,619	1,993
Indiana	425	503	3,562	1,342
Iowa	152	166	1,327	414
Kansas	213	180	1,480	601
Kentucky	120	259	2,558	1,087
Louisiana	93	130	2,388	1,129
Maine	177	514	1,067	733
Maryland	227	456	4,767	1,810
Massachusetts	281	609	5,950	3,290
Michigan	866	858	7,125	2,583
Minnesota	860	644	3,552	1,222
Mississippi	87	97	1,247	631
Missouri	327	251	2,236	856
Montana	142	95	1,014	402
Nebraska	336	198	1,453	510
Nevada	69	44	419	142
New Hampshire	75	34	399	175
New Jersey	157	190	2,310	1,040
New Mexico	103	143	1,442	652
New York	771	672	11,778	6,474
North Carolina	186	296	4,105	2,472
North Dakota	193	127	723	252
Ohio	406	497	4,256	1,818
Oklahoma	222	279	2,436	1,080
Oregon	318	418	4,080	1,423
Pennsylvania	442	399	4,870	1,638
Rhode Island	97	124	1,004	483
South Carolina	148	344	2,100	780

Table 24 (continued)
Age of Alcoholism Clients in Treatment on September 30, 1980

State	CLIENTS 18 AND UNDER Number	CLIENTS 19–20 Number	CLIENTS 21–44 Number	CLIENTS 45–59 Number
South Dakota	122	91	1,073	522
Tennessee	120	271	2,404	1,298
Texas	1,553	1,757	4,280	2,304
Utah	143	110	897	545
Vermont	84	111	801	244
Virginia	439	513	5,064	1,986
Washington	411	687	4,066	1,407
West Virginia	75	63	818	401
Wisconsin	727	773	5,830	2,103
Wyoming	60	58	584	189
Washington, D.C.	463	26	1,087	370
Puerto Rico	18	44	3,335	1,871
National Total	15,526	19,199	163,868	73,439
Number of States Included	52	52	52	52
Virgin Islands	0	0	26	4
Guam	0	0	8	3
American Samoa	0	0	0	1
T.T. Pacific Islands	0	2	20	1
N. Mariana Islands	--	--	--	--

General Table Notes

The last five island territories are not included in calculations of summary statistics.

Two dashes (--) indicate that data are not available.

The sum or row amounts may not equal the total due to rounding.

Notes for Table 24

The data in the table are the number of alcoholism clients in each category reported to be in treatment on September 30, 1980. Data are taken from the 1980 NDATUS. While it might be desirable to examine these data in terms of total populations within each category in each state, census estimates at that level of detail are not sufficiently valid to permit such analysis. In addition, the rates of alcohol abuse and alcoholism for these groups have not been estimated, either nationally or on a state-by-state basis, with sufficient accuracy to make any comparisons meaningful.

Table 24 (continued)
Age of Alcoholism Clients in Treatment on September 30, 1980

State	CLIENTS 60–64 Number	CLIENTS 65 AND OVER Number	TOTAL CLIENTS* Number
Alabama	89	44	2,411
Alaska	27	17	941
Arizona	213	139	5,317
Arkansas	246	89	3,336
California	1,841	664	54,482
Colorado	209	145	8,626
Connecticut	161	85	4,000
Delaware	14	15	461
Florida	605	304	8,998
Georgia	344	193	6,656
Hawaii	2	7	281
Idaho	66	26	1,738
Illinois	246	153	8,115
Indiana	210	115	6,169
Iowa	77	59	2,274
Kansas	120	48	2,635
Kentucky	162	74	4,244
Louisiana	177	86	4,089
Maine	74	79	2,658
Maryland	310	137	7,867
Massachusetts	652	358	11,422
Michigan	328	207	11,992
Minnesota	281	356	6,975
Mississippi	140	58	2,260
Missouri	129	69	4,173
Montana	82	40	1,778
Nebraska	82	40	2,611
Nevada	19	7	693
New Hampshire	32	20	745
New Jersey	160	75	3,945
New Mexico	108	105	2,553
New York	779	508	22,404
North Carolina	409	236	7,990
North Dakota	68	45	1,622
Ohio	230	104	8,419
Oklahoma	286	130	4,573
Oregon	308	161	7,185
Pennsylvania	260	105	7,742
Rhode Island	43	46	1,807
South Carolina	171	76	3,629
South Dakota	93	75	1,983
Tennessee	235	85	4,426

Table 24 (continued)
Age of Alcoholism Clients in Treatment on September 30, 1980

State	CLIENTS 60–64 Number	CLIENTS 65 AND OVER Number	TOTAL CLIENTS* Number
Texas	859	268	11,617
Utah	65	28	1,792
Vermont	57	42	1,340
Virginia	293	159	8,804
Washington	281	121	6,980
West Virginia	60	55	1,481
Wisconsin	289	202	9,979
Wyoming	51	17	965
Washington, D.C.	60	5	2,244
Puerto Rico	361	211	5,835
National Total	12,464	6,493	307,262
Number of States Included	52	52	52
Virgin Islands	1	0	31
Guam	0	0	11
American Samoa	0	0	1
T.T. Pacific Islands	1	2	27
N. Mariana Islands	--	--	--

Source: SAPIS, *National Status Report,* pp. 88–91.

General Table Notes

The last five island territories are not included in calculations of summary statistics.

Two dashes (--) indicate that data are not available.

The sum or row amounts may not equal the total due to rounding.

Notes for Table 24

The data in the table are the number of alcoholism clients in each category reported to be in treatment on September 30, 1980. Data are taken from the 1980 NDATUS. While it might be desirable to examine these data in terms of total populations within each category in each state, census estimates at that level of detail are not sufficiently valid to permit such analysis. In addition, the rates of alcohol abuse and alcoholism for these groups have not been estimated, either nationally or on a state-by-state basis, with sufficient accuracy to make any comparisons meaningful.

*Note that age was not reported for 16,273 of the total 307,262 alcoholism clients reported to be in treatment.

Table 25
Distribution of Clients in Treatment and Treatment Capacity by Type of Care in
Alcoholism Only and Combined Treatment Units
National Drug and Alcoholism Treatment Utilization Survey (NDATUS)
September 30, 1980

| | CLIENTS IN TREATMENT | | | | | |
| | ALCOHOL-ISM ONLY | | COMBINED | | TOTAL | |
Type of Care	Number	%	Number	%	Number	%
Detox medical model	5,787	2.5	1,563	2.1	7,350	2.4
Detox social setting	3,879	1.7	417	0.6	4,296	1.4
Rehab model	32,333	13.9	4,838	6.5	37,171	12.1
Custodial domiciliary model	3,958	1.7	757	1.0	4,715	1.5
Ambulatory medical detox	2,075	0.9	334	0.5	2,409	0.8
Limited care (including day care)	2,922	1.3	722	1.0	3,644	1.2
Outpatient services	182,328	78.2	65,429	88.4	247,747	80.6
TOTAL	233,272	100.0	74,060	100.0	307,332	100.0

| | TREATMENT CAPACITY | | | | | |
| | ALCOHOL-ISM ONLY | | COMBINED | | TOTAL | |
Type of Care	Number	%	Number	%	Number	%
Detox medical model	8,611	3.1	2,297	2.6	10,908	3.0
Detox social setting	5,114	1.8	725	0.8	5,839	1.6
Rehab model	37,879	13.6	6,172	6.9	44,051	12.0
Custodial domiciliary model	5,354	1.9	992	1.1	6,346	1.7
Ambulatory medical detox	2,646	1.0	685	0.8	3,331	0.9
Limited care (including day care)	3,366	1.2	1,199	1.3	4,565	1.2
Outpatient services	215,682	77.4	77,499	86.5	293,181	79.6
TOTAL	278,652	100.0	89,569	100.0	368,221	100.0

Source: NIAAA, *Drug & Alcoholism Treatment Survey*, p. 9.

Figure 5

Distribution of Clients in Treatment by Type of Care and Facility Location in Alcoholism Only and Combined Treatment Units

**National Drug and Alcoholism Treatment Utilization Survey
(NDATUS)
September 30, 1980**

TYPE OF CARE

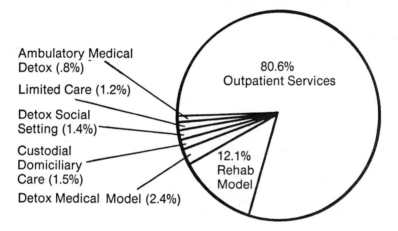

Ambulatory Medical Detox (.8%)

Limited Care (1.2%)

Detox Social Setting (1.4%)

Custodial Domiciliary Care (1.5%)

Detox Medical Model (2.4%)

80.6% Outpatient Services

12.1% Rehab Model

FACILITY LOCATION

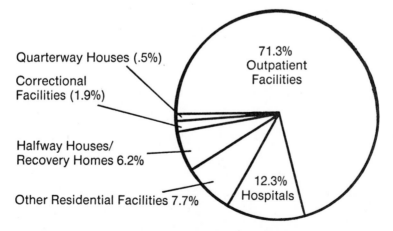

Quarterway Houses (.5%)

Correctional Facilities (1.9%)

Halfway Houses/ Recovery Homes 6.2%

Other Residential Facilities 7.7%

71.3% Outpatient Facilities

12.3% Hospitals

Source: NIAAA, *Drug & Alcoholism Treatment Survey*, p. 11.

Table 26
Distribution of Clients in Treatment and Treatment Capacity by Facility Location in
Alcoholism Only and Combined Treatment Units
National Drug and Alcoholism Treatment Utilization Survey (NDATUS)
September 30, 1980

| Facility Location | CLIENTS IN TREATMENT | | | | | |
| | ALCOHOLISM ONLY | | COMBINED | | TOTAL | |
	Number	%	Number	%	Number	%
Hospital	31,856	13.7	5,157	7.0	37,013	12.0
Quarterway house	1,332	0.6	309	0.4	1,641	0.5
Halfway house/recovery home	17,353	7.4	1,613	2.2	18,966	6.2
Other residential facility	19,113	8.2	2,933	4.0	22,046	7.2
Outpatient facility	158,421	67.9	62,802	84.8	221,223	72.0
Correctional facility	5,197	2.2	1,246	1.7	6,443	2.1
TOTAL	233,272	100.0	74,060	100.0	307,332	100.0
	TREATMENT CAPACITY					
Hospital	38,556	13.8	6,819	7.6	45,375	12.3
Quarterway house	1,649	0.6	352	0.4	2,001	0.5
Halfway house/recovery home	20,904	7.5	2,075	2.3	22,979	6.2
Other residential facility	24,077	8.6	4,195	4.7	28,272	7.7
Outpatient facility	188,265	67.6	74,402	83.1	262,667	71.3
Correctional facility	5,201	1.9	1,726	1.9	6,927	1.9
TOTAL	278,652	100.0	89,569	100.0	368,221	100.0

Source: NIAAA, *Drug & Alcoholism Treatment Survey*, p. 12.

Table 27
Demographic Characteristics of Clients in Alcoholism Only and Combined Treatment Units
National Drug and Alcoholism Treatment Utilization Survey (NDATUS)
September 30, 1980

Client Characteristics	ALCOHOLISM ONLY		COMBINED		TOTAL	
	Number	%	Number	%	Number	%
Race/Ethnicity						
American Indian	10,135	4.6	2,096	2.9	12,231	4.2
Asian	598	.3	197	.3	795	.3
Black	34,277	15.6	9,289	13.0	43,566	15.0
Hispanic	29,712	13.5	2,656	3.7	32,368	11.1
White	144,654	65.9	57,009	80.0	201,663	69.4
TOTAL	219,376	100.0	71,247	100.0	290,623	100.0
Sex						
Male	169,891	78.5	52,492	73.8	222,383	77.3
Female	46,586	21.5	18,606	26.2	65,192	22.7
TOTAL	216,477	100.0	71,098	100.0	287,575	100.0
Age						
18 and under	10,173	4.8	5,178	7.3	15,351	5.4
19–20	12,768	6.0	6,017	8.5	18,785	6.6
21–44	118,435	55.6	41,149	58.2	159,584	56.2
45–59	56,412	26.5	14,354	20.3	70,766	24.9
60–64	10,652	5.0	2,727	3.9	13,379	4.7
65 and over	4,752	2.2	1,338	1.9	6,090	2.1
TOTAL	213,192	100.0	70,763	100.0	283,955	100.0

Source: NIAAA, *Drug & Alcoholism Treatment Survey,* p. 14.

Table 28
Principal Population Served in Alcoholism Only and Combined Treatment Units
National Drug and Alcoholism Treatment Utilization Survey (NDATUS)
September 30, 1980

Population	ALCOHOLISM ONLY		COMBINED		TOTAL	
	Number	%	Number	%	Number	%
Inner city	666	22.1	130	9.0	796	17.8
Other urban	1,069	35.4	475	32.8	1,544	34.6
Suburban	550	18.2	233	16.1	783	17.5
Rural	731	24.2	611	42.2	1,342	30.1
TOTAL	3,016	100.0	1,449	100.0	4,465	100.0

Source: NIAAA, *Drug & Alcoholism Treatment Survey*, p. 20.

Table 29
Percentage of 10th–12th Graders in Each Volume of Drinking Group from 1978 National Survey

Drinking Group	Percentage
Abstainers—don't drink or drink less often than once a year.*	25.0
Infrequent drinkers—drink once a month at most and drink small amounts per typical drinking occasion.**	7.6
Light drinkers—drink once a month at most and drink medium amounts per typical drinking occasion or drink no more than three to four times a month and drink small amounts per typical drinking occasion.	18.8
Moderate drinkers—drink at least once a week and small amounts per typical drinking occasion or three to four times a month and medium amounts per typical drinking occasion or no more than once a month and large amounts per typical drinking occasion.	16.6
Moderate/heavier drinkers—drink at least once a week and medium amounts per typical drinking occasion or three to four times a month and large amounts per typical drinking occasion.	17.3
Heavier drinkers—drink at least once a week and large amounts per typical drinking occasion.	14.8
	(4,918)

Source: John R. DeLuca, ed., *Fourth Special Report*, p. 22.

Note: Percentages are based on "weighted" observations.

*Those who drank less than once a year were classified as abstainers because the absolute alcohol consumed per day was essentially "0." Of those classified as abstainers above, 4.5% in 1974 and 4.0% in 1978 were "former drinkers"; i.e., they had had at least 2 or 3 drinks at some time in the past but not in the preceding year.

**Small, medium and large amounts refer to 1 drink or less per drinking occasion, 2 to 4 drinks per drinking occasion, and 5 or more drinks per drinking occasion, respectively. A drink is equivalent to the following: 12 fluid ounces of beer, 4 fluid ounces of wine or 1 fluid ounce of distilled spirits.

310

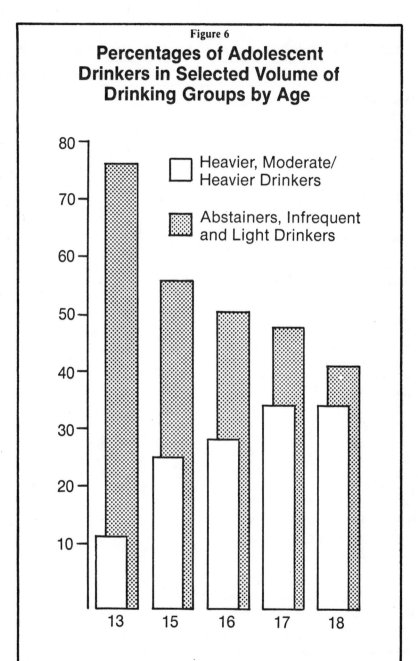

Figure 6

Percentages of Adolescent Drinkers in Selected Volume of Drinking Groups by Age

☐ Heavier, Moderate/Heavier Drinkers

▨ Abstainers, Infrequent and Light Drinkers

Source: John R. De Luca, ed., *Fourth Special Report*, p. 23.

Note: Data for 13-year-olds are drawn from 1974 survey results. Data for all other ages are from 1978 survey results. Care must be taken in interpreting the rapid increase from age 13 to age 15 since the data are from two separate surveys conducted at different points in time.

Table 30
Estimated Economic Cost of Alcohol Abuse in the United States in 1975

Economic Cost	Estimated Cost (in millions)	
ECONOMIC COST DUE TO ALCOHOL ABUSE		
● Lost production:		
Lost market production in 1975	$15,457.8	
Lost military production in 1975	411.3	
Present value in 1975 of lost future production due to		
excess mortality in 1975	3,768.3	$19,637.4
● Health care costs		12,743.4
● Motor vehicle crash losses:	5,198.5	
Total		
Less double-counted items:		
Lost production in 1975	3.1	
Lost future production	50.5	
Health care costs	1.5	
	55.1	5,143.4
● Fire losses:		
Total	604.4	
Less double-counted items:		
Lost production in 1975	6.5	
Lost future production	112.3	
Health care costs	51.5	
	170.3	434.1
● Social responses:		
Social welfare system	1,273.8	
Alcohol programs	74.7	
Highway safety	29.2	
Fire protection	392.0	
Criminal justice system (nonviolent crime)	170.1	1,939.8
Total economic cost due to alcohol abuse		$39,898.1
ECONOMIC COST ASSOCIATED WITH ALCOHOL		
● Violent crime		$ 2,097.7
● Criminal justice system (violent crime)		759.6
Total economic cost associated with alcohol		$ 2,857.3
Total economic cost due to alcohol abuse and associated with alcohol		$42,755.4

Source: NIAAA, *The Economic Cost of Alcoholism 1975* (Rockville, Md.), p. 211.

Table 31
Tentative Estimates of the Economic Cost of Fire in 1975 That Might Be Attributable to Alcohol Abuse

Type of Loss	Estimated Cost of Fire (millions)	Proportions That Might Be Attributable to Alcohol Abuse	Tentative Estimates of Economic Cost Due to Alcohol Abuse (millions)
Present value in 1975 of lost future production due to premature death	$ 435.5	59.7	$260.0
Medical treatment of personal injuries	712.7	16.8 35.0	119.7 249.4
Lost production due to personal injury	89.9	16.8 35.0	15.1 31.4
Property damage			
Building fires	3,436.6	6.1	209.6
Nonbuilding fires	734.0	0.0	0.0
TOTAL	$5,408.6		
Low Estimate	$604.4		
High Estimate	$750.4		

Source: NIAAA, *The Economic Cost of Alcoholism 1975*, p. 146.

Table 32
An Estimate of the Economic Cost of Crime Where Alcohol Is Associated with the Crime

Offense	Estimated Cost of Crime (millions)	Proportion of Offenses Where Alcohol Is Associated (percent)	Estimated Cost of Crime Where Alcohol Is Associated (millions)
Homicide	$3,091.6	67	$2,071.4
Forcible rape	9.3	24	2.2
Robbery	77.2	not known	0.0
Aggravated assault	80.4	30	24.1
	$3,258.5		$2,097.7

Source: NIAAA, *The Economic Cost of Alcoholism 1975*, p. 172.

Table 33
Estimated Economic Costs of Motor Vehicle Crashes Attributable to Alcohol Abuse in 1975, by Type of Crash

Type of Crash	Estimated Economic Costs (in billions)	Estimated Net Percentage of Crashes due to Alcohol Abuse at or above		Estimated Economic Costs (in billions) due to Alcohol Abuse at or above	
		BAC = .05%	BAC = .10%	BAC = .05%	BAC = .10%
Fatality	$ 9.854	41.5	32.5	$4.089	$3.203
Personal injury					
● Minor/moderate	8.550	13.0	8.5	1.112	.727
● Severe/critical	2.473	12.0	7.5	.297	.185
Property damage only	7.840	7.0	3.0	.549	.235
All crashes	$28.717			$6.047	$4.350

Source: NIAAA, *The Economic Cost of Alcoholism 1975*, p. 130.

Table 34
Estimated Present Value in 1975 of Lost Future Production due to Excess Mortality among Alcohol Abusers in 1975, by Sex and Age

Age Group	MALES		FEMALES		TOTAL	
	Excess Mortality	Present Value of Lost Production (in millions)	Excess Mortality	Present Value of Lost Production (in millions)	Excess Mortality	Present Value of Lost Production (in millions)
20–29	3,007	$ 588.8	759	$ 82.7	3,766	$ 671.5
30–39	3,563	708.4	962	93.1	4,525	801.5
40–49	7,829	1,223.5	1,697	128.3	9,526	1,351.8
50–59	8,712	834.8	445	21.1	9,157	855.9
60–69	2,202	72.5	160	3.1	2,362	75.6
70+	1,933	11.8	—	—	1,933	11.8
All Ages	27,246	$3,439.8	4,023	$328.3	31,269	$3,768.1

Sources: Present value of lost production is derived from earnings data discounted at 6% in B. S. Cooper and W. Brody, *1972 Lifetime Earnings by Age, Sex, Race, and Education Level*, Research and Statistics Note no. 12 (Washington, D.C.: Office of Research and Statistics, Social Security Administration, May 20, 1976), reprinted in NIAAA, *The Economic Cost of Alcoholism 1975*, p. 55.

Table 35
Estimated Consumption of Taxed Alcoholic Beverages:
U.S. Gallons of Absolute Alcohol Per Person
(Calendar Year 1979)

State	DISTILLED SPIRITS		WINE		BEER		TOTAL	
	Amount	(Rank)	Amount	(Rank)	Amount	(Rank)	Amount	(Rank)
Alabama	0.63	38	0.09	45	0.84	49	1.56	47
Alaska	1.22	4	0.34	11	1.23	23	2.79	6
Arizona	0.81	26	0.27	18	1.43	6	2.51	16
Arkansas	0.43	50	0.08	48	0.80	51	1.31	50
California	0.99	10	0.54	3	1.25	19	2.78	7
Colorado	0.98	12	0.35	9	1.32	12	2.66	10
Connecticut	0.98	12	0.32	15	1.02	40	2.32	21
Delaware	1.02	8	0.21	24	1.19	26	2.42	17
Florida	1.08	7	0.28	17	1.41	8	2.77	8
Georgia	0.86	23	0.13	38	0.95	43	1.95	40
Hawaii	0.94	16	0.32	15	1.30	13	2.56	14
Idaho	0.57	46	0.20	26	1.24	21	2.01	34
Illinois	0.91	17	0.25	19	1.25	19	2.42	17
Indiana	0.61	41	0.12	41	1.05	37	1.78	41
Iowa	0.56	48	0.09	45	1.24	21	1.90	39
Kansas	0.57	46	0.10	43	1.05	37	1.72	43
Kentucky	0.58	44	0.07	49	0.92	45	1.57	47
Louisiana	0.78	30	0.19	27	1.11	33	2.08	31
Maine	0.83	25	0.22	21	1.14	32	2.19	28
Maryland	1.09	6	0.25	19	1.21	24	2.55	15
Massachusetts	1.01	9	0.34	11	1.29	14	2.65	11
Michigan	0.80	29	0.21	24	1.18	28	2.19	28
Minnesota	0.91	17	0.19	27	1.18	28	2.28	23
Mississippi	0.65	35	0.07	49	0.93	46	1.65	45
Missouri	0.62	40	0.16	31	1.21	24	1.98	36
Montana	0.80	29	0.33	14	1.78	1	2.91	4
Nebraska	0.70	33	0.14	36	1.34	11	2.19	28
Nevada	2.26	2	0.60	2	1.77	2	4.64	2

Table 35 (continued)
Estimated Consumption of Taxed Alcoholic Beverages:
U.S. Gallons of Absolute Alcohol Per Person
(Calendar Year 1979)

State	DISTILLED SPIRITS		WINE		BEER		TOTAL	
	Amount	(Rank)	Amount	(Rank)	Amount	(Rank)	Amount	(Rank)
New Hampshire	1.99	3	0.47	4	1.68	3	4.14	3
New Jersey	0.88	19	0.34	11	1.05	37	2.28	23
New Mexico	0.65	35	0.22	21	1.36	10	2.23	26
New York	0.95	15	0.36	6	1.10	34	2.41	19
North Carolina	0.66	34	0.16	31	0.92	47	1.74	42
North Dakota	0.88	19	0.13	38	1.29	14	2.29	22
Ohio	0.58	44	0.15	35	1.18	28	1.91	39
Oklahoma	0.64	37	0.11	42	0.94	45	1.69	44
Oregon	0.73	31	0.36	6	1.18	28	2.27	25
Pennsylvania	0.59	42	0.18	30	1.26	18	2.03	32
Rhode Island	0.88	19	0.40	5	1.29	14	2.57	13
South Carolina	0.87	22	0.13	38	1.02	40	2.02	33
South Dakota	0.81	26	0.14	36	1.07	35	2.01	34
Tennessee	0.56	48	0.09	45	0.97	43	1.61	46
Texas	0.63	38	0.16	31	1.43	6	2.22	27
Utah	0.40	51	0.10	43	0.72	52	1.21	51
Vermont	1.14	5	0.35	9	1.27	17	2.76	9
Virginia	0.72	32	0.19	27	1.07	35	1.98	36
Washington	0.84	24	0.36	6	1.19	26	2.39	20
West Virginia	0.59	42	0.07	49	0.82	49	1.48	49
Wisconsin	0.99	10	0.22	21	1.66	4	2.87	5
Wyoming	0.96	14	0.16	31	1.52	5	2.64	12
Washington, D.C.	2.53	1	0.83	1	1.37	9	4.73	1
Puerto Rico	--	--	--	--	--	--	--	--
National Value	0.81		0.25		1.18		2.25	

Source: SAPIS, *National Status Report*, pp. 126–127.

316

Table 36
Reported Deaths from Selected Alcohol-Related Causes and Total Deaths from All Causes
(Calendar Year 1978)

State	ALCOHOLIC PSYCHOSIS Number	ALCOHOLISM Number	CIRRHOSIS OF THE LIVER, ALCOHOLIC MENTION Number	ACCIDENTAL POISONING DUE TO ALCOHOL* Number
Alabama	10	82	126	....
Alaska	1	16	20	.....
Arizona	2	126	192	--
Arkansas	3	34	57	--
California	18	530	2,561	--
Colorado	2	80	123	--
Connecticut	4	94	207	--
Delaware	0	23	29	--
Florida	16	281	577	--
Georgia	17	241	230	--
Hawaii	1	8	23	--
Idaho	2	21	31	--
Illinois	9	177	449	--
Indiana	4	99	172	--
Iowa	5	43	83	--
Kansas	3	33	62	--
Kentucky	8	87	126	--
Louisiana	14	67	112	--
Maine	1	31	73	--
Maryland	5	175	187	--
Massachusetts	4	70	251	--
Michigan	10	143	483	--
Minnesota	2	90	177	--
Mississippi	9	43	72	--
Missouri	5	95	185	--
Montana	5	20	60	--
Nebraska	1	12	82	--
Nevada	4	32	71	--
New Hampshire	0	13	53	--
New Jersey	12	79	358	--
New Mexico	4	148	103	--
New York	17	471	2,023	--
North Carolina	16	332	346	--
North Dakota	1	16	57	
Ohio	13	154	436	--
Oklahoma	2	112	123	--
Oregon	1	74	170	--
Pennsylvania	14	182	566	--
Rhode Island	1	45	61	--
South Carolina	4	102	116	--

Table 36 (continued)
Reported Deaths from Selected Alcohol-Related Causes and Total Deaths from All Causes
(Calendar Year 1978)

State	ALCOHOLIC PSYCHOSIS Number	ALCOHOLISM Number	CIRRHOSIS OF THE LIVER, ALCOHOLIC MENTION Number	ACCIDENTAL POISONING DUE TO ALCOHOL* Number
South Dakota	1	25	39	--
Tennessee	7	122	142	--
Texas	8	211	456	--
Utah	1	40	54	--
Vermont	0	17	24	--
Virginia	15	161	237	--
Washington	7	107	211	--
West Virginia	4	55	80	--
Wisconsin	7	102	209	--
Wyoming	0	19	27	--
Washington, D.C.	0	22	116	--
Puerto Rico	--	--	--	--
National Total	300	5,362	12,828	0*
Number of States Included	51	51	51	0
Virgin Islands	--	--	--	--
Guam	--	--	--	--
American Samoa	--	--	--	--
T.T. Pacific Islands	--	--	--	--
N. Mariana Islands	--	--	--	--

General Table Notes

The last five island territories are not included in calculations of summary statistics.

Two dashes (--) indicate that data are not available.

The sum or row amounts may not equal the total due to rounding.

Notes for Table 36

The data in the table represent the number of all deaths in calendar year 1978 attributed to one of the four alcohol-related causes listed. The "Total" column indicates the total number of deaths from all causes within each state. Statistics are provided by the National Center for Health Statistics (NCHS). Data are obtained directly from copies of original death certificates provided to NCHS by the registration offices of the 50 states and the District of Columbia and the Cooperative Health Statistics System (CHSS). Data from 1978 are the most recent available. Cause of death was classified using the *Eighth Revision International Classification of Diseases, Adopted for Use in the United States.* When more than one cause was reported, the cause designated by the certifying physician as the underlying cause of death was tabulated. ICDA codes included are the following: 291, Alcoholic Psychosis; 303, Alcoholism; 571.0, Cirrhosis of the Liver, Alcoholic Mention; and 860, Accidental Poisoning due to Alcohol.

*Note that for 1978, figures on accidental poisoning due to alcohol were not available on a state-by-state basis. Nationally, 363 deaths were reported in this category.

Table 36 (continued)
Reported Deaths from Selected Alcohol-Related Causes and Total Deaths from All Causes
(Calendar Year 1978)

State	TOTAL OF ALL DEATHS ATTRIBUTED TO ALCOHOL-RELATED CAUSES Number	TOTAL DEATHS, ALL CAUSES Number	PERCENTAGE OF TOTAL DEATHS ATTRIBUTED TO ALCOHOL-RELATED CAUSES Percent	(Rank)
Alabama	218	34,680	0.60	32
Alaska	37	1,690	2.10	2
Arizona	320	19,198	1.60	6
Arkansas	94	21,898	0.40	48
California	3,109	176,069	1.70	5
Colorado	205	18,361	1.10	12
Connecticut	305	26,078	1.10	12
Delaware	52	4,957	1.00	17
Florida	874	95,595	0.90	22
Georgia	488	43,298	1.10	12
Hawaii	32	4,563	0.70	29
Idaho	54	6,507	0.80	25
Illinois	635	103,026	0.60	32
Indiana	275	47,548	0.50	44
Iowa	131	27,450	0.40	48
Kansas	98	21,665	0.40	48
Kentucky	221	33,421	0.60	32
Louisiana	193	35,242	0.50	44
Maine	105	10,179	1.00	17
Maryland	367	33,130	1.10	12
Massachusetts	325	52,660	0.60	6
Michigan	636	74,968	0.80	25
Minnesota	269	33,316	0.80	25
Mississippi	124	23,350	0.50	44
Missouri	285	49,442	0.50	44
Montana	85	6,488	1.30	8
Nebraska	95	14,443	0.60	32
Nevada	107	5,056	2.10	2
New Hampshire	66	10,179	0.60	6
New Jersey	449	65,993	0.60	6
New Mexico	255	8,456	3.00	1
New York	2,511	167,572	1.40	7
North Carolina	694	47,322	1.40	7
North Dakota	74	5,491	1.30	8
Ohio	603	96,569	0.60	6
Oklahoma	237	27,943	0.80	25
Oregon	245	20,895	1.10	12
Pennsylvania	762	120,074	0.60	32

Table 36 (continued)
Reported Deaths from Selected Alcohol-Related Causes and Total Deaths from All Causes
(Calendar Year 1978)

State	TOTAL OF ALL DEATHS ATTRIBUTED TO ALCOHOL-RELATED CAUSES	TOTAL DEATHS, ALL CAUSES	PERCENTAGE OF TOTAL DEATHS ATTRIBUTED TO ALCOHOL-RELATED CAUSES	
	Number	Number	Percent	(Rank)
Rhode Island	107	8,873	1.20	10
South Carolina	222	24,112	0.90	22
South Dakota	65	6,492	1.00	17
Tennessee	271	38,745	0.60	32
Texas	675	103,845	0.60	32
Utah	95	7,892	1.20	10
Vermont	41	4,426	0.90	22
Virginia	413	40,767	1.00	17
Washington	325	30,490	1.00	17
West Virginia	139	19,646	0.70	29
Wisconsin	318	40,324	0.70	29
Wyoming	46	3,112	1.40	7
Washington, D.C.	138	7,065	1.90	4
Puerto Rico	--	--	--	--
National Total	18,490	1,930,561	0.96	
Number of States Included	51	51	51	
Virgin Islands	--	--	--	
Guam	--	--	--	
American Samoa	--	--	--	
T.T. Pacific Islands	--	--	--	
N. Mariana Islands	--	--	--	

Source: SAPIS, *National Status Report,* pp. 128–131.

General Table Notes

The last five island territories are not included in calculations of summary statistics.

Two dashes (--) indicate that data are not available.

The sum or row amounts may not equal the total due to rounding.

Notes for Table 36

The data in the table represent the number of all deaths in calendar year 1978 attributed to one of the four alcohol-related causes listed. The "Total" column indicates the total number of deaths from all causes within each state. Statistics are provided by the National Center for Health Statistics (NCHS). Data are obtained directly from copies of original death certificates provided to NCHS by the registration offices of the 50 states and the District of Columbia and the Cooperative Health Statistics System (CHSS). Data from 1978 are the most recent available. Cause of death was classified using the *Eighth Revision International Classification of Diseases, Adopted for Use in the United States.* When more than one cause was reported, the cause designated by the certifying physician as the underlying cause of death was tabulated. ICDA codes, included are the following: 291, Alcoholic Psychosis; 303, Alcoholism; 571.0, Cirrhosis of the Liver, Alcoholic Mention; and 860, Accidental Poisoning due to Alcohol.

*Note that for 1978, figures on accidental poisoning due to alcohol were not available on a state-by-state basis. Nationally, 363 deaths were reported in this category.

Table 37
Number of Reported Arrests for Selected Alcohol-Related Causes and Total Arrests for All Causes
(Calendar Year 1979)

State	DRIVING UNDER INFLUENCE	DRUNKENNESS	LIQUOR LAW VIOLATIONS	DISORDERLY CONDUCT
	Number	Number	Number	Number
Alabama	33,036	34,209	10,954	13,048
Alaska	2,974	586	2,389	1,115
Arizona	30,937	0	6,784	9,550
Arkansas	22,747	23,998	5,641	5,749
California	289,553	234,697	35,465	18,103
Colorado	16,619	165	6,293	12,589
Connecticut	2,401	214	760	20,172
Delaware	357	210	964	1,468
Florida	43,254	21,466	11,326	12,214
Georgia	62,120	53,114	2,660	14,634
Hawaii	2,487	0	364	905
Idaho	5,808	187	3,632	1,841
Illinois	19,827	2,124	32,267	152,151
Indiana	15,986	27,616	11,051	8,309
Iowa	11,498	12,720	6,704	3,922
Kansas	9,224	221	4,180	5,823
Kentucky	36,172	66,927	6,083	9,949
Louisiana	13,868	22,317	791	15,837
Maine	8,305	143	3,276	3,893
Maryland	10,118	1	4,604	11,328
Massachusetts	20,035	511	8,772	15,126
Michigan	40,981	1,023	30,663	17,365
Minnesota	14,666	1	8,281	6,555
Mississippi	9,626	13,509	1,371	4,601
Missouri	19,783	997	7,354	11,987
Montana	2,428	625	2,155	3,297
Nebraska	9,384	143	3,560	3,428
Nevada	6,690	10,764	3,233	2,460
New Hampshire	7,272	3,221	1,478	2,974
New Jersey	17,076	98	8,375	39,234
New Mexico	5,842	0	2,816	4,176
New York	35,963	0	5,328	53,885
North Carolina	75,034	0	8,325	13,540
North Dakota	4,644	1	6,473	1,330
Ohio	32,945	34,443	11,044	25,843
Oklahoma	23,363	46,956	4,974	5,656
Oregon	28,550	40	13,751	4,824
Pennsylvania	18,911	48,057	56,884	54,889
Rhode Island	1,381	139	901	3,346
South Carolina	18,724	31,334	4,340	12,568

Table 37 (continued)
Number of Reported Arrests for Selected Alcohol-Related Causes and Total Arrests for All Causes
(Calendar Year 1979)

State	DRIVING UNDER INFLUENCE Number	DRUNKENNESS Number	LIQUOR LAW VIOLATIONS Number	DISORDERLY CONDUCT Number
South Dakota	3,620	304	2,080	1,518
Tennessee	26,875	67,509	3,270	10,840
Texas	85,808	230,124	11,107	39,929
Utah	6,743	7,017	5,367	2,012
Vermont	298	13	80	316
Virginia	35,798	55,952	4,906	11,873
Washington	10,021	374	11,343	3,874
West Virginia	6,323	34,882	399	1,527
Wisconsin	28,982	0	15,471	31,237
Wyoming	3,835	3,284	2,894	1,907
Washington, D.C.	0	12	213	3,260
Puerto Rico	--	--	--	--
National Total	1,238,892	1,092,248	403,396	717,977
Number of States Included	51	51	51	51
Virgin Islands	--	--	--	--
Guam	--	--	--	--
American Samoa	--	--	--	--
T.T. Pacific Islands	--	--	--	--
N. Mariana Islands	--	--	--	--

General Table Notes

The last five island territories are not included in calculations of summary statistics.

Two dashes (--) indicate that data are not available.

The sum or row amounts may not equal the total due to rounding.

Notes for Table 37

This table presents the number of arrests for calendar year 1979 for selected offenses. Arrest statistics are provided by the Federal Bureau of Investigation's Uniform Crime Reporting (UCR) Program. UCR data are obtained either from State Uniform Crime Reporting programs (43 presently operational) or directly from participating law enforcement agencies. States with operational UCRs usually have mandatory reporting requirements and are able to provide assistance to local agencies to ensure completeness and quality of data.

In one respect, these data may be considered conservative estimates of alcohol-related arrests. Arrests are classified by a single offense, using a hierarchical rule. Consequently, if a person commits a crime while intoxicated, the arrest is categorized according to the primary offense and not recorded as an alcohol-related arrest. On the other hand, "Driving Under the Influence" includes arrests for impairment due to any type of drug; it is not limited to impairment due to alcohol.

Table 37 (continued)
Number of Reported Arrests for Selected Alcohol-Related Causes and Total Arrests for All Causes
(Calendar Year 1979)

State	VAGRANCY Number	TOTAL ARRESTS, ALL CAUSES Number	PERCENTAGE OF ALL ARRESTS DUE TO ALCOHOL-RELATED CAUSES Percent	(Rank)
Alabama	153	191,920	47	10
Alaska	3	18,627	37	22
Arizona	508	121,678	39	19
Arkansas	914	114,510	51	6
California	11,963	1,328,577	44	13
Colorado	63	148,058	24	41
Connecticut	239	93,481	25	40
Delaware	181	20,887	15	49
Florida	811	398,451	22	43
Georgia	409	283,264	46	11
Hawaii	1	32,013	11	50
Idaho	17	37,100	30	34
Illinois	107	530,886	38	21
Indiana	65	155,566	40	16
Iowa	150	85,118	41	15
Kansas	318	70,048	28	37
Kentucky	137	211,248	56	1
Louisiana	251	188,121	28	37
Maine	29	41,582	37	22
Maryland	641	165,938	16	47
Massachusetts	139	148,710	29	35
Michigan	1,049	277,378	32	28
Minnesota	71	95,246	31	31
Mississippi	67	63,051	46	11
Missouri	484	170,212	23	42
Montana	32	26,604	32	28
Nebraska	344	50,898	33	27
Nevada	2,597	70,204	36	25
New Hampshire	16	37,044	40	16
New Jersey	1,516	307,564	21	44
New Mexico	21	40,686	31	31
New York	10,063	880,580	11	50
North Carolina	325	330,681	29	35
North Dakota	30	25,877	48	9
Ohio	198	327,278	31	31
Oklahoma	0	149,319	54	2
Oregon	1	119,882	39	19
Pennsylvania	543	400,814	44	13

Table 37 (continued)
Number of Reported Arrests for Selected Alcohol-Related Causes and Total Arrests for All Causes
(Calendar Year 1979)

State	VAGRANCY Number	TOTAL ARRESTS, ALL CAUSES Number	PERCENTAGE OF ALL ARRESTS DUE TO ALCOHOL-RELATED CAUSES Percent	(Rank)
Rhode Island	140	34,469	17	46
South Carolina	27	127,848	52	4
South Dakota	35	18,661	40	16
Tennessee	532	206,870	52	4
Texas	655	746,728	49	7
Utah	127	64,958	32	28
Vermont	10	4,449	16	47
Virginia	2	285,807	37	22
Washington	185	97,169	26	39
West Virginia	77	79,056	54	2
Wisconsin	49	207,805	36	25
Wyoming	20	24,334	49	7
Washington, D.C.	15	16,682	20	45
Puerto Rico	--	--	--	--
National Total	36,330	9,673,937		
Number of States Included	51	51		
Virgin Islands	--	--	--	
Guam	--	--	--	
American Samoa	--	--	--	
T.T. Pacific Islands	--	--	--	
N. Mariana Islands	--	--	--	

Source: SAPIS, *National Status Report,* pp. 132–135.

General Table Notes

The last five island territories are not included in calculations of summary statistics.

Two dashes (--) indicate that data are not available.

The sum or row amounts may not equal the total due to rounding.

Notes for Table 37

This table presents the number of arrests for calendar year 1979 for selected offenses. Arrest statistics are provided by the Federal Bureau of Investigation's Uniform Crime Reporting (UCR) Program. UCR data are obtained either from State Uniform Crime Reporting programs (43 presently operational) or directly from participating law enforcement agencies. States with operational UCRs usually have mandatory reporting requirements and are able to provide assistance to local agencies to ensure completeness and quality of data.

In one respect, these data may be considered conservative estimates of alcohol-related arrests. Arrests are classified by a single offense, using a hierarchical rule. Consequently, if a person commits a crime while intoxicated, the arrest is categorized according to the primary offense and not recorded as an alcohol-related arrest. On the other hand, "Driving Under the Influence" includes arrests for impairment due to any type of drug; it is not limited to impairment due to alcohol.

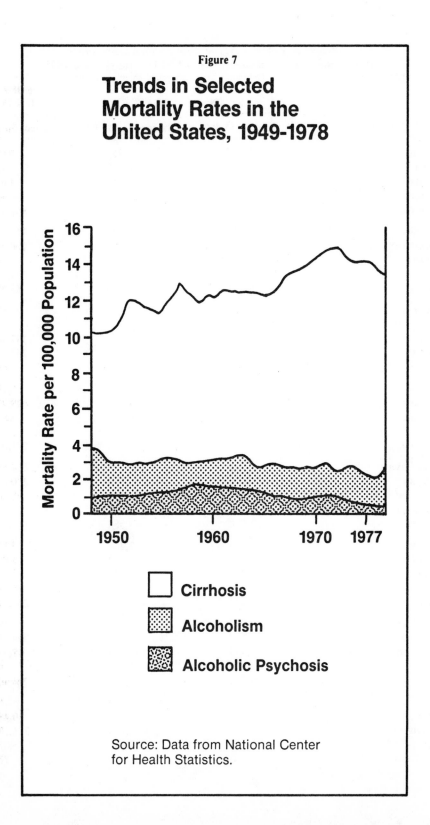

Figure 7

**Trends in Selected
Mortality Rates in the
United States, 1949-1978**

Source: Data from National Center
for Health Statistics.

Table 38
Amount of Public Revenue from Alcoholic Beverages
(Local and State—Calendar Year 1978; Federal—Fiscal 1978)

State	LOCAL (CY 78) Amount (in $1,000)	STATE (CY 78) Amount (in $1,000)	FEDERAL (FY 78)* Amount (in $1,000)
Alabama	6,953	114,359	3,593
Alaska	0	8,616	133
Arizona	7,255	42,257	4,674
Arkansas	397	27,159	447
California	60,000	390,199	804,373
Colorado	17,539	45,937	115,151
Connecticut	0	70,254	126,588
Delaware	0	4,977	48
Florida	0	338,391	137,737
Georgia	66,931	113,180	53,222
Hawaii	1,990	24,888	668
Idaho	781	19,483	74
Illinois	57,722	160,509	347,362
Indiana	0	71,897	237,483
Iowa	0	68,166	491
Kansas	317	26,116	5,409
Kentucky	4,772	36,197	629,213
Louisiana	19,191	70,005	38,871
Maine	0	31,747	3,578
Maryland	9,809	67,325	241,023
Massachusetts	4,925	100,786	154,695
Michigan	0	226,574	370,035
Minnesota	15,791	81,123	52,168
Mississippi	144	51,982	183
Missouri	5,880	49,582	165,154
Montana	233	22,254	5,122
Nebraska	2,940	20,163	2,833
Nevada	3,933	25,752	73
New Hampshire	0	32,532	28,302
New Jersey	9,878	112,533	287,045
New Mexico	997	18,145	1,590
New York	98,100	315,667	304,330
North Carolina	6,498	135,946	98,335
North Dakota	1,500	10,166	90
Ohio	5,340	234,314	294,401
Oklahoma	1,779	40,699	185
Oregon	0	61,705	30,486
Pennsylvania	0	252,250	271,186
Rhode Island	1,055	18,957	6,070
South Carolina	0	101,430	770

Table 38 (continued)
Amount of Public Revenue from Alcoholic Beverages
(Local and State—Calendar Year 1978; Federal—Fiscal 1978)

State	LOCAL (CY 78) Amount (in $1,000)	STATE (CY 78) Amount (in $1,000)	FEDERAL (FY 78)* Amount (in $1,000)
South Dakota	1,560	11,775	80
Tennessee	49,153	68,820	83,516
Texas	25,783	271,275	187,367
Utah	1,248	22,406	40
Vermont	171	15,870	72
Virginia	6,466	123,342	32,611
Washington	5,461	147,213	65,407
West Virginia	6,001	35,140	7,024
Wisconsin	3,503	87,375	186,593
Wyoming	401	7,569	41
Washington, D.C.	0	24,521	--
Puerto Rico	--	--	--
National Total	512,397	4,459,528	5,385,942
Number of States Included	51	51	50
Virgin Islands	--	--	--
Guam	--	--	--
American Samoa	--	--	--
T.T. Pacific Islands	--	--	--
N. Mariana Islands	--	--	--

Source: SAPIS, *National Status Report*, pp. 138–139.

General Table Notes

The last five island territories are not included in calculations of summary statistics.

Two dashes (--) indicate that data are not available.

The sum or row amounts may not equal the total due to rounding.

Notes for Table 38

The local and state revenues were compiled by the Distilled Spirits Council of the United States (DISCUS) and reflect tax collections on beverage alcohol for calendar year 1978. This is the most recent year for which estimates are available on such revenues.

Federal revenues represent excise taxes collected on alcoholic beverages. The data were compiled by the Internal Revenue Service and reflect collections during fiscal year 1978. The 1978 federal figure is presented in the table for comparison with the state and local figures.

*Federal revenues for Washington, D.C. are included in those for the state of Maryland.

Table 39
Per Capita Amount of Public Revenue from Alcoholic Beverages
(Local and State—Calendar Year 1978; Federal—Fiscal Year 1978)

State	LOCAL (CY 78) Amount	STATE (CY 78) Amount	FEDERAL (FY 78)* Amount
Alabama	1.80	29.60	0.93
Alaska	0.00	21.52	0.33
Arizona	2.67	15.57	1.72
Arkansas	0.17	11.91	0.20
California	2.55	16.60	34.21
Colorado	6.09	15.96	40.01
Connecticut	0.00	22.68	40.88
Delaware	0.00	8.37	0.08
Florida	0.00	35.32	14.38
Georgia	12.40	20.97	9.86
Hawaii	2.06	25.80	0.69
Idaho	0.83	20.66	0.08
Illinois	5.10	14.17	30.67
Indiana	0.00	13.18	43.54
Iowa	0.00	23.43	0.17
Kansas	0.13	11.09	2.30
Kentucky	1.31	9.94	172.76
Louisiana	4.58	16.69	9.27
Maine	0.00	28.26	3.18
Maryland	2.34	16.06	57.48
Massachusetts	0.86	17.60	27.02
Michigan	0.00	24.53	40.06
Minnesota	3.88	19.94	12.82
Mississippi	0.06	20.77	0.07
Missouri	1.20	10.12	33.69
Montana	0.30	28.40	6.54
Nebraska	1.88	12.89	1.81
Nevada	4.93	32.27	0.09
New Hampshire	0.00	35.40	30.80
New Jersey	1.35	15.34	39.13
New Mexico	0.77	14.06	1.23
New York	5.61	18.06	17.41
North Carolina	1.11	23.25	16.82
North Dakota	2.30	15.59	0.14
Ohio	0.50	21.78	27.36
Oklahoma	0.59	13.57	0.06
Oregon	0.00	23.57	11.65
Pennsylvania	0.00	21.33	22.93
Rhode Island	1.12	20.04	6.42
South Carolina	0.00	33.07	0.25

Table 39 (continued)
Per Capita Amount of Public Revenue from Alcoholic Beverages
(Local and State—Calendar Year 1978; Federal—Fiscal Year 1978)

State	LOCAL (CY 78) Amount	STATE (CY 78) Amount	FEDERAL (FY 78)* Amount
South Dakota	2.27	17.12	0.12
Tennessee	10.83	15.16	18.40
Texas	1.82	19.17	13.24
Utah	0.86	15.40	0.03
Vermont	0.33	31.04	0.14
Virginia	1.22	23.18	6.13
Washington	1.33	35.82	15.92
West Virginia	3.11	18.22	3.64
Wisconsin	0.75	18.63	39.79
Wyoming	0.86	16.14	0.09
Washington, D.C.	0.00	38.60	--
Puerto Rico	--	--	--
National Value	2.27	19.80	23.91
Number of States Included	51	51	50
Virgin Islands	--	--	--
Guam	--	--	--
American Samoa	--	--	--
T.T. Pacific Islands	--	--	--
N. Mariana Islands	--	--	--

Source: SAPIS, *National Status Report,* p. 141.

General Table Notes

The last five island territories are not included in calculations of summary statistics.

Two dashes (--) indicate that data are not available.

The sum or row amounts may not equal the total due to rounding.

Notes for Table 39

The local and state revenues were compiled by the Distilled Spirits Council of the United States (DISCUS) and reflect tax collections on beverage alcohol for calendar year 1978. This is the most recent year for which estimates were available on such revenues.

Federal revenues represent excise taxes collected on alcoholic beverages. The data were compiled by the Internal Revenue Service and reflect collections during fiscal year 1978. The 1978 federal figure is presented in the table for comparison with the state and local figures.

Per capita calculations are based on population counts for April 1980 provided by the Bureau of the Census.

*Federal revenues for Washington, D.C., are included in those for the state of Maryland.

Table 40
Number of Citizen Self-Help and Information Groups Offering Alcohol Services
(December 1980)

State	ALCOHOLICS ANONYMOUS INC. GROUPS Number	AL-ANON GROUPS Number	ALATEEN GROUPS Number	NATIONAL COUNCIL ON ALCOHOLISM INC. AFFILIATED COUNCILS Number
Alabama	141	112	16	6
Alaska	76	28	6	15
Arizona	291	147	20	4
Arkansas	130	86	11	0
California	2,759	835	114	31
Colorado	302	153	18	6
Connecticut	589	187	36	4
Delaware	75	28	7	1
Florida	813	346	50	2
Georgia	324	196	22	3
Hawaii	106	20	3	1
Idaho	101	56	9	3
Illinois	1,213	492	77	10
Indiana	446	200	39	1
Iowa	268	199	46	4
Kansas	213	177	37	2
Kentucky	229	127	16	2
Louisiana	200	127	23	2
Maine	143	90	15	3
Maryland	498	226	27	2
Massachusetts	726	300	52	7
Michigan	736	377	63	10
Minnesota	824	649	100	0
Mississippi	104	80	11	1
Missouri	365	199	33	2
Montana	135	98	22	2
Nebraska	268	147	26	5
Nevada	84	30	5	2
New Hampshire	143	48	9	1
New Jersey	631	250	52	6
New Mexico	119	75	4	3
New York	1,446	557	111	19
North Carolina	360	187	23	6
North Dakota	119	111	16	0
Ohio	884	361	63	6
Oklahoma	198	168	17	4
Oregon	230	104	13	4
Pennsylvania	752	308	61	12
Rhode Island	102	34	4	1
South Carolina	120	67	10	1

Table 40 (continued)
Number of Citizen Self-Help and Information Groups Offering Alcohol Services
(December 1980)

State	ALCOHOLICS ANONYMOUS INC. GROUPS	AL-ANON GROUPS	ALATEEN GROUPS	NATIONAL COUNCIL ON ALCOHOLISM INC. AFFILIATED COUNCILS
	Number	Number	Number	Number
South Dakota	120	89	16	1
Tennessee	230	148	19	3
Texas	693	436	88	4
Utah	111	55	5	0
Vermont	75	33	6	0
Virginia	451	198	24	3
Washington	492	225	29	9
West Virginia	104	52	8	0
Wisconsin	571	376	67	6
Wyoming	64	44	7	0
Washington, D.C.	83	29	3	1
Puerto Rico	90	38	6	0
National Total	20,347	9,705	1,565	221
Number of States Included	52	52	52	52
Virgin Islands	4	4	0	1
Guam	0	3	1	0
American Samoa	0	0	0	0
T.T. Pacific Islands	0	0	0	0
N. Mariana Islands	0	0	0	0

Source: SAPIS, *National Status Report,* pp. 122–123.

General Table Notes

The last five island territories are not included in calculations of summary statistics.

The sum or row amounts may not equal the total due to rounding.

Notes for Table 40

The data in the table are the number of affiliated groups or programs in each state. Data on the number of programs were provided by the specific organizations.

Figure 8

A Chart of Alcohol Addiction and Recovery
To be read from left to right

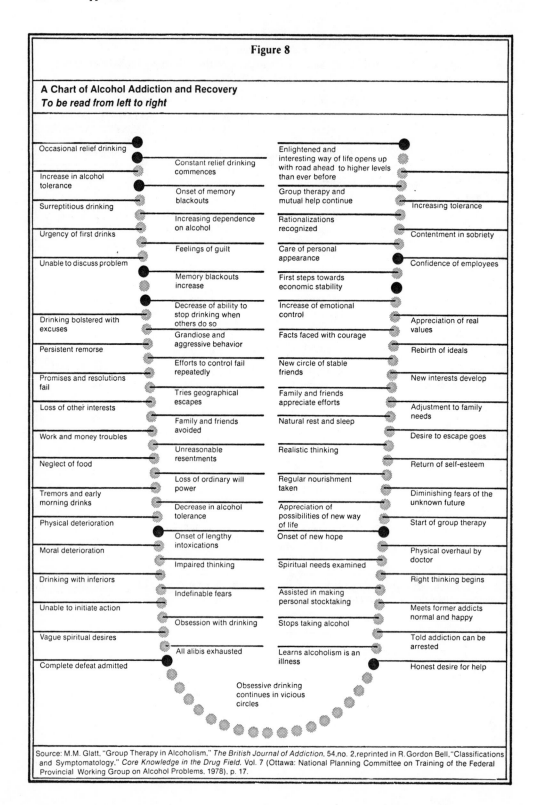

Source: M.M. Glatt, "Group Therapy in Alcoholism," *The British Journal of Addiction,* 54,no. 2,reprinted in R. Gordon Bell, "Classifications and Symptomatology," *Core Knowledge in the Drug Field,* Vol. 7 (Ottawa: National Planning Committee on Training of the Federal Provincial Working Group on Alcohol Problems, 1978), p. 17.

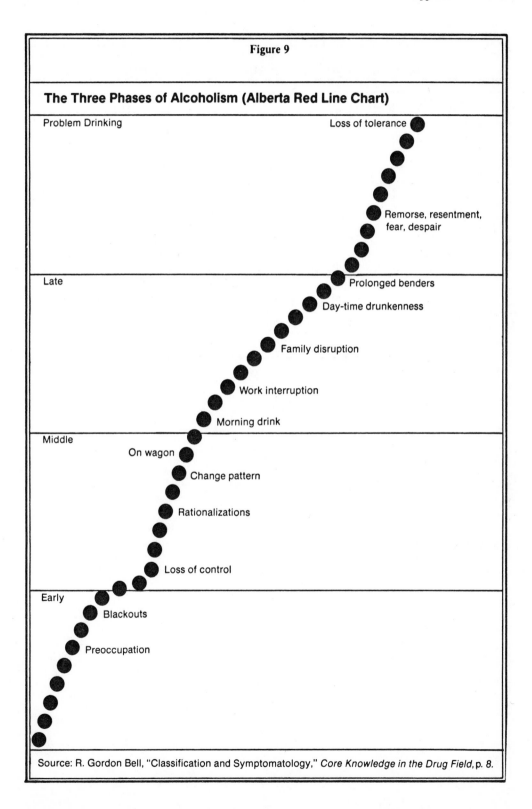

Figure 9

The Three Phases of Alcoholism (Alberta Red Line Chart)

Problem Drinking — Loss of tolerance

Remorse, resentment, fear, despair

Late — Prolonged benders

Day-time drunkenness

Family disruption

Work interruption

Morning drink

Middle

On wagon

Change pattern

Rationalizations

Loss of control

Early

Blackouts

Preoccupation

Source: R. Gordon Bell, "Classification and Symptomatology," *Core Knowledge in the Drug Field,* p. 8.

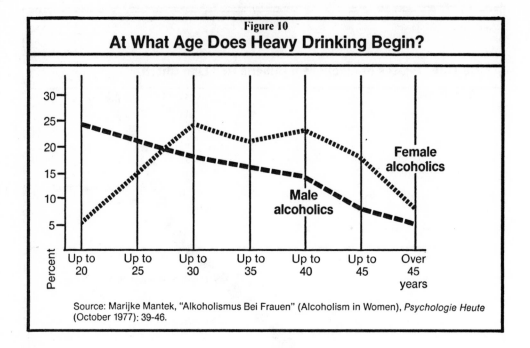

Figure 10
At What Age Does Heavy Drinking Begin?

Source: Marijke Mantek, "Alkoholismus Bei Frauen" (Alcoholism in Women), *Psychologie Heute* (October 1977): 39-46.

Table 41
Use of Other Drugs among Current Drinkers and Those Who Are Not Current Drinkers*

Use of Other Drugs	PERCENTAGE OF YOUTH: AGES 12 to 17 YEARS		PERCENTAGE OF ADULTS: AGES 18+ YEARS	
	Current Drinkers	Not Current Drinkers	Current Drinkers	Not Current Drinkers
Size of sample (unweighted base)	302	684	1622	968
Nonmedical psychotherapeutic pill user				
Yes	18.8	6.5	18.9	9.4
No	81.2	93.5	81.1	90.6
Ever used marijuana				
Yes	44.3	11.8	31.4	6.9
No	55.7	88.2	68.6	93.1
Ever used other illicit drugs				
Yes	36.7	10.2	19.7	4.7
No	63.3	89.8	80.2	94.6

Source: H. I. Abelson and P. M. Fishburne, *Nonmedical Use of Psychoactive Substances* (Princeton, NJ: Response Analysis Co., 1976), reprinted in Ernest P. Noble, ed., *Third Special Report,* p. 197.

*Those who report drinking alcoholic beverages within the past month.

Table 42
Most Consistent Features of the Fetal Alcohol Syndrome

Growth and Performance

- Prenatal onset growth deficiency, more pronounced in length than in weight
- Concomitant microcephaly (small head circumference) even when corrected for small body weight and length
- Postnatal growth deficiency in weight and length, usually below 3rd percentile
- Delay of intellectual development and/or mental deficiency (mean IQ from Seattle study = 64, range 16–92)
- Fine motor dysfunction (poor coordination)

Head and Face

- Microcephaly
- Short palpebral fissures (narrow eye slits)
- Midfacial (maxillary) hypoplasia (underdevelopment of midfacial region)
- Flattened, elongated philtrum (middle of upper lip) associated with thin, narrow vermilion lip borders (highly specific to FAS)
- Minor ear anomalies including low set ears

Limbs

- Abnormal creases in the palm of the hand
- Minor joint anomalies
  —syndactyly (fingers or toes joined together)
  —clinodactyly (abnormal bending of fingers or toes)
  —camptodactyly (one or more fingers constantly flexed at one or more phalangeal joints)

Heart

- Ventricular atrial septal defect (valve defects)

Brain

- Absence of corpus callosum
- Hydrocephalus (excess fluid in cranium)
- Brain cell migratory abnormalities

Other

- Minor genital anomalies
- Hemangiomas (benign tumors made up of blood vessels) in infancy

Source: Data from Kenneth L. Jones and David W. Smith, "The Fetal Alcohol Syndrome," *Teratology* 12, no. 1 (1975):1–10, reprinted in Ernest P. Noble, ed., *Third Special Report*, p. 172.

Figure 11

Factors That Can Lead to Alcoholism in Women

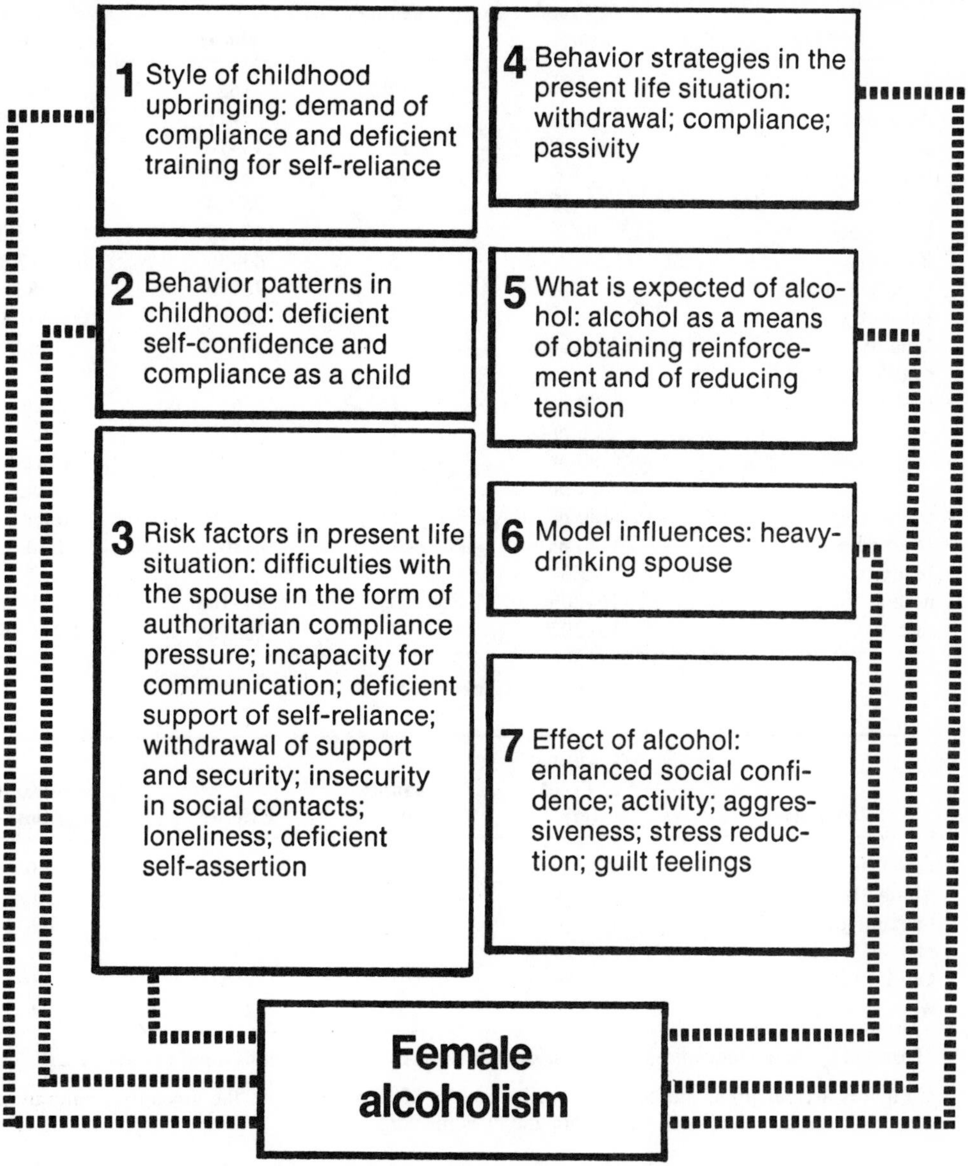

1 Style of childhood upbringing: demand of compliance and deficient training for self-reliance

4 Behavior strategies in the present life situation: withdrawal; compliance; passivity

2 Behavior patterns in childhood: deficient self-confidence and compliance as a child

5 What is expected of alcohol: alcohol as a means of obtaining reinforcement and of reducing tension

3 Risk factors in present life situation: difficulties with the spouse in the form of authoritarian compliance pressure; incapacity for communication; deficient support of self-reliance; withdrawal of support and security; insecurity in social contacts; loneliness; deficient self-assertion

6 Model influences: heavy-drinking spouse

7 Effect of alcohol: enhanced social confidence; activity; aggressiveness; stress reduction; guilt feelings

Female alcoholism

The more these risk factors are present, the greater becomes the danger of female alcoholism.

Source: Marijke Mantek, "Alkoholismus Bei Frauen," *Psychologie Heute*, pp. 39-46.

Table 43
Calories and Carbohydrates in Selected Alcoholic Beverages

Beverage	% Alcohol or Proof (pr)	Quantity (oz)	Calories	Carbohydrates (grams)
ale	5%	12	162	13.8
Anisette	42–60 pr	1	64–111	7.5–13.9
beer	4.6–4.9%	12	144–165	11.0–14.1
beer, 3.2 low gravity	3.8%	12	142	13.6
beer, low carbohydrate	4.6%	12	96–145	0.2–4.2
beer, near	0.4%	12	62–73	13.7–15.0
Bordeaux	11.5–12.5%	3	63–96	trace–7.5
brandy, flavored	70 pr	1	72–100	1.0–8.9
burgundy	12–14%	3	12–82	trace–1.8
Chianti	12–13%	3	59–90	0.1–6.3
distilled spirits*				
	80 pr	1	65	trace
	86 pr	1	70	trace
	90 pr	1	74	trace
	94 pr	1	77	trace
	100 pr	1	83	trace
Drambuie	80 pr	1	110	11.0
Madeira	19%	3	120	6.3
port	16–20%	3	94–165	2.0–11.8
sherry	16–20%	3	76–158	1.2–11.6

Cocktails**

Beverage	% Alcohol or Proof (pr)	Quantity (oz)	Calories	Carbohydrates (grams)
daiquiri	52.5 pr	3	177	12.0
Manhattan	55 pr	3	147	3.0
martini, gin	67.5 pr	3	168	0.6
martini, vodka	65 pr	3	147	0
Old Fashioned	62 pr	3	165	3.0
whiskey sour	12.5%	8	256	17.6

*Distilled spirits include all hard liquors, such as whiskey, gin, rum, unflavored brandies etc.

**Figures are for premixed cocktails (with alcohol). The potency and the amount of calories and carbohydrates in cocktails mixed in bars and at home vary.

Appendix 2
Sources of Information

This section contains selected major sources of information on alcohol abuse and alcoholism.

The sources do *not* include listings of treatment centers. Detailed lists of these are generally available from national or local governments. In addition it was not possible to provide information sources for every foreign country, since many countries failed to or chose not to supply such information despite repeated requests.

CONTENTS

UNITED STATES

NATIONAL ORGANIZATIONS

AL-ANON FAMILY GROUP
  HEADQUARTERS
P. O. Box 182
Madison Square Station
New York, New York 10010

ALCOHOL AND DRUG PROBLEMS
  ASSOCIATION OF NORTH
  AMERICA
1101 Fifteenth Street, N. W. #204
Washington, D. C. 20005

ALCOHOLICS ANONYMOUS
General Service Office
468 Park Avenue South
New York, New York 10016

NATIONAL CLEARINGHOUSE FOR
  ALCOHOL INFORMATION
(Information service of the National
  Institute on Alcohol Abuse and
  Alcoholism)
P. O. Box 2345
Rockville, Maryland 20852

NATIONAL COUNCIL ON
  ALCOHOLISM
733 Third Avenue
New York, New York 10017

NATIONAL INSTITUTE ON
  ALCOHOL ABUSE AND
  ALCOHOLISM
(same address as its information service,
  National Clearinghouse for Alcohol
  Information)

STATE AND TERRITORIAL AGENCIES

Alabama
Division of Alcoholism and Drug Abuse
Department of Mental Health
502 Washington Avenue
Montgomery, Alabama 36104
Tel: (205) 834-4350

Alaska
Department of Health & Social Services
Office of Alcoholism and Drug Abuse
Pouch H-05-F
231 South Franklin
Juneau, Alaska 99811
Tel: (907) 586-6201

Arizona
Alcohol Section
Arizona Department of Health Services
2500 East Van Buren
Phoenix, Arizona 85008
Tel: (602) 271-3009

Arkansas
Arkansas Office on Alcohol and Drug
  Abuse Prevention
1515 West 7th Avenue, Suite 300
Little Rock, Arkansas 72202
Tel: (501) 371-2604

California
Department of Alcohol and Drug
  Programs
111 Capitol Mall
Suite 450
Sacramento, California 95814
Tel: (916) 445-1940

Colorado
Alcohol and Drug Abuse Division
Department of Health
4210 East 11th Avenue
Denver, Colorado 80220
Tel: (303) 320-6137

Connecticut
Connecticut Alcohol and Drug Abuse
  Council
90 Washington Street, Room 312
Hartford, Connecticut 06115
Tel: (203) 566-4145

Delaware
Bureau of Alcoholism and Drug Abuse
Division of Mental Health

1901 North Dupont Highway
Newcastle, Delaware 19720
Tel: (302) 421-6101

Florida
Alcoholic Rehabilitation Program
Department of Health & Rehabilitation
  Services
1323 Winewood Boulevard
Tallahassee, Florida 32301
Tel: (904) 488-0900

Georgia
Alcohol and Drug Abuse Section
Division of Mental Health & Mental
  Retardation
Georgia Department of Human Resources
618 Ponce De Leon Avenue, N.E.
Atlanta, Georgia 30308
Tel: (404) 894-4785

Hawaii
Department of Health
State Substance Abuse Agency
Alcohol and Drug Abuse Branch
1270 Queen Emma Street, Room 505
Honolulu, Hawaii 96813
Tel: (808) 548-7655

Idaho
Bureau of Substance Abuse
Department of Health & Welfare
450 West State Street, 4th Floor
Boise, Idaho 83720
Tel: (208) 334-4368

Illinois
Alcohol Division
Illinois Department of Mental Health &
  Developmental Disabilities
160 North Lasalle Street, Room 1500
Chicago, Illinois 60601
Tel: (312) 793-2907

Indiana
Division of Addiction Services
Department of Mental Health
5 Indiana Square
Indianapolis, Indiana 46204
Tel: (317) 232-7818

Iowa
Department of Substance Abuse
Insurance Exchange Building, Suite 202
505 5th Avenue
Des Moines, Iowa 50319
Tel: (515) 281-3641

Kansas
Alcoholism and Drug Abuse Section
Department of Social Rehabilitation
  Service
2700 West Sixth Street
Biddle Building
Topeka, Kansas 66606
Tel: (913) 296-3925

Kentucky
Alcohol and Drug Branch
Bureau of Health Services
Department of Human Resources
275 East Main Street
Frankfort, Kentucky 40621
Tel: (502) 564-7450

Louisiana
Office of Mental Health & Substance
  Abuse
Department of Health & Human
  Resources
655 North 5th Street
Baton Rouge, Louisiana 70829
Tel: (504) 342-2590

Maine
Office of Alcoholism and Drug Abuse
  Prevention
Department of Human Services
32 Winthrop Street
Augusta, Maine 04330
Tel: (207) 289-2781

Maryland
Alcoholism Control Administration
201 West Preston Street
4th Floor
Baltimore, Maryland 21201
Tel: (301) 383-2781, 2782, 2783

Massachusetts
Massachusetts Division of Alcoholism
755 Boylston Street

Boston, Massachusetts
Tel: (617) 727-1960

Michigan
Office of Substance Abuse Services
Department of Public Health
3500 North Logan Street
Lansing, Michigan 48909
Tel: (517) 373-8600

Minnesota
Chemical Dependency Program Division
Department of Public Welfare
4th Floor Centennial Building
658 Cedar Street
St. Paul, Minnesota 55155
Tel: (612) 296-4610

Mississippi
Division of Alcohol and Drug Abuse
Department of Mental Health
619 Robert E. Lee State Office Building
Jackson, Mississippi 32901
Tel: (601) 354-7031

Missouri
Division of Alcoholism and Drug Abuse
Department of Mental Health
2002 Missouri Boulevard
Jefferson City, Missouri 65102
Tel: (314) 751-4942

Montana
Alcohol and Drug Abuse Division
Department of Institutions
1539 11th Avenue
Helena, Montana 59601
Tel: (406) 449-2827

Nebraska
Nebraska Department of Public
  Institutions
Nebraska Division of Alcoholism & Drug
  Abuse
801 West Van Dorn
Box 94728
Lincoln, Nebraska 68509
Tel: (402) 471-2851

Nevada
Bureau of Alcohol and Drug Abuse
Department of Human Resources

505 East King Street
Carson City, Nevada 89710
Tel: (702) 885-4790

New Hampshire
Office of Alcohol & Drug Abuse
  Prevention
Health and Welfare Building
Hazen Drive
Concord, New Hampshire 03301
Tel: (603) 271-4626, 4630

New Jersey
New Jersey Division of Alcoholism
129 East Hanover Street
Trenton, New Jersey 08625
Tel: (609) 292-8947

New Mexico
Substance Abuse Bureau
Behavioral Health Service Division
Health and Environment Department
P. O. Box 968
Santa Fe, New Mexico 87503
Tel: (505) 827-5271 Ext. 226

New York
New York Office of Alcoholism and
  Substance Abuse
Division of Substance Abuse Services
Executive Park South
Box 8200
Albany, New York 12203
Tel: (518) 488-4270

North Carolina
Alcohol and Drug Abuse Services
Division of MH/MR and Substance
  Abuse
325 North Salisbury Street
Albermarle Building, Room 1100
Raleigh, North Carolina 27611
Tel: (919) 733-4670

North Dakota
Division of Alcoholism & Drug Abuse
State Department of Health
909 Basin Avenue
Bismarck, North Dakota 58505
Tel: (701) 224-2768

Ohio
Division of Alcoholism
Ohio Department of Health
246 North High Street
Columbus, Ohio 43215
Tel: (614) 466-3425

Oklahoma
Division of Alcoholism and Drug Abuse
    Programs
Department of Mental Health
4545 North Lincoln Boulevard
Suite 100
P. O. Box 53277
Oklahoma City, Oklahoma 73152
Tel: (405) 521-2811

Oregon
Program for Alcohol and Drug Problems
Oregon Mental Health Division
2575 Bittern Street, N. E.
Salem, Oregon 97310
Tel: (503) 378-2163

Pennsylvania
Governor's Council on Drug & Alcohol
    Abuse
2101 North Front Street
Harrisburg, Pennsylvania 17120
Tel: (717) 787-9857

Rhode Island
Division of Substance Abuse
General Hospital
Building 303
Rhode Island Medical Center
Cranston, Rhode Island 02920
Tel: (401) 464-2091

South Carolina
South Carolina Commission on Alcohol
    and Drug Abuse
3700 Forest Drive
Landmark East, Suite 300
Columbia, South Carolina 29204
Tel: (803) 758-2183

South Dakota
South Dakota Division of Alcoholism
Joe Foss Building
Pierre, South Dakota 57501
Tel: (605) 773-4806

Tennessee
Division of Alcohol and Drug Abuse
Tennessee Department of Mental Health
501 Union Building
Nashville, Tennessee 37219
Tel: (615) 741-1921

Texas
Texas Commission on Alcoholism
809 Sam Houston State Office Building
Austin, Texas 78701
Tel: (512) 475-2725

Utah
Division of Alcoholism and Drugs
150 West North Temple, Suite 350
P. O. Box 2500
Salt Lake City, Utah 84110
Tel: (801) 533-6532

Vermont
Alcohol and Drug Abuse Division
Department of Social and Rehabilitation
    Services
103 South Main Street
State Office Building
Waterbury, Vermont 05676
Tel: (802) 241-2170

Virginia
Division of Substance Abuse
Virginia Department of Mental Health
    and Mental Retardation
P. O. Box 1797
109 Governor Street
Richmond, Virginia 23214
Tel: (804) 786-5313

Washington
Bureau of Alcoholism and Substance
    Abuse
Washington Department of Social &
    Health Services
Mailstop OB-44W
Olympia, Washington 98504
Tel: (206) 753-3073

West Virginia
Department of Health
Alcoholism and Drug Abuse Program
State Capitol
1800 Kanawha Boulevard E

Charleston, West Virginia 25305
Tel: (304) 348-3616

Wisconsin
State Bureau of Alcohol and Other Drug
   Abuse
One West Wilson Street
Room 523
Madison, Wisconsin 53702
Tel: (608) 266-3442

Wyoming
Alcohol and Alcohol Abuse Programs
Hathaway Building
Cheyenne, Wyoming 82002
Tel: (307) 777-7115

District of Columbia
D. C. Department of Human Resources
Mental Health, Alcohol and Addiction
   Services Branch
421 8th Street, NW
2nd Floor
Washington, D. C. 20004
Tel: (202) 724-5637

Puerto Rico
Department of Addiction Control Services
P. O. Box B-Y

Piedras Station
Puerto Rico 00928
Tel: (809) 764-5014

American Samoa
Mental Health Clinic
Government of American Samoa
Pago Pago, American Samoa 96799

Guam
Mental Health and Substance Abuse
   Agency
P. O. Box 20999
Guam, Guam 96921
Tel: (404) 477-9704

Trust Territories
Department of Health Services
Office of the High Commissioner
Saipan, Trust Territories 96950
Tel: (615) 741-1921

Virgin Islands
Division of Mental Health, Alcoholism
   and Drug Dependency
P. O. Box 520
Christiansted
St. Croix, Virgin Islands
Tel: (809) 773-1192, 774-4888

CANADA

PROVINCIAL AND
TERRITORIAL AGENCIES

Alberta
Alberta Alcoholism & Drug Abuse
   Commission
10909 Jasper Ave.
Edmonton, Alberta T5J 3M9
Tel: (403) 427-4275

British Columbia
The Alcohol & Drug Commission of
   British Columbia
805 West Broadway, 8th Floor
Vancouver, British Columbia V5Y 1P9
Tel: (604) 731-9121

Manitoba
Alcoholism Foundation of Manitoba
1580 Dublin Ave.

Winnipeg, Manitoba R3E 0L4
Tel: (204) 775-8601

New Brunswick
Alcoholism & Drug Dependency
   Commission
103 Church Street
P. O. Box 6000
Fredericton, New Brunswick E3B 5H1
Tel: (506) 453-2136

Newfoundland
Department of Health
Confederation Building
St. John's, Newfoundland A1C 5T7
Tel: (709) 737-2300

Alcohol & Drug Addiction Foundation of
   Newfoundland

3 Blackmarsh Road
St. John's, Newfoundland A1E 1S2
Tel: (709) 579-4041

Nova Scotia
Nova Scotia Commission on Drug
  Dependency
5668 South Street
Halifax, Nova Scotia B3J 1A6
Tel: (902) 424-4270

Ontario
Ministry of Health
9th Floor, Hepburn Block
Queen's Park
Toronto, Ontario M7A 1S2
Tel: (416) 965-5167

Alcoholism & Drug Addiction Foundation
33 Russell Street
Toronto, Ontario M5S 2S1
Tel: (416) 595-6000

Prince Edward Island
Addiction Foundation of Prince Edward
  Island
Box 37
Charlottetown, Prince Edward Island
C1A 7K2
Tel: (902) 892-4265

Quebec
Department of Social Affairs
Information Centre on Alcoholism and
  Other Addictions
1075. Chemin ste-Foy
Quebec, P. Q. G1S 2M1
Tel: (418) 643-9621

Saskatchewan
Alcoholism Commission of Saskatchewan
3475 Albert Street
Regina, Saskatchewan S4S 6X6
Tel: (306) 565-4085

Northwest Territories
Alcohol & Drug Program
Department of Social Services
Government of the Northwest Territories
Yellowknife, N.W.T. X1A 2L9
Tel: (403) 873-7155
Alcohol & Drug Coordinating Council
Box 1769
Yellowknife, N.W.T. X0E 1H0
Tel: (403) 873-7155

Yukon Territory
Alcohol & Drug Services
Box 2703
Whitehorse, Y. T. Y1A 2C6
Tel: (403) 667-5777

FOREIGN SOURCES

INTERNATIONAL

World Health Organization
1121 Geneva 27,
Switzerland

NATIONAL

Argentina
Ministerio de Salud Publica
Defensa 120
Buenos Aires
Argentina

Australia
Australian Council of Social Services, Inc.
149 Castelereagn Street

Sydney, New South Wales 2000
Australia

Australian Foundation on Alcoholism &
  Drug Dependence
2nd Floor
T and G Building
London Circuit
Canberra City, A. C. T. 2601
Australia

New South Wales
Health Commission
9-13 Young Street
Sydney, New South Wales 2000
Australia

Queensland
Department of Health
Alcohol and Drug Dependence Service
"BIALA"
270 Roma Street
Brisbane, Queensland 4000
Australia

South Australia
Alcohol & Drug Addicts Treatment
    Board
1st Floor
3/161 Greenhill Road
Parkside, South Australia 5063
Australia

Tasmania
Department of Health Services
Public Buildings
Davey Street
Hobart, Tasmania 7000
Australia

Victoria
Alcohol and Drug Services
Mental Health Division
Health Commission of Victoria
Enterprise House
555 Collins Street
Melbourne, Victoria 3000
Australia

Western Australia
Western Australia Alcohol and Drug
    Authority
Greenchurch House
25 Richardson Street
West Perth
Western Australia, 6005
Australia

Austria
Republik Oesterreich
Bundeministerium fuer Gesundheit und
    Umweltschutz
Stubenring 1
1010 Wein
Austria

Belgium
Comite National pour l'Etude et
la Prevention de l'Alcoolisme
et des Autres Toxicomanies

Ministry of Public Health
Ministere de Sante Publique
Cabinet du Ministre
Rue Joseph II 30
Brussels 1040
Belgium

Colombia
Corporacion Colombiana contra
    Alcoholismo
Carrera 50C # 60-13
Bogota,
Colombia

Ministerio de Salud
Calle 16 No. 7-39
Bogota,
Colombia

Denmark
Ministry of Education
Frederiksholms Kanal 21
1220 Copenhagen K
Denmark

National Board of Health
1, St. Kongensgade
DK-1264 Copenhagen K
Denmark

Egypt
Ministry of Health
People's Assembly Street
Lazogli
Cairo,
Egypt

Finland
State Alcohol Monopoly
Social Research Institute of Alcohol
    Studies
Kalevankatu 12
00100 Helsinki 10
Finland

France
Haut Comite d'Etude et d'Information sur
    l'Alcoolisme
27, Rue Oudinot
75700 Paris
France

Germany, East
Ministerium fuer Gesundheitswesen der
   DDR
Hauptabt. Int. Beziehg
GDR 1020 Berlin
Rathausstr.
German Democratic Republic

Hygiene Museum
GDR 8010 Dresden
Julius—Fucik—Allee
German Democratic Republic

German, West
Deutsche Hauptstelle gegen die
   Suchtoefahren
Westring 2 4700
Hamm
German Federal Republic

Hungary
Alkolizmus Elleni Orszagos Bizottsag
Budapest, V.,
Arany Janos v. 31
1051
Hungary

Egeszsegugyi Miniszterium
Budapest, V.,
Akademia v. 10
1055
Hungary

Iceland
Liquor Prevention Council
Eiriksgata 5
101 Reykjavik
Iceland

India
Indian Council on Medical Research
Ansari Nagar,
Post Box 4508
New Delhi—110029
India

Ireland
The Economic and Social Research
   Institute
4 Burlington Road
Dublin 4,
Republic of Ireland

Department of Health
Customs House
Dublin 1,
Republic of Ireland

Israel
Department of Alcoholism Treatment
   Services
Ministry of Labour and Social Affairs
10 Yad Harutzim Street, Talpiot
P. O. Box 1260
Jerusalem 91000
Israel

Italy
Ministero della Sanita'
D. G. Servizi Medicina Sociale
Viale della Civilta' Romana (EUR)
00144 Roma, Italy

Jamaica
The Permanent Secretary
Ministry of Health
10 Caledonia Avenue
Kingston 5, Jamaica WI

Japan
Mental Health Division
Public Health Bureau
Ministry of Health and Welfare
1—2—2 Kasumigaseki
Chiyoda-ku, Tokyo, Japan

Mexico
Instituto Mexicano de Psiquiatria
Antiguo Camino a Xochimilco 101
Mexico 22, D. F.
Mexico

Secretaria de Salubridad y Asistencia
Direccion General de Control de
   Alimentos Bebidas y Medicamentos
Liverpoool 6, D. F.
Mexico

New Zealand
National Society on Alcoholism and Drug
   Dependence New Zealand (Inc.)
Box 1642
Wellington
New Zealand

Alcoholic Liquor Advisory Council
P. O. Box 5023
Wellington
New Zealand

Poland
Spoteczny Komitet Przeciwalkoholowy
    (Committee to Fight Alcoholism)
UL. Kopernika 36/40
00—328 Warszawa
Poland

South Africa
The Department of Health, Welfare &
    Pensions
Private Bag X88
Pretoria 0001
Republic of South Africa

Sweden
Centralforbundet for Alkohol
Karlavagen 117
Box 27302
10254 Stockholm, Sweden

Switzerland
Schweizerische Fachstelle
fuer Alkoholprobleme
avenue Ruchonnet 14
CH—1003 Lausanne/Switzerland

L'Institut suisse de prophylaxie de
    l'alcoolisme
ISPA, Case postale 203
1000 Lausanne 13
Switzerland

United Kingdom
Alcoholics Anonymous
11 Redcliffe Gardens
London SW 10
United Kingdom

Government Advisory Committee on
    Alcoholism
Dept. of Health and Social Security
Alexander Fleming House
Elephantine and Castle
London SE1
United Kingdom

Institute of Psychiatry
Addiction Research Unit
DeCrespigny Park
London SE5
United Kingdom

Medical Council on Alcoholism
3 Grosvenor Crescent
London SW1
United Kingdom

National Council on Alcoholism
(Same as the Medical Council on
    Alcoholism)

Venezuela
Division de Higiene Mental
Ministerio de Sanidad
Edificio Sur, Picso 8,
Centro Simon Bolivar
Caracas 1010,
Venezuela

SELECTED ENGLISH-LANGUAGE JOURNALS AND PERIODICALS

Alcohol Health and Research World
(Publication of the National Institute on
    Alcohol Abuse and Alcoholism)
P. O. Box 2345
Rockville, MD 20852
Quarterly

Alcoholism: The National Magazine
P. O. Box C19051
Queen Anne Station

Seattle, WA 98109
Bimonthly

The Alcoholism Report
(Newsletter for professionals in the field of
    alcoholism)
744 National Press Building
Washington, DC 20045-1753
Twice monthly

American Journal of Drug and Alcohol Abuse
Marcel Dekker, Inc.
270 Madison Avenue
New York, NY 10016
Four times a year

British Journal of Addiction
(Publication of The Society for the Study of Addiction to Alcohol and Other Drugs)
Longman Group, Ltd.
43/45 Annandale Street
Edinburgh, Scotland EH7 4AT
United Kingdom
Quarterly

British Journal on Alcohol and Alcoholism
(Publication of the Medical Council on Alcoholism)
3 Grosvenor Crescent
London SW1X 7EE
United Kingdom
Quarterly

Digest of Alcoholism Theory and Application (DATA)
(Publication of the Johnson Institute)
10700 Olson Memorial Highway
Minneapolis, MN 55441-6199
Quarterly

Drug and Alcohol Dependence
(Published under the auspices of the International Council on Alcohol and Alcoholism)
Elsevier Sequoia, S. A.
P. O. Box 851
1001 Lausanne 1, Switzerland
Monthly

The Forum
(International monthly journal of Al-Anon)

Al-Anon Family Group Headquarters, Inc.
1 Park Avenue
New York, NY 10016
Monthly

The Grapevine
(International monthly journal of Alcoholics Anonymous)
The Alcoholics Anonymous Grapevine, Inc.
468 Park Avenue South
New York, NY 10016
Monthly

The Journal
(Newspaper)
Addiction Research Foundation
33 Russell Street
Toronto, Ontario M5S 2S1
Canada
Monthly

Journal on Alcohol and Drug Education
(Publication of the Education Section of the Alcohol and Drug Problems Association of North America)
1120 East Oakland, P. O. Box 10212
Lansing, MI 48901
Four times a year

Journal of Studies on Alcohol
(Publication of the Center of Alcohol Studies, Rutgers University)
P. O. Box 969
Piscataway, NJ 08854
Monthly

U. S. Journal of Drug and Alcohol Dependence
(Newspaper)
2119-A Hollywood Boulevard
Hollywood, FL 33020
Monthly

BIBLIOGRAPHY

Ackerman, Robert J. *Children of Alcoholics*. Hollywood, Fla.: Health Communications, 1978.

Ackoff, R. L.; Gupta, S.; and Minas, J. S. *Scientific Method: Optimizing Applied Research Decisions*. New York: John Wiley and Sons, 1969.

Addeo, Edmund G., and Addeo, Jovita R. *Why Our Children Drink*. Englewood Cliffs, N.J.: Prentice-Hall, 1975.

Addiction Research Foundation. *Alcohol, Drugs and Traffic Safety*. Toronto, 1976.

———. *Alcohol—Public Education and Social Policy*. Toronto, 1981.

———. *The Forgotten Children*. Toronto, 1969.

———. *Halfway Houses for Alcoholics*. Toronto, 1978.

———. *Proposal for a Comprehensive Health-Oriented Alcohol Control Policy in Ontario*. Toronto, 1973.

———. *R.I.D.E.—A Driving-While-Impaired Countermeasure Program*. Toronto, 1979.

———. *Statistical Supplement to the ARF Annual Report*. Toronto, 1982.

———. *The Treatment of Alcoholics: An Ontario Perspective*. Toronto, 1978.

Ahlstrom, Salme. *Trends in Drinking Habits among Finnish Youth from the Beginnings of the 1960s to the Late 1970s*. Helsinki: Social Research Institute of Alcohol Studies, 1979.

Aitken, P. P. *Ten-to-Fourteen-Year-Olds and Alcohol: A Development Study in the Central Region of Scotland*. Edinburgh: Scottish Health Education Unit, 1978.

Akins, Carl, and Beschner, George. *Ethnography: A Research Tool for Policymakers in the Drug and Alcohol Fields*. Rockville, Md.: National Institute on Drug Abuse, 1980.

Al-Anon Family Group Headquarters. *Al-Anon Faces Alcoholism*. New York, 1973.

———. *Alateen—Hope for Children of Alcoholics*. New York, 1973.

———. *The Dilemma of the Alcoholic Marriage*. New York, 1967.

———. *Living with an Alcoholic*. New York, 1978.

———. *Youth and the Alcoholic Parent*. New York, 1960.

Alcoholics Anonymous World Services. *The Alcoholic Husband*. New York, 1954.

———. *The Alcoholic Wife*. New York, 1954.

———. *Alcoholics Anonymous*. New York, 1955.

———. *Alcoholics Anonymous Comes of Age: A Brief History of A.A.* New York, 1957.

———. *Alcoholism—The Illness*. New York, 1959.

———. *As Bill Sees It*. New York, 1967.

———. *Dr. Bob and the Good Oldtimers: A Biography with Recollections of Early A.A. in the Midwest*. New York, 1980.

———. *Sedatives, Stimulants, and the Alcoholic*. New York, 1964.

———. *The Story of How Many Thousands of Men and Women Have Recovered from Alcoholism*. New York, 1955.

———. *Twelve Steps and Twelve Traditions*. New York, 1952.

Allen, H. W. *A History of Wine*. London: Faber and Faber, 1961.

American Medical Association. *Manual on Alcoholism.* Chicago, 1977.

Anastasi, Anne. *Psychological Testing.* New York: Macmillan Co., 1961.

Anderson, D. S., and Gadaleto, A. F. *That Happy Feeling: An Innovative Model for a Campus Alcohol Education Program.* Atlanta: Southern Area Alcohol Education and Training Program, 1979.

Anderson, J. R., and Bower, G. H. *Human Associative Memory.* Washington, D.C.: Winston and Sons, 1973.

Angmann and Associates. *Health Insurance Coverage of Alcoholism Benefits: Results of a National Survey and Implications for California.* San Francisco: California State Senate Committee on Health and Welfare, n.d.

Ansbacher, H., and Ansbacher, R. *The Individual Psychology of Alfred Adler.* New York: Basic Books, 1946.

Archard, Peter. *Vagrancy, Alcoholism and Social Control.* London: Macmillan and Co., 1979.

Armor, David J.; Polich, J. Michael; and Stambul, Harriet B. *Alcoholism and Treatment.* New York: John Wiley and Sons, 1978.

Asbury, Herbert. *The Great Illusion, an Informal History of Prohibition.* Garden City, N.Y.: Doubleday and Co., 1950.

Asimi, A. A. D. *Teenage Drinking Behavior: Report of a Survey in Northwestern Ontario.* Thunder Bay, Ont.: Lakehead University, 1971.

Australian Foundation on Alcoholism and Drug Dependence. *National Alcohol and Drug Dependence Multidisciplinary Institute, August 27 to September 1, 1978.* Canberra, 1978.

Ausubel, David P. *Drug Addiction: Physiological, Psychological and Sociological Aspects.* New York: Random House, 1958.

Avogaro, P.; Sirtori, C. R.; and Tremoli, E. *Metabolic Effects of Alcohol.* New York: Elsevier, 1979.

Ayars, Albert L., and Milgram, Gail G. *The Teenager and Alcohol.* New York: Richards Rosen Press, 1970.

Bacon, Margaret, and Jones, Mary Brush. *Teen-Age Drinking.* New York: Thomas Y. Crowell, 1968.

Bacon, Selden D. *Alcoholism: Nature of the Problem.* New York: National Council on Alcoholism, 1964.

————. *Understanding Alcoholism.* Philadelphia: American Academy of Political and Social Science, 1958.

Bahr, Howard M. *Skid Row: An Introduction to Disaffiliation.* New York: Oxford University Press, 1973.

Bailey, C. B.; Ginter, D. J.; and Woodlock, B. K. *Handbook for Alcoholism Counselors.* Cleveland: Alcoholism Services of Cleveland, 1978.

Bain, D.; Taylor, L.; Bohm, P. E.; Boudreau, R. J.; Chaudron, D. C.; and Sharma, N. *Counseling Skills for Alcoholism Treatment Services: A Literature Review and Experience Survey.* Ottawa: Health Promotion Directorate, Health and Welfare Canada, 1980.

Bandura, Albert. *Principles of Behavior Modification.* New York: Holt, Rinehart and Winston, 1969.

Barnard, Charles P. *Families, Alcoholism and Therapy.* Springfield, Ill.: Charles C. Thomas, 1981.

Barnes, G. M.; Abel, E. L.; and Ernst, C. A. S. *Alcohol and the Elderly: A Comprehensive Bibliography.* Westport, Conn.: Greenwood Press, 1980.

Barnes, T., and Price, S. *Interaction of Alcohol and Other Drugs—Supplement.* Toronto: Addiction Research Foundation, 1973.

Barr, H. L., and Cohen, A. *The Problem-Drinking Drug Addict.* Washington, D.C.: National Institute on Drug Abuse, 1979.

Bean, Margaret H., and Zinberg, Norman E. *Dynamic Approaches to the Understanding and Treatment of Alcoholism.* New York: Free Press, 1981.

Beauchamp, Dan E. *Beyond Alcoholism: Alcohol and Public Health Policy.* Philadelphia: Temple University Press, 1980.

Begleiter, H. *Biological Effects of Alcohol.* New York: Plenum Press, 1980.

Bell, Judith, and Billington, D. Rex. *Annotated Bibliography of Health Education Research Completed in Britain from 1948–1978.* Edinburgh: Scottish Health Education Unit, 1980.

Bemko, Jane. *Substance Abuse Book Review Index 1980.* Toronto: Addiction Research Foundation, 1981.

Benjamin, F. B. *Alcohol, Drugs and Traffic Safety: Where Do We Go from Here?* Springfield, Ill.: Charles C. Thomas, 1980.

Bergin, A. E., and Strupp, H. H. *Changing Frontiers in the Science of Psychotherapy.* Chicago: Aldine Atherton, 1972.

Billings, J. S. *The Liquor Problem.* Boston: Houghton Mifflin and Co., 1905.

Birnbaum, Isabel M., and Parker, Elizabeth S. *Alcohol and Human Memory.* Hillsdale, N.J.: Lawrence Erlbaum Associates, 1977; dist. John Wiley and Sons.

Black, Claudia. *My Dad Loves Me, My Dad Has a Disease.* Newport Beach, Calif.: ACT, 1980.

Blakeslee, Alton, and Sullivan, Brian. *Alcohol: The New Teen-Age Turn-On.* New York: Associated Press, 1975.

Blane, H. T. *The Personality of the Alcoholic: Guises of Dependency.* New York: Harper and Row, 1968.

———. *The Role of the Nurse in the Care of the Alcoholic Patient in the General Hospital.* Boston: Division of Alcoholism, Massachusetts Department of Public Health, 1960.

———, and Chafetz, M. E. *Youth, Alcohol, and Social Policy.* New York: Plenum Press, 1979.

Bloch, Sidney. *An Introduction to the Psychotherapies.* Oxford: Oxford University Press, 1979.

Block, Jean Libman. *Alcohol and the Adolescent.* New York: National Council on Alcoholism, n.d.

Block, Marvin, A. *Alcohol and Alcoholism: Drinking and Dependence.* Belmont, Calif.: Wadsworth, 1970.

———. *Could Your Child Become an Alcoholic?* New York: National Council on Alcoholism, 1960.

———. *Guide Lines for Admission of Alcoholics to Hospitals.* New York: Smithers, Christopher D., Foundation, 1968.

Blocker, Jack S., Jr. *Alcohol, Reform and Society: The Liquor Issue in Social Context.* Westport, Conn.: Greenwood Press, 1979.

Blomberg, R. D.; Preusser, D. F.; Hale, A.; and Ulmer, R. G. *A Comparison of Alcohol Involvement in Pedestrians and Pedestrian Casualties.* Springfield, Va.: National Technical Information Service, 1979.

Blum, Eva M., and Blum, Richard H. *Alcoholism, Modern Psychological Approaches to Treatment.* San Francisco: Jossey-Bass, 1967.

Blumberg, Leonard; Shipley, T. E.; and Shandler, I. W. *Skid Row and Its Alternatives.* Philadelphia: Temple University Press, 1973.

————, and Barsky, Stephen F. *Liquor and Poverty: Skid Row as a Human Condition.* monograph no. 13. New Brunswick, N.J.: Rutgers Center of Alcohol Studies, 1978.

Blume, Sheila B. *Fetal Alcohol Syndrome: Task Force Report to the Governor.* Albany: New York State Division of Alcoholism and Alcohol Abuse, 1979.

Bogue, Donald. *Skid Row in American Cities.* Chicago: University of Chicago Press, 1963.

Bolger, J. *A Study of the Legal Drinking Age Policy in Ontario.* Toronto: Centre for Urban and Community Studies and The Child in the City Programme, University of Toronto, 1979.

Bortenstein, R. F.; Crowther, R. F.; Shumate, R. P.; Ziel, W. B.; and Zylman, R. *The Role of the Drinking Driver in Traffic Accidents.* Bloomington: Department of Police Administration, Indiana University, 1964.

Brandsma, Jeffrey M.; Maultsby, M. C.; and Welsh, R. J. *Outpatient Treatment of Alcoholism: A Review and Comparative Study.* Baltimore: University Park Press, 1980.

Brasch, R. *How Did It Begin?* New York: David McKay Co., 1965.

Brill, Leon, and Winick, Charles. *The Yearbook of Substance Use and Abuse.* Vol. II. New York: Human Sciences Press, 1980.

Brisolara, Ashton. *The Alcoholic Employee: A Handbook of Useful Guidelines.* New York: Human Sciences Press, 1979.

British Royal College of Psychiatrists. *Alcohol and Alcoholism.* Report of a Special Committee of the Royal College of Psychiatrists. London: Tavistock Publications, 1979.

Bronetto, J. *Alcohol Price, Alcohol Consumption and Death by Liver Cirrhosis.* Toronto: Addiction Research Foundation, 1960–63.

Brooks, Cathleen. *The Secret Everyone Knows.* San Diego: Operation Cork, 1981.

Bruun, Kettil, and Hauge, Kagnar. *Drinking Habits among Northern Youth.* Helsinki: Finnish Foundation for Alcohol Studies, 1963.

————; Koura, E.; Popham, R. E.; and Seeley, J. R. *Liver Cirrhosis Mortality as a Means to Measure the Prevalence of Alcoholism.* Helsinki: Finnish Foundation for Alcohol Studies, 1960.

Bureau of National Affairs. *Alcoholism and Employee Relations: A BNA Special Report.* Washington, D.C., 1978.

Bush, Patricia J. *Drugs, Alcohol & Sex.* New York: Richard Marek, 1980.

Busse, S.; Mulloy, C. T.; Weise, C. E.; Chamberlain, C. M.; and Tetera, D. R. *Disulfiram in the Treatment of Alcoholism: An Annotated Bibliography.* Toronto: Addiction Research Foundation, 1978.

Butters, Nelson, and Cermak, Laird S. *Alcoholic Korsakoff's Syndrome: An Information-Processing Approach to Amnesia.* New York: Academic Press, 1980.

Cahalan, Donald. *Implications of American Drinking Practices and Attitudes for Prevention and Treatment of Alcoholism.* Berkeley: Social Research Group, School of Public Health, University of California, n.d.

————. *Problem Drinkers.* San Francisco: Jossey-Bass, 1970.

————, and Room, Robin. *Problem Drinking among American Men.* New Brunswick, N.J.: Rutgers Center of Alcohol Studies, 1974.

————; Cisin, I. H.; and Crossley, H. M. *American Drinking Practices.* New Haven: College and University Press, 1969.

————. *American Drinking Practices: A National Survey of Behavior and Attitudes.* monograph no. 6. New Brunswick, N.J.: Rutgers Center of Alcohol Studies, 1969.

California Department of Public Health. *Alcoholism and California: Follow-up Studies of Treated Alcoholics; Description of Studies.* Berkeley, 1961.

Callaway, E.; Jones, R. T.; Stone, G. C.; Peeke, S. C.; and Doyle, J. *Neuropsychological Studies of Alcohol: Final Report.* Springfield, Va.: National Technical Information Service, 1978.

Camberwell Council on Alcoholism. *Women and Alcohol.* New York: Methuen, 1980.

Carroll, Charles R. *Alcohol: Use, Non-Use, and Abuse.* Dubuque: William C. Brown, 1970.

Carroll, R. S. *What Price Alcohol?* New York: Macmillan Co., 1941.

Catanzaro, Ronald J. *Alcoholism.* Springfield, Ill.: Charles C. Thomas, 1968.

Catlin, C. E. G. *Liquor Control.* New York: Henry Holt and Co., 1931.

Cavan, S. *Liquor License: An Ethnography of Bar Behavior.* Chicago: Aldine Publishing Co., 1966.

Chafetz, Morris E., *Liquor: The Servant of Man.* Boston: Little, Brown and Co., 1965.

————. *Why Drinking Can Be Good for You.* New York: Stein and Day, 1976.

————. and Demone, Harold W., Jr. *Alcoholism and Society.* New York: Oxford University Press, 1962.

————; Blane, Howard T.; and Hill, Marjorie J. *Frontiers of Alcoholism.* New York: Science House, 1970.

Chalfant, H. Paul; Roper, B. S.; and Rivera-Worley, C. *Social and Behavioral Aspects of Female Alcoholism: An Annotated Bibliography.* Westport, Conn.: Greenwood Press, 1980.

Cherrington, Ernest H. *The Evolution of Prohibition in the United States of America.* Westerville, Ohio: American Issue Press, 1920.

Cicchinelli, L.; Potter, A.; and Halpern, J. *The Relationship between Yearly Earnings and Client Characteristics for Persons Receiving Alcoholism Treatment.* Springfield, Va.: National Technical Information Service, 1978.

Clark, P. M. S., and Kricka, L. J. *Medical Consequences of Alcohol Abuse.* New York: Halsted Press, and John Wiley and Sons, 1980.

Clinebell, Howard J. *Understanding and Counseling the Alcoholic.* New York: Abingdon Press, 1968.

Cohen, Sidney. *The Substance Abuse Problems.* New York: Haworth Press, 1981.

Coleman, James S. *The Adolescent Society.* New York: Free Press, 1961.

Collier, D. F., and Somfay, S. A. *Ascent from Skid Row: the Bon Accord Community 1967–1973.* Toronto: Addiction Research Foundation, 1974.

Collins, James J., Jr. *Drinking and Crime: Perspectives on the Relationships between Alcohol Consumption and Criminal Behavior.* New York: Guilford Publications, 1981.

Colvin, D. L. *Prohibition in the United States.* New York: George H. Doran Co., 1926.

Connecticut State Department of Mental Health, Alcoholism Division. *Teaching about Alcohol in Connecticut Schools.* Hartford, 1966.

Cook, Jim, and Lewington, Mike. *Images of Alcoholism.* London: British Film Institute, 1979; New York: New York Zoetrope, 1980.

Cooper, M. L. *Private Health Insurance Benefits for Alcoholism, Drug Abuse and Mental Illness.* Washington, D.C.: Intergovernmental Health Policy Project, 1979.

Cooper, W. E.; Schwar, T. G.; and Smith, L. S. *Alcohol, Drugs and Road Traffic.* Cape Town: Juta and Co., 1979.

Corrigan, Eileen M. *Alcoholic Women in Treatment.* New York: Oxford University Press, 1980.

Corsini, Raymond J. *Current Psychotherapies,* 2nd ed. Itasca, Ill.: F. E. Peacock Publishers, 1979.

Costales, Clare, and Berry, Jo. *Alcoholism: The Way Back to Reality.* Glendale, Calif.: Regal Books Division, G/L Publications, 1980.

Cox, Ann E. *Training Guidelines and Workbook for the Behavioral Management of Intoxicated and Disruptive Clients.* Toronto: Addiction Research Foundation, 1981.

Cronbach, Lee J. *Essentials of Psychological Testing.* New York: Harper and Row, 1960.

Cross, Wilbur. *Kids & Booze: What You Must Know to Help Them.* New York: Dutton and Co., 1979.

Crowder, R. G. *Principles of Learning and Memory.* Hillsdale, N.J.: Lawrence Erlbaum Associates, 1976.

Crumbaugh, James C.; Wood, William M.; and Wood, W. Chadwick. *Logotherapy: New Help for Problem Drinkers.* Chicago: Nelson-Hall, 1980.

Curlee-Salisbury, Joan. *When the Woman You Love Is an Alcoholic.* St. Meinrad, Ind.: Abbey Press, 1978.

Cutler, R., and Storm, T. *Drinking Practices in Three British Columbia Cities. II. Student Survey.* Vancouver: Alcoholism Foundation of British Columbia, 1973.

Czechowicz, D. *Detoxification Treatment Manual.* Washington, D.C.: U.S. Government Printing Office, 1979.

Dahlstrom, W. G., and Welsch, G. S. *An MMPI Handbook: A Guide to Use in Clinical Practice and Research.* Minneapolis: University of Minnesota Press, 1965.

David, Kenneth, and Cowley, James. *Pastoral Care in Schools and Colleges.* London: Edward Arnold, n.d.

Dawkins, Marvin P. *Alcohol and the Black Community: Exploratory Studies of Selected Issues.* Saratoga, Calif.: Century Twenty-One, 1980.

Demone, Harold W. *Alcohol Education: What Does a Teacher Need to Know to Teach?* Montpelier, Vt.: Vermont State Department of Education, 1960.

Dennison, Darwin; Prevet, T.; and Affleck, M. *Alcohol and Behavior: An Activated Education Approach.* St. Louis: Mosby, 1980.

Diehm, A. P.; Seaborn, R. F.; and Wilson, G. C. *Alcohol in Australia: Problems and Programmes.* New York: McGraw-Hill Book Co., 1978.

Dimas, George C. *Alcohol Education in Oregon Schools.* Portland: Alcohol Studies and Rehabilitation Section, Oregon State Mental Health Division, 1964.

Distilled Spirits Council of the United States. *DISCUS Facts Book 1979. The Beverage Alcohol Industry: Public Attitudes and Economic Patterns.* Washington, D.C., 1980.

————. *Distilled Spirits Industry Annual Statistical Review 1979.* Washington, D.C., 1980.

Dollard, John, and Miller, Neal E. *Personality and Psychotherapy.* New York: McGraw-Hill Book Co., 1950.

Dorchester, Daniel. *The Liquor Problem in All Ages.* New York: Phillips and Hunt, 1884.

Douglass, R. L.; Wagenarr, A. C.; and Barkey, P. M. *Alcohol Availability, Consumption and the Incidence of Alcohol-Related Social and Health Problems in Michigan.* Ann Arbor: Highway Safety Research Institute, University of Michigan, 1979.

Downard, William L. *Dictionary of the History of the American Brewing and Distilling Industries.* Westport, Conn.: Greenwood Press, 1980.

Drews, Toby R. *Getting Them Sober.* Plainfield, N.J.: Haven Books, 1980.

Durfee, C. H. *To Drink or Not to Drink.* New York: Longmans and Green, 1937.

Durkheim, Emile. *Suicide.* New York: Free Press, 1962.

Du-Torr, B. M. *Drugs, Rituals, and Altered States of Consciousness.* Rotterdam: A. A. Balkema, 1977.

Eddy, Cristen C., and Ford, John L. *Alcoholism in Women.* Dubuque: Kendall/Hunt, 1980.

Edwards, Griffith, and Grant, Marcus. *Alcohol Treatment in Transition.* Baltimore: University Park Press, 1980.

————. *Alcoholism: New Knowledge and New Responses.* London: Crown Helm, 1977.

Efron, Daniel E., ed. *Psychopharmacology: A Review of Progress.* Public Health Service Publication, no. 1836. Washington, D.C.: Public Health Service, 1968.

Emerson, Edward Randolph. *Beverages, Past and Present.* New York: G. P. Putnam's Sons, 1908.

Emerson, Haven. *Alcohol: Its Effects on Man.* New York: Appleton-Century-Crofts, 1934.

Emerson, Vivian J.; Holleyhead, R.; Isaacs, M. D. J.; Fuller, N. A.; and Hunt, D. J. *The Measurement of Breath Alcohol: The Laboratory Evaluation of Substantive Breath Test Equipment and the Report of an Operational Police Trial.* Harrogate, England: Forensic Society; Edinburgh, Scotland; Scottish Academic Press, 1980.

Engelmann, Larry. *Intemperance: The Lost War against Liquor.* New York: Free Press, 1979.

Englebardt, Stanley L. *Kids and Alcohol—the Deadliest Drug.* New York: Lothrop, Lee and Shepard Co., 1975.

Engs, Ruth C. *Responsible Drug and Alcohol Use.* New York: Macmillan Co., 1979.

Entine, A. D. *The Relationship between the Number of Sales Outlets and the Consumption of Alcoholic Beverages in New York and Other States.* Albany: New York State Moreland Commission of the Alcoholic Beverage Control Law, 1963.

Erdoes, Richard. *Saloons of the Old West.* New York: Alfred A. Knopf, 1979.

Eriksson, K.; Sinclair, J. D.; and Kiianmaa, K. *Animal Models of Alcohol Research.* New York: Academic Press, 1980.

Estes, Nada J.; Smith-DiJulio, K.; and Heinemann, M. E. *Nursing Diagnosis of the Alcoholic Person.* St. Louis: Mosby, 1980.

Everest, Allan S. *Rum across the Border: The Prohibition Era in Northern New York.* Syracuse: Syracuse University Press, 1978.

Ewing, John A. *Drinking to Your Health.* n.p. Reston, Va., 1981.

————, and Rouse, Beatrice A. *Drinking. Alcohol in American Society—Issues and Current Research.* Chicago: Nelson-Hall, 1978.

Fann, William E.; Karacan, I.; Pokorny, A. D.; and Williams, R. L. *Phenomenology and Treatment of Alcoholism.* New York: SP Medical and Scientific Books, 1980.

Faris, Robert E. L., and Dunham, H. Warren. *Mental Disorders in Urban Areas.* New York: Hofner, 1939.

Feit, Marvin D. *Management and Administration of Drug and Alcohol Programs.* Springfield, Ill.: Charles C. Thomas, 1979.

Fenichel, Otto. *The Psychoanalytic Theory of Neurosis.* New York: W. W. Norton and Co., 1945.

Fields, W. C. *Never Trust a Man Who Doesn't Drink.* Compiled by Paul Mason. New York: Stonyan Books, 1971.

Fillmore, K. M.; Bacon, S. D.; and Hyman, M. *The 27-Year Longitudinal Panel Study of Drinking by Students in College, 1949–1976. Final Report.* Springfield, Va.: National Technical Information Service, 1979.

Fitzgibbon, Constantine. *Drink.* New York: Doubleday and Co., 1979.

Fleit, L. *Alcohol and Sexuality: A Handbook for the Counselor/Therapist.* Arlington, Va.: H/P Publishing Co., 1979.

Fleming, Alice. *Alcohol, the Delightful Poison.* New York: Dell Publishing Co., 1975.

Follmann, Joseph F., Jr. *Helping the Troubled Employee.* New York: Amacom, 1978.

Forbes, Thomas Rogers. *Crowner's Quest.* The American Philosophical Society, *Transactions,* vol. 68, part I. Philadelphia, 1978.

Ford, J. C. *Depth Psychology, Morality and Alcoholism.* Weston, Mass.: Weston College Press, 1951.

Fort, Joel. *Alcohol: Our Biggest Drug Problem.* New York: McGraw-Hill Book Co., 1973.

Fowler, R. D., Sr. *Studies in Alcoholism.* Montgomery: Alabama Commission on Alcoholism, 1960.

Fox, Ruth. *The Alcoholic Spouse.* New York: National Council on Alcoholism, 1956.

———. *Alcoholism: Behavioral Research and Therapeutic Approaches.* New York: Springer Publishing Co., 1967.

———, and Lyon, Peter. *Alcoholism: Its Scope, Cause and Treatment.* New York: Random House, 1955.

Freed, Earl X. *An Alcoholic Personality?* Thorofare, N.J.: Charles B. Slack, 1979.

Freedman, M., and Kaplan, H. I. *Comprehensive Textbook of Psychiatry.* Baltimore: Williams and Wilkins, 1967.

Freeman, K. M., and Koegler, R. R. *From Skid Row to the Olympics.* Castaic, Calif.: Institute of Creative Leisure, 1978.

Freudenberger, Herbert J., and Richelson, Geraldine. *The High Cost of High Achievement.* Garden City, N.Y.: Anchor Press, 1980.

Furnas, J. C. *The Life and Times of the Late Demon Rum.* New York: G. P. Putnam's Sons, 1965.

Galanter, Marc. *Alcohol and Drug Abuse in Medical Education.* Rockville, Md.: National Institute on Drug Abuse, 1980.

———. *Currents in Alcoholism. Vol. VI: Treatment and Rehabilitation and Epidemiology.* Ontario: Academic Press, 1979.

———. *Currents in Alcoholism. Vol. VII: Recent Advances in Research and Treatment.* Ontario: Academic Press, 1980.

Gastineau, Clifford F.; Darby, W. J.; and Turner, T. B. *Fermented Food Beverages in Nutrition.* New York: Academic Press, 1979.

Gerard, D. L., and Saenger, G. *Out-Patient Treatment of Alcoholism: A Study of Outcome and Its Determinants.* Toronto: University of Toronto Press, 1966.

Gerstel, E. K.; Mason, R. E.; Piserchia, P. V.; and Kristiansen, P. L. *A Pilot Study of the Social Contexts of Drinking and Correlates.* Research Triangle Park, N.C.: Research Triangle Institute, 1975.

Gibbins, R. I. *Chronic Alcoholism.* Brookside Monograph, no. I. Ontario: Alcoholism Research Foundation, 1953.

Gibbins, Robert J; Israel, Yedy; Kalant, Harold; Popham, Robert E.; Schmidt, Wolfgang; and Smart, Reginald G. *Research Advances in Alcohol and Drug Problems, Vol. 1.* New York: John Wiley and Sons, 1974.

———. *Research Advances in Alcohol and Drug Problems, Vol. 2.* New York: John Wiley and Sons, 1975.

———. *Research Advances in Alcohol and Drug Problems, Vol. 3.* New York: John Wiley and Sons, 1976.

Gitlow, Stanley E., and Peyser, Herbert S. *Alcoholism: A Practical Treatment Guide.* New York: Grune and Stratton, 1980.

Glaser, Frederick B.; Greenberg, Stephanie W.; and Barrett, Morris. *A Systems Approach to Alcohol Treatment*. Toronto: Addiction Research Foundation, 1978.

Gonzalez, Gerardo M. *Procedures and Resource Materials for Developing a Campus Alcohol Abuse Prevention Program: A Tested Model*. Gainesville: University of Florida, 1978.

Goodman, Donald. *Is Alcoholism Hereditary?* Oxford, New York and London: Oxford University Press, 1976.

Goodman, L., and Gilman, A. *The Pharmacological Basis of Therapeutics*. 2nd ed. New York: Macmillan Co., 1955.

Goodwin, Donald W., and Erickson, Carlton K. *Alcoholism and Affective Disorders: Clinical, Genetic, and Biochemical Studies*. New York: SP Medical and Scientific Books, 1979.

Gottheil, Edward; McLellan, A. Thomas; and Druley, Keith A. *Substance Abuse and Psychiatric Illness: Proceedings of the Second Annual Coatsville-Jefferson Conference on Addiction, 1978*. New York: Pergamon Press, 1980.

————, and Alterman, Arthur I. *Addiction Research and Treatment: Converging Trends*. London: Pergamon Publishing Co., 1979.

Grant, Marcus; Plant, Martin; and Saunders, W. *Drinking and Alcohol Problems in Scotland*. Edinburgh: Scottish Health Education Unit, 1980.

Greeley, Andrew M.; McCready, William C.; and Theisen, G. *Ethnic Drinking Subcultures*. New York: Bergin Publishers, 1980.

Griffin, Tom, and Svendsen, Roger. *The Student Assistance Program: How It Works*. Center City, Minn.: Hazelden, 1980.

Grimm, Anne C., and Huber, Kristina R. *Alcohol/Safety Public Information Materials Catalog, No. 5*. Ann Arbor: University of Michigan, 1981.

Gross, Milton M., ed. *Alcohol Intoxication and Withdrawal, Experimental Studies*. New York: Plenum Press, 1973.

————. *Alcohol Intoxication and Withdrawal, Experimental Studies II*. New York: Plenum Press, 1975.

————. *Alcohol Intoxication and Withdrawal—IIIA. Biological Aspects of Ethanol*. New York: Plenum Press, 1976.

————. *Alcohol Intoxication and Withdrawal—IIIB. Studies in Alcohol Dependence*. New York: Plenum Press, 1976.

Group Health Association of America. *Alcoholism Services Handbook for Prepaid Group Plans*. Springfield, Va.: National Technical Information Service, 1979.

Groupe, Vincent. *Alcoholism Rehabilitation: Methods and Experiences of Private Rehabilitation Centers*. New Brunswick, N.J.: Rutgers Center of Alcohol Studies, 1978.

Groves, W. E.; Rossi, P. H.; and Grafstein, D. *Study of Life Styles and Campus Communities: Preliminary Report*. Baltimore: Johns Hopkins University, 1970.

Gusfield, Joseph R. *The Culture of Public Problems: Drinking-Driving and the Symbolic Order*. Chicago: University of Chicago Press, 1981.

————. *Symbolic Crusade: Status Politics and the American Temperance Movement*. Urbana: University of Illinois Press, 1963.

Guthrie, D. *A History of Medicine*. London: Nelson and Sons, 1945.

Gwinner, Paul, and Grant, Marcus. *What's Your Poison*. London: British Broadcasting Corp., n.d.

Hackwood, Frederick W. *Inns, Ales and Drinking Customs of Old England*. New York: Sturgiss and Walton Co., 1909.

Hamer, John, and Steinbring, Jack. *Alcohol and Native Peoples of the North*. Lanham, Md.: University Press of America, 1980.

Hammond, R. L. *Almost All You Ever Wanted to Know about Alcohol but Didn't Know Who to Ask*. Lansing: American Business Men's Research Foundation, 1978.

Harper, Frederick D. *Alcoholism Treatment and Black Americans*. Rockville, Md.: National Clearinghouse for Alcohol Information, 1979.

———. *Jogotherapy: Jogging as a Therapeutic Strategy*. Alexandria, Va.: Douglass Publishers, 1979.

Harris, D. H., and Howlett, J. B. *Visual Detection of Driving While Intoxicated*. Springfield, Va.: National Technical Information Service, 1979.

Hartford, T. C.; Parker, D. A.; and Light, L. *Normative Approaches to the Prevention of Alcohol Abuse and Alcoholism*. Rockville, Md.: National Institute on Alcohol Abuse and Alcoholism, 1980.

Haskins, James. *Teen-age Alcoholism*. New York: Hawthorn Books, 1976.

Heath, Dwight B., and Cooper, A. M. *Alcohol Use and World Cultures: A Comprehensive Bibliography of Anthropological Sources*. Toronto: Addiction Research Foundation, 1981.

Himwich, H. E. *Alcoholism: Basic Aspects and Treatment*. Washington, D.C.: American Association for the Advancement of Science, 1951.

Hofmann, Frederick G. *A Handbook on Drug and Alcohol Abuse: The Biomedical Aspects*. New York: Oxford University Press, 1975.

Hollingshead, A. B., and Redlich, F. C. *Social Class and Mental Illness*. New York: John Wiley and Sons, 1958.

Hollis, S. *Casework: a Psychosocial Therapy*. New York: Random House, 1965.

Hooton, C. *What Shall We Say about Alcohol?* New York: Abingdon Press, 1960.

Hore, Brian D., and Plant, Martin A. *Alcohol Problems in Employment*. London: Croom Helm, 1981.

Hornik, Edith Lynn. *You and Your Alcoholic Parent*. New York: Association Press, 1974.

Houthakker, H. S., and Taylor, Lester D. *Consumer Demand in the United States: Analyses and Projections*. Cambridge, Mass.: Harvard University Press, 1970.

Howard, Marion. *Did I Have a Good Time? Teenage Drinking*. New York: Continuum, 1980.

Huelke, D. F., and Davis, R. A. *Pedestrian Fatalities*. Ann Arbor: Highway Safety Research Institute, University of Michigan, 1969.

Hughes, H. E., and Schneider, D. *The Man from Ida Grove: A Senator's Personal Story*. Lincoln, Va.: Chosen Books, 1979.

Hugunin, M. B. *Helping the Impaired Physician. Proceedings of the AMA Conference on "The Impaired Physician: Answering the Challenge," February 4–6, 1977: Atlanta, Georgia*. Chicago: American Medical Association, 1979.

Hyde, Margaret O. *Alcohol: Drink or Drug?* New York: McGraw-Hill Book Co., 1974.

Idestrom, Carl-Magnus, ed. *Alcohol and Brain Research*. Copenhagen: Munksgaard, 1980.

Institute of Medicine, Division of Health Promotion and Disease Prevention. *Alcoholism, Alcohol Abuse and Related Problems: Opportunities for Research*. Washington, D.C.: Academy Press, 1980.

Israel, Yedy, and Mardones, Jorge, eds. *Biological Basis of Alcoholism*. New York: John Wiley and Sons, 1971.

Jackson, Michael. *The World Guide to Beer*. New York: Ballantine Books, 1978.

Jacobs, Michael R. *Problems Presented by Alcoholic Clients*. Toronto: Addiction Research Foundation, 1981.

Jaffe, Jerome H.; Peterson, Robert; and Hodgson, Ray. *Addictions: Issues and Answers.* London: Harper and Row, 1980.

Jellinek, E. M. *The Alcoholism Complex.* New York: Smithers, Christopher D., Foundation, 1960.

———. *The Disease Concept of Alcoholism.* New Haven: Hillhouse Press, 1960.

———. *Government Programs on Alcoholism: A Review of the Activities in Some Foreign Countries.* Ottawa: Department of National Health and Welfare, 1963.

Jessor, Richard; Graves, T. D.; Hanson, R. C.; and Jessor, S. L. *Society, Personality, and Deviant Behavior.* New York: Holt, Rinehart and Winston, 1968.

Johns, T. R., and Pascarella, E. A. *An Assessment of the Limited Driving License Amendment to the North Carolina Statutes Relating to Drunk Driving.* Chapel Hill, N.C.: Highway Safety Research Center, University of North Carolina, 1971.

Johnston, Lloyd. *Drugs and American Youth.* Ann Arbor: Institute for Social Research, 1973.

Joint Commission on Accreditation of Hospitals. *Consolidated Standards for Child, Adolescent, and Adult Psychiatric Alcoholism and Drug Abuse Programs.* Chicago, 1979.

Jones, D. C.; Schlenger, W. E.; and Zelon, H. S. *Alcoholism Manpower Information System. Final Report.* Research Triangle Park, N.C.: Center for Health Studies, Research Triangle Institute, 1979.

Jones, R. K., and Joscelyn, K. B. *Alcohol and Highway Safety 1978: A Review of the State of Knowledge. (Summary Volume).* Springfield, Va.: National Technical Information Service, 1978.

Jordan, Donald K. *Alcohol Abuse Prevention: A Comprehensive Guide for Youth Organizations.* Boys' Club of America Project TEAM, 1978.

Josephson, E. *An Assessment of Statistics on Alcohol-Related Problems.* Washington, D.C.: Distilled Spirits Council of the United States, 1980.

Kalant, Oriana Josseau. *Alcohol and Drug Problems in Women.* Vol. 5. New York: Plenum Publishing Corp., 1980.

———, and Kalant, H. *Drugs, Society and Personal Choice.* Toronto: General Publishing, 1971.

Kane, Geoffrey P. *Inner-City Alcoholism: An Ecological Analysis and Cross-Cultural Study.* New York: Human Sciences Press, 1981.

Kant, F. *The Treatment of the Alcoholic.* Springfield, Ill.: Charles C. Thomas, 1954.

Kaufman, Edward, and Kaufmann, Pauline N. *Family Therapy of Drug and Alcohol Abuse.* New York: Gardner Press, 1979.

Keithahn, C. F. *The Brewing Industry: Staff Report of the Bureau of Economics, Federal Trade Commission.* Springfield, Va.: National Technical Information Service, 1978.

Keller, Mark, and McCormick, M. *A Dictionary of Words about Alcohol.* New Brunswick, N.J.: Rutgers Center of Alcohol Studies, 1968.

———, and Seeley, John R. *The Alcohol Language: With a Selected Vocabulary.* Toronto: University of Toronto Press, 1958.

Kellermann, Joseph L. *A Guide for the Family of the Alcoholic.* New York: National Council on Alcoholism, 1960.

Kemper Insurance Co. *A Neglected Area of Loss Reduction: What to Do about the Employee with a Drinking Problem.* Chicago, 1966.

Keniston, Kenneth. *Youth and Dissent: The Rise of a New Opposition.* New York: Harcourt Brace Jovanovich, 1971.

Kent, Patricia. *An American Woman and Alcohol.* New York: Holt, Rinehart and Winston, 1967.

Kerlinger, Frederick N. *Foundations of Behavioral Research*. New York: Holt, Rinehart and Winston, 1964.

————, and Pedhazur, E. J. *Multiple Regression in Behavioral Research*. New York: Holt, Rinehart and Winston, 1973.

King, F. A. *Beer Has a History*. New York: Hutchinson's Scientific and Technical Publications, 1947.

Kinney, Jean, and Leaton, Gwen. *Loosening the Grip: A Handbook of Alcohol Information*. Center City, Minn.: Hazelden, 1978.

Kinsey, Barry A. *The Female Alcoholic: A Social Psychological Study*. Springfield, Ill.: Charles C. Thomas, 1966.

Kissin, Benjamin, and Begleiter, Henri, eds. *The Biology of Alcoholism, Vol. I, Biochemistry*. New York: Plenum Press, 1972.

————. *The Biology of Alcoholism, Vol. 2, Physiology and Behavior*. New York: Plenum Press, 1972.

————. *The Biology of Alcoholism, Vol. 3, Clinical Pathology*. New York: Plenum Press, 1974

————. *The Biology of Alcoholism, Vol. 4, Social Aspects of Alcoholism*. New York: Plenum Press, 1976.

————. *The Biology of Alcoholism, Vol. 5, Treatment and Rehabilitation of the Chronic Alcoholic*. New York: Plenum Press, 1977.

Klausner, S. Z.; Foulks, E. F.; and Moore, M. H. *The Inupiat: Economics and Alcohol on the Alaskan North Slope*. Philadelphia: Center for Research on the Acts of Man, 1979.

————. *Social Change and the Alcohol Problem on the Alaskan North Slope*. Philadelphia: Center for Research on the Acts of Man, 1980.

Krasnegor, N. A. *Behavioral Analysis and Treatment of Substance Abuse*. Washington, D.C.: National Institute on Drug Abuse, 1979.

Kricka, L. J., and Clark, P. M. S. *Biochemistry of Alcohol and Alcoholism*. New York: Halsted Press, 1979.

Krout, J. A. *The Origins of Prohibition*. New York: Alfred A. Knopf, 1924.

Kruse, H. D., and Grob, Gerald N. *Alcoholism as a Medical Problem*. New York: Hoeber-Harper, 1956.

Kurtz, Ernest. *Not-God: A History of Alcoholics Anonymous*. Center City, Minn.: Hazelden, 1979.

Kuusi, P. *Alcohol Sales Experiment in Rural Finland*. Helsinki: Finnish Foundation for Alcohol Studies, 1957.

Kyvig, David E. *Repealing National Prohibition*. Chicago: University of Chicago Press, 1979.

Langone, John, and Langone, Dolores deN. *Women Who Drink*. Reading, Mass.: Addison-Wesley, 1980.

Lanu, K. E. *Control of Deviating Drinking Behavior: An Experimental Study of Formal Control over Drinking Behavior*. Helsinki: Finnish Foundation for Alcohol Studies, 1956.

Larkin, E. J. *The Treatment of Alcoholism: Theory, Practice, and Evaluation*. Ontario: Addiction Research Foundation, 1974.

Lee, Essie E. *Alcohol—Proof of What?* New York: Julian Messner, 1976.

Lee, John Parks. *What Shall We Tell Our Children about Drinking?* New York: National Council on Alcoholism, 1960.

Leiberman, M. A., and Borman, L. D. *Self-Help Groups for Coping with Crises: Origins, Members, Processes, and Impact*. San Francisco: Jossey-Bass, 1979.

Leigh, C. D. *Prohibition in the United States: A History of the Prohibition Party and of the Prohibition Movement.* New York: George H. Doran, Co., 1926.

Leite, Evelyn. *To Be Somebody.* Center City, Minn.: Hazelden, 1979.

Lemert, E. W. *Alcohol and the Northwest Coast Indians.* Berkeley: University of California Press, 1954.

Lennard, Henry, and Bernstein, A. *The Anatomy of Psychotherapy: Systems of Communication and Expectation.* New York: Columbia University Press, 1960.

Levy, H. *Drink: An Economic and Social Study.* London: Routledge and Kegan Paul, 1951.

Levy, J. E., and Kunitz, S. J. *Indian Drinking: Navajo Practices and Anglo-American Theories.* New York: John Wiley and Sons, 1974.

Li, T. K.; Schenker, S.; and Lumeng, L. *Alcohol and Nutrition: Proceedings of a Workshop, September 26–27, 1977, Indianapolis, Indiana.* Washington, D.C.: U.S. Government Printing Office, 1979.

Liban, Carolyn B., and Smart, Reginald G. *The Value of the Informant Method for Studying Drinking Habits.* Toronto: Addiction Research Foundation, 1980.

Lichine, Alexis. *Encyclopedia of Wines and Spirits.* New York: Alfred A. Knopf, 1968.

Lingeman, Richard R. *Drugs from A to Z.* New York: McGraw-Hill Book Co., 1974.

Linn, R. *You Can Drink and Stay Healthy: A Guide for the Social Drinker.* New York: Franklin Watts, 1979.

Little, J. W., and Hartman, B. S. *Review of Legal Literature Published between July 1974 and July 1978 Pertaining to Alcohol and Drug Involvement in Highway Safety.* Springfield, Va.: National Technical Information Service, 1978.

Lockhard, Sir R. B. *Scotch: The Whisky of Scotland in Fact and Story.* London: Putnam and Co., 1971.

Lockhart, D. L. *The Swinging Door: An Evaluation of Services to and Needs of Street People in Downtown Salinas.* Salinas: Sun Street Centers, Community Alcoholism Programs, 1979.

Lolli, Giorgio. *Social Drinking, the Effects of Alcohol.* New York: Collier Books, 1961.

————; Serianni, E.; Golder, G.; and Luzzatto-Fegiz, P. *Alcohol in Italian Culture: Food and Wine in Relation to Sobriety among Italians and Italian Americans.* New Haven: Yale Center of Alcohol Studies, 1958.

Lord, Luther, and Lord, Eileen. *Here's How to Sobriety.* Center City, Minn.: Hazelden, 1977.

Lotter, J. M. *Social Problems in the RSA.* Pretoria: Institute for Sociological, Demographic and Criminological Research, South African Human Sciences Research Council, 1979.

Louria, D. B. *The Drug Scene.* New York: McGraw-Hill Book Co., 1968.

Lovell, H. W. *Hope and Help for the Alcoholic.* Garden City, N.Y.: Doubleday and Co., 1951.

Lowinson, Joyce H., and Ruiz, Pedro. *Substance Abuse: Clinical Problems and Perspectives.* Easton, Md.: Williams and Wilkins Co., 1981.

Lucia, Salvatore P. *Alcohol and Civilization.* New York: McGraw-Hill Book Co., 1960.

————. *A History of Wine as Therapy.* Philadelphia: J. B. Lippincott Co., 1963.

Luks, Alan. *Having Been There.* New York: Charles Scribner's Sons, 1979.

MacAndrew, Craig, and Edgerton, Robert B. *Drunken Comportment: A Social Explanation.* Chicago: Aldine Publishing Co., 1969.

MacLennan, Anne. *Women: Their Use of Alcohol and Other Legal Drugs.* Toronto: Addiction Research Foundation, 1976.

Macurdy, E. A., and Hollander, M. J. *A Survey of Drinking Practices and Attitudes to Alcohol Use in B.C.* Vancouver: Alcohol and Drug Commission, Ministry of Health, 1978.

Madden, J. S. *Guide to Alcohol and Drug Dependence.* Bristol, England: J. Wright and Sons, 1979.

————; Walker, Robin; and Kenyon, W. H. *Aspects of Alcohol and Drug Dependence.* Kent, England: Pitman Medical Limited, 1980.

Maddox, George L. *The Domesticated Drug: Drinking among Collegians.* New Haven: College and University Press, 1970.

————, and McCall, Bevode C. *Drinking among Teen-Agers.* New Brunswick, N.J.: Rutgers Center of Alcohol Studies, 1964.

Madsen, William. *The American Alcoholic: The Nature-Nurture Controversy in Alcoholic Research and Therapy.* Springfield, Ill.: Charles C. Thomas, 1974.

Majchrowicz, Edward, and Noble, Ernest P. *Biochemistry and Pharmacology of Ethanol.* 2 vols. New York and London: Plenum Publishing Corp., 1979.

Makela, Klaus. *Prices of Alcoholic Beverages in Finland, 1950–1975.* Helsinki: Social Research Institute of Alcohol Studies, 1980.

————. *Unrecorded Consumption of Alcohol in Finland, 1950–1975.* Helsinki: Social Research Institute of Alcohol Studies, 1979.

————; Room, Robin; Single, Eric; Sulkunen, Pekka; and Walsh, Brendan. *Alcohol, Society and the State. Vol. 1: A Comparative Study of Alcohol Control.* Toronto: Addiction Research Foundation, 1982.

Malzberg, Benjamin. *The Alcoholic Psychosis.* New Haven: Yale Center of Alcohol Studies, 1960.

Mandell, W. *Youthful Drinking.* New York: Wakoff Research Center, 1962.

Manello, Timothy A.; Paddock, J. A.; Wick, W.; and Seaman, F. J. *Problem Drinking among Railroad Workers: Extent, Impact and Solutions.* Washington, D.C.: University Research Corp., 1979.

Mann, George A. *Recovery of Reality: Overcoming Chemical Dependency.* New York: Harper and Row, 1979.

Mann, Marty. *New Primer on Alcoholism.* New York: Holt, Rinehart and Winston, 1963.

————. *Primer on Alcoholism.* New York: Holt, Rinehart and Winston, 1958.

Manning, William O., and Vinton, Jean. *Harmfully Involved.* Center City, Minn.: Hazelden, 1978.

Marden, P. G., and Kolodner, K. *Alcohol Abuse among Women: Gender Differences and Their Implications for the Delivery of Services.* Springfield, Va.: National Technical Information Service, 1979.

Marr, D. *From Liquor and Loneliness to Love and Laughter.* Kansas City, Kan.: Sheed Andrews and McMeel, 1978.

Marshall, Mac. *Beliefs, Behaviors, and Alcoholic Beverages: A Cross-Cultural Survey.* Ann Arbor: University of Michigan Press, 1979.

————. *Weekend Warriors: Alcohol in a Micronesian Culture.* Palo Alto: Mayfield Publishing Co., 1979.

Martin, J. P. *Violence and the Family.* New York: John Wiley and Sons, 1978.

Marvin, D. *World's Original Social Drinker's Almanac.* Oceanside, Calif.: Marvin, 1979.

Mass Observation. *The Pub and the People.* London: Gollancz, 1943.

Maultsby, Maxie C., Jr. *A Million Dollars for Your Hangover.* Lexington, Ky.: Rational Self-Help Books, 1978.

————, and Welsh, Richard J. *Outpatient Treatment of Alcoholism.* Baltimore: University Park Press, 1979.

Mayer, John E., and Filstead, William J. *Adolescence and Alcohol.* Cambridge, Mass.: Ballinger Publishing Co., 1980.

McCarthy, Raymond G. *Alcohol Education for Classroom and Community: A Source Book for Educators.* New York: McGraw-Hill Book Co., 1964.

————. *Discussion Guides for Questions about Alcohol.* New York: National Council on Alcoholism, 1956.

————. *Drinking and Intoxication.* New Haven: Yale Center of Alcohol Studies, 1959.

————. *Exploring Alcohol Questions.* New York: National Council on Alcoholism, 1962.

————. *What Shall Our Schools Teach about Alcohol?* New York: National Council on Alcoholism, 1964.

McClelland, David C.; Davis, W. N.; Kalin, R.; and Wanner, E. *The Drinking Man.* New York: Free Press, 1972.

McCord, William, and McCord, Joan. *Origins of Alcoholism.* Stanford, Calif.: Stanford University Press, 1960.

Mecca A. M. *Alcoholism in America: A Modern Perspective.* San Rafael: California Health Research Foundation, 1980.

Mello, Nancy K. *Advances in Substance Abuse: Behavioral and Biological Research.* Greenwich, Conn.: JAI Press, 1980.

————, and Mendelson, Jack H., eds. *Recent Advances in Studies of Alcoholism.* publication no. (HSM) 71-9045. Washington, D.C.: U.S. Government Printing Office, 1971.

Meltzoff, Julian, and Kornreich, Melvin. *Research in Psychotherapy.* New York: Atherton Press, 1970.

Mendelson, Jack H., and Mello, Nancy K. *The Diagnosis and Treatment of Alcoholism.* New York: McGraw-Hill Book Co., 1979.

Mendlewicz, J., and Van Praag, H. M. *Alcoholism: A Multidisciplinary Approach.* Basel: Karger, 1979.

Menninger, Karl A. *Man against Himself.* New York: Harcourt, Brace and Co., 1938.

Metropolitan Life Insurance Co. *Alcoholism.* New York, 1967.

Michigan Department of Education. *A Curriculum Guide on Alcohol Education.* Lansing, 1970.

Milgram, Gail Gleason. *Alcohol Education Materials 1973–1978: An Annotated Bibliography.* New Brunswick, N.J.: Rutgers Center of Alcohol Studies, 1980.

————. *Coping with Alcohol.* New York: Richards Rosen Press, 1980.

————. *What Is Alcohol? And Why Do People Drink?* New Brunswick, N.J.: Rutgers Center of Alcohol Studies, 1975.

Miller, Merlene; Gorski, Terence T.; and Miller, David K. *Learning to Live Again: A Guide for Recovery from Alcoholism.* Hazel Crest, Ill.: Human Ecology Systems, 1980.

Miller, P. M. *Behavioral Treatment of Alcoholism.* Toronto: Pergamon Press, 1976.

————. *Personal Habit Control.* New York: Simon and Schuster, 1978.

Miller, William R. *The Addictive Behaviors: Treatment of Alcoholism, Drug Abuse, Smoking and Obesity.* Elmsford, N.Y.: Pergamon Press, 1980.

Mishara, Brian L., and Kastenbaum, Robert. *Alcohol and Old Age.* New York: Grune and Stratton, 1980.

Mississippi State Department of Education. *Alcohol Education Handbook.* Mississippi School Bulletin, no. 141. Jackson, n.d.

Morewood, Samuel. *Inebriating Liquors.* Dublin: W. Curry, Jun. and Company, and W. Carson, 1838.

Morrison, L. W. *Wines and Spirits.* Baltimore: Penguin Books, 1968.

Moser, Joy. *Prevention of Alcohol-Related Problems.* Toronto: Alcoholism and Drug Addiction Research Foundation for World Health Organization, 1980.

———. *Problems and Programmes Related to Alcohol and Drug Dependence in 33 Countries.* Geneva: World Health Organization, 1974.

Mulford, H. A. *Meeting the Problems of Alcohol Abuse: A Testable Action Plan for Iowa.* Cedar Rapids: Iowa Alcoholism Foundation, 1970.

Mullan, Hugh, and Sangiuliano, Iris. *Alcoholism: Group Psychotherapy and Rehabilitation.* Springfield, Ill.: Charles C. Thomas, 1966.

Nathan, Peter E.; Marlatt, G. Alan; and Loberg, Tor. *Alcoholism: New Directions in Behavioral Research and Treatment.* New York: Plenum Press, 1978.

National Center for Alcohol Education. *Services for Alcoholic Women: Foundations for Change. Trainer Manual.* Washington, D.C.: U.S. Government Printing Office, 1979.

National Clergy Conference on Alcoholism. *The Blue Book, Vol. XXXI. Proceedings of the 31st National Clergy Conference on Alcoholism, Omaha, Nebraska, May 22–26, 1979.* n.d.

The National Council of Women Working Party on Alcohol Problems. *Alcohol and the Unborn Child—The Fetal Alcohol Syndrome.* London: National Council of Women, 1980.

National Council on Alcoholism. *Do's and Don'ts for the Wives of Alcoholics.* New York, 1960.

———. *Facts on Alcoholism.* New York, 1966.

———. *The Rights of Alcoholics and Their Families.* New York, 1976.

National DWI Conference. *Proceedings of the Second National DWI Conference, Rochester, Minnesota, May 30–June 1, 1979.* Falls Church, Va.: AAA Foundation for Traffic Safety, 1980.

National Industrial Conference Board. *The Alcoholic Worker.* New York, 1958.

National Institute on Alcohol Abuse and Alcoholism. *Alcohol and Health.* First Special Report to the U.S. Congress from the Secretary of Health, Education and Welfare. Washington, D.C.: U.S. Government Printing Office, 1971.

———. *Alcohol and Health: New Knowledge.* Second Special Report to the U.S. Congress from the Secretary of Health, Education and Welfare. Washington, D.C.: U.S. Government Printing Office, 1974.

———. *Alcohol and Health.* Third Special Report to the U.S. Congress from the Secretary of Health, Education and Welfare. Washington, D.C.: U.S. Government Printing Office, 1978.

———. *Alcoholism and Alcohol Abuse among Women: Research Issues.* Washington, D.C.: U.S. Government Printing Office, 1980.

———. *Alcoholism Prevention: Guide to Resources and References.* Rockville, Md., 1979.

———. *The Public Health Approach to Problems Associated with Alcohol Consumption.* Rockville, Md., 1980.

———. *Recent Advances in Studies of Alcoholism.* Washington, D.C., 1970.

Navin, R. B. *Analysis of a Slum Area.* Washington, D.C.: Catholic University Press, 1934.

Newlove, Donald. *Those Drinking Days: Myself and Other Writers.* New York: Horizon Press, 1981.

Newman, Henry W. *Acute Alcoholic Intoxication: A Critical Review.* Stanford, Calif.: Stanford University Press, 1979.

Newman, I. M. *Dissemination and Utilization of Alcohol Information.* Lincoln: Nebraska Alcohol Information Clearinghouse and Health Education Department, University of Nebraska, 1980.

Newman, J. *Time for Change in Alcoholism Treatment? Traditional and Emerging Concepts.* Pittsburgh: University of Pittsburgh, 1979.

Nicholi, Armand M., Jr. *The Harvard Guide to Modern Psychiatry.* Cambridge, Mass.: Harvard University Press, 1979.

Norback, Judith. *The Alcohol and Drug Abuse Yearbook/Directory 1979–80.* New York: Van Nostrand Reinhold Co., 1979.

North, Robert, and Orange, Richard, Jr. *Teenage Drinking.* New York: Macmillan Co., 1980.

O'Gorman, P. A., and Lacks, H. *Aspects of Youthful Drinking.* New York: National Council on Alcoholism, 1979.

Olive, G. *Drug-Action Modifications—Comparative Pharmacology.* Oxford: Pergamon Publishing Corp., 1979.

Ontario Department of Health. *Report on the Activities of the Ontario Council of Health.* 1969.

Opperman, D. J. *Spirit of the Vine.* Cape Town: Human and Rousseau, 1968.

Orford, Jim, and Edwards, Griffith. *Alcoholism.* Oxford: Oxford University Press, 1977.

Osterberg, E. *Alcohol Policy Measures and the Consumption of Alcoholic Beverages in Finland, 1950–1975.* Helsinki: Social Research Institute of Alcohol Studies, 1980.

Ottenberg, J. F. X. Carroll, and Bolognese, C. *Treating Mixed Psychiatric-Drug Addicted and Alcoholic Patients.* Eagleville, Pa.: Eagleville Hospital and Rehabilitation Center, 1979.

Palmer, Charles E. *Inebriety: Its Source, Prevention and Cure.* Philadelphia: Union Press, 1912.

Paolino, Thomas J., and McGrady, Barbara S. *The Alcoholic Marriage: Alternative Perspectives.* New York: Grune and Stratton, 1977.

Paredes, Alfonso, ed. *The Alcoholism Services Delivery System.* San Francisco: Jossey-Bass, 1981.

Partanen, J. *Our National Commodity Consumption Patterns and the Use of Alcohol.* Helsinki: Social Research Institute of Alcohol Studies, 1979.

————; Bruun, K.; and Markkanen, T. *Inheritance of Drinking Behavior: A Study of Intelligence, Personality, and Use of Alcohol of Adult Twins.* Helsinki: Finnish Foundation for Alcohol Studies, 1966.

Pasciutti, J. *Mental Health Aspects of Alcohol Education.* Boston: Massachusetts Office of the Commissioner of Alcoholism, 1958.

Patrick, Clarence H. *Alcohol, Culture and Society.* Durham: Duke University Press, 1952.

Pattison, E. Mansell; Sobell, Mark B.; and Sobell, Linda Carter. *Emerging Concepts of Alcohol Dependence.* New York: Springer, 1977.

Pearl, Raymond. *Alcohol and Longevity.* New York: Alfred A. Knopf, 1926.

Pearson, Charles C., and Hendricks, James Edwin. *Liquor and Anti-Liquor in Virginia 1619–1919.* Durham: Duke University Press, 1967.

Peele, Stanton. *How Much Is Too Much.* Englewood Cliffs, N.J.: Prentice-Hall, 1981.

Pekkanen, L. *Nutritional Factors in the Regulation of Voluntary Ethanol Drinking in the*

Laboratory Rat. Helsinki: Research Laboratories of the State Alcohol Monopoly (Alko), 1980.

Perrine, M. W.; Waller, J. A.; and Harris, L. S. *Alcohol and Highway Safety: Behavioral and Medical Aspects*. U.S. Department of Transportation NHTSA Technical Report. Washington, D.C., 1971.

Petrie, Asenath. *Individuality in Pain and Suffering*. Chicago: University of Chicago Press, 1967.

Pfeffer, Arnold Z. *Alcoholism*. Modern Monographs in Industrial Medicine, no. 2. New York: Grune and Stratton, 1958.

Pickett, D. *Alcohol and the New Age*. New York: Methodist Book Concern, 1926.

Pittman, David Joshua. *Primary Prevention of Alcohol Abuse and Alcoholism: An Evaluation of the Control Consumption Policy*. St. Louis: Social Science Institute, Washington University, 1980.

————. *Society, Culture, and Drinking Patterns*. New York: John Wiley and Sons, 1962.

————. *World Health Organization Committee of Experts in Alcoholism*. New York: Harper and Row, 1967.

————, and Gordon, C. W. *Revolving Door: A Study of the Chronic Police Case Inebriate*. Glencoe, Ill.: Free Press, 1958.

Plant, Martin A. *Drinking Careers—Occupations, Drinking Habits and Drinking Problems*. London: Tavistock Publications, 1979.

Plaut, Thomas F. *Alcohol Problems: A Report to the Nation by the Cooperative Commission on the Study of Alcoholism*. New York: Oxford University Press, 1967.

Polacsek, E.; Barnes, T.; Turner, N.; Hall, R.; and Weise, C. *Interaction of Alcohol and Other Drugs*. Toronto: Addiction Research Foundation, 1972.

Poley, Wayne; Lea, Gary; and Vibe, Gail. *Alcoholism: A Treatment Manual*. New York: Gardner Press, 1979.

Polich, J. Michael, and Armor, David J. *The Course of Alcoholism: Four Years after Treatment*. Santa Monica: Rand Corp., 1980.

————, and Orvis, B. R. *Alcohol Problems: Patterns and Prevalence in the U.S. Air Force*. Santa Monica: Rand Corp., 1979.

Polk, K. *Drinking and the Adolescent Culture*. Eugene, Ore.: Lane County Youth Project, 1964.

Pollack, S.; Didenko, O. R.; McEachern, A. W.; and Berger, R. M. *Drinking Driver and Traffic Safety Project*. U.S. Department of Transportation NHTSA Technical Report. Washington, D.C., 1972.

Popham, R. E. *Alcohol and Alcoholism*. Toronto: University of Toronto Press, 1970.

Powell, David J. *Clinical Supervision, Skills for Substance Abuse Counselors: Manual*. New York: Human Sciences Press, 1980.

————. *Clinical Supervision, Skills for Substance Abuse Counselors: Trainees Workbook*. New York: Human Sciences Press, 1980.

Pratt, Arthur. *How To Help and Understand the Alcoholic or Drug Addict*. Louisville: Love Street Books, 1980.

Presnall, Lewis F. *The Modern Approach to Alcoholism*. New York: National Council on Alcoholism, 1965.

Province of Ontario. *Effective Management through P.P.B.S.* Treasury Board of Ontario, 1969.

Purich, D. J. *Drinking and Driving: What to Do If You're Caught*. Vancouver: International Self-Counsel Press, 1978.

Rachman, S., and Teasdale, J. *Aversion Therapy and Behavior Disorders*. London: Routledge and Kegan Paul, 1969.

Rankin, J. G., ed. *Alcohol, Drugs and Brain Damage*. Toronto: Alcoholism and Drug Addiction Research Foundation of Ontario, 1975.

Rathod, N. H.; Caldwell, D.; and Glatt, M. M. *Abuse of Alcohol amongst Medical Practitioners: Proceedings of a Symposium Organized Jointly by the Medical Council on Alcoholism and the Society for the Study of Addiction, 26th January, 1977*. London: Society for the Study of Addiction, 1979.

Rea, F. B. *Alcoholism: Its Psychology and Cure*. London: Epworth Press, 1956.

Regier, Marilyn. *Social Policy in Action: Perspectives on the Implementation of Alcoholism Reforms*. Lexington, Mass.: Lexington Books, 1979.

Regional Council on Alcoholism of Cuyahoga, Geauga, Lake and Lorain Counties. *Guidelines for the Establishment of a Residential Program for the Treatment of Alcoholism*. Cleveland, 1978.

Reid, J. *A Social and Legal Profile of Saskatchewan Impaired Drivers: Final Report*. Regina: Saskatchewan Alcoholism Commission, 1978.

Reuss, C. *History of Beer Consumption in Belgium 1900–1957*. Louvain: Universitaire de Louvain, 1959.

Richter, Derek. *Addiction and Brain Damage*. Baltimore: University Park Press, 1980.

Rigter, H., and Crabbe, J. C., Jr. *Alcohol Tolerance and Dependence*. New York: Elsevier/North-Holland Biomedical Press, 1980.

Rittenhouse, J. D. *Consequences of Alcohol and Marijuana Use: Survey Items for Perceived Assessment*. Rockville, Md.: National Institute on Drug Abuse, 1979.

Rix, Keith J. B. *Alcohol: Questions and Answers*. Edinburgh: Scottish Council on Alcoholism, 1977.

Robe, Lucy Barry. *Haunted Inheritance*. Minneapolis: CompCare Publications, 1980.

Robertson, J. J. *The Impaired Physician: Proceedings of the Third AMA Conference on the Impaired Physician, September 29–October 1, 1978, Minneapolis, Minnesota*. Chicago: American Medical Association, 1980.

Robinson, David. *Alcohol Problems: Reviews, Research and Recommendations*. New York: Holmes and Meier, 1979.

———. *From Drinking to Alcoholism: A Sociological Commentary*. New York: John Wiley and Sons, 1976.

———. *Talking Out of Alcoholism: The Self-Help Process of Alcoholics Anonymous*. London: Croom Helm, 1979.

Robinson, Robert R. *On the Rocks*. Ontario: Scholastic-TAB Publications, 1979.

Roe, Daphne. *Alcohol and the Diet*. Westport, Conn.: AVI Press, 1981.

Room, Robin. *Governing Images and Prevention of Alcohol Problems*. Berkeley: University of California, n.d.

———. *Minimizing Alcohol Problems*. Berkeley: University of California, n.d.

———. *Prevention—Of What?* Berkeley: University of California, n.d.

Rorabaugh, W. J. *The Alcoholic Republic: An American Tradition*. New York: Oxford University Press, 1979.

Rossi, Peter H.; Freeman, Howard E.; and Wright, Sonia R. *Evaluation: A Systematic Approach*. Beverly Hills: Sage Publications, 1979.

Roueche, Berton. *The Neutral Spirit*. Boston: Little, Brown and Co., 1960.

Royce, James E. *Alcohol Problems and Alcoholism*. New York: Free Press, 1981.

Ruggels, W. L. et al. *A Follow-up Study of Clients at Selected Alcoholism Treatment Centers Funded by NIAAA*. Stanford, Calif.: Stanford Research Institute, May 1975.

Rutledge, B., and Kaye, Fulton E. *International Collaboration: Problems and Opportunities*. Toronto: Addiction Research Foundation, 1977.

Ryan, L. C., and Mohler, S. R. *Current Role of Alcohol as a Factor in Civil Aircraft Accidents*. Springfield, Va.: National Technical Information Service, 1980.

Saltman, J. *The New Alcoholics: Teenagers*. New York: Public Affairs Pamphlet, 1973.

Sandler, Merton. *Psychopharmacology of Alcohol*. New York: Raven Press, 1980.

Sandmaier, Marian. *The Invisible Alcoholics: Women and Alcohol Abuse in America*. New York: McGraw-Hill Book Co., 1980.

Sargent, Margaret. *Drinking and Alcoholism in Australia: A Power Relations Theory*. Melbourne: Longman Cheshire, 1979.

Schecter, Arnold J., ed. *Drug Dependence and Alcoholism, Vol. 1, Biomedical Issues*. New York: Plenum Press, 1980.

———. *Drug Dependence and Alcoholism, Vol. 2, Social and Behavioral Issues*. New York: Plenum Press, 1980.

Schmidt, W., and Kornaczewski, A. *A Note on the Effect of Lowering the Legal Drinking Age on Alcohol Related Motor Vehicle Accidents*. Toronto: Addiction Research Foundation, 1973.

Schuckit, M. A. *Drug and Alcohol Abuse: A Clinical Guide to Diagnosis and Treatment*. New York: Plenum Medical Book Co., 1979.

Schulberg, A.; Sheldon, A.; and Baker, F. *Program Evaluation in the Health Fields*. New York: Behavioral Publications, 1969.

Scoles, P., and Fine, E. W. *Alcohol and Traffic Safety: Proceedings of the First Conference on Alcohol-Highway Safety Programs in the Commonwealth of Pennsylvania, Lancaster, Pennsylvania, October 5, 6, 7, 1977*. Philadelphia: Michael C. Prestegord and Co., 1978.

Scrimgeour, G. J.; Palmer, J. A.; Edwards, L.; Goldspiel, S.; and Logan, A. B. *Comparative Analysis of Alcohol Highway Safety Judicial Standards and Existing Professional Standards. Vol. I: Technical Report*. Springfield, Va.: National Technical Information Service, 1978.

Seeger, Francis M. D. *Until My Last Breath*. Hollywood, Fla.: Health Communications, 1980.

Seltman, C. *Wine in the Ancient World*. London: Routledge and Kegan Paul, 1957.

Shadwell, A. *Drink in 1914–1922: A Lesson in Control*. London: Longsman, Green and Co., 1923.

Shain, Martin, and Groeneveld, Judith. *Employee Assistance Programs: Philosophy, Theory and Practice*. Toronto: Lexington, 1980.

———; Suurvali, Helen; and Kilty, H. L. *The Parent Communication Project*. Toronto: Addiction Research Foundation, 1980.

Shapiro, L., and Mortimer, R. G. *Literature Review and Bibliography of Research and Practice in Pedestrian Safety*. Ann Arbor: Highway Safety Research Institute, University of Michigan, 1969.

Silverstein, Alvin, and Silverstein, Virginia B. *Alcoholism*. Philadelphia: J. B. Lippincott Co., 1975.

Silverstein, Lee M.; Edelwich, Jerry; and Flanagan, Donald. *High on Life*. Hollywood, Fla.: Health Communications, 1981.

Sinclair, Andrew. *Prohibition: The Era of Excess*. Boston: Atlantic Monthly Press Book; Little, Brown and Co., 1962.

Single, Eric, and Giesbrecht, Norman. *Rates of Alcohol Consumption and Patterns of Drinking in Ontario 1950–1975*. Toronto: Addiction Research Foundation, 1979.

———; Morgan, Patricia; and de Lint, Jan. *Alcohol, Society, and the State. Vol. 2: The Social History of Control in Seven Countries*. Toronto: Addiction Research Foundation, 1982.

Small, Jacquelyn. *Transformers*. Hollywood, Fla.: Health Communications, 1982.

Smart, Reginald G. *The New Drinkers: Teenage Use and Abuse of Alcohol*. 2nd ed. Toronto: Addiction Research Foundation, 1980.

———; Storm, T.; Baker, E. F. W.; and Solursh, L. *Lysergic Acid Diethylamide (LSD) in the Treatment of Alcoholism: An Investigation of Its Effects on Drinking Behavior, Personality Structure and Social Functioning*. Toronto: University of Toronto Press, 1967.

Smith, Cedric M. *Alcoholism, Treatment*. Vol. 2. Edinburgh: Churchill Livingstone, 1977.

Smith, W. H., and Helwig, F. C. *Liquor, the Servant of Man*. Boston: Little, Brown and Co., 1939.

Smithers, Christopher D., Foundation. *Alcohol and Alcoholism: A Police Handbook*. New York, 1966.

———. *Alcoholism—A Family Illness*. New York, 1967.

———. *Arresting Alcoholism*. New York, 1962.

———. *Biochemical and Nutritional Aspects of Alcoholism*. New York, 1964.

———. *A Company Program on Alcoholism—Basic Outline*. New York, 1959.

———. *Experimentation*. New York, 1965.

———. *Pioneers We Have Known in the Field of Alcoholism*. Mill Neck, N.Y.: 1979.

———. *Understanding Alcoholism: For the Patient, the Family, and the Employer*. New York, 1968.

Snyder, Charles R. *Alcohol and the Jews*. New Brunswick, N.J.: Rutgers Center of Alcoholic Studies, 1958.

Sobell, Linda Carter; Sobell, Mark B.; and Ward, Elliott. *Evaluating Alcohol and Drug Abuse Treatment Effectiveness*. New York: Pergamon Press, 1980.

Sobell, Mark B., and Sobell, Linda Carter. *Behavioral Treatment of Alcohol Problems*. New York: Plenum Press, 1978.

Solomon, Joel. *Alcoholism and Clinical Psychiatry*. New York: Downstate Medical Center, 1982.

Southerby, Norm, and Southerby, Alexandra. *Twelve Young Women*. Long Beach, Calif.: Southerby and Associates, 1975.

Spahr, John Howard. *Sober Life*. Ardmore, England: Dorrance and Co., 1979.

Spicer, Jerry. *Program Management. Outcome Evaluation: How to Do It*. Center City, Minn.: Hazelden, 1980.

Stanton, Alfred H., and Schwartz, Morris S. *The Mental Hospital*. New York: Basic Books, 1954.

Steiner, Claude. *Games Alcoholics Play*. New York: Grove Press, 1974.

———. *Healing Alcoholism*. New York: Grove Press, 1979.

Stewart, Ernest I., and Malfetti, James L. *Rehabilitation of the Drunken Driver*. New York: Teachers College Press, 1970.

Stewart, George R. *American Ways of Life*. New York: Doubleday and Co., 1954.

Straus, R. *Escape from Custody: A Study of Alcoholism and Institutional Dependency as Reflected in the Life Record of a Homeless Man.* New York: Harper and Row, 1974.

Straus, Robert, and Bacon, Selden D. *Drinking in College.* New Haven: Yale University Press, 1953.

Stroh, Carl M. *Addiction, Society and Self.* Vancouver: Alcohol and Drug Commission, 1980.

Sulkunen, P. *Abstainers in Finland 1946–1976: A Study in Social and Cultural Transition.* Helsinki: Social Research Institute of Alcohol Studies, 1979.

Tahka, V. *The Alcoholic Personality.* Helsinki: Finnish Foundation for Alcohol Studies, 1966.

Talland, George A. *Deranged Memory.* New York: Academic Press, 1965.

————, and Waugh, N. C., eds. *The Pathology of Memory.* New York: Academic Press, 1969.

Tarter, Ralph E., and Sugerman, A. Arthur. *Alcoholism.* Reading, Mass.: Addison-Wesley, 1976.

Taylor, William B. *Drinking, Homicide and Rebellion in Colonial Mexican Villages.* Stanford, Calif.: Stanford University Press, 1979.

Terhune, William B. *The Safe Way to Drink: How to Prevent Alcohol Problems Before They Start.* New York: Pocketbooks, 1969.

Tessler, Diane Jane. *Drugs, Kids, and Schools: Practical Strategies for Educators and Other Concerned Adults.* Rockville, Md.: National Institute on Drug Abuse, 1980.

Thompson, J. *Alcohol and Drug Research in Saskatchewan, 1970–1978: Subject, Index and Abstracts.* Regina: Saskatchewan Alcoholism Commission, 1978.

Thomsen, Robert. *Bill W.* New York: Harper and Row, 1975.

Thurman, Ronald G. *Alcohol and Aldehyde Metabolizing Systems—IV.* New York: Plenum Publishing Corp., 1980.

Todd, J. E. *Drunkenness a Vice, Not a Disease.* Hartford: Case, Lockwood and Brainard, 1882.

Towery, O. B.; Seidenberg, G. R.; and Santoro, V. *Quality Assurance for Alcohol, Drug Abuse, and Mental Health Services: An Annotated Bibliography.* Rockville, Md.: U.S. Alcohol, Drug Abuse, and Mental Health Administration, 1979.

Towle, L. H. et al. *Alcoholism Program Monitoring System Development: Evaluation of the ATC Program.* Stanford, Calif.: Stanford Research Institute, 1973.

Trice, Harrison M. *Alcoholism in America.* New York: McGraw-Hill Book Co., 1966.

————. *Alcoholism in Industry—Modern Procedures.* New York: Smithers, Christopher D., Foundation, 1962.

Truax, Lyle H. *Judge's Guide for Alcohol Offenders.* New York: National Council on Alcoholism, 1972.

Twerski, Abraham J. *Caution: "Kindness" Can Be Dangerous to the Alcoholic.* Englewood Cliffs, N.J.: Prentice-Hall, 1981.

Tyrrell, Ian R. *Sobering Up: From Temperance to Prohibition in Antebellum America, 1800–1860.* Westport, Conn.: Greenwood Press, 1979.

Ullman, A. D. *To Know the Difference.* New York: St. Martin's Press, 1960.

U.K., Home Office. *Habitual Drunken Offenders.* Report of the Working Party. London: Her Majesty's Stationery Office, 1971.

U.S., Congress, Senate, Committee on Labor and Human Resources. *Comprehensive Alcohol Abuse and Alcoholism Prevention, Treatment, and Rehabilitation Act Amendments of 1979.* Washington, D.C.: U.S. Government Printing Office, 1979.

————. *Report on Consumer Health Warnings for Alcoholic Beverages and Related Issues, 96th Congress.* Washington, D.C.: U.S. Government Printing Office, 1979.

U.S., Department of Health, Education and Welfare. *Alcohol and Health.* Washington, D.C.: U.S. Government Printing Office, 1971.

————. *Alcohol and Health: New Knowledge.* Washington, D.C.: U.S. Government Printing Office, 1974.

U.S., Department of Transportation. *The 1968 Alcohol and Highway Safety Report.* Washington, D.C.: U.S. Government Printing Office, 1968.

U.S., General Accounting Office. *The Drinking-Driver Problem—What Can Be Done about It?* Springfield, Va.: National Technical Information Service, 1979.

U.S., National Center for Alcohol Education. *Services for Alcoholic Women: Foundations for Change: Resource Book.* Rockville, Md.: U.S. Government Printing Office, n.d.

U.S., National Clearinghouse for Alcohol Information and Division of Special Treatment and Rehabilitation. *Classification of Alcoholism Treatment Settings.* Rockville, Md., 1978.

Valle, Stephen K. *Alcoholism Counseling: Issues for an Emerging Profession.* Springfield, Ill.: Charles C. Thomas, 1979.

Vischi, T. R.; Jones, K. R.; Shank, E. L.; and Lima, L. H. *The Alcohol, Drug Abuse, and Mental Health National Data Book.* Washington D.C.: U.S. Alcohol, Drug Abuse and Mental Health Administration, 1980.

Vuylsteek, K. *Health Education: Smoking, Alcoholism, Drugs.* Albany: WHO Publications Centre, 1979.

Waddell, Jack O., and Everett, Michael W. *Drinking Behavior among Southwestern Indians: An Anthropological Perspective.* Tucson: University of Arizona Press, 1980.

————, and Watson, O. Michael. *The American Indian in Urban Society.* Boston: Little, Brown and Co, 1971.

Wagner, Robin S. *Sarah T: Portrait of a Teen-age Alcoholic.* New York: Ballantine Books, 1976.

Walker, Lenore E. *The Battered Woman.* New York: Harper and Row, 1979.

Wallerstein, R. S. *Hospital Treatment of Alcoholism: A Comparative Experimental Study.* Menninger Clinic Monograph Series, no. 11. New York: Basic Books, 1957.

Wallgren, H. *On the Relationship of the Consumption of Alcoholic Beverages to the Genesis of Alcoholic Disorders.* Helsinki: Alkon Keskuslaboratorio, 1970.

————, and Barry, H. *Actions of Alcohol.* Vol. II. Amsterdam: Elsevier, 1970.

Warburton, Clark. *The Economic Results of Prohibition.* New York: Columbia University, 1932. ,

Ward, David A. *Alcoholism: Introduction to Theory and Treatment.* Dubuque: Kendall/Hunt, 1980.

Washburne, Chandler. *Primitive Drinking.* New Haven: College and University Press, 1961.

Waterbury, J. *Your Thoughts and Feelings.* Knoxville: St. Mary's Medical Center, 1979.

Wechsler, Henry. *Minimum-Drinking-Age Laws.* Lexington, Mass.: Lexington Books, 1980.

Weiner, Jack B. *Drinking.* New York: W. W. Norton and Co., 1976.

Weise, C. E. *Behavior Modification for the Treatment of Alcoholism.* Toronto: Addiction Research Foundation, 1975.

Weiss, Mildred H. *What We Know about Alcohol.* Cleveland: Cleveland Health Museum, 1957.

Weiss, Richard M. *Dealing with Alcoholism in the Workplace.* Ottawa: Conference Board in Canada, 1980.

West, Elliot. *The Saloon on the Rocky Mountain Mining Frontier.* Lincoln: University of Nebraska Press, 1979.

West, L. H. T., and Hore, T. *An Analysis of Drink Driving Research.* Clayton, Victoria, Australia: Higher Education Advisory and Research Unit, Monash University, 1980.

Western Electric. *Policy and Program—Employees with Drinking Problems (A Guide for Supervisors).* New York, 1962.

Whitney, Elizabeth D. *The Lonely Sickness.* Boston: Beacon Press, 1965.

Wiener, Carolyn. *The Politics of Alcoholism: Building an Arena around a Social Problem.* New Brunswick, N.J.: Transaction Books, Rutgers University, 1981.

Wilerson, D. *Sipping Saints.* Old Tappan, N.J.: Fleming H. Revell Co., 1978.

Wilkinson, Rupert. *The Prevention of Drinking Problems: Alcohol Control and Cultural Influences.* New York: Oxford University Press, 1970.

Williams, Roger J. *Alcoholism: The Nutritional Approach.* Austin: University of Texas Press, 1959.

Williams, T. K. *The Ethanol-Induced Loss of Control Concept in Alcoholism.* Kalamazoo: Western Michigan University, 1970.

Willoughby, Alan. *The Alcohol-Troubled Person: Known & Unknown.* Chicago: Nelson-Hall, 1979.

W[ilson], Bill. *The AA Way of Life.* New York: Alcoholics Anonymous World Services, 1967.

Wilson, Lois. *Lois Remembers: Memoirs of the Co-Founder of Al-Anon and Wife of the Co-Founder of Alcoholics Anonymous.* New York: Al-Anon Family Group Headquarters, 1979.

Wisconsin Department of Health and Social Services. *Youth, Alcohol, and the Law: Final Report. Wisconsin 1933–1978.* Madison, 1978.

Wiseman, Jacqueline P. *Stations of the Lost: The Treatment of Skid Row Alcoholics.* Chicago: University of Chicago Press, 1979.

Woititz, Janet G. *Marriage on the Rocks.* New York: Delacorte Press, 1979.

Wolpe, Joseph. *Psychotherapy of Reciprocal Inhibition.* Stanford, Calif.: Stanford University Press, 1958.

World Health Organization. *Alcohol-Related Disabilities.* Geneva, 1977.

———. *Expert Committee on Mental Health, Alcoholism Subcommittee, Second Report.* World Health Organization Technical Report Series, no. 48. Geneva, 1952.

———. *Problems Related to Alcohol Consumption.* Albany: WHO Publications Centre, 1980.

———. *Public Health Aspects of Alcohol and Drug Dependence: Report of a WHO Conference, Dubrovnik, 21–25 August 1978.* Copenhagen: WHO Regional Office for Europe, 1979.

Youcha, Geraldine. *A Dangerous Pleasure.* New York: Hawthorn Books, 1978.

Young, M. E. *Drinking Drivers (A Bibliography with Abstracts).* Springfield, Va.: National Technical Information Service, 1979.

Zador, P. *Statistical Evaluation of the Effectiveness of "Alcohol Safety Action Programs."* Washington, D.C.: Insurance Institute for Highway Safety, 1974.

Zimberg, Sheldon; Wallace, John; and Blume, Sheila B. *Practical Approaches to Alcoholism Psychotherapy.* New York and London: Plenum Press, 1978.

INDEX